HANDBOOK OF COMPUTATIONAL SOCIAL SCIENCE, VOLUME 2

The *Handbook of Computational Social Science* is a comprehensive reference source for scholars across multiple disciplines. It outlines key debates in the field, showcasing novel statistical modeling and machine learning methods, and draws from specific case studies to demonstrate the opportunities and challenges in CSS approaches.

The Handbook is divided into two volumes written by outstanding, internationally renowned scholars in the field. This second volume focuses on foundations and advances in data science, statistical modeling, and machine learning. It covers a range of key issues, including the management of big data in terms of record linkage, streaming, and missing data. Machine learning, agent-based and statistical modeling, as well as data quality in relation to digital trace and textual data, as well as probability, non-probability, and crowdsourced samples represent further foci. The volume not only makes major contributions to the consolidation of this growing research field, but also encourages growth into new directions.

With its broad coverage of perspectives (theoretical, methodological, computational), international scope, and interdisciplinary approach, this important resource is integral reading for advanced undergraduates, postgraduates, and researchers engaging with computational methods across the social sciences, as well as those within the scientific and engineering sectors.

Uwe Engel is Professor at the University of Bremen, Germany, where he held a chair in sociology from 2000 to 2020. From 2008 to 2013, Dr. Engel coordinated the Priority Programme on "Survey Methodology" of the German Research Foundation. His current research focuses on data science, human-robot interaction, and opinion dynamics.

Anabel Quan-Haase is Professor of Sociology and Information and Media Studies at Western University and Director of the SocioDigital Media Lab, London, Canada. Her research interests include social media, social networks, life course, social capital, computational social science, and digital inequality/inclusion.

Sunny Xun Liu is a research scientist at Stanford Social Media Lab, USA. Her research focuses on the social and psychological effects of social media and AI, social media and well-being, and how the design of social robots impact psychological perceptions.

Lars Lyberg was Head of the Research and Development Department at Statistics Sweden and Professor at Stockholm University. He was an elected member of the International Statistical Institute. In 2018, he received the AAPOR Award for Exceptionally Distinguished Achievement.

The purpose of the EAM book series is to advance the development and application of methodological and statistical research techniques in social and behavioral research. Each volume in the series presents cutting-edge methodological developments in a way that is accessible to a broad audience. Such books can be authored, monographs, or edited volumes.

Sponsored by the European Association of Methodology, the EAM book series is open to contributions from the Behavioral, Social, Educational, Health and Economic Sciences. Proposals for volumes in the EAM series should include the following: (1) Title; (2) authors/editors; (3) a brief description of the volume's focus and intended audience; (4) a table of contents; (5) a timeline including planned completion date. Proposals are invited from all interested authors. Feel free to submit a proposal to one of the members of the EAM book series editorial board, by visiting the EAM website http://eam-online.org. Members of the EAM editorial board are Manuel Ato (University of Murcia), Pamela Campanelli (Survey Consultant, UK), Edith de Leeuw (Utrecht University) and Vasja Vehovar (University of Ljubljana).

Volumes in the series include

For more information about this series, please visit: www.routledge.com/European-Association-of-Methodology-Series/book-series/LEAEAMS

HANDBOOK OF COMPUTATIONAL SOCIAL SCIENCE, VOLUME 2

Data Science, Statistical Modelling, and Machine Learning Methods

Edited by Uwe Engel, Anabel Quan-Haase,
Sunny Xun Liu and Lars Lyberg

Routledge
Taylor & Francis Group

LONDON AND NEW YORK

First published 2022
by Routledge
2 Park Square, Milton Park, Abingdon, Oxon OX14 4RN

and by Routledge
605 Third Avenue, New York, NY 10158

Routledge is an imprint of the Taylor & Francis Group, an informa business

British Library Cataloguing-in-Publication Data
A catalogue record for this book is available from the British Library

Library of Congress Cataloging-in-Publication Data
A catalog record for this book has been requested

ISBN: 9780367457808 (hbk)
ISBN: 9781032077703 (pbk)
ISBN: 9781003025245 (ebk)

DOI: 10.4324/9781003025245

Typeset in Bembo
by Apex CoVantage, LLC

Lars E. Lyberg

December 1, 1944 – March 1, 2021

Lars E. Lyberg had a passion for methods and statistics and made many contributions to these fields. During his career he was a prolific writer and active member of the research community, working across disciplines including statistics, sociology, public opinion, and survey methodology, but his recent contributions to computational social science made him an innovative and much respected scholar. In May 2018, Lars Lyberg received the American Association for Public Opinion Research (AAPOR) Award for Exceptionally Distinguished Achievement. This award is given for outstanding contribution to the field of public opinion research. We quote from this laudation to appreciate once again Lars' many outstanding contributions to the field of survey methodology and statistics.

"For more than five decades, Lars Lyberg has made significant and important contributions to the field of survey research. Lars' career started at Stockholm University where he earned a Doctorate in Statistics. In 1966, Lars began his professional work career at Statistics Sweden where he spent more than 40 years, culminating in his appointment as Head of the Research and Development Department."

Lars was the founder of the *Journal of Official Statistics* and served as its Chief Editor for more than 25 years. Lars is a prolific author having written or edited many books and numerous journal articles in top journals including *Survey Methodology, Public Opinion Quarterly, and Survey Research Methods*. Lars was an elected member of the International Statistical Institute, past president of the International Association of Survey Statisticians, and a fellow of the Royal Statistical Society and American Statistical Association.

Lars is co-editor of the present *Handbook of Computational Social Science* and therein a co-author of a chapter on a changing survey landscape. On March 1, 2021, Lars passed away. We dedicate Volume 1 of this Handbook to the memory of Lars E. Lyberg, a pioneer in statistics, survey methodology, and computational social science.

On occasion of the 2018 AAPOR Award, Steve Everett produced a video that is publicly available at https://www.youtube.com/watch?v=Gi_P86lf3IY. The video starts with Lars talking about himself, his life, his career, continues with showing the moment he receives the award, and ends with a speech by Lars to commemorate the occasion. The video provides an opportunity to remember Lars, and his many personal and academic accomplishments.

March 15, 2021   Uwe Engel, Anabel Quan-Haase, Sunny Xun Liu

CONTENTS

CONTRIBUTORS

Nazanin Alipourfard is a PhD candidate of computer science at University of Southern California Information Sciences Institute. Her doctoral dissertation focuses on "Emergence and Mitigation of Bias in Heterogeneous Data", including multidimensional data and networked data. She published papers on mitigation of biases in multidimensional data using Simpson's paradox in ICWSM and WSDM conferences, as well as perception bias in directed networks in *Nature Communications* journal. https://orcid.org/0000-0001-9971-2179. (nazanina@isi.edu)

Rebecca Andridge is an associate professor of biostatistics at The Ohio State University College of Public Health. She received her PhD from the University of Michigan. She conducts methodologic work in imputation methods for missing data, primarily in large-scale probability samples, and measures of selection bias for nonprobability samples. She teaches introductory graduate and undergraduate biostatistics, primarily to public health students, and won the college's Outstanding Teaching Award in 2011. She is a fellow of the American Statistical Association and is an associate editor of the *Journal of Official Statistics* and the *Journal of Survey Statistics and Methodology*. https://orcid.org/0000-0001-9991-9647

Thomas Augustin is Professor of Statistics at the University of Munich (LMU), Germany. There he is head of the "Foundations of Statistics" group and dean of study for the bachelor and master programs in statistics and data science. Thomas has a diploma and a PhD in statistics from LMU Munich. He had worked at LMU and Bielefeld University before he became professor at LMU in 2003. His primary research interests are related to the foundations of statistics and data science, including imprecise probabilities, (generalized) measurement error and missing data models, classification under complex uncertainty, decision theory, and history of statistical thinking. He is also interested in issues of data quality in empirical social research and official statistics. https://orcid.org/0000-0002-1854-6226

Johann Bacher studied sociology at the Johannes Kepler University of Linz (Austria). In 1986 he finished his PhD, and in 1994 his habilitation. From 1998 to 2004, he was full professor of sociology at the Friedrich-Alexander University Erlangen-Nuremberg. Since 2004, he is full professor of sociology and empirical research and head of the Department of Empirical Research at the Johannes Kepler University Linz. His current research interests include research methods, youth unemployment, value orientations, and social structure. Recent publications appeared in *Quality and Quantity* and *Journal of Human Values*. https://orcid.org/0000-0002-8151-8922

Jelke Bethlehem studied mathematical statistics at the University of Amsterdam. After obtaining his pre-doctoral degree he was employed as a research worker at the Statistical Department of the Mathematical Centre in Amsterdam. In 1978 he joined the Department for Statistical Methods of Statistics Netherlands, first as a research worker and later as a senior statistician. His main research topics were the treatment of nonresponse in sample surveys, in which he obtained his PhD, and disclosure control of survey data. From 1987 to 1996 he was head of the Statistical Informatics Department of Statistics Netherlands, which developed standard software for collecting and processing survey data. From 1997 to 2014, he was a senior survey methodologist of the Methodology Department of Statistics Netherlands. He was involved in research projects in the area of survey methodology, including some European research projects. From 1991 to 2011, he was also a part-time professor in statistical information processing at the University of Amsterdam (Faculty of Economics). From 2012 to 2017 he was a professor of survey methodology (with a focus on online surveys) at the Faculty of Social Sciences of the Leiden University. https://orcid.org/0000-0002-6088-5512

Stefan Bosse is an interdisciplinary physicist and computer scientist. Since 2016 he has been teaching and researching as a senior researcher and private lecturer (Privatdozent) at the University of Bremen, Department of Mathematics and Computer Science, and in 2018–2019 he was an interim professor and lecturer at the University of Koblenz-Landau, Department of Computer Science, Institute of Software Technologies. Since 2020, he has been Scientific Director of the interregional and interdisciplinary DFG Research Group 3022. His main research area is distributed artificial intelligence in general and information processing in massive parallel and distributed systems with agent-based approaches combined with machine learning and agent-based simulation. He addresses a broad range of application fields like smart cities, materials, and crowd sensing, all covered by data science methodologies. http://orcid.org/0000-0002-8774-6141

Pierson Browne is a PhD candidate in the Department of Sociology and Legal Studies at the University of Waterloo. He completed his master's degree at Concordia University, where he wrote his thesis on how independent game development entrepreneurs negotiate risk and ideate non-collocative communities of practice and labour. His dissertation research examines applied quantitative methodology and the uptake of the Bayesian statistical paradigm in the discipline of sociology. Specifically, it explores the theoretical and practical implications of explicit engagement with Bayesian thinking, generative modelling, and probabilistic programming. During his time at Netlab, Pierson has focused on designing and developing Python and R packages for computational social science and network analysis. https://orcid.org/0000-0002-3073-2603

Keith Burghardt is a computer scientist at USC Information Sciences Institute who specializes in understanding human behavior with physics-inspired models. Burghardt received numerous awards including a 2018 Award for Excellence in Postdoctoral Research (UC Davis), the 2016 ISI Director's Intern Award, and the 2012 Best Undergraduate Physics Thesis Award at the University of Maryland. Burghardt received a BS in physics (magna cum laude with high honors) and PhD in physics at the University of Maryland in 2012 and 2016, respectively. https://orcid.org/0000-0003-1164-9545. (keithab@isi.edu)

Jesse Chandler is a researcher at Mathematica, a US policy research firm. He completed his PhD in social psychology at the University of Michigan and postdoctoral training in psychology and public policy at Princeton University. Jesse's research focuses on best practices in data collection and communication of research findings to data users. An important part of this research concerns how measurement error (caused by careless or fraudulent responses) impacts the quality of survey data. https://orcid.org/0000-0001-8151-0915

Tyler Crick is a PhD student in the Department of Sociology and Legal Studies at the University of Waterloo. His master's research was focused on rhetoric, discourse analysis, digital literacy, and misinformation, with his major research project being the development of a browser toolbar to assist internet users with assessing the credibility of online content. His current research interests continue to be focused on misinformation, with an emphasis on its production, patterns of dissemination, and social impact. This research includes large-scale data analysis using computational social science methods such as social network analysis, machine learning, and natural language processing. His work with Netlab has been focused on Python development, as well as research and development in a broad range of computational methodologies. https://orcid.org/0000-0003-1559-9936

Lena Dahlhaus is a lecturer at the University of Bremen, where she teaches statistical data analysis using R to undergraduate level sociology students. Following a bachelor's degree in sociology, she received a master's degree in social research with distinction from the University of Bremen in 2020. Previously, Lena has been working at the Social Science Methods Centre and the Working Group Statistics and Social Research at the University of Bremen, where she was involved in research projects about the role of artificial intelligence in society. Her research interests include survey methodology, natural language processing, research ethics, and integrating traditional and new forms of data. https://orcid.org/0000-0003-4244-5545

Richard D. De Veaux is the C. Carlisle and M. Tippit Professor of Statistics in the Department of Mathematics and Statistics at Williams College. He is a fellow of the American Statistical Association (ASA) and was its 2018–2021 vice president. He received his PhD in statistics from Stanford University under the direction of Persi Diaconis. Dick's research interests include applications of statistics to real-world problems in science and industry. He is the co-author of several textbooks, including *Intro Stats, 6th ed.*, *Stats, Data and Models, 5th ed.*, and *Business Statistics, 3rd ed.* https://orcid.org/0000-0002-0319-0423. (rdeveaux@williams.edu)

Adam Eck is an assistant professor of Computer Science and leads the Social Intelligence Lab at Oberlin College. He received his PhD in computer science from the University of Nebraska-Lincoln, where he was also a postdoc in the Survey Research and Methodology Program. Adam's research interests include interdisciplinary applications of artificial intelligence and machine learning to solve real-world problems, such as data science and machine learning for improving data collection and analysis in the computational social sciences (e.g., survey informatics), as well as decision-making for intelligent agents and multi-agent systems in complex environments. https://orcid.org/0000-0001-7651-6984. (aeck@oberlin.edu)

Ted Enamorado is an assistant professor of political science at Washington University in St. Louis, and a faculty affiliate at the Center for the Study of Race, Ethnicity, and Equity and the Division of Computational and Data Sciences. Ted holds a PhD in politics (Political Economy program) from Princeton University, where he was affiliated with the Program for Quantitative and Analytical Political Science (Q-APS) and the Research Program in Political Economy. His fields of specialization are political economy and political methodology. https://orcid.org/0000-0002-2022-7646

Uwe Engel is Professor Emeritus at the University of Bremen (Germany) where he held a chair in sociology from 2000 to 2020. In 2007 he founded the Social Science Methods Centre of Bremen University and has since directed this institution. Prior to this he held a professorship for social sciences at the University of Potsdam and an assistant professorship at the Department of Philosophy, Religious Studies, and Social Sciences at the University of Duisburg. From 2008 to 2013 Uwe coordinated the Priority Programme 1292 "Survey Methodology" of the German Research Foundation (DFG). His research focuses on survey methodology, data science, longitudinal and multilevel modeling, and field research (experiments, surveys). Sociological interests include human-robot interaction, artificial intelligence, and opinion dynamics. Uwe is a founding member of the European Association of Methodology (EAM) and the Bremen International Graduate School of Social Sciences (BIGSSS). He earned a doctorate in sociology at Leibniz University of Hannover in 1986 with a PhD thesis on multivariate data analysis in status inconsistency research. http://orcid.org/0000-0001-8420-9677

Cornelia Fedtke is currently finalizing her MA in sociology at the University of Hamburg, Germany. In her studies, she focuses on discourse, digitalization, and computational social science. Apart from her studies, she worked in research projects on hate speech and counter-speech in social media at the University of Hamburg as well as on digitalization in organizations in cooperation with researchers of the Helmut-Schmidt-University, Hamburg. In her master thesis, she analyzes discourses in social media using qualitative and computational approaches in a mixed-methods design. https://orcid.org/0000-0002-4869-2814

Fabian Flöck is Head of the data science team at the Computational Social Science Department at GESIS. He is researching how to build data science methods that precisely and reliably measure social phenomena and are at the same time transparent and accessible for researchers. This includes natural language processing with ML methods, HCI, and human computation. He has a background in computer sciences and communication sciences. https://orcid.org/0000-0002-0727-1319

Thomas Gschwend (PhD, State University of New York at Stony Brook, 2001) is Professor of Political Science and Chair of Quantitative Methods in the Social Sciences at the Department of Political Science, University of Mannheim (Germany), where his research focuses on comparative politics, judicial politics, public opinion, political psychology, as well as political methodology. He is particularly interested in the processes by which institutions pre-structure an individual's decision-making process and its consequences for voters, party strategies, and election outcomes. Gschwend is the co-recipient of the 2012 Gosnell Prize for Excellence in Political Methodology. His scholarly articles have been published in *Political Analysis*, *Journal of Politics*, *British Journal of Political Science*, *Electoral Studies*, and the *European Journal of Political Research*, among others. His most recent English book publications are *Multi-Level Electoral Politics: Beyond the Second-Order Election Model* (Oxford University Press, 2017; co-authored with Sona N. Golder, Ignacio Lago, André Blais, and Elisabeth Gidengil), *Research Design in Political Science: How to Practice What They Preach* (Palgrave Macmillan, 2011; co-edited with Frank Schimmelfennig), and *Strategic Voting in Mixed-Electoral Systems* (SFG-Elsevier 2004). https://orcid.org/0000-0002-8656-9622

Raphael H. Heiberger is Tenure-Track Professor at the Institute for Social Sciences of the University of Stuttgart. He is head of the newly founded lab on computational social science. He received his PhD (summa cum laude) from the University of Bamberg (Germany) and was visiting scholar at UCLA and a Fulbright Fellow at UC Berkeley. He is a permanent member of the McFarland Lab at Stanford University. Besides various aspects of natural language processing, his research interests focus on social network analysis, Bayesian statistics (esp. machine learning), and, more generally, the application of computational methods on social phenomena like markets, media discourse, and science's structural properties. https://orcid.org/0000-0003-3465-7214

Lianne Ippel holds a PhD from Tilburg University for her thesis titled "Multilevel Modeling for Data Streams with Dependent Observations". In 2018, she won the "best PhD thesis award" at the General Online Research conference in Cologne. After a two-year postdoc at the Institute of Data Science at Maastricht University where she mainly worked on privacy preserving methods, she now works at Statistics Netherlands, the national statistics institute of the Netherlands. Here, she continues to work on privacy preserving methods in addition to studying innovations in questionnaire research. Topics of interest include but are not limited to studying whether smartphone applications, sensor data, or even data donations are viable options to reduce respondent burden. https://orcid.org/0000-0001-8314-0305

Jakob Jünger is a postdoctoral researcher at the Institute of Political Science and Communication Studies in Greifswald, Germany, and at the Digital Academy of Sciences in Mainz, Germany. His work focuses on online platforms and on the theoretical foundations of communication at the intersection of public and private settings. He utilizes and promotes automated methods of data collection and analysis, such as the scientific use of application programming interfaces, network analysis, and computer simulation. Further, by contributing to digital humanities projects, he fosters building knowledge infrastructures based on semantic web technologies. In the field of computational communication science, he is particularly concerned with the epistemological and social consequences of automated methods. https://orcid.org/0000-0003-1860-6695

Maurits Kaptein is a professor of data science and health at the Jheronimus Academy of Data Science (JADS) and the Tilburg University (both in The Netherlands). At JADS, Maurits runs the computational personalization lab (see www.nth-iteration.com). Maurits' recent research focuses on data-driven methods for treatment personalization in healthcare. Maurits has published papers in impactful journals in various fields such as the *Journal of Interactive Marketing*, *Psychometrika*, the *Journal of Statistical Software*, and the *Journal of Machine Learning Research*. Maurits is also a co-founder of Scailable and author of several books. https://orcid.org/0000-0002-6316-7524

Christoph Kiefer studied psychology and mathematics at the FernUniversität Hagen and TU Braunschweig. After finishing his master's degree in psychology (2016), he pursued his doctoral studies at the unit of Psychological Methods at the RWTH Aachen. In 2020, he received his PhD at the RWTH Aachen for a dissertation on causal and statistical inference on count outcomes. Currently, he is a postdoctoral researchers at the unit of Psychological Methods at Bielefeld University. In his research, he is interested in developing new methods for investigating average and conditional (causal) effects of an intervention, such as a cognitive training, based on nonlinear regression models and models for latent change. http://orcid.org/0000-0002-9166-400X

Benedikt Langenberg studied statistical data analysis, psychology, and computer science at the Ghent University (Belgium) and RWTH Aachen University (Germany). In 2018, he started his doctoral studies at the RWTH Aachen University and currently is finishing his studies at the Bielefeld University (Germany). His PhD thesis is on "Repeated Measures ANOVA with Latent Variables: A New Approach Based on Structural Equation Modeling" supervised by Dr. Axel Mayer (Bielefeld University). His research interests include the analysis of causal effects and effect size estimators in experimental designs in the field of psychology and social sciences. His methodological interests concern the intersection of analysis of variance, structural equation modeling, and hierarchical models. He further focuses on methods and algorithms for model selection and data mining in structural equation models. https://orcid.org/0000-0002-4757-0698

Florian Lemmerich received his PhD from the University of Würzburg in 2014 with a thesis on efficient and effective approaches for subgroup discovery, a data mining technique for extracting interesting patterns from data. After being a postdoc at GESIS Leibniz Institute for the Social Sciences in Cologne and at RWTH Aachen University, he is currently working as a tenured professor for Applied Machine Learning at the University of Passau, Germany. His research interests include the development of interpretable, reliable, and responsible data mining and machine learning algorithms as well as applications of such techniques for the analysis of behavioral data, specifically digital trace data from the web. https://orcid.org/0000-0001-7620-1376

Kristina Lerman is a principal scientist at the USC California Information Sciences Institute and holds a joint appointment as a full research professor in the USC Computer Science Department. Trained as a physicist, she now applies network analysis, data science, and machine learning techniques to problems in computational social science, including crowdsourcing, social network, and social media analysis. Her recent work on modeling and understanding biases in heterogeneous data and in social networks has been covered by the *Washington Post*, *Wall Street Journal*, and *MIT Technology Review*. https://orcid.org/0000-0002-5071-0575.

Sunny Xun Liu is a social science research scientist and associate director at Stanford Social Media Lab. Liu earned her PhD in mass communication and media from Michigan State University. Her research focuses on the social and psychological effects of social media and AI, social media and well-being, and how the design of social robots impact psychological perceptions. Before joining Stanford, she was an associate professor at California State University, Stanislaus. She has won top three faculty paper awards from ICA and AEJMC and published in communication and psychology journals. Her research has been funded by Google Research and Stanford HAI. https://orcid.org/0000-0001-8910-9384

Lars Lyberg has made significant and important contributions to the field of survey research for more than five decades. Lars' career started at Stockholm University where he earned a doctorate in statistics. In 1966, Lars began his professional work career at Statistics Sweden where he spent more than 40 years, culminating in his appointment as head of the Research and Development Department. Lars was the founder of the *Journal of Official Statistics* and served as its chief editor for more than 25 years. Lars has written or edited numerous books and is author of numerous journal articles. Lars was an elected member of the International Statistical Institute, past president of the International Association of Survey Statisticians, and a fellow of the Royal Statistical Society and American Statistical Association. In 2018, he received the AAPOR Award for Exceptionally Distinguished Achievement of the American Association for Public Opinion Research.

Axel Mayer obtained his PhD in 2013 from the University of Jena, Germany, with a thesis on latent variables and causal mediation models in structural equation modeling. In 2014–2016, he was a postdoctoral researcher in the Department of Data Analysis at Ghent University, and in 2016–2020 he was a junior professor at the Department of Psychology, RWTH Aachen

University (Germany). Currently, he is a professor for Psychological Methods and Evaluation at Bielefeld University. In his research, he is interested in developing new methods for investigating if, how, and for whom an intervention, such as a psychotherapeutic treatment or a health training, has an effect. His methodological research emphasis is on development and application of models for analyzing average and conditional (causal) effects, causal mediation models, and models for latent change. An important aspect of his research is the development of user-friendly statistical software to make modern statistical methods and models available for a broader audience. https://orcid.org/0000-0001-9716-878X

John McLevey is an associate professor in the Departments of Knowledge Integration and Sociology & Legal Studies and the principal investigator of Netlab at the University of Waterloo, Canada. His research interests are primarily in the areas of network science, computational social science, affect and cognitive social science, political sociology, and environmental sociology. He is the author of *Doing Computational Social Science* (Sage), *Industrial Development and Eco-Tourisms* (with Stoddart and Mattoni, Palgrave MacMillan), and *The Face-to-Face Principle: Science, Trust, Truth, and Democracy* (with Collins, Evans, Innes, Mason-Wilkes, and Kennedy, Cardiff University Press). He is co-editor of the second edition of the Sage Handbook of Social Network Analysis (with John Scott and Peter Carrington) and special issues of *Social Networks* (2021, on social networks and climate change) and *Society & Natural Resources* (2020, on climate change and energy futures). His current research on influence, deception, and polarization in political discussion networks is funded by an Insight Grant from the Social Sciences and Humanities Research Council of Canada. https://orcid.org/0000-0002-8512-1308

Sebastian Munoz-Najar Galvez is the Bluhm Family Assistant Professor of Data Science and Education at the Harvard Graduate School of Education. Sebastian received a doctoral degree in sociology of education from the Graduate School of Education at Stanford University. He is a sociologist of science who uses computational linguistics and network analysis to study the ebb and flow of research agendas. His scholarship leverages large collections of dissertations, scientific papers, patents, and event logs from digital libraries to show how changes in knowledge production systems affect the careers of scholars and the public value of science. His most recent publications include "Paradigm Wars Revisited" (*American Educational Research Journal*, 2019) and the "The Innovation-Diversity Paradox" (*Proceedings of the National Academy of Sciences*, 2020). https://orcid.org/0000-0002-4402-9564

Dominic Nyhuis is DAAD Visiting Assistant Professor at the Department of Political Science and at the Center for European Studies, University of North Carolina at Chapel Hill. He received his PhD in 2015 from the University of Mannheim. In his research on European and German politics, he focuses on party politics, legislatures, and subnational politics. With a background in quantitative methods, he is particularly interested in how the digital transformation impacts upon research practices in the social sciences. To this end, he has worked on the automated collection of large-scale web data, as well as on tools for the analysis of text and video data. https://orcid.org/0000-0001-6790-4117

Gabriele Paolacci is an associate professor of marketing at Rotterdam School of Management, Erasmus University. He joined RSM after graduate studies at Ca' Foscari University of Venice (where he got his PhD) and at Ross School of Business, University of Michigan (where he was a visiting scholar). Gabriele's research investigates substantive and methodological questions in behavioral research. Within the substantive domain, he conducts research in the field of consumer judgment and decision-making. In particular, he studies how people's decisions seemingly contradict the assumptions and prescriptions of rational choice theory. He also conducts empirical research on the practice of online data collection in the behavioral sciences. He has investigated whether crowdsourced samples (e.g., MTurk workers) provide data of high quality, and how to attenuate their distinctive threats to experimental validity (e.g., nonnaive participants, study impostors). https://orcid.org/0000-0002-9938-7940

Andreas Pöge studied sociology, history, and politics at the University of Münster. From 2002 to 2016 he was research assistant at the Universities of Trier and Bielefeld. From 2011 to 2012 he had an interim professorship at the University of Gießen, from 2015 to 2016 at the University of Hamburg, and from 2017 to 2018 at the University of Münster. Since 2016 he has been a senior researcher in the field of quantitative methods of empirical social research at the Faculty of Sociology at the University of Bielefeld. His research focuses on the methodology and application of structural equation models, latent class, and cluster analysis. His current substantive research focuses on juvenile delinquent behavior and values. https://orcid.org/0000-0002-2074-2816

Anabel Quan-Haase is a full professor of sociology and information and media studies at Western University. She is the coeditor of *the Handbook of Social Media Research Methods* (Sage, 2017), coauthor of *Real-Life Sociology* (Oxford University Press, 2020), author of *Technology and Society* (Oxford University Press, 2020), and coeditor of the *Handbook of Computational Social Science* (Routledge, forthcoming). https://orcid.org/0000-0002-2560-6709

Jost Reinecke is a professor of quantitative methods of empirical social research at the Faculty of Sociology at the University of Bielefeld. His research focuses on the methodology and application of structural equation models and latent class analysis both cross-sectionally and longitudinally. His current methodological research focuses on growth curve and growth mixture models and the development of techniques related to multiple imputation of missing data in complex survey designs. His current substantive research focuses on the longitudinal development of adolescents' delinquent behavior and on the application of the situational action theory in panel designs. https://orcid.org/0000-0001-9171-8066

Tobias Ringwald is a research assistant at the Institute for Anthropomatics and Robotics (IAR) at the Karlsruhe Institute of Technology (KIT), where he also received his MSc in computer science in 2018. His current research interests focus on large-scale automatic image and video analysis of political speeches through machine learning methods. Further research efforts span deep learning and computer vision, particularly transfer learning, unsupervised domain adaptation, and domain generalization, especially in the context of learning from synthetic data. https://orcid.org/0000-0001-8216-7645

Oliver Rittmann is a PhD candidate at the Center for Doctoral Studies in Social and Behavioral Sciences at the University of Mannheim and a research associate at the chair of Quantitative Methods in the Social Sciences at the University of Mannheim. He holds a master's degree in political science from the University of Mannheim and a bachelor's degree in social sciences from the Heinrich-Heine University of Düsseldorf. His research focuses on legislative debates, political representation, and the measurement of structural inequalities within legislative bodies. Methodologically, he is interested in statistical modeling, causal inference, and the automated analysis of text, audio, and video. https://orcid.org/0000-0001-7707-9835

Fernando Sancho-Caparrini earned his PhD in computer science from the University of Seville and is a professor of computer science and artificial intelligence at the University of Seville. He has participated in more than 25 national and international projects, has more than 100 scientific publications in journals and conferences, has supervised/co-supervised seven doctoral theses and more than 50 end of master and degree works. His research has been mainly focused on the field of application of artificial intelligence and machine learning techniques to the analysis and modeling of complex systems, with special emphasis on their temporal evolution (through dynamic systems) and their structural evolution (through complex networks). Website: www.cs.us.es/~fsancho. https://orcid.org/0000-0003-1660-4098. Scopus: 22434438600. Dialnet: 3281626.

Indira Sen is a doctoral researcher at GESIS Leibniz Institute for Social Sciences, Cologne. Her interest lies in understanding biases in inferential studies from digital traces, with a focus on computational linguistics and natural language processing. Before GESIS, she completed her bachelor's and master's degrees in India and has interned at NTU, Singapore, and EPFL, Switzerland. https://orcid.org/0000-0003-3475-0371

Itay Sisso is currently affiliated with Facebook Research and spent two years as the lead data scientist at Kayma Labs while receiving his PhD in cognitive science from the Hebrew University. His background is in aerospace engineering (BSc and MSc) and military operations research (major in the Israeli Air Force). His main fields of research are in the intersection of emotions, personality, and decision-making, as well as online research methods and data quality. More specifically, he studied individual differences and the mechanism behind the choice overload phenomenon, with a focus on regret and opportunity cost. Nowadays he uses his knowledge in research methods, data science, and behavioral science to conduct applied behavioral research in the industry. https://orcid.org/0000-0002-2650-3891

Martin Spiess is Professor for Psychological Methods and Statistics at the University of Hamburg, Germany. He studied psychology and received his doctoral degree in statistics at the Department of Economics, University of Konstanz, Germany, working on semi-parametric estimation of categorical panel models. For his postdoctoral qualification he worked on the estimation of panel models and techniques to compensate for missing data, for example, weighting and multiple imputation at the Faculty of Economics of the University of Regensburg, Germany, the German Institute for Economic Research (DIW), and the International Institute of Management, University Flensburg, Germany. He completed his postdoctoral thesis to qualify as a professor at the Faculty of Social Sciences at the University of Bremen, Germany. His current research interests are the foundations of psychological research methods in light of the replication crisis, robust multiple imputation and semi-parametric estimation of general regression models integrating various sources of external information. https://orcid.org/0000-0003-1855-643X

Rainer Stiefelhagen (Dr.-Ing., Universität Karlsruhe TH, 2002) is a full professor at the Karlsruhe Institute of Technology (KIT) where he directs the Computer Vision for Human-Computer Interaction Lab at the Institute for Anthropomatics and Robotics as well as KIT's Study Center for Visually Impaired Students. His research interests include image and video understanding and in particular the perception of people in image and video, including their gestures, actions, identities, etc. He has authored more than 250 papers in leading conferences and journals. He has been awarded several best paper awards (ICPR'12, ICPR'14, BMVC'15, BMVC'19, IEEE FG'19), a Google Research Faculty award (2013), and a Fraunhofer Attract grant (2007–2012). https://orcid.org/0000-0001-8046-4945

Juan Luis Suárez earned his PhD in philosophy at the University of Salamanca in 1996 and his PhD in Hispanic literatures at McGill University (2000). He became a full professor at Western University in 2007. In 2014 he completed his Global Executive MBA at I.E. Business School.

He has authored four books, co-authored seven monographs, and published over 80 articles. Since 2010 he has run the Canada Foundation for Innovation–funded CulturePlex Lab (cultureplex.ca) at Western University, a multidisciplinary lab on digital transformation that works with banks, technology start-ups, and other organizations in designing and implementing their digital future. https://orcid.org/0000-0001-9302-2986

Richard Valliant is Research Professor Emeritus at the University of Michigan and the Joint Program for Survey Methodology at the University of Maryland. He received his PhD from Johns Hopkins University. He has over 40 years of experience in survey sampling, estimation theory, and statistical computing. He was formerly an associate director at Westat, a US research firm, and a mathematical statistician with the US Bureau of Labor Statistics. He has a range of applied experience in survey estimation and sample design on a variety of establishment, institutional, and household surveys. He is also a fellow of the American Statistical Association, an elected member of the International Statistical Institute, and has been an associate editor of the *Journal of the American Statistical Association*, *Survey Methodology*, and the *Journal of Official Statistics*. He is a co-author of the books *Practical Tools for Designing and Weighting Survey Samples* (2nd edition), *Survey Weights: A Step-by-Step Guide to Calculation*, and *Finite Population Sampling and Inference: A Prediction Approach*. https://orcid.org/0000-0002-9176-2961

Jeroen K. Vermunt received his PhD from Tilburg University in the Netherlands in 1996 and is currently a full professor at this university. In 2005, he received the Leo Goodman award from the American Sociological Association methodology section. His work has been published in the main journals in statistics and social science methodology, as well as in applied social science journals. His research interests include latent class and finite mixture models, item response theory modeling, longitudinal and event history data analysis, multilevel analysis, and generalized latent variable modeling. He is the co-developer (with Jay Magidson) of the Latent GOLD software package. https://orcid.org/0000-0001-9053-9330

Claudia Wagner is a full professor (W3) for Applied Computational Social Science at RWTH Aachen and the scientific director of the department Computational Social Science at GESIS Leibniz Institute for the Social Sciences. Before that she was a W1 professor for data science at the University Koblenz-Landau and the team lead of team Data Science at GESIS that investigates social phenomena in offline and online social networks and social media. She received her PhD from Graz University of Technology in 2013, before joining GESIS as a postdoctoral researcher (2013–2016). https://orcid.org/0000-0002-0640-8221

Bernd Weiß is the head of the GESIS Panel and deputy head of the department Survey Design and Methodology at GESIS Leibniz Institute for the Social Sciences. His research interests focus on methods of empirical research in the social sciences, family sociology, and juvenile delinquency. https://orcid.org/0000-0002-1176-8408

Katrin Weller is an information scientist working at GESIS Leibniz Institute for the Social Sciences in Köln (Cologne, Germany), Department Computational Social Science. She leads the Social Analytics and Services team and is responsible for new approaches to using social media data in social science research. In 2015, she was a digital studies fellow at the Library of Congress' John W. Kluge Center in Washington, DC (USA). Until 2012 she worked at the Department of Information Science at Heinrich-Heine-University Düsseldorf (Germany). Within the fields of computational social science, internet research, and web science, her research focus is on emerging practices of using social media as new types of research data, data management, and preservation, as well as new forms of measuring scholarly communication including altmetrics. https://orcid.org/0000-0003-3799-1146

Knut Wenzig studied social sciences at the Friedrich-Alexander-Universität Erlangen-Nürnberg (FAU). After some years as a research assistant at two universities he worked at the Research Data Center (RDC) of the National Educational Panel Study (now Leibniz Institute for Educational Trajectories, Bamberg, Germany). In 2014 he joined the RDC of the Socio-Economic Panel Study (SOEP) at DIW Berlin. He is interested in data science and research infrastructure for the social sciences, like metadata, occupational classification, and cluster analysis. Together with others he founded blog.surveydata.org, a blog for RDC staff in Germany, Switzerland, and Austria. https://orcid.org/0000-0002-2259-0203

Gregor Wiedemann is working as Senior Researcher at the Leibniz Institute for Media Research | Hans Bredow Institute (HBI), where he heads the Media Research Methods Lab. His work focuses on computational social science, in particular the development of methods and applications of natural language processing and text mining for empirical social and media research. Gregor studied political science and computer science in Leipzig and Miami, USA. In 2016, he received his doctorate from the Department of Computer Science at the University of Leipzig for his thesis on the automation of discourse and content analysis using text mining and machine learning methods. Afterward, he worked as a postdoc in the Department of Computer Science at the University of Hamburg, where he researched NLP methods for information extraction, hate speech detection, and argument mining. https://orcid.org/0000-0002-4239-295X

Camilla Zallot is currently a PhD candidate in consumer behavior in the Marketing Department of the Rotterdam School of Management, Erasmus University. Her current research projects revolve around how moral concerns and information about the morality of others influence markets. https://orcid.org/0000-0003-2078-4984

PREFACE

Digitization has revolutionized society, including the realm of social science. We are currently in the midst of a digital paradigm where digital technology evolves at unprecedented rates and impacts ever more domains of life. With the seamless integration of digital technology, from mobile phones to AI, into the rhythms of everyday life, there is also greater generation and accumulation of related behavioral data of prime interest to the social sciences. Digitization is changing the object of social science research. Public life and human behavior increasingly take place in digital environments both within and beyond social media. Robots, autonomous vehicles, and conversational agents are gaining considerably in importance. Advances in data science and artificial intelligence create behavioral opportunities but also challenge privacy protection, ethical norms, and common ways of life. In short, social science is changing because digitization is changing its focus.

Digitization is also changing the very methods of social research. If life takes place in digital environments, novel methods are needed for reaching target populations. Similarly, different kinds of data need different methods of data collection, processing, and analysis. The past decade has seen continued efforts toward the development and application of computational methods to let social science follow people to where they are – in digital environments ranging from social media to video gaming to AI. "Computational social science" (CSS) has become the umbrella term for all such efforts. CSS is both a rapidly developing field and a field in need of professional and institutional consolidation. This concerns its theoretical and methodological foundations, issues of research ethics and data policy, and further development of statistical and computational methods.

While the dynamic development of CSS observed in recent years is largely due to the digitization of society, it is important to remember that the roots of CSS are in mathematical sociology, statistical modeling, and social simulation. The field is much broader than the efforts around the study of popular digital trace data lets us assume. Furthermore, CSS represents a genuinely interdisciplinary field of study, not just a subfield of social science.

Against this background, the *Handbook of Computational Social Science* aims to make a major contribution to the consolidation of CSS while also moving it into new directions. The editors developed the idea of the handbook at the Digital Traces Workshop, which took place in 2018 at the University of Bremen, Germany. The three-day workshop was organized by the University's Social Science Methods Centre and funded by the German Research Foundation

(DFG), the federal state of Bremen, and the Bremen International Graduate School of Social Sciences (BIGSSS). During the workshop, an interdisciplinary group of scholars shared recent advancements in CSS research and established new transatlantic research collaborations. Forty-four participants from Canada, the United States, and eight countries in Europe took part in the invited talks on key debates in the field, showcasing novel statistical modeling and machine learning methods and also drawing from specific case studies to demonstrate the opportunities and challenges in CSS approaches. While not all the authors of the present handbook were a part of the initial workshop, the idea for the handbook was born out of this event.

Computational social science is a field at the intersection of different disciplines, such as social science, computing, and data science. The editors thus deliberately invited authors to contribute from diverse disciplines and fields of study to showcase the interdisciplinary nature of computational social science research. We very much appreciate that so many colleagues accepted this invitation: they carefully drafted and revised their chapters and participated in the peer-review process. This is a particularly impressive achievement, as the COVID-19 pandemic has created new work-life balance challenges for many academics. We would also like to express our sincere thanks to Lucy McClune, psychology editor at Routledge, Taylor & Francis Group, and her assistant, Akshita Pattiyani, for their encouragement and continued support. A big thanks goes also to Silke Himmel at the University of Bremen for her invaluable assistance in the organization of the Digital Traces Workshop and her invaluable administrative assistance in this handbook project.

We end this preface with a heavy heart. On March 1, 2021, our co-editor Lars Lyberg passed away. Lars was a lead participant of the Digital Traces Workshop in 2018 and has been a valued collaborator in shaping the direction of the handbook. With his parting, the field of computational social science loses an influential scientist and visionary. We mourn a friend.

March 15, 2021

Uwe Engel, Anabel Quan-Haase, Sunny Xun Liu

1

INTRODUCTION TO THE *HANDBOOK OF COMPUTATIONAL SOCIAL SCIENCE*

Uwe Engel, Anabel Quan-Haase, Sunny Xun Liu and Lars Lyberg

We write the introduction to the two-volume *Handbook of Computational Social Science* with excitement and awe. The handbook brings together a considerable corpus of research and insight, with 22 contributions for volume 1 "Theory, Case Studies, and Ethics" and 22 contributions for volume 2 "Data Science, Statistical Modelling, and Machine Learning Methods." Over 90 experts contributed from a wide range of academic disciplines and institutions to provide a mosaic of the diversity of computational social science (CSS) scholarship. They lay out the foundation for what CSS is today and where it is heading, outlining key debates in the field, showcasing novel statistical modeling and machine learning methods, and also drawing from specific case studies to demonstrate the opportunities and challenges presented by CSS approaches.

Our goal with the handbook is to reach a wide readership by taking a multidisciplinary and multimethod approach. The handbook includes foundational chapters for up-and-coming scholars and practitioners, who are interested in consolidating their understanding of key terms, methods, and means of data interpretation as well as more advanced analytical approaches that serve as a learning resource for current experts in CSS. The handbook is aimed at a wide range of scholars with backgrounds in technical fields such as statistics, methods, and computer science, as well as scholars in the social and behavioral sciences, the latter notably including psychology, cognitive science, sociology, communication, new media studies, and political science, among others. The handbook also allows practitioners and policymakers who are tasked with analyzing a specific data set to adopt a set of best practices to guide their research efforts.

Computational social science is an exciting field of research that is growing rapidly and in diverse directions. In 2018, Springer started the publication of its dedicated journal, the *Journal of Computational Social Science*, which is broad in scope and interdisciplinary in nature and aims "to understand social and economic structures and phenomena from a computational point of view" (https://www.springer.com/journal/42001, para. 2). For example, its volume 3, issue 2, special issue was on "Misinformation, Manipulation and Abuse in the Era of COVID-19," bringing together top modeling and simulation experts on the topic. This demonstrates how CSS is having a direct impact on our understanding of pressing societal research questions and advancing novel methodological approaches. Computational social science research has an important role to play in society by providing unique and policy-relevant insights through its capability to apply computational approaches to large data sets. Besides, many special issues with

DOI: 10.4324/9781003025245-1

a CSS focus are being proposed, such as the 2021 call for papers by the journal *Chinese Sociological Review*. The call requests manuscripts that "offer important theoretical and empirical insights to advance our understanding of the development in CSS and help move forward the field in Chinese societies" (https://think.taylorandfrancis.com/special_issues/computational-social-science/, para. 3). This shows that there is an invisible college of the kind that Diana Crane (1972) described in her earlier work forming around the topic, with a rapid "proliferation of conferences, workshops, and summer schools across the globe, across disciplines, and across sources of data" (Lazer et al., 2020, p. 1060). As the field grows, CSS collaborations and research clusters are emerging globally. The field is not only growing but also consolidating, and our handbook represents an important step forward in this process.

The chapters in the two-volume handbook provide a deep understanding of theory as well as methodological opportunities and challenges. The main aims include:

- *Theoretical debates*: Key theoretical debates are presented from different perspectives to show how the field is gaining strength and evolving.
- *Showcasing novel statistical modeling and machine learning methods*: The chapters describe cutting-edge methodological developments and their application to a range of data sets.
- *Ethical debates and guidelines*: The chapters demonstrate the dimensions of data ethics and the need for guidelines and appropriate pedagogy.
- *State-of-the-art artificial intelligence*: The chapters highlight the use of various AI systems as methodological tools, data sets, and a combination of both.
- *Demonstrating cross-disciplinary applications of CSS*: The chapters promote the development of new interdisciplinary research approaches to answer new and pressing research questions.
- *Computational methods of data collection and data management*: The chapters support our understanding and application of such methods in the field.

1 Computational social science and the digitization of everyday life

Computational social science is an interdisciplinary field of study at the intersection of data science and social science that pursues causal and predictive inference as its main objective. With historical roots in mathematical modeling and social simulation, the recent digitization of all aspects of everyday life has turned CSS into a dynamically developing and rapidly growing research field. With the seamless integration of digital technology, from mobile phones to AI, into the rhythms of everyday life, there is also a greater generation and accumulation of related behavioral data of prime interest to the social sciences. Because most of these data are digital, CSS calls for computational methods of data collection, data management, data processing, and data analysis (Lazer et al., 2020). Computational social science is, thus, an evolving field with a mix of big-data, computational-methods, and data-science facets, as will be further detailed in this handbook (Engel, volume 1: chapter 9).

While it is true that computational methods are becoming increasingly relevant to the social sciences, it is equally true that the social sciences have participated in the development of a range of computational methods from the outset: some examples include statistical data analysis, social simulation, and mathematical modeling. For example, Coleman's (1964) seminal book *Introduction to Mathematical Sociology* constitutes one of the precursors of contemporary analytical sociology by explaining the unique challenges in attempting to quantify social behavior: "Because behavior is usually expressed in qualitative terms, any mathematical language which can serve for social science must in some fashion mirror this discrete, nonquantitative behavior" (p. 102). Also included in these early developments was Columbia University's Bureau of Applied Social Research (Barton, 1979) with its pioneering work on multivariate analysis, measurement, the analysis of change, and multilevel methodology. Additionally, we can also highlight the contributions to CSS made in the area of social simulation and its multilevel approach toward social complexity (Cioffi-Revilla, 2017). Hox (2017, p. 3) similarly identifies the social simulation branch as critical in the development of CSS as a unique field of study when reviewing "three important elements" of CSS, listing "big data, analytics, and simulation."

The very interdisciplinary nature of CSS and its diverse historical roots make this field difficult to define and delimit. While some scholars narrow the scope of CSS to "big data," harvested through computational methods from social media platforms – often referred to as digital trace data – this narrow approach is perhaps questionable (Cioffi-Revilla, volume 1: chapter 2; Lorenz, volume 1: chapter 10). "Big data" are not only available through social media data extraction; many other sources of "big data" are available, including location-based data collected via mobile phones, bank transaction data, e-health records, and e-commerce transactions. Another important point is that the development of artificial intelligence (AI) and its integration into daily life through robotics with smart speaker assistants (SSA) is another source of data for CSS. As SSAs like Google Home and Amazon Echo (Alexa) support a range of activities from e-commerce to information provision, they also generate increasing amounts of data (Brause & Blank, 2020). As our society advances toward sensor-rich computational environments in the future, smartphone, smart office, and smart city devices will also be primary data sources.

Another approach to delimiting the field of CSS is by looking at its relation to data science. Hox (2017, p. 3), for instance, regards CSS as an interdisciplinary field that combines mathematics, statistics, data science, and social science. In this view, data science is a central tool, among others, in CSS. Some proponents of data science go as far as to subsume CSS under data science, in which case it is regarded as a "new interdisciplinary field that synthesizes and builds on statistics, informatics, computing, communication, management, and sociology . . . to transform data to insights and decisions" (Cao, 2017, p. 43:8). In contrast, Kelleher and Tierney (2018) move away from any kind of taxonomy and instead stress the commonalities that exist between data science and CSS such as the focus on improving decision-making through a reliance on data. For Kelleher and Tierney, all these concepts are used in the literature interchangeably – data science, machine learning, and data mining – although data science can be broader in scope. While machine learning "focuses on the design and evaluation of algorithms for extracting patterns from data" and "data mining generally deals with the analysis of structured data," data science "also takes up other challenges, such as the capturing, cleaning, and transforming of unstructured social media and web data; the use of big-data technologies to store and process big, unstructured data sets; and questions related to data ethics and regulation" (Kelleher & Tierney, 2018, p. 1f.). Hence, these terms are often used interchangeably, and as our discussion shows, how they relate to each other remains a subject of debate.

If CSS is regarded as an emerging scientific field, this trend should be reflected in suitable indicator variables. Here, we look at the number of publications making explicit reference to CSS. This represents only one such indicator; a few others are covered in later chapters (see Engel & Dahlhaus, volume 1: chapter 20, Bosse et al., volume 2: chapter 4). Figure 1.1 draws a rough picture of the trends in CSS in recent years, as reflected in the *Web of Science* Core Collection for the period 2010 to 2020. The figure displays the results of three separate searches: the number of publications in response to a search for (1) "computational social science," (2) "data science" *in conjunction with* "computational social science," and (3) "agent-based modeling" (considering both spellings: modeling and modelling) in conjunction with "computational social science." It is noteworthy that a search for "data science" and "agent-based modeling" reveals considerably higher numbers *if each is used alone* as a search term. This simply indicates that both appear to also be of great importance far beyond the narrower field of CSS.

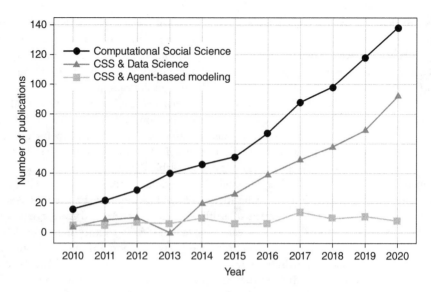

Figure 1.1 Computational social science, data science, and agent-based modeling

Figure 1.1 demonstrates an increasing interest in core CSS questions as well as in combination with data science. The lack of publications combining CSS and agent-based modeling is noteworthy, the latter taken as an example of a prominent approach in the simulation branch of CSS. Also of great importance is the advancement of research that combines agent-based modeling with empirical research (Lorenz, volume 1: chapter 10; Bosse, volume 2: chapter 13).

2 Balanced scope, modeling perspectives, and a basic multilevel orientation

We asked a group of notable scientists to delineate the scope and boundaries of CSS in relation to theory and methodology (see Table 1.1). First, *Claudio Cioffi-Revilla* outlines the scope of CSS (volume 1: chapter 2), which, for him, is understood as a field that integrates the study of humans and groups at all scales through the formal methodology of computational and mathematical models. The chapter aims to offer a balanced view of CSS, not slanted toward a version "driven by 'big data' from social media, and progress in algorithms from computer science, eschewing theory, mathematical models, and computational simulations."[1] Instead, Cioffi-Revilla specifies the scope of CSS as "theoretically and methodologically guided by theory, enriched by analytical models, and enabled by computer simulations; all three drawing on empirical data, be it big or small" (volume 1, chapter 2).

A key advantage of the interdisciplinary nature of CSS is its connections with theoretical terrains in multiple areas. Analytical sociology involves three defining characteristics: a basic multilevel orientation towards the modeling of social processes and a methodological realism which rejects "as-if" explanations and instead pursues a mechanism-based explanation of aggregate outcomes (Keuschnigg et al., 2018). Against this background, *Benjamin F. Jarvis, Marc Keuschnigg*, and *Peter Hedström* highlight and discuss the relationship between CSS and analytical sociology (volume 1: chapter 3). They "highlight the ways in which analytical sociologists are using CSS tools to further social research" using "agent-based modelling, large-scale online experiments, digital trace data, and natural language processing" to identify "how large-scale properties of social systems emerge from the complex interactions of networked actors at lower scales." The authors also discuss how computational social scientists can, conversely, take advantage of analytical sociology.

Table 1.1 Overview of topics covered in volume 1 "Theory, Case Studies, and Ethics"

Volume 1			
Scope		*Ethics/policy*	*Case studies*
Methodology & research		*Self-commitments*	*Subject areas*
Topics			
The balanced scope of CSS	Cognitive modeling	Open computational science	Face-to-face interaction
Analytical sociology	Agent-based modeling	Privacy	Affective science
Causal and predictive modeling	Survey landscape	Big data regulations	Political sentiment
Communication science	Digital trace data	Principled AI framework	Bots & social media
			Social robots
			Propaganda & extremism

Sociological explanations of aggregate outcomes assign an elementary role to the individual human agent (Coleman, 1990). Individuals act and interact and that way intentionally or inadvertently produce the phenomena we observe at the aggregate level. The behavior of agents represents accordingly an essential part of the micro-foundations of aggregate outcomes and, thus, should be understood properly. This is the starting point of the chapter on cognitive modeling (volume 1: chapter 4) in which *Holger Schultheis* presents computational cognitive modeling as an approach to a deeper understanding of the individuals involved in social processes.

A vital discussion concerns the issue of whether social science should be targeted at prediction or explanation (Hofman et al., 2017). Cautiously worded, practicing social science unguided by theory is presumed to be unimaginable to many social scientists. This places an emphasis on explanation. On the other hand, data science lays much stress on just the opposite pole, prediction. A balanced concept of CSS should accordingly strive for a solution to the explanation vs. prediction debate, too. As *Uwe Engel* sets out in his chapter on causal and predictive modeling (volume 1: chapter 9), one such solution is offered by taking advantage of CSS being a *computational* science which translates an abstract debate into precise models, with the inclusive choice of exploiting the complete causal–predictive modeling spectrum.

Social science may be conceived of as an umbrella term for disciplines such as sociology, political science, and communication science. *Stephanie Geise* and *Annie Waldherr* devote their chapter to an overview of one such subfield of CSS, computational communication science (CCS) (volume 1: chapter 5). Based on lessons from working group sessions with experts, the chapter addresses recent challenges of CCS while reflecting upon its future development and expansion.

3 Survey research

The textual and digital trace data collected in social media represent an undoubtedly extremely relevant source for social research. However, even though such data have gained considerable importance in recent years and even though CSS research uses social media as a major data source, it would be misleading to regard survey research as a field outside of CSS and decoupled from its dynamic development. The digitization of life has changed the opportunity structure *for both* research branches. To this can be added the observation that both are exposed to similar threats to data quality and the combined use of their data in integrated research designs. The handbook, thus, covers relevant survey aspects as well.

First, *Lars Lyberg* and *Steven G. Heeringa* draw a picture of a changing survey landscape (volume 1: chapter 6). They start with the "golden age of survey research" and continue by providing insight into the changes survey research underwent since that golden age. The exposition includes the "new data sources such as types of big data, administrative data, Paradata, and other process data," highlights the role of model-assisted surveys and survey-assisted models, and amongst others, draws attention to combinations of probability and non-probability sampling and the enrichment of traditional survey work by artificial intelligence and machine learning.

Other chapters take up the sampling topic as well. *Rebecca Andridge* and *Richard Valliant* (volume 2: chapter 11) set out the statistical foundations for inference from probability and non-probability samples. They review the fundamentals of probability sampling, describe two main approaches to inference for non-probability samples, and provide examples of non-probability samples that have worked and others that have failed. Second, *Jelke Bethlehem* centers on the challenges of online non-probability surveys (volume 2: chapter 12). He draws attention to the fact that the lack of proper sampling frames causes many surveys to be de facto self-selection surveys. In this connection, he also addresses the role of online panels if taken as sampling frames. The chapter compares online surveys recruited using random sampling with those based on self-selection. Some simulations and examples show the perils of non-probability-based online surveys. Third, *Camilla Zallot*, *Gabriele Paolacci*, *Jesse Chandler*, and *Itay Sisso* address crowd-sourced samples in observational and experimental research using Amazon Mechanical Turk (MTurk) as an example of "what has become the most popular sampling frame in the social sciences" (volume 2: chapter 10). The chapter asks how MTurk samples compare to traditional samples in survey and experimental research, highlights the ethical concerns involved, and asks what challenges researchers can expect to face on this platform.

4 Digital trace data

"Digital traces left by individuals when they act or interact online provide researchers with new opportunities for studying social and behavioral phenomena." *Florian Keusch* and *Frauke Kreuter* (volume 1: chapter 7) review digital trace data and the variety of technical systems such data comes from. The authors point to the fine-grained nature of such data and the virtue of enabling observations of individual and social behavior at high frequencies and in real time. The authors also draw attention to a feature similarly addressed in other chapters, in fact, a non-intrusive measurement in which "the data collection happens without the observed person having to self-report." While the original definition of digital trace data is limited to data that are found, that is, "data created as a by-product of activities not stemming from a designed research instrument," the authors argue "that digital traces can and should sometimes be collected in a designed way to afford researchers control over the data-generating process and to expand the range of research questions that can be answered with these data."

5 Data collection

Digital trace data come from a variety of technical systems. *Florian Keusch* and *Frauke Kreuter* (volume 1: chapter 7) provide a not-exhaustive list: business transaction systems, telecommunication networks, websites, social media platforms, smartphone apps, sensors built into wearable devices, and smart meters. Several chapters address accordingly related forms of data collection. *Stefan Bosse*, for instance, covers crowdsensing for large-scale agent-based simulation in his concept of fusing real and virtual worlds by "creating augmented virtuality by using mobile agents and agent-based simulation technologies" (volume 2: chapter 13). Social media data take center stage in chapters on data collection via application programming interfaces (APIs) and web mining. First, *Jakob Jünger* traces a brief history of APIs and discusses the opportunities and limitations of their use for online research (volume 2: chapter 2), while the subsequent chapter focuses more on a demonstration of how to access data practically using an API (volume 2: chapter 3). In this chapter, *Dominic Nyhuis* discusses the value of APIs for social research and provides an overview of basic techniques for accessing data from web interfaces. Then, *Stefan Bosse, Lena Dahlhaus*, and *Uwe Engel* draw attention to web data mining (volume 2: chapter 4). The chapter highlights the steps involved and threats to data quality, outlines how to extract content from web pages via an alternative method to the use of APIs, namely, web scraping, and addresses the legal implications of this method of data collection.

6 Data quality

Several chapters address the data-quality theme by some means or another, including the chapters referred to in the preceding three sections. Two prominent points of origin help in introducing the data quality topic in CSS: the well-known total survey error approach (Biemer & Lyberg, 2003) and the classic concept of unobtrusive measures (Webb et al., 2000). *Indira Sen, Fabian Flöck, Katrin Weller, Bernd Weiß,* and *Claudia Wagner* present their total error framework for digital traces of humans online (TED), an approach inspired by existing error frameworks in survey methodology, such as the total survey error framework (TSE) (volume 2: chapter 9).

A prominent argument assumes that improved data quality is already achievable by passive forms of data collection because "found" data replace error-prone self-reports on behavior by the unnoticed direct observation of this behavior itself. At first glance this argument appears convincing indeed: if people are not asked for a response at all, neither such a response nor any inadvertent survey-related side effect can occur. This, however, does not preclude the potency of other sources of social influence if opinions are expressed in public contexts where platform-specific terms of service, higher-ranking legal rules, and the potential fear of undesirable personal consequences may shape the way opinions in blogs and discussion lists are expressed. *Michael Adelmund* and *Uwe Engel* use the example of public opinion formation on the far right of the political spectrum to discuss this case (volume 1: chapter 22). Also, *Uwe Engel* and *Lena Dahlhaus* draw attention to a further factor that may impair the quality of digital trace data, the systematic protection against tracking on the internet (volume 1: chapter 20).

7 Open science

The direction of numerous science fields has been moving toward an open science paradigm. *Stephanie Geise* and *Annie Waldherr* (volume 1: chapter 5) describe how CSS researchers from multiple disciplines see both opportunities and challenges for open science practices. For example, "content and data sharing activities connected with 'best practice' exchange also are associated with additional ethical and legal challenges – including the acknowledgement of privacy requirements and terms of service, as well as an increased risk of data misuse by third parties." In the chapter "Open Computational Social Science" (volume 1: chapter 8), *Jan G. Voelkela* and *Jeremy Freesea* set out four principles of open science: open practices, open data, open

Table 1.2 Overview of topics covered in volume 2 "Data Science, Statistical Modeling, and Machine Learning Methods"

Volume 2			
Data collection, management, cleaning	Data quality	Statistical modeling & simulation	Machine learning
Topics			
History of APIs	Total error approach	Crowdsensing & data mining	ML methods for CSS
API use	Crowdsourced samples	Agent-based modeling	Principal component analysis
Web content mining	Inference from probability & non-probability surveys	Subgroup discovery and latent growth modeling	Clustering methods
Online learning for data streams	Challenges	Robust analysis of heterogeneous data	Topic modeling
Handling missing data in large databases			Contextualized word embeddings
Probabilistic record linkage			Automated video analysis

tools, and open access. These principles have direct relevance for the achievable data quality and validity of scientific inference because the replicability of results may depend strongly on the way these principles are implemented in research practice. The chapter provides theoretical definitions and concrete practical examples for each principle. It describes the main challenges of the implementation of the principles and the computational approaches to address these challenges. *Lars Lyberg and Steven G. Heeringa* (volume 1: chapter 6) provide a unique perspective on the open science movement when they discuss the changing landscape of the survey method. They point out that technological innovations, such as the internet and cloud computing, are "influencing not only how significant amounts of survey data are being collected but also the standards and expectations for the transparency, access and usability of survey products." Also, as to the "tools and norms required to formalize transparent, replicable research," especially in "the context of team-based collaborative research," *John McLevey, Pierson Browne, and Tyler Crick* (volume 2: chapter 8) introduce a principled-data-processing framework (Table 1.2).

8 Privacy, ethics, and policy

Ethical considerations are a key part of any research project, and CSS projects have unique challenges when it comes to ethics. First, the many ethical considerations that need to be taken into account are only now becoming more apparent. As these projects are complex, ethics are also complex. Ethical guidelines for conducting survey research and experimental studies are well established and well known, yet guidelines linked to CSS projects are still in their infancy and only slowly emerging. There are, for example, large discrepancies in ethical expectations across disciplines, institutions, and private vs. academic environments. Three chapters in volume 1 highlight central ethical debates and suggest approaches to better integrate data stewardship in ways that are equitable and just.

The chapter by *William Hollingshead, Anabel Quan-Haase,* and *Wenhong Chen* (volume 1: chapter 11) focuses on four major challenges that CSS scholars confront concerning ethical questions and dilemmas: (1) data representativeness, (2) aggregation and disaggregation, (3) research data archiving, and (4) data linkage. One topic the authors highlight is the impact of data representativeness because it is not well understood to what extent the social media user base of any given platform reflects a nationally representative sample or what biases may be present. Drawing on case studies of exemplary research, the authors provide a roadmap for CSS to address these issues. They conclude that what is needed is a commitment to pedagogy, to teaching the principles of ethics in computational social science projects.

To explore ethical dimensions in CSS scholarship further, *James Popham, Jennifer Lavoie, Andrea Corradi,* and *Nicole Coomber* (volume 1: chapter 12) examine the challenges involved in using big data technologies to provide valuable insights for and ultimately inform decision-making in municipalities, based on a case study of public engagement through a symposium Big Data in Cities: Barriers and Benefits, which was held in May of 2017 in Ontario, Canada. From the insights gained from the public engagement, they propose a set of best practices on how to address privacy and ethics, data-sharing protocols, the motives for using data, and how they are used.

Chapter 13 by *Daniel Varona* and *Juan Luis Suárez* looks critically at the use of artificial intelligence, and specifically machine learning, in decision-making processes. Through a detailed analysis of existing guidelines for the use of artificial intelligence, the authors propose a regulatory framework that follows the merits of "principled artificial intelligence" to move toward design-based trustworthy AI. Through their analysis, they identify potential barriers that could prevent the framework from becoming a methodological reference during the AI project life-cycle, such as references to passive skills. The authors also highlight the digital gap that exists between developed and developing countries in creating trustworthy AI.

9 Research examples and case studies

A significant advantage of CSS research is its interdisciplinarity. Computational social science can borrow theories, methodologies, and data from multiple disciplines, especially the disciplines that rarely talked to each other beforehand. This interdisciplinary advantage can bring challenges. Grasping a fitting theory, an appropriate computational approach, and an available data set that best answer a research question is tough, especially for new CSS researchers. Several chapters provide concrete examples to explore this process.

Social media is a popular data source in CSS studies, especially in the fields of psychology, political science, and communication. *Max Pellert, Simon Schweighofer,* and *David Garcia* (volume 1: chapter 15) focus on emotional dynamics and summarize methods to collect, classify, quantify, and analyze social media data to trace and measure emotion dynamics, collective emotions, and affective expression in various social and cultural contexts. The chapter presents theoretical thinking on the role, meaning, and functionality of affective expression in social media and practical examples and case studies from previous studies.

Several case studies focus on the applications of CSS in political domains. *Séraphin Alava* and *Rasha Nagem* (volume 1: chapter 21) present a detailed roadmap, method descriptions, and a modeling toolkit for detecting ISIS extremist discourse online. A few chapters focus on Twitter data. Developments in data mining and machine learning have advanced the approaches we take to use the data to understand and even predict human behavior and important outcomes, such as the state of a pandemic or an outcome of an election. *Niklas M. Loynes* and *Mark J. Elliot* (volume 1: chapter 16) attend to a forecasting aspect of Twitter-based public opinion research.

They showcase how sentiment analysis was use to predict the US 2016 Democratic presidential primary elections in New Hampshire, South Carolina, and Massachusetts. *Ho-Chun Herbert Chang, Emily Chen, Meiqing Zhang, Goran Muric,* and *Emilio Ferrara* (volume 1: chapter 18) summarize recent studies using Twitter data on the COVID-19 pandemic and the 2020 US presidential election. The chapter provides a nuanced analysis of the impact of bots on the manipulation of the issues and describes how a health issue can be confounded with political agendas to distort the public sphere. In the chapter, the authors further provide reflections on a sensible balance between advancing social theory and concrete, timely reporting of ongoing events, which has been the subject of a debate in the CSS community. *Yimin Chen* (volume 1: chapter 17) also focuses on bots, but his discussion of trolls and bots is oriented from a broad cultural and historical perspective. The chapter argues, "trolls and bots are products of internet culture, but internet culture is shaped by our broader societal cultures. A kinder, gentler internet can only be achieved through striving for a kinder, gentler society."

Sensing technology and machine learning represent key links to both data analytics and human-robot interaction. The Royal Society (2017) locates machine learning at the intersection of artificial intelligence, data science, and statistics, with applications in robotics. Machine learning in society is a topic of central relevance to CSS because it changes both the object and methods of social science. *Johann Schaible, Marcos Oliveira, Maria Zens,* and *Mathieu Génois* (volume 1: chapter 14) provide a review on how to use sensors to study face-to-face interaction and how to align proxies from sensing data with social interaction constructs. The chapter lays out the steps for using sensors to study human interactions: from operationalization of the face-to-face interaction concept, to link the concept with a physical entity that can be detected by sensors, to choose the useful sensors to measure the concept, and finally to work out strategies to resolve the issues related to the collection and quality of the data. *Uwe Engel* and *Lena Dahlhaus* (volume 1: chapter 20) set out various theoretical and methodological thinking about data quality and privacy concerns of digital tracing data. The chapter offers empirical findings from a Delphi survey and a population survey in the context of human-robot interactions to further explore the intricate balance between data analytics and human-robot interaction. *Sunny Xun Liu, Elizabeth Arredondo, Hannah Miezkowski, Jeff Hancock,* and *Byron Reeves* (volume 1: chapter 19) present an experimental design study to investigate the effects of social robot characteristics (warm vs. competent) and design features (physical appearance, narratives describing these characteristics, and combinations of appearance and characteristic narratives) on people's perceptions of warmth, competence, job suitability, and overall first-impression evaluations of social robots.

10 Machine learning methods and statistical and computational advancements

A first point of reference is the popular "big data" concept because it defines the characteristic features data may possess. Often, big data are described in terms of the four Vs of big data: volume (scale of data), velocity (analysis of streaming data), variety (different forms of data), and veracity (uncertainty of data) (IBM, 2012). To this original list, two additional Vs have been added: virtue (ethics) and value (knowledge gain) (Quan-Haase & Sloan, 2017). All these *V*s make great demands on data collection and statistical analysis. *Volume* matters because large data sets can make analysis more complicated. Accordingly, *Martin Spiess* and *Thomas Augustin* cover in their chapter one such complicating factor, the handling of missing data in large databases (volume 2: chapter 6). Then, the collection and analysis of streaming data may require special computational tools. Referring to this, *Lianne Ippel, Maurits Kaptein,* and *Jeroen K. Vermunt* present *online learning* as an analysis method that updates parameter estimates instead of re-estimating them to analyze large or streaming data (volume 2: chapter 5).

In CSS, *variety* is a challenge through the simultaneous use of quite different kinds of data, such as the user-generated content in social media and the digital marks people leave when surfing the web. Such textual and digital trace data complement survey data and make great demands on their separate and combined analysis. In any case, the combination of information from multiple data sources represents a challenge. *Ted Enamorado* discusses in his chapter on probabilistic record linkage in R how "new computational algorithms have reduced the computational resources and time needed to merge large data sets" and illustrates "the power of these new algorithms through a guided example using the open-source R package fastLink" (volume 2: chapter 7).

Finally, *veracity* refers to the whole spectrum of data-quality criteria as known in social science methodology. Statistical advancements in this regard involve, for instance, the sampling topic as covered in the chapter on inference from probability and non-probability samples already referred to earlier by *Rebecca Andridge* and *Richard Valliant* (volume 2: chapter 11).

Statistical modeling is taken as a second point of reference to statistical and computational advancements. A first strand refers to the conjunction of simulation and empirical data. *Jan Lorenz* discusses in his chapter how agent-based modeling can be driven by data (volume 1: chapter 10). He views the "strength of agent-based modeling" in the "quantitative causal understanding of emergence through complex nonlinear dynamics on the macro-level" and raises the query of validation with empirical data. He points out, "agent-based models are to explain real-world phenomena, and thus a useful model should have a reflection in empirical data and the other way round." In a similar vein, *Stefan Bosse* seeks the conjunction of agent-based modeling and crowd sensing in his exposition of multi-agent systems (volume 2: chapter 13). Also, *Fernando Sancho-Caparrini* and *Juan Luis Suárez* (volume 2: chapter 14) present a model based on cultural agents, "that is, human-like agents whose main framework of interactions is defined by its belonging to cultural networks."

Advanced statistical modeling in the presence of heterogeneity is the third point of reference taken in the present context. First, *Axel Mayer, Christoph Kiefer, Benedikt Langenberg*, and *Florian Lemmerich* integrate methods of growth curve modeling and state-of-the-art pattern mining techniques to identify unusual developmental trajectories (volume 2: chapter 15). Then, *Nazanin Alipourfard, Keith Burghardt*, and *Kristina Lerman* (volume 2: chapter 16) cover disaggregation via Gaussian regression for heterogeneous data. They propose a method "that discovers latent confounders by simultaneously partitioning the data into overlapping clusters (disaggregation) and modeling the behavior within them (regression)."

Machine learning methods represent an extremely significant point of reference for statistical and computational advancements. *Richard D. De Veaux* and *Adam Eck* give a systematic and detailed overview of this field of advanced methods (volume 2: chapter 17). In their chapter, they "introduce two fundamental problems in supervised machine learning – classification and regression" and explain the supervised machine learning process. The authors "also describe and contrast several fundamental types of supervised machine learning models" and "conclude by highlighting the strengths of both the various approaches and popular software resources for utilizing and applying these valuable tools." Following this exposition of supervised methods, two chapters cover the most important unsupervised methods of machine learning. First, *Andreas Pöge* and *Jost Reinecke* (volume 2: chapter 18) introduce principal component analysis (PCA) as belonging to a group of statistical procedures "that are used to reduce the complexity of a given set of variables." The authors offer a brief overview of the basic concepts, history, and statistical fundamentals of the original PCA, compare PCA with factor analysis, and list some software programs and packages that offer PCA. Then, *Johann Bacher, Andreas Pöge*, and *Knut Wenzig* (volume 2: chapter 19) provide an overview of clustering methods. The chapter covers topics such as the steps toward an appropriate cluster solution, clustering methods, criteria to determine the number of clusters, methods to validate cluster solutions, and relevant computer programs.

Textual data represent a data source of great and growing importance for the social sciences. Such data make high demands on data analysis. *Raphael H. Heiberger* and *Sebastian Munoz-Najar Galvez* (volume 2: chapter 20) deal with text mining and a popular tool therein – topic modeling. They point out, "topic models are a popular tool to reduce texts' complexity and find meaningful themes in large corpora." The chapter addresses the methodological challenges the method is faced with, particularly the selection of an appropriate number of topics and its relation to preprocessing decisions. Then, *Gregor Wiedemann* and *Cornelia Fedtke* (volume 2: chapter 21) address the research interests that "go beyond topics that are limited to broad discourse-level semantics." They refer to the "interest that arguments, stances, frames, or discourse positions are expressed in what specific contexts and how they emerged in the first place." In their chapter, they "elaborate on how basic text mining and new neural network-based embedding technologies such as BERT relate to linguistic structuralism as the theoretical and methodological foundation of discourse analysis and many other qualitative research methods."

Video data represent another resource of great importance for the social sciences. *Dominic Nyhuis, Tobias Ringwald, Oliver Rittmann, Thomas Gschwend*, and *Rainer Stiefelhagen* (volume 2: chapter 22) cover automated video analysis for social science research. They provide an overview of technical solutions for common classification scenarios in video data, discuss current studies and "a sample application on video footage from a German state-level parliament in greater detail," and close "with a discussion of potentials and challenges for automated video analysis in social science research."

11 Conclusions

This introductory chapter provides an overview of some of the cutting-edge and innovative work occurring in CSS across disciplines and geographic boundaries. The handbook makes numerous contributions to consolidating CSS while also moving it into new directions. First, the handbook brings together current understandings of what CSS is and the opportunities it provides to scholars and policymakers. The handbook also showcases novel approaches as they are being developed and tested. State-of-the-art machine learning tools and models have been applied to tackle critical social, political, and health issues, such as misinformation, extremist propaganda, and COVID-19. Computational social science has been applied to study interpersonal interactions, human-robot interaction, and various human-AI communications. The handbook also creates awareness around challenges that CSS confronts moving forward. Computational social science projects cannot be neatly aligned within a single discipline and often require multidisciplinary teams. This multidisciplinary model does not always conveniently align with institutional expectations and resources (Lazer et al., 2020) and, thus, calls for a rethinking of how academic institutions, funding agencies, and tenure and promotion guidelines work. Another challenge of CSS projects is the role of ethics. Where do data originate? How can we guarantee individuals' data self-determination? The handbook starts an important debate around how to best implement ethics best practices, but it also shows the need for more work to identify critical questions and develop robust guidelines.

In our aim to be comprehensive, we brought together more than 90 experts from over 40 institutions in North America, Europe, and the Middle East. Certainly, there is the opportunity for future projects in CSS to expand the geographic reach and diversity of topics. Furthermore, gender representation in CSS is critical. We call for further analysis of how the interdisciplinary nature of CSS can contribute to greater gender equity in the selection of collaborators and thereby have a lasting effect on the technical fields, in a way that impacts *what* is studied and *how*.

Note

1 Quotations refer to the respective chapter abstracts.

References

Barton, A. (1979). Paul Lazarsfeld and applied social research: Invention of the university applied social research institute. *Social Science History*, *3*(3/4), 4–44. https://doi:10.2307/1170954

Biemer, P. B., & Lyberg, L. E. (2003). *Introduction to survey quality*. Wiley.

Brause, S. R., & Blank, G. (2020). Externalized domestication: Smart speaker assistants, networks and domestication theory. *Information, Communication & Society*, *23*(5), 751–763.

Cao, L. (2017). Data science: A comprehensive overview. *ACM Computing Surveys*, *50*(3), 43.1–43.42. https://doi.org/10.1145/3076253

Chinese Sociological Review. Call for papers on "computational social science". https://think.taylorandfrancis.com/special_issues/computational-social-science/

Cioffi-Revilla, C. (2017). *Introduction to computational social science: Principles and applications* (2nd ed.). Springer.

Coleman, J. S. (1964). *Introduction to mathematical sociology*. The Free Press of Glencoe.

Coleman, J. S. (1990). *Foundations of social theory*. Belknap Press of Harvard University Press.

Crane, D. (1972). *Invisible colleges: Diffusion of knowledge in scientific communities*. The University of Chicago Press.

Hofman, J. M., Sharma, A., & Watts, D. J. (2017). Prediction and explanation in social systems. *Science*, *355*(6324), 486–488. https://doi.org/10.1126/science.aal3856

Hox, J. J. (2017). Computational social science methodology, anyone? *Methodology*, *13*, 3–12. https://doi.org/10.1027/1614-2241/a000127

IBM Big Data & Analytics Hub. (2012). *The four V's of big data*. Retrieved December 30, 2020, from www.ibmbigdatahub.com/infographic/four-vs-big-data

Kelleher, J. D., & Tierney, B. (2018). *Data science*. MIT Press.

Keuschnigg, M., Lovsjö, N., & Hedström, P. (2018). Analytical sociology and computational social science. *Journal of Computational Social Science*, *1*, 3–14. https://doi.org/10.1007/s42001-017-0006-5

Lazer, D. M. J., Pentland, A., Watts, D. J., Aral, S., Athey, S., Contractor, N., . . . Wagner, C. (2020). Computational social science: Obstacles and opportunities. *Science*, *369*(6507), 1060–1062. https://doi.org/10.1126/science.aaz8170

Quan-Haase, A., & Sloan, L. (2017). Introduction to the handbook of social media research methods: Goals, challenges and innovations. In L. Sloan & A. Quan-Haase (Eds.), *The Sage handbook of social media research methods* (pp. 1–9). Sage.

The Royal Society. (2017). *Machine learning: The power and promise of computers that learn by example*. https://royalsociety.org/~/media/policy/projects/machine-learning/publications/machine-learning-report.pdf

Webb, E. J., Campbell, D. T., Schwartz, R. D., & Sechrest, L. (2000). *Unobtrusive measures*. Sage.

SECTION I

Data in CSS

Collection, management, and cleaning

2
A BRIEF HISTORY OF APIS
Limitations and opportunities for online research

Jakob Jünger

1 Introduction

Online platforms such as Facebook, YouTube and Twitter offer a wide range of data for scientific research. Since many of the social media providers have set up application programming interfaces (APIs), extensive volumes of data can be collected automatically (Jünger, 2018; Keyling & Jünger, 2016). Social media data are attractive, *inter alia*, because they not only include already available communication, such as that from public media, but they also make organisational and interpersonal communication visible (Ledford, 2020). In addition, these data are process-generated (Baur, 2011, p. 1234), meaning that they are generated independently of scientific research and thus promise an authentic insight into human behaviour.[1] A wide range of studies in the social sciences exploit APIs for data collection and analysis. Thus, the establishment and development of APIs has significant implications for science.

This chapter starts by tracing the development of APIs, with a focus on the relationship of YouTube, Facebook and Twitter to science. Based on an extensive review of press releases, change logs and API references, three periods are distinguished. During the first period, of construction, the platforms established their APIs. An ecosystem of mashups, clients and organisations then evolved. In the following period, of conquest, the providers worked on securing their influence by strategic acquisitions and by placing restrictions on their APIs. For example, Twitter bought Tweetie and restricted the development of third-party clients by changing the terms of its services and API. In the third period, of concern, the political dimension of the APIs became apparent. For example, the events around the U.S. election in 2016 were reflected in changes in APIs and policies.

Comparing different services and historical epochs reveals both the variable and the constant principles of the APIs. Available endpoints, necessary skills and, not least, the regulation of the providers all play decisive roles in determining who can do what kind of research. This poses the threat of a divide between the data-haves and the data-have-nots (boyd & Crawford, 2012; Bruns, 2013). In the second part of the chapter, the different shapes of the APIs are evaluated from a social science perspective. Looking at APIs in relation to scientific demands reveals the factors that have to be considered when doing API-based research.

DOI: 10.4324/9781003025245-3

2 Tracing the development of APIs

An application programming interface works like a plug and a socket. For example, the USB specification defines the dimensions of the plugs and sockets, thus every plug should fit into a socket, whether it is a computer mouse, a storage stick or a fan for hot days. An API is the software counterpart of a hardware interface, and it defines how two software components will interoperate (Jacobson et al., 2012, p. 5). Many different functions of the computer system can be exposed by an API. On one hand, the *API provider* allows access to resources such as showing pictures on a monitor (output), the geolocated position of a device (input) or data on a hard drive (throughput). On the other hand, an *API consumer* uses these resources to create an application such as a computer game, an online map or a search machine. With regard to the collection and analysis of scientific data, web-based APIs are increasingly important. Here, the different parties are distributed over a network and communicate using the Hypertext Transfer Protocol (HTTP). These APIs implement the principles of representational state transfer (REST). Entities can be accessed by name (URLs), and data can be represented in different formats such as HTML, XML or JSON (Fielding, 2000). Typical actions include fetching and posting content, and these actions are called verbs or methods. Furthermore, cloud computing services, for example Amazon Web Services, provide data storage, machine learning capabilities and much more via web-based APIs. In a broad sense, every website server provides some sort of programming interface that is consumed by web browsers to display web pages. Furthermore, APIs can be implemented on network protocols other than HTTP, such as the WebSocket protocol, which allows faster bidirectional asynchronous transmission (Internet Engineering Task Force [IETF], 2011) or protocols for specific tasks such as MTProto, as used in the Telegram Messenger (Telegram, 2020).

Application programming interfaces are not only a type of software, but they constitute a contract between provider and consumer (Jacobson et al., 2012, p. 4). The contract assures the consumer that the interface will always work in the same way. In contrast to a standard web page, the core functionality of an API is relatively stable, and the data is structured. On this basis, it is reasonable to build software or hardware on an infrastructure provided by third parties. In consequence, an ecosystem may emerge around the central API provider. Social media providers introduced their APIs quite early, and Facebook, YouTube and Twitter, three of the most influential players, are the focus of this chapter. While not primarily developed for scientific research, their APIs, to some extent, allow access to the content and usage data on their platforms.

Thus, documentation of these interfaces is crucial for third-party developers. At the same time, the documentation and related policies give insights into the organising principles and are the basis for the historical reconstruction given in the following section. Media reporting, API references, platform and developer policies, press releases, weblogs and scientific literature are systematically analysed and accompanied by field research, that is, by testing the APIs. The internet archive was used to access API references from the earlier years (see Jünger, 2022, in press, for methodological details).

3 Three periods of API evolution

Software development is an ongoing process and not easily sliced into historical periods. With regard to APIs, the version numbers assigned by the operators can provide an initial orientation as they reflect changes in the technical infrastructure. Nevertheless, from a social science perspective, political and organisational changes are more important, and aiming at an overview

Table 2.1 Main issues in the evolution of APIs

Phase	Key issues
~2005: Period of Construction	Web 2.0
Main perspective: technology	Linking processes
	Authorisation services
	Data access
~2010: Period of Conquest	Acquisitions
Main perspective: economy	Competition
	Standardisation
	Access restrictions
~2015: Period of Concern	Intermediation
Main perspective: politics	Regulation
	Partnerships

of the different APIs and the consequences for research, the analysis needs to abstract from the many small steps of development. When looking at extensions and restrictions over the course of time, roughly three periods can be distinguished (see Table 2.1). The three providers were all founded around the year 2005, acquiring businesses and building their APIs to allow them to link into the diverse landscape of online services. Moving five years forward, to around 2010, more and more restrictions were introduced as the APIs matured. These restrictions controlled how third-party organisations could interact and profit from Facebook, YouTube and Google. While the providers opened their business in the first period, later they seemed to focus on conquering the ecosystem that had evolved around their APIs. In the third period, beginning around 2015, political issues increasingly arose, most prominently the role of the platforms and their APIs in the U.S. election. Thus, in addition to technological changes, the main issues changed as well. The three periods described as construction, conquest and concern, with their main issues, are briefly summarised in the following sections. What we will see is how organisations, technology and data became deeply intertwined with human communication behaviour and society. The interactivity of users, providers and platforms challenges the sciences (Marres, 2017, p. 33) and is reflected in the later development of the APIs. Therefore, the timeline in Table 2.1 will serve as the basis for distilling the principles that affect research.

3.1 Construction: linking technical processes (~2005)

The first APIs are said to have originated in the year 2000 from eBay and Salesforce (Lane, 2016). While eBay provided access to its marketplace (eBay, 2000), Salesforce sold what today is called cloud computing. Their API provided customer relationship management as a software service (Salesforce, 2000). Thus, from the beginning, APIs were related to commercial business operations. Some years later, at the end of September 2005, O'Reilly's article "What Is Web 2.0" elicited an echo that continues to this day. One of the key concepts associated with the term Web 2.0 is web services that allow for data-driven development and the mixing of applications (O'Reilly, 2005). An essential component of Web 2.0 mashups was Google Maps, which had been reverse-engineered by different users to integrate it into their own pages. Later, an official API was introduced by Google (Google, 2005).

Three key players entered the field at that time in relation to user-generated content, another component of Web 2.0. These were Facebook (2004), YouTube (2005) and Twitter (2006).

YouTube was the first of the three to publish an API. Only six months after their foundation, an XML-based API was made accessible. Two years later, after Google had acquired YouTube, the API was migrated to the JSON-based Google Data API in 2007. This version lasted for about five years. In the meantime, several functions were added to the API, for example an upload function (2008) and analytics (2012).

Two and a half years after its foundation, Facebook followed in 2006 with the Facebook API, Version 1.0. In the early years, they invested heavily in functionality and laid the cornerstones for their API. Access to the user feed (streams) and analytics allowed page providers to gain insights into their users' behaviour. An SQL-style language, the Facebook Query Language (2007), was established in addition to fixed endpoints. Facebook even published its source code, "initiating an industry-wide practice of controlled openness" (Bodle, 2011, p. 329).[2] In contrast to the other services, Facebook promoted integration in two ways. On the one hand, third parties could now integrate their applications into the Facebook website; on the other hand, Facebook services could be integrated into external applications. Furthermore, Facebook was gaining ground as an identity provider. Facebook Connect (2008) allowed users to log into third-party services with their Facebook account. While promoted as a comfort tool, at the same time Facebook acquired usage data about a broad variety of websites. These API-based technologies deeply embedded Facebook into the infrastructure of website providers.

Twitter also released an API only six months after the first tweet was posted. The API remained stable over a period of four years, and in fact, the API seemed to drive the development of Twitter from the beginning. Many third-party vendors built on this API, such as Summize, a search engine for product reviews. Summize would soon be acquired by Twitter and, as a result, a search API was added in 2008.

During this early phase, linking services through APIs was established as a basic principle of the web. While the hyperlink, as a core technology of the web, connects static resources, described by metaphors of space (Rogers, 2013, p. 46), APIs linked dynamic processes and flows of information. During this time, the companies became increasingly important for the internet economy (Doerrfeld et al., 2016), and the commercialisation of internet technology began to take place.[3]

3.2 Conquest: conquering the ecosystem (~2010)

After an ecosystem had emerged around the APIs, the providers reclaimed control. In 2011, Twitter had more than 750,000 registered third-party apps (Sarver, 2011). Instead of developing apps of their own, Twitter acquired some of the most popular clients. This included Tweetie, an unofficial app for using Twitter on iPhones (2010), and the social media dashboard application TweetDeck (2011). Moreover, the social media aggregation service Gnip was acquired (2014). At the same time, the opportunities for third-party clients were limited by the terms of the services and some changes in the architecture: "We've already begun to more thoroughly enforce our Developer Rules of the Road with partners, for example with branding, and in the coming weeks, we will be introducing stricter guidelines around how the Twitter API is used" (Sippey, 2012). The first version of the API was shut down in early 2013 after the possible impact had been evaluated with blackout tests (Twitter, 2013).

Three types of access restriction were implemented, step by step. First, with open authorisation, a new mechanism for logging into the API was introduced (#oauthcalypse). All requests now needed to be authorised, which broke with the former policy of more open access (Twitter, 2010). Second, third-party apps on mobile and entertainment devices, as well as apps with more than 100,000 users, needed to go through app reviews before they could go into production mode (Twitter, 2012). This effectively prevented the development of new clients without the collaboration of Twitter. Third, rate limits were imposed on all endpoints. Only fixed amounts of data could be requested based on sliding time frames (Twitter, 2012). Access, therefore, became more complicated, causing some negative reactions from the ecosystem. Twitter was laying the foundation for their API, essentially as it continues to exist today.

At Facebook, the API was also being transformed into the form that it still has today. Some changes related to apps integrated into the Facebook website, in particular, Facebook Markup Language (FBML) was replaced with iframes. As with Twitter, the access rules were also worked out. From 2011 on, all requests had to go through open authorisation, and (presumably automated) app reviews were introduced. Nevertheless, one year later, the number of apps was over nine million (Facebook, 2012). With the introduction of the Graph API 2.0 in 2014, which was even before the first wave of the Cambridge Analytica scandal, Facebook introduced changes that limited access of third-party apps to friends who had the same app installed (Facebook, 2014, 2020). YouTube's situation was similar: the third version of the YouTube Data API, introduced in 2012, stipulated that all requests had to be authenticated with OAuth2. The older access methods, based on developer keys only, continued to exist in parallel until 2015 (YouTube, 2013). Eventually, older devices from third-party vendors such as Panasonic's smart TVs no longer worked (Golem, 2015). Furthermore, around this time, Google blocked a YouTube app developed by Microsoft. Microsoft had developed the app because there were no apps for Windows Phones, only for Android and iOS (Golem, 2013).

In parallel, another issue related to securing influence arose: standardisation. Already in 2007, Google had launched the provider-independent interface specification OpenSocial (Kraus, 2007). Over the years, several social networking organisations joined, among them LinkedIn, MySpace, the Google-owned Orkut, the German networking site StudiVZ and Xing. The project was later continued by the World Wide Web Consortium (W3C) (Jacobs, 2014), and in 2017, the W3C recommendation, Activity Streams 2.0, was published (W3C, 2017). Another initiative was launched by Mozilla in 2012. Their Social API was intended to provide a better integration of social web applications into browsers (Mozilla, 2019). Facebook joined and provided an extension for Firefox. One of the goals was to reduce the number of share buttons on websites.

Nevertheless, few of the providers built on the concepts of standardisation, and little is heard about these projects now. Furthermore, depending on who sets the standard, the dominant platforms can become even more dominant:

> Yet, this interoperability comes at a price as a handful of dominant SNSs utilise Open APIs and a growing number of social applications to solicit, collect, and open up user data for advertisers and data brokers that have much to gain from users' valuable data.
>
> (Bodle, 2011, p. 321)

For example, Facebook took a 30% slice off payments made through apps on its platform (Glaser, 2018). Thus, standardisation activities cannot hide the fact that suppliers are engaged in aggressive competition. For example, in 2012, Twitter blocked API access to images hosted by the Facebook-owned Instagram (Hernandez, 2012). In response, Instagram prevented the display of their images on the Twitter feed (Twitter, 2012). YouTube focused on a fight in the field of copyrights and took action, for example, against the MP3 conversion services (Zota, 2012). Common to all providers was the establishment of stronger access mechanisms and competition to play a dominant role in the internet economy. Providing APIs pays off when the apps built on the APIs create users, attention and revenue.

3.3 Concern: the political dimension of technology (~2015)

The increasing economic influence of technology brought political consequences. Especially in recent years, it has become apparent that internet companies do not simply provide technology but are deeply embedded in societal contexts. Discussions regarding the rights and obligations relating to dealing with data are particularly controversial. On the one hand, actors outside the companies claim access for socio-political reasons. For example, Politwoops permanently monitors Twitter and archives the deleted tweets of politicians. Politwoops is run by the Open State Foundation in 30 countries. In 2015, Twitter stopped access to their API, stating, "Preserving deleted Tweets violates our developer agreement. Honoring the expectation of user privacy for all accounts is a priority for us, whether the user is anonymous or a member of Congress" (Twitter, 2015, cited from Trotter, 2015). The decision was subsequently heavily criticised by human rights organisations and internet activists (e.g. Accessnow, 2015). Eventually, Twitter reopened the access. In an opposing case, another nongovernmental organisation (NGO) enforced the blocking of data access for the third-party provider, GeoFeedia. According to the American Civil Liberties Union, GeoFeedia had offered U.S. authorities a product for monitoring protests that was based on geodata from Twitter. In consequence, data access was revoked not only by Twitter but also by Facebook and Instagram (Cagle, 2016).

These two cases demonstrate how the platforms have evolved from service providers to information intermediaries (Newman & Fletcher, 2018). Their role as intermediaries is intensively discussed in relation to the U.S. elections, the two anchor points being the data analytics firm Cambridge Analytica (CA) and the Russian company, Internet Research Agency (IRA). The first critical reports on Cambridge Analytica appeared in the *Guardian* on 1.12.2015. However, the wave did not really start rolling until over two years later when the *New York Times* and the *Guardian* took up the matter again (Cadwalladr & Graham-Harrison, 2018; Dachwitz et al., 2018; Rosenberg et al., 2018). Facebook was primarily affected by this. Aleksandr Kogan, an assistant professor of psychology in Cambridge, had collected data under the auspices of scientific purposes. Users had participated voluntarily in a personality quiz; however, the data was passed on to Cambridge Analytica. The psychometric services of Cambridge Analytica were then used by Steve Bannon in the Trump election campaign to target voters. Later, Facebook referred to the fact that, according to the terms of its service, such a transmission was not allowed. Nevertheless, against a backdrop of common practices and rules, an API was used, in the way APIs are used, to connect different businesses. Until recent years, the architecture of Facebook was explicitly designed for the integration of different services. For example, browser games such as Cow Clicker were directly embedded in the user interface but were served from third-party servers. For these games and apps to operate, some access to user data was crucial for authorisation (Bogost, 2018).

Furthermore, Google, Facebook and Twitter came under pressure because they did not stop the potential influence of the Russian Internet Research Agency in the 2016 U.S. election (Dawson & Innes, 2019). That company, also known as the "Trolls from Olgino", created polarising fake comments and booked political advertisements on the platforms. Although real people were acting here, the issue of bot communication gained popularity in the news. Thus, in the context of the IRA and CA, the role of APIs in data analysis became contested. In consequence, the organisation of the APIs was changed quite drastically (Reselman, 2018). While app reviews were not new at that time, they became obligatory for all developers on the platforms. Policies were revised and, for example, the scope of data access was restricted around 2018. These changes were intensively discussed in the social sciences under the terms "post-API age" (Freelon, 2018) and "APIcalypse" (Bruns, 2019). Indeed, independent research is becoming harder as researchers also need to go through app review when accessing platform data (Bruns, 2018, 2019; Venturini & Rogers, 2019). While the dependencies increased, the companies also started explicit cooperations with science, for example with the Social Science One initiative (Puschman, 2019; Social Science One, 2020).

4 Consequences for science

The establishment and development of APIs is not without consequences for science. Platform providers are data intermediaries who base their business models on the datafication of user behaviour (Dorfer, 2016; Cukier & Mayer-Schoenberger, 2013). Therefore, organisations like Facebook, Twitter and Google are embedded in an ecology of actors, expectations and discourse. Such "ecologies of communication" have been analysed from the perspectives of media logic (Altheide, 2013; van Dijck & Poell, 2013; Klinger & Svensson, 2014), mediatisation (Couldry & Hepp, 2013) and mediation (Livingstone, 2009). One of the basic assumptions of media ecology is that technology frames the behaviour of actors and thus formats the resulting communication artefacts (Altheide, 1994, p. 670). These artefacts, in turn, influence the following activities, for example when users comment on other users' comments, using the means provided by the platform. This results in a circular process in which users and platform operators work on the co-production of data (Vis, 2013). Scientists can be seen as a special kind of user, analysing data that is mediated by the platforms (Figure 2.1). Therefore, APIs are not neutral research instruments but rather what Marres and Gerlitz call interface-methods: "methods that we – as social and cultural researchers – can't exactly call our own, but which resonate sufficiently with our interests and familiar approaches to offer a productive site of empirical engagement with wider research contexts, practices, and apparatuses" (Marres & Gerlitz, 2016, p. 27). The following section builds on these concepts with a focus on the ecology of data. Analysing the mediating mechanisms reveals how user and platform behaviours are intertwined and also the conditions of scientific knowledge production.

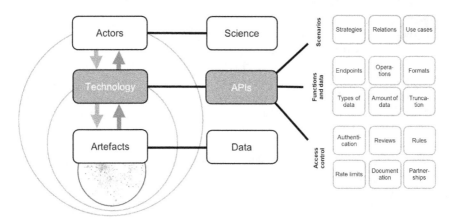

Figure 2.1   The ecology of data and the shapes of APIs

By comparing the development of APIs over the course of time and between platforms, 15 organising principles describing the APIs were inductively developed and then grouped into three categories (Table 2.2):

- *Scenarios*: The API providers publish use cases on their websites. These use cases, for example, encompass curating content or marketing and analysis. Furthermore, the providers follow different strategies. For example, when features appear in the API first, this points to an API-driven development. With regard to apps developed by third-party vendors, some of these provide core functionality, substituting for the user interfaces of the providers, while others enhance the platforms. All of these different aspects illustrate how the APIs are integrated into the data ecology.
- *Functions and data types*: The APIs differ in their endpoints and data formats. Some give access to historic data while most APIs are designed for (near) real-time access. The returned data are formatted, ordered and truncated in different ways, containing only minimal data, on the one hand, and fully hydrated objects on the other.
- *Access control mechanisms*: Authentication, authorisation and the rules of data access change over time. Moreover, documentation plays a key role in determining how easily social scientists find their way into the world of APIs. Reflecting on the different access control mechanisms highlights the limitations of social science research.

Each of these principles, and thus different API designs, presents both opportunities and limitations for online research, as discussed later.

4.1 Scenarios

The use cases for APIs promoted by the providers include both displaying content in third-party applications and generating content. Priority is given to marketing-related goals that promote interaction between organisations and customers. The APIs also enable integration of features such as "like" buttons or authentication functions ("Login with . . ."). Although the range of possible applications is broad, scientific analysis is not very prominent. However, Twitter, in particular, now lists research as a target group. Nevertheless, they point out that academic research is a means to "improve our service" (Twitter, 2020a). Scientific research usually needs only read-only access to APIs and is therefore covered by the scenarios, despite the many access restrictions (see section 4.3).

Based on the providers' own communication (blogs) and media coverage, it can be assumed that the providers have different strategies according to whether the development is API-driven or whether the API is rather a reaction to external requirements. In some cases, functions are available via the API earlier than via the web interface; for example, in 2009, the Twitter geotagging API was available before it was supported in the official client (Twitter, 2009). In contrast, before any API was made available for Instagram or Google+, users reverse-engineered the platform and developed unofficial APIs.[4]

With regard to the scientific use of APIs, another aspect of development is interesting: for cross-platform applications, the standardisation of APIs would be helpful. Two development approaches can be noted here. First, in some cases, the providers rely on semantic web technologies such as Microdata, which is embedded in web pages and thus allows structured access. The dominance of the platforms has probably contributed to the fact that media providers, for example, use the OpenGraphProtocol, which is preferred by Facebook and supported by other providers such as Twitter and many more (Facebook, 2020). On this basis, the preview images

Table 2.2 Shapes of APIs and the main scientific demands

Category	Implementation	Main scientific demands
Scenarios		
Use cases	• Generate and view content • Marketing and analysis • Authentication and infrastructure	View content
Strategies	• API-driven development • Reactive implementation of APIs • Standardisation	Standardisation
Relations	• Substitutional clients • Complementary clients	Complementary clients
Functions and data types		
Endpoints	• Content: e.g. user-generated content • Analytics: e.g. metadata • Functionality: e.g. authentication methods	Content
Operations	• Post and get: HTTP methods • Query languages: SQL-like interface	Get and query
Data formats	• Structured snippets: e.g. JSON • Data(base) files: e.g. RSS feeds or data dumps	Structured
Types of data	• Live vs. historic data • Aggregated vs. non-aggregated data • Anonymised vs. personalised data	Non-aggregated complete historic data
Amount of data	• Fields: explicitly requested data • Hydrated objects: all available data included • Paginated data and streams: slice by slice	Garden hose & fire hose
Truncations	• Recency: only the last messages • Privacy: only unprotected messages • Ranking: only "relevant" messages	Differentiation between ranking information and creation time
Access control		
Authentication	• Open authorisation: standardised access • Key-based: dedicated authentication tokens • Open access: no authentication necessary	Key-based
Reviews	• Proposals • Screencasts	Institutional access
Rules	• Terms of services • Developer terms (+robots.txt)	Scientific rules
Rate limits	• Load-based • User-based • Request-based • Money-based	Pricey load-based access
Documentation	• Playgrounds & explorers • Software development kits • References	References
Partnerships	• Privileges • Bans	Privileges

are extracted when sharing links, and this basically also allows scientific web scrapers to access structured content.

The second approach concerns the standardisation of the APIs themselves (beyond the REST principle). Basic data structures and actions on social media platforms are very similar.

The development of the Open Social protocol, which was initially supported by Google, has now been promoted by the W3C under the name "Activity Streams" without, however, having a significant influence on the platforms as far as is traceable (Jacobs, 2014). Instead, own standards have been set. Here, it becomes clear that the providers prevent substitutive use of their APIs. Initially, clients developed by third parties, especially for Twitter, achieved a high degree of distribution; but now, third-party apps are limited to complementary usage scenarios. Not only do the usage guidelines prescribe this, but the limitations to access rates also effectively hinder growth in user numbers beyond the official clients.

Thus, if one considers use cases, presumed strategies and the relationships between operators and third parties, APIs appear to be a control instrument used for economic growth. Scientific criteria play only a marginal role at best, and therefore it is necessary to consider to what extent the data collection yields findings about the users investigated and to what extent it reflects the platform operators.

4.2 Functions and data types

Social media APIs not only provide data but they also expose functions such as the authentication of users or the provision of ad analytics to businesses. Nevertheless, for science, data access endpoints are the most important. While analytics could provide information not easily visible in the user interface, academic analyses mostly follow their own research questions and, thus, mostly require non-aggregated data. In contrast, analytic features are potential marketing mechanisms for the providers. While there are no "raw" data (Gitelman & Jackson, 2013, p. 2), every additional stage in the data-generating process challenges transparency, which is a core value for science. If scientists understand themselves as observers measuring the world, data analyses will usually only need read access, and therefore, only a limited set of operations is important. Write access changes the underlying world but can be helpful for recruiting participants through automatic invitation comments (e.g. Courtois & Mechant, 2014). This example highlights how APIs are not hidden backdoors, but rather, they are part of the social interaction infrastructure.

From this perspective, two principles must be weighed against each other. On the one hand, low-level access and low-level data allow flexibility, even for innovative research questions that require creative solutions for the operationalisation of theoretical concepts. On the other hand, using predefined query languages and endpoints not only enhances efficiency but also improves validity because the platform logic is transferred to the research procedures. However, since we do not know the effects of the platform logic in advance, usually the more comprehensive low-level data access is preferred. Ideally, we can use both to handle the amount of data, where a "garden hose" approach will use preselected cases and fields, and a "fire hose" approach will access all available data at once.

In relation to the formats, types and amount of data, the API designs are in stark contrast with academic research. Social media APIs are mostly designed to foster real-time interaction between users. For scientific research, on the other hand, it makes more sense to have access to historical data in defined periods of time to make it possible to compile a controlled sample from which to generalise to populations. Otherwise, inference statistics become unreliable. The truncation, sorting and aggregation of data based on largely unknown criteria is a particular challenge to research. For example, Facebook limits access to 600 posts per page, at maximum (Ho, 2020). Moreover, the unseen data is problematic, not only with regard to deleted data. For example, without knowing at what point in time a follower started following a page, the evolution over time can only be traced by ongoing live data collection. Moreover, scientists have to decide which perspective they will take: from the users' perspective, data should be ordered and truncated in the same way that a user sees it. From the platform perspective, the data should be ordered by creation time and not truncated if custom analyses are to be implemented.

4.3 Access control

Access control mechanisms have become increasingly restrictive over time (see also Perriam et al., 2020), but at the same time, they have been standardised. In the field of social media APIs, there are hardly any open access options without authentication. Presumably, there are two explanations for this increasingly restricted access. First, the data is often personal data and must be protected against inappropriate access (Puschmann, 2019, p. 3). Especially in recent years, this has become particularly evident against the background of political discussion, and it has also been codified in corresponding regulatory documents such as the General Data Protection Regulation of the European Union. Second, these data are to be regarded as an economic asset of commercial enterprises, which thus not only protect their resources but also market them systematically.

The commercial property protection is particularly evident from the rate limits. A load-based limitation is quite reasonable when the operators bear the corresponding costs. Twitter offers higher contingents and more extensive access points for money (Twitter, 2020b). However, operators also often impose limits based on requests per time frame, which is not readily understandable given the strong economic position of the operators and the potential benefits they receive from third-party attention attribution. Limiting the number of requests to short time windows, such as 15 or 60 minutes, is inhibiting for scientific projects that rely less on continuous data access and more on one-off large-scale data collection.

As authentication mechanisms, on the one hand, personalised API keys are employed, and on the other, open authorisation has been established. OAuth allows very different access scenarios, particularly in a role separation between application developer and user (IETF, 2012). Thus, API-based third-party applications can make requests on behalf of users. In terms of scientific use for data collection, however, this procedure complicates the process, as corresponding methods must first be implemented. From a scientific point of view, authentication via API keys would be preferable if, for research projects, the developers of the API application (e.g. when used via Python or R scripts) were also the users of the application. However, open authorisation does allow for a division of labour, so that corresponding clients can be made available for non-programming projects, for example in applications such as NVivo, NodeXL or Facepager.

One of the changes in recent years has been the expansion of proactive reviews. Without an evaluation, which can also lead to complete rejection, only a small amount of (own) data can be accessed in a sandbox mode. From the scientific point of view, in principle, reviews are to be welcomed as a quality management mechanism; however, such reviews follow the criteria of the providers and not scientific criteria (Bruns, 2019, p. 10). While legal regulations such as the German copyright law acknowledge the special position of scientific analyses (e.g. §60d UrhG), this is hardly found among the platforms' rules. In addition, media companies or other commercial enterprises have the resources to enter into privileged partnerships, but individual scientific projects rarely do. The application process is a challenge, as is the process of going through app reviews, for example, when screencasts have to be created or sample analyses submitted, as is the case with YouTube. Against this background, the establishment of specific scientific partner programmes triggers a twofold response (Bruns, 2019; Puschman, 2019). On the one hand, the appreciation of scientific work is certainly welcome, but on the other hand, higher-resource research institutions are again being favoured. A more general access for academic institutions would be valuable.

Low-threshold access would also be helpful for teaching purposes. Moreover, when learning how to use APIs, the documentation is important. All social media providers offer extensive support in the form of software development packages (SDKs) or web interfaces for testing the APIs (API explorers). In the social science context, however, the reference of the endpoints is especially important, first, because appropriate programming knowledge for the integration of SDKs cannot always be assumed, and second, because the transparency of the collection and analysis is a crucial scientific requirement. This is especially significant from an external perspective, as the providers are closed systems with numerous unknown internal mechanisms.

Overall, it turns out that the access control of APIs is not exactly science-friendly. Specific access requirements should be considered in advance when designing data collection projects, although they may already have changed between the time a project is planned and implemented.

5 Conclusion

Programming interfaces have become an integral part of certain areas of social science research. Among other things, these interfaces allow structured and comparatively convenient access to communication data on online platforms. Nevertheless, certain peculiarities have to be considered, in particular because the APIs are under the full control of the providers and are not always compatible with scientific criteria. There is the possibility that scientific research may be based on the availability of data rather than on substantive criteria. One reason for the considerable prominence of Twitter studies in comparison to studies on other platforms such as Instagram, YouTube or WhatsApp could be, for example, Twitter's ease of availability (see Jünger, 2022, in press).

From a comparative perspective – both between different platforms and over time – it is possible not only to identify the variations and characteristics of the different APIs but also to benchmark these against scientific criteria. The construction period starting around the year 2005 is characterised by the providers building and extending their interfaces. In this way, they became anchored in the ecosystem of the internet, which became even more apparent in the years after 2010. The APIs were consolidated and access restrictions were established that fostered complementary use while hindering substitutive use. Finally, a few years later, and especially in the context of the first reports on Cambridge Analytica in 2015, the political dimension of interfaces became increasingly evident. Overall, a transformation has taken place from a technical, via an economic, to a political perspective on APIs.

A consideration of usage scenarios, functionality and access mechanisms reveals that the scientific use of APIs must always be reflected epistemologically. It is only in recent years that science has been increasingly perceived as a partner. However, the scientific requirements for data access continue to contrast with current implementation. Data are often not as comprehensively accessible as would be necessary to assess the quality of samples and the derived findings. Nevertheless, working with APIs enables otherwise virtually impossible insights to be gained into the processes on online platforms. It is important to recognise that the results reflect not only user behaviour, but also the platforms' mechanisms and the scientists' decisions. APIs are both a research tool and a research object. In this respect, it would be advisable in future to conduct more comparative or cross-platform studies.

Acknowledgement

We acknowledge support for the open access publication from the University of Greifswald.

Notes

1 For a critical discussion of this assumption see Jensen (2014), Webster (2011) and Vis (2013).
2 See https://github.com/facebookarchive/platform for an old snapshot of the Facebook platform's PHP code.
3 For a critical discussion of commercialisation see Fuchs (2014).
4 See https://github.com/mislav/instagram for an example of an unofficial Instagram API or https://github.com/jmstriegel/php.googleplusapi for an unofficial Google+ API.

References

Accessnow. (2015). *Hey @twitter! Bring back #politwoops*. https://act.accessnow.org/ea-action/action?ea.client.id=1921&ea.campaign.id=42617

Altheide, D. L. (1994). An ecology of communication: Toward a mapping of the effective environment. *The Sociological Quarterly*, *35*(4), 665–683. https://doi.org/10.1111/j.1533-8525.1994.tb00422.x

Altheide, D. L. (2013). Media logic, social control, and fear. *Communication Theory*, *23*(3), 223–238. https://doi.org/10.1111/comt.12017

Baur, N. (2011). Mixing process-generated data in market sociology. *Quality & Quantity*, *45*(6), 1233–1251. https://doi.org/10.1007/s11135-009-9288-x

Bodle, R. (2011). Regimes of sharing. *Information, Communication & Society*, *14*(3), 320–337. https://doi.org/10.1080/1369118X.2010.542825

Bogost, I. (2018, March 22). My cow game extracted your Facebook data. *The Atlantic*. www.theatlantic.com/technology/archive/2018/03/my-cow-game-extracted-your-facebook-data/556214/

boyd, d., & Crawford, K. (2012). Critical questions for big data. *Information, Communication & Society*, *15*(5), 662–679. https://doi.org/10.1080/1369118X.2012.678878

Bruns, A. (2013). Faster than the speed of print: Reconciling 'big data' social media analysis and academic scholarship. *First Monday*, *18*(10). https://doi.org/10.5210/fm.v18i10.4879

Bruns, A. (2018, April 25). Facebook shuts the gate after the horse has bolted, and hurts real research in the process. *Internet Policy Review*. https://policyreview.info/articles/news/facebook-shuts-gate-after-horse-has-bolted-and-hurts-real-research-process/786

Bruns, A. (2019). After the 'APIcalypse': Social media platforms and their fight against critical scholarly research. *Information, Communication & Society*, *22*(11), 1544–1566. https://doi.org/10.1080/13691 18X.2019.1637447

Cadwalladr, C., & Graham-Harrison, E. (2018, March 17). Revealed: 50 million Facebook profiles harvested for Cambridge Analytica in major data breach. *The Guardian*. www.theguardian.com/news/2018/mar/17/cambridge-analytica-facebook-influence-us-election

Cagle, M. (2016). *Facebook, Instagram, and Twitter provided data access for a surveillance product marketed to target activists of color*. www.aclunc.org/blog/facebook-instagram-and-twitter-provided-data-access-surveillance-product-marketed-target

Couldry, N., & Hepp, A. (2013). Conceptualizing mediatization: Contexts, traditions, arguments. *Communication Theory*, *23*(3), 191–202. https://doi.org/10.1111/comt.12019

Courtois, C., & Mechant, P. (2014). An evaluation of the potential of Web 2.0 APIs for social research. In G. Patriarche, H. Bilandzic, J. L. Jensen, & J. Jurišić (Eds.), *Audience research methodologies: Between innovation and consolidation* (pp. 212–224). Routledge.

Cukier, K., & Mayer-Schoenberger, V. (2013). The rise of big data: How it's changing the way we think about the world. *Foreign Affairs*, *92*(3), 28–40.

Dachwitz, I., Rudl, T., & Rebiger, S. (2018, March 21). Was wir über den Skandal um Facebook und Cambridge Analytica wissen [What we know about the Facebook and Cambridge Analytica scandal]. *Netzpolitik.org*. https://netzpolitik.org/2018/cambridge-analytica-was-wir-ueber-das-groesste-datenleck-in-der-geschichte-von-facebook-wissen/

Dawson, A., & Innes, M. (2019). How Russia's internet research agency built its disinformation campaign. *The Political Quarterly*, *90*(2), 245–256. https://doi.org/10.1111/1467-923X.12690

Doerrfeld, B., Sandoval, K., Wood, C., Lauret, A., & Anthony, A. (2016). The API economy: Disruption and the business of APIs. *Nordic APIs*. https://nordicapis.com/api-ebooks/the-api-economy/

Dorfer, L. (2016). Datenzentrische Geschäftsmodelle als neuer Geschäftsmodelltypus in der Electronic-Business-Forschung: Konzeptionelle Bezugspunkte, Klassifikation und Geschäftsmodellarchitektur [Data-centric business models as a new business model type in electronic business research: Conceptual reference points, classification and business model architecture]. *Schmalenbachs Zeitschrift Für Betrieb-swirtschaftliche Forschung, 68*(3), 307–369. https://doi.org/10.1007/s41471-016-0014-9

eBay. (2000). *Ebay launches new initiative to provide expanded e-commerce solutions.* https://web.archive.org/web/20050208210046/https://pages.ebay.com/aboutebay/thecompany/2000/november.html

Facebook. (2012). *Amendment No. 4 to Form S-1.* www.sec.gov/Archives/edgar/data/1326801/000119312512175673/d287954ds1a.htm

Facebook. (2014). *Facebook platform changelog.* https://web.archive.org/web/20140714133607/https://developers.facebook.com/docs/apps/changelog/

Facebook. (2020). *Facebook platform migrations.* https://developers.facebook.com/docs/graph-api/changelog/archive/migrations

Fielding, R. T. (2000). *Architectural styles and the design of network-based software architectures* (Dissertation). University of California, Irvine.

Freelon, D. (2018). Computational research in the post-API age. *Political Communication, 35*(4), 665–668. https://doi.org/10.1080/10584609.2018.1477506

Fuchs, C. (2014). *Social media: A critical introduction.* Sage.

Gitelman, L., & Jackson, V. (2013). Introduction. In L. Gitelman (Ed.), *"Raw data" is an oxymoron* (pp. 1–14). The MIT Press.

Glaser, A. (2018, March 20). Another whistleblower says Facebook knew for years that its data-sharing policies were a huge problem. *Slate.* https://slate.com/technology/2018/03/another-whistleblower-says-facebook-knew-for-years-its-data-sharing-policies-were-a-huge-problem.html

Golem. (2013). Google blockiert Youtube-App für windows phone [Google blocks Youtube app for Windows Phone]. *Golem.* https://www.golem.de/news/microsoft-google-blockiert-youtube-app-fuer-windows-phone-1301-96636.html

Golem. (2015). Youtube-App auf manchen Geräten nicht mehr nutzbar [Youtube app no longer functional on some devices]. *Golem.* https://www.golem.de/news/api-update-youtube-app-auf-manchen-geraeten-nicht-mehr-nutzbar-1504-113628.html

Google. (2005). *The world is your JavaScript-enabled oyster.* https://googleblog.blogspot.com/2005/06/world-is-your-javascript-enabled_29.html

Hernandez, B. A. (2012, July 26). Instagram: Twitter to blame for broken 'find friends' feature. *Mashable.* https://mashable.com/2012/07/26/instagram-twitter-to-blame-for-broken-find-friends-feature/

Ho, J. C.-T. (2020). How biased is the sample? Reverse engineering the ranking algorithm of Facebook's graph application programming interface. *Big Data & Society, 7*(1). https://doi.org/10.1177/2053951720905874

Internet Engineering Task Force. (2011). *The WebSocket protocol. RFC 6455.* https://tools.ietf.org/html/rfc6455

Internet Engineering Task Force. (2012). *The OAuth 2.0 Authorization framework. RFC 6749.* https://tools.ietf.org/html/rfc6749

Jacobs, I. (2014, December 16). Opensocial foundation moves standards work to W3C social web activity. *W3C Blog.* www.w3.org/blog/2014/12/opensocial-foundation-moves-standards-work-to-w3c-social-web-activity/

Jacobson, D., Brail, G., & Woods, D. (2012). *Apis: A strategy guide: Creating channels with application programming interfaces.* O'Reilly.

Jensen, K. B. (2014). Audiences, audiences everywhere: Measured, interpreted, and imagined. In G. Patriarche, H. Bilandzic, J. L. Jensen, & J. Jurišić (Eds.), *Audience research methodologies: Between innovation and consolidation* (pp. 227–239). Routledge.

Jünger, J. (2018). Mapping the field of automated data collection on the web. Data types, collection approaches and their research logic. In M. Welker, C. Stützer, & M. Egger (Eds.), *Computational social science in the age of big data: Concepts, methodologies, tools, and applications* (pp. 104–130). Halem.

Jünger, J. (2022, in press). Die Macht der APIs. Online-Plattformen als Kontextfaktoren wissenschaftlicher Forschung [The power of the APIs. Online platforms as context factors of scientific research]. In A. Kostiučenko & M. Kuhnhenn (Eds.), *Die Macht des Kontextes.* de Gruyter.

Jünger, J. (2022, in press). Verhaltens-, Forschungs- oder Datenschnittstellen? Drei Perspektiven auf die sozialwissenschaftliche Bedeutung von Application Programming Interfaces (APIs) [Behavioural, research or data interfaces? Three perspectives on the significance of Application Programming Interfaces (APIs) for social science]. In E. Koenen, T. Birkner, C. Pentzold, C. Katzenbach, & C. Schwarzenegger (Eds.), *Digital communication research. Digitale Kommunikation und Kommunikationsgeschichte.* DGPuK.

Keyling, T., & Jünger, J. (2016). Observing online content. In G. Vowe & P. Henn (Eds.), *Political communication in the online world: Theoretical approaches and research designs* (pp. 183–200). Routledge.

Klinger, U., & Svensson, J. (2014). The emergence of network media logic in political communication: A theoretical approach. *New Media & Society*, *17*(8), 1241–1257. https://doi.org/10.1177/1461444814522952

Kraus, J. (2007, November 2). OpenSocial makes the web better. *Google Official Blog*. https://googleblog.blogspot.com/2007/11/opensocial-makes-web-better.html

Lane, K. (2016). *API evangelist history of APIs*. https://history.apievangelist.com/

Ledford, H. (2020). How Facebook, Twitter and other data troves are revolutionizing social science. *Nature*, *582*(7812), 328–330. https://doi.org/10.1038/d41586-020-01747-1

Livingstone, S. (2009). On the mediation of everything: ICA presidential address 2008. *Journal of Communication*, *59*(1), 1–18. https://doi.org/10.1111/j.1460-2466.2008.01401.x

Marres, N. (2017). *Digital sociology: The reinvention of social research*. Polity.

Marres, N., & Gerlitz, C. (2016). Interface methods: Renegotiating relations between digital social research, STS and sociology. *The Sociological Review*, *64*(1), 21–46. https://doi.org/10.1111/1467-954X.12314

Mozilla. (2019). *Social API*. https://developer.mozilla.org/en-US/docs/Archive/Social_API

Newman, N., & Fletcher, R. (2018). Platform reliance, information intermediaries, and news diversity. A look at the evidence. In M. Moore & D. Tambini (Eds.), *Digital dominance: The power of Google, Amazon, Facebook, and Apple* (pp. 133–152). Oxford University Press.

O'Reilly, T. (2005). *What is web 2.0: Design patterns and business models for the next generation of software*. www.oreilly.com/pub/a/web2/archive/what-is-web-20.html

Perriam, J., Birkbak, A., & Freeman, A. (2020). Digital methods in a post-API environment. *International Journal of Social Research Methodology*, *23*(3), 277–290. https://doi.org/10.1080/13645579.2019.1682840

Puschmann, C. (2019). An end to the wild west of social media research: A response to Axel Bruns. *Information, Communication & Society*, *22*(11), 1582–1589. https://doi.org/10.1080/1369118X.2019.1646300

Reselman, B. (2018, July 5). It's the end of the API economy as we know it. *Programmableweb*. https://www.programmableweb.com/news/its-end-api-economy-we-know-it/analysis/2018/07/05

Rogers, R. (2013). *Digital methods*. The MIT Press.

Rosenberg, M., Confessore, N., & Cadwalladr, C. (2018, March 17). How Trump consultants exploited the Facebook data of millions. *The New York Times*. www.nytimes.com/2018/03/17/us/politics/cambridge-analytica-trump-campaign.html

Salesforce. (2000). *Products & services*. https://web.archive.org/web/20000303134956/www.salesforce.com/info/products.html

Sarver, R. (2011, March 11). Twitter development talk: Consistency and ecosystem opportunities. https://groups.google.com/forum/#!topic/twitter-development-talk/yCzVnHqHIWo

Sippey, M. (2012, June 29). Delivering a consistent Twitter experience. *Twitter Developers Blog*. https://web.archive.org/web/20120630064926/https://dev.twitter.com/blog/delivering-consistent-twitter-experience

Social Science One. (2020). *Our Facebook partnership*. https://socialscience.one/our-facebook-partnership

Telegram. (2020). *MTProto mobile protocol*. https://core.telegram.org/mtproto

Trotter, J. K. (2015, June 3). Twitter just killed politwoops. *TKTK*. http://tktk.gawker.com/twitter-just-killed-politwoops-1708842376

Twitter. (2009, November 19). Think globally, tweet locally. *Twitter Blog*. https://blog.twitter.com/official/en_us/a/2009/think-globally-tweet-locally.html

Twitter. (2010, August 30). Twitter applications and OAuth. *Twitter Blog*. https://blog.twitter.com/official/en_us/a/2010/twitter-applications-and-oauth.html

Twitter. (2012, December 5). Instagram photo-rendering issue. *Twitter*. https://web.archive.org/web/20121208053613/http://status.twitter.com/post/37258637900/instagram-photo-rendering-issue

Twitter. (2013, March 29). API v1 retirement: Final dates. *Twitter Developers Blog*. https://web.archive.org/web/20130502185948/https://dev.twitter.com/blog/api-v1-retirement-final-dates

Twitter. (2020a). *Twitter data for academic research*. https://developer.twitter.com/en/use-cases/academic-researchers

Twitter. (2020b). *Pricing. API access that scales with you and your solution*. https://developer.twitter.com/en/pricing

Van Dijck, J., & Poell, T. (2013). Understanding social media logic. *Media and Communication, 1*(1), 2–14. https://doi.org/10.12924/mac2013.01010002

Venturini, T., & Rogers, R. (2019). "API-based research" or how can digital sociology and journalism studies learn from the Facebook and Cambridge Analytica data breach. *Digital Journalism, 7*(4), 532–540. https://doi.org/10.1080/21670811.2019.1591927

Vis, F. (2013). A critical reflection on big data: Considering APIs, researchers and tools as data makers. *First Monday, 18*(10). https://doi.org/10.5210/fm.v18i10.4878

Webster, J. G. (2011). The duality of media: A structurational theory of public attention. *Communication Theory, 21*(1), 43–66. https://doi.org/10.1111/j.1468-2885.2010.01375.x

World Wide Web Consortium. (2017). *Activity streams 2.0: W3C recommendation 23 May 2017.* www.w3.org/TR/activitystreams-core/

YouTube. (2013). *Implementing OAuth 2.0 authentication.* https://web.archive.org/web/20150316081145/https://developers.google.com/youtube/v3/guides/authentication

Zota, V. (2012, June 20). YouTube geht gegen MP3-Konvertierungsdienst vor [YouTube takes action against MP3 conversion service]. *Heise.* www.heise.de/newsticker/meldung/YouTube-geht-gegen-MP3-Konvertierungsdienst-vor-1621474.html

3

APPLICATION PROGRAMMING INTERFACES AND WEB DATA FOR SOCIAL RESEARCH

Dominic Nyhuis

1 Introduction: what are APIs and what are they good for?

Web data has become increasingly important for social research. Countless web services are amassing an enormous wealth of data of every conceivable kind. Not least the many social network sites collect data on human behavior and human interactions on an unprecedented scale, which can shed light on any number of social phenomena. Realizing the value of this information for the general public and for social research specifically, many services have decided to make their data publicly accessible – by setting up dedicated application programming interfaces (APIs).

This chapter offers a brief introduction to APIs, so researchers can learn how to benefit from these opportunities. In addition to discussing the general principles of APIs, we will provide some pointers on how to access data from a technical point of view. For these parts of the chapter, we rely on the programming language R. While R may not strike the more tech-savvy readers as the obvious choice, we believe that R offers many advantages for a social science audience. R has become enormously popular among social scientists for statistical analyses. Along with this growth, the functionality of R has expanded into various neighboring fields and now includes functionality for web interactions. This expansion holds particular promise for social scientists who are more likely to be familiar with R than with a more conventional programming language. Moreover, the ability to carry out the data collection parts of a research project in the same computing environment as the data management and analysis components ensures a smoother workflow.

Before turning to the technical elements of this introduction, we begin by defining the subject of interest and by discussing the relative merits of APIs over web scraping. Application programming interfaces have a fairly broad meaning in computer science. They can be understood as routines that structure machine interactions. When social scientists speak of APIs, they typically refer to Web APIs, which are employed in client-server interactions. But even within the subset of Web APIs, the social science interest is typically restricted to those APIs that allow querying data from a service, while Web APIs have considerably wider applications in modern web development. For the remainder of this chapter, we refer to this narrow subset of Web APIs when we speak of APIs.

DOI: 10.4324/9781003025245-4

One way to understand APIs is to consider how collecting data using APIs is different from and similar to web scraping. Web scraping ordinarily means accessing an HTML document and extracting the relevant pieces of information from the document. Ignoring the details, we can think of web scraping as a two-step process. In a first step, we send a query to a server to request a particular resource, frequently an HTML document. In a second and often considerably more cumbersome step, we extract the relevant information from the HTML document.

When interacting with an API, the first step is quite similar to the first step in web scraping. The curators of an API define what kind of information can be requested, as well as the format of a valid query. As we will see later, the components of such a query are no different from the components of an ordinary URL. The main difference lies in the response from the server. Whereas the response in web scraping is often an HTML document, we receive the information in a simple data format when interacting with an API, thus mostly doing away with the second step.

Collecting data from APIs comes with a number of advantages over web scraping. First, the availability of an API suggests that our collection efforts are explicitly encouraged by the curators of a service and the API documentation typically spells out rules and limitations, allowing us to sidestep some of the ethical murkiness of scraping data. Because our collection efforts are welcomed, APIs make their data more easily accessible. This means that many of the hurdles we frequently encounter in web scraping, such as dynamic web architectures, do not arise in API interactions. What is more, the provision of information in dedicated data formats not only simplifies matters for researchers, who do not have to dig through heaps of irrelevant and often unstructured information, it also lessens the burden on the server side – something we should always strive for when engaging in automated web data collection.

Particularly for researchers who are less familiar with the minutiae of web technologies, one additional benefit of collecting data from APIs are the so-called wrappers. Due to the predefined format of valid queries, it is simple enough to write a program that turns the search parameters into a valid query, sends it to the server, collects and interprets the response, and presents it to the user. For example, developers have written wrappers in R for many of the most popular web services, which gather data from these APIs and store them in a native R data format.

Despite the many benefits of APIs over web scraping, there are several downsides of APIs that should not be left unmentioned. First, many APIs require users to register with a service and provide their credentials along with their query. In most cases, this constitutes more of a hassle than a true limitation, and requiring users to register is perfectly reasonable from the perspective of service providers. The ease of sending countless requests to an API makes disruptive and potentially costly behavior very easy. To identify and ban actors engaging in such bad behavior, user authentication is a simple and effective strategy. User authentication is also typically required when the service is not free of charge.

While user registration is not problematic per se, it is often tied to another, more severe downside of APIs – service limitations. In a further attempt to lessen the burden that any individual user can create on the server, providers frequently limit the number of service requests that a user can make in a given period. Occasionally, such limitations are used to incentivize users to sign up for paid accounts of a service.

One additional challenge of collecting data via APIs stems from the fact that each service provider is free to make design choices in setting up their systems. Therefore, to collect data from an API requires users to engage with the API documentation. This hurdle is less problematic when a wrapper for an API exists, because users can rely on the wrapper to turn their search parameters into a valid service request. Similarly, changes in the API definition can easily break user-written code. To be sure, this concern is no different from changes in the source code of websites, which can break the code used for web scraping. What is more, there is a tacit understanding that service providers should ensure the consistency of their APIs as much as possible, such that changes in the source code of a website may even be more likely than changes in the definition of an API.

These challenges notwithstanding, in most cases the benefits of APIs greatly outweigh their downsides. Therefore, whenever users are looking to collect web data, they should ascertain whether the information is available via an API. Indeed, in some cases it might not even be possible to access data any other way.

We begin the remainder of this chapter with a very brief overview of the most important web technologies and data formats to equip readers with some core concepts. Section 3 highlights general principles of APIs with an example from the UK police. Subsequently, we elaborate how to access data from the Twitter API.

2 A very short primer on web technologies and data formats

To understand APIs, it is helpful to be aware of some basic web technologies and common data formats on the web. Due to space constraints, many details and technical features are disregarded here. For an extended introduction, see Munzert et al. (2014).

2.1 The hypertext transfer protocol

The first and crucial web technology is the so-called hypertext transfer protocol (HTTP), which is commonly used to transfer messages between client and server. For example, when accessing a website in the browser, we typically request an HTML document that resides at a particular location on a server. If all goes well, the resource is provided by the server and the document is interpreted and displayed by the browser. Additional resources that are needed to correctly display the document, say, images, are automatically requested from the server without explicit user input. Therefore, a single user request typically results in a series of messages between client and server, all of which conform to the HTT protocol.

There are two aspects of these messages that we want to highlight, as they are relevant for querying data via APIs. The first is the address that we use for requesting a particular resource, the well-known uniform resource locator (URL), such as the following example of a URL to a specific Wikipedia page:

```
https://en.wikipedia.org/wiki/Mannheim
```

We can distinguish three components of the URL, the protocol (`https`), the domain (`en.wikipedia.org`), and the path to the specific location of the resource (`/wiki/Mannheim`). While no path information is needed to construct a valid address, the key point here is that we will come across these three components all over the web and being able to distinguish between them is useful for constructing API queries. In addition to these three components, there is one more element that we frequently encounter in dealing with APIs. Consider the following example:

```
https://en.wikipedia.org/w/index.php?search=mannheim
```

In this case, we typed "mannheim" into the Wikipedia search bar.[1] The search term was appended to the URL as a parameter. The first two elements of the URL remain the same, but the location of the resource has changed (/w/index.php). The specific query is introduced with a question mark (?) and the parameters always come in the form of key-value pairs, which are separated by equal signs (=). The possible keys are arbitrarily defined by each site. In the common case of multiple parameters, they are separated by an ampersand (&), such as in the following example, where we ask Wikipedia to return a list of articles containing the search term:

```
https://en.wikipedia.org/w/index.php?
search=mannheim&fulltext=1
```

The last two examples relate to a second aspect of HTTP messages that should be noted. In the HTT protocol, only a handful of message types can be exchanged between client and server, and we basically only ever encounter two: the GET and the POST methods. For our purposes, the key difference between the two methods is how they incorporate query parameters. This is important for interacting with APIs, as we typically need to specify one or more variables when we request data from an API. In the more common GET method, the query parameters are appended to the URL as shown in the earlier examples. In case of the POST method, the parameters are included in the body of the message. We will return to this idea in the case study in section 4.

2.2 Web data formats

In addition to the key technologies for querying data, we need to familiarize ourselves with the structure of the responses that we typically receive from APIs. As the exchange of data is crucial for many web applications, several data formats have been developed. Among them, XML and JSON are currently the most popular, and most APIs will provide their data in one of these two formats. Both formats are similar in that they store the data as plain text. Therefore, it is possible to open XML and JSON documents in any text editor to inspect and edit them, or even create a new document from scratch.

Figure 3.1 displays an example of a very simple XML document. If you have ever looked at an HTML document, it is easy to spot the similarities between XML and HTML documents. Like HTML, XML documents are composed of markup elements (<>, </>) which structure the content of the document. We also note the hierarchical structure of the document, where content is nested between an opening (<>) and a closing tag (</>) and the entire node is nested inside other nodes.[2] The hierarchical structure helps extract specific pieces of information from the document.

It is important to note that data providers are free to choose the names of the tags to best fit their data. Only the general characteristics of XML documents are prescribed, not the

```
▼<dataformats>
  ▼<format>
      <name>XML</name>
      <file_extension>.xml</file_extension>
    </format>
  ▼<format>
      <name>JSON</name>
      <file_extension>.json</file_extension>
    </format>
  </dataformats>
```

Figure 3.1 A sample XML document

```
▼<dataformats>
    <format name="XML" file_extension=".xml"/>
    <format name="JSON" file_extension=".json"/>
</dataformats>
```

Figure 3.2   A variant of the XML document

```
{"dataformats":[
    {"name":"XML","file_extension":".xml"},
    {"name":"JSON","file_extension":".json"}
]}
```

Figure 3.3   A sample JSON document

substance. Beyond that, providers are also free to structure the document in a way that works best for their data. As an example, Figure 3.2 presents an alternative way to structure the same two pieces of information on the two data formats. In this case, the information about name and file extension is provided as two attributes associated with the format nodes.

The same information is also provided in Figure 3.3. In this case, the document conforms to the JSON format. As before, despite the standards for structuring JSON documents, a number of different documents could have been created to store the information, some of which are better suited to store the information with as little overhead as possible. Once again, it is up the data provider to choose the most suitable document variant for the data they are providing.

Like the XML format, the JSON format is fairly straightforward and human-readable – although one might argue that XML documents are a little easier to parse with human eyes than documents in the JSON format. At their core, JSON documents consist of name-value pairs, separated by a colon. Objects in the JSON format are created with curly braces and the individual data points are separated by a comma. We can also identify the hierarchical document structure in the sample document presented in Figure 3.3. In this case, the two pieces of information are combined in two objects ({ }), which, in turn, are combined in an array of length two, indicated by the square brackets ([ ]). This array serves as the value to the data-formats variable.

3 Some simple API queries: the case of data.police.uk

To showcase the general principles of APIs and to highlight how web technologies and data formats are used in practice, we begin by studying a simple API provided by the UK police. The contents of the API are documented at `https://data.police.uk/docs/`. Most importantly, the API provides a number of current and geolocated crime statistics that could be relevant for studying a variety of social science questions.

We begin by accessing a list of the territorial police forces in the UK that, according to the API documentation, is located at `https://data.police.uk/api/forces`. We could access this document by typing this address into our browser, which would yield the result displayed in Figure 3.4. The data is provided in the JSON format. In this case, the document simply contains an ID variable and a name variable for the different police forces, which are combined in individual objects and further bracketed by an array.

```
[{"id":"avon-and-somerset","name":"Avon and Somerset Constabulary"},
{"id":"bedfordshire","name":"Bedfordshire Police"},
{"id":"cambridgeshire","name":"Cambridgeshire Constabulary"},
{"id":"cheshire","name":"Cheshire Constabulary"},{"id":"city-of-london","name":"City of
London Police"},{"id":"cleveland","name":"Cleveland Police"},{"id":"cumbria","name":"Cumbria
Constabulary"},{"id":"derbyshire","name":"Derbyshire Constabulary"},{"id":"devon-and-
cornwall","name":"Devon & Cornwall Police"},{"id":"dorset","name":"Dorset Police"},
{"id":"durham","name":"Durham Constabulary"},{"id":"dyfed-powys","name":"Dyfed-Powys
Police"},{"id":"essex","name":"Essex Police"},
{"id":"gloucestershire","name":"Gloucestershire Constabulary"},{"id":"greater-
manchester","name":"Greater Manchester Police"},{"id":"gwent","name":"Gwent Police"},
{"id":"hampshire","name":"Hampshire Constabulary"},
{"id":"hertfordshire","name":"Hertfordshire Constabulary"},
{"id":"humberside","name":"Humberside Police"},{"id":"kent","name":"Kent Police"},
{"id":"lancashire","name":"Lancashire Constabulary"},
{"id":"leicestershire","name":"Leicestershire Police"},
{"id":"lincolnshire","name":"Lincolnshire Police"},{"id":"merseyside","name":"Merseyside
Police"},{"id":"metropolitan","name":"Metropolitan Police Service"},
{"id":"norfolk","name":"Norfolk Constabulary"},{"id":"north-wales","name":"North Wales
Police"},{"id":"north-yorkshire","name":"North Yorkshire Police"},
{"id":"northamptonshire","name":"Northamptonshire Police"},
{"id":"northumbria","name":"Northumbria Police"},
{"id":"nottinghamshire","name":"Nottinghamshire Police"},{"id":"northern-
ireland","name":"Police Service of Northern Ireland"},{"id":"south-wales","name":"South
Wales Police"},{"id":"south-yorkshire","name":"South Yorkshire Police"},
{"id":"staffordshire","name":"Staffordshire Police"},{"id":"suffolk","name":"Suffolk
Constabulary"},{"id":"surrey","name":"Surrey Police"},{"id":"sussex","name":"Sussex
Police"},{"id":"thames-valley","name":"Thames Valley Police"},
{"id":"warwickshire","name":"Warwickshire Police"},{"id":"west-mercia","name":"West Mercia
Police"},{"id":"west-midlands","name":"West Midlands Police"},{"id":"west-
yorkshire","name":"West Yorkshire Police"},{"id":"wiltshire","name":"Wiltshire Police"}]
```

Figure 3.4   Screenshot of the JSON file – UK police forces (February 2021)

```
> library(rvest)
Loading required package: xml2
> library(jsonlite)
> (html <- read_html("https://data.police.uk/api/forces"))
{html_document}
<html>
[1] <body><p>[{"id":"avon-and-somerset","name":"Avon and Somerset Constabulary"},{"id":"bedfordshire","name":"Bedfordshire Police"},
{"id":"cambridges ...
> json <- html_text(html)
> forces_dat <- fromJSON(json)
> (N <- nrow(forces_dat))
[1] 44
> forces_dat[sample(N, 10),]
                   id                          name
21         lancashire         Lancashire Constabulary
15 greater-manchester      Greater Manchester Police
6           cleveland                Cleveland Police
42       west-midlands            West Midlands Police
32   northern-ireland Police Service of Northern Ireland
8           derbyshire          Derbyshire Constabulary
17           hampshire           Hampshire Constabulary
29    northamptonshire        Northamptonshire Police
38              sussex                   Sussex Police
12          dyfed-powys             Dyfed-Powys Police
```

Figure 3.5   R code snippet – UK police forces

To access this information in R requires only the few lines of code displayed in Figure 3.5. We begin by loading the two modules `rvest` and `jsonlite`. The `rvest` module provides functions for interacting with the web, and the `jsonlite` module is used for dealing with data in the JSON format. Next, we load the HTML file containing the police forces data and store it in the (arbitrarily named) object `html`. Checking the contents of the HTML file that is now stored in the working memory of R, we find that the document has very little structuring information. The document simply consists of a `<p>` node, nested inside a `<body>` node, nested inside an `<html>` node. The `<p>` node wraps around the JSON document displayed in Figure 3.4. To convert the JSON document into a conventional rectangular data matrix, we first extract the content of the HTML file and store the output in the object `json`, before converting it into a data matrix using the `fromJSON()` function provided by the `jsonlite` package. Finally, we check the number of entries in the resulting data matrix (44) and have R output 10 random entries.

So far, our interaction with the police API is little impressive and unnecessarily burdensome, as the resulting data could have been provided and accessed in a much more straightforward way. The real power of APIs comes from our ability to make repeated calls to an API, while varying the parameters of the request. For example, the police API provides data on the number of reported stops and searches for the various territorial police forces. The general API query looks as follows:

```
https://data.police.uk/api/stops-force?
force=force-id&date=year-month
```

Before making a specific query, be sure to note the typical components of a URL, which we introduced in the previous section. The query contains the protocol (`https`), the domain (`data.police.uk`), the path to the location of the resource (`/api/stops-force`), and the key-value pairs of the query (`force=force-id` and `date=year-month`), separated by an ampersand. To request data for a specific police force and time period, we simply replace the variable names with specific values and send the resulting query to the server. For example, to request data on the stops and searches reported by the Greater Manchester police force in January 2018, we use the `force-id` variable for the Manchester police from the previous API call (`greater-manchester`), which yields the following query:

```
https://data.police.uk/api/stops-force?
force=greater-manchester&2018-01
```

Querying the data from the server using the thus-defined API call is done in much the same way as before. Using the code displayed in Figure 3.6, we extract the JSON file with the sought-after information and convert the resulting character vector into a conventional rectangular data matrix. The data set holds 242 entries in 16 variables. As we are only interested in the data collection process and not in the actual data, we do not discuss the variables here and simply provide a tabulation of the `object_of_search` variable for illustrative purposes.

With the few lines of code presented earlier, it is possible to amass a data set of considerable size, simply by changing the police force, year, and month parameters in the query. For example, there are 3,857 stops and searches on record for the Greater Manchester police force in the year 2018, a sufficient number of data points to highlight patterns. As an example, Figure 3.7

```
> html <- read_html("https://data.police.uk/api/stops-force?force=greater-manchester&date=2018-01")
> json <- html_text(html)
> stops_dat <- fromJSON(json)
> dim(stops_dat)
[1] 242  16
> colnames(stops_dat)
 [1] "age_range"                          "outcome"        "involved_person"
 [4] "self_defined_ethnicity"             "gender"         "legislation"
 [7] "outcome_linked_to_object_of_search" "datetime"       "removal_of_more_than_outer_clothing"
[10] "outcome_object"                     "location"       "operation"
[13] "officer_defined_ethnicity"          "type"           "operation_name"
[16] "object_of_search"
> table(stops_dat$object_of_search)

Anything to threaten or harm anyone    Article for use in theft  Articles for use in criminal damage
                                 19                          41                                    6
                  Controlled drugs                    Firearms                     Offensive weapons
                               125                           2                                    15
                      Stolen goods
                                34
```

Figure 3.6   R code snippet – Greater Manchester stops and searches

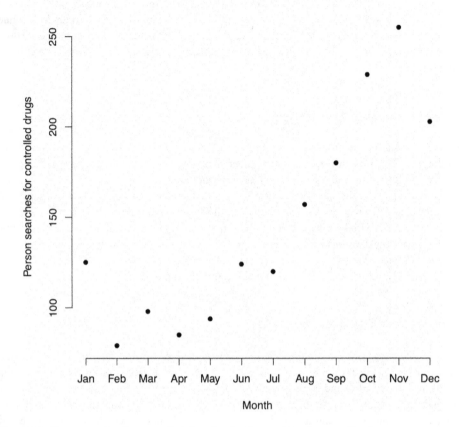

Figure 3.7 Person searches for controlled drugs by the Greater Manchester police force

displays the absolute number of police stops and searches for suspected controlled drugs by the Greater Manchester police.

To be sure, while we observe an uptick of the relevant stops and searches in the second half of 2018, it would require both social science theorizing and case knowledge to make sense of this empirical pattern. Are we observing a general shift in drug use or a seasonal trend, have police reporting standards changed, has the police instituted a new policy against drug use, or are we observing an altogether different phenomenon? Some of these questions could be answered by adding more data points to our descriptive analysis, but they also underscore that social science theorizing is as essential as ever, even in the age of big data. We close this section by encouraging you to retrace the steps of the API interaction we sketched previously to familiarize yourself with the technical aspects of gathering data from APIs, but also to collect and analyze the data yourself to identify patterns in UK policing.

We should note that the API provides a range of other interesting data that we did not discuss in this section. At the time of writing, the API distinguishes between crime-related, neighborhood-related, and stops-and-searches-related data. Now that you know how to collect data from the API in principle, it is just a matter of inspecting the API documentation for the different query types and figuring out which variables need to be defined by the user to formulate a valid API request. For example, to access the crime statistics for a particular point on the map, three parameters are needed – date, longitude, and latitude – to construct a valid query with the following general pattern:

```
https://data.police.uk/api/crimes-at-location?
date=year-month&lat=latitude&lng=longitude
```

You can easily spot the similarities between this query for accessing geolocated crime data and the query that we used earlier to access data on stops and searches, which we reproduce here to simplify the comparison:

```
https://data.police.uk/api/stops-force?
force=force-id&date=year-month
```

The differences are the path on the server where the resources are located (`/crimes-at-location` vs. `/stops-force`) and the key-value pairs to specify the parameters (`date`, `lat`, `lng` vs. `force`, `date`).

4 A more complex example: collecting data from Twitter

Social networks are particularly valuable sources of data for social science research. Not only have social networks fundamentally changed the way that humans interact in the digital age, social networks also record human interactions on an unprecedented scale. Twitter in particular has been highly influential in social research. The platform has left its mark on many different disciplines, in such diverse areas as public health (Broniatowski et al., 2013; Chew & Eysenbach, 2010; Eichstaedt et al., 2015), criminology (Gerber, 2014), economics (Bollen et al., 2011), and politics (Barberà, 2015; Colleoni et al., 2014; Himelboim et al., 2013; Tumasjan et al., 2011).

One of the reasons why Twitter has had such an impact on social research compared to other platforms like Facebook is the relative ease with which Twitter makes its data available to the public. While many observers have faulted Facebook for being so restrictive about making their data available for social science research, the greater accessibility of Twitter data arguably reflects the nature of the two platforms. Whereas communication on Twitter is public by default, private interactions are at the core of Facebook. From this point of view, it is perfectly reasonable that Facebook is more restrictive in providing access to data resulting from private interactions.

In the remainder of this section, we outline how to automatically collect data from Twitter. To do so, we rely on the `rtweet` package in R, which simplifies some of the more challenging aspects of accessing Twitter data. One of the key differences between the Twitter API and the API that we studied in the previous section is the need to register with Twitter before querying the API. Unfortunately, the process of setting up an account is somewhat complex, and we cannot document it here in detail. You can find the details at `https://developer.twitter.com/en/docs/basics/getting-started`. At the time of writing, Twitter distinguishes between a Standard, a Premium, and an Enterprise account for accessing their API. The key difference between the two paid account types and the free standard version is the extent to which data access is limited. After applying for a developer account, it is necessary to register an app and generate a set of access keys that need to be supplied to the API in order to make queries.

Assuming you followed the steps for registering an app, you can replace the app name and the four variables in the code snippet displayed in Figure 3.8 to authenticate yourself with the

```
> create_token(
+        app = "MyTwitterApp",
+        consumer_key = "CONSUMER_KEY",
+        consumer_secret = "CONSUMER_SECRET",
+        access_token = "ACCESS_TOKEN",
+        access_secret = "ACCESS_SECRET"
+ )
```

Figure 3.8 R code snippet – Twitter authentication

```
> tweets <- get_timeline("HamillHimself", n = 50)
> ncol(tweets)
[1] 90
> tweets$created_at[1]
[1] "2021-02-03 18:19:38 UTC"
> tweets$favorite_count[1]
[1] 12789
> tweets$retweet_count[1]
[1] 1904
> tweets$followers_count[1]
[1] 4490935
```

Figure 3.9 R code snippet – Timeline Mark Hamill (February 2021)

Twitter API. Fortunately, when you authenticate yourself this way, you do not have to explicitly supply your credentials in subsequent queries.

Quite a number of options are provided by the Twitter API, some of which are irrelevant for the purposes of collecting data. An overview of the API functionality can be found at `https://developer.twitter.com/en/docs/api-reference-index`. In the example in Figure 3.9, we query the 50 most recent tweets that were sent from the account of Mark Hamill (@HamillHimself) using the function `get_timeline()` from the `rtweet` package. We find that the resulting data set has no less than 90 variables for each tweet with various pieces of meta information in addition to the content of the tweets themselves. To highlight some of the available meta information, we output the time of creation and the number of favorites and retweets for the most recent tweet in the data set ([1]), as well as the overall follower count for the account of Mark Hamill (approximately 4.5 million at the time of writing).

Other API methods are similarly easy to use. For example, a search for tweets containing a particular search term looks as simple as `search_tweets(q = "searchterm")`. Note that the API restricts the number of tweets that can be requested and severely limits the possibility of searches for tweets from the past. At the time of writing, the standard account is limited to searches for tweets from the past seven days. On a more positive note, many of the functions have quite a large number of parameters to refine search queries. Once again, we encourage you to set up an account and play around with the various possibilities that the API offers.

Instead of documenting additional and mostly self-explanatory functions from the `rtweet` package, we believe it is more valuable to take a peak under the hood of the function calls to highlight how similar the queries to the Twitter API are to the queries from the previous section. Unfortunately, due to the need for authentication, you cannot copy and run the code displayed in Figure 3.10 on your machine. To do so, you have to replace the `access_token`

```
> library(httr)
> library(stringr)
>
> hamill_raw <- GET(
+         "https://api.twitter.com/1.1/statuses/user_timeline.json?screen_name=HamillHimself&count=50",
+         add_headers(Authorization = str_c("Bearer ", access_token))
+ )
> parsed_hamill <- content(hamill_raw, as = "parsed")
> length(parsed_hamill)
[1] 50
```

Figure 3.10   R code snippet – Timeline Mark Hamill (February 2021)

```
> baby_yoda <- GET(
+         "https://api.twitter.com/1.1/search/tweets.json?q=baby%20yoda&result_type=popular&count=10",
+         add_headers(Authorization = str_c("Bearer ", access_token))
+ )
> parsed_yoda <- content(baby_yoda, as = "parsed")
> names(parsed_yoda$statuses[[1]])
 [1] "created_at"              "id"                     "id_str"                  "text"
 [5] "truncated"               "entities"               "metadata"                "source"
 [9] "in_reply_to_status_id"   "in_reply_to_status_id_str" "in_reply_to_user_id"   "in_reply_to_user_id_str"
[13] "in_reply_to_screen_name" "user"                   "geo"                     "coordinates"
[17] "place"                   "contributors"           "is_quote_status"         "retweet_count"
[21] "favorite_count"          "favorited"              "retweeted"               "possibly_sensitive"
[25] "lang"
```

Figure 3.11   R code snippet – Tweet searches (February 2021)

variable with your own authentication credentials, specifically the Bearer Token, which can be accessed in a process that is described at `https://developer.twitter.com/en/docs/basics/authentication/oauth-2-0/bearer-tokens`. In this case, we use the `GET()` function from the `httr` package, which mimics the functionality of the HTTP method GET that was briefly introduced in section 2. Consider the API query:

```
https://api.twitter.com/1.1/statuses/
user_timeline.json?screen_name=HamillHimself&count=50
```

This query is identical to the query that was sent by the function `get_timeline()` to the Twitter API in Figure 3.9. Note how we can easily identify the four common URL components: protocol (`https`), domain (`api.twitter.com`), path (`/1.1/statuses/user_time-line`), and the two query parameters as key-value pairs (`screen_name=HamillHimself` and `count=50`).

A second call to the Twitter API is presented in Figure 3.11. In this case, we request 10 popular tweets from the past seven days that contain the search term "baby yoda". Note that empty spaces are not allowed in URLs, so they are replaced by the character string "%20". We can use the same function as before to send our query to the API; only the URL changes:

```
https://api.twitter.com/1.1/search/tweets.json?
q=baby%20yoda&result_type=popular&count=10
```

Once again, we simply adapt the path (`/1.1/search/tweets.json`) and the key-value pairs (`q=baby%20yoda`, `result_type=popular`, `count=10`) to request the new data. This query also underscores the need to study the API documentation to figure out which parameters are available. For example, we could further restrict the results to tweets that were sent in a certain geographic area (`geocode`) or sent in a particular language (`lang`). In the same way, it is important to study the API documentation to ensure that we choose reasonable parameter values. While the possible parameter values might be obvious in case of the `count` parameter – although an upper limit likely applies, it is not obvious which values can be selected for the `result_type` parameter.

5 Conclusion

Application programming interfaces are a crucial element of modern web design. Many services establish links with one another by providing dedicated access points for the systematic information exchange. For example, a weather service might sell their data to a third party that wants to incorporate this information on their site. To exchange the information on a continuous basis, an API is the best solution.

But the sharp increase in the number of available APIs has also had an enormous impact on noncommercial interests, not least on academic research. It has become increasingly common for organizations to make their data publicly accessible by setting up an API. Whereas APIs used to be most common among companies who possessed the necessary technical expertise to support an API, application programming interfaces are ever more frequently provided by civil society actors.

At the same time, we have witnessed a big push by governments to make their data available to the general public as part of the open data/open government movement. A prominent example is `data.gov`, a website hosted by the US government that provides an overview of data and APIs collected by different government branches. Similar efforts can be identified in Canada (`open.canada.ca`), the United Kingdom (`data.gov.uk`), and the European Union (`data.europa.eu`).

These efforts are set to have a major impact on academic research. The largest impact may well be expected on social research, where the traditional data sparsity problem has given way to a wealth of data. These days, the social sciences are faced with an abundance of easily available data to shed light on any number of social science questions. To check whether there is an API that might provide data for your particular research problem, you might consider `www.programmableweb.com`, which compiles an index of available APIs.[3]

In closing, we hope that this chapter has demonstrated how simple it is to collect data via APIs – and that the examples may have sparked some idea on how the available data might be employed for a substantive research application.

Notes

1 We slightly simplified the URL for the purposes of illustration. Note that there are other, but less common, components of URLs that we do not discuss here.
2 Note that the indentation of the document only serves to improve the human readability of the document. The substance of the document would not change if we had written the document as a single line of text.
3 If you are familiar with R and would like to make use of the available wrappers that have been written in R to access an API, you can find an overview of the available wrappers at https://cran.r-project.org/web/views/WebTechnologies.html.

References

Barberà, P. (2015). Birds of the same feather tweet together: Bayesian ideal point estimation using Twitter data. *Political Analysis, 23*(1), 76–91.
Bollen, J., Mao, H., & Zeng, X. (2011). Twitter mood predicts the stock market. *Journal of Computational Science, 2*(1), 1–8.

Broniatowski, D. A., Paul, M. J., & Dredze, M. (2013). National and local influenza surveillance through Twitter: An analysis of the 2012–213 influenza epidemic. *PLoS One, 8*(12), 1–8.

Chew, C., & Eysenbach, G. (2010). Pandemics in the age of Twitter: Content analysis of tweets during the 2009 H1N1 outbreak. *PLoS One, 5*(11), 1–13.

Colleoni, E., Rozza, A., & Arvidsson, A. (2014). Echo chamber or public sphere? Predicting political orientation and measuring political homophily in Twitter using big data. *Journal of Communication, 64*(2), 317–332.

Eichstaedt, J. C., Schwarz, H. A., Kern, M. L., Park, G., Labarthe, D. R., Merchant, R. M., Jha, S., Agrawal, M., Dziurzynski, L. A., Sap, M., Weeg, C., Larson, E. E., Ungar, L. H., & Seligman, M. E. P. (2015). Psychological language on Twitter predicts county-level heart disease mortality. *Psychological Science, 26*(2), 159–169.

Gerber, M. S. (2014). Predicting crime using Twitter and kernel density estimation. *Decision Support Systems, 61*, 115–125.

Himelboim, I., McCreery, S., & Smith, M. (2013). Birds of a feather tweet together: Integrating network and content analyses to examine cross-ideology exposure on Twitter. *Journal of Computer-Mediated Communication, 18*(2), 40–60.

Munzert, S., Rubba, C., Meißner, P., & Nyhuis, D. (2014). *Automated web data collection with R: A practical guide to web scraping and text mining*. Wiley.

Tumasjan, A., Sprenger, T. O., Sander, P. G., & Welpe, I. M. (2011). Election forecasts with Twitter: How 140 characters reflect the political landscape. *Social Science Computer Review, 29*(4), 402–418.

4

WEB DATA MINING[1]

Collecting textual data from web pages using R

Stefan Bosse, Lena Dahlhaus and Uwe Engel

1 Introduction: textual data in computational social science

Today much social interaction and interpersonal communication takes place on the internet. This produces large amounts of both textual data and the behavioral marks people leave when surfing the web. Social media has gained considerably in importance in recent years and represents a rich and indispensable data source for social research. Moreover, much data is available *only on the internet*. This raises the questions of how to identify appropriate methods to collect such data and how to process it to gain the desired insights. In answering these questions, the chapter focuses on the digital collection of *textual* data. Web scraping, also known as web harvesting, describes the extraction of information from web pages. Normally this information is the text published thereon. Although such an extraction may be done manually by copying and pasting, the usual rule is, increasingly, the automatic extraction of information by parsing techniques and software bots (search engines). For this chapter, current techniques are drafted before the setting up of a web page that explains how to extract the information published on it. A fictitious example page is built to cover a use case of special social science interest: the analysis of textual data published on *blogs on scientific* topics. The website of the European Commission, for instance, practices such a blog on artificial intelligence and acts as a reference in the present case.

Data collection undergoes a clear trend toward applying digital methods to do other than survey data. This is largely due to both the availability of relevant data and steady further development of relevant computational methods. This extends the scope and analytical capabilities of practicing social research enormously, but it also produces special demands and challenges. In the first place, unlike the common closed-ended survey questions, textual data requires further processing steps to arrive at an analyzable structure. Although a detailed exposition of this preprocessing step of content analysis is beyond the scope of this chapter on data collection, the chapter provides at least some aid to orientation in this regard. Second, the trend toward the use of textual data from social media comes along with the question of how far such data and related research designs permit the researcher to draw generalizable inferences. A section accordingly takes on the involved validity perspective. Finally, the legal aspect of web mining is addressed.

DOI: 10.4324/9781003025245-5

2 Quantitative content analysis

Next to the more common structured forms of data obtained in surveys or official statistics, the scientific analysis of textual data, referred to as content analysis, dates back to the 1960s (Krippendorff, 2018). Social scientists take an interest in the exploration of textual data because of its unique conveyance of human thoughts and behavior and its high density of information. Before the rise of databases and the World Wide Web, the process of analyzing written human communication relied heavily on the time-consuming collection and processing of the textual data itself. Content analysis was, therefore, often limited regarding the quantity of collected data. A consequence of the increased availability of digital technologies has been a shift in how human interaction and communication are documented and, as such, are progressively more available to researchers (Gentzkow et al., 2019). Data sources on the internet are as diverse as their communicational context, ranging from searchable databases designed specifically to convey information to their users to structured contexts like message boards and single websites of blogs of companies or private individuals. Textual data are used by researchers from a variety of scientific disciplines to conduct both qualitative and quantitative content analysis and are expected to grow further in importance. Current fields of application, for example, are the use of textual data to analyze political discourses, campaigns, and voter behavior (e.g., Stier et al., 2018; Yang & Kim, 2017), the exploration of changes and dynamics in public opinion formation (e.g., Flores, 2017; Das et al., 2019), and the detection of social media users facing mental health issues (Coppersmith et al., 2018). Completing the collection of textual data is, in a way, an intermediate target. Harvesting data on the internet via web scraping is a method commonly chosen to obtain such amounts of data that were too extensive to evaluate by use of qualitative methods. Quantitative content analysis requires experience in the field of natural language processing (NLP) methods. The objective of NLP is to process textual, human-generated communication into data formats that are accessible by computers (Eisenstein, 2019). Unlike numeric data, words, as the smallest possible unit of communication, are symbolic by nature and contain meaningful, albeit country- and language-specific, information. Regardless of the source of the data itself – be it a news website, blog, social network, or message board, understanding how to process written communication is the key to the statistical analysis of text. It is important to first consider the variability of textual data before proceeding in further analysis of the material obtained. The quality of data on the internet varies heavily depending on the context it is produced for and the objective of its communication. The World Wide Web is used in both professional and private contexts; therefore, depending on the purpose of the text, the effort spent on orthography and grammar can be expected to differ. In more informal contexts, like social networks, parts of the sentiment of a sentence may not even be conveyed through text but through emoticons. Additionally, despite recent developments in NLP methods aiming to better extract and interpret the underlying structures of communication (e.g., argumentation mining; Lytos et al., 2019), it is still not possible for computers to access the even more complex nuances of human communication like irony and ambiguity. Methods of NLP require words with identical meaning to be spelled identically. Since computers access text in a different way than a human interpreter can do, preprocessing in a sense of unifying the text as much as possible before using computational methods is often necessary. Typical steps of preprocessing include splitting sentences into single words, removing punctuation, converting words to lower case, and removing the frequently occurring so-called stop words (e.g., conjunctions and articles) from the analysis (Bird et al., 2009; Kannan et al., 2014). In its most basic form, results of NLP resemble the computation of more traditional descriptive statistics, for example, frequency distributions of words occurring in a particular text. Over recent decades more sophisticated NLP methods have emerged, such as text classification,

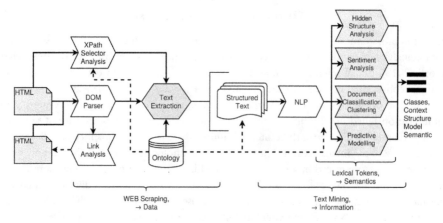

Figure 4.1   Principle functional and data flow diagram of the entire web mining task

linguistic approaches, and unsupervised learning models. Figure 4.1 highlights a selection of such methods: sentiment analysis, the identification of hidden structures and clusters, document classification, and the use of text for predicting outcomes (Kwartler, 2017). Quantitative content analysis can be performed using a variety of programming languages and tools. Common strategies to process text include using the Natural Language Toolkit (NLTK) platform for conducting NLP in Python (Bird et al., 2009) or the packages quanteda (Benoit et al., 2018) or tidytext (Silge & Robinson, 2017) available in R.

3 Is web scraping legal?

As far as we know, but not without further ado. Though one might argue that published content may be extracted from a website in question *simply because of being published there intentionally*, it depends on further factors as well. As far as we understand the discussion, the list of relevant requirements involves the free accessibility *to the web page* itself and the adherence to data privacy laws and copyright (including the neighboring right under copyright protecting investments in databases). *Free access* means access without the need for a web crawler to *bypass effective technical safety devices* if installed for guarding a page/site from being trawled through. It also means that an extraction of information from a web page does not infringe liabilities incurred by a scraper crawler beforehand. This applies to *terms of service*, which precludes the scraping of content if the website operator and the scraper have entered into such terms of service in a legally binding way. The latter usually requires that a person working for a screen scraper has had a chance to read the terms and expressed consent in the incorporation of the terms into an agreement, for example by accessing the website personally and/or logging in to it. The mere automatic crawling of a website by a robot should normally not result in the incorporation of terms of service; however, terms may be expressed in a machine-readable format such as robots.txt.

This file is often part of a website to regulate the behavior of search engines; that is, of bots acting as *web crawlers*. Google's use of this file may be regarded as the internet standard, as to the involved page- and text-level settings (https://developers.google.com/search/reference/robots_txt). Relevant entries in this regard involve "disallow" vs. "allow" ([no] content may be crawled) and "noindex" vs. "index" ([not] to show the page in search results). Since modern web browsers provide an easy way of inspecting the underlying HTML source code of a web page via the navigation to the web developer area involved, a look at the robots.txt specification may reveal a basic website owner's orientation toward/against giving possible permission for reading given web page content out. Note, however, that some website operators take the position that what they express through robots.txt is not legally decisive but rather the human-readable terms of service.

The use of internet platforms may require an adherence to their terms of service, which in this case may be a requisite for visiting the website. If such terms of service become binding between the website operator and a scraper (e.g., since the scraper has visited the website or logged into it and expressed consent to terms of service in a legally binding way) and if they forbid data scraping, the researcher is well advised to seek explicit permission for data scraping. Alternatively, if a digital platform grants access via the use of APIs, this might be a reasonable alternative to scraping the web content.

Web scraping must not infringe *data privacy* laws, neither of the website operator and its staff nor of any other persons whose data may be accessible on the website. In this regard, often the best solution is the full anonymization of data which removes the personal quality of the data and, therefore, the data privacy regime does not apply to data once anonymized (anonymization, however, is itself subject to data privacy laws).

Also, web scraping must not infringe *copyright*. In this regard, one of the relevant factors is the reasons data are scraped, whether for noncommercial scientific use or financial gain. Scientific research conducted for the public benefit is likely to be treated differently than is data collection for commercial reasons among competitors in a market. The overall situation is complex indeed, so in cases of doubt, legal advice should be sought before any attempt at extracting web page content. Regarding the European Union, for instance, FAQs on copyright are dealt with by the European Union Intellectual Property Office Observatory (EUIPO) at https://euipo.europa. eu/ohimportal/en/web/observatory/faqs-on-copyright. A further relevant source is the General Data Protection Regulation (https://ec.europa.eu/info/law/law-topic/data-protection_en).

Because *copyright* regulations must be adhered to, it is recommended to check if the owner of a website in question has issued any license in this respect. The European Commission, for instance, permits the reuse of its website content under a particular Creative Commons license (https://ec.europa.eu/info/legal-notice_en) which then provides the relevant details; for example, the permission to share and adapt the material (e.g., https://creativecommons.org/ licenses/by/4.0/). Similar rights are granted, for instance, by the World Health Organization (www.who.int/about/who-we-are/publishing-policies/copyright). If no such declaration can be found on a website in question, or if a declaration exists but leaves questions open concerning a given web scraping project, then it is best and possibly even unavoidable to ask the website owner for explicit permission before any attempt at extracting information from this site. Such an explicit permission is especially advantageous because it eliminates ambiguity and may additionally bear on *informed consent*, a core principle in *data privacy* laws – if the website operator is in a position to consent to the use of data on the website.

Klawonn (2020) concludes from his inquiry that web scraping is normally permissible for noncommercial empirical research if only an unessential share of data were extracted from the database underlying a web page/site. For one's own research, the limit is set to 75 percent. The author refers to German law when he writes that, in the case of databases, noncommercial scientific research should be allowed to create but not disseminate the resulting text corpora. Always forbidden should be the copying of complete databases without the consent of the database owner. He notes too that the bypassing of technical safety devices is forbidden. The author also mentions under which conditions resulting text corpora must be deleted at the end of a research project. In any case, the database source is to be cited. If such rules are adhered to, web scraping for research for the public benefit appears legal if restricted only to data in the public domain.

It is important to acknowledge possible country-specific regulations. Waterman (2020), for instance, refers to a decision of the United States Court of Appeals for the Ninth Circuit (California) from late 2019 (concerning, *inter alia*, the Californian Computer Fraud and Abuse Act ["CFAA"], the Digital Millennium Copyright Act, and the common law of trespass) and writes that this decision "showed that any data that is *publicly available* and *not copyrighted* is fair game for web crawlers" (emphasis in original, https://law.justia.com/cases/federal/appellate-courts/ca9/17-16783/17-16783-2019-09-09.html). He continues in pointing to the limits for *commercial* use of scraped data and that some forms of web scraping are illegal under US law. This applies, for instance, to data from sites that require authentication "because users must agree to the site's Terms of Service before logging in to the site" and

> because those terms of service typically forbid activity like automated data collection. But since publicly available sites cannot require a user to agree to any Terms of Service before accessing the data, users are free to use web crawlers to collect data from the site.

A potentially helpful development for the scientific community in Europe is the recent opinion of the advocate general at the European Court of Justice *Maciej Szpunar* on the requirements for an infringement of the so-called sui generis right under the copyright that protects databases (http://curia.europa.eu/juris/document/document.jsf?text=&docid=236430&pageIndex=0&doclang=EN&mode=req&dir=&occ=first&part=1). This opinion in the matter Case C-762/19, SIA "CV-Online Latvia" v SIA "Melons" shows a substantially more permissive tendency than earlier decisions of the court. The advocate general argues that a search engine which copies and indexes the whole or a substantial part of the contents of databases that are freely accessible on the internet and then allows its users to carry out searches in those databases effects an extraction and a reutilization of those contents within the meaning of the database right. The maker of a database is entitled to prevent such an extraction/reutilization only on the condition that it adversely affects the database maker's investment in obtaining, verifying, or presenting those contents. The extraction/reutilization must constitute a risk for the possibilities of recouping that investment. Whether this is the case must be examined by the court that decides on such a matter, but even if the court affirms such a finding, this does not automatically result in a finding of infringement. The advocate general emphasizes that the courts must still ensure that the exercise of the right to prevent the extraction/reutilization does not result in an abuse of a dominant position of the maker of that database in the market concerned or a secondary market.

If the court follows the advocate general's opinion – which it does more often than not – an indexing or other extraction of a third-party database would constitute an infringement of the database right only if it harms the database maker economically in a way that threatens the recouping of the maker's investment. If the database is the only source of the data, the database maker must make sure that interested parties can use it for alternative products. Such a ruling will probably have a bearing on screen-scraping cases other than an indexing by a metasearch engine and make it altogether easier to collect data on the open internet.

4 The validity of published web content

Shadish et al. distinguish the four well-known *standard concepts of validity* and list threats pertaining to each of them (2002). Two of these concepts cover aspects of generalizability of inference. While external validity designates the generalizability of inferences over variations in persons, settings, treatment, and outcomes, construct validity refers to inferences about what is being measured by outcome measurements and, thus, covers the generalizability to the higher-order constructs they represent. Even though the use of "found data" (Hox, 2017) replaces carefully designed measurement instruments, the nonreactive nature of found data is sometimes regarded as advantageous when used as *unobtrusive measures* (Webb et al., 1966/2000). When doing so, the argument is that such data replace error-prone self-reports on behavior (for example as obtained in surveys) by the unnoticed direct observation of this behavior itself. At first glance, this argument appears convincing indeed: if people are not asked for a response at all, no such response nor any inadvertent survey-related side effect can occur. This, however, does not preclude the potency of other sources of influence. The crucial point is that "motivated misreporting" (Tourangeau et al., 2015) is not confined to survey research. As Lazer and Radford (2017) put it, "people systematically lie about everything from whether they voted, to what their weight and height are." Found *textual* data are, accordingly, not error-free only because they are obtained unobtrusively. Salganik (2018) illustrates this point using the example of self-reports on Facebook. Such self-reports are *published* posts in public contexts and accordingly motivated, for instance, by gaining acceptance and influence in respective communities. In general, posts are formed also by adherence to platform-specific terms of service, higher-ranking legal rules, and the potential fear of undesirable personal consequences that may let users avoid the expression of too extreme opinions in blogs and discussion lists. Furthermore, another source of measurement error may result from the use of automated forms of collecting textual data. The meaning of words and sentences may be complex indeed, and their meaning may depend on the context within which they were expressed. Then only highly advanced forms of automated data collection may avoid distorting this context-dependency and the related capability of adequately recognizing, for instance, insinuations, slang, and satirical or humorous expressions.

External validity is threatened, too. Platform-specific user populations, for instance, are likely to impair the generalizability of results across different such populations. Also, selection effects due to technical (API) restrictions, privacy settings, guards against tracking, and the potential requirement of informed consent in digital forms of data collection matter (e.g., Keyling & Jünger, 2016).

5 Web data

The World Wide Web is an enormous source of information consisting of services (using the Hypertext Transfer Protocol, HTTP) providing HTML documents. The HTML content format is designed for presenting information to humans, not computers. Therefore, automated information extraction from the web (aka web scraping) has to address the gap between HTML structure and textual structure related to humans' speech semantics.

The source of web-based data is related to web content and web services that can be categorized in:

- Static and dynamic content of web pages (HTML)
- Dialogue and discussion databases (social blogs, chats)
- Digital communication
- Search engine databases
- Personalized data (statistics of user access of web pages and services)
- Video media (containing oral and written language) and audio data (containing oral language)
- Any meta information of media (web pages, browser cookies, video, audio media)

5.1 Feature selection in web data

Feature selection in web data is the general process to extract relevant data from web data sources. If these web data sources are publicly visible web pages, then web scraping can be applied to get data from text documents with layout, discussed later (first-class data). If data is hidden in databases, for example message databases of social media messenger services like Facebook or Twitter (secondary-class data), then often a dedicated web application programming interface (API) can be used. The general process and data flow in web data mining is shown in Figure 4.1.

Features of a web page can be classified in:

- The server domain (address) hosting the web page
- Textual content
- Metadata
- Link references (to other web pages)
- Layout of the web page
- Placement of external and secondary content (e.g., advertisement)
- User and personal data (e.g., author information not contained in metadata of web page)
- Statistical data
- Numerical data (e.g., contained in tables)

5.2 Web scraping and crawling

Depending on the research objective, two main approaches to data collection on the internet can be considered. Social network providers, companies, and organizations may allow users and researchers to access and download data via an API. Popular networks such as the Facebook and Instagram APIs are cases in point, where both the access to data and its scope and diversity have become more restricted for users and academic research. Providers increasingly lean toward requesting a summary of the research plan and further contact information before granting access to data (Perriam et al., 2020; Lomborg & Bechmann, 2014). Web data mining is engineered to access publicly available web content, whereas APIs, while requiring authentication, can provide access to otherwise non-public information too (Lomborg & Bechmann, 2014). Web APIs enable filtered access to the underlying database content, in contrast to web scraping that gets access to the meta-level of the data with a visual representation. The use of APIs offers advantages, for example legality of the obtained data, but, depending on the required data, also holds several drawbacks compared with the web scraping process addressed in this chapter primarily:

- Web API often causes monetary costs, and the amount to be paid determines the data filter (e.g., maximal number of messages that can be accessed, data quality, data variables)
- Web API can change without any notice and at any time, mostly changing the filter function
- Web API can be biased for commercial reasons (i.e., a source of error in sentiment analysis)
- Web API provides directly structured data based on an ontology or schema; getting structured data from web scraping is a challenge and requires user interaction
- Web API can be accessed by any client software; web scraping can require a web browser and user interaction

In the following section, the web scraping basics are introduced.

5.3 Web scraping and crawling

Web scraping is widely known from search engine crawler robots and is the task to extract relevant data from web pages via generic HTTP requests.

5.4 HTML websites as a data source

The Hypertext Markup Language (HTML) is a common and widely used standard for the representation of originally text content, structure, and layout, in recent years extended to the representation of multimedia content, including audio and video (HTML5), too. HTML is a domain-specific subset of the generalized Extensible Markup Language (XML) model, and XML is a subset of the Standard Generalized Markup Language (SGML). XML is a standard for creating languages that meet XML criteria like structural organizations and strict conformity to schemas (a language ontology). HTML is defined by its own schema.

XML, as does HTML, consists of tagged elements (tag) that can be nested. Nested tag elements create a tree structure. A tag consists of a tag name, optional attributes, and content (if any). Content of a tag element can be either a list of other tag elements (children elements) or plain text (including so-called entities, discussed later). XML as well as HMTL group information in hierarchies. The elements in documents relate to each other in parent/child and sibling/sibling relationships. The element names and their structural relationships are defined in a schema.

The content of a tag element (children elements) is enclosed between a tag specifier and an anti-tag specifier, shown as follows:

1: <**tag** *attribute=value.. >*
2: . . . *children content* . . .
3: </**tag**>

Definition 4.1 XML/HTML tag element
   The nesting of elements creates document trees composing the Document Object Model (DOM). Each node of the tree is an HTML tag element; children of an HTML element spawn sub-trees.

   To understand how web scraping functions, a description of the basic composition of a website and its pages and how a reader can inspect this composition, using modern browsers and some helper utilities, is introduced. A website is commonly identified by a URL and is organized in pages that are linked.

   An HTML file is plain text with a specific character encoding (e.g., UTF8 or ASCII with national code pages associating characters to numerical code). HTML markup enables the definition of structure, layout, and style formats. HTML defines the positioning (layout) of web pages, their content, and their visual styles. An HTML file consists of a header defining meta-attributes, styles, and script code, discussed later. The body consists of a page structure tree defining the order, position, and content of visuals. Visual styling can be defined by style classes or by individual styling of page content.

   Here is an example of different representations of the name "John Doe" (with the first word as the surname and the second word as the family name) using different formats and languages (CSV: comma separated values, JSON: JavaScript Object Notation):

```
Text:  "John Doe"
CSV:   John, Doe
```

```
JSON: {FirstName:'John', LastName:'Doe'}
XML:  <name><first>John</first><last>Doe</last></name>
HTML: <html><head><title>Name</title></head><body>
      <p>John Doe</p>
      </body></html>
```

As well as the plain text representation of the name, the HTML format loses the semantic relationship (first and last name), too. This can be an important side effect and challenge in web data mining to extract structured content related to a more or less precisely defined ontology. An ontology defines semantic associations and structural relationships. The interpretation of XML or JSON content relies on ontologies giving tag names a meaning and context.

A web browser and HTML support basically the following visuals (content boxes):

1. Text
2. Images
3. Audio and video media and players

HTML supports the following structuring layouts for text visuals:

1. Section headings
2. Paragraphs
3. Ordered lists (numbered)
4. Unordered lists (unnumbered)
5. Tables
6. Frames

The languages used to build web pages are basically HTML, CSS (cascading style sheets), and JavaScript, which are the technical targets of web scraping. In the beginning of the Web, a web page was organized as a paper with sections starting with a heading line and followed by content or subsections. For this purpose, the heading tags exist (h1, h2 . . .). Today, modern websites are not organized in this one-dimensional layout style anymore; they now use a two- or three-dimensional dynamic layout.

5.4.1 From text content to structured data

Typically, text mining tasks are tasks that map plain text documents on structured and hierarchical feature records. There are structural and semantic features that must be extracted from the raw text data. For example, a book is structured in chapters and sections. Chapters and sections can be considered as nested sub-documents.

Formally, the web data mining task *map* aims to map a text document T structured for visualization and navigation and described by a document model schema $\mathbb{S}$ on a data record structure D related to information semantics that can be described by an ontology model $\mathbb{O}$:

$$\textbf{\textit{map}}(T): T|\mathbb{S} \rightarrow D|\mathbb{O} \tag{4.1}$$

That means, the primary task to be solved is the derivation of a mapping relation function M (the model transformation function) that maps $\mathbb{S}$ on $\mathbb{O}$, commonly a domain- and problem-specific function that cannot be derived automatically.

$$M(T) : \mathbb{S} \rightarrow \mathbb{O} \tag{4.2}$$

The web data mining function consists of three chained functions:

1. A parser function P that structures the plain text document by arranging text elements in an abstract text tree structure (ATT) in compliance with the document schema $\mathbb{S}$ (e.g., HTML)
2. A compiler function C that transforms the abstract text tree ATT to an abstract data structure format, commonly a data tree ADT, in compliance to the ontology $\mathbb{O}$
3. A data formatter function F that transforms the abstract data tree ADT in the desired output data format $\mathbb{Y}$, e.g., JSON

$$\boldsymbol{map}(T) = F_{\mathbb{Y}}\left(C_{\mathbb{O}}\left(P_{\mathbb{S}}(T)\right)\right) \tag{4.3}$$

The data record structure D consists of a set of attributes a_i, that is, $D = \{a_i\}$, containing nested records and lists of elements. The document schema and the target data information ontology are typically lowly correlated.

In the following, a short example shows the large gap between the document schema (here consisting of formatting elements like section headings or paragraphs) and the target data type (a bibliography data structure) as part of ontology "Publication."

```
1: 𝕊   := head, body
2:      head := styles
3:      styles := highlight | color | emphasis | footnote
4:      body := heading | paragraph | list | table
5: ⇒
6: 𝕆   := Novel | Science | News | Advertisement
7:      Science :=
8:      { title        : text,
9:        affiliation  : text,
10:       homepage     : text,
11:       main-author  : boolean,
12:       abstract     : text,
13:       doi          : text}
```

Example 1: Comparison of a document schema describing the elements of a text document (e.g., an HTML document) and an information ontology describing a publication database with different classes of papers.

5.4.2 HTML elements

There are a few HTML elements that are associated with language semantics, summarized in the Table 4.1.

Further tag elements like lists (<ul><li>, <ol><li>) provide only weak semantical and structural correlation of the web page with the extracted structured data.

Table 4.1 HTML elements associated with language semantics

HTML Tag	Semantic
`<title>`	The title of the page (header section)
`<meta>`	The meta tag defines variables (header section), e.g., keywords, characterset
`<h1>`	Heading and start of a main section
`<h2>, <h3>, . .`	Deeper nested document sections
`<dl><dt><dd>`	A definition list assigning a descriptive text to headline or topic (keyword)
`<table><th><tr><td>`	A structured table organising text in rows and columns. If there is a separate header row, the columns can be assigned to attribute names creating a record table.
`<a href=URL>`	The anchor tag provides (named) links to other documents or parts of the current page
`<link href=URL>`	External content is referenced and included in the current document
`<iframe src=URL>`	External content is referenced and included in the current document in a separate and encapsulated frame

Beside the tag element type, a tag element can be attributed by formatting styles (commonly not relevant for text mining) and style classes. Style classes can be used as a semantic mapper, although the style class name (not its associated style formats) is only an opportunistic indicator for document structure and element semantics. Style class to semantic or structure mapping have to be constructed for each new website and in the worst case for every web page to be scanned.

Content can be hidden and only displayed on specific events (e.g., by click events performed by the user).

5.4.3 Feature selection: selecting content

The main challenge of extracting structured data from HTML documents is the selection of relevant elements and their mapping on feature types and hierarchies. Tree-structured documents are typically parsed and analyzed using paths of nodes along DOM node elements until nodes containing the relevant data are found.

Two different main data classes have to be distinguished:

1. Table and numerical data (organized in rows and columns with a mostly regular structure)
2. Text data (organized in sections)

Typically, content is extracted by using descriptive methods, that is, by providing patterns to select parts of the document. Common descriptive methods with pattern matching are regular expressions and XPath expressions, explained in the following subsection. Dynamic content (e.g., a sub-range of lists with varying number of elements) is difficult to handle with patterns and pattern matching. State-based and problem-specific parsers that search desired content iteratively can be a better choice to extract data from web pages. Pattern matching can mostly only be applied to context-free problems (i.e., the absolute position of elements is not relevant). Context-dependent search requires a state-based parser programmed for each specific search problem.

Table 4.2 Regular expressions

Expression	Description
.	Matches any character
\s	Matches a space or tabulator character
\d	Matches a digit character
?ε	Matches the expression one or zero times
[α-β]	Matches a character in the range α to β
[^α,..]	Matches a character without the ones following
ε★	Matches an expression ε zero, one, or more times
ε+	Matches an expression ε one, two, or more times
(ε)	Defines a capturing group that can be referenced
ε|ε	Alternation expression

5.4.3.1 REGULAR EXPRESSIONS

Regular expressions are patterns used to match parts of text (e.g., sentences, keywords, numbers) associated with character combinations in strings. Regular expressions can solve a broad range of text pattern matching and text extraction processes and are specially encoded text strings.

A regular expression consists of terminals (i.e., characters, character ranges, decimal numbers) that can only match one character or a static text string, or literals describing placeholders for dynamic content, shown in Table 4.2.

Regular expressions cannot be used primarily for content extraction from HTML pages. But they can be used in a second step to extract or find relevant textual information from previously extracted text (that can contain a lot of nonrelevant information). Regular expressions must be used in conjunction with text function, for example, a match or replace function, shown in principle in Example 2.

```
1: text="The brown fox hunts white eggs"
2: text.match(/brown/)? ⇒ true
3: text.match(/white/)? ⇒ true
4: text.match(/brown[ ]+([^ ]+)/)? ⇒ ["fox"]
5: text.replace(/fox|egg/g,"animal")
6: ⇒ "the brown animal hunts white animals"
```

Example 2: Regular expressions applied to a sentence

5.4.3.2 XPATH EXPRESSIONS

XPath is a language for matching paths and patterns in tree-structured documents, that is, XML or HTML documents. The XPath patterns address structure as well as data values. An XPath query uses a search pattern to return a list of matching nodes. An XPath is just a string descriptor composed of expressions, shown in Table 4.3.

Referencing content of an HTML web page with XPath selectors is a nontrivial task. HTML tag elements can be referenced by:

1. Their (unique) identity (*id*) attribute (on one hand producing the best matching, but sequences or lists of elements require exact details of all single element identity names)

2. Their style classes (if there is any meaningful relation between style names and content structure)
3. Their relative or absolute position in element lists
4. Their relative or absolute position in the DOM tree

In Example 3, some typical XPath expressions are shown. They will be used in the next section dealing with text extraction of a simple web page.

```
1: //*[contains(\@class,"author")]
2: //span
3: //*[contains(\@class,"blog") and
4:    (((count(preceding-sibling::*) + 1) = 2) and
5:    parent::*)]
6: //*[contains(\@class,"date")] |
7: //*[contains(\@class,"author")]
8: //*[(((count(\preceding-sibling::*) + 1) = 1) and parent::*)]
9: //*[contains(\@class,"date")]
```

Example 3: Examples of XPath expressions

Mapping the DOM content structure on the target data structure is a challenge. HTML element classes describe commonly formatting styles, not semantics or data structure. An extensive commonly handcrafted analysis of the web pages is mandatory.

5.4.4 *Automatized extraction and machine learning*

The derivation of suitable selection patterns, for example using XPath expressions, can be a time-consuming and error-prone task, shown in the practical section 5.7. After deriving a suitable set of pattern expressions, these pattern expressions must be associated with data mapping functions that map the raw extracted content to data structure. This task typically requires extensive scripting and programming. Finally, XPath expressions are contextless and stateless and pose some limitations.

In Grasso et al. (2013), the extraction pattern and the data structure mapping are merged by an advanced but minimalistic wrapping language OXPath. OXPath extends XPath expressions

Table 4.3 XPath expressions

Expression	Description
nodename	Selects all nodes with the name "nodename"
/	Selects from the root node
//	Selects nodes in the document from the current node that match the selection no matter where they are
.	Selects the current node
..	Selects the parent of the current node
@	Selects attributes
⋆	Any matching element
[*n*]	Selects *n*-th element of a list
last()	Selects last element of a list

with more advanced conditional expressions reducing under- and over-fitting of content extraction. OXPath handles patterns and actions on patterns together. Finally, OXPath enable multipage navigation. Most web pages are split over multiple pages.

Beside the content extraction, validation is required to ensure a high data quality of the extracted content (avoiding under- and over-mapping). In Thomsen et al. (2012), a complete web scraping framework is introduced, decomposing the web scraping process in selection, validation, and reinduction functions with a high degree of reusability.

But all presented approaches require a significant amount of user and expert interaction. Automated data extraction from web content can utilize machine learning to extract structure from flat and noisy content. Using such methodology, the web page content is extracted as a contiguous block of text (linear text), for example, discussed by Zhou and Mashuq (2014). An either supervised or unsupervised trained model *M* performs a block clustering of the linear text with a final classification and selection of the text blocks with respect to the target data structure.

5.4.5 *Dynamic versa static content*

In the beginning of the Web, the pages were static text files stored on a file server. Each web request got an exact copy of the stored files. In the last decades, the server-based dynamic creation of HTML pages raises significantly, and today most web pages are created dynamically by using SQL databases storing the content (data) and PHP frameworks creating the HTML document format and styling (Figure 4.2). This content is called server-based content.

By introducing the JavaScript programming language that can be embedded in any HTML document and executed by the browser, another class of documents were created: client-based dynamic content. JavaScript was primarily used to create interactive documents with dynamic layouts and visibility of content. JavaScript code can modify the DOM and therefore can load and present data from remote sources at viewing time. This capability makes it more difficult to

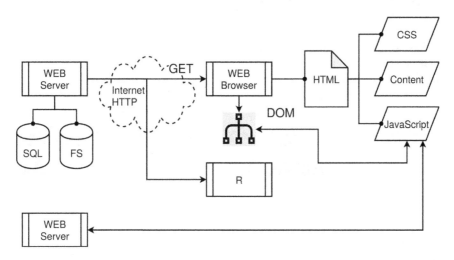

Figure 4.2 A web server provides HTML files. An HTML file consists of style definitions, document content, and JavaScript code. The web server can create the HTML sources from a static file (system) or dynamically by using a database and HTML templates (typically composed by PHP code). On the client side, JavaScript can modify the document content and can load external content or data, too, e.g., from a different web server.

get and extract desired content from a web page. Moreover, only requesting the web page is not sufficient. The code must be executed prior to content extraction.

Finally, the dynamically code-created content of the web page can depend on:

1.   The web browser identification (the so-called user-agent identification, e.g., "Mozilla/5.0 (X11; SunOS i86pc; rv:45.0) Gecko/20100101 Firefox/45.0")
2.   The location (internet network address or geospatial location)
3.   Cookies stored by the code of the web page (or by code of another web page from the same domain)
4.   User (log-in) credentials
5.   User interactions (multimodal: mouse, keyboard, etc.)

5.6 Using R for data collection: how to parse web pages with a simple example[2]

In this section, two practical examples of web data mining are demonstrated using the widely used statistical and data analysis software R. These examples show the programmatical implementation of the three mining functions introduced formally in section 5.4. The first example shows the extraction of table data (primarily numerical data), and the second example performs extraction of structured text content.

5.7 Demonstration

5.7.1 The visual appearance

Figure 4.3 shows an example page containing table structured data, and Figure 4.4 shows an example page containing structured text in the form of news snippet blocks arranged in a linear list. Both demonstration pages embed the relevant content in a navigation frame, typical for modern website layouts.

The basis DOM structure of the first page is shown in Example 4. A challenge is the mixed layout of the table with header and data rows and two stacked sub-tables (for years 2021 and 2020).

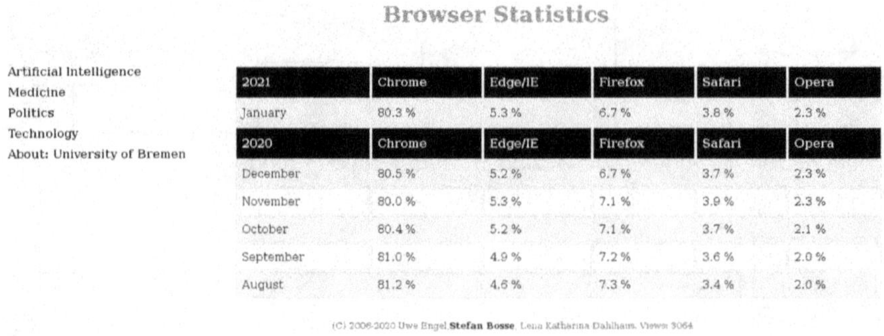

Browser Statistics

Artificial Intelligence
Medicine
Politics
Technology
About: University of Bremen

2021	Chrome	Edge/IE	Firefox	Safari	Opera
January	80.3 %	5.3 %	6.7 %	3.8 %	2.3 %
2020	Chrome	Edge/IE	Firefox	Safari	Opera
December	80.5 %	5.2 %	6.7 %	3.7 %	2.3 %
November	80.0 %	5.3 %	7.1 %	3.9 %	2.3 %
October	80.4 %	5.2 %	7.1 %	3.7 %	2.1 %
September	81.0 %	4.9 %	7.2 %	3.6 %	2.0 %
August	81.2 %	4.6 %	7.3 %	3.4 %	2.0 %

(C) 2006-2020 Uwe Engel **Stefan Bosse**, Lena Katharina Dahlhaus. Views 3064

Figure 4.3   Table data mining demo 1: the visually and rendered appearance of the example web page shown by a typical web browser

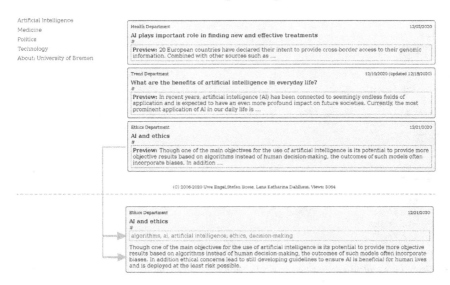

Figure 4.4   Text mining demo 2: (top) the visually and rendered appearance of the example web page shown by a typical web browser; (bottom) expanded hidden content

The second demonstration page shows a list of news blog entries. Each news blog snippet contains a date, an author name, a headline, a keyword list, and a shortened preview of the news text. The preview and the news text can be switched in place by user interaction (clicking on the preview text field). The keyword list also opens only by user interaction (hovering over the keyword field).

5.7.2 The Document Object Model

The basic structure of the demonstration DOM is shown in Example 4 (showing irrelevant content) and Examples 5 and 6 (showing relevant content containing the target data to be extracted).

```
html
 ├──head
 ├────style
 ├──body
 ├────script
 ├────h1#text
 ├────div(flex-container)
 ├──────div(column-left)
 ├────────ul
 ├──────────li
 ├────────────a(href="demo02.html")#text
 ├──────────li
 ├────────────a(href="demo03.html")#text
 ...
```

Example 4: Start of DOM tree of both demonstration pages (up to here no relevant content)

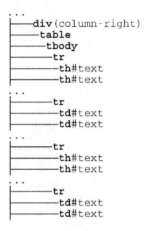

```
...
├────div(column-right)
├───────table
├────────tbody
├─────────tr
├───────────th#text
├───────────th#text
...
├─────────tr
├───────────td#text
├───────────td#text
...
├─────────tr
├───────────th#text
├───────────th#text
...
├─────────tr
├───────────td#text
├───────────td#text
```

Example 5: First content relevant part of DOM tree of the demonstration page 1 containing a data table

```
...
├────div(column-right)
├──────div(blog)
├───────span(author)#text
├───────span(headline)#text
├───────span(tags-button)#text
├───────span(tags)#text
├───────span(id=preview1)#text
├───────span(id=text1)#text
├──────div(blog)
├───────span(author)#text
├───────span(headline)#text
├───────span(tags-button)#text
├───────span(tags)#text
├───────span(id=preview2)#text
├───────span(id=text2)#text
...
```

Example 6: First content relevant part of DOM tree of the demonstration page 2 containing a news list

The target data must be extracted from HTML *div* and *span* tag elements. The relevant data structure mapping can be achieved here by unique style classes (e.g., author, headline). This is commonly not the case, and ambiguous data content types must be resolved either by HTML tag positions (relative and absolute), by an automatic posterior text analysis, or by hand.

5.7.3 R preparation

The following code snippet Code 1 shows a basic R setup loading required libraries and finally parsing the DOM tree of a web page. The libraries must be previously installed. The central library is *rvest*. The installation of the rvest packages via the install.packages("rvest") command has a lot of dependencies that require attention and in particular the installation of additional system packages (e.g., development libraries with support for SSL, XML, HTTP to access and process HTML pages).

The HTML pages can be loaded via remote HTTP communication or from files stored previously in the local file system (e.g., by using a generic web browser). Accessing remote web pages via R and HTTP is performed without providing user credentials and a user-agent. This anonymous request can be rejected by the remote web server.

```
1: # General-purpose data wrangling
2: library(tidyverse)
3: # Parsing of HTML/XML files
4: library(rvest)
5: # String manipulation
6: library(stringr)
7: # Verbose regular expressions
8: library(rebus)
9: # Eases DateTime manipulation
10: library(lubridate)
11: # JSON formatting
12: library(jsonlite)
```

Code 1: R setup for web scraping

5.7.4 R data extraction

```
1: # Load and parse DOM of HTML file
2: html <- read_html('demo01.html')
3: rows <- html %>% html_nodes(xpath='//tr')
4: tables <- c()
5: table  <- c()
6:
7: for (row in rows) {
8:   th <- row %>% html_nodes('th')
9:   td <- row %>% html_nodes('td')
10:  if (!(th %>% rlang::is_empty())) {
11:    # Start of a new table
12:    if (!( table %>% is_empty)) {
13:      tables <- append(tables,list(table))
14:    }
15:    table <- c();
16:    table <- append(table,list(th %>% html_text()));
17:  }
18:  if (!(td %>% rlang::is_empty())) {
19:    # Append row to current table
20:    table <- append(table,list(td %>% html_text()));
21:  }
22: }
```

```
23: # Append last table to tables list
24: if (!( table %>% is_empty)) {
25:   tables <- append(tables,list(table))
26: }
27: # Format tables in JSON format
28: json <- toJSON(tables)
```

Code 2: Demo 1, table extraction: Parse the HTML document and extract content finally coded in JSON format

```
 1: # Load and parse DOM of HTML file
 2: html <- read_html('demo02.html')
 3: # Selecting headline nodes
 4: headlines <-
 5:   html %>% html_nodes(xpath='//*[contains(@class,"headline")]')
 6:        %>% html_text()
 7: # Selecting authors/source nodes
 8: sources <-
 9: html %>% html_nodes(xpath='//*[contains(@class,"author")]')
10:        %>% html_text()
11: # Selecting date nodes
12: dates <-
13:   html %>% html_nodes(xpath='//*[contains(@class,"date")]')
14:        %>% html_text()
15: # Create a compound data structure
16: data <- c();
17: for (i in 1:length(headline)) {
18:   data <- append(data, list(list(headline=headlines[i],
19:                       source=sources[i], date=dates[i])))
20: }
21: # Format mining results in JSON format
22: json <- toJSON(data);
```

Code 3: Demo 2, text extraction: Parse the HTML document and extract content finally coded in JSON format

The following tasks are to be performed:

1. Analyze the web page for relevant content and create XPath selectors by visual inspection by using a web browser to extract the content from the web page
2. Parse and analyze web page for external links; store all web links in a list
3. Demo 1: Extract all tables as a list (array)
4. Demo 2: Extract all news blog snippets as a record list (array)

   • Each record should contain information about the author, date of publication, the headline, and the preview text

5. Demo 2: Analyze linked web content contained in the news snippet
6. Create a content tree with all the referenced sub-documents (both demonstrations)
7. Create a JSON data object from the extracted content.

Program Codes 2 and 3 produce a JSON object with the following type signature:

```
type table = table []
type table = (number|string) [][]
type news = {headline: string [],
             source: string [],
             date: string []} []
```

The date attribute of each entry must be further processed to create a uniform date format. Some date entries contain auxiliary text like "updated on".

The output from demo #1 is:

```
[[["2021","Chrome","Edge/IE","Firefox","Safari","Opera"],
["January","80.3 %","5.3 %","6.7 %","3.8 %","2.3 %"]],
[["2020","Chrome","Edge/IE","Firefox","Safari","Opera"],
["December","80.5 %","5.2 %","6.7 %","3.7 %","2.3 %"],
["November","80.0 %","5.3 %","7.1 %","3.9 %","2.3 %"],
["October","80.4 %","5.2 %","7.1 %","3.7 %","2.1 %"],
["September","81.0 %","4.9 %","7.2 %","3.6 %","2.0 %"],
["August","81.2 %","4.6 %","7.3 %","3.4 %","2.0 %"]]]
```

The output from demo #2 is:

```
[{"headline":["Solidarity with Members of Boğaziçi University"],
  "source":["Health Department"],
  "date":["12/02/2020"]},
 {"headline":["Arctic Climate Change: From Greenhouse to Icehouse "],
  "source":["Trend Department"],
  "date":["12/10/2020 (updated 12/18/2020)"]},
 {"headline":["Workshop: Cognitive Architectures for Robots"],
  "source":["Ethics Department"],
  "date":["12/21/2020"]}]
```

More details using R and rvest performing web scraping and data mining can be found in Munzert et al. (2015).

5.8 XPath selection

XPath content filters have to be defined to extract parts of the HTML DOM tree that contain the desired data content. The XPath selectors provide automatic filtering of HTML element nodes. They are not able to extract the text content (except in some simple cases) and perform the mapping to the target data structure.

XPath selectors have to be created by visual inspection of the web page(s) under test. A naive way to specify an XPath selector is inspecting the DOM tree by using the DOM inspector tool contained in any modern web browser. But this can be a highly complex and time-consuming process considering modern blown-up web pages created by client- and server-side code.

Another more efficient and reliable way is using a dedicated XPath inspector written in JavaScript and executed in the target web page context (Figure 4.5). By sideloading injection and content framing, it is possible to analyze arbitrary web pages by using a web browser and the inspector framework contained in a (locally stored) HTML wrapper document (named frame. html). The HTML wrapper document loads the target web page in an HTML frame and injects the inspector software.

Due to cross-origin access policy restrictions, the target web page must be downloaded first (e.g., by using the web browser itself).

After the inspector is loaded in the target page context, HTML DOM elements can be selected visually by clicking on the elements. An appropriate HTML and XPath selector is created that can be used in R and rvest.

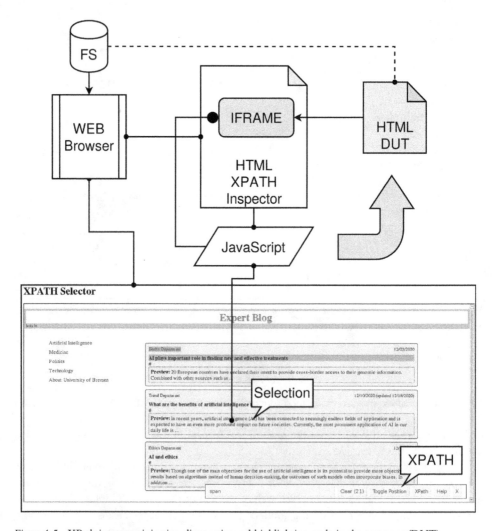

Figure 4.5 XPath inspector injecting diagnostics and highlighting code in the test page (DUT)

6 The real world and challenges

In the previous section, web data mining was demonstrated with a simple static web page. Accessing data from today's real-world web pages has to address different difficulties:

1. The web server delivers browser-specific content. A generic HTTP request, that is, by R, provides no user-agent information, that is, an identification of the web browser that requests the page. The result of the request is unpredictable and ranges from a default web page notification (web browser not supported) to the desired content. Furthermore, modern websites support mobile devices with limited user interaction capabilities and targeting small screen size layouts. Without proper user-agent information, the web server can also return a limited version of the web page with reduced content.
2. The access of a web page requires user authentication (access-restricted content).
3. The content is built dynamically by client-side JavaScript code.
4. The content is blocked due the usage of cookie storage violating German/European privacy restrictions and requires user interaction to allow exceptions. The content blocking is mostly limited to the visual representation and does not affect the DOM of the HTML page, but there is no guarantee that the desired data content is available before user interaction.
5. The data content structure is not related with unique HTML tag elements and styles (style classes), that is, there is no bijective mapping function *map*: $T \Leftrightarrow D$. This is a typical problem in dynamically created content, e.g., by using database-driven server frameworks like TYPO3.
6. The structural HTML elements like headings h1, h2, and so on are used in a misleading context with a high degree of ambiguity. The following real-world example demonstrates this issue. Heading elements are often used to ease recognition of relevant highlighted content for search engine crawlers (like news headlines).

6.1 Complex example web page

To demonstrate the challenges of web scraping of complex dynamically server-created web pages, a final example with the widely used TYPO3 content management system (CMS) created web page from the University of Bremen is shown in Figure 4.6 and analyzed. This web page shows complex and nested content layout. In TYPO3, like any other CMS, content management is completely separated from content layout and styles. This leads to a significant decorrelation of HTML DOM structure and styles from content and data structure (loss of semantic relation).

The data mining task consists of the extraction of news entries with date, headline, and short text message fields. A first overview analysis of the web page shows that

1. The date fields can be accessed with a `//time` XPath expression
2. The news headlines can be accessed with a `//h3` XPath expression
3. The news short text message can be accessed with `//p` XPath expression

Applying these simple filters to the content extraction delivers 20 date entries, 35 headline entries, and 48 message entries. The filter is insufficient to extract the desired content (only 20 news messages are visible; the rest is hidden by code) correctly. The list of the entire news blocks (containing date, headline, and message child elements) can be extracted by using a

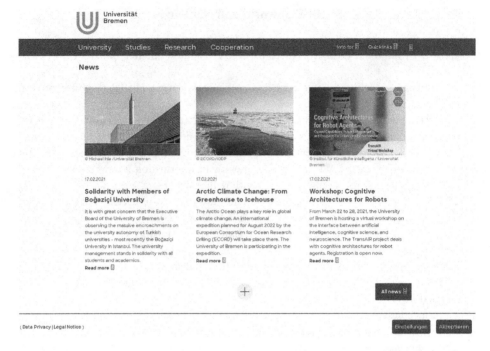

Figure 4.6 The real-world test page from the University of Bremen (home page) accessed at 22.2.2021 (shown is a part of the viewport of the page content with relevant news content snippets to be extracted)

more specific XPath `//*[contains(@class,"news-link")]` referencing division elements with the specific style class attribute. This list is finally divided in the subparts with additional XPath selectors applied to each block list.

This example shows the difficulties of extracting the data from complex web pages. Typically, this process cannot be automatized and requires a lot of handcrafted work.

7 Data quality

The previous demonstration showed different query results depending on the accuracy of the query patterns. This uncertainty can reduce the data quality with respect to completeness and wrongly extracted and classified data.

Further issues can affect the data quality and the data extraction process, which must be addressed by the web scraping software:

1. Blocking of content based on the internet address, requiring proxy server support
2. Blocking of content due to human-bot tests (CAPTCHA), requiring support for CAPTCHA-based scraping and proxy supports (CAPTCHA appearance can relate to internet address, too)
3. Point-and-click user interfaces for identifying content is error prone and can result in under- or over-fitted content matching, requiring validation tools
4. Irregular text formats, for example different date and time formats mixed with auxiliary text; reduces text-data mapping quality

5. Different views of a page based on web browser (user-agent) identification and personalization of web page can invalidate extraction patterns or change the data. Most web services provide a mobile version with a different layout and reduced content. Practically, unknown or older browsers are considered as mobile software, obfuscating the data mining process.

To summarize, the quality of data derived from web scraping technologies can vary significantly and requires validation and quality evaluation by expert interaction.

Notes

1 Acknowledgements. The section on "Is web scraping legal?" benefited much from an exchange with Fabian Seip at Hengeler Mueller (https://www.hengeler.com/en). We greatly appreciate this support.
2 Availability and implementation: The inspector software, the demonstration scripts (in R), and the data sets are available at https://github.com/bsLab/webscraping.

References

Benoit, K., Watanabe, K., Wang, H., Nulty, P., Obeng, A., Müller, S., & Matsuo, A. (2018). quanteda: An R package for the quantitative analysis of textual data. *The Journal of Open Source Software, 3*(30), 774.

Bird, S., Loper, E., & Klein, E. (2009). *Natural language processing with Python.* O'Reilly Media.

Coppersmith, G., Leary, R., Crutchley, P., & Fine, A. (2018). Natural language processing of social media as screening for suicide risk. *Biomedical Informatics Insights, 10.* https://doi.org/1178222618792860

Das, S., Dutta, A., Lindheimer, T., Jalayer, M., & Elgart, Z. (2019). YouTube as a source of information in understanding autonomous vehicle consumers: Natural language processing study. *Transportation Research Record, 2673*(8), 242–253.

Eisenstein, J. (2019). *Introduction to natural language processing.* MIT Press.

Flores, R. D. (2017). Do anti-immigrant laws shape public sentiment? A study of Arizona's SB 1070 using Twitter data. *American Journal of Sociology, 123*(2), 333–384.

Gentzkow, M., Kelly, B., & Taddy, M. (2019). Text as data. *Journal of Economic Literature, 57*(3), 535–574.

Grasso, G., Furche, T., & Schallhart, C. (2013). Effective web scraping with oxpath. In *Proceedings of the 22nd International Conference on World Wide Web* (pp. 23–26).

Hox, J. J. (2017). Computational social science methodology, anyone? *Methodology, 13,* 3–12. https://doi.org/10.1027/1614-2241/a000127

Kannan, S., Gurusamy, V., Vijayarani, S., Ilamathi, J., & Nithya, M. (2014). Preprocessing techniques for text mining. *International Journal of Computer Science & Communication Networks, 5*(1), 7–16.

Keyling, T., & Jünger, J. (2016). Observing online content. In G. Vowe & P. Henn (Eds.), *Political communication in the online world: Theoretical approaches and research designs* (pp. 183–200). Routledge.

Klawonn, T. (2020, January 1). Grenzen des "Web scrapings". *Forschung & Lehre.* www.forschung-und-lehre.de/recht/grenzen-des-web-scrapings-2421/

Krippendorff, K. (2018). *Content analysis: An introduction to its methodology.* Sage.

Kwartler, T. (2017). *Text mining in practice with R.* Wiley.

Lazer, D., & Radford, J. (2017). Data ex machina: Introduction to big data. *Annual Review of Sociology, 43,* 19–39. https://doi.org/10.1146/annurev-soc-060116-053457

Lomborg, S., & Bechmann, A. (2014). Using APIs for data collection on social media. *The Information Society, 30*(4), 256–265.

Lytos, A., Lagkas, T., Sarigiannidis, P., & Bontcheva, K. (2019). The evolution of argumentation mining: From models to social media and emerging tools. *Information Processing & Management, 56*(6), 102055.

Munzert, S., Rubba, C., Meißner, P., & Nyhuis, D. (2015). *Automated data collection with R: A practical guide to web scraping and text mining.* John Wiley & Sons.

Perriam, J., Birkbak, A., & Freeman, A. (2020). Digital methods in a post-API environment. *International Journal of Social Research Methodology, 23*(3), 277–290.

Salganik, M. J. (2018). *Bit by bit: Social research in the digital age.* Princeton University Press.

Shadish, W. R., Cook, T. D., & Campbell, D. T. (2002). *Experimental and quasi-experimental designs for generalized causal inference.* Houghton Mifflin.

Silge, J., & Robinson, D. (2017). *Text mining with R: A tidy approach.* O'Reilly Media.

Stier, S., Bleier, A., Lietz, H., & Strohmaier, M. (2018). Election campaigning on social media: Politicians, audiences, and the mediation of political communication on Facebook and Twitter. *Political Communication, 35*(1), 50–74.

Thomsen, J. G., Ernst, E., Brabrand, C., & Schwartzbach, M. (2012, July). WebSelF: *A web scraping framework*. In *International Conference on Web Engineering* (pp. 347–361). Springer.

Tourangeau, R., Kreuter, F., & Eckman, S. (2015). Motivated misreporting: Shaping answers to reduce survey burden. In U. Engel (Ed.), *Survey measurement: Techniques, data quality and sources of error* (pp. 24–41). Campus.

Waterman, T. (2020, January 29). *Web scraping is now legal.* https://medium.com/@tjwaterman99/web-scraping-is-now-legal-6bf0e5730a78

Webb, E. J., Campbell, D. T., Schwartz, R. D., & Sechrest, L. (2000). *Unobtrusive measures*. Sage. (Original work published 1966)

Yang, J., & Kim, Y. M. (2017). Equalization or normalization? Voter – candidate engagement on Twitter in the 2010 US midterm elections. *Journal of Information Technology & Politics, 14*(3), 232–247.

Zhou, Z., & Mashuq, M. (2014). Web content extraction through machine learning. *Stanford University*, 1–5.

5

ANALYZING DATA STREAMS FOR SOCIAL SCIENTISTS

Lianne Ippel, Maurits Kaptein and Jeroen K. Vermunt

1 Introduction

One of the new challenges of our current digital age is processing and analyzing the vast amounts of data (Gaber, 2012; Gaber et al., 2005; L'Heureux et al., 2017). Data are collected via many different devices, for example smartphones and wearables, and in various contexts like at home, while navigating, or in a hospital. The common characteristic of these data is that the data are often too large to be processed at once and/or have an accumulative nature where new data points continue to augment the data set. Even though computational power is increasing exponentially, the storage, processing, and analysis of such data remains challenging (Ippel et al., 2016a, 2019; Yang et al., 2017). Storing all data might be expensive, and computations of complex models can be time consuming. Even the computations of 'simple' models like linear regressions can become too time consuming when using large or, even worse, growing data sets. Moreover, methods typically used to analyze such large data sets are often black boxes, making it difficult to explain the results of these methods (Rudin, 2019).

In this chapter, we address several approaches to analyzing large data sets or even data streams using methods frequently used by social scientists, which are both computationally feasible to analyze large data and maintain their explainable character. In the next section, we identify four approaches to analyzing large data. We continue this chapter with some examples of models for independent observations, illustrating one of these approaches in particular, namely online learning (Bifet et al., 2010; Shalev-Shwartz, 2011). After these examples, we introduce SEMA, an algorithm to estimate generalized linear models for analyzing dependent observations using online learning. This chapter ends with a discussion of future developments and further readings.

2 Approaches to analyze large volumes of data

In this section, we detail four approaches to analyzing large and/or streaming data. We start with two techniques, which are especially beneficial for analyzing large data: subsampling and parallel computing. We end this section with two techniques that are tailored to analyzing streams of data, namely sliding windows and online learning.

DOI: 10.4324/9781003025245-6

2.1 Processing large data

Given that the data are either large and/or computational time is lengthy, one can choose to select only a smaller number of observations to analyze. This process is called subsampling, where one randomly samples observations (i.e., the rows) from the entire data set and uses this subsample of observations for their analysis (Wang et al., 2018, 2019). This is an appropriate method when the aim of the analysis is to obtain insights of the associations between a set of variables. Repeating the process of subsampling several times will in addition provide insights into the stability of the parameter estimates. However, when using this technique for prediction purposes, much information about the unit of analysis is lost due to subsampling. This might negatively affect prediction performances and at the very least increases standard errors (due to the smaller number of observations).

An alternative method for dealing with lengthy computations is dividing the data over several machines. The computations, which would previously be done sequentially, are now done in parallel (Böse & Högqvist, 2010; Chu et al., 2007). The results of the computations of each of the separate machines are combined afterwards. Parallel computing is an efficient method to deal with large data, when the methods used allow for parallel computing, that is, the computations of one part of the data should not depend on other parts of the data. In addition, when data are streaming in, the demand for more or more powerful machines remains and the overhead caused by combining the results from several machines will grow.

2.2 Processing data (as) streams

Instead of processing all data at once, whether it is a subsample or divided across several machines, data might also be analyzed sequentially, either out of necessity, for the data is arriving over time, or because data are stored in a cloud solution and are processed sequentially. A sliding window comes down to a subsample of data of either a certain time interval or a certain number of data points, that is, the window (Gaber, 2012). As new data are streaming in, a sliding window 'moves' forward excluding the oldest data points and including the new or yet unseen data points. While this method has several strong advantages, such as user control about exactly how many resources are used for the analysis and well-accommodated temporal fluctuations, it also comes with an important downside. It requires domain knowledge to determine the appropriate size of the window. While large windows will increase the chances of capturing enough significant events, it will also increase the demand on the resources. Especially in a situation with reoccurring fluctuations of events, a sliding window approach can easily miss these patterns due to a too narrow window.

The last approach we discuss is called online learning. This approach updates parameter estimates with information from the most recent data points, instead of computing the parameter estimates again every time new data enter. In doing so, this approach never returns to historical data, thereby speeding up computations vastly and lowering the burden of data storage. Obviously, online learning also does not go without domain knowledge. First, one has to ensure all required variables are included in the analysis as additional information will be 'forgotten', and hence, lost. Second, deciding how much weight the new information is given is not always straightforward. Especially in situations with concept drift (Elwell & Polikar, 2011), one needs to make a decision in the bias-variance trade off (Belkin et al., 2019) in terms of how close to follow changes in the data. Following the changes too closely, that is, relatively much weight is on the most recent data points, or not close enough both will negatively affect the prediction performances as well as the estimates of the associations between variables.

3 Online estimation with independent observations

In this section, we will go into more detail of online learning for independent observations by illustrating the estimation of several parameters. Some of these online estimated parameters are identical to their offline (i.e., computed using all data at once) counterparts (more examples can be found here, Ippel et al., 2016a). Other parameters have to be estimated iteratively, for example the regression coefficients of logistic regression. For these kinds of parameters, the online approach might not always give the exact same result. This might be due to the order in which the data were entered, the weight given to new observations, or the number of iterations set in the offline setting. First, we discuss some of the identical estimators, followed by an online learning approach to estimate logistic regression coefficients, which is an approximate solution.

3.1 Exact estimators

One of the keystone statistics used in most models used by social scientists is the covariance between two variables. We now illustrate how to compute this parameter online. Let X and Y be data vectors with n entries. Now, the covariance between X and Y is denoted by:

$$S_{xy} = \frac{\sum_{i=1}^{n}\left(X_i - \bar{X}\right)\left(Y_i - \bar{Y}\right)}{n-1} \tag{5.1}$$

where i is the index of an entry of the data vector and $\bar{X}$ and $\bar{Y}$ are respectively the averages of X and Y. The first step, however plain perhaps, is keeping the count, n. In online learning, we often use the following notation

new state := previous state + new information,

where ':=' is an assignment sign, replacing the previous state with a new state. Hence, writing an online counter, n, using this online learning formulation, we write

$$n := n + 1$$

Second, we compute the average of the variable. Assuming that the number of observations is already updated, we write the online estimation of the mean as follows:

$$\bar{X} := \bar{X} + \frac{X_n - \bar{X}}{n}, \tag{5.2}$$

where subscript n denotes the most recent data point. Here, the weight of the new observation is given by $\frac{1}{n}$, that is, each data point receives an equal weight. However, when one chooses to alter this weight, for instance $\frac{1}{min(n,1000)}$, more recent data points receive relatively a higher weight and will therefore influence the parameter estimates more than the older data points will. The last part for the online computation of the covariance is more complicated and exists of multiple steps. Assuming the counter n is already updated:

$$\bar{X} := \bar{X} + \frac{X_n - \bar{X}}{n},$$

$$\sum xy := \sum xy + \left(X_n - \bar{X}\right)\left(Y_n - \bar{Y}\right), \tag{5.3}$$

$$\bar{Y} := \bar{Y} + \frac{Y_n - \bar{Y}}{n},$$

$$s_{xy} := \frac{\sum xy}{n-1},$$

where $\sum xy$ is the sum of cross products. While $\bar{X}$ is updated first in Equation 5.3, the result is the same whether one chooses to update $\bar{Y}$ first (Pébay, 2008). This equation can also be used to compute the variance of a variable, however with a minor adjustment. Line 2 of Equation 5.3 in words is, 'new sum of cross products is the previous sum of cross products plus the difference between the last data point and a mean that includes this last data point multiplied by the differences between the last data point and a mean that excludes this last data point'. Now, if one wants to compute the variance, one has to resort to an auxiliary variable to temporarily store that difference between the last data point and the mean excluding the most recent data point:

$$d = X_n - \bar{X},$$

$$\bar{X} := \bar{X} + \frac{X_n - \bar{X}}{n},$$

$$\sum xx := \sum xx + d(X_n - \bar{X}), \qquad (5.4)$$

$$s_x^2 := \frac{\sum xx}{n-1},$$

where d is an auxiliary variable, $\sum xx$ the sum of squares, and s_x^2 the sample variance. In combining Equation 5.3 and Equation 5.4, one can also compute correlation estimates in an online manner. Now, let us move to an analysis often used by social scientists: linear regression.

This analysis, like covariance estimates, yields identical parameter estimates in both the traditional offline approach, using all data at once, and an online learning approach. To briefly remind the reader, linear regression coefficients are computed as follows:

$$\hat{\beta} = (X'X)^{-1} X'Y \qquad (5.5)$$

where X is a $n \times p$ data matrix, where p is the number of variables, including a column of 1s for the intercept. Once there are enough observations available for $X'X$ to be invertible (i.e., $X'X$ should be positive definite), one only needs to invert this $X'X$ matrix once, and afterwards directly update the inverted matrix as follows, using the formulation of Sherman-Morrison:

$$(X'X)^{-1} := (X'X)^{-1} - \frac{(X'X)^{-1} x_n x_n' (X'X)^{-1}}{1 + x_n (X'X)^{-1} x_n'} \qquad (5.6)$$

where x_n is the most recent data point or vector with p entries. The second part of Equation 5.5 is computed online similar to Equation 5.3 line 2:

$$X'Y := X'Y + X_n Y_n \qquad (5.7)$$

Next, multiplying the results of Equation 5.6 and Equation 5.7 yields identical regression coefficient estimates to the offline estimated coefficients. Unfortunately, not all parameters can be estimated using a closed form expression, and therefore not all parameter estimates are identical in their online and offline estimation approach. We now continue with the discussion of stochastic gradient descent, an online estimation approach to fit, for instance, logistic regression models.

3.2 Approximating estimators

While data scientists often use logistic regression as a classification method, social scientists are often more interested in the regression coefficients of the logistic regression. Now, even fitting a logistic regression using all data at once is an optimization problem, since there is no closed form expression. This even amplifies the demand for an online estimation procedure, as iterative procedures for model fitting quickly become infeasible when data are streaming in. The iterations required to obtain a stable solution for the regression coefficients will require more time as more data are entering, and with the new data entering, one has to redo the analysis to remain up to date.

Various estimation methods and algorithms can be used to estimate a logistic regression model (Hilbe, 2009; Heinze, 2006), and for the purpose of this chapter we look into the maximum likelihood framework and use the (stochastic) gradient descent algorithm (Bottou, 2010). In general, gradient descent entails the following: derive the first order derivative of the log-likelihood function and set it equal to zero. Then, iteratively update the parameter estimates until convergence is reached. To illustrate gradient descent, we provide the example of logistic regression. The log-likelihood function of logistic regression is:

$$\ell = \sum_{i=1}^{n} Y_i log\left(\frac{\exp(X_i\beta)}{1+\exp(X_i\beta)}\right) + (1-y_i) log\left(1-\frac{\exp(X_i\beta)}{1+\exp(X_i\beta)}\right) \tag{5.8}$$

with the first order derivative:

$$\frac{\delta\ell}{\delta\beta} = \sum_{i=1}^{n} \left(y_i - \frac{exp(X_i\beta)}{1+exp(X_i\beta)}\right) X_i \tag{5.9}$$

Equation 5.9 is a summation of the contributions of each of the rows in the data set to the derivative. Instead of summing over the entire data set at once, the summative nature can be exploited by taking intermediate steps towards a more likely solution after adding the contribution of each data point:

$$\hat{\beta} := \hat{\beta} + \lambda\left(y_n - \frac{\exp(X_n\beta)}{1+\exp(X_n\beta)}\right) X_n \tag{5.10}$$

where λ is the learning rate giving weight to new observations. Similar to Equation 5.2, the learning rate can be decided upon by the researcher.

The parameters estimated in this section, whether they are obtained through approximations or in closed form solution, all have in common that the parameters are estimated using data from which we assume the data rows are independent of each other. This implies that there is no correlation between data points. However, in social science practice, we often deal with situations where this assumption is violated because we have repeated observations of individuals or other kinds of groupings such as employees nested within companies, children in classrooms within schools, or citizens in countries. In the next section, we detail how to fit a multilevel model using online learning.

4 Streaming expectation maximization approximation

In this section, we focus on the online estimation with dependent observations. Commonly, dependent observations are analyzed with multilevel models. For the online estimation of these models, we introduce the streaming expectation maximization approximation (SEMA) algorithm, an online learning algorithm based on the EM algorithm (Ippel et al., 2019, 2016b). Multilevel models have several advantages, such as better out-of-sample predictions, over models that assume a fixed effect; they are also easier to interpret as the models only exist of three types of parameters (i.e., regression coefficients, variance parameters, and residual variance) (Raudenbush & Bryk, 2002; Skrondal & Rabe-Hesketh, 2004). However, the downside of these models is that they rely on iterations to fit the model, similar to the logistic regression. When data are either large (i.e., long) or augmented with new observations, the estimation time of such a multilevel model quickly becomes infeasible, as does the required computational power to do the series of matrix inversions necessary to estimate the model parameters. While we assume data to enter over time, using SEMA for model estimation can still be beneficial in the case of stationary data. While in a data stream, SEMA will not revisit previously seen observations; that is not to say that it is impossible. In a stationary data set, SEMA can be used to iterate over the data set more efficiently than the offline method, using fewer iterations in order to converge (Ippel et al., 2016b). In this section, we first detail the multilevel model and highlight one of the commonly used estimation algorithms to fit the model, that is, EM algorithm. We then continue with the discussion of SEMA.

4.1 Multilevel model

When the assumption of independent observations is violated, social scientists often resort to multilevel models to account for these dependencies (Raudenbush & Bryk, 2002; Skrondal & Rabe-Hesketh, 2004). For instance, assuming that a school effect on student performance is normally distributed and within a school the children's performances are also normally distributed, we can estimated a 'normal × normal' model; however, other distributions that fall within the framework of the exponential family (e.g., beta binomial or negative binomial) can be accounted for similarly. In multilevel modeling, we refer to level 1 as the lower level, for example observations, and level 2 as the higher level, for example individuals. Instead of assuming a fixed effect, which is the same for each individual, in this model we estimate individual effects. These individual effects are not directly observable as they are coming from (a) latent variable(s). Assuming normally distributed individual effects and normally distributed errors, the model formulation is then as follows:

$$y_{ij} = x_{ij}\beta + z_{ij}b_j + \varepsilon_{ij} \tag{5.11}$$

where y_{ij} is observation i of person j, x_{ij} is a vector of p fixed effect covariates, z_{ij} is a vector of r random or individual effect covariates, β is the fixed effect regression coefficient, b_j are individual effects and $b_j \sim N(0, \tau^2)$, ε_{ij} is the error term per observation, and $\varepsilon_{ij} \sim N(0, \sigma^2)$, where $b_j \perp \varepsilon_{ij}$. Additionally, let J be the number of individuals, n the number of observations, and n_j the number of observations from one individual.

4.2 Model estimation using EM algorithm

An option to estimate the coefficients of Equation 5.11 is by using the 'expectation maximization' algorithm. In short, the algorithm works as follows: in the first step, the expectation step, the unobserved values (of the latent variable) are predicted, given the current set of parameter estimates. The second step, the maximization step, then maximizes the (log-)likelihood given these predictions, thereby updating the estimates of the parameters. Alternating between these two steps, EM algorithm will obtain the maximum likelihood estimates.

4.2.1 E step

The E step consists of three equations, one for each type of parameter: β, τ^2, and σ^2 to compute the complete data sufficient statistics, CDSS. We use the term complete data because we treat the predicted values as if they were observed. We refer to the CDSS as T_1, T_2, and T_3, for respectively β, τ^2, and σ^2. Each will be discussed in turn, starting with T_1:

$$T_{1(k)} = \sum_{j=1}^{J} X_j' Z_j \hat{b}_{j(k)} \tag{5.12}$$

where X_j is an $n_j \times p$ matrix, Z_j is an $n_j \times r$ matrix, k indexes the current iteration, $T_{1(k)}$ is an $p \times 1$ vector, and $\hat{b}_{j(k)}$ is an $r \times 1$ vector and defined as:

$$\hat{b}_{j(k)} = C_{j(k)}^{-1} \left(Z_j' y_j - Z_j' X_j \hat{\beta}_{(k-1)} \right) \tag{5.13}$$

where $C_{j(k)}$ is an $r \times r$ matrix which quantifies the uncertainty of $\hat{b}_j$, and is given by:

$$C_{j(k)} = Z_j' Z_j + \hat{\sigma}_{(k-1)}^2 \hat{\tau}_{(k-1)}^{-1} \tag{5.14}$$

Second, $T_{2(k)}$ is computed as follows:

$$T_{2(k)} = \sum_{j=1}^{J} \hat{b}_{j(k)} \hat{b}_{j(k)}' + \hat{\sigma}_{(k-1)}^2 \sum_{j=1}^{J} C_{j(k)}^{-1}, \tag{5.15}$$

where $T_{2(k)}$ is an $r \times r$ matrix. Lastly, $T_{3(k)}$ is given by:

$$T_{3(k)} = \sum_{j=1}^{J} u'u + \hat{\sigma}_{(k-1)}^2 tr\left(\sum_{j=1}^{J} C_{j(k)}^{-1} Z_j' Z_j \right) \tag{5.16}$$

where $u = y_j - X_j \hat{\beta} - Z_j \hat{b}$ is the residual.

4.2.2 M step

Using the updated CDSS, in the M step the parameter estimates are updated. In iteration k, β is computed as follows:

$$\hat{\beta}_{(k)} = \left(\sum_{j=1}^{J} X_j' X_j \right)^{-1} \sum_{j=1}^{J} X_j' Y_j - T_{1(k)} \tag{5.17}$$

The $\hat{\tau}_{(k)}^2$ is equal to:

$$\hat{\tau}_{(k)}^2 = \frac{T_{2(k)}}{J}, \tag{5.18}$$

Lastly, $\hat{\sigma}_{(k)}^2$ is given by:

$$\hat{\sigma}_{(k)}^2 = \frac{T_{3(k)}}{n} \tag{5.19}$$

4.3 Online model estimation using SEMA

Several operations presented in the previous sections would make the online estimation of the multilevel model infeasible in a growing data set. For instance, the matrix multiplication and inversion $((X' X)^{-1})$ is a costly operation, which would have to be computed again every time an update is desired. In this section, we will detail the adaptations that allow for online estimation. However, note that the online estimation will not result in the exact same parameter estimates when only a few observations have been processed as the offline estimation procedure. When more (i.e., tens of thousands) observations have been processed, the estimates of the parameters will be the same or at least highly similar.

4.4 Online E step

In this section, we will use the '~' to differentiate between the offline and online estimated parameters. We refer to the individual that is generating the most recent data point as j_t, where t indexes the most recent data point. Since all three CDSS are sums over individuals, the online update for each of the CDSS follows this logic:

CDSS:= CDSS − previous contribution + updated contribution

The online computation of $\tilde{T}_1$ is as follows:

$$\tilde{T}_1 := \tilde{T}_1 - T_{1 j_{t(t-1)}} + T_{1 j_t} \tag{5.20}$$

where $T_{1 j_t}$ is defined as:

$$T_{1 j_t} = X'_j Z_j \hat{b}_j, \tag{5.21}$$

where the online computation of $X'_j Z_j$ equals:

$$X'_j Z_j := X'_j Z_j + X_{tj} Z'_{tj}. \tag{5.22}$$

Second, the CDSS $\tilde{T}_2$ is computed as follows:

$$\tilde{T}_2 := \tilde{T}_2 - T_{2 j_{t(t-1)}} + T_{2 j_t} \tag{5.23}$$

where $T_{2 j_t}$ is given by:

$$T_{2 j_t} = \hat{b}_j \hat{b}'_j + \hat{\sigma}^2 C_j^{-1} \tag{5.24}$$

where $\hat{b}_j$ is computed online exactly the same as offline (Equation 5.13), where the product of $Z'_j Y_j$ is computed similar online to Equation 5.22 and $Z'_j X_j$ is the transpose of that same equation. The online computation of C_j online requires the online matrix multiplication presented earlier in Equation 5.22. Lastly, the computation of $\tilde{T}_3$,

$$\tilde{T}_3 := \tilde{T}_3 - T_{3 j_{t(t-1)}} + T_{3 j_t} \tag{5.25}$$

where the individual contribution is given by:

$$T_{3 j_t} = Y'_j Y_j + \hat{\beta}' X'_j X_j \hat{\beta} + \hat{b}'_j Z'_j Z_j \hat{b}_j - 2 Y'_j X_j \hat{\beta} - 2 Y'_j Z_j \hat{b}_j + 2 \hat{\beta}' X'_j Z_j \hat{b}_j + \hat{\sigma}^2 tr(C_j^{-1}) \tag{5.26}$$

For Equation 5.26, we have to store several components to ensure we do not have to redo the computations when new observations come in. For instance, we have to store $X'_j X_j$ matrix, similar to $Z'_j Z_j$, $Y'_j X_j$, $Y'_j Z_j$, and lastly $X'_j Z_j$. All these matrix and vector products are updated like Equation 5.22. When the new contribution is computed, these matrices are multiplied with the relevant parameters.

4.5 Online M step

In the case of fitting a multilevel model where both the random effects and the error terms are assumed to be normally distributed, the M step of EM algorithm is computationally simple. Adapting this step to fit in an online learning algorithm is therefore rather straightforward: the maximization of τ^2 and σ^2 remain exactly the same. The estimation of the fixed effect regression coefficients, β, is altered slightly to fit the online framework. The main adaptation is in the matrix inversion of $X' X$. While the inverse of C_j matrix has to be computed for the most recent individual to update the model, the $(X' X)^{-1}$ can be updated directly (Ippel et al., 2016a, 2019; Sherman & Morrison, 1950; Plackett, 1950). The reason for this difference is that the computation of C_j depends on continuously changing estimates of the model parameters and the values of the latent variables, while $X' X$ only depends on the values of the observed covariates. Once $X' X$ is invertible, the inverse of this matrix can be updated using the formulation presented in Equation 5.6. You can find an R package with the SEMA algorithm at https://github.com/L-Ippel/SEMA.

5 Discussion

This chapter introduces several approaches to analyzing data streams with independent and dependent observations. Four approaches were suggested in how to process large and/or streaming data. We introduced online learning estimation procedure for models commonly used by social scientists, such as correlations and linear regression. However, for many models online learning approaches have not yet been developed. For instance, commonly used machine learning algorithms, for example random forest, and neural networks are challenging to estimate in an online learning manner. The research field of analyzing data streams is growing vastly.

In addition to exploring new methods to analyze data streams, methodological issues regarding analyzing data streams is a pioneering research field. Currently, open questions are, for instance, the treatment of (temporarily) missing data. To illustrate, it is yet unclear how one should handle data streams where not all covariates are observed at once, resulting in missing values. While randomly missing values can cause an increase of the standard error, the problem becomes even more challenging when values are missing due to attrition: a particular subgroup of observations drops out of the stream. This will likely lead to biased estimates.

Related to the issue of systematic dropout is concept drift (e.g., Zliobaite, 2009), where the data-generating model fluctuates over the data collecting period. There are several approaches for handling such fluctuations over time. One branch of research is focused on the auto-correlation models where previous observations are taken into account for new predictions (e.g., Cappé, 2011). Another branch of research focuses on forgetting factors also known as learning rates. This learning or forgetting parameter determines the weight of the newly observed data compared to the weight of the historical data. A simple example is the computation of the sample mean: $\dfrac{1}{min(n; 1000)} \sum_{i=1}^n x_i$. Computing the sample mean like this gives equal weight to all observations, until $n = 1000$. When additional observations augment the data set, these observations will influence the sample mean more than the historic data, allowing the mean to fluctuate more with the recent data.

An additional complication in analyzing data streams with fluctuations over time arises when observations from an individual are collected at highly skewed time intervals. Observations closer in time are more strongly correlated than are observations spread out over a longer time interval. These differences in time intervals might therefore cause bias in the individual predictions as dependencies between close-in-time observations compared to distance-in-time observations might not be picked up adequately by the model.

Lastly, analyzing data streams, similar to analyzing static data sets, requires a well-designed research plan. This plan should entail which method and model will be used and which variables will be collected. Moreover, it should also contain which tests will be done at which point in time, to prevent type 1 error inflation. In data streams, this research plan is even more important than in the case of static data analysis, since data that were not stored are lost. It also means that prior to the data collection, one has to consider the purpose of the study, for example different strategies apply for a prediction of whether someone will click on an advertisement versus understanding the influence of sentiment after a match of a national soccer match on stock market behavior, and how long or how many observations will be collected.

Using data streams to understand social behavior is an exciting new research area. It allows novel research questions to be asked using innovative research methods. More and more tools are becoming available for the interested researcher such as RapidMiner (Hofmann & Klinkenberg, 2013) and Massive Online Analysis (Bifet et al., 2010) that allow mining and learning from these data streams.

References

Belkin, M., Hsu, D., Ma, S., & Mandal, S. (2019). Reconciling modern machine learning practice and the classical bias – variance trade-off. *Proceedings of the National Academy of Sciences*, *116*(32), 15849–15854. doi:10.1073/pnas.1903070116

Bifet, A., Holmes, G., Kirkby, R., & Pfahringer, B. (2010). MOA: Massive Online Analysis. *The Journal of Machine Learning Research*, *11*, 1601–1604.

Böse, J.-H., & H¨ogqvist, M. (2010). *Beyond online aggregation: Parallel and incremental data mining with online map-reduce*.

Bottou, L. (2010). Large-scale machine learning with stochastic gradient descent. In *Proceedings of the 19th international conference on computational statistics (compstat'2010)* (pp. 177–187). Physica-Verlag HD. doi: https://doi.org/10.1007/978-3-7908-2604-3_16

Cappé, O. (2011). Online expectation-maximisation. In K. Mengersen, M. Titterington, C. Robert, & P. Robert (Eds.), *Mixtures: Estimation and applications* (pp. 1–20). Wiley.

Chu, C., Kim, S. K., Lin, Y., & Ng, A. Y. (2007). Map-reduce for machine learning on multicore. In B. Schölkopf, J. C. Platt, & T. Hoffman (Eds.), *Advances in neural information processing systems* (19th ed., Vol. 19, p. 281). Massachusetts Institute of Technology. doi:10.1234/12345678

Elwell, R., & Polikar, R. (2011). Incremental learning of concept drift in nonstationary environments. *IEEE Transactions on Neural Networks*, *22*(10), 1517–1531. doi:10.1109/TNN.2011.2160459

Gaber, M. M. (2012). Advances in data stream mining. *Wiley Interdisciplinary Reviews: Data Mining and Knowledge Discovery*, *2*(1), 79–85. doi:10.1002/widm.52

Gaber, M. M., Zaslavsky, A., & Krishnaswamy, S. (2005). Mining data streams: A review. *SIGMOD*, *34*(2), 18–26.

Heinze, G. (2006). A comparative investigation of methods for logistic regression with separated or nearly separated data. *Statistics in Medicine*, *25*(24), 4216–4226. doi:10.1002/sim.2687

Hilbe, J. M. (2009). *Logistic regression models*. Chapman and Hall/CRC. doi:10.1201/9781420075779

Hofmann, M., & Klinkenberg, R. (2013). *RapidMiner: Data mining use cases and business analytics applications*. Chapman & Hall/CRC.

Ippel, L., Kaptein, M. C., & Vermunt, J. K. (2016a). Dealing with data streams: An online, row-by-row, estimation tutorial. *Methodology*, *12*(4). doi:10.1027/1614-2241/a000116

Ippel, L., Kaptein, M. C., & Vermunt, J. K. (2016b). Estimating randomIntercept models on data streams. *Computational Statistics & Data Analysis*, 169–182. doi:10.1016/j.csda.2016.06.008

Ippel, L., Kaptein, M. C., & Vermunt, J. K. (2019, March 1). Estimating multilevel models on data streams. *Psychometrika*, *84*(1), 41–64. doi:10.1007/s11336-018-09656-z

L'Heureux, A., Grolinger, K., Elyamany, H. F., & Capretz, M. A. M. (2017). Machine learning with big data: Challenges and approaches. *IEEE Access*, *5*, 7776–7797. doi:10.1109/ACCESS.2017.2696365

Pébay, P. (2008, September). Formulas for robust, one-pass parallel computation of covariances and arbitrary-order statistical moments. *Sandia Report, SAND2008–6*, 1–18. www.ntis.gov/search/product.aspx?ABBR=DE20111028931%5Cninfoserve.sandia.gov/sand_doc/2008/086212.pdf

Plackett, R. (1950). Some theorems in least squares. *Biometrika*, *37*, 149–157.

Raudenbush, S., & Bryk, A. (2002). *Hierarchical linear models: Applications and data analysis methods* (2nd ed., J. de Leeuw, Ed.). Thousand Oaks, CA: Sage.

Rudin, C. (2019). Stop explaining black box machine learning models for high stakes decisions and use interpretable models instead. *Nature Machine Intelligence*, *1*(5), 206–215. doi:10.1038/s42256-019-0048-x

Shalev-Shwartz, S. (2011). Online learning and online convex optimization. *Foundations and TrendsR in Machine Learning*, *4*(2), 107–194. doi:10.1561/2200000018

Sherman, J., & Morrison, W. J. (1950). Adjustment of an inverse matrix corresponding to a change in one element of a given matrix. *The Annals of Mathematical Statistics*, *21*(1), 124–127. doi:10.1214/aoms/1177729893

Skrondal, A., & Rabe-Hesketh, S. (2004). *Generalized latent variable models: Multilevel, longitudinal, and structural equation models* (Vol. 17). doi:10.1007/BF02295939

Wang, H., Yang, M., & Stufken, J. (2019). Information-based optimal subdata selection for big data linear regression. *Journal of the American Statistical Association*, *114*(525), 393–405. doi:10.1080/01621459.2017.1408468

Wang, H., Zhu, R., & Ma, P. (2018). Optimal subsampling for large sample logistic regression. *Journal of the American Statistical Association*, *113*(522), 829–844 (PMID: 30078922). doi:10.1080/01621459.2017.1292914

Yang, C., Huang, Q., Li, Z., Liu, K., & Hu, F. (2017). Big data and cloud computing: Innovation opportunities and challenges. *International Journal of Digital Earth*, *10*(1), 13–53. doi:10.1080/17538947.2016.1239771

Zliobaite, I. (2009). Learning under concept drift: An overview. *Training*, abs/1010.4, 1–36.

6

HANDLING MISSING DATA IN LARGE DATABASES

Martin Spiess and Thomas Augustin

1 Introduction

Missing data often occur even in carefully planned studies. Hence, this chapter deals with methods for handling missing values with an emphasis on large data sets. We avoid the term 'big data' because its use is ambiguous and appears in rather different contexts, from more or less clearly defined and, with standard techniques and equipment, manageable data situations up to data sets with a huge number of units and/or variables requiring up to multiples of petabytes or more of storage space and specific processing technology. Even more broadly, the term 'big data' often denotes not only the data set itself but also the whole process from data collection and editing to analysis and interpretation (e.g. Gandomi & Haider, 2015).

Missing data are not a specific problem of certain sizes or types of data sets, and large data sets are no exception. To avoid a treatment of predominantly computational topics, we will assume in the sequel that the data sets are structured in the sense that variables are defined, that is, that each possible observation can be assigned to exactly one variable in the data set. For most statistical analyses of scientific interest, it is moreover crucial to define what the variables ought to measure. We also assume that statistical units, possibly independent, can be identified. In addition we only consider situations in which data sets do not grow too fast but are stable long enough so that the required techniques can be applied.

Assigning observed values to variables and variables to units may reveal missing values not obvious in the unstructured data set. In addition, large data sets are often the result of merging two or more data sets from different sources, where possibly different types of variables are supposed to measure the same construct, but other variables are collected in only one or a few data sets. We will assume throughout that the problem of identifying variables measuring the same construct is solved, and the corresponding variables are already transformed into variables that can be analysed over different data sets. Variables not collected in a subsample are said to be missing by design. Finally, we presuppose throughout that inferences are intended about a population, based on a sample from that population, and mostly assume that the sampling design can be ignored for the analyses of interest.

Associated with the availability of increasingly larger data sets, techniques for analysing these data sets became popular or have been (further) developed, like classification and regression trees or artificial neural networks, mainly optimized with respect to their prediction properties

DOI: 10.4324/9781003025245-7

(e.g. Breiman, 2001; Gandomi & Haider, 2015) as opposed to more traditional approaches in the social sciences, being mainly interested in structural aspects of a model. The focus of these two approaches on different goals comes along with a differing quality of their theoretical justification. For example, theoretically justified methods to handle missing data are developed within the latter framework (e.g. Robins et al., 1995; Rubin, 1987, 1996), whereas theoretically well-justified techniques to compensate for missing data in the prediction framework seem not to be available. In fact, within the prediction context either ad hoc methods which are known to lead to invalid inferences within the structure modelling framework or (derivatives of) well-justified techniques developed within this same approach are adopted. These techniques are then evaluated using criteria, often based on simulations, with respect to their predictive accuracy (e.g. Moorthy et al., 2014).

This chapter does not deal with methods to handle missing data in the context of inferential techniques justified solely on their prediction properties. Instead, we discuss available methods to compensate for missing data in large data sets, developed and justified within the structure modelling framework. If a researcher is interested in the structural aspects of a model, then – given the necessary assumptions are met – the methods discussed later allow valid inferences, if necessary after suitable technical modifications to analyse large data sets.

One prominent compensation method is imputation, where missing values or items are replaced by somehow plausible values. Thus, a tempting idea is to generate these imputations using methods optimized with respect to their predictive properties. Whether adopting this strategy is theoretically justified in a structure modelling framework is the topic of a substantial part of this chapter. A first crucial step, dealt with in the following section, is to identify the intention associated with inferences from data sets and the corresponding criteria to evaluate various methods and techniques. Following these fundamental considerations, phenomenological aspects of missing data are described in section 3 and the process leading to missing values, the missing data mechanism, is introduced in section 4. In section 5, two prominent methods are described – weighting to compensate for missing units and imputation to handle missing items. In the light of the foregoing discussion, we argue in section 6 that particularly in large data sets the naive strategy of using imputation techniques, optimized with respect to their predictive properties, may lead to invalid inferences within the structure modelling context. Some final remarks complete the chapter.

2 Subject of inferences and evaluation criteria

Similar to the distinction between structure modelling and prediction, Breiman (2001) differentiates between the algorithmic and the data modelling culture. The former is deliberately agnostic about the structure of the data-generating process (DGP) and instead tries to find an algorithm that, based on predictors, for example vector x, generates predictions for a dependent variable, for example the scalar variable y. The data modelling approach aims at learning about a DGP, the basic structure of which is assumed to be known. For that purpose, a model is formulated that 'explains' in a statistical sense how variables y are generated from independent variables x. Similarly, the explanatory modelling approach in Shmueli (2010) starts with a theoretical causal model, adopts a statistical model and tries to learn about the stated causal effects of x on y.

If predictions are of main interest, then the statistical methods are usually evaluated based on their prediction accuracy. The expected prediction error (EPE) is defined as $E[D(y, m(x))]$, where $m(x)$ is a function to predict y, and $D(y, m(x))$ is a loss function quantifying the deviation of the prediction $m(x)$ from y. Consider the prediction for a new variable y_0 given a new value $\boldsymbol{x}_0$. Then $E[D(y_0, \hat{m}(\boldsymbol{x}_0))]$, where estimator $\hat{m}(\cdot)$ is a function of y and $\boldsymbol{x}$ usually observed in a (training) sample, is taken with respect to $(y \, \boldsymbol{x}^T)^T$ and y_0 conditional on $\boldsymbol{x}_0$, and $(y_0 \, \boldsymbol{x}_0^T)^T$ is assumed to be independent from $(y \, \boldsymbol{x}^T)^T$. Finally, the expectation of EPE with respect to $\boldsymbol{x}_0$ is taken to get the mean EPE over all possible prediction cases (Hastie et al., 2009). In case of a continuous scalar variable y, a popular loss function is the squared error loss leading to EPE $= E[(y - m(\boldsymbol{x}))^2]$. If y is discrete, then a popular loss function is based on the zero-one loss function, $D(y, m(\boldsymbol{x})) = [1 - I(y = m(\boldsymbol{x}))]$, where $I(c)$ is the indicator function, which is one if c is true and zero otherwise. Thus, EPE $= E[1 - I(y = m(\boldsymbol{x}))]$. Within the prediction framework, the method with the smallest prediction error would be chosen.

If the focus is on modelling the DGP, then there is no immediate evaluation criterion. Instead, the properties of an estimator adopted to estimate unknown aspects of the DGP and the fit of the estimated model to the data are relevant. The estimator results from the chosen estimation method which in turn depends on the adopted statistical model, the associated assumptions about the DGP and the underlying statistical inference paradigm.

In a frequentist context, an estimator is evaluated based on its properties over a hypothetically infinite number of repetitions of exactly the same random DGP, given a finite sample size of n units or for $n \to \infty$. An important property is unbiasedness in finite samples or asymptotically for $n \to \infty$, which guarantees that the estimator varies around the true value of the unknown parameter in a non-systematic way only. To be able to account for the uncertainty inherent in the estimator, an additional requirement is that its variance estimator is (asymptotically) unbiased. Finally, distributional assumptions are often made to justify distributions – which may be replaced by numerical techniques like the bootstrap – of estimators and functions thereof, like test statistics. With these ingredients, approximate confidence intervals can be calculated and hypotheses can be tested.

A standard estimation method is based on the likelihood function. Let $\boldsymbol{u}$ be a random variable, $f(\boldsymbol{u} \mid \boldsymbol{\theta})$ its assumed probability or density function depending on some unknown parameter $\boldsymbol{\theta}$. Then the likelihood function $L(\boldsymbol{\theta} \mid \boldsymbol{u})$ is this same function, but with $\boldsymbol{u}$ fixed at its realized values and $\boldsymbol{\theta}$ taking on values in $\boldsymbol{\omega}$, an appropriate parameter space. The unknown aspects of the model are then estimated given an observed sample by maximizing the log-likelihood function $l(\boldsymbol{\theta}) = \log L(\boldsymbol{\theta} \mid \boldsymbol{u})$ with respect to $\boldsymbol{\theta}$, leading to the maximum likelihood estimator (ML estimator or MLE). ML methods require strong distributional assumptions, whereas semi- or non-parametric approaches work with weaker assumptions. Given a set of substantiated assumptions and acceptable coverage rates of confidence intervals, estimators in the classical model-based framework are evaluated based on their (asymptotic) properties, trading-off bias against variance, and estimated models are validated by descriptive residual analyses and goodness-of-fit tests.

The likelihood function is also at the heart of parametric Bayesian inference, where prior knowledge (or ignorance) about model parameters in form of a prior distribution is combined with observed data information via the likelihood function to form the so-called posterior distribution of the parameter. This posterior distribution reflects the knowledge about the parameters of scientific interest in the light of new data and is used to draw inferences. Bayesian inferences, like direct-likelihood inferences, are generally not evaluated from a frequentist perspective but are based on their plausibility or their support from the observed data (Rubin, 1976). To evaluate models, the posterior distribution of the parameter may be inspected and Bayes factors comparing different models can be calculated. There is, however, also a demand to evaluate Bayesian inferences from a frequentist point of view (e.g. Rubin, 1996). In case of direct-likelihood inferences, models are compared via likelihood ratios, that is, relations of likelihood functions based on different models at their respective maximum.

Inferences may also be made on a design-based approach, which would be adopted if interest is about totals, proportions or means of characteristics in available finite populations. In an ideal design-based approach, the only random variables are sample selection indicators that indicate which of the population elements are selected into the sample. Functions of the interesting characteristics, the selection indicators and their probabilities, usually known from the sampling design, are used to estimate the population statistics of interest. Interpreting the assumed sampling design as a statistical model, this model and the adopted estimator are again evaluated within a frequentist framework preliminary with respect to bias and variance of the estimator.

3 Missing data

Not observing units selected into the sample is often denoted as unit non-response, not observing single responses or items as item non-response. Although these labels seem to imply that unit and item non-response are distinct concepts, this is not the case: unit non-response is just an extreme form of item non-response. And even if a unit is not observed, information may be available on an aggregate level, for example about the neighbourhood of a household or the distance of a company from public transport. Depending on whether information is missing as unit or item non-response, different methods have been proposed to compensate missing data in statistical analyses.

Another phenomenological aspect that has an effect on how to deal with missing values is the pattern of missing values. The main distinction is between a monotone and a non-monotone missing data pattern. A missing data pattern is monotone if the rows and columns of a rectangular data set can be arranged in such a way that, in each row going from left to right, if there is a column with a missing value, all following values in this row are also missing. If the missing data pattern is monotone, then assumptions simplifying the analysis are easier to justify. Unfortunately, often the missing data pattern is not monotone.

4 The missing data mechanism

Theoretically justified approaches to compensate for missing values are developed within the structure modelling framework. The decision about how to deal with missing values depends on the missing data mechanism (MDM). A widely accepted classification (Rubin, 1976; Little & Rubin, 2002) differentiates between missing values that are missing completely at random (MCAR), missing at random (MAR) or missing not at random (MNAR). Roughly, missing values are MCAR if the probability of the observed pattern of missing and observed values is independent from all variables included in the model of scientific interest. Note that the phrase 'model of scientific interest' is used here in a wide sense including simple models, like a mean model, but also more complex models, like structural equation models. Missing values are MAR if this probability may depend on observed values but not on variables with missing values. Values missing by design are usually MCAR or MAR. Finally, missing values are MNAR if the probability of the observed pattern of missing and observed values depend on variables whose values are not observed.

The process from the selected sample to the observed (sub-)sample can be interpreted as a second selection step. The corresponding selection indicator is considered a random response indicator r_{ij}, where

$$r_{ij} = \begin{cases} 1 & \text{if variable } j \text{ of unit } i \text{ is observed,} \\ 0 & \text{otherwise.} \end{cases}$$

The response probabilities are usually unknown. An important question is then whether the MDM can be ignored in downstream analyses, thus avoiding an error-prone step of explicitly taking the MDM into account.

It can be shown that if missing data are MCAR, the MDM can be ignored because then the observed part of the data set is a simple random sample from the selected sample. On the other hand, if missing values are MNAR then, generally, the MDM has to be modelled explicitly. If missing values are MAR, then it depends. Roughly, if estimators are evaluated from a fre-quentist perspective, like in classical model-based inferential statistics, then the MDM cannot generally be ignored. Otherwise, under a non-frequentist evaluation regime like in Bayesian or direct-likelihood analyses, the MDM can be ignored if in addition the parameters of the MDM and the model of scientific interest are distinct, that is, not linked to each other (Rubin, 1976). Despite these seemingly clear boundaries, there are gray zones with respect to ignorability of the MDM. For example, MLEs are often evaluated from a frequentist perspective. And although calculation of the MLE is not affected by the MDM if missing values are MAR, its distribution is. However, in large samples the MDM can usually be ignored if the observed instead of the expected information (ignoring the MDM) is used to estimate its variance (Laird, 1988).

It should be noted that sometimes stronger versions of MCAR and MAR are adopted, assuming that the aforementioned definitions hold for all possible patterns of observed and miss-ing values, denoted as everywhere MCAR and MAR, respectively (cf. Seaman et al., 2013). Further, ignorability of the MDM means neither that missing values can generally be ignored nor that standard analysis software for completely observed data sets can safely be used.

5 Methods to compensate for missing data

Since unit non-response is just an extreme form of item non-response, the same methods can in principle be used to compensate for missing information in both cases. Sometimes proposed simple 'rule-of-thumb' or ad hoc methods, like using only completely observed units or replac-ing each missing value by the (un)conditional mean of observed values and then proceeding as if these values were observed, are in most cases theoretically not justified and lead to invalid inferences in the structure modelling framework (e.g. Little & Rubin, 2002).

Theoretically justified methods can be divided into methods intended to work in specific situations where missing value compensation and data analyses are conducted by the same entity, for example based on the ML method, and more generally applicable methods that can be adopted even if the final analysis of scientific interest is not exactly known. Weighting and the method of multiple imputation (MI) are approaches developed following the latter idea.

ML methods require specification of the joint distribution of all observed variables treated as random conditional on variables fixed at their observed values. Generally, not only y and $\boldsymbol{x}$ but also response indicators r, indicating which elements in $(y\,\boldsymbol{x}^T)^T$ are observed or missing, have to be considered. The likelihood simplifies considerably if the MDM is ignorable. If in addition the missing data pattern is monotone, then the likelihood function factors into terms that are easier to handle. ML methods as well as other methods for specific models requiring weaker assumptions and allowing missing data to be MNAR are described, for example in Little and Rubin (2002) or Cameron and Trivedi (2005). However, since available software solutions apply to specific models and situations only, we will discuss the more generally applicable methods of weighting and MI in the following sections.

5.1 *Weighting*

The underlying idea in design-based statistics is to weight the contribution of each selected and observed unit to the estimating function for the unknown statistic or parameter with the inverse of its known selection probability. The same strategy can be adopted to compensate for missing units in both the design- and the model-based context, in which case the unknown response probabilities have to be estimated.

For example, given $i = 1, \ldots, n$ independent copies $(r_i \; y_i \; \mathbf{x}_i^T \; \mathbf{v}_i^T)^T$ of $(r \; y \; \mathbf{x}^T \; \mathbf{v}^T)^T$, consider the least squares problem $\min_\theta \sum_{i=1}^n (y_i - m(\mathbf{x}_i))^2$, where y_i is the dependent and $\mathbf{x}_i$ is a vector of independent variables. Assume that the model of scientific interest, $m(\mathbf{x})$, is correctly specified up to unknown parameter θ, $r = 1$ if $(y \mathbf{x}^T)$ is observed and $r = 0$ otherwise, and $\mathbf{v}$ is an additional variable that is observed for all units selected into the sample. Then one might consider the estimating equations:

$$0 = \sum_{i=1}^n m'(\mathbf{x}_i) \frac{r_i (y_i - m(\mathbf{x}_i))}{g(r_i = 1 \mid \mathbf{x}_i, \mathbf{v}_i, y_i)} \tag{6.1}$$

to estimate θ, where $m'(\mathbf{x}_i)$ is the first derivative of $m(\mathbf{x}_i)$ with respect to θ, $g(r_i = 1 \mid \mathbf{x}_i, \mathbf{v}_i, y_i)$ is the probability of observing unit i conditional on $(\mathbf{x}_i^T \; \mathbf{v}_i^T \; y_i)^T$ and $r_i / g(r_i = 1 \mid \mathbf{x}_i, \mathbf{v}_i, y_i)$ weights each individual contribution to (6.1). Thus, selected and observed units with a lower probability of being observed receive higher weights in the analysis. Note that instead of $m'(\mathbf{x}_i)(y_i - m(\mathbf{x}_i))$, other contributions could be considered.

To see when (6.1) allows valid inferences in a frequentist model-based sense for $n \to \infty$, consider the expectation:

$$0 = \sum_{i=1}^n m'(\mathbf{x}_i) E\{ E[\frac{E(r_i \mid \mathbf{x}_i, \mathbf{v}_i, y_i)(y_i - m(\mathbf{x}_i))}{g(r_i = 1 \mid \mathbf{x}_i, \mathbf{v}_i, y_i)} \mid \mathbf{x}_i, \mathbf{v}_i] \mid \mathbf{x}_i \} \tag{6.2}$$

where $E(r_i \mid \mathbf{x}_i, \mathbf{v}_i, y_i) = \Pr(r_i = 1 \mid \mathbf{x}_i, \mathbf{v}_i, y_i)$. If $g(r_i = 1 \mid \mathbf{x}_i, \mathbf{v}_i, y_i)$ were known, it could be plugged into (6.2), which would then equal the (conditional) expectation $\sum_{i=1}^n m'(\mathbf{x}_i) E[(y_i - m(\mathbf{x}_i)) \mid \mathbf{x}_i]$ for the complete data set. In real-world applications $g(r \mid \mathbf{x}, \mathbf{v}, y)$ is unknown and has to be estimated. However, only $\mathbf{v}$ is observed for all selected units. Thus, if $g(r = 1 \mid \mathbf{v}) = E(r \mid \mathbf{v}) = E(r \mid \mathbf{x}, \mathbf{v}, y)$, that is, missing units are everywhere MAR, then (6.2) is equal to the expectation based on unweighted estimation if all cases are observed and leads to the same solution θ_0. Under this MAR assumption, replacing (6.2) by its sample analogue allows consistent estimation of θ. Additionally, the asymptotic variance and normal distribution of the estimator $\hat{\theta}$ can be derived (e.g. Wooldridge, 2007). In this scenario, unweighted estimation allows valid inferences for θ up to the constant, for example in the linear model, in which case $\mathbf{v}$ need not be observed and missing units would be MNAR. See results in Heckman (1979), Terza (1998) and McCulloch et al. (2016). Note that the assumption that $E[E(y \mid \mathbf{x}, \mathbf{v}) \mid \mathbf{x}]$ is correctly specified by $m(\mathbf{x})$ does not imply that $E(y \mid \mathbf{x}, \mathbf{v})$ is equal to $E(y \mid \mathbf{x})$.

Consider unweighted estimation if r is independent from y and v given x. Then (6.2) reduces to

$$0 = \sum_{i=1}^{n} m'\left(x_i\right) E[r_i \mid x_i][E(y_i \mid x_i) - m\left(x_i\right)]$$

which is solved by the true parameter value θ_0. In this situation, weighted analyses using $g(r \mid v)$ allow valid inferences as well. Note that the MDM may depend on variables x which are not observed for all units.

If $E(r \mid x, v, y) = E(r \mid x, v)$ then inferences of unweighted analyses are generally invalid unless $E(y \mid x) = E(y \mid x, v)$. On the other hand, if we can include those x variables that have an effect on $E(r \mid x, v)$ into our model to estimate weights, that is, if they are always observed, then weighted analyses will allow valid inferences.

Weighted estimation requires response probabilities to be estimated. Fortunately, it turns out that for valid inferences it is not required to adapt estimation of the model of scientific interest correspondingly. Ignoring that response probabilities are estimated leads to an overestimation of variances and hence to conservative inferences. However, the variances of the estimators of scientific interest tend to be smaller as compared to using the true response probabilities (Robins et al., 1995). Additionally, to minimize the risk of missing units being MNAR, one might include as many variables and functions thereof as possible, like polynomial terms or interactions, into the response model that is to be estimated. Robins et al. (1995) show that this strategy does not increase the asymptotic variance of estimators of scientific interest in the context of weighted estimating equations. However, there are limits to this general statement because the maximum possible number of predictors in the response model is restricted by convergence requirements with respect to the estimators of the response model as $n \to \infty$ (Robins et al., 1995). Including a large number of variables may lead to estimated response probabilities close to zero even for the observed units and as a consequence to large standard errors and even biased estimators in finite samples (Kang & Schafer, 2007). Thus, if variables v are available for all selected units and missing values are MAR, $g(r \mid v)$ may be estimated either by rich standard logit, probit, more robust robit models including many variables and functions thereof or, in large samples, by more flexible approaches like the generalized boosted model as described in McCaffrey et al. (2004).

The unweighted approach should be adopted if the probability of observing units depends only on predictor variables included in the model of scientific interest or in specific cases as discussed previously. Hence, rich models of scientific interest that include predictors explaining response behaviour can protect against invalid inferences due to missing units. See, for example, Wooldridge (2002, 2007) or Kang and Schafer (2007) for more discussion.

If both weighted and unweighted analyses allow valid inferences in a specific situation, then unweighted estimation should be preferred, as unweighted analyses tend to lead to smaller standard errors and thus more precise statements in general and avoid invalid inferences due to a possibly misspecified MDM.

Often, however, additional variables v are not available and it may not be justified to assume that the probability of observing units solely depends on x. In these situations, sensitivity analyses realizing different plausible scenarios can give an impression of the robustness of inferences with respect to various assumptions about the MDM. This approach is particularly appealing in large data sets, where variances of estimators almost vanish and even overestimated variances may not mask biased estimates. Promising approaches are either based on worst case bounds which are derived without imposing assumptions on the MDM or running through a continuum of increasingly strong assumptions, from worst case bounds to ignorability (e.g. Kline &

Santos, 2013; Manski, 2016). However, derivation of the bounds are challenging and solutions are not yet available for many practically relevant situations.

5.2 *Multiple imputation*

Although the weighting approach can be generalized to compensate for missing values in general regression models, the method of MI was specifically developed to compensate for item non-response in analyses not only confined to regression models. The basic idea underlying the method of MI is to generate several, say M, plausible values for each missing value and then analyse these M versions of the completed data set M times with standard software for completely observed data sets (Rubin, 1987, 1996). The theory of MI was derived within a Bayesian framework. Starting point for inferences is the posterior distribution of the parameter θ of scientific interest given the variables whose values have been observed:

$$\int p(\theta \mid \boldsymbol{u}_{(1)}, \boldsymbol{u}_{(0)}, \boldsymbol{r}) f(\boldsymbol{u}_{(0)} \mid \boldsymbol{u}_{(1)}, \boldsymbol{r}) d\boldsymbol{u}_{(0)}, \tag{6.3}$$

where $\boldsymbol{u}_{(1)}$ is the vector of variables whose values are observed, $\boldsymbol{u}_{(0)}$ is the vector of variables whose values are not observed, $\boldsymbol{r}$ is the corresponding vector of binary response variables and integration has to be replaced by summation if corresponding elements in $\boldsymbol{u}_{(0)}$ are discrete. Note that (6.3) is the distribution of θ conditional on the observed values but marginal not only with respect to the variables whose values are not observed but also with respect to the parameter of the missing data mechanism. Further, in the previous formulation we assumed the sample selection mechanism to be ignorable.

If in addition the missing values are MAR and the parameter θ of the model of scientific interest and the parameter governing the missing data mechanism are independent, then the MDM can be ignored and the first distribution under the integral in (6.3), $p(\theta \mid \boldsymbol{u}_{(1)}, \boldsymbol{u}_{(0)}, \boldsymbol{r})$, does not depend on $\boldsymbol{r}$. Let $f(\boldsymbol{u}_{(1)} \mid \boldsymbol{\theta})$ be the distribution of the observed part of $\boldsymbol{u}$ given unknown parameter $\boldsymbol{\theta}$, which is usually not identical to θ, and $p(\boldsymbol{\theta})$ the prior distribution of $\boldsymbol{\theta}$. Then the second distribution in (6.3) simplifies to:

$$f(\boldsymbol{u}_{(0)} \mid \boldsymbol{u}_{(1)}, \boldsymbol{r}) = \int (f(\boldsymbol{u}_{(0)} \mid \boldsymbol{u}_{(1)}, \boldsymbol{\theta}) p(\theta \mid \boldsymbol{u}_{(1)}) d\theta \tag{6.4}$$

(Rubin, 1987), where $p(\theta \mid \boldsymbol{u}_{(1)})$ is the posterior distribution of $\boldsymbol{\theta}$ given the observed values in $\boldsymbol{u}$,

$$p(\theta \mid \boldsymbol{u}_{(1)}) \propto f(\boldsymbol{u}_{(1)} \mid \theta) p(\theta)$$

and $\propto$ denotes proportionality.

Hence, (6.4) together with (6.3) implies a procedure to generate imputations: Select values for $\boldsymbol{\theta}$ from its posterior distribution based on the observed part of $\boldsymbol{u}$, insert them in $f(\boldsymbol{u}_{(0)} \mid \boldsymbol{u}_{(1)}, \boldsymbol{\theta})$ to generate values for $\boldsymbol{u}_{(0)}$. Repeat these steps M times. These values can be interpreted as being realizations from the marginal distribution $f(\boldsymbol{u}_{(0)} \mid \boldsymbol{u}_{(1)}, \boldsymbol{r})$ with respect to $\boldsymbol{\theta}$, also denoted as the posterior predictive distribution of $\boldsymbol{u}_{(0)}$. Inserting these possible values into $p(\theta \mid \boldsymbol{u}_{(1)}, \boldsymbol{u}_{(0)}, \boldsymbol{r})$, the completed-data posterior distribution of $\boldsymbol{\theta}$ in (6.3) generates M values for $\boldsymbol{\theta}$ from its marginal posterior distribution with respect to $\boldsymbol{u}_{(0)}$, given the observed values in $\boldsymbol{u}_{(1)}$.

Thus (6.4) describes the idea of how to generate MIs if the MDM is ignorable and (6.3) shows the way to conduct statistical inferences. The two separate steps are originally understood to be performed by different entities: The database producer and the analyst. The former is assumed to have access to information, for example to sensitive data which are not publicly available, statistical knowledge and computational resources to generate imputations. The latter is assumed to have basic programming skills and access to standard software to analyse completely observed data sets (Rubin, 1996).

The task of the database user is to estimate the parameter of interest $\hat{\boldsymbol{\theta}}_m$ and its variance $\widehat{\operatorname{Var}}(\hat{\boldsymbol{\theta}}_m)$, both available from the analyst's standard software for completely observed data sets, for each of the $m = 1,\ldots,M$ completed versions of the data set and then combine the estimation results using the rules for frequentist model-based inferences derived from (6.3) via

$$\bar{\hat{\boldsymbol{\theta}}}_M = \sum_{m=1}^{M}, \hat{\boldsymbol{\theta}}_m, \widehat{\operatorname{Var}}\left(\bar{\hat{\boldsymbol{\theta}}}_M\right) = \bar{W}_M + \left(1 - M^{-1}\right)B_M,$$

$$\bar{W}_M = M^{-1}\sum_{m=1}^{M}\widehat{\operatorname{Var}}\left(\hat{\boldsymbol{\theta}}_m\right) \text{ and } B_M = (M-1)^{-1}\sum_{m=1}^{M}\left(\hat{\boldsymbol{\theta}}_m - \bar{\hat{\boldsymbol{\theta}}}_M\right)\left(\hat{\boldsymbol{\theta}}_m - \bar{\hat{\boldsymbol{\theta}}}_M\right)^T,$$

where $\bar{W}_M$ is denoted as the 'within'- and B_M as the 'between'-variance (Rubin, 1987). Under standard assumptions, $\bar{\hat{\boldsymbol{\theta}}}_M$ is consistent, approximately normally distributed with variance that can be estimated by $\widehat{\operatorname{Var}}\left(\bar{\hat{\boldsymbol{\theta}}}_M\right)$ in large samples and for a sufficiently large M. With these results, inferences can proceed as in case of completely observed data sets. Hence, once the imputations are generated, the additional effort for the database user to compensate for non-response is low.

The generation of imputations is more demanding. As (6.4) is still too general to be practicable, in a first step both terms under the integral sign are simplified. First note that in many cases a so-called non-informative or flat prior for $\boldsymbol{\theta}$, $p(\boldsymbol{\theta}) \propto c$, is chosen, which is generally interpreted as modelling the absence of any prior information and is usually an improper distribution, that is, a distribution with a probability function whose integral over the parameter space is not finite. However, in many practically relevant situations a well-defined proper posterior distribution exists. Of course, other prior distributions may be chosen as well (e.g. Bernardo, 2003). Further, the distributions involved are often based on independent units given $\boldsymbol{\theta}$, so that

$$f(\boldsymbol{u}_{(1)} \mid \boldsymbol{\theta}) = \prod_{i=1}^{n} (f(\boldsymbol{u}_{(1),i} \mid \boldsymbol{\theta}).$$

After having derived $p(\boldsymbol{\theta} \mid \boldsymbol{u}_{(1)}) \propto \prod_{i=1}^{n} (f(\boldsymbol{u}_{(1),i} \mid \boldsymbol{\theta})p(\boldsymbol{\theta})$ for a particular problem, a value for $\boldsymbol{\theta}$ can be generated based on the observed part of the sample. In a next step, the randomly selected value $\boldsymbol{\theta}^*$ is plugged into $f(\boldsymbol{u}_{(0)} \mid \boldsymbol{u}_{(1)}, \boldsymbol{\theta})$ to independently draw a value $\boldsymbol{u}^*$ for $\boldsymbol{u}_{(0)}$ (cf. (6.3)). Repeating the steps of generating $\boldsymbol{\theta}^*$ and $\boldsymbol{u}^*$ $m = 1,\ldots,M$ times generates M imputations for $\boldsymbol{u}_{(0)}$ from its posterior predictive distribution (see (6.3)). Although $f(\boldsymbol{u}_{(1),i} \mid \boldsymbol{\theta})$ is often still rather complicated, there do exist practically relevant situations where it simplifies considerably.

As an example, consider a simple linear regression model with y the always observed dependent variable and x the predictor affected by non-response, an ignorable MDM and $(y\,x)^{\mathrm{T}}$ bivariate normally distributed. As a consequence, the model required for generating the imputations is a normal linear homoscedastic regression model from x on y and can be estimated using the completely observed part of the sample. Starting with a uniform prior distribution for the parameters of this imputation model, their posterior distribution can easily be simulated and $m = 1,\ldots,M$ imputations can be generated following Rubin (1987, pp. 166–167).

Finally, the M imputed data sets, where M has been proposed to range between 5 and 100 (e.g. Kleinke et al., 2020), would then be used to estimate the model of interest M times, thus approximating (6.3). Inferences can be based on the aforementioned combining rules (Rubin, 1987).

Within a Bayesian framework, the previously described procedure allows valid inferences if all assumptions are met. However, often at least some assumptions may only approximately be met and very often statistical results are evaluated from a frequentist perspective. Hence Rubin (1987, 1996) gives general conditions under which inferences based on a MI method tends to be (confidence-) valid in more general settings, where confidence-valid means that, for example, $(1-\alpha)$ -confidence intervals cover the true values with probability of at least $1-\alpha$. Basically, inferences are confidence-valid if the statistical method, which would have been applied to the data set if it were not affected by non-response, would have been confidence-valid and the MI method is confidence-proper for the complete-data statistic, that is, the estimate $\hat{\boldsymbol{\theta}}$ based on the complete data set, and its variance. Following Rubin (1996), an MI method is confidence-proper if, for $M \rightarrow \infty$, $\bar{\hat{\boldsymbol{\theta}}}_m$ is approximately unbiased for the complete-data statistic $\hat{\boldsymbol{\theta}}$ and $\widehat{\text{Var}}\left(\bar{\hat{\boldsymbol{\theta}}}_M\right) \geq \text{Var}\left(\bar{\hat{\boldsymbol{\theta}}}_M\right)$. Overestimation of the variance of $\bar{\hat{\boldsymbol{\theta}}}_m$ may result from an overestimation of the within- or the between-variance, for example due to a moderately misspecified imputation model (Rubin, 2003).

Following Rubin (1987, 1996), an MI method tends to be frequentist confidence-proper in large samples if the imputations are independent draws from an appropriate Bayesian model. Two general ways to generate imputations have been proposed: by modelling the joint distribution of all variables with missing values conditional on the observed values (e.g. Schafer, 1997) and by modelling univariate conditional distributions (fully conditional specification, FCS, e.g. van Buuren and Groothuis-Oudshoorn, 2011). The former procedure, although being close to theoretical requirements, is not very flexible and may imply a misspecified imputation model in many situations with different types of incompletely observed variables, as the number of available multivariate distributions is restricted. In the latter case, there may not exist a proper common distribution implied by the marginal models, but its advantage is its flexibility to deal with different types of variables and generate imputations, using many different models.

Non-Bayesian imputation models may allow confidence-valid inferences as well (e.g. Rubin, 1987). Hence, many different imputation techniques have been proposed and implemented in publicly available software within the FCS framework. However, not all of the implied imputation methods are confidence-proper such that inferences based on the multiply imputed data sets are confidence-valid, using the earlier combining rules.

6 Pitfalls of imputation in predictive settings

Within the prediction framework, imputation techniques are justified implicitly, referring to the ability of techniques to deal with missing values, and/or, in simulation studies, based on their prediction accuracy. In the context of predictors being MCAR, Hastie et al. (2009), for example, note that some learning methods deal automatically with missing predictors during the training phase, for example by replacing an incompletely observed predictor variable with a surrogate variable and its split-point, as is done in classification and regression trees. Alternatively, ad hoc methods are adopted, using the mean or median of observed values or individual predictions from a fitted flexible model as imputations. In simulation studies, imputation methods are evaluated, using their prediction accuracy, that is, some function of the deviations of the imputations from the true (but deleted) values.

How imputations should be generated depends on the desired evaluation criteria of the applied inferential methods, which are obvious under both the structure modelling and the predictive approach. A theoretical link between the evaluation criteria and the mechanism creating the imputations exists only for the former. Thus, techniques proposed to generate imputations in large databases often mimic the theory of MI (Rubin, 1987, 1996) as outlined earlier, which is developed within the structure modelling approach, but are often evaluated using, for example, the root mean squared error of imputations and functions thereof (e.g. Li et al., 2014).

However, a simple example shows that the predictive accuracy is not informative with respect to whether an imputation method is proper in the structure modelling sense (cf. Rubin, 1996): Suppose not all values of a binary variable y are observed. Somehow, the imputer gets to know the true probability that $y = 1$, $\Pr(y = 1) = 0.6$, and, ignoring the DGP, imputes $y^* = 1$ for each missing value. The EPE of the imputations based on the zero-one loss function is $\text{EPE} = E[1 - I(y = y^*)] = 1 - (1 \cdot 0.6 + 0 \cdot 0.4) = 0.4$. Using the true DGP to generate imputations, $\text{EPE} = 1 - (0.6^2 + 0.4^2) = 0.48$. Clearly, according to the EPE, the former imputation method would be preferred.

Let the probability of observing y be $\Pr(r = 1) = 0.7$. If the data, sorted such that the first $i = 1, \ldots, n_{(1)}$ values are observed, would later be used to estimate the true, but to the analyst unknown, probability that $y = 1$ by $\hat{\pi}_1 = [n_{(0)} + \sum_{i=1}^{n_{(1)}} I(y_i = 1)] / (n_{(0)} + n_{(1)})$, where $n_{(0)}$ is the number of missing y-values, then for fixed $n = n_{(0)} + n_{(1)}$, $E(\hat{\pi}_1) = E(n_{(0)} / n) + 0.6 \cdot E(n_{(1)} / n) = 0.3 + 0.6 \cdot 0.7 = 0.72$. Hence $\hat{\pi}_1$ is a biased estimator. In addition, the standard variance estimator can be shown to be upward biased. If the imputer generated the imputations according to the DGP, then $E(\hat{\pi}_2) = E[\sum_{i=1}^{n_{(1)}} I(y_i = 1) + \sum_{i=n_{(1)}+1}^{n} I(y_i = 1)] / n = 0.6$, that is, $\hat{\pi}_2$ and its variance estimator would be unbiased. Hence, the first imputation method would be preferable within the predictive framework but would be misleading in the structure modelling framework.

It should be noted that this is not an isolated example. In linear regression, for example, it can be shown that a model with fewer predictors than in the correct model may have lower EPE than the latter, but may imply biased estimators (Wu et al., 2007). An imputation model optimized with respect to the EPE may thus lead to biased estimation in the model of scientific interest. Similarly, robust imputation methods that, for example, reduce the influence of outliers as proposed by Templ et al. (2011) may have a low EPE but can lead to severely biased inferences (Salfrán et al., 2016).

Inferences, using slightly misspecified imputation models, may still be confidence-valid. This 'self-correcting' property of MI (Rubin, 2003) is due to a tendency of increased variation in the imputations if the imputation model is misspecified, leading to exaggerated within- and between-variance, like in the previous example with binary y. Consequently, the large standard errors tend to mask biases of estimators of scientific interest. With increasing sample size, however, standard errors get smaller and biased estimators tend to lead to invalid inferences within the structure modelling framework. These results underpin the importance of the (approximately) correct specification of all aspects of the posterior predictive distribution of the variables with missing values. Whether or under which conditions inferences are still valid in the sense of a minimum EPE within the predictive approach is not clear, due to a missing theoretical framework.

7 Final remarks

Theoretically well justified compensating for missing units seems not to be widespread in analyses of large databases outside the survey context. Hence, either the observed subsamples are assumed to be non-selective samples from the population of interest or all predictors affecting the response probability which are informative with respect to the research questions are assumed to be included as covariates into the models of scientific interest.

On the other hand, the problem of missing values has been addressed in the literature on large data sets mainly in the context of the predictive approach. Unfortunately, the EPE as a popular criterion within this framework is not appropriate to evaluate an imputation method within the structure modelling framework. Due to the lack of theoretical arguments, it is not known whether it is an appropriate general criterion for the predictive approach either. Hence, if imputations need to be generated and the intention is to learn about the DGP, then they should either be generated from an appropriate posterior predictive distribution or, taking advantage of a more flexible strategy, using techniques which are demonstrated, for example in extensive simulations, to allow (confidence-)valid inferences in a broad range of situations with respect to bias of estimators and coverage rates of confidence intervals.

References

Bernardo, J. M. (2003). Bayesian statistics. In R. Viertl (Ed.), *Probability and statistics. Encyclopedia of life support systems (EOLSS), Developed under the Auspices of the UNESCO*. Eolss Publishers. www.eolss.net

Breiman, L. (2001). Statistical modeling: The two cultures. *Statistical Science, 16*(3), 199–231. https://doi.org/10.1214/ss/1009213726

Cameron, A. C., & Trivedi, P. K. (2005). *Microeconometrics. Methods and applications*. Cambridge University Press.

Gandomi, A., & Haider, M. (2015). Beyond the hype: Big data concepts, methods, and analytics. *International Journal of Information Management, 35*, 137–144. https://doi.org/10.1016/j.ijinfomgt.2014.10.007

Hastie, T., Tibshirani, R., & Friedman, J. (2009). *The elements of statistical learning: Data mining, inference, and prediction* (2nd ed.). Springer.

Heckman, J. J. (1979). Sample selection bias as a specification error. *Econometrica, 47*(1), 153–161. https://doi.org/10.2307/1912352

Kang, J. D. Y., & Schafer, J. L. (2007). Demystifying double robustness: A comparison of alternative strategies for estimating a population mean from incomplete data. *Statistical Science, 22*(4), 523–539. http://dx.doi.org/10.1214/07-STS227

Kleinke, K., Reinecke, J., Salfrán, D., & Spiess, M. (2020). *Applied multiple imputation. Advantages, new developments and pitfalls*. Springer.

Kline, P., & Santos, A. (2013). Sensitivity to missing data assumptions: Theory and an evaluation of the U.S. Wage structure. *Quantitative Economics, 4*, 231–267. https://doi.org/10.3982/QE176

Laird, N. M. (1988). Missing data in longitudinal studies. *Statistics in Medicine, 7*, 305–315. https://doi.org/10.1002/sim.4780070131

Li, Y., Li, Z., & Li, L. (2014). Missing traffic data: Comparison of imputation methods. *IET Intelligent Transportation Systems, 8*(1), 51–57. https://doi.org/10.1049/iet-its.2013.0052

Little, R. J. A., & Rubin, D. B. (2002). *Statistical analysis with missing data* (2nd ed.). John Wiley & Sons.

Manski, C. F. (2016). Credible interval estimates for official statistics with survey nonresponse. *Journal of Econometrics, 191*, 293–301. https://doi.org/10.1016/j.jeconom.2015.12.002

McCaffrey, D. F., Ridgeway, G., & Morral, A. R. (2004). Propensity score estimation with boosted regression for evaluating causal effects in observational studies. *Psychological Methods, 9*, 403–425. https://doi.org/10.1037/1082-989x.9.4.403

McCulloch, C. E., Neuhaus, J. M., & Olin, R. L. (2016). Biased and unbiased estimation in longitudinal studies with informative visit processes. *Biometrics, 72*, 1315–1324. https://doi.org/10.1111/biom.12501

Moorthy, K., Mohamad, M. S., & Deris, S. (2014). A review on missing value imputation algorithms for microarray gene expression data. *Current Bioinformatics, 9*, 18–22. https://doi.org/10.2174/1574893608999140109120957

Robins, J. M., Rotnitzky, A., & Zhao, L. (1995). Analysis of semiparametric regression models for repeated outcomes in the presence of missing data. *Journal of the American Statistical Association, 90*(429), 106–121. https://doi.org/10.1080/01621459.1995.10476493

Rubin, D. B. (1976). Inference and missing data. *Biometrika, 63*(3), 581–592. https://doi.org/10.1093/biomet/63.3.581

Rubin, D. B. (1987). *Multiple imputation for nonresponse in surveys*. John Wiley & Sons.

Rubin, D. B. (1996). Multiple imputation after 18+ years. *Journal of the American Statistical Association*, *91*(434), 473–489. https://doi.org/10.1080/01621459.1996.10476908

Rubin, D. B. (2003). Discussion on multiple imputation. *International Statistical Review*, *71*(3), 619–625.

Salfrán, D., Jordan, P., & Spiess, M. (2016). *Missing data: On Criteria to evaluate imputation methods*. Discussion Paper, no. 4. www.psy.uni-hamburg.de/arbeitsbereiche/psychologische-methoden-und-statistik/discussion-papers.html

Schafer, J. L. (1997). *Analysis of incomplete multivariate data*. Chapman & Hall.

Seaman, S., Galati, J., Jackson, D., & Carlin, J. (2013). What is meant by "missing at random"? *Statistical Science*, *28*(2), 257–268. http://dx.doi.org/10.1214/13-STS415

Shmueli, G. (2010). To explain or to predict? *Statistical Science*, *25*(3), 289–310. http://dx.doi.org/10.1214/10-STS330

Templ, M., Kowarik, A., & Filzmoser, P. (2011). Iterative stepwise regression imputation using standard and robust methods. *Computational Statistics and Data Analysis*, *55*, 2793–2806. https://doi.org/10.1016/j.csda.2011.04.012

Terza, J. V. (1998). Estimating count data models with endogenous switching: Sample selection and endogenous treatment effects. *Journal of Econometrics*, *84*, 129–154. https://doi.org/10.1016/S0304-4076(97)00082-1

van Buuren, S., & Groothuis-Oudshoorn, K. (2011). MICE: Multivariate imputation by chained equations in R. *Journal of Statistical Software*, *45*(3), 1–67. http://hdl.handle.net/10.18637/jss.v045.i03

Wooldridge, J. M. (2002). Inverse probability weighted m-estimators for sample selection, attrition, and stratification. *Portuguese Economic Journal*, *1*, 117–139. https://doi.org/10.1007/s10258-002-0008-x

Wooldridge, J. M. (2007). Inverse probability weighted estimation for general missing data problems. *Journal of Econometrics*, *141*, 1281–1301. https://doi.org/10.1016/j.jeconom.2007.02.002

Wu, S., Harris, T. J., & McAuley, K. B. (2007). The use of simplified or misspecified models: Linear case. *The Canadian Journal of Chemical Engineering*, *85*, 386–398. https://doi.org/10.1002/cjce.5450850401

7

A PRIMER ON PROBABILISTIC RECORD LINKAGE

Ted Enamorado

1 Introduction

Modern social science research often relies on bringing together information from different sources to advance our understanding about questions of interest. From studies that seek to explain the differences between self-reported and actual behavior (Ansolabehere & Hersh, 2012; Barbera, 2015; Meredith & Morse, 2015; Berent et al., 2016; Hill & Huber, 2017; Jackman & Spahn, 2019; Bonica, 2019) and the effects of the national news media on mass public and elite behavior (DellaVigna & Kaplan, 2007; Hopkins & Ladd, 2014; Arceneaux et al., 2016; Martin & Yurukoglu, 2017) to studies on clientelism and redistributive politics (De La O, 2013; Zucco, 2013, 2015; Rueda, 2016), scholars have spent considerable amounts of time and effort assembling detailed data sets from multiple sources to conduct sound empirical analyses.

When merging data, the main difficulty faced by the researcher is that oftentimes a unique identifier that unambiguously links records across two data sets, such as the social security number, does not exist or is not available. Under this scenario the true match status of all pairwise comparisons across two data sets is unknown and merging data is prone to misclassifications; in particular, we might fail to find true matches in the data (false negatives) or classify as matches observations that do not refer to the same entity (false positives). This problem is more pronounced when the data are noisy, either due to missing information or typographical errors.

Since the work of Fellegi and Sunter (1969), who formalized the notion of probabilistic record linkage (PRL), a growing literature in statistics, computer science, and more recently in the social sciences has aimed to solve this problem via a principled framework that uses variables in common between data sets as potential identifiers. The goal is to produce a probabilistic estimate for the latent matching status across pairs of records. The advantages of such an approach are that it is devised specifically as a mechanism to control for possible error rates and to account for any remaining uncertainty when conducting post-merge analysis.

In this chapter, I present a brief introduction to the standard approach of probabilistic record linkage and the computational improvements recently introduced by Enamorado et al. (2019) and implemented in fastLink, an R package for PRL (Enamorado et al., 2017). Then, I illustrate these methods using a hands-on coding example for a common task among social scientists, that is, creating a unique identifier within a data set that contains duplicates. This chapter concludes with a discussion of avenues for future research in this important area of computational social science.

DOI: 10.4324/9781003025245-8

2 Probabilistic record linkage

In this section, I present the standard approach of probabilistic record linkage. I start by describing how to construct an agreement pattern, which will be our vehicle to make comparisons possible. Then, I explain the classification process (based on the results from the probabilistic model) that adjudicates which pairs of records are more likely to be matches than non-matches. Finally, I discuss the computational improvements brought into the probabilistic record literature by fastLink.

2.1 Representing comparisons as agreement patterns

Suppose that we wish to merge two data sets, A and B, with sample sizes N_A and N_B, respectively. The problem is that the true matching status for all the $N_A \times N_B$ distinct pairs is unknown. Therefore, the best strategy to conduct a merge under those circumstances is to use the variables that are common to both data sets as potential identifiers. Unfortunately, in practice, most data are noisy, which means that if the variables in common (let's assume that there are $K \geq 1$ such variables) are recorded with error, for example misspellings, missing information, and so on. The latter means that an exact match on these fields would classify many true matches as non-matches due to the noise in the data.

To make comparisons possible, we use the agreement value, denoted by $\gamma_k(i, j)$, which is a function that represents the level of similarity for the kth variable between the ith observation of data set A and the jth observation of data set B. To each pair of records, the collection of agreement values across all the variables in common is called an agreement pattern. Thus, an agreement pattern denoted by $\boldsymbol{\gamma}(i, j) = \{\gamma_1(i, j), \gamma_2(i, j), \ldots, \gamma_k(i, j), \ldots, \gamma_K(i, j)\}$ represents a sequence of similarity levels across all the K variables used to link files. Thus, the agreement pattern is a key component of probabilistic record linkage, as many models work on the intuitive basis that the higher the level of agreement across fields as recorded in $\boldsymbol{\gamma}(i, j)$, the more likely a pair of records is to be a match.

To construct each $\gamma_k(i, j)$, we first need to calculate a measure of similarity $S_k(i, j)$ between the observed values for variable k that the ith and jth observations take. Consequently, the smaller the value of $S_k(i, j)$, the closer are the values being compared. In the case of string-valued variables, there are three prominent options for $S_k(\cdot)$: Levenshtein (also known as "edit distance"), Jaro, and Jaro-Winkler, all involving character-wise comparisons of two strings (see Cohen et al., 2003; Yancey, 2005 for a detailed description of each measure). For numeric-valued variables, $S_k(\cdot)$ can be represented by an L1 (absolute value of the difference) or an L2 norm (Euclidean distance) as measures of distance between two values.

Let the number of agreement levels in the kth variable be denoted by L_k, then, for example, if $L_k = 2$ we have that:

$$\gamma_k(i,j) = \begin{cases} 1 & \text{if } S_k(i,j) \leq \tau \quad \text{``identical (or nearly so)''} \\ 0 & \text{otherwise} \quad\quad\quad \text{``different''} \end{cases}$$

where τ is a threshold value that allows us to move from a continuous measure $S_k(i, j)$ to a discrete one $\gamma_k(i, j)$. The value of τ is set at the discretion of the researcher – see Jaro (1989) and Winkler (1990) for examples of threshold values commonly used by the U.S. Census Bureau.[1]

Of course, not all data at our disposal is perfectly recorded, and missing values are common features of social science data. The latter means that some components of $\boldsymbol{\gamma}(i, j)$ might be missing. That is why we define a missingness vector of length K, denoted by $\delta(i, j)$, where its kth element $\delta_k(i, j)$ is equal to 1 if at least one record in the pair (i, j) has a missing value in the kth variable and is equal to 0 otherwise.

Figure 7.1 presents an illustrative example on how agreement patterns are constructed. The top panels represent two artificial data sets, A and B, of five and four records, respectively. As noted earlier, the first step to obtain each $\gamma(i, j)$ is to compare the values of a pair of records for a given variable. In this example, such an operation translates into 20 comparisons per variable.

Data set A

| | Name | | | | Address | |
	First	Middle	Last	Date of birth	House	Street
A.1	Karla	V	Smith	12-12-1927	780	Devereux St.
A.2	Gabriele	NA	Martin	01-15-1942	780	Devereux St.
A.3	Amanda	NA	Martines	09-10-1992	60	16th St.
A.4	Jimmy	NA	Landregan	02-03-1957	1122	Boland Ct.
A.5	Samantha	NA	Parkington	05-26-1895	345	Madison Ave.

Data set B

| | Name | | | | Address | |
	First	Middle	Last	Date of birth	House	Street
B.1	Emma	NA	Chow	06-01-1987	10	Nassau St.
B.2	Mia	V	Love	08-18-1995	120	Hibben Magie Rd.
B.3	Gabriela	D	Martin	01-15-1942	780	Dvereux St.
B.4	Lorna	F	Pine	10-02-1988	250	Lemonick Cr.

⇓

Step 1: Comparisons
Jaro-Winkler for first, middle, last, and street name; L1 norm for date of birth and house number

| | Name | | | | Address | |
	First	Middle	Last	Date of birth	House	Street
A.1-B.1	0.52	NA	1.00	21721	770	0.40
A.1-B.2	0.49	0.00	1.00	24721	660	0.62
			⋮			
A.2-B.2	0.54	NA	1.00	19573	660	0.62
A.2-B.3	0.07	NA	0.00	0	0	0.09
			⋮			
A.5-B.4	0.62	NA	0.29	34097	95	0.62

⇓

Step 2: From Comparisons to Agreement Patterns
$\tau = 0.10$ for first, middle, last, and street name; $\tau = 1$ for date of birth and house number

| | Name | | | | Address | | |
	First	Middle	Last	Date of birth	House	Street	Agreement Pattern
A.1-B.1	0	NA	0	0	0	0	{ 0, NA, 0, 0, 0, 0 }
A.1-B.2	0	1	0	0	0	0	{ 0, 1, 0, 0, 0, 0 }
				⋮			
A.2-B.2	0	NA	0	0	0	0	{ 0, NA, 0, 0, 0, 0 }
A.2-B.3	1	NA	1	1	1	1	{ 1, NA, 1, 1, 1, 1 }
				⋮			
A.5-B.4	0	NA	0	0	0	0	{ 0, NA, 0, 0, 0, 0 }

Figure 7.1 An illustrative example on how to construct agreement patterns. The top panels show two artificial data sets with five and four records, respectively. The third panel shows how the comparisons across values for the different variables are made. The bottom panel shows how we can move from comparisons to agreement values, and consequently to agreement patterns.

The third panel of Figure 7.1 presents the first step of the process where pairwise similarity measures across six variables: first, middle, and last name, date of birth, house number, and street name. String-valued variables are compared using the Jaro-Winkler string distance – a value of 0 represents that the two values being compared are the same and a value of 1 means that they are different. In the case of numeric-valued variables, the absolute value of the difference (L1 norm) is used. For example, if we compare observations $A.1$ and $B.2$, we obtain a normalized Jaro-Winkler score of 0.49 for first name, 0 for middle name, 1 for last name, and 0.62 for street name; in addition, those two observations are 24,721 days apart in terms of age and their house numbers differ in 660 units.

For all the variables, let $L_k = 2$ and $\tau = 0.10$ for string-valued variables and $\tau = 1$ for numeric-valued variables. Then, for example, we get an agreement pattern for observations $A.1$ and $B.2$ equal to $\gamma(A.1, B.2) = \{0, 1, 0, 0, 0, 0\}$, that is, only the middle names are identical for those observations – see the last panel of Figure 7.1. Note that a comparison involving at least one missing value is indicated by NA, and in our notation this is described by the vector $\delta(i, j)$. For example, $\delta(A.2, B.3) = \{0, 1, 0, 0, 0, 0\}$ indicates the middle name comparison is not possible due to a missing value when comparing records $A.2$ and $B.3$.

Without a doubt, constructing agreement patterns is the most computational expensive step of any record linkage task as the number of comparisons grows in a quadratic fashion with the size of the data sets. To reduce the number of comparisons, a common technique used in the related literature is blocking, that is, making comparisons only for observations that share the same value in a variable, treating as non-matches observations that differ on that variable. For example, a researcher may only make comparisons for observations that share the same gender.[2] To facilitate exposition, no blocking scheme is assumed when discussing analytical results. However, all the concepts we discuss later can be incorporated into any blocking scheme.

2.2 The Fellegi-Sunter model

Fellegi and Sunter (1969) formalized the intuition behind the ideas of Newcombe et al. (1959) and Newcombe and Kennedy (1962) and proposed what is today the workhorse model of probabilistic record linkage. The Fellegi-Sunter model is a two-class mixture model, where the unobserved variable $M(i, j)$ indicates whether the ith record in the data set A and the jth record in the data set B is a match.

The model has the following structure:

$$\gamma_\kappa(i, j) \mid M(i, j) = m \overset{\text{indep.}}{\sim} \text{Discrete}(\pi_{km}) \tag{7.1}$$

$$M(i, j) \overset{\text{i.i.d.}}{\sim} Bernoulli(\lambda) \tag{7.2}$$

where π_{km} is a vector of length L_k, containing the probability of each agreement level for the kth variable given that the pair is a match ($m = 1$) or a non-match ($m = 0$), and λ represents the probability of a match across all pairwise comparisons. Through the parameter π_{k0}, the model allows the possibility that two records can have identical values for some variables even when they do not represent a match.

The model relies on three key independence assumptions: (1) the latent matching status $M(i, j)$ is assumed to be independently and identically distributed; (2) conditional independence of the agreement levels across merging variables; and (3) the data is missing at random (MAR). This last assumption was recently introduced in the record linkage literature by Sadinle (2017) and Enamorado et al. (2019) to avoid ad hoc decisions about how to represent comparisons involving a missing value.[3]

Under these assumptions, the observed-data likelihood function of the model defined in Equations (7.1) and (7.2) is given by,

$$
l_{obs}\left(\lambda,\pi\,|\,\delta,\gamma\right) \propto \prod_{i=1}^{N_A}\prod_{j=1}^{N_B}\left\{\sum_{m=0}^{1}\lambda^m\left(1-\lambda\right)^{1-m}\prod_{k=1}^{K}\left(\prod_{l=0}^{L_k-1}\pi_{kml}^{1\{\gamma k(i,j)=1\}}\right)^{1-\delta_k(i,j)}\right\}
$$

where π_{kml} represents the lth element of probability vector π_{km}, that is,

$$
\pi_{kml} = \Pr(\gamma_k(i,j) = l \mid M(i,j) = m).
$$

Following the work of Winkler (1988), the model parameters are estimated using the expectation maximization (EM) algorithm (Dempster et al., 1977).

2.3 *Fellegi-Sunter decision rules*

Fellegi and Sunter (1969) propose an optimal classification plan, where the goal is to separate pairs of records into three groups: matches, non-matches, and cases where the model had problems in terms of classification. It is in this last group, known as the clerical review region, where the matching status of each pair of records is adjudicated by *human judgment* in an ex-post manner.

Figure 7.2 presents the intuition behind the Fellegi-Sunter decision rules on how to separate records into groups. The idea is to select two thresholds so that the false positive and false negative rates are controlled, in other words, keep them below a certain predetermined value by the researcher. Formally, to separate records into one of the aforementioned classes, the first step

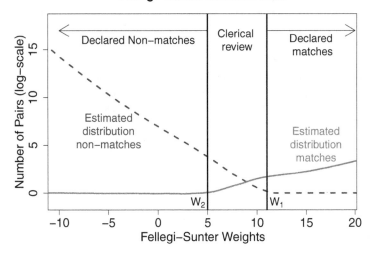

Figure 7.2 Illustration of the Fellegi-Sunter decision rules. Pairwise comparisons with agreement patterns to the left (right) of W_2 (W_1) are classified as non-matches (matches). Adjudication of the matching status of pairwise comparisons between W_2 and W_1 is left for clerical review. Note that W_2 (W_1) is selected such that the area below the solid (dashed) line which represents the estimated distribution of matches (non-matches) is small.

Fellegi and Sunter (1969) take is to rank observations according to their likelihood of being a match. To do so, they introduce the following weights for each agreement pattern:

$$W_h = log\left(\frac{Pr\left(\gamma_h|M_h = 1\right)}{Pr\left(\gamma_h|M_h = 0\right)}\right) \tag{7.3}$$

where $h \in \{1, \ldots, H\}$ indexes unique instances of an agreement pattern and H represents the total number of distinct agreement patterns we observe in the data. Note that larger Fellegi-Sunter weights imply more support in favor of the hypothesis that the pairs of records (i, j) with agreement pattern γ_h are a match.

The next step in the process is to order pairs and obtain an upper threshold W_1 and a lower threshold W_2 such that the values for the false positive and false negative rates are small. Fellegi and Sunter (1969) proved that the area between W_1 and W_2, the clerical review region, is optimal in the sense that there is no other decision rule, for the same level of error tolerance, that will include fewer observations. In practice, however, most researchers focus on W_1 as clerical reviews tend to be time consuming and expensive, but see Enamorado, 2020 for new approaches on how to conduct a more efficient clerical review and improve the overall precision of the linkage process.

2.4 Scaling the process

In Enamorado et al., 2019, the authors compare the computational performance of fastLink with that of the RecordLinkage package in R (Sariyar & Borg, 2016) in terms of running time. These are the only other open-source packages in R that implement a probabilistic model of record linkage in the Fellegi-Sunter tradition. To mimic a standard computing environment of applied researchers, all the calculations are performed on a Macintosh laptop computer with a 2.4 GHz Quad-Core Intel Core i5 processor and 16 GB of RAM.

As mentioned earlier, it is well known that the bottleneck in terms of computations is the large number of required comparisons (e.g., Jaro, 1972; Christen, 2012), for which a hashing technique is used – see Enamorado et al., 2019, for more details. To illustrate the computational gains from fastLink, I consider the setup in which the comparisons are made for two data sets of equal size with 50% overlap (observations in common between data sets), 10% missing proportion under missing completely at random (MCAR). The linkage variables are first name, middle initial, last name, house number, street name, and year of birth. The size of each data set is varied from 1,000 records to 200,000 observations. Each data set is a random sample (without replacement) based on the 341,160 female registered voters in 2006 in the state of California – for these records complete information in each linkage field is available (see Enamorado et al., 2019, for more details about these data). To build the agreement patterns, the Jaro-Winkler string distance is used with a cutoff of 0.94 for first name, last name, and street name. For the remaining fields, a binary comparison based on exact matches is used to construct the agreement values.

Figure 7.3 presents the results of this running time comparison. Although fastLink and RecordLinkage take a similar amount of time for data sets of 1,000 records, the running time increases exponentially for the other packages in contrast to fastLink (black solid circles connected by a solid line), which exhibits a near linear increase. When making the comparisons for data sets of 150,000 records each, fastLink takes under three hours. In contrast, it takes more than 22 hours for RecordLinkage (solid triangles connected by a dotted line), to make the comparisons for two data sets of only 20,000 observations each. As the size of the data sets increases,

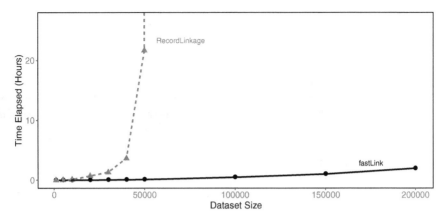

Figure 7.3 Running time comparison. The plot presents the results of making the comparisons for data sets of equal size. The data sets were constructed from a sample of female registered voters in California. The amount of overlap between data sets is 50%, and, for each data set, there are 10% missing observations in each linkage variable: first name, middle initial, last name, house number, street name, and year of birth. The missing data mechanism is missing completely at random (MCAR). The most recent version of fastLink (black solid dots connected by a solid line) is significantly faster than the other open-source R package.

Figure 7.3 illustrates that the differences in running time become many orders of magnitude larger, emphasizing the value of the development of new algorithms to scale PRL methods.

3 Hands-on example

In this section, we illustrate via a hands-on example one of the most common record linkage tasks, that is, deduplication. In practice, deduplication can be quite consequential and useful when the researcher is interested in creating a unique identifier that allows tracking multiple instances of the same entity and/or in removing duplicated records from the data set.

We use the synthetic data set RLdata10000 from the RecordLinkage package in R, a data set that has been widely used to assess the accuracy of many PRL approaches (Enamorado & Steorts, 2020). RLdata10000 contains 10,000 total records of individuals and 10% of those records are duplicated. As noted previously, the focus will be in identifying the duplicates in the data set via probabilistic record linkage. To do so, we will link RLdata10000 against itself.

Our first step will be to load the data and inspect the first four observations to get a sense of how the data are structured.

```
## Read the RLdata1000 dataset
records <- read.csv("RLdata10000.csv")

## First 4 records in RLdata10000
head(records, 4)
##   fname_c1 fname_c2 lname_c1 lname_c2   by bm bd ent_id
## 1 FRANK      <NA>   MUELLER    <NA>   1967  9 27   3606
## 2 MARTIN     <NA>   SCHWARZ    <NA>   1967  2 17   2560
## 3 HERBERT    <NA>   ZIMMERMANN <NA>   1961 11  6   3892
## 4 HANS       <NA>   SCHMITT    <NA>   1945  8 14    329
```

We will focus our attention on the following identifying fields: first (fname c1) and last name (lname c1), day (bd), month (bm), and year of birth (by). We will not use the middle name (fname c2) and second last name (lname c2), as these fields are mostly filled with missing values. In addition, one unique feature of RLdata10000 is that it contains a unique identifier (ent id) such that one can evaluate the accuracy of any record linkage method when compared against the truth.

As noted earlier, RLdata10000 contains 10,000 records, among which 8,000 of them are unique and have no duplicate and 1,000 are duplicated once. Thus, these data contain 9,000 unique records. Note that duplicated records are introduced by randomly perturbing one linkage field.

```
## Count the number of unique ids
length(unique(records$ent_id))
```

```
## [1] 9000
```

To establish a baseline, we will use exact matching, which is one of the most popular approaches by applied researchers to merge records when a unique identifier is missing. Exact matching has the great advantage of being conservative against false positives but the disadvantage of not being robust to the presence of missing values and typographical errors in the data; moreover, exact matching, as many other rule-based (deterministic) record linkage approaches, gives equal weight to each variable used when determining if a pair of records corresponds to the same entity.

```
## Linkage Fields
linkageFields <- c("fname_c1", "lname_c1", "by", "bm", "bd")
```

```
## Exact matching
exact.match <- merge(records, records, by = linkageFields)
nrow(exact.match)
```

```
## [1] 10016
```

Exact matching returns 10,000 self-matches, that is, each record is perfectly matched against itself, but it only identifies eight records (the excess over 10,000) that are duplicated. The latter means that for these records, RLdata10000 does not contain perturbed information in the five linkage fields we use to conduct the merge − actually these corresponds records were perturbed in the middle and second last name.

As it can be noted, not surprisingly, by resorting to exact matching, we are still missing 992 records for which a duplicate exists due to the noise introduced in the linkage fields.

In contrast to exact matching, fastLink represents a more flexible and principled approach. Not only does the probabilistic model behind fastLink weight each variable differently when estimating the match probabilities, it is also robust to the occurrence of typographical errors and missing information across the linkage fields.

We now explain how a deduplication task can be conducted via fastLink. First, we will load the package.

```
## Load fastLink
library(fastLink)
```

```
## Note that as of July 2021, the most recent
```

```
## version of fastLink is 0.6.0.
packageVersion("fastLink")
## [1] '0.6.0'
```

Next, we will use the same linkage fields as in the exact matching case but will use string similarity measures for the string-valued fields: first and last name. In particular, we will use three
agreement levels, that is, agreement (or nearly agreement), partial agreement, and disagreement,
based on the Jaro-Winkler string distance with 0.94 (cut.a) and 0.84 (cut.p) as the threshold values. For the numeric-valued fields (day, month, and year of birth), we use a binary comparison,
based on exact matches.

```
## Fields that we will compare based on
## a string similarity measure
stringDistFields <- c("fname_c1", "lname_c1")

## Fields for which we have 3
## possible agreement values
## Agree, Partially Agree, Disagree
partialMatchFields <- c("fname_c1", "lname_c1")
```

Based on the match probability obtained from fastLink, we use 0.90 as the matching threshold to produce the set of likely duplicates in the RLdata10000 data set. To do so, we call the
fastLink() function as follows:

```
out <- fastLink(dfA = records, dfB = records,
                varnames = linkageFields,
                stringdist.match = stringDistFields,
                partial.match = partialMatchFields,
                cut.a = 0.94, cut.p = 0.84,
                threshold.match = 0.90
            )
##
## =====================
## fastLink(): Fast Probabilistic Record Linkage
## =====================
##
```

We save in the object out all the results from fastLink. After having fit fastLink to the data,
we proceed to extract and store our deduplicated data. We do so as follows:

```
## Deduplicated dataset:
recordsfL <- getMatches(dfA = records, dfB = records,
                        fl.out = out)

## The deduplicated data looks like this:
head(recordsfL, 4)
## fname_c1 fname_c2 lname_c1 lname_c2 by bm bd ent_id dedupe.ids
```

```
## 1 FRANK    <NA>    MUELLER    <NA> 1967  9 27 3606    1
## 2 MARTIN   <NA>    SCHWARZ    <NA> 1967  2 17 2560 1038
## 3 HERBERT  <NA>    ZIMMERMANN <NA> 1961 11  6 3892 1999
## 4 HANS     <NA>    SCHMITT    <NA> 1945  8 14 329  2942
```

The object recordsfL contains a new data set with 10,000 records but with a new unique identifier dedupe.ids obtained using fastLink. If fastLink predicts that a pair of records is duplicated, then these records will have the same value for dedupe.ids.

```
## Let's count how unique records fastLink finds:
length(unique(recordsfL$dedupe.ids))
```

```
## [1] 8983
```

fastLink finds that there are 8,983 unique records in the data — just 17 records shy of the 9,000 mark. Next we present two examples of records that we know are duplicates based on the unique identifier (ent id) in RLdata10000. For both pairs of records, we can see that fastLink also classified them as matches even when there was a typographical error in the last name of the first example and in the birth year of the second case.

```
## Some examples of known duplicates
recordsfL[recordsfL$ent_id == 20,]
## fname_c1 fname_c2 lname_c1 lname_c2 by bm bd ent_id dedupe.ids
## 2461 PAUL <NA> SCHAEFER <NA>  1942 7 2 20 1481
## 3612 PAUL <NA> SCHAECFER <NA> 1942 7 2 20 1481

recordsfL[recordsfL$ent_id == 77,]
## fname_c1 fname_c2 lname_c1 lname_c2 by bm bd ent_id dedupe.ids
## 1056 JENS <NA> WAGNER   <NA> 1976 8 14 77   65
## 2763 JENS <NA> WAGNER   <NA> 1986 8 14 77   65
```

Now, to evaluate the overall performance of fastLink, we will use a confusion table. The confusion table will allow users to compare the results of fastLink to truth and assess how large the misclassification errors are. To construct the confusion table, we will create indicator variables that will tell us if a record was a true (estimated) duplicate based on the unique identifier from RLdata10000 (fastLink). In this scenario, a confusion table is just the cross table between these two binary variables.

```
## Duplicate indicator based on the true unique id
recordsfL$dupTrue <- ifelse(duplicated(recordsfL$ent_id),
                            "Duplicated", "Not duplicated")

## Duplicate indicator based on fastLink
recordsfL$dupfL <- ifelse(duplicated(recordsfL$dedupe.ids),
                          "Duplicated", "Not duplicated")
```

```
## Confusion table
confusion <- table("fastLink" = recordsfL$dupfL,
                   "True Matching Status" = recordsfL$dupTrue)
confusion
##                     True Matching Status
## fastLink           Duplicated Not duplicated
## Duplicated         82                     35
## Not duplicated     18                     8965
```

As we can see in this table, out of the 1,000 duplicated records, fastLink correctly found 982 (true positives) of them. However, fastLink misclassified as duplicates 35 records that were not duplicates in truth (false positives) and classified as non-duplicates 18 records that were duplicates (false negatives). To translate these numbers into metrics that are widely used when assessing the accuracy of any classifier, we calculate the false discovery and false negative rates. The false discovery rate tells us that among all the declared duplicates by fastLink only 3.4% were non-duplicates. The false negative rate, on the other hand, tells us that among the pool of duplicates fastLink only missed (fail to find) 1.8% of them. In contrast, the false discovery rate for exact matching is 0% but the false negative rate is 99.5%.

```
## True Positives, False Positives, and False Negatives:
TP <- confusion[1, 1]
FP <- confusion[1, 2]
FN <- confusion[2, 1]

## False Discovery Rate:
FDR <- round(FP/(FP + TP), 3)
FDR

## [1] 0.034

## False Negative Rate:
FNR <- round(FN/1000, 3)
FNR

## [1] 0.018
```

In sum, the goal of this hands-on example illustrates how fastLink finds a good balance when dealing with the trade-off between controlling error rates (false positives and false negatives) and how it outperforms other deterministic approaches such as exact matching. Moreover, it provides a simple template that researchers can use when conducting a similar task.

4 Concluding remarks and future work

Incorporating information from multiple sources is at the core of social science research. In scenarios where a unique identifier is missing, the Fellegi-Sunter model of probabilistic record linkage has been proven to be a useful tool. In this paper, we have discussed the standard approach of probabilistic record linkage and illustrated how new algorithms have facilitated the implementation of techniques that did not scale to even moderately sized data sets.

While the Fellegi-Sunter model offers a robust approach to probabilistic record linkage, incorporating such a technique with generative models that aim to model comparisons in a more flexible way, that is, beyond agreement patterns, could be an interesting avenue of future research. In addition, to further improve the probabilistic record linkage, it is critical to find ways to improve its accuracy, as discussed in Enamorado, 2020; active learning combined with a probabilistic approach appears to be such an avenue. Finally, scalability is still a big concern without the assistance of blocking when the number of records is large (millions of records), therefore, more data-driven and principled blocking techniques are much needed.

Notes

1 Note that comparisons can be classified using more than two levels, for example using three agreement levels, we can classify comparisons into identical (or nearly so), similar, and different; the only requirement is that we need to set the number of threshold values to be equal to the number of levels the agreement values can take minus one.
2 Christen (2012) and Steorts et al. (2014) are two excellent reviews of blocking techniques.
3 For example, a common practice in the record linkage literature has been to categorize comparisons involving a missing value as different values (see e.g., Sariyar et al., 2012).

References

Ansolabehere, S., & Hersh, E. (2012). Validation: What big data reveal about survey misreporting and the real electorate. *Political Analysis*, *20*(4), 437–459.

Arceneaux, K., Johnson, M., Lindsta¨dt, R., & Vander Wielen, R. J. (2016). The influence of news media on political elites: Investigating strategic responsiveness in congress. *American Journal of Political Science*, *60*(1), 5–29.

Barbera, P. (2015). Birds of the same feather tweet together. Bayesian ideal point estimation using Twitter data. *Political Analysis*, *23*(1), 76–91.

Berent, M. K., Krosnick, J. A., & Lupia, A. (2016). Measuring voter registration and turnout in surveys. *Public Opinion Quarterly*, *80*(3), 597–621.

Bonica, A. (2019). Are donation-based measures of ideology valid predictors of individual-level policy preferences? *Journal of Politics*, *81*(1), 327–333.

Christen, P. (2012). *Data matching. Concepts and techniques for record linkage, entity resolution, and duplicate detection.* Springer.

Cohen, W. W., Ravikumar, P., & Fienberg, S. (2003). A comparison of string distance metrics for name-matching tasks. *International Joint Conference on Artificial Intelligence (IJCAI)*, 18.

De La O, A. (2013). Do conditional cash transfers affect electoral behavior? Evidence from a randomized experiment in Mexico. *American Journal of Political Science*, *57*(1), 1–14.

DellaVigna, S., & Kaplan, E. (2007). The fox news effect: Media bias and voting. *Quarterly Journal of Economics*, *122*(3), 1187–1234.

Dempster, A. P., Laird, N. M., & Rubin, D. B. (1977). Maximum likelihood from incomplete data Via the EM algorithm (with discussion). *Journal of the Royal Statistical Society, Series B, Methodological*, *39*(1), 1–37.

Enamorado, T. (2020). Active learning for probabilistic record linkage. *Social Science Research Network (SSRN)*. https://ssrn.com/abstract=3257638

Enamorado, T., Fifield, B., & Imai, K. (2017). *fastLink*. R package version 0.4. https://CRAN.R-project.org/package=fastLink

Enamorado, T., Fifield, B., & Imai, K. (2019). Using a probabilistic model to assist merging of large-scale administrative records. *American Political Science Review*, *113*(2), 353–371.

Enamorado, T., & Steorts, R. C. (2020). Probabilistic blocking and distributed Bayesian entity resolution. In *Lecture notes in computer science* (pp. 253–268). Privacy in Statistical Databases.

Fellegi, I. P., & Sunter, A. B. (1969). A theory for record linkage. *Journal of the American Statistical Association, 64*(328), 1183–1210.

Hill, S. J., & Huber, G. A. (2017). Representativeness and motivations of the contemporary donorate: Results from merged survey and administrative records. *Political Behavior, 39*(1), 3–29.

Hopkins, D. J., & Ladd, J. M. (2014). The consequences of broader media choice: Evidence from the expansion of fox news. *Quarterly Journal of Political Science, 9*(1), 115–135.

Jackman, S., & Spahn, B. (2019). Why does the American national election study overestimate voter turnout? *Political Analysis, 27*(2), 193–207.

Jaro, M. (1972). *UNIMATCH-A computer system for generalized record linkage under conditions of uncertainty*. Technical Report, Spring Joint Computer Conference.

Jaro, M. (1989). Advances in record-linkage methodology as applied to matching the 1985 census of Tampa, Florida. *Journal of the American Statistical Association, 84*(406), 414–420.

Martin, G. J., & Yurukoglu, A. (2017). Bias in cable news: Persuasion and polarization. *American Economic Review, 107*(9), 2565–2599.

Meredith, M., & Morse, M. (2015). The politics of the restoration of Ex-Felon voting rights: The case of Iowa. *Quarterly Journal of Political Science, 10*(1), 41–100.

Newcombe, H. B., & Kennedy, J. M. (1962). Record linkage: Making maximum use of the discriminating power of identifying information. *Communications of Association for Computing Machinery, 5*(11), 563–567.

Newcombe, H. B., Kennedy, J. M., Axford, S. J., & James, A. P. (1959). Automatic linkage of vital records. *Science, 130*, 954–959.

Rueda, M. (2016). Small aggregates, big manipulation: Vote buying enforcement and collective monitoring. *American Journal of Political Science, 61*(1), 163–177.

Sadinle, M. (2017). Bayesian estimation of bipartite matchings for record linkage. *Journal of the American Statistical Association, 112*(518), 600–612.

Sariyar, M., & Borg, A. (2016). Record linkage in R. R package. Version 0.4–10. http://cran.r-project.org/package=RecordLinkage

Sariyar, M., Borg, A., & Pommerening, K. (2012). Missing values in deduplication of electronic patient data. *Journal of the American Medical Informatics Association, 19*, e76–e82.

Steorts, R. C., Ventura, S. L., Sadinle, M., & Fienberg, S. E. (2014). A comparison of blocking methods for record linkage. In *Lecture Notes in Computer Science* (Vol. 8744, pp. 253–268). Privacy in Statistical Databases.

Winkler, W. E. (1988). Using the EM algorithm for weight computation in the Fellegi – Sunter model of record linkage. In *Proceedings of the Section on Survey Research Methods* (pp. 667–671). American Statistical Association.

Winkler, W. E. (1990). String comparator metrics and enhanced decision rules in the Fellegi-Sunter model of record linkage. In *Proceedings of the Section on Survey Research Methods*. American Statistical Association. www.iser.essex.ac.uk/research/publications/501361

Yancey, W. (2005). Evaluating string comparator performance for record linkage. *Research Report Series*. Statistical Research Division U.S. Census Bureau.

Zucco, C. (2013). When payouts pay off: Conditional cash transfers and voting behavior in Brazil 2002–10. *American Journal of Political Science, 57*(4), 810–822.

Zucco, C. (2015). The impacts of conditional cash transfers in four presidential elections (2002–2014). *Brazilian Journal of Political Science, 9*(1), 135–149.

8

REPRODUCIBILITY AND PRINCIPLED DATA PROCESSING

John McLevey, Pierson Browne and Tyler Crick

1 Introduction

Scientific research continues to be plagued by a replication crisis, wherein results from published academic literature are found to be impossible to replicate, even by the teams responsible for arriving at said findings (Baker, 2016; Christensen et al., 2019; Collins, 1992; Freese, 2007; Freese & Peterson, 2017; King, 1995; Pridemore et al., 2018). In response to this crisis, many highly ranked academic journals have become signatory to initiatives designed to enforce high standards for replication (Gleditsch et al., 2003; e.g. Joint Statement by Political Science Journal Editors, 2015). Although there are many such initiatives – the specifics of which vary – most are concerned with ensuring that all published material is accompanied by an exhaustive, accessible copy of the data as well as the code used to arrive at the conclusions presented in the finished paper.

In this chapter, we consider the much-discussed replication crisis to be only one dimension of the more general project of doing research – and computational social science specifically – in reproducible and transparent ways. Later, we discuss the importance of reproducibility and transparency in computational social science, followed by a discussion of how these ideals are complicated by the realities of doing rigorous collaborative research in our field. We then present an overview of a framework called 'principled data processing' (PDP) which offers a core set of principles and practices that demand a commitment to reproducibility and transparency, on the one hand, and improving the quality and efficiency of collaborative research on the other (Ball, 2016a, 2016b). Finally, we show one powerful way of organizing and managing computational social science research projects within this PDP framework using pdpp – a simple and lightweight command line tool.

Our primary motivation with this chapter is to contribute to collective efforts to facilitate greater reproducibility and transparency in our field. As such, we use a number of vignettes and other hypothetical examples to connect high-level discussions of principles and ideals with concrete research practices. We also present some minimal examples of code that are sufficient for using pdpp in computational social science research projects, even though this breaks with the conventional emphasis on high-level literature reviews in handbook chapters. Finally, the pragmatically oriented portions of this chapter assume that researchers have already implemented version control (using tools such as git) into their workflows and view it as a necessary – but by no means sufficient – cornerstone of doing reproducible and transparent research.

DOI: 10.4324/9781003025245-9

2 Reproducibility and transparency

At risk of stating a truism, the volume of data available to computational social scientists has grown rapidly and is likely to continue to do so for the foreseeable future. This unprecedented wealth of data has emerged in lockstep with increasingly inexpensive access to more computing power than ever. To collect, manage, and process data at the scale that is currently available, researchers need to work in teams with diverse expertise, adopt new programming techniques and computational infrastructure, and apply new methods and models that are suitable for the types of data that are increasingly available. In contexts such as these, doing research that meets a high standard of reproducibility and transparency can be as challenging as it is scientifically and ethically imperative.

Until relatively recently, the opacity of data analysis was widely accepted: since it was usually impossible to examine the code and data one's colleagues were using to derive their findings, it was assumed that most researchers could reproduce their own work if necessary. There continue to be few professional incentives to do replication studies in science: they are generally devalued, require striving for conformity rather than novelty, can be perceived as hostile or threatening, and are extremely challenging to execute properly (e.g. Christensen et al., 2019; Collins, 1998). Furthermore, some types of research design, including mixed-methods designs that include qualitative components, do not lend themselves well to a narrow focus on replication. With the potential payoffs stacked against reproduction studies, very few scientists have made systematic attempts to reaffirm the reliability of published findings. Ongoing concerns over the replicability of scientific results have prompted certain academic journals to take action. For example, in 2012, the *American Journal of Political Science* began implementing a reproducibility standard for article acceptance. They propose, "[by] requiring scholars to provide access to their data and conducting our own replications on those data, we confirm the rigour of, and promote public confidence in, the studies we publish" (Jacoby et al., 2017).

Although there is a great deal of discussion about the 'replication crisis' in the academy and even in popular media, we see replication as just one important part of a larger and more pressing challenge: making reproducibility, transparency, and openness into cornerstones of our scientific cultures (Christensen et al., 2019; Collins, 1998; McLevey, 2020, 2021). Doing so would help make replication easier and more common, as one of the main barriers to successful replication is that published articles and methodological appendices contain only a fraction of the information and *craft knowledge* necessary to execute even an imperfect replication (Collins, 1974, 2016; Freese & Peterson, 2017). An emphasis on reproducibility and transparency makes replication easier and less threatening, allows researchers to learn more quickly from one another's work, can accelerate discovery and innovation, and can be adapted when faced with the different sets of constraints imposed when working with sensitive data or qualitative methods.

Beyond scientific benefits, a lack of reproducibility and transparency in computational social science is, in many cases, *unethical*. O'Neil (2016) provides a powerful argument along these lines in *Weapons of Math Destruction*, which critiques computational models that are opaque, unregulated, and incontestable, yet are widely used in contexts that have tangible effects on people's lives and well-being. Through a series of case studies on the use of computational models in domains such as policing and education, she shows how algorithms that were considered by some to be more impartial or 'fair' ways of making decisions actually replicated deeply ingrained biases and, due to their opacity, were beyond reproach by those affected. In many situations, the problem lies with algorithmic feedback loops; a tangible example of this can be seen in policing, where predictive models exacerbate inequalities based on race and class (Brayne, 2017, 2020; O'Neil, 2016).

In the context of computational social science, reproducibility and transparency are the twin cornerstones of scientific validity – they are necessary but not sufficient components of doing research with high ethical standards. Opaque models and important research decisions made behind closed lab doors can exacerbate social inequalities and other injustices, and if estimates from a model impact life and well-being, the model should *at the very least* be open to interrogation and rectification. As computational social scientists, we should default to openness, reproducibility, and transparency as much as possible, but especially when using complex computational models or when we have any expectation that our work may have an impact beyond the knowledge we build in our immediate scientific communities. In other words, we must be mindful of the ethical problems posed by doing work that is not open, transparent, and reproducible and ensure we do not worsen social inequalities by fuelling harmful algorithmic feedback loops of the kind described in detail by O'Neil (2016).

Computational social science projects (and, indeed, all scientific projects) should also be auditable: reviewers unfamiliar with the project should be able to rapidly and easily determine how the various pieces of code in the project work together, at a high level, to produce the final output. Reviewers, moreover, should be able to dig into said code and identify problem areas based on discrepancies or anomalies observed in the output. Although traditional documentation (in the form of in-code comments and external written manuals) – if properly maintained – can help the project be auditable, the shifting scope and requirements of any computational social science project will often render such documentation obsolete. Wherever possible, teams should rely on self-documenting code: a paradigm in which directories, scripts, variables, functions, and data files are given succinct, descriptive names (Gentzkow & Shapiro, 2014). If correctly implemented, measures such as these can help facilitate rapid and effective external reviews of the data and code used to develop and articulate findings.[1]

The practical challenges of reproducibility and transparency, then, are ensuring that data processing workflows are automated and auditable. Automated workflows eliminate the need for reviewers or other interested parties to become familiar with any kind of documentation before results are forthcoming. As long as the automation is foregrounded, reviewers can determine for themselves whether the project produces the results as presented. Gentzkow and Shapiro (2014), for instance, recommend writing a shell script that runs a series of other scripts in the correct order and produces a finalized PDF, DOCX, or HTML output.

Many researchers and organizations have begun to innovate in response to the challenges presented by the need for collaboration and transparency in computational social science. The *American Journal of Political Science* (*AJPS*), for example, makes use of Harvard's Dataverse project, which is an open data platform for academic research data and has seen nearly five million data set downloads at the time of writing. To reproduce the analysis, the *AJPS* requires that the commands used to analyze the data be included on the Dataverse. These guidelines, however, are chiefly aimed at the syntax files used in statistical software such as Stata and R, with the main suggestion being that researchers intuitively name their syntax file(s) to match up with specific analyses in the submitted article. Computational social science workflows are not always structured in such a one-to-one translatable fashion. As such, we propose the adoption of an intuitive framework for compartmentalizing the pieces of computational social science projects and have developed a simple but powerful command line tool to help researchers more easily build their projects to fit such a process.

By focusing on reproducibility and transparency generally, rather than replication specifically, we emphasize practices and principles that can be used to greatly improve the quality of any research project, regardless of whether it is ever replicated, and to support more ethical research practices. In a sense, it is more important that all projects are auditable and reproducible rather than replicable, which is also more realistic, and can include research ethics as part of the equation. However, before we describe this framework and the accompanying Python package, we will take a closer look at how collaboration – essential though it is – can introduce many challenges to doing reproducible and transparent work.

3 Adhocracy, black boxes, and the collaboration problem

It is likely that most computational social scientists reading this chapter have experienced the feeling of dread that manifests when the prospect of making changes to old code is raised. Perhaps new data have been gathered, or the research team wishes to make use of a previously overlooked variable, or the time has come to scale up the existing project to account for a broader range of cases and applications. Despite previously having everything working and being confident that the project accurately and responsibly processes the data sets your team is using, you are far less confident in your team's ability to extend or make changes to your existing code base without breaking everything.

Perhaps you think you're overreacting and take a peek at code that – despite being regularly relied upon – hasn't been thoroughly examined since it was originally written and tested months or even years ago. Instead of a well-organized, easily understandable procession of discrete steps in a sensible data processing pipeline, you're greeted by an incomprehensible primordial soup of data and code – dozens of files languidly suspended in the same directory with no organizing principles in sight.

The aforementioned experience – or experiences akin to it – are endemic in our trade. Gentzkow and Shapiro (2014) describe how writing and debugging code has become an indispensable and routine practice in computational social science. They also recognize that most social scientists are self-taught programmers and lack deep knowledge of relevant computer science and engineering practices. This, they claim, leads researchers and research assistants to adopt a 'seat-of-your-pants' approach to generating and organizing code, data, and results. For example, Figure 8.1 is a graphical representation of a data processing pipeline our team of six researchers created over time, using such a 'seat-of-your-pants' approach. Sorting out the horrible mess we created when developing the first version of this data processing pipeline prompted us to (a) start from the beginning again and (b) use the principled data processing framework described later in this chapter. The experience of working within this framework has been so positive that it led us to develop the pdpp tool to make it easier for our team, and others, to use this approach.

Our team developed Figure 8.1 by hand in an effort to clarify which scripts (developed by which researchers) were responsible for producing which dependencies. While the specifics are irrelevant, the meandering, disorganized structure should be familiar to anyone who has attempted to develop a collaborative data processing project. Of particular note here:

- *Too complicated and vague*: Even though each component of this project was developed carefully and tested rigorously on its own, the overall data processing pipeline is nearly impossible to understand as a result of its convoluted structure and equally convoluted conventions (or lack thereof) used to name scripts and their outputs.
- *Expired references*: Several scripts in the data processing pipeline either create or read in files (including some intermediate data sets) that are no longer formally part of the data processing pipeline. For example, a script might create a file to be read in by another script, but one of those scripts changes and the project directory becomes messier and more complex over time, and the processing pipeline becomes harder to understand because the actual files used in the pipeline are mixed in with other files that are not actually used.

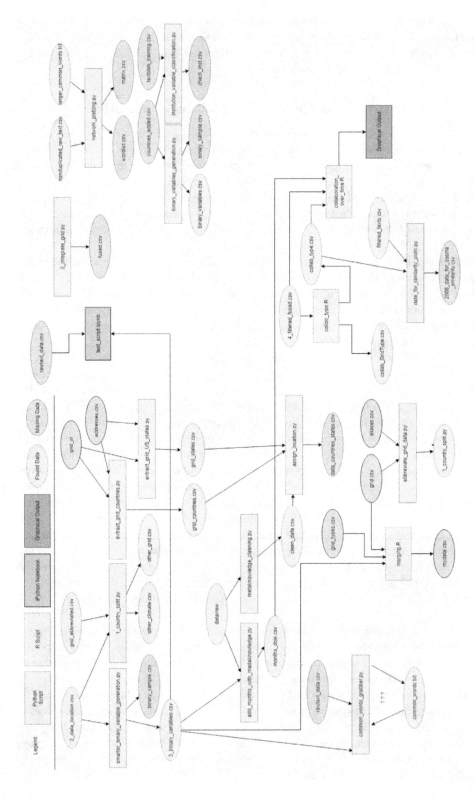

Figure 8.1 Project-level chaos resulting from a lot of reasonable context-specific decisions by experienced developers and researchers

- *Islanded tasks*: The diagram's upper-right corner contains several tasks that – for reasons we were never able to fully understand – make no contribution to the data processing pipeline or the overall project. They simply exist inside the project, doing nothing.
- *Circular dependencies*: In the lower left corner, a task produces its own input file; the file's only purpose in the project is to be fed back into the task that created it. While we can determine who created these files and when, all knowledge of their original purpose or previous connections to the larger data processing pipeline has been lost.

At this point, readers might be under the impression that the primordial soup of code and data that is revealed when 'pulling back the curtain' is the result of researchers' carelessness, neglect, or incompetence. Not so. We contend that – more frequently than not – these Gordian knots of data and code are the result of a series of well-intentioned decisions made by intelligent researchers who are well equipped to complete the tasks they are charged with. In the earlier example, the researchers' decisions were sensible at the time and included many 'best practices' from engineering and data science, such as unit testing. Moreover, the project itself worked: provided that the handcrafted list of step-by-step instructions for executing the pipeline was followed exactly, the project depicted in the diagram was – astoundingly – capable of producing the desired outputs from the data set gathered for the project. When we set out to adapt the pipeline to a different data set, however, our team was intractably stymied by the convoluted, incomprehensible morass we had built.

The pipelines that computational social scientists use are often developed following an 'adhocratic' (or 'seat-of-the-pants,' in Gentzkow and Shapiro's words) logic. The term 'adhocracy' describes multidisciplinary teams of experts that have dynamic membership from project to project, non-hierarchical structures, and a relative lack of 'rules' (Mintzberg & McHugh, 1985). The field of organizational management has recently had cause to re-examine adhocracy; despite its archaic origins, the structure it describes maps well onto the agile development processes frequently employed by contemporary technology firms (Birkinshaw & Ridderstråle, 2010). As far as organizing principles go, adhocracy can enable teams of individuals with diverse skills and expert knowledge to meaningfully contribute to a project and produce results in a relatively short time frame. If the only objective is to finish the data analysis and move on to something else, the kludged-together, on-the-fly style of problem solving that adhocracy engenders is an ideal means of completing the project's goals.

Adhocracy is also a pretty good model of what happens on many computational social science research teams: one or more principal investigators develop a research project that may include, for example, a series of related papers as output. First, the project itself, the papers, and the outputs that make it up are planned; then, some division of labour is agreed upon for the faculty investigators as well as student members of the research team. Although all members of the team generally contribute at least some code, it is fairly normal for student members of the team to take on responsibility for developing and testing a significant portion of the project's codebase. In a typical academic effort, research assistants will need to write code capable of collecting, screening, cleaning, summarizing, organizing, analyzing, and visualizing the project's data (Gentzkow & Shapiro, 2014). Even for small teams, say of two to three people, collaboration brings together researchers with different backgrounds, preferences, strengths, weaknesses, and idiosyncrasies, which can introduce just as many problems as it solves.

University-based research teams carry a high risk of rapid collaborator turnover; as time passes, any given contributor's schedule can shift, their availability can change, and students graduate. Thus, academic projects need to be capable of unexpectedly losing collaborators and bringing new collaborators onto the team, all without paying the prohibitive cost of getting every new collaborator up to speed with every piece of code written for the project to that point. Unlike software development, where agile teams are only producing code and have dedicated staff groups devoted to documentation and oversight, academic research teams are producing code as only a portion of their work. It is unusual to have a student doing only documentation or code oversight; even if this were the case, those students would still need to be working towards graduation.

By allowing anyone to contribute to a project as best they can without forcing each contributor to learn in detail how every piece of the project's code works, adhocratic projects often fall victim to rampant 'black boxing.' In a heavily 'black-boxed' project, most team members know what any given piece of the project's code does and are aware that it works reliably, but they do not know how the code works or how the small pieces of code fit together to form an integrated multi-step data analysis workflow. What's more, black-boxed code often defies understanding and cannot be altered or repaired: everyone except the authors (and, in some cases, the authors themselves) might find it difficult to comprehend what a piece of code does. Gentzkow and Shapiro describe how their attempts to understand their research assistants' coding work were often abortive: in many cases, they found it more efficient to painstakingly rewrite the code themselves.

Aside from incomprehensibility, excessively black-boxed code can deleteriously impact the scientific rigour of a computational social science research project. It is often impossible, not to mention undesirable, for principal investigators to micromanage the work their collaborators – student or faculty – are doing. As such, contributors will inevitably make mistakes which, due to the many impenetrable layers of code written by many different contributors, will be difficult to detect, let alone locate or rectify. Gentzkow and Shapiro describe how coding errors led to their regression models producing incomplete, inaccurate results, or situations where discrepancies in definitions of samples between various pieces of code weren't detected until after the results had been submitted to a scholarly journal. Gentzkow and Shapiro's accounts mirror our own experiences: we were forced, at one point, to redesign and implement a data processing pipeline that was functional but which we could no longer understand or generalize to other parts of our research project.

In sum, adhocracy is often dropped into an academic environment but does not thrive therein – it needs some modification or structure that is, itself, reproducible. Without structure, the highly competent and well-intentioned members of research teams can make many individual decisions that are reasonable at the time – and for some small portion of a larger project – but in the big picture this often results in incomprehensible data processing pipelines and an excessive amount of black boxing. In other words, reasonable decisions made by experts about some specific component of a project can still result in a code base that is incomprehensible even to members of the team and far from the ideals of reproducible and transparent science. The core struggle of adhocracy generally, and collaborative computational science specifically, is to convince all members of the team to voluntarily adopt a set of principles designed to structure their combined work without hampering the teams' capacity for flexibility and adaptability.

Researchers are aware of the issues we have discussed in the two preceding sections. In the section that follows, we will introduce a framework developed by Patrick Ball (2016a, 2016b) to ameliorate the struggles inherent to collaboratively producing auditable, transparent data processing pipelines.

4 Principled data processing

This principled data processing (PDP) framework was initially proposed by sociologist and statistician Patrick Ball of the Human Rights Data Analysis Group (Ball, 2016a, 2016b) in the context of their statistical research on mass killings and other acts of political violence. Ball outlines a set of core principles that, as we have argued to this point, should be explicitly adopted in research workflows:

1. *Transparency*: Every portion of the project is visible, and the role it plays can be easily derived from its name (in broad terms, at least).
2. *Auditability*: The project (or components thereof) can be successfully executed on different platforms and in different software environments by analysts who were not necessarily involved in its creation.
3. *Reproducibility*: The project's expected results can be generated by anyone with the same data, code, and software dependencies.
4. *Scalability*: The project's constituent elements are capable of being used for a larger number and wider variety of inputs, outputs, and purposes than originally intended.

Ball describes the system as one designed to ensure that the structure and functionality of a project and its constituent parts are easily understood: not only by other members of a team, but also by the researchers who wrote the code in the first place. If followed by all members of a team, a data processing framework that is anchored in these four principles can buttress against the collaboration and transparency problems facing computational social scientists.

The first – and arguably most fundamental – portion of the PDP framework calls for projects to be split up into a series of discrete tasks, each of which is stored in its own separate, dedicated directory. Each task's directory should have a succinct name that allows newcomers to rapidly ascertain the task's role in the project's overall structure.

Second, each task directory should follow the same organizational scheme. Rather than allowing data, source code, and results to freely mingle, Ball recommends organizing the contents of each task directory into three subdirectories: (a) the 'input' directory, which contains all of the data required by the task; (b) the 'output' directory, which is where all of the task's results are stored; and (c) the 'src' directory, which holds all of the source code necessary to properly and reliably transform the inputs into new outputs.[2]

The small tasks that make up a larger project are interconnected. Aside from the first and final tasks in any given project, every task retrieves its input data from the output of another task, and the output it produces is the input of some other task. The relationships between tasks are formalized by a series of symbolic links (or 'symlinks'), which are lightweight placeholders in a computer's filesystem that, when accessed, point the accessor to a different file or location elsewhere on disk. Each task's input directory contains one or more symlinks pointing to files in other tasks' output directories. This serves three purposes: first, the use of symlinks allows for the separated directory structure to be maintained without necessitating the use of duplicate files; second, the symlinks allow users to determine the project's overall dependency structure (i.e., which tasks are executed in what order); third, the use of symlinks ensures that any changes made to any task's output file will be propagated to the tasks for whom that file is a dependency, ensuring that all tasks stay up to date without any need for manual oversight.

The final critical aspect of Ball's PDP framework is the use of GNU Make via a Makefile. A Makefile is a general-purpose tool used to intelligently execute a series of shell commands – it is commonly employed to compile complex software. GNU Make allows users to split the commands they wish their Makefile to execute into a series of discrete steps, each with their own set of 'dependencies,' 'targets,' and 'actions.'[3] 'Dependencies' are what a task needs before it can run, 'targets' are what a task produces, and 'actions' are the specific steps a task takes (usually in the form of shell commands) to turn the 'dependencies' into the 'targets.' Once properly established, a project-level Makefile allows users to run the entire project using a single command – make. Once invoked, GNU Make will determine how the various tasks should be executed – and in what order – based on the chain of dependencies defined therein. GNU Make also determines whether a task needs to be rerun; tasks are only executed if their dependencies have changed since the last time they were run (if the dependencies haven't changed, then the targets should be identical and do not need to be generated again).

In our view, Ball's principled data processing is an excellent protocol that directly addresses the problems outlined in our previous sections on transparency and collaboration. Using a series of automated tasks as the quanta of an analytical workflow is immensely helpful in ameliorating many of the pitfalls inherent to data processing, including onboarding new collaborators, documentation, writing transparent code, and ensuring reproducible outputs.

4.1 Potential drawbacks

As useful as Ball's principled data processing is, some might encounter difficulties implementing the protocol. Strictly following Ball's recommendations would require every member of a team to familiarize themselves with GNU Make, Linux/Unix, and YAML. While these requirements are sensible in contexts where everyone can be reasonably expected to have some background in some or all of the aforementioned areas, these same requirements can present an onerous or even insurmountable barrier in others.

On a more practical level, the very act of creating and maintaining Makefiles can become prohibitively costly. In projects featuring a comparatively large number of files spread across a large number of tasks, the amount of menial labour (in the form of typing or copying file and directory names with exacting precision) required to simply create a Makefile can significantly impact the time it takes to automate a project. Even for those familiar with GNU Make, the spectre of updating a Makefile after a relatively minor change in a large project's dependency structure can be daunting.

When we first adopted the PDP framework, we used the same tools in the same configuration that Ball (2016a) proposes using. However, we found that the use of highly complex tools like Make actually made aspects of our collaborative projects *more* opaque to some members of the team, especially those who have expertise in statistical and computational models but know little about open source computing culture and tools. This caused an unofficial divide on the team where some collaborators were more capable of making contributions within the PDP framework than others were. To reduce the amount of necessary technical training, we developed a command line tool that dramatically simplifies working within the PDP framework.

5 Introducing pdpp

pdpp is a command-line tool for Python3.6+ that simplifies principled data processing for computational social science projects. Although it is written in Python, it can be used to manage projects written in any programming language whose scripts can be run from the command line (e.g. R). pdpp views analytical projects as being composed of many small, granular, interconnected tasks: each task takes an input, runs the input through one or more pieces of source code, and produces one or more output files. The outputs from most tasks serve as the input for other tasks. In aggregate, the tasks form a chain that takes the project-level input (e.g. a. csv file with data) and produces one or more forms of project-level output (which can take the form of papers, visualizations, statistical model results, other data sets, and so on).

pdpp offers a number of advantages over a strict interpretation of Ball's original principled data processing framework.

5.1 Ease of use

Our primary motivation for developing pdpp was to give a broader range of researchers easier access to the benefits of principled data processing. As such, while developing the package, ease-of-use was one of our chief priorities; we wanted to ensure that even new and inexperienced programmers would find our package simple to learn and apply. After all, the principles are more important than the tools. We also designed pdpp to reduce the amount of menial labour necessary to implement Ball's recommendations for principled data processing. When projects get very large and involve shuffling around vast numbers of individual data files, the simple act of copying and pasting filenames into your automation suite of choice can become prohibitively time consuming. The pdpp package handles all of this automatically and allows you to rapidly assemble and reconfigure complicated projects.

5.2 Suitable for non-expert programmers

When working with pdpp, a basic understanding of Python can be helpful in some edge cases, but it is far from necessary: all of pdpp's functionality can be applied without the need for any direct code alteration or scripting. Knowledge of the command line from your operating system of choice is all that is needed. This stands in contrast to Ball's principled data processing, which requires users to be familiar with syntax for GNU Make, YAML, and Unix/Linux.

5.3 Cross-platform, cross-language

Another benefit of using pdpp is its cross-platform, cross-language compatibility: pdpp can be used by most platforms, with most languages, on any of the major operating systems, and for most projects involving the preparation and analysis of data sets. While pdpp is written in Python, it smoothly interfaces with other languages without requiring users to write (or even understand) Python code. As such, pdpp is an excellent choice for researchers who are familiar with, for example, R but have little to no experience with any other programming environments.

5.4 Minimal downstream workflow

We wanted to ensure that the projects developed using pdpp can be shared, iterated upon, and reproduced without forcing end users (such as journal reviewers, colleagues, etc.) to familiar-ize themselves with pdpp. To run projects built using pdpp, all that is required is an installation of pdpp.

6 How to use pdpp

Every pdpp project consists of one _import_ directory, one _export_ directory, a dodo.py file, and one or more tasks (each contained in their own descriptively named directory). The _import_ directory is used as the common starting point for all locally stored data used through-out the project: all of the project's input data should be stored in the _import_ directory.[4] The _export_ directory is used as the common terminus for all project-level end products and provides a convenient centralized location for gathering all needed output files. The dodo.py file is used by the doit package, upon which pdpp's automation suite is built.

As previously described, pdpp is designed to separate data analysis pipelines into a series of discrete tasks. Each of these tasks should be descriptively named and are usually accompanied by three pieces of functional metadata:

1. Dependencies – the files a task will need to execute properly.
2. Actions – the commands a task will execute.
3. Targets – the files a task will produce as a result of the actions it will take.

The pdpp package and Ball's original formulation of the PDP framework share similar goals, but the routes they take to achieve them differ. pdpp makes three assumptions which abstract away much of what must be explicitly stated in Ball's framework: the first assumption is that tasks will typically be small in scope, self-contained, and written in Python or R.[5] Note that this is merely pdpp's default behaviour. pdpp can be used with scripts written in any language, provided those scripts can be executed using shell commands. By default, pdpp assumes that each task's source code will be composed of a single script, as tasks that require multiple scripts are probably an indication that the task needs to be split further into multiple tasks. pdpp can still automatically handle tasks whose source code consists of multiple scripts, provided each script is written in the same language and has the same file extension. Tasks with two or more scripts written in different languages must be manually implemented. When a project is run, pdpp will execute all of the scripts (written in languages it recognizes) contained in each task's src folder in an arbitrary order.

The second assumption is that any files in one task's output directory can be considered its targets if – and only if – they are dependencies for other tasks. Each task's targets are dynamically determined at runtime based on other tasks' dependencies. This means that rather than having to explicitly list each task's targets, pdpp infers what each task's targets are based on what files other tasks expect to be able to get from it. From a conceptual standpoint, this assumption may seem tautological, but in practical terms, it removes a remarkable amount of menial upkeep.

The third and final assumption is that anything identified as neither a dependency nor source code is unimportant to the project and can be safely ignored.

In typical use cases, the assumptions previously enumerated permit pdpp to rapidly build robust, reliable dependency structures based only on users' indications of which tasks depend on which files elsewhere in the project.

pdpp is built around five main shell commands, each of which handles one aspect of the package's functionality. Note that the following commands must be entered in a project-level directory (either the main project directory or one of the subproject directories). pdpp commands will fail to resolve if the console's current working directory is a non-project location. In alphabetical order, the commands are:

6.1 *pdpp graph*

The pdpp graph command can be used to visualize your project's dependency structure and, in line with Ball's original vision, document the project's structure dynamically without requiring keeping written documentation up to date. It has four modes:

1. sparse – graphs only the dependencies between tasks.
2. source – graphs task dependencies alongside representations of each task's source code.

3. file – graphs the dependencies between tasks and individual files.
4. all – includes all elements from both source and file modes.[6]

In all cases, pdpp graph will produce a graph of your project's dependency structure in either the. pdf,. png, or. jpg format (Figures 8.2–8.5).

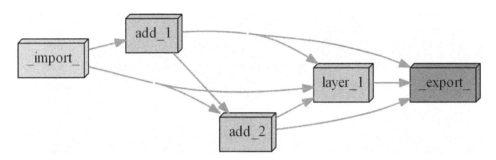

Figure 8.2 Sparse mode

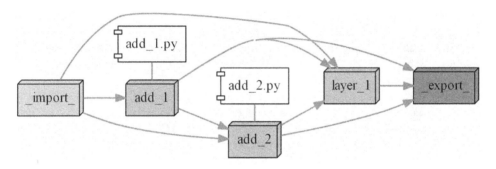

Figure 8.3 Source mode

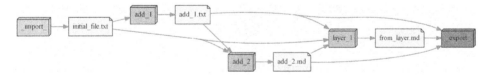

Figure 8.4 File mode

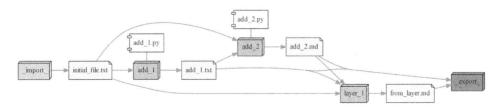

Figure 8.5 All mode

6.2 *pdpp init*

The first step in creating a pdpp-compliant project involves creating an empty directory, navigating to it, and executing the pdpp init command from within. This command populates the directory (which we will refer to from now on as the 'project directory') with all the infrastructure necessary to support pdpp. The pdpp init command does the following:

- Creates an _import_ directory and an _export_ directory, used for storing the entire project's input data and outputs, respectively.
- Creates a generic. gitignore file used by version control to selectively exclude certain files.
- Creates a dodo.py file used by the doit package, which pdpp uses to handle automation.

6.3 *pdpp new*

The pdpp new command is used to create a new directory structure corresponding to one task. Upon executing the command, the user will be asked to supply the task's name, which should follow the following conventions: unique within the project, no upper case characters, no spaces, and no non-underscore special characters (underscores should be used in place of spaces).[7] For example, clean_tweets is a valid name for a task, whereas CleanTweets and Clean tweets are not.

The command creates a task directory, which itself contains input, output, and src directories, as well as a task-specific pdpp_task.yaml file, which pdpp uses to store execution metadata about the task. By default, a blank Python script will be added to the src directory, and. gitkeep files will be included in each of the created directories to ensure their preservation via version control software. Users should feel free to begin writing code in the provided blank Python script or replace it with a script in a language of their choosing.[8]

After the new task has been named and its directory structure populated, pdpp will prompt users to indicate which files contained elsewhere in the project are dependencies for the new task. This is done in a two-step process: first, pdpp asks users to indicate which of the project's other task directories contain dependencies for the new task; second, pdpp presents users with the outputs[9] from the selected tasks (alongside all of the files in the _import_ directory), and prompts users to choose which of the individual files are needed by the new task. Recall that all the pre-existing data files used by – but not produced by – the project's tasks should be stored in the project's _import_ directory.

6.4 *pdpp rig*

The pdpp rig command is identical to the pdpp new command, except that it is intended for use with existing tasks. The rig command allows users to reconfigure the dependencies of any task: after entering pdpp rig, users will be prompted to select which task they wish to 'rig,' at which point users will be first prompted to indicate which other tasks (including _import_) contain dependencies for the task being rigged, and then asked to identify which of the other tasks' files are dependencies. pdpp rig can be used to configure the _export_ task, which is necessary to ensure that the project's overall output files (visualizations, statistical models, etc.) are properly identified as targets of their respective tasks.

6.5 *pdpp run*

The pdpp run command is used to execute each of the tasks in the user's project from start to finish. It is the equivalent to running Make in Ball's original implementation.

7 Sample workflow

In this section, we present a sample workflow designed to familiarize users with the pdpp package's basic functionality and to make the preceding discussion more concrete. For this example, we'll use a modified version of Karan Bhanot's "Dataset Creation and Cleaning: Web Scraping Using Python" project (Bhanot, 2018). Bhanot's project is designed to serve as an example of how one might use information scraped from a web page to create a data set for analysis. It begins by gathering information from Wikipedia, converting the retrieved HTML data into the pandas dataframe format, and then saving the resulting dataframe to disk as a CSV (comma separated values) file. The second step in the process involves loading the saved CSV, cleaning the data set, altering covariates, and saving the results to disk in another CSV, ready for further analysis.

Readers are encouraged to replicate the workflow described later: all that is required is an installation of Python (version 3.6 or greater), pandas, pdpp, and access to the example scripts in the public pdpp_example repository at https://github.com/pbrowne88/pdpp_example.

The best way to start a new project using pdpp is to create an empty directory, navigate to it, and execute the pdpp init command. In the following example, the project directory is named example_project, but the name is unimportant. It should now contain the _import_ and _export_ directories.

Many projects will begin with one or more pre-existing dataset(s) saved to disk; in such cases, all relevant data should be stored in the newly created _import_ directory, which can be found inside the project directory configured by pdpp init. This example, however, does not rely on extant data: the scrape.py script is responsible for collecting and storing data.

This example project consists of two tasks – 'scrape' and 'clean' – which will gather and process our data set, respectively. Now that our project directory is configured, we can proceed by creating a directory for our first task – 'scrape.' Execute the pdpp new command and type 'scrape' when prompted to name the new task. pdpp will then inquire about which of the project's other tasks contain dependencies for the newly created task. Since this is the project's first task and the project doesn't require us to store any data in the _import_ folder, the 'scrape' task has no dependencies; all of the other tasks should be left deselected.

When creating a new task, pdpp automatically creates a Python script with the same name as the task directory and places it in the task's src directory. At this point, that placeholder script should be replaced with the scrape.py script from the example repository. Once the script is in place, navigate to the src directory in the scrape task's directory and run the script with your Python interpreter from the command line.

You can confirm that the script ran correctly by listing the contents of the scrape/output directory: it should contain a file called dataset.csv – this file should contain one row for each United Nations member state and columns for 'Country,' 'Total Area,' 'Percentage Water,' 'Total Nominal GDP,' and 'Per Capita GDP.' While examining dataset.csv, you might notice that much of the data collected and stored by the scrape.py script is riddled with non-numerical symbols and that these symbols are prevalent enough to seriously complicate computational analysis. Fortunately, the clean step is designed to ameliorate this issue.

After navigating back to the project directory, execute the pdpp new command – this time, use 'clean' as the name of the new task. The new clean task is designed to take in the dataset.csv file produced by scrape and prepare it for use in an analytical workflow: as such, dataset.csv is a dependency of the clean task. When pdpp prompts us to indicate which other tasks contain dependencies for the clean task, we can select the scrape task (and only this task) by highlighting it with the spacebar.

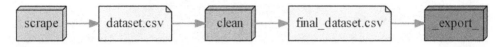

Figure 8.6   The project's final structure as visualized by pdpp graph

At this point, pdpp will present us with another menu of all the eligible output files contained in all of the tasks we indicated earlier. Since we only indicated one task (scrape) and that task's output directory contains only one file (dataset.csv), we are given only one option. Select it and proceed!

Once this is done, pdpp will proceed by creating a hard link to dataset.csv in the scrape/output directory and placing the link in the clean/input directory. This means that the dataset.csv file can now be accessed by the clean task, and any changes made to scrape/output/dataset.csv will be automatically reflected in clean/input/dataset.csv.

As previously, replace the placeholder clean.py script with the complete version from the repository, navigate to the clean/src directory, and run the script with your interpreter. If everything worked as intended, there should be a file titled final_dataset.csv in the clean task's output directory. The entries in each of the columns should be much cleaner now, though not necessarily correct: the Australian landmass, for example, is almost certainly not 76% water! If you're feeling bold, try digging into this example project's code and the dataset.csv file to see if you can isolate where the issue is coming from. In a small example project such as this one, it should be a relatively easy task; in larger projects with dozens of tasks, structural clarity will be indispensable when tracking down and ameliorating error sources.

Now that we have implemented both of the project's tasks, we can finalize the project. First, to ensure that all of the project's end products are stored in the same location, ready to be easily accessed by other scripts or projects, use pdpp rig on the _export_ task and list clean/output/final_dataset.csv as a dependency.

Finally, we can use pdpp graph to produce a graphical representation of our project's structure, shown in Figure 8.6.

Now that the project's structure is in place, you can use pdpp run to rerun 'stale' tasks. This will be useful in cases where changes have been made to input data or a piece of source code.

8 Conclusion

In this chapter, we highlighted the ongoing struggle to embed adherence to reproducibility and transparency into the practice of computational social science, which we see as a superset of – and requiring much bigger changes than what is called for in – the ongoing discussion of the role of replication in the sciences. A strong emphasis on reproducibility and transparency in computational social science would make replications easier and likely more successful while also being compatible with mixed-methods research that does not lend itself well to the replication model. In addition to its many intellectual benefits for our community and other individual investigators and teams, reproducible and transparent research practices also enable us to do more ethical computational analyses, especially when our methods and models may have tangible impacts on individuals' lives and well-being. We introduced a framework – principled data processing – that can help accomplish this and demonstrated one way of adopting this framework that relies on a new command line tool called pdpp.

Notes

1 It should be noted that transparent code and data will not facilitate reproducibility tests that implicate the data-generating process itself; for example, the push for transparent data and code will not help in cases where researchers employ flawed or intentionally mendacious techniques for gathering or generating data.

2 While 'input,' 'src,' and 'output' should be the only project-relevant directories found inside any given task, Ball allows that other directories may be included. One such directory Ball mentions by name is the 'hand' directory, which is used to develop new source code in an interactive environment such as a Jupyter Notebook. Ball recognizes that Jupyter Notebooks can be remarkably useful for developing new code, but they are not suitable for use with the overall project and as such should not be placed in the 'src' directory.

3 GNU Make has many more features and is capable of much more than what is detailed here. For the purposes of focus and brevity, our description of GNU Make only covers those aspects pertinent to Ball's PDP framework.

4 This requirement to store does not apply to dynamically retrieved or generated data; data pulled from a URL or queried from a database does not need to be stored in the _import_ directory. This also does not apply to data files created as part of the project's execution. The _import_ requirement exists to ensure that the dependency structure between tasks is preserved for all project-level input data files.

5 Although pdpp only has automated support for Python and R at the time of this chapter's publication, more languages will be added in post-release updates.

6 Be warned: the 'all' graphs can become unreasonably messy, even for modestly sized projects.

7 These conventions are necessary to avoid the complications that arise from how various languages and operating systems interpret special characters and capitalization.

8 Note that at the time of writing, pdpp does not support tasks that have multiple scripts written in different languages. This is because pdpp directly runs project scripts from the shell and needs to know which shell command is appropriate to use on which files in an src directory. Advanced users will be able to create custom workarounds, but most users should avoid creating tasks that rely on multiple pieces of source code from multiple languages. If your task has two pieces of source code, it is almost always more appropriate to split it into two separate tasks.

9 Defined as files in the task's output directory.

References

Baker, M. (2016). 1,500 scientists lift the lid on reproducibility. *Nature, 533*, 452–454.

Ball, P. (2016a). Principled data processing. *Data & Society Talks: Small Group Session.* https://hrdag.org/talks-discussions/

Ball, P. (2016b). The task is a quantum of workflow. *Human Rights Data Analysis Group.* https://hrdag.org/2016/06/14/

Bhanot, K. (2018). Dataset creation and cleaning: Web Scraping using Python – Part 1. *Towards Data Science.* https://towardsdatascience.com/dataset-creation-and-cleaning-web-scraping-using-python-part-1-33afbf360b6b

Birkinshaw, J., & Ridderstråle, J. (2010). Adhocracy for an agile age. *Organization Science, 22*(5), 1286–1296.

Brayne, S. (2017). Big data surveillance: The case of policing. *American Sociological Review, 82*(5), 977–1008.

Brayne, S. (2020). *Predict and surveil: Data, discretion, and the future of policing.* Oxford University Press.

Christensen, G., Freese, J., & Miguel, E. (2019). *Transparent and reproducible social science research: How to do open science.* University of California Press.

Collins, H. (1974). The TEA set: Tacit knowledge and scientific networks. *Science Studies, 4*(2), 165–185.

Collins, H. (1992). *Changing order: Replication and induction in scientific practice.* University of Chicago Press.

Collins, H. (1998). The meaning of data: Open and closed evidential cultures in the search for gravitational waves. *American Journal of Sociology, 104*(2), 293–338.

Collins, H. (2016). Reproducibility of experiments: Experimenters' regress, statistical uncertainty principle, and the replication imperative. In H. Atmanspacher & S. Maasen (Eds.), *Reproducibility: Principles, problems, practices, and prospects.* John Wiley & Sons.

Freese, J. (2007). Replication standards for quantitative social science: Why not sociology? *Sociological Methods & Research, 36*(2), 153–172.

Freese, J., & Peterson, D. (2017). Replication in social science. *Annual Review of Sociology, 43*, 147–165.

Gentzkow, M., & Shapiro, J. M. (2014). *Code and data for the social sciences: A practitioner's guide.* University of Chicago.

Gleditsch, N. P., James, P., Ray, J. L., & Russett, B. (2003). Editors' joint statement: Minimum replication standards for international relations journals. *International Studies Perspectives, 4*(1), 105.

Jacoby, W. G., Lafferty-Hess, S., & Christian, T.-M. (2017). Should journals be responsible for reproducibility? *Inside Higher Ed, 17*. www.insidehighered.com/blogs/rethinking-research/should-journals-be-responsible-reproducibility

Joint Statement by Political Science Journal Editors. (2015). Data access and research transparency (DART): A joint statement by political science journal editors. *Political Science Research and Methods, 3*.

King, G. (1995). Replication, replication. *PS: Political Science and Politics, 28*(3), 444–452.

McLevey, J. (2020). Epistemic and evidential cultures. In S. Delmont & P. Atkinson (Eds.), *Sage research methods fundamentals*. SAGE Publications Limited.

McLevey, J. (2021). *Doing computational social science*. Sage.

Mintzberg, H., & McHugh, A. (1985). Strategy formation in an adhocracy. *Administrative Science Quarterly*, 160–197.

O'Neil, C. (2016). *Weapons of math destruction: How big data increases inequality and threatens democracy.* Broadway Books.

Pridemore, W. A., Makel, M. C., & Plucker, J. A. (2018). Replication in criminology and the social sciences. *Annual Review of Criminology, 1*, 19–38.

SECTION II

Data quality in CSS research

9

APPLYING A TOTAL ERROR FRAMEWORK FOR DIGITAL TRACES TO SOCIAL MEDIA RESEARCH

Indira Sen, Fabian Flöck, Katrin Weller,
Bernd Weiß and Claudia Wagner

1 Introduction

Thanks to social media, conversations that happened in (semi-)private settings around the world have moved online. Now, the collective banter, arguments, entreaties, and even hostilities that took place offline are found on multiple platforms such as Twitter, Facebook, Instagram, and more, at a much larger scale. On the one hand, this represents a treasure trove of data that social scientists can leverage to learn about the "ABCs" of humans: attitudes, behaviors, and characteristics. These data can help in (i) assessing theories developed and tested using more traditional methods of studying humans, such as surveys, as well as (ii) conceptualizing new theories, especially those that explain digital aspects of human existence. Although such enormous amounts of observational traces have never before been available and promises for answers to new and old questions abound, they are certainly not a panacea for learning about human ABCs. Studying online human behavior comes with its own set of methodological and technical challenges. It also raises issues of representation and external validity – regarding other online contexts, but specifically to offline settings. Such studies may not only be unfit to (in)validate previously established theories, but when their findings or insights are applied to real-world applications such as policymaking within or beyond sociotechnical systems, biases can be both conceived and reinforced (boyd & Crawford, 2012; Olteanu et al., 2019). Therefore, it is essential to understand the differences between two paradigms of studying human behavior: survey-based methods (SB) and digital trace data (DTD)–based methods.

The benefits of massive data sets have been discussed in detail (e.g., Mayer-Schönberger & Cukier, 2013), but some attention has also been devoted to its drawbacks (e.g., Olteanu et al., 2019). One caveat is that firsthand analysis of all (or even most) raw data at this scale is beyond human capacity. Therefore, researchers often depend on automated methods for preprocessing, annotating, and aggregating, raising concerns of validity. For example, while surveys usually rely on coding systems that have been developed in advance and are applied by human coders, DTD methods count on either fully automated solutions such as machine learning or a combination of human and automated solutions, often developing labeling approaches based on one particular data set. One effect of different platforms producing very heterogeneous types of data

DOI: 10.4324/9781003025245-11

is that each necessitates a tailored approach. Further, platform-specific norms affect how people express or record attitudes, behaviors, or characteristics. Researchers collect very specific subsets of the data of their choosing, and they construct (proxy) variables used for measurement in very distinct ways.

Which humans are selected into the sample of study is another issue. Survey researchers, again hindered by the infeasibility of reaching a large number of people or responses, typically use probabilistic samples for the estimation of unbiased statistics and/or employ reweighting strategies. With DTD being large scale, researchers can bypass the infeasibility of accessing large populations due to social media platforms containing the digital traces of millions of people; yet *which* populations they reach on a given platform is often unclear. Even studies that focus on platform-specific phenomena (in contrast to inferring to general populations beyond the platform) face limitations, as computational tools for most researchers are still constrained. Therefore, typically only a relevant subset of the platform data is queried. The choice of query terms can affect the representativity of the final sample further. Without knowledge of the mechanisms driving the selection of certain types of individuals, reweighting strategies may fail.

The prevalence of the aforementioned problems highlights issues of similar impact that plague both SB and DTD approaches. Building on this insight, we leverage the error diagnosis tools provided by the total survey error framework (TSE) (e.g., Groves et al., 2011) to categorize systematically and concisely name the errors and biases present in DTD approaches. Building bridges between survey methodology and DTD methods serves two purposes: first, it provides researchers a common vocabulary to interpret and record issues with social science studies irrespective of the data source they use, fostering interdisciplinary collaboration. Second, it allows us to translate and apply error mitigation strategies developed in survey methodology to DTD studies. Both of these help in it laying the foundation for improving estimates from web and social media data by encouraging more emphasis on research design.

2 The total error framework for digital traces of humans (TED)

To shed light on how measurement and representation errors manifest in estimates derived from digital traces, we make use of the total error framework for digital traces of humans (TED) (Sen et al., 2019). We link errors to the following design decision steps inherent to conducting observational studies using digital traces, as listed by TED (see Figure 9.1).

Like in a survey, a researcher working with digital traces needs to *define the theoretical construct and a conceptual link to the ideal measurement* that will quantify it (cf. "construct definition" in the center strand of Figure 9.1). However, in SB research, as the outcome of this step, the measurement instrument can be usually concretely tailored to the research question before data is generated,[1] including one or several stimuli (questions). In contrast, non-designed but "found" (or "organic") digital traces are *non-reactive*, that is, the researcher is neither defining nor administering a stimulus but is observing the behavioral traces of participants in the field. In this step, a non-definition or under-definition of the construct or a mismatch between the construct and the envisioned ideal measurement corresponds to issues of *validity*.

The second design step of *selecting one or more platforms* as sources for digital traces is often done in conjunction with the construct definition step and is further directly linked to the definition of the target population. The chosen platform(s) set(s) a specific "sampling frame" for both traces and users.

Traces refer to content (e.g., tweets on Twitter), or (inter)actions (e.g., likes) on digital platforms, typically generated by identifiable users (such as a user account) that can be reasonably believed to represent a human actor (or sometimes a group of human actors). Users representing

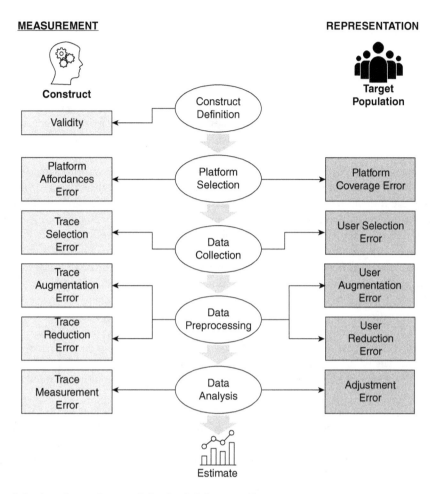

Figure 9.1 A total error framework for the digital traces of humans

(commercial) organizations or automated programs run the risk of being mistaken as suitable proxies for human actors. They usually have to be filtered out for research questions aiming at measuring individual persons' ABCs. Users typically emit various traces over time.

The behavior of users and the traces generated by them are impacted by (i) platform-specific sociocultural norms (e.g., posting rules) as well as (ii) the platform's design and technical constraints (e.g., length restrictions for messages), leading to measurement errors which we together summarize as *platform affordances error*.

In addition to measurement errors, the mismatch between the individuals in the target population and those being represented on the platform is the *platform coverage error*, a representation error.

For *data collection*, and in contrast to surveys, researchers (i) can then choose to either sample traces *or* users and (ii) frequently have access to the entire sampling frame of a platform. Therefore, there is generally no need for sampling due to logistical infeasibility, as is typically done in surveys. Depending on their needs and the theoretical construct, the researcher devises a data collection strategy, which usually involves a set of concise *queries* (e.g., keyword searches) that *select* a specific portion of the platform data, producing the final data subset that will be studied.

These query choices determine on what basis the construct of interest is quantified and thus may lead to measurement errors. The difference between traces required for establishing the ideal measurement and trace collected due to the researcher-specified query is termed *trace selection error*. The representation error incurred due to the gap between the selection of users and the sampling frame that the platform provides (its user base) is called the user *selection error*.

The traces and the users that make up this subset are usually further filtered or *preprocessed*, including labeling. In this regard, digital traces – particularly of textual nature – are similar to survey data based on open-ended questions, which require a considerable amount of preprocessing before they can be statistically analyzed. However, due to commonly huge volumes of digital traces, preprocessing of digital traces is almost exclusively done via automated methods. Second, preprocessing for users in digital traces is much more relevant than for survey respondents. For the former, many important attributes (demography, bot-vs-human, etc.) have to be inferred at this step. Just as free text survey responses are coded to ascertain categories and inadequately trained coders can assign incorrect labels, *trace augmentation error* occurs often because of inaccurate categorization due to the usage of pretrained machine learning methods or other predefined heuristics, frequently designed for different contexts. On the other hand, the measurement error incurred due to the removal of potentially eligible traces – and the non-removal of ineligible traces – is termed the *trace reduction error*. Similarly, representation errors in the form of user *augmentation* and user *reduction* errors are incurred when users are preprocessed.

Depending on the subject of analysis, final metrics for the main construct to be measured (and auxiliary variables) are then calculated (e.g., a "presidential approval score" per tweet, from 0 to 1) and data points are aggregated to produce a final estimate for the target population, as is done for survey estimates. Additionally, modeling of the data on top of the final indicators is done to unearth patterns of underlying processes.

As per TED, two main errors can plague this last step in the study process. Any error that distorts how the final trace is constructed due to modeling choices is denoted as *trace measurement error*. The (un)availability of accurate demographic information – or other features to be considered for adjustment – as well as the choice of method (e.g., post-stratification) can also cause errors which fall under *adjustment error*, in line with the adjustment error in the TSE (Groves et al., 2011).

3 Case studies

To help understand the utility of the error framework for digital traces of humans, we apply it to diagnose, document, and illustrate errors in existing computational social science (CSS) studies. TED is mainly motivated by – but not limited to – social media data such as Twitter, Facebook, and Reddit data as well as other data collected on web platforms such as search engine queries used in social sensing studies. Therefore, we examine existing literature that has leveraged digital traces for social sensing or nowcasting.

3.1 Case 1: Presidential Approval From Tweets

Our first example is the case of measuring *presidential approval*, which can be understood as a subtask of measuring public opinion from social media. In the 1930s, the Gallup organization began asking Americans, "Do you approve or disapprove of the way [the incumbent] is handling his job as president?"[2] and since then this question for gauging presidential approval has become a regular fixture in political opinion polling. Political scientists have been interested in different aspects of presidential approval: demographic leaning (Gilens, 1988), the effect of issues on it (Andrade & Young, 1996), and the "rally round the flag effect" (Newman & Force-himes, 2010), among others. Survey methodology has developed methods to precisely measure presidential approval. An approval rating is a percentage determined by a polling that indicates the percentage of respondents to an opinion poll who approve of a particular person or program. O'Connor et al. (2010) were one of the first to explore how tweets could complement polls used for assessing public opinion. Since then, many attempts have been made to measure the construct of presidential approval, or political outcomes in general, through digital traces (Barberá, 2016; Pasek et al., 2019), ranging from search engine queries (Stephens-Davidowitz, 2012) to Wikipedia article views (Smith & Gustafson, 2017), with mixed success. Our first case study reviews and summarizes practices in various publications that attempt to measure *presidential approval from tweets*. We shed light on the various issues that could potentially arise in these studies, by analyzing them through the lens of TED.

3.1.1 Construct definition

In a questionnaire one can rather directly measure the construct of presidential approval by asking a question such as, "Do you approve or disapprove of the way Donald Trump is handling his job as president?" A researcher working with digital trace data, on the other hand, cannot apply such a stimulus and collect the resulting response. They may instead consider the act of tweeting positively about the president to be equivalent to approval and tweeting negatively about them as disapproval (O'Connor et al., 2010; Pasek et al., 2019). This in itself might lead to inaccurate measurements. Regarding precision, it is often difficult to disentangle if a tweet specifically comments on how the president is handling their job or if it refers to the president's private or past life (which is not necessarily a related construct). Regarding recall, not all (dis)approval is expressed through sentiment but might be uttered in a neutral tone. Moreover, the way the concept "tweeting positively about the president" is operationalized in detail varies a lot and can be error prone. For example, mentions of the president alongside positively connoted words may indicate approval, but could also be effects of sarcasm or (nonfavorable) jokes. It may also be that the positive sentiment is directed at another target in the tweet. What constitutes a "positive" word might also be subjective and depends on the method used. Lastly, researchers have to be confident that the envisioned, ideal measurement for their construct is likely to be applicable to different strata of users (or users) on the platform. If a certain populace is much less likely to use sentiment expressions in tweets, this might lead to grave distortions in the measurement.

3.1.2 Platform selection

In posting their opinion on Twitter, users have to adhere to the *affordances* of the platform as well as its explicit and unspoken norms. Users may have to write terse tweets or a thread consisting of multiple tweets to express their opinion about the president on Twitter. Users may also be less likely to expose an opinion that they assume to be unpopular on the platform and beyond, given that posts are potentially seen by a wide audience. Twitter's "trends" feature, showing popular (including political) hashtags, might moreover motivate users to post an opinion mimicking others. All of these constraints affect how a user will (not) express their opinion towards the president and can therefore distort the overall measurement, causing a *platform affordance error*.

If we assume that full access to all relevant data on Twitter is given for research purposes, the sampling frame includes all users who have self-selected to register and to openly express their opinion on Twitter. These respondents are most likely not a representation of the target population (e.g., US voters) which causes a *platform coverage error* – mostly due to undercoverage – that may lead to highly misleading estimates (Fischer & Budescu, 1995). Also, nonhumans (e.g., bots, businesses) may hold user accounts and are therefore part of the sampling frame that is defined by the platform, which, in this case, can be regarded as overcoverage. In reality, this platform-specific sampling frame is further restricted by deliberate technological impediments and terms of use set forth by Twitter as the monopolistic data provider, which only allow free access to a 1% sample of all tweets in a given time frame. The randomness of this secondary, "imposed sampling" is disputed and can lead to added representation errors (Morstatter et al., 2013). In this specific form, it is idiosyncratic to Twitter, although other providers might adopt similar measures in the future.[3]

3.1.3 Data collection

Assume that we aim to capture all tweets about the – as of writing – current US president. If solely and exactly tweets that mention the keyword "Trump" are collected, tweets unrelated to Donald Trump, which for example refer to Melania Trump or "playing a trump card," could be included and lead to noise. Likewise, relevant queries might be excluded that simply refer to "the president," "Donald," or acronyms. Not excluding ineligible or excluding eligible traces in this way can severely harm the soundness of the measurement instrument. And while more complex query strategies and heuristics are of course possible, they always come with a trade-off between false positives and false negatives, affecting the measurement by causing a *trace selection error*.

The selection defined by keywords also entails a second frame for the sampling of Twitter users, that is, users in addition to the one induced by platform selection: since the chosen keywords (e.g., the full spelling of "Trump") are only used by a subgroup of users, only those users are represented in the study, by extension of their tweets. Certain groups of users, like Spanish-speaking people living in the US or younger liberal voters, may be underrepresented if profiles are included based on keywords that mainly capture how adult English-speaking Americans refer to political topics, leading to a misrepresentation of the target population and causing a user *selection error*. Another form of user selection error can occur if users are actively sampled because of their profile data or appearance on a list, not because of, or through, their tweets. Since only specific types of users might provide profile information used for selection (foremost, demographics and geolocation), or be prolific enough to appear on other users' lists, this can bias the user selection as well.

3.1.4 Data preprocessing

After data collection, the obtained sample of tweets may be preprocessed in two ways: *augmentation*, where auxiliary information about each data point is generated, and *reduction*, where some data points or components of data are removed. If traces are incorrectly preprocessed, it may lead to measurement errors. Political tweets are often annotated with sentiment to understand opinions towards the president (O'Connor et al., 2010; Barberá, 2016). However, the users of Twitter might have adopted very different vocabularies (e.g., "Web-born" slang and abbreviations) than those covered in popular sentiment lexica and even use words in different contexts, leading to misidentification or under-coverage of sentiments, resulting in *trace augmentation error*. Recent work has also shown that sentiment analysis methods are often racially biased, treating occurrences of sentiment words alongside African American names and terms differently from those without (Kiritchenko & Mohammad, 2018). Unintended racial bias in classifiers can also contribute to the mismeasurement of the construct and constitutes a trace augmentation error.

Further, researchers might decide to use a classifier that removes spam but is too aggressive (high false positive rate) removing non-spam tweets as well. They might likewise discard tweets that do not contain any natural language content, thereby ignoring relevant statements made through hyperlinks or embedded pictures and videos, leading to a *trace reduction error.*

Besides tweets (traces), the accounts of the tweet authors (users) may also be preprocessed. For example, Twitter users' gender, ethnicity, or location may be inferred to understand how presidential approval differs across demographics. Yet these methods often exhibit distinct error rates for different subgroups of users. For instance, automated gender inference methods based on images have higher error rates for African Americans (Buolamwini & Gebru, 2018), while name-based methods perform worse on non-Westernized names (Karimi et al., 2016); therefore, gender inferred through such means would cause the over- or underestimation of approval rates among African American or Asian populaces downstream, causing a *user augmentation error.*

While estimating presidential approval from tweets, researchers are usually not interested in posts that are created by bots or organizations. One can detect such accounts (Wang et al., 2019; Alzahrani et al., 2018) at the risk of removing users that show bot- or organization-like behavior and/or retaining bot accounts that produce large amounts of tweets relevant to the construct, leading to a *user reduction error.*

3.1.5 *Data analysis*

Eventually, the researcher annotates the tweets with the proxy or score variable that measures presidential approval and calculates the final estimate (either per tweet or in aggregate). Based on how this proxy is inferred, they incur *trace measurement errors.* If the construct was defined and operationalized as "sentiment towards the president," and trace augmentation was performed by using sentiment lexicons, the researcher obtains counts of positive and negative words for the collected tweets. Now they must define a final link function if they aim to combine all traces into a single aggregate estimate for the construct of "approval." They may choose to count the normalized positive words in a day (Barberá, 2016), determine the ratio of positive and negative words per tweet, or add the ratio of all tweets in a day (Pasek et al., 2019). The former calculation of counting positive words in a day may underestimate negative sentiments of a particular day, while in the latter aggregate, negative and positive mentions in tweets which contain both would neutralize each other, resulting in such a tweet effectively having "no sentiment."

When comparing presidential approval on Twitter with survey data, Pasek et al. (2019) reweight the survey estimates with aggregate Twitter usage demographics (obtained from earlier surveys) but fail to find alignment between the two measures. In this case, the researchers assume that the demographics of Twitter users are the same as that of subset of Twitter users tweeting about the president, an assumption which might lead to *adjustment error.* Previous research has indeed shown that users who talk about politics on Twitter tend to have different characteristics than random Twitter users (Cohen & Ruths, 2013) and that they tend to be younger and have a higher chance of being white men (Bekafigo & McBride, 2013). It might thus be necessary to infer demographics of all individuals in the selection to reweight it, which means that possible errors are inherited from the user augmentation step. Yet, another adjustment error can then be committed by choosing the wrong reweighting approach, for example post-stratifying on only one characteristic instead of using joint distributions of demographic features (Wang et al., 2019).

3.2 Case 2: Google's Perspective API

CSS studies often make use of off-the-shelf, "ready-made" data sets or tools developed by other researchers for their own study (Salganik, 2019). This contrasts with the procedure outlined in the previous case study, where a researcher "customizes" most of their design steps.[4] In our second case study, we apply the TED on the construction of a particular measurement tool, the Perspective API,[5] rather than on a study of a specific target population via social media. The Perspective API is based on a machine learning model that was developed for detecting "toxicity" in text documents on the Web, such as tweets or article comments.

While the Perspective API itself was first launched by Google in 2018, the underlying model was described by Wulczyn et al. (2017). The model, trained on a massive data set of personal attacks in Wikipedia edits and news article comments, achieved a high performance of 97.19%. Area under the curve (AUC) on an in-domain test set. Since then, variations of this model (with not all alterations made transparent to the public) have been applied for a variety of content moderation tasks as well as detecting hate speech in different types of content ranging from newspaper articles to blog comments (Hua et al., 2020). The most widely used models currently available from the Perspective API score textual content across several categories such as "toxicity," "severe toxicity," and "identity attack." In this work, we focus on the toxicity model since it is widely used.

A researcher using the Perspective API to study, say, hate speech in tweets would not only have to contend with the biases introduced by their own design choices but, they would also have to deal with the bias encoded into this measurement instrument, which itself has been subject to design decisions along the pipeline described by the TED and is prone to the related errors. In the following sections, we look at the construction of the Perspective API, the errors and biases that are "baked into it" due to the design choices, and the implications of these errors on a potential DTD study that a researcher might want to conduct using the API.

3.2.1 Construct definition

The developers of the Perspective API describe a toxic comment as "a rude, disrespectful, or unreasonable comment that is likely to make you leave a discussion." First, note that the definition is particularly focused on *conversational* structures, while single utterances such as speeches by politicians or news articles may be one-sided rather than conversational.

The use of the Perspective API for measuring related but somewhat distinct constructs is of particular concern. A popular application scenario is, for instance, detecting hate speech. First, the definition of toxicity does not include any reference to hate speech, which is a complex construct with contested definitions that vary by country, legal systems, and cultural context (Fortuna & Nunes, 2018). While toxicity might be construed as a "sub-construct" of hate speech, it could also describe acts of speech that are not per se hateful but still detrimental to a conversation. In that vein, the relation of these constructs is by no means consensually defined among experts in this field.

Consequently, a researcher should closely analyze to what extent a model captures hate speech or a related construct they want to quantify, otherwise risking issues of *validity*. Researchers should also note that the toxicity score is *undirected*. This means an overall measure of toxicity may fail as a measure of toxicity directed towards a predefined user, when multiple users are mentioned.

3.2.2 Platform selection and data collection

The data for building the toxicity models were themselves obtained from "online forums such as Wikipedia . . . and *New York Times*."[6] Therefore, a researcher who wants to use the Perspective

API should note that the models are first and foremost suited for these particular platforms or those which have similar conversational structures. Twitter, where a number of studies related to hate speech detection using the API have been conducted (Qayyum et al., 2018; ElSherief et al., 2018, among others), diverges from online forums in several ways, mainly that it is used to broadcast terse textual information of an idiosyncratic style. Further, in addition to rules laid out by the platforms in their community guidelines or terms of service, different platforms adhere to varying unspoken norms of civility and politeness. The language used in some subreddits is distinct from a news or finance forum, not only by what is allowed in the particular space, but also by what meaning certain ("rude") terms carry for both speaker and audience. These settings all amount to very particular *platform affordances*. Researchers applying the Perspective API for measuring toxic attitudes and content moderation on platforms should accordingly note the differences between the affordances of the targeted platform and the often *very distinct data used to train the underlying models* powering the API.

Platform selection can also induce potential *coverage* issues, if only specific individuals are represented in the training data. Since for the Perspective API not all details of the training data are available, we conflate coverage issues due to platform selection (platform coverage error) and data collection (entity selection error). Similar to our previous example regarding sentiment classifiers, several researchers have noted racial bias in the Perspective API's performance (Sap et al., 2019). Sap et al. find that the Perspective API's toxicity scores are significantly higher for sentences with African American English (AAE) dialect markers, compared to their non-AAE counterparts (see Figure 9.2). If the training data is not sufficiently representative of the population the system is (supposed) to be applied to, it can lead to potentially high misclassification or "disparate mistreatment" (Zafar et al., 2017) for underrepresented subpopulations. While we do not know the demographic composition of the data sample used, the general demographics of Wikipedia almost certainly influenced the training of the toxicity models, where the majority of editors are "mainly technically inclined, English-speaking, white collar men living in majority-Christian, developed countries in the Northern hemisphere."[7]

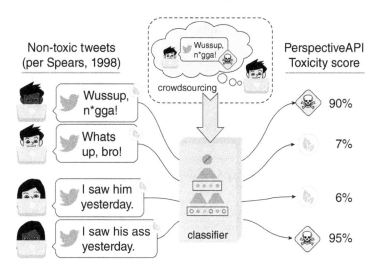

Figure 9.2   Previous research has shown that the Toxicity API provides higher toxicity scores for tweets in the African American English (AAE) dialect compared to their non-AAE counterparts (taken from Sap et al., 2019)

In addition to racial bias, the toxicity models are also susceptible to other forms of unintended bias based on various user types, including gender and sexual minorities. The creators of the model find that since a number of identity terms co-occur with toxic data points (toxic comments directed at minorities), automated models may associate the presence of such terms with toxicity (Dixon et al., 2018). This is problematic as accusations or disclosure of being victims of toxicity may be labeled toxic.

Researchers should perform error analysis to understand potential issues of the API for their data set, paying close attention to expressions by minorities.

3.2.3 Data preprocessing

The data sample for building the toxicity models was augmented in several ways, primary of which is the annotation of toxicity, and related constructs such as stereotypes, by several crowdworkers based on an expanded definition of toxicity.[8]

As some of the creators of the API describe (Aroyo et al., 2019), toxicity is a subjective construct that different people perceive in different ways. How data points are annotated for toxicity can depend on the annotators' personal beliefs and interactions as well as the ambiguity of instructions. Other work in natural language processing (NLP) indicates that crowdsourced data sets often end up capturing a narrower understanding of the construct, that is, what the *annotators* perceive about it (Geva et al., 2019). Therefore, *trace augmentation error* in toxicity detection can creep in due to annotator biases and can lead to automatic models detecting a subset of toxicity.

3.2.4 Data analysis

Finally, the creators of the model, according to the Model card,[9] use a convolutional neural network (CNN) (LeCun & Bengio, 1995) trained with a specialized NLP technique, namely word embeddings (GloVe), which is fine-tuned during training on the annotated data. Word embeddings are resulting from an unsupervised method that automatically learns the semantic associations between words by discovering them from large unstructured data sets. Therefore, GloVe embeddings, trained on a large corpus of web data including tweets (Li et al., 2017), often show "human-like" biases such as gender and racial stereotypes (Caliskan et al., 2017). In the section Platform Selection and Data Collection, we saw that the data sampling technique can inadvertently introduce bias in the data set, depending on which kind of users are represented in the data set. *Trace measurement error*, in the form of biases of tools like GloVe, can exacerbate these stereotypes even further.

To summarize, the Perspective API is exemplary of "ready-made," powerful tools available for computational social scientists. While the proprietary toxicity model is not available for inspection, many details of its conceptualization and construction are open-sourced. At the same time, researchers should be aware of the shortcomings of the model when used on novel data. Analysing the API through TED not only surfaces these issues in a systematic manner but also advances a more precise diagnosis of errors.

4 Conclusion

To make research on human ABCs – that is based on digital traces, surveys, or both – more comparable and to increase the reproducibility of digital trace-based research, it is important to describe potential error sources and mitigation strategies systematically. We have therefore explained and applied our framework TED for disentangling the various kinds of errors that may originate in the unsolicited nature of this data, in effects related to specific platforms, as well as in the data collection and analysis strategies.

Our case studies demonstrate how TED can be applied not only to document errors in CSS pipelines (Case 1) but also to instruments used in CSS studies, such as the Perspective API, whose design choices encode certain errors into it (Case 2). These case studies stand as prototypical examples that showcase the broad applicability of TED to a range of similar – and popular – CSS approaches to studying DTD and employing novel out-of-the-box machine learning tools.

Just as survey methodology has benefited from understanding potential limitations in a systematic manner, TED acts as a set of recommendations for researchers on *what* to reflect on and on *how* they might use digital traces for studying social indicators. It does so (i) by drawing from concepts developed and refined in survey research to pinpoint and mitigate errors and, maybe more importantly, (ii) by developing a shared vocabulary to enhance the dialogue among scientists from heterogeneous disciplines working in the area of computational social science. We recommend researchers not only to use TED to think about the various types of errors that may occur, but also to use it to more systematically document limitations if they cannot be avoided. These design documents should be shared with research results where possible.

Notes

1 This is not always the case, especially nowadays when secondary analyses of existing survey data is common.
2 Trump job approval – Gallup poll. Retrieved June 25, 2020, from https://news.gallup.com/poll/203207/trump-job-approval-weekly.aspx
3 Facebook, for example, currently restricts access to public posts over its CrowdTangle platform, but no known access forms based on a (random) sampling strategy are known to us at this time.
4 Aside from sentiment lexica or demographic inference methods employed, our aforementioned example(s) designed all other steps in the research pipeline autonomously.
5 Perspective API. Retrieved June 23, 2020, from www.perspectiveapi.com/
6 Increasing transparency in perspective's machine learning. . . . (2019, January 30). Retrieved June 25, 2020, from https://medium.com/the-false-positive/increasing-transparency-in-machine-learning-models-311ee08ca58a
7 Racial bias on Wikipedia – Wikipedia. Retrieved June 25, 2020, from https://en.wikipedia.org/wiki/Racial_bias_on_Wikipedia
8 https://github.com/conversationai/conversationai.github.io/blob/master/crowdsourcing_annotation_schemes/toxicity_with_subattributes.md
9 https://developers.perspectiveapi.com/s/about-the-api-model-cards

References

Alzahrani, S., Gore, C., Salehi, A., & Davulcu, H. (2018, July). Finding organizational accounts based on structural and behavioral factors on Twitter. In *International conference on social computing, behavioral-cultural modeling and prediction and behavior representation in modeling and simulation* (pp. 164–175). Springer.
Andrade, L., & Young, G. (1996). Presidential agenda setting: Influences on the emphasis of foreign policy. *Political Research Quarterly, 49*(3), 591–605.
Aroyo, L., Dixon, L., Thain, N., Redfield, O., & Rosen, R. (2019). May. Crowdsourcing subjective tasks: The case study of understanding toxicity in online discussions. In *Companion proceedings of the 2019 World Wide Web conference (WWW '19)* (pp. 1100–1105). Association for Computing Machinery. https://doi.org/10.1145/3308560.3317083
Barberá, P. (2016). *Less is more? How demographic sample weights can improve public opinion estimates based on Twitter data*. Work Pap NYU.

Bekafigo, M. A., & McBride, A. (2013). Who tweets about politics? Political participation of Twitter users during the 2011gubernatorial elections. *Social Science Computer Review, 31*(5), 625–643.

boyd, d., & Crawford, K. (2012). Critical questions for big data: Provocations for a cultural, technological, and scholarly phenomenon. *Information, Communication & Society, 15*(5), 662–679.

Buolamwini, J., & Gebru, T. (2018, January). Gender shades: Intersectional accuracy disparities in commercial gender classification. Proceedings of the 1st conference on fairness, accountability and transparency. *PMLR, 81,* 77–91.

Caliskan, A., Bryson, J. J., & Narayanan, A. (2017). Semantics derived automatically from language corpora contain human-like biases. *Science, 356*(6334), 183–186.

Cohen, R., & Ruths, D. (2013, June). Classifying political orientation on Twitter: It's not easy! In *Seventh international AAAI conference on weblogs and social media.* AAAI.

Dixon, L., Li, J., Sorensen, J., Thain, N., & Vasserman, L. (2018, December). Measuring and mitigating unintended bias in text classification. In *Proceedings of the 2018 AAAI/ACM conference on AI, ethics, and society* (pp. 67–73). ACM.

ElSherief, M., Nilizadeh, S., Nguyen, D., Vigna, G., & Belding, E. (2018, June). Peer to peer hate: Hate speech instigators and their targets. In *Twelfth international AAAI conference on web and social media.* AAAI.

Fischer, I., & Budescu, D. V. (1995). Desirability and hindsight biases in predicting results of a multi-party election. In J.-P. Caverni, M. Bar-Hillel, F. H. Barron, & H. Jungermann (Eds.), *Contributions to decision making—I* (pp. 193–211). North-Holland/Elsevier Science Publishers.

Fortuna, P., & Nunes, S. (2018). A survey on automatic detection of hate speech in text. *ACM Computing Surveys (CSUR), 51*(4), 1–30.

Geva, M., Goldberg, Y., & Berant, J. (2019). Are we modeling the task or the annotator? an investigation of annotator bias in natural language understanding datasets. arXiv preprint arXiv:1908.07898.

Gilens, M. (1988). Gender and support for Reagan: A comprehensive model of presidential approval. *American Journal of Political Science,* 19–49.

Groves, R. M., Fowler Jr, F. J., Couper, M. P., Lepkowski, J. M., Singer, E., & Tourangeau, R. (2011). *Survey methodology* (Vol. 561). John Wiley & Sons.

Hua, Y., Ristenpart, T., & Naaman, M. (2020, May). Towards measuring adversarial Twitter interactions against candidates in the US midterm elections. In *Proceedings of the international AAAI conference on web and social media* (Vol. 14, pp. 272–282). AAAI.

Karimi, F., Wagner, C., Lemmerich, F., Jadidi, M., & Strohmaier, M. (2016, April). Inferring gender from names on the web: A comparative evaluation of gender detection methods. In *Proceedings of the 25th international conference companion on World Wide Web* (pp. 53–54).

Kiritchenko, S., & Mohammad, S. M. (2018). Examining gender and race bias in two hundred sentiment analysis systems. arXiv preprint arXiv:1805.04508.

LeCun, Y., & Bengio, Y. (1995). Convolutional networks for images, speech, and time series. *The Handbook of Brain Theory and Neural Networks, 3361*(10), 1995.

Li, Q., Shah, S., Liu, X., & Nourbakhsh, A. (2017, May). Data sets: Word embeddings learned from tweets and general data. In *Eleventh international AAAI conference on web and social media.* AAAI.

Mayer-Schönberger, V., & Cukier, K. (2013). *Big data: A revolution that will transform how we live, work, and think.* Houghton Mifflin Harcourt.

Morstatter, F., Pfeffer, J., Liu, H., & Carley, K. M. (2013, June). Is the sample good enough? comparing data from twitter's streaming api with twitter's firehose. In *Seventh international AAAI conference on weblogs and social media.* AAAI.

Newman, B., & Forcehimes, A. (2010). "Rally round the flag" events for presidential approval research. *Electoral Studies, 29*(1), 144–154.

O'Connor, B., Balasubramanyan, R., Routledge, B. R., & Smith, N. A. (2010, May). From tweets to polls: Linking text sentiment to public opinion time series. In *Fourth international AAAI conference on weblogs and social media.* AAAI.

Olteanu, A., Castillo, C., Diaz, F., & Kiciman, E. (2019). Social data: Biases, methodological pitfalls, and ethical boundaries. *Frontiers in Big Data, 2,* 13.

Pasek, J., McClain, C. A., Newport, F., & Marken, S. (2019). Who's tweeting about the president? What big survey data can tell us about digital traces? *Social Science Computer Review.* doi:10.1177/0894439318822007

Qayyum, A., Gilani, Z., Latif, S., & Qadir, J. (2018, December). Exploring media bias and toxicity in south Asian political discourse. In *2018 12th international conference on open source systems and technologies (ICOSST)* (pp. 01–08). IEEE.

Salganik, M. J. (2019). *Bit by bit: Social research in the digital age.* Princeton University Press.

Sap, M., Card, D., Gabriel, S., Choi, Y., & Smith, N. A. (2019, July). The risk of racial bias in hate speech detection. In *Proceedings of the 57th annual meeting of the association for computational linguistics* (pp. 1668–1678). ACL.

Sen, I., Flöck, F., Weller, K., Weiss, B., & Wagner, C. (2019). A total error framework for digital traces of humans. arXiv preprint arXiv:1907.08228.

Smith, B. K., & Gustafson, A. (2017). Using Wikipedia to predict election outcomes: Online behavior as a predictor of voting. *Public Opinion Quarterly, 81*(3), 714–735.

Stephens-Davidowitz, S. I. (2012). The effects of racial animus on a black presidential candidate: Using Google search data to find what surveys miss. SSRN 2050673.

Wang, Z., Hale, S., Adelani, D. I., Grabowicz, P., Hartman, T., Floeck, F., & Jurgens, D. (2019, May). Demographic inference and representative population estimates from multilingual social media data. In *The World Wide Web conference* (pp. 2056–2067). Association for Computing Machinery. https://doi.org/10.1145/3308558.3313684

Wulczyn, E., Thain, N., & Dixon, L. (2017, April). Ex machina: Personal attacks seen at scale. In *Proceedings of the 26th international conference on World Wide Web* (pp. 1391–1399). International World Wide Web Conferences Steering Committee, Republic and Canton of Geneva. https://doi.org/10.1145/3038912.3052591

Zafar, M. B., Valera, I., Gomez Rodriguez, M., & Gummadi, K. P. (2017, April). Fairness beyond disparate treatment & disparate impact: Learning classification without disparate mistreatment. In *Proceedings of the 26th international conference on World Wide Web* (pp. 1171–1180). International World Wide Web Conferences Steering Committee, Republic and Canton of Geneva. https://doi.org/10.1145/3038912.3052660

10

CROWDSOURCING IN OBSERVATIONAL AND EXPERIMENTAL RESEARCH

Camilla Zallot, Gabriele Paolacci, Jesse Chandler and Itay Sisso

A substantial fraction of the observational and experimental data collected in the social sciences is now coming from crowdsourcing platforms. The steady shift towards crowdsourced samples that has occurred over the last decade means that it is more important than ever to be acquainted with the characteristics and dynamics of such samples. This chapter aims to familiarize computational social scientists with crowdsourced samples, and in particular with what has become the most popular source of such samples across the social sciences: Amazon Mechanical Turk (MTurk). This chapter will answer several questions: Who joins the MTurk platform as a worker and why? How do MTurk samples compare to traditional samples in survey and experimental research such as undergraduate students? What challenges can researchers expect to face on MTurk? What are the ethical concerns that these online workplaces bring to the surface? We hope the answers to these questions will be useful to a variety of computational social scientists: aspiring survey and experimental researchers who want to familiarize themselves with the main characteristics of crowdsourcing; experienced researchers who seek a deeper understanding of the implications of their methodological choices; and outsiders who want to take a peek at how social science is conducted in the present and will be conducted in the future.

1 Why so successful? An introduction to MTurk

MTurk is an online labor market, founded by Amazon in 2005, that connects a large pool of businesses and individuals that need tasks to be completed with workers (MTurkers) who are willing to complete them. Originally, MTurk was designed as an "artificial artificial intelligence" platform that performed tasks that are difficult for computers yet simple for people to do. These activities included tagging pictures or coding text for content or sentiment, creating the human-annotated data sets necessary for machine learning algorithms, and transcribing audio files. Since 2008, MTurkers have increasingly been used by academics as participants for survey and experimental research. After little more than a decade, studies using MTurk samples are widespread if not routine in social science. Reviews of sample composition in top-tier journals suggest that more than a third of all published papers in social psychology (Anderson et al., 2019), consumer psychology (Goodman & Paolacci, 2017), cognitive psychology (Stewart et al., 2017), and some subspecialties of clinical psychology (Miller et al., 2017) rely on at least some MTurk data.

DOI: 10.4324/9781003025245-12

Compared to traditional student samples or commercial online samples, MTurk offers advantages in terms of population size and diversity, cost, speed, and flexibility. First and foremost, MTurk can connect researchers instantly with thousands of participants. Prior to MTurk, most social scientists relied on college student samples, which were often smaller, slower to recruit, and only readily available at specific times in the year. In contrast, MTurk can guarantee to the average researcher a large population at any given time (about 16,000, according to a conservative estimate) and a similar turnover to a university pool (Stewart et al., 2015); the overall MTurk population might be well over 100,000 (Difallah et al., 2018), and depending on the research design it is feasible to recruit tens of thousands of unique participants within a reasonable time frame.

Relative to traditional convenience samples composed of college students or residents of college towns, the MTurk population is also remarkably diverse in terms of age, education, income, race, profession, political affiliation, and many other characteristics (Casey et al., 2017). This means that researchers not only have easy access to a diverse sample of the (US) population, but also that it is possible to recruit relatively large samples of hard-to-find populations. In the past researchers have been able to reach populations of specific theoretical, social, or methodological interest on MTurk, for example people of a certain ethnicity, people with particular life experiences such as veterans, or those with specific psychopathological symptoms (Chandler & Paolacci, 2017).

MTurk also presents considerable logistical advantages for observational and experimental research conducted using surveys. Foremost among these is that it provides a secure and far more flexible platform by which to easily manage recruitment and payment. Research conducted in physical labs (and by extension, online samples that recruit from the same pool) usually employs participants for set increments of time (e.g., a half hour). In contrast, MTurk workers are paid by the minute, allowing researchers to avoid paying for time they will not use.

1.1 Replicability

While the practical advantages of MTurk ensured a quick expansion of its use in academic research, many have questioned the reliability, validity, and more generally the quality of data collected on MTurk. As a first step to ensure its legitimacy as a data source, many researchers started comparing results between MTurk and more traditional subject pools, either by replicating classic experiments with MTurk samples or by running parallel identical experiments in multiple subject pools (Bartneck et al., 2015; Behrend et al., 2011; Casler et al., 2013; Coppock, 2018; Goodman et al., 2013; Mullinix et al., 2015; Paolacci et al., 2010; Smith et al., 2016).

In studies running parallel experiments, MTurk samples have produced results comparable to student samples, campus samples, and other online samples (Goodman et al., 2013; Paolacci et al., 2010). Importantly for concerns about generalizability, results obtained on MTurk also compare favorably to those observed in more representative samples of the population, obtaining effects that are consistently in the same direction and usually of the same approximate magnitude (Coppock, 2018; Mullinix et al., 2015; Weinberg et al., 2014). For example, Mullinix and colleagues (2015) found that 29 out of 36 experimental effects were statistically significant in the same direction on MTurk and within a nationally representative sample. In general, correlations between variables observed on MTurk are very similar to those observed in the population as a whole (Snowberg & Yariv, 2018), though relationships between political views and other variables do frequently differ (Zack et al., 2019).

Overall, these results suggest that MTurk samples can be compared favorably to samples used for academic research in the past; on the other hand, there are still a number of characteristics and respondent dynamics unique to MTurk that researchers must be aware of in order to maximize validity and data quality. In the remainder of this chapter, we will provide a description of who MTurk workers are, addressing the ways in which they are similar to and the ways in which they differ from the general population; furthermore, we will discuss the reasons they are on the platform and what the main drivers of their behavior on the platform are. Next, we will focus on the characteristics unique to MTurk that threaten the reliability, validity, and quality of the data collected and provide corresponding solutions. We finish with a discussion of ethical concerns related to carrying out academic research on MTurk in a responsible manner.

2 MTurkers: who are they and why do they work?

2.1 Demographic characteristics of MTurk workers

Recent estimates show that most of the workers on MTurk are from the US (75%) followed by India (16%) and in much smaller proportions Canada, Great Britain, Philippines, and Germany (1.1%–2.7%; Difallah et al., 2018). For a description and comparison of the Indian MTurk demographics, see Boas et al. (2018). As virtually all HITs (i.e., human intelligence tasks, the way tasks are labeled on MTurk) with keyworks "survey", "research", or "psychology" are restricted to the US population (Difallah et al., 2015), the remainder of this description of MTurk demographics will focus on the US subject pool.

Like any Internet sample, MTurk workers tend to be younger on average than the adult population they are drawn from. To illustrate, 20%, 60%, and 80% of US MTurk workers are born after 1990, 1980, and 1970 respectively. In the broader US population, these proportions are 20%, 40%, and 60%. The two populations also differ on other characteristics that are correlated with age: MTurkers tend to have lower household income and higher levels of education (Casey et al., 2017; US Census Bureau, 2016).

Compared to the US population, MTurk workers are both more likely to be unemployed (Casey et al., 2017) and more likely to have a white-collar rather than a blue-collar job (Castille et al., 2019). In terms of distribution across industries, however, the occupations among MTurkers are representative of the general population (Huff & Tingley, 2015). Finally, compared to the US population, MTurk workers tend to be less religious (Lewis et al., 2015), on the Democratic side of the political spectrum (c.f. Levay et al., 2016), less likely to be married (Berinsky et al., 2012), and more likely to identify as LGBTQ (Casey et al., 2017).

While age and other demographic traits explain many of the differences between MTurk samples and the general US population, it may be difficult, conceptually and statistically, to explain all of them. Levay et al. (2016) administered the ANES (American National Election Studies) questionnaire to an MTurk sample and found that, while MTurk workers do differ significantly from the national sample on a wide range of socioeconomic, political, personal, religious, and behavioral characteristics, most differences are not entirely eliminated when controlling for age, gender, race, and ethnicity, and some differences are not explained at all. Importantly, it is possible to obtain an MTurk sample that is more representative of the US population, by under- or oversampling workers with specific demographic characteristics to meet representative quotas; however, as the presence of unexplained differences between MTurk and the general population suggests, true "representativeness" may be conceptually elusive and operationally difficult to achieve.

2.2 Psychographic characteristics of MTurk workers

Along with demographic differences, there are also psychographic differences between MTurk workers and other samples and the general US population. In a large sample of MTurk workers ($N = 10,000$), Casey and colleagues (2017) found workers to be less extroverted, slightly less conscientious and emotionally stable, and more open to experience than the general US population. MTurk workers also score higher on clinical measures of social detachment, implying social isolation and aversion (Hargittai & Shaw, 2020; McCredie & Morey, 2018), and report higher levels of social anxiety (Arditte et al., 2016; Shapiro et al., 2013). Likewise, there is suggestive evidence that workers may score higher on autism spectrum disorder features (for a discussion see J. Chandler & Shapiro, 2016). Independent of whether these differences can be explained by the younger age of the sample, these results emphasize that one should be cautious while generalizing from MTurk research on social interactions to people in general.

MTurk workers also score differently on several other clinical measures. They demonstrated higher scores on depression, phobia, suicidal ideation, and traumatic stress scales. Ophir et al. (2019) find that, in comparison to responses to the CDC National Health survey, MTurk workers display a higher incidence of what would qualify as major depression (11.0% vs 3.6%). For depression at least, differences between workers and the population as a whole cannot be explained by mere demographic differences. Various sociodemographic and health and lifestyle variables (e.g., income, work status, exercise) explain only 42.7% of the difference in depression prevalence between the two samples (Ophir et al., 2019; see also Walters et al., 2018). Again, these results warn against attempts to achieve representativeness by matching samples based on demographic quotas.

Workers also differ from the general population on a number of other behavioral and attitudinal measures. As might be expected from people who use a specialized online platform, they are more likely to be more skilled at using the Internet and more likely to adopt technologies (Hargittai & Shaw, 2020). Relatedly, Walters et al. (2018) found that MTurk workers were less likely to be vaccinated or smoke and more likely to exercise, even after adjusting for demographic covariates.

2.3 Understanding worker motivation

It is important to understand why people are motivated to participate in MTurk and the contextual factors that define their experience on the platform. MTurk is rarely a workers' primary source of income, with only 13.8% reporting it as such (Paolacci et al., 2010). Almost 60% of workers spend less than 12 hours weekly on the platform (Kaufmann & Schulze, 2011), consistent with the large segment of the pool that reports to be employed full time. However, earning money is in fact the primary reason workers use the MTurk platform (Chen et al., 2019; Kaplan et al., 2018; Litman et al., 2015), and likely for this reason workers wish more work was available to them (Berg, 2015; Yang et al., 2018).

While workers largely participate for money, they also have other motivations that may influence how much they participate or (more likely) the kinds of tasks they prioritize. Workers report a variety of intrinsic motivations, such as developing skills, "gaining self-knowledge" (Litman et al., 2015), community identification (Kaufmann & Schulze, 2011), and simply "killing time" (Paolacci et al., 2010). These motivations seem to drive the kinds of tasks that workers decide to complete. For example, workers motivated to develop competence report that they are more likely to select challenging tasks, while those with social motives report that they prefer tasks requiring coordination or cooperation with other workers (Pee et al., 2018).

Research has also explored the effect of intrinsic motivation on worker productivity. Chandler and Kapelner (2013) find that portraying work as meaningful (i.e., the work was necessary to assist medical researchers) resulted in higher likelihood of participation and higher quantity of output; when the same work was portrayed as meaningless (i.e., it was not going to be used), quality of work decreased. Rogstadius and colleagues (2011) find that framing the task as "helping others" resulted in better quality output. On the other hand, Shaw and colleagues (2010) tested a number of intrinsic incentives (nonfinancial competition with other workers, reminders of the importance of the work, being thanked in advance for doing the work, being primed for good work by answering a questionnaire, being told they were trusted to do the work to the best of their ability) and found that they did not result in better performance than a control condition or financial incentives.

3 Data quality

Understanding workers' motivation has important consequences for data quality. The quality control mechanism that is built into MTurk hinges upon workers' motivation to earn money: requesters can reject workers' submissions if they consider them not to be of sufficient quality, which results in foregone payment. Workers are also assigned a reputation score based on the proportion of their work that is approved, and this score determines access to future tasks when these tasks select for approval rate. While simple, this kind of reputation score enables people to participate in economic transactions with strangers with relative confidence. As implied by studies of MTurk replicability, it also motivates most workers to make a good faith effort when completing studies. However, data quality remains one of the chief concerns among those who consider crowdsourcing their samples. The separation between researcher and participants is a unique challenge: There is no easy way to verify whether people are who they say they are (or even that they are people – see section on "Fraudulent Worker Profiles"), and it is difficult to control where, how, and why MTurk workers participate in research. Though the MTurk reward system can reduce misbehavior, potential quality issues exist as a logical consequence of workers' motivations to earn as much as possible while managing their reputation. We discuss some of these implications later.

3.1 Fraudulent survey responses

Since workers are highly motivated to complete HITs, they will do their best to qualify for tasks. This is a major concern for studies that select workers on self-reported characteristics, because workers may lie to gain access to them. Most studies find that only a minority of workers will lie about their identity to gain access to a study; however, minimal rates of misreporting at the broader MTurk population level can translate into substantial fraudulent responses in a study that targets a rare subpopulation (Chandler & Paolacci, 2017). For example, when recruiting a specific kind of worker with an incidence rate of 5%, a 1% fraud rate will lead to almost 17% $(0.01/(0.05+0.01))$ of responses being fraudulent.

Fraud can have a serious impact on data quality. Importantly, impostors may try to adjust their responses in a manner that is consistent with how they believe they should respond given their claimed identity. In some cases, this can contribute to obscure true effects, similar to what non-systematic measurement error does. The political attitudes of people who fraudulently claim affiliation with a political party are less extreme than the attitudes of those who are truly affiliated with that party (Siegel & Navarro, 2019). Likewise, fraudulently depressed workers report more depressive symptoms than nondepressed workers but fewer depressive symptoms than truly depressed people (Chandler et al., 2020, Study 1). In other circumstances, including fraudulent responses can lead to spurious effects. For example, people who report to be red-blue colorblind (which is biologically impossible) claim to be unable to distinguish blue numbers on a red background (Kan & Drummey, 2018), and men who claim to be women report a preference for pink products not held by actual women (Sharpe Wessling et al., 2017).

Given this tendency, explicitly stating screening criteria and asking workers to self-select into studies is the worst way to recruit workers with specific characteristics. Instead, workers should be unobtrusively screened for desired characteristics. However, if workers learn that they have been screened out, some may attempt the HIT again and change their responses to gain eligibility. Some of these workers can be blocked (e.g., through placing a cookie in the users' browser[1] or by blocking multiple attempts from the same IP address[2]). However, the easiest way to minimize fraud is to conceal decisions about study eligibility from the worker. One way of doing this is running a large-scale pretest to measure the variables of interest (or obtain these from existing data sources[3]) and to then recontact the eligible workers with the focal research. Another option is to recruit workers for a survey that includes measures of the characteristics of interest and then immediately invite workers with the desired characteristics to complete a second survey in exchange for an additional "bonus" payment.

3.2 Fraudulent worker profiles

Some workers will also lie about certain characteristics when setting up their account in order to gain access to more or better paying HITs (Chandler et al., 2020). Survey tasks are particularly desirable to workers, but most of them require US residency. This creates a strong incentive to fake US residency. A first line of defense against this type of misreport is that to confirm US residency, workers must acquire a US bank account and social security number, which undergoes an unknown verification process by Amazon. More recently, researchers seeking US workers have used tools to require a US IP address as well.

In 2018 there was a surge in US-based human-generated, but extremely low-quality, responses (Chmielewski & Kucker, 2020). The increase was caused in part by non-native (and non-language-proficient) English speakers that originate mostly in India and Venezuela (Kennedy, Clifford, Burleigh, Waggoner et al., 2018) (though these workers may also have made use of automated form-fillers to provide responses). These workers are able to avoid IP restrictions by logging on to virtual machines located in US data centers to simulate US IP addresses (Dennis et al., 2018). Fortunately, these type of workers' access to studies can be reduced using tools that compare worker IP addresses or geolocations to a database of known fraudulent addresses (Prims et al., 2018). As fraudulent profiles, by definition, generate low-quality responses, researchers can minimize their impact by employing measures to identify poor-quality data (discussed in the "Data Quality" section).

3.3 Attrition

Compared to experiments conducted in physical labs, where participants are supervised, MTurk workers can leave a study at any time. This has given rise to concerns about attrition, that is, that participants begin a study but do not complete it. Attrition on MTurk is highly dependent on study characteristics, with levels obtained by faculty members in a single department ranging from 0% to 77.6% (Zhou & Fishbach, 2016). The potential impact of attrition on study results is determined by the overall attrition rate of a study, the difference in attrition rates between conditions, and the correlation between the probability that a study participant will drop out and their response on the dependent variable (for a detailed discussion see Deke & Chiang, 2017). Attrition can be particularly problematic when differential attrition rates are high and act disproportionally on participants with particular characteristics, creating confounds (Deke & Chiang, 2017).

It is particularly important for researchers to minimize attrition in their studies. The most common reasons workers abandon a task is that it requires more time than anticipated (reducing the effective hourly rate) and that it includes unclear instructions and "glitches" (Han et al., 2019; Kaplan et al., 2018). This suggests that researchers should be clear upfront about the effort and time it takes for participants to complete the task and should ensure that the task is pilot tested before launching it.

Researchers can also try to avoid (or at least measure) differential attrition across experimental conditions. Some experimental studies require more effort out of participants, or require them to consider more unpleasant topics, in some conditions than in others (Rinderknecht, 2019). When differential attrition across conditions is a concern, participants could be exposed to all experimental conditions (albeit in different orders) and the analysis restricted to those who complete the entire study (Hauser et al., 2018). Finally, researchers should collect and report measures of attrition; they can also collect individual difference measures early in the experiment, so that they can test whether certain characteristics contributed to attrition and check that final experimental groups do not differ on key variables (Hauser et al., 2018).

3.4 Non-naïveté

Another difference between MTurk workers, lab samples, and to an extent also other online samples is that MTurk workers are likely to have participated in many more studies. This concern is compounded by the fact that a majority of the studies on MTurk are actually taken by a small and highly active proportion of the overall population. Illustratively, Chandler and colleagues (2014) found that 10% of workers completed 41% of the HITs, and that especially the most productive ones were familiar with paradigmatic experiments in the social sciences (e.g., the trolley problem). This suggests that, if participant naivete is an important requirement for the interpretation of results of the study, certain common paradigms may not be suitable for use on MTurk.

Experiences in prior studies can also change participant responses. Returning to the issue of participant fraud, there is some evidence that participants who learned information about eligibility criteria in one study (owning a VR headset) applied this information when answering the first question of a later study, leading to a dramatic increase in the number of participants who claimed to own VR headsets (Chandler & Paolacci, 2017). Prior experience can also influence responses to questions not directly tied to incentives. One area of substantial concern is the impact of repeated experience on some tasks leading to improved performance on measures of ability. Practice effects have been repeatedly observed on measures of cognitive ability (e.g., Chandler et al., 2014; Stagnaro et al., 2018; Woike, 2019) but may also extend to other measures (e.g., tests of creativity, Oppenlaender et al., 2020). These kinds of practice effects can undermine the predictive power of measures if they lead workers of even moderate ability to score perfectly on the measure (a ceiling effect) and can cause spurious correlations between over-practiced measures that are themselves correlated with worker experience (Woike, 2019, but not always; for a discussion see Stagnaro et al., 2018). For studies that use measures of ability as an outcome measure, the increased variation of scores that results from including a mix of people who have and have not been exposed to the items could make it harder to detect the impact of experimental treatments, because most tests of statistical significance assess differences in average scores between treatments relative to differences in individual scores within treatment groups.

Practice effects can also lead people to mindlessly apply "correct" answers above and beyond any improvement in underlying ability. Woike (2019) observed that workers would apply the correct answer from a previous exposure to measures of ability to superficially similar later questions with different answers. Similarly, Chandler and colleagues (2015) find that multiple exposures to the same experimental material can reduce effect sizes, especially when participants are assigned to a different condition the second time. One interpretation of this finding is that information from prior experimental treatments comes to mind, regardless of whether it is explicitly contained within a study. In its most extreme form, people can simply cut and paste responses to difficult or unpleasant questions to avoid answering them. In one study, around 5% of participants seemed to copy and paste responses to a commonly used experimental text prompt used to induce a feeling of powerlessness (Rinderknecht, 2019), making it unlikely that this writing task had the desired psychological effect. Importantly, and consistent with the previous discussion, repeated participation seems not to be a concern for studies that rely on automatic processes (Zwaan et al., 2018).

It is therefore important to ensure that workers do not repeatedly participate in the same or similar studies. Workers cannot be relied upon to correctly report having completed a certain study before. Large proportions of workers who had completed a study before claimed that they had not, and self-reporting of prior participation is not a reliable predictor of attenuated effects in a later study (Chandler et al., 2015). However, researchers can limit the number of non-naïve workers in their study. When conducting a series of related experiments, workers who have completed earlier studies can be excluded from completing later studies. Likewise, workers with extensive prior experience can be excluded from participating if there are concerns that this experience is problematic (e.g., it makes it likely that participants are familiar with a study procedure and this familiarity might threaten validity). Amazon allows requesters to limit the number of prior tasks eligible workers have completed. Likewise, Cloud Research allows researchers to exclude workers who are known to have completed many research studies.

3.5 Cross talk

To the frustration of many workers, Amazon's reputational system is designed to ensure that requesters can find high-quality workers, but not vice versa. As a result, workers have created a number of communities in which they can share information about specific requesters and tasks. These communities raise the concern that participants could share details of studies that researchers do not want revealed until after the study is complete, such as different experimental treatments, the use of deception, or the availability of bonus payments for specific workers. The presence of discussions about posted studies is potentially concerning, because it both influences readers' perceptions of the study and quickly drives them to complete it: one study of a large sample of tasks found that when a HIT is posted in a discussion forum, participation rates increase by nearly 60% (Yang et al., 2018).

Edlund and colleagues (2017) analyzed the discussions posted on a forum about posted studies and found that 9% of the comments included key information and an additional 30% important information or information about qualification. However, it is unclear how likely a given study is to end up in a discussion board and how many workers may in fact stumble upon this information, especially in absence of an incentive to do so. In fact, Chandler and colleagues (2014) find that, in a survey of 300 participants, only 13% report ever seeing the content of a study discussed online. Furthermore, Edlund and colleagues (2017) found that simply asking the participants not to discuss the experiment online was successful in eliminating the problem. Monitoring MTurk forums (e.g., on Reddit) is still a sensible recommendation when cross talk might threaten the validity of one's study.

3.6 Distraction

Since workers complete surveys in an unsupervised environment, researchers cannot ensure that they are paying attention – MTurk workers have reported that they often complete multiple surveys at the same time or that they complete surveys while doing other activities, such as watching TV (Chandler et al., 2014). Moreover, because MTurk workers are paid per HIT, there is a concern that they may rush through surveys without paying close attention to survey materials. Indeed, Smith and colleagues (2016) find that compared to a US panel, MTurk workers completed a survey about 50% faster. This has led to many concerns about "satisficing" behavior, straight-lining (giving the same answer to all questions), answering at random, or answering without reading the materials (called, among others, careless or insufficient effort responding) (Berinsky et al., 2014; Curran, 2016; Huang et al., 2015; Kim et al., 2017; Meade & Craig, 2012).

Importantly, through an extensive review of the literature and further experiments, Thomas and Clifford (2017) find that MTurk workers display rates of inattention no higher than student samples or other online samples. Exclusion rates based on screener items (i.e., questions used to identify and subsequently exclude problematic respondents) range from 2% to 52% depending on the difficulty and extent of screener question – no different from the range observed in the lab (6%–46%) or in other online panels and samples (5%–63%). These findings are consistent with the finding that distractions in web surveys do not necessarily impact data quality (Wenz, 2019). However, that average rates do not differ does not imply that MTurkers will be invariably attentive, and inattention is likely to remain a reason of concern for many researchers. We describe next a number of methods that, alone or in conjunction with one another, have been reliably shown to improve data quality.

3.7 Identifying and removing poor-quality responses

Poor data responses are often assumed to introduce noise into data. When a source of noise is uncorrelated with a variable of interest, it makes it more difficult to observe the potential effect of that variable. For example, in experimental studies where treatment condition is randomly assigned, careless participants tend to decrease observed treatment effects (Kennedy, Clifford, Burleigh, Jewell et al., 2018). However, the effects of including poor-quality responses is not as predictable. In the context of correlational data (e.g., observed associations between participants' responses to different questions), random responses can add noise as they do to experiments, reducing observed effect sizes. This is especially true when sets of items with opposite meanings are collapsed together to form a single score (Chmielewski & Kucker, 2020). In practice, however, careless responses to different questions are non-independent (because they come from the same person; Presser, 1984) and are thus correlated, which can inflate observed correlations. To complicate matters further, differences in the means and the distributions of the true and careless responses are also captured by these analyses, which can suppress, inflate, or in some cases even reverse the sign of correlations observed within each group (for a detailed discussion see Chandler et al., 2020). For example, Chandler and colleagues (2020) found that in an uncleaned data set, higher educational attainment is associated with increased social anxiety and depression, but when poor-quality responses are removed, more education is associated with decreased social anxiety and depression. Therefore, poor-quality responses cannot be necessarily offset by increasing the statistical power of a study. We provide here some suggestions for identifying poor-quality responses.

3.7.1 Response speed

One option is to identify workers who have completed the task implausibly quickly. Researchers have developed a number of different benchmarks based on reading speed or benchmarked survey data. Recommendations for surveys with any (offline) population are to use a two-second per item rule (based on four to seven word items with a five-point Likert scale; Huang et al., 2012) or 300 milliseconds per word (Zhang & Conrad, 2014). However, because MTurk workers may complete surveys faster than other samples for benign reasons such as experience with the format (Kees et al., 2017; Smith et al., 2016), Wood and colleagues (2017) suggest a more conservative limit of one second per item. Since items can vary in length, and some pages may include a lot of text in addition to/instead of the items, we recommend using a rule based on a words-per-minute reading speed. Following Carver (1992), we suggest 600 words per minute (100 milliseconds per word) as the maximal speed for text comprehension. In practice, this means one should count the words on a page, divide it by 10, and flag every participant completing that page in less than the resulted number of seconds (e.g., on a 173-word page, the cutoff would be 17.3 seconds). Our rule is consistent with Wood et al. (2017) assuming an average item length of about 10 words.

3.7.2 Analysis of response patterns

Researchers can also identify workers who provide illogical or unlikely responses, for which several methods exist (see Curran, 2016, for a review). Researchers can identify problematic respondents informally by inspecting data for unusual values (e.g., more than eight children) or combinations of values (e.g., unemployed with a household income >$150k). Open-ended responses can also be a valuable source of data. Responses that are irrelevant, appear to be copied from elsewhere, are only one or two words long, or are written in all caps are all indications of potential data quality issues.

Some researchers have developed more quantitative methods of identifying unusual data such as counting strings of questions with the same response to identify participants who straight-line (that is, give the same answers to all items in a scale); examining the consistency between different scales or parts of scales (Curran, 2016); and examining intra-individual response variability, which measures the standard deviation of responses for each participant, whereby high standard deviations denote random responding, while low standard deviations imply straight-lining (Marjanovic et al., 2015).

3.7.3 Screener questions

It is much easier to assess data quality when questions are included in the survey that have patterns of responses that can be verified as logical, plausible, internally consistent, or sensitive to the content of the study. These "screener" questions have been shown to be effective at increasing the power of the experiment and reducing noise in the data without introducing significant sampling bias (Thomas & Clifford, 2017). A variety of different types of screener questions exist. Researchers have included factual questions to verify that workers paid attention to critical instructions (Kane & Barabas, 2019; Oppenheimer et al., 2009), questions with logically impossible responses (e.g., "while watching the television, have you ever had a fatal heart attack?"; Paolacci et al., 2010), and batteries of questions with unlikely responses (assuming that reporting many rare experiences or beliefs is a signal of data quality; Maniaci & Rogge, 2014).

The design and content of each individual study determine which techniques are used to achieve data quality; however, generally, we recommend a combination of a speed check, a screener item (e.g., an infrequency question), a specific screener such as a comprehension check, and an IP test for suspicious IPs. See Chandler et al. (2020) for an exhaustive description of each technique and where and when it will work best.

4 Beyond convenience samples

Most researchers use MTurk to conduct simple survey experiments. However, workers are used to complete a much wider variety of tasks, and the platform is easily linked to external sites. This facilitates the implementation of study designs that are more complex than questionnaires. For example, many researchers conduct studies in which small or even large groups of workers interact with one another (cf. Arechar et al., 2018). Researchers have also experimented with using MTurkers as research assistants in various parts of the research process, including screening articles for literature reviews (Krivosheev et al., 2017; Mortensen et al., 2017), acting as "sensors" to collect data on behalf of researchers (Lukyanenko & Parsons, 2018), stimulus creation (Sina et al., 2014), survey item creation (Holland et al., 2016), testing (Edgar et al., 2016), and content coding (Benoit et al., 2016; Conley & Tosti-Kharas, 2014; Leeper, 2016). Moreover, researchers leveraged MTurk to conduct labor field experiments, observing how actual workers respond to different forms of incentives (Fest et al., 2019).

5 Ethics

Especially in the early years of the platform, the lack of rules and regulations and the anonymity of workers led to a situation in which strong norms about the ethical treatment of MTurk workers were not in place. First and foremost, researchers are encouraged to not let anonymity and distance from their research participant allow them to relax common standards. These include seeking the approval of institutional review boards, ensuring participants read and agree to a consent form, and that they are correctly debriefed if necessary. More uniquely to MTurk, efforts have been made to examine and understand the ethical issues surrounding the worker-requester relationship. Guidelines have been suggested, for example by the Dynamo Initiative (Salehi et al., 2015). Fair compensation, fairness in the extent to which work is accepted or rejected, and privacy are three main ethical concerns that we discuss in this section.

5.1 Compensation

Completing HITs on MTurk is considered to be a form of self-employment; as labor laws have been slow to update to the unfamiliar nature of the crowdsourcing format, the working relationship between requesters and the "crowd" is almost entirely unregulated, and MTurk workers have very little or no benefits or protection (Felstiner, 2011). This has been reflected in the level of compensation – researchers, especially in the past, often underpaid workers (as little as $0.01 per HIT) or even asked them to complete HITs for free (Hara et al., 2018; Mason & Suri, 2012; Mason & Watts, 2009), perhaps revealing beliefs that voluntarily completing surveys is not necessarily equivalent to work. Importantly, working on MTurk entails a lot more than just taking a HIT – it includes searching for HITs, informing oneself on the reputation of unfamiliar requesters, communicating with other workers and requesters, spending additional time deciphering unclear HIT descriptions or instructions, etc. Taking this unpaid "overtime" into account, Hara et al. (2018) find that only 4% of workers earn more than the federal minimum wage, while the average wage amounts to $2/h.

Complaints by workers have led to many calls to conform HIT payments to minimum wage levels (e.g., $7.25/h; Pittman & Sheehan, 2016; Salehi et al., 2015; Williamson, 2016). Payments on the site have increased over time (Difallah et al., 2015), and recent analyses suggest that MTurk workers are now more positive about their interactions with academic requesters (Moss et al., 2020).

There are many voluntary steps that researchers can take to maximize the extent to which workers are compensated fairly for their work. First and foremost, one should carefully measure and honestly communicate completion times for the HIT, setting payment rates accordingly at a minimum of $0.12 per minute ($7.25/h). Researchers should ensure the HIT instructions are clear and there are no problems that will take additional worker time to solve. Finally, returning (rejecting) HITs is one of the biggest factors driving down real wages (Hara et al., 2018), underlying the need for HIT instructions to be designed to minimize mistakes that will lead to rejections.

5.2 Rejection

Requesters have full control over whether to accept a worker's HIT submission; as requesters do not have to forfeit the work if it is rejected, there is an incentive to reject more than the strictly necessary. Requesters rejecting good work is one of the most-voiced complaints, mentioned in a 2016 study by 52% of workers (Brawley & Pury, 2016). Workers also complained about mass rejections, being rejected due to technical difficulties, and being rejected or blocked from HITs without being given a reason.

In contrast to these complaints, Matherly (2018) highlights a positivity bias in the use of the reputation system on MTurk. Data quality in academic research is more of a subjective judgment; leniency and reciprocity principles, and fear of retaliation, sway researchers in favor of accepting all work. Moreover, some IRBs' guidelines demand full payment for all participants. Since (currently) rejecting a participant's work automatically denies their payment, some researchers are bound to accept all work regardless of data quality. Finally, identifying and rejecting low-quality work is time consuming – rejected workers also tend to contact requesters to complain or find out why they were rejected, resulting in additional time costs. The result is that the reputation system may become only mildly diagnostic of worker quality and then only at the very highest levels (contrary to earlier indications that a 95% acceptance rate threshold suffices, Peer et al., 2014). There is an argument for researchers to reject work more often, in order to allow the reputation system to function. If researchers do choose to reject low-quality respondents, they should keep in mind to only reject when the data quality is poor beyond a reasonable doubt and to provide explicit reasons for rejection to the workers that are aligned to expectations.

5.3 Privacy

Researchers can undermine MTurk workers' privacy by asking directly for sensitive information, aggregating data from various HITs, unauthorized information sharing, phishing/malware, etc. (Xia et al., 2017). Despite being concerned for their own privacy (e.g., Kang et al., 2014), workers may provide personal information to avoid the consequences of noncompliance

(Sannon & Cosley, 2019). Importantly, WorkerIDs cannot be directly linked to personal information. However, perhaps they might point to a specific individual when they are linked through multiple experiments with data that is granular enough (e.g., postal code, age, sex, etc.). It is thus particularly important for researchers to ensure that they never store identifiable information (e.g., while posting data on public repositories).

6 Conclusion

Crowdsourced samples, of which MTurk is the foremost example, are inexpensive, convenient, and plentiful. It is likely that they will be a feature of academic research for a long time to come, and as such, researchers are advised to acquaint themselves with the unique characteristics and dynamics of such samples. Crowdsourced samples are perhaps less different from more traditional student and online samples than we have been led to believe, and most of the best practices that have been successful in the past at ensuring study subjects are attentive and conscientious carry over seamlessly to studies run on a crowdsourcing platform. On the other hand, anonymity, distance, and lack of researcher oversight on participants give rise to a number of concerns and unique challenges that we have detailed and addressed in this chapter.

MTurk is a continuously evolving marketplace that responds to changing social forces and incentives. An awareness of these dynamics is essential to ensure academics have a deeper understanding of their methodological choices and can continue to use this valuable resource to its full potential.

Notes

1 The Qualtrics survey-building platform has this as an available feature named "prevent ballot box stuffing" under survey options.
2 Some third-party platforms that run experiments on MTurk, such as CloudResearch (formerly Turk Prime) and Positly, have this as an available feature.
3 Both Amazon and Cloud Research maintain data sets of workers with specific characteristics. Researchers can also select eligible participants from studies they have conducted in the past.

References

Anderson, C. A., Allen, J. J., Plante, C., Quigley-McBride, A., Lovett, A., & Rokkum, J. N. (2019). The MTurkification of social and personality psychology. *Personality and Social Psychology Bulletin*, *45*(6), 842–850. https://doi.org/10.1177/0146167218798821

Arditte, K. A., Çek, D., Shaw, A. M., & Timpano, K. R. (2016). The importance of assessing clinical phenomena in Mechanical Turk research. *Psychological Assessment*, *28*(6), 684–691. https://doi.org/10.1037/pas0000217

Arechar, A. A., Gächter, S., & Molleman, L. (2018). Conducting interactive experiments online. *Experimental Economics*, *21*(1), 99–131. https://doi.org/10.1007/s10683-017-9527-2

Bartneck, C., Duenser, A., Moltchanova, E., & Zawieska, K. (2015). Comparing the similarity of responses received from studies in Amazon's Mechanical Turk to studies conducted online and with direct recruitment. *PloS One*, *10*(4), e0121595. https://doi.org/10.1371/journal.pone.0121595

Behrend, T. S., Sharek, D. J., Meade, A. W., & Wiebe, E. N. (2011). The viability of crowdsourcing for survey research. *Behavior Research Methods*, *43*(3), 800–813. https://doi.org/10.3758/s13428-011-0081-0

Benoit, K., Conway, D., Lauderdale, B. E., Laver, M., & Mikhaylov, S. (2016). Crowd-sourced text analysis: Reproducible and agile production of political data. *American Political Science Review*, *110*(2), 278–295. https://doi.org/10.1017/S0003055416000058

Berg, J. (2015). Income security in the on-demand economy: Findings and policy lessons from a survey of crowdworkers. *Comparative Labor Law & Policy Journal*, *37*(3), 543–576.

Berinsky, A. J., Huber, G. A., & Lenz, G. S. (2012). Evaluating online labor markets for experimental research. *Political Analysis*, *20*(3), 351–368. https://doi.org/10.1093/pan/mpr057

Berinsky, A. J., Margolis, M. F., & Sances, M. W. (2014). Separating the shirkers from the workers? Making sure respondents pay attention on self-administered surveys. *American Journal of Political Science, 58*(3), 739–753.

Boas, T. C., Christenson, D. P., & Glick, D. M. (2018). Recruiting large online samples in the United States and India: Facebook. *Mechanical Turk and Qualtrics, 32.*

Brawley, A. M., & Pury, C. L. S. (2016). Work experiences on MTurk. *Computers in Human Behavior, 54,* 531–546. https://doi.org/10.1016/j.chb.2015.08.031

Carver, R. P. (1992). Reading rate: Theory, research, and practical implications. *Journal of Reading, 36*(2), 84–95.

Casey, L. S., Chandler, J., Levine, A. S., Proctor, A., & Strolovitch, D. Z. (2017). Intertemporal differences among MTurk workers. *SAGE Open, 7*(2).

Casler, K., Bickel, L., & Hackett, E. (2013). Separate but equal? *Computers in Human Behavior, 29*(6), 2156–2160. https://doi.org/10.1016/j.chb.2013.05.009

Castille, C. M., Mahmoud, B. H., Williamson, R. L., & Buckner, J. E. (2019). *Comparing MTurk and the US population's occupational diversity.*

Chandler, D., & Kapelner, A. (2013). Breaking monotony with meaning. *Journal of Economic Behavior & Organization, 90,* 123–133. https://doi.org/10.1016/j.jebo.2013.03.003

Chandler, J. J., Mueller, P., & Paolacci, G. (2014). Nonnaïveté among Amazon Mechanical Turk workers. *Behavior Research Methods, 46*(1), 112–130. https://doi.org/10.3758/s13428-013-0365-7

Chandler, J. J., & Paolacci, G. (2017). Lie for a dime. *Social Psychological and Personality Science, 8*(5), 500–508. https://doi.org/10.1177/1948550617698203

Chandler, J. J., Paolacci, G., Peer, E., Mueller, P., & Ratliff, K. A. (2015). Using nonnaive participants can reduce effect sizes. *Psychological Science, 26*(7), 1131–1139. https://doi.org/10.1177/0956797615585115

Chandler, J., & Shapiro, D. (2016). Conducting clinical research using crowdsourced convenience samples. *Annual Review of Clinical Psychology, 12,* 53–81. https://doi.org/10.1146/annurev-clinpsy-021815-093623

Chandler, J., Sisso, I., & Shapiro, D. (2020). Participant carelessness and fraud: Consequences for clinical research and potential solutions. *Journal of Abnormal Psychology, 129*(1), 49–55. https://doi.org/10.1037/abn0000479

Chen, W.-C., Suri, S., & Gray, M. L. (2019). More than money: Correlation among worker demographics, motivations, and participation in online labor market. *Proceedings of the International AAAI Conference on Web and Social Media, 13,* 134–145.

Chmielewski, M., & Kucker, S. C. (2020). An MTurk crisis? Shifts in data quality and the impact on study results. *Social Psychological and Personality Science, 11*(4), 464–473. https://doi.org/10.1177/1948550619875149

Conley, C., & Tosti-Kharas, J. (2014). *Crowdsourcing content analysis for managerial research* [Text]. https://doi.org/info:doi/10.1108/MD-03-2012-0156

Coppock, A. (2018). Generalizing from survey experiments conducted on Mechanical Turk: A replication approach. *Political Science Research and Methods,* 1–16.

Curran, P. G. (2016). Methods for the detection of carelessly invalid responses in survey data. *Journal of Experimental Social Psychology, 66,* 4–19. https://doi.org/10.1016/j.jesp.2015.07.006

Deke, J., & Chiang, H. (2017). The WWC attrition standard: Sensitivity to assumptions and opportunities for refining and adapting to new contexts. *Evaluation Review, 41*(2), 130–154. https://doi.org/10.1177/0193841X16670047

Dennis, S. A., Goodson, B. M., & Pearson, C. (2018). *MTurk workers' use of low-cost "virtual private servers" to circumvent screening methods: A research note.*

Difallah, D. E., Catasta, M., Demartini, G., Ipeirotis, P. G., & Cudré-Mauroux, P. (2015). *The dynamics of micro-task crowdsourcing* (A. Gangemi, S. Leonardi, & A. Panconesi, Eds.; pp. 238–247). ACM Press. https://doi.org/10.1145/2736277.2741685

Difallah, D. E., Filatova, E., & Ipeirotis, P. (2018). Demographics and dynamics of Mechanical Turk workers. In *Proceedings of WSDM 2018.* Marina Del Rey.

Edgar, J., Murphy, J., & Keating, M. (2016). Comparing traditional and crowdsourcing methods for pretesting survey questions. *SAGE Open, 6*(4), 2158244016671770. https://doi.org/10.1177/2158244016671770

Edlund, J. E., Lange, K. M., Sevene, A. M., Umansky, J., Beck, C. D., & Bell, D. J. (2017). Participant crosstalk. *The Quantitative Methods for Psychology, 13*(3), 174–182. https://doi.org/10.20982/tqmp.13.3.p174

Felstiner, A. (2011). Working the crow: Employment and labor law in the crowdsourcing industry. *Berkeley Journal of Employment and Labor Law, 143.*

Fest, S., Kvaloy, O., Nieken, P., & Schöttner, A. (2019). *Motivation and incentives in an online labor market* (SSRN Scholarly Paper ID 3343857). Social Science Research Network. https://papers.ssrn.com/abstract=3343857

Goodman, J. K., Cryder, C. E., & Cheema, A. (2013). Data collection in a flat world. *Journal of Behavioral Decision Making, 26*(3), 213–224. https://doi.org/10.1002/bdm.1753

Goodman, J. K., & Paolacci, G. (2017). Crowdsourcing consumer research. *Journal of Consumer Research, 44*(1), 196–210. https://doi.org/10.1093/jcr/ucx047

Han, L., Roitero, K., Gadiraju, U., Sarasua, C., Checco, A., Maddalena, E., & Demartini, G. (2019). All those wasted hours: On task abandonment in crowdsourcing. In *Proceedings of the twelfth ACM international conference on web search and data mining* (pp. 321–329). Association for Computing Machinery.

Hara, K., Adams, A., Milland, K., Savage, S., Callison-Burch, C., & Bigham, J. (2018). A Data-Driven Analysis of Workers' Earnings on Amazon Mechanical Turk. In *Proceedings of the 2018 CHI conference on human factors in computing systems* (pp. 1–14). Association for Computing Machinery.

Hargittai, E., & Shaw, A. (2020). Comparing internet experiences and prosociality in Amazon Mechanical Turk and population-based survey samples. *Socius, 6*, 2378023119889834. https://doi.org/10.1177/2378023119889834

Hauser, D., Paolacci, G., & Chandler, J. J. (2018). *Common concerns with MTurk as a participant pool: Evidence and solutions.* https://doi.org/10.31234/osf.io/uq45c

Holland, S. J., Simpson, K. M., Dalal, R. S., & Vega, R. P. (2016). I can't steal from a coworker if I work from home: Conceptual and measurement-related issues associated with studying counterproductive work behavior in a telework setting. *Human Performance, 29*(3), 172–190. https://doi.org/10.1080/08959285.2016.1160094

Huang, J. L., Bowling, N. A., Liu, M., & Li, Y. (2015). Detecting insufficient effort responding with an infrequency scale: Evaluating validity and participant reactions. *Journal of Business and Psychology, 30*(2), 299–311. https://doi.org/10.1007/s10869-014-9357-6

Huang, J. L., Curran, P. G., Keeney, J., Poposki, E. M., & DeShon, R. P. (2012). Detecting and deterring insufficient effort responding to surveys. *Journal of Business and Psychology, 27*(1), 99–114.

Huff, C., & Tingley, D. (2015). Who are these people? *Research and Politics, 2*(3), 205316801560464.

Kan, I. P., & Drummey, A. B. (2018). Do imposters threaten data quality? *Computers in Human Behavior.* https://doi.org/10.1016/j.chb.2018.02.005

Kane, J. V., & Barabas, J. (2019). No harm in checking: Using factual manipulation checks to assess attentiveness in experiments. *American Journal of Political Science, 63*(1), 234–249. https://doi.org/10.1111/ajps.12396

Kang, R., Brown, S., Dabbish, L., & Kiesler, S. (2014). *Privacy attitudes of Mechanical Turk workers and the U.S. public.* Tenth Symposium on Usable Privacy and Security (SOUPS).

Kaplan, T., Saito, S., Hara, K., & Bigham, J. P. (2018, June 15). Striving to earn more: A survey of work strategies and tool use among crowd workers. In *Sixth AAAI conference on human computation and crowdsourcing.* www.aaai.org/ocs/index.php/HCOMP/HCOMP18/paper/view/17920

Kaufmann, N., & Schulze, T. (2011). *Worker motivation in crowdsourcing and human computation.* /paper/Worker-Motivation-in-Crowdsourcing-and-Human-Kaufmann-Schulze/8ac303322f73d6d0ae32b374476f82b47e5cb982

Kees, J., Berry, C., Burton, S., & Sheehan, K. (2017). An analysis of data quality. *Journal of Advertising, 46*(1), 141–155. https://doi.org/10.1080/00913367.2016.1269304

Kennedy, R., Clifford, S., Burleigh, T., Jewell, R., & Waggoner, P. (2018). The shape of and solutions to the MTurk quality crisis. *SSRN Electronic Journal.* https://doi.org/10.2139/ssrn.3272468

Kennedy, R., Clifford, S., Burleigh, T., Waggoner, P., & Jewell, R. (2018). How Venezuela's economic crisis is undermining social science research – About everything. *Washington Post.*

Kim, D. S., McCabe, C. J., Yamasaki, B. L., Louie, K. A., & King, K. M. (2017). Detecting random responders with infrequency scales using an error-balancing threshold. *Behavior Research Methods.* https://doi.org/10.3758/s13428-017-0964-9

Krivosheev, E., Casati, F., Caforio, V., & Benatallah, B. (2017, September 21). Crowdsourcing paper screening in systematic literature reviews. In *Fifth AAAI conference on human computation and crowdsourcing.* Fifth AAAI Conference on Human Computation and Crowdsourcing. www.aaai.org/ocs/index.php/HCOMP/HCOMP17/paper/view/15921

Leeper, T. J. (2016). Crowdsourced data preprocessing with R and Amazon Mechanical Turk. *The R Journal, 8*(1), 276–288.

Levay, K. E., Freese, J., & Druckman, J. N. (2016). The demographic and political composition of Mechanical Turk samples. *SAGE Open, 6*(1), 215824401663643. https://doi.org/10.1177/2158244016636433

Lewis, A. R., Djupe, P. A., Mockabee, S. T., & Su-Ya Wu, J. (2015). The (non) religion of Mechanical Turk workers. *Journal for the Scientific Study of Religion, 54*(2), 419–428. https://doi.org/10.1111/jssr.12184

Litman, L., Robinson, J., & Rosenzweig, C. (2015). The relationship between motivation, monetary compensation, and data quality among US- and India-based workers on Mechanical Turk. *Behavior Research Methods, 47*(2), 519–528. https://doi.org/10.3758/s13428-014-0483-x

Lukyanenko, R., & Parsons, J. (2018, January 1). *Beyond Micro-Tasks: Research Opportunities in Observational Crowdsourcing* [Article]. Journal of Database Management (JDM). https://doi.org/10.4018/JDM.2018010101

Maniaci, M. R., & Rogge, R. D. (2014). Caring about carelessness: Participant inattention and its effects on research. *Journal of Research in Personality, 48*, 61–83. https://doi.org/10.1016/j.jrp.2013.09.008

Marjanovic, Z., Holden, R., Struthers, W., Cribbie, R., & Greenglass, E. (2015). The inter-item standard deviation (ISD): An index that discriminates between conscientious and random responders. *Personality and Individual Differences, 84*, 79–83. https://doi.org/10.1016/j.paid.2014.08.021

Mason, W., & Suri, S. (2012). Conducting behavioral research on Amazon's Mechanical Turk. *Behavior Research Methods, 44*(1), 1–23. https://doi.org/10.3758/s13428-011-0124-6

Mason, W., & Watts, D. J. (2009). *Financial incentives and the "performance of crowds"* (P. Bennett, R. Chandrasekar, M. Chickering, P. Ipeirotis, E. Law, A. Mityagin, F. Provost, & L. Ahn, Eds., p. 77). ACM Press. https://doi.org/10.1145/1600150.1600175

Matherly, T. (2018). A panel for lemons? Positivity bias, reputation systems and data quality on MTurk. *European Journal of Marketing, 53*(2), 195–223. https://doi.org/10.1108/EJM-07-2017-0491

McCredie, M. N., & Morey, L. C. (2018). Who are the Turkers? A characterization of MTurk workers using the personality assessment inventory. *Assessment*. https://doi.org/10.1177/1073191118760709

Meade, A. W., & Craig, S. B. (2012). Identifying careless responses in survey data. *Psychological Methods, 17*(3), 437–455. https://doi.org/10.1037/a0028085

Miller, J. D., Crowe, M., Weiss, B., Maples-Keller, J. L., & Lynam, D. R. (2017). Using online, crowdsourcing platforms for data collection in personality disorder research: The example of Amazon's Mechanical Turk. *Personality Disorders, 8*(1), 26–34. https://doi.org/10.1037/per0000191

Mortensen, M. L., Adam, G. P., Trikalinos, T. A., Kraska, T., & Wallace, B. C. (2017). An exploration of crowdsourcing citation screening for systematic reviews. *Research Synthesis Methods, 8*(3), 366–386. https://doi.org/10.1002/jrsm.1252

Moss, A. J., Rosenzweig, C., Robinson, J., & LItman, L. (2020). *Is it ethical to use Mechanical Turk for behavioral research? Relevant data from a representative survey of MTurk participants and wages*. PsyArXiv. https://doi.org/10.31234/osf.io/jbc9d

Mullinix, K. J., Leeper, T. J., Druckman, J. N., & Freese, J. (2015). The generalizability of survey experiments. *Journal of Experimental Political Science, 2*(02), 109–138.

Ophir, Y., Sisso, I., Asterhan, C. S. C., Tikochinski, R., & Reichart, R. (2019). The Turker Blues: Hidden factors behind increased depression rates among Amazon's Mechanical Turkers. *Clinical Psychological Science, 1*(19). https://doi.org/10.1177/2167702619865973

Oppenheimer, D. M., Meyvis, T., & Davidenko, N. (2009). Instructional manipulation checks. *Journal of Experimental Social Psychology, 45*(4), 867–872. https://doi.org/10.1016/j.jesp.2009.03.009

Oppenlaender, J., Milland, K., Visuri, A., Ipeirotis, P., & Hosio, S. (2020). Creativity on paid crowdsourcing platforms. arXiv:2001.06798 [Cs]. https://doi.org/10.1145/3313831.3376677

Paolacci, G., Chandler, J., & Ipeirotis, P. G. (2010). Running experiments on MTurk. *Judgment and Decision Making, 5*(5).

Pee, L. G., Koh, E., & Goh, M. (2018). Trait motivations of crowdsourcing and task choice: A distal-proximal perspective. *International Journal of Information Management, 40*, 28–41. https://doi.org/10.1016/j.ijinfomgt.2018.01.008

Peer, E., Vosgerau, J., & Acquisti, A. (2014). Reputation as a sufficient condition for data quality on Amazon Mechanical Turk. *Behavior Research Methods, 46*(4), 1023–1031.

Pittman, M., & Sheehan, K. (2016). Amazon's Mechanical Turk a digital sweatshop? Transparency and accountability in crowdsourced online research. *Journal of Media Ethics, 31*(4), 260–262. https://doi.org/10.1080/23736992.2016.1228811

Presser, S. (1984). Is inaccuracy on factual survey items item-specific or respondent-specific? *Public Opinion Quarterly, 48*(1B), 344–355. https://doi.org/10.1093/poq/48.1B.344

Prims, J. P., Sisso, I., & Bai, H. (2018). *Suspicious IP online flagging tool*. https://itaysisso.shinyapps.io/bots/

Rinderknecht, R. G. (2019). Effects of participant displeasure on the social-psychological study of power on Amazon's Mechanical Turk. *SAGE Open, 9*(3), 2158244019876268. https://doi.org/10.1177/2158244019876268

Rogstadius, J., Kostakos, V., Kittur, A., Smus, B., Laredo, J., & Vukovic, M. (2011). An assessment of intrinsic and extrinsic motivation on task performance in crowdsourcing markets. In *Proceedings of the international AAAI conference on web and social media* (Vol. 5, No. 1). Association for the Advancement of Artificial Intelligence. Retrieved from https://ojs.aaai.org/index.php/ICWSM/article/view/14105

Salehi, N., Irani, L. C., Bernstein, M. S., Alkhatib, A., Ogbe, E., Milland, K., & Clickhappier. (2015). *We are dynamo* (B. Begole, J. Kim, K. Inkpen, & W. Woo, Eds., pp. 1621–1630). ACM Press.

Sannon, S., & Cosley, D. (2019). Privacy, power, and invisible labor on Amazon Mechanical Turk. In *Proceedings of the 2019 CHI conference on human factors in computing systems* (pp. 1–12). Association for Computing Machinery. https://doi.org/10.1145/3290605.3300512

Shapiro, D. N., Chandler, J., & Mueller, P. A. (2013). Using Mechanical Turk to study clinical populations. *Clinical Psychological Science, 1*(2), 213–220. https://doi.org/10.1177/2167702612469015

Sharpe Wessling, K., Huber, J., & Netzer, O. (2017). MTurk character misrepresentation. *Journal of Consumer Research, 44*(1), 211–230. https://doi.org/10.1093/jcr/ucx053

Shaw, A. D., Horton, J. J., & Chen, D. L. (2010). Designing incentives for inexpert human raters. In *Proceedings of the 2010 ACM conference on computer supported cooperative work* (pp. 275–284). Association for Computing Machinery. https://doi.org/10.1145/1958824.1958865

Siegel, J. T., & Navarro, M. (2019). A conceptual replication examining the risk of overtly listing eligibility criteria on Amazon's Mechanical Turk. *Journal of Applied Social Psychology, 12*(12), 964. https://doi.org/10.1111/jasp.12580

Sina, S., Kraus, S., & Rosenfeld, A. (2014). Using the crowd to generate content for scenario-based serious-games. arXiv:1402.5034 [Cs]. http://arxiv.org/abs/1402.5034

Smith, S. M., Roster, C. A., Golden, L. L., & Albaum, G. S. (2016). A multi-group analysis of online survey respondent data quality. *Journal of Business Research, 69*(8), 3139–3148. https://doi.org/10.1016/j.jbusres.2015.12.002

Snowberg, E., & Yariv, L. (2018). *Testing the waters: Behavior across participant pools* (No. w24781). National Bureau of Economic Research. https://doi.org/10.3386/w24781

Stagnaro, M. N., Pennycook, G., & Rand, D. (2018). Performance on the cognitive reflection test is stable across time. *Judgment and Decision Making, 13*(3), 260–267.

Stewart, N., Chandler, J., & Paolacci, G. (2017). Crowdsourcing samples in cognitive science. *Trends in Cognitive Sciences, 21*(10), 736–748. https://doi.org/10.1016/j.tics.2017.06.007

Stewart, N., Ungemach, C., Harris, A., Bartels, D. M., Newell, B. R., Paolacci, G., & Chandler, J. (2015). The average laboratory samples a population of 7300 MTurk workers. *Judgment and Decision Making, 10*(5), 479.

Thomas, K. A., & Clifford, S. (2017). Validity and Mechanical Turk: An assessment of exclusion methods and interactive experiments. *Computers in Human Behavior, 77*, 184–197. https://doi.org/10.1016/j.chb.2017.08.038

US Census Bureau. (n.d.). *American fact finder.* American Fact Finder. Retrieved January 12, 2016, from https://factfinder.census.gov/faces/nav/jsf/pages/index.xhtml

Walters, K., Christakis, D. A., & Wright, D. R. (2018). Are Mechanical Turk worker samples representative of health status and health behaviors in the U.S.? *PLoS One, 13*(6), e0198835. https://doi.org/10.1371/journal.pone.0198835

Weinberg, J., Freese, J., & McElhattan, D. (2014). Comparing data characteristics and results of an online factorial survey between a population-based and a crowdsource-recruited sample. *Sociological Science, 1*, 292–310. https://doi.org/10.15195/v1.a19

Wenz, A. (2019). Do distractions during web survey completion affect data quality? Findings from a laboratory experiment. *Social Science Computer Review.* https://doi.org/10.1177/0894439319851503

Williamson, V. (2016). On the ethics of crowdsourced research. *PS: Political Science & Politics, 49*(01), 77–81. https://doi.org/10.1017/S104909651500116X

Woike, J. K. (2019). Upon repeated reflection: Consequences of frequent exposure to the cognitive reflection test for Mechanical Turk participants. *Frontiers in Psychology, 10.* https://doi.org/10.3389/fpsyg.2019.02646

Wood, D., Harms, P. D., Lowman, G. H., & DeSimone, J. A. (2017). Response speed and response consistency as mutually validating indicators of data quality in online samples. *Social Psychological and Personality Science, 8*(4), 454–464. https://doi.org/10.1177/1948550617703168

Xia, H., Wang, Y., Huang, Y., & Shah, A. (2017). "Our privacy needs to be protected at all costs": Crowd workers' privacy experiences on Amazon Mechanical Turk. In *Proceedings of the ACM on human-computer interaction, 1(CSCW)* (pp. 1–22). Association for Computing Machinery. https://doi.org/10.1145/3134748

Yang, J., van der Valk, C., Hossfeld, T., Redi, J., & Bozzon, A. (2018). How do crowdworker communities and microtask markets influence each other? A data-driven study on Amazon Mechanical Turk. *Proceedings of the AAAI Conference on Human Computation and Crowdsourcing, 6*(1), 193–202. Retrieved from https://ojs.aaai.org/index.php/HCOMP/article/view/13335

Zack, E. S., Kennedy, J., & Long, J. S. (2019). Can nonprobability samples be used for social science research? A cautionary tale. *Survey Research Methods, 13*(2), 215–227. https://doi.org/10.18148/srm/2019.v13i2.7262

Zhang, C., & Conrad, F. G. (2014). Speeding in web surveys- the tendency to answer very fast and its association with straightlining. *Survey Research Methods, 8*(2).

Zhou, H., & Fishbach, A. (2016). The pitfall of experimenting on the web: How unattended selective attrition leads to surprising (yet false) research conclusions. *Journal of Personality and Social Psychology, 111*(4), 493–504. https://doi.org/10.1037/pspa0000056

Zwaan, R. A., Pecher, D., Paolacci, G., Bouwmeester, S., Verkoeijen, P., Dijkstra, K., & Zeelenberg, R. (2018). Participant Nonnaiveté and the reproducibility of cognitive psychology. *Psychonomic Bulletin & Review, 25*(5), 1968–1972. https://doi.org/10.3758/s13423-017-1348-y

11

INFERENCE FROM PROBABILITY AND NONPROBABILITY SAMPLES

Rebecca Andridge and Richard Valliant

1 Introduction

Although probability samples have been the standard for finite population estimation for decades, they often require complex designs, extended field periods, and high expense to achieve the goal of collecting high-quality data. A concern with some types of probability samples is that response rates may be so low that they are tantamount to nonprobability samples. In contrast to probability surveys, nonprobability surveys can be faster and cheaper to conduct. A serious question is whether they can produce accurate estimates for the populations that are target of inference. In this chapter, we describe probability and nonprobability sampling techniques and the methods of inference that can be used for both. Section 2 reviews techniques used in probability sampling, which for decades have been the standard, particularly for official statistics. Section 3 enumerates the types of nonprobability samples, based on a classification by the American Association for Public Opinion Research, that practitioners have used. Examples of nonprobability samples that have failed to produce good estimates, along with a few that have succeeded, are in section 4. In section 5, we describe the potential problems with nonprobability samples that can bias inferences. The general problems of inference with these samples is described in section 6. Section 7 gives some of the details of approaches to estimation with nonprobability samples, including how information from probability samples can be used to potentially improve inference from nonprobability samples. We concentrate on surveys of households or persons, but the issues raised here apply to other types of units like businesses or schools.

2 Probability sampling

Both probability and nonprobability sampling concern the problem of making inference about a population based on a sample. In general, both assume that there is a finite population and, in the absence of time and monetary constraints, measurements could be taken on every member of this population, producing a *census*. In lieu of a census, a *sample* is used wherein a subset of the population is selected for measurement. How that sample is selected is the key difference between probability and nonprobability sampling. In a probability sample, each unit in the population has a known, positive (non-zero) probability of being selected into the sample, and randomness is involved in the selection of which units actually get included in one particular sample. Many

DOI: 10.4324/9781003025245-13

textbooks describe in detail the features of and inference methods for probability samples (e.g., Cochran, 1977; Levy & Lemeshow, 2008; Lohr, 2010); in this section we briefly review the key design features of probability samples which are the building blocks that, when combined, create sampling schemes ranging from simple random samples to complex multistage designs.

2.1 Vocabulary

Table 11.1 summarizes terminology used to describe the components of probability sampling. An *observation unit* is what we measure, which is often a person as in a household survey, but could alternatively be a business as in an establishment survey or even an animal as in wildlife surveys. By definition observation units are distinct, and the complete collection of observation units makes up the *target population*. Through a known process that involves randomization, a *sample* of observation units is taken through selection of *sampling units*. Importantly, sampling units can be the same as the observation unit (e.g., one person) but can also be a collection of observation units (e.g., a household). When sampling is conducted in multiple stages, there may be multiple sampling units – for example, first sampling schools and then sampling students within schools. The phrase *primary sampling unit (PSU)* is often used to describe the sampling unit that is selected first (e.g., the school). The enumeration of the complete set of sampling units creates the *sampling frame*, from which the sampling units will be selected.

There are many types of sampling frames, and often in practice there can be a mismatch between observation units available on the sampling frame and the observation units in the population. An address-based sampling frame or sampling frame consisting of telephone numbers might be incomplete or contain outdated information. This gives rise to the notion of the *sampled population*, which is the group of observation units that could actually be included in the sample. Mismatch between the target population and sampled population is referred to as a *coverage error*. This mismatch can take two forms: *undercoverage* is when some of the target population does not appear on the sampling frame, and *overcoverage* is when the sampling frame contains units that are not part of the target population. Coverage is just one type of error that can occur in probability sampling; for a complete treatment of the so-called total survey error framework, see Biemer et al. (2017).

Table 11.1 The vocabulary of probability sampling

Observation unit (or element)	One (non-overlapping) unit on which a measurement is taken
Target population	Complete collection of observation units
Sample	A subset of a population (that will be/has been measured)
Sampling unit	A unit that can be selected for a sample (might be an observation unit or a collection of observation units)
Sampling frame	A list of all sampling units
Sampled population	All observation units that could possibly be in the sample (the population from which the sample was actually taken)
Strata (singular: Stratum)	Set of mutually exhaustive and exclusive subgroups of the population, with known subgroup membership for all sampling units *before* sampling occurs (e.g., dividing address-based sample into geographic regions)
Clusters	Aggregation of individual sampling units into larger sampling units (e.g., households containing individual people; census tracts containing individual residences)

2.2 Types of probability samples (how to select the sample)

The simplest form of sampling is the *simple random sample (SRS)*. In an SRS, every possible subset of *n* units in the population has the same chance of being in the sample. Importantly, while in an SRS every unit has an equal chance of being selected into the sample, equal probability of selection is a necessary but not sufficient condition for an SRS. Simple random sampling can be done *with replacement (SRSWR)*, such that a unit can be selected into the sample more than once (also referred to as unrestricted random sampling, or URS), or *without replacement (SRSWOR)*, such that each unit can only be selected once. In practice, a simple SRS is not often used, but rather simple random sampling is used in conjunction with more complicated design features as described later.

In a *stratified random sample*, the population is first divided into *H* distinct subgroups called *strata*. Importantly, stratum membership must be known in advance of sample selection, that is, stratum membership must be available on the sampling frame. Then, an SRS is selected from each stratum, with each SRS taken independently. Strata must be mutually exclusive (each unit only belongs to one stratum) and exhaustive (all units belong to a stratum). Strata are often subgroups of interest, because the stratified design ensures elements are selected from each subgroup. Often strata are chosen such that units in the same stratum tend to be more similar than randomly selected units across strata are. If constructed in this way, estimates of population-level attributes can be made with increased precision relative to an SRS if a significant proportion of the variability in the attribute of interest is due to differences among strata. However, it is important to note that not all stratified designs result in precision gains; some stratification schemes can actually lead to decreased overall precision relative to an SRS.

In a *cluster sample*, individual units in the population are aggregated into larger sampling units called *clusters*, and a sample of clusters is selected. Cluster sampling is often used when you do not have a full list of individual units in the population, but you do have a list of all clusters in the population, for example when you can enumerate housing units but not the occupants of the housing units. If all observation units in a selected cluster are measured, it is called a *one-stage cluster sample*. Alternatively, a random sample of the observation units in the selected clusters might be measured, referred to as a *two-stage cluster sample*, because random selection occurs in two stages. Cluster sampling tends to cause a decrease in precision relative to SRS, because individual units within a cluster tend to be similar – so there's not as much information in a cluster sample of, say, 100 individual units that come from five clusters of size 20 as there is in an SRS of 100 individual units.

In a *systematic sample*, a starting point is chosen from a list of population units (sampling frame), and that unit and each *k*th unit after that one on the list is chosen. If the list is randomly ordered, systematic sample will behave like an SRS and you can use analysis methods appropriate for an SRS. But, a systematic sample is *not* an SRS, because all possible subsets of *n* units do not have the same probability of being sampled. For example, if the 100th unit is chosen, the 101st unit cannot be chosen – so the probability of a sample that contains both of these units is 0 (but the probability of other samples is >0).

Another important type of sampling is *probability proportional to size (PPS) sampling*. In a PPS sample, the probability a unit is selected into the sample is directly proportional to a size measure that is known for all units before sampling (i.e., is available on the sampling frame). This type of sampling is often used in conjunction with cluster sampling, where the size measure is the size of the cluster, such that larger clusters (with more observation units) have a higher chance of being selected.

These design features are often combined to create more complex designs, for example a stratified cluster sample (e.g., households stratified by geographic region) or a multistage cluster sample (e.g., children within schools within districts). Depending on how these features are combined and the specific implementations of each component, the resulting sample selection method may or may not be an *equal probability of selection method* (*EPSEM*). EPSEM refers to using a sampling technique that results in each population unit having the same probability of selection, and samples obtained with this property are often called *self-weighting samples*. The most obvious EPSEM sampling is taking an SRS; if a sample of size n is drawn with replacement from a population of size N, the probability of selection for any one unit is n/N. But more complex designs can be EPSEM as well, for example using PPS at the first stage to sample clusters and then at the second stage sampling exactly the same number of observation units per cluster. In this scenario, larger clusters have a bigger probability of being sampled, but then observation units in large clusters have a smaller probability of being sampled. Thus overall, the second stage sampling compensates for the first stage, so that each observation unit in the population has equal probability of selection. Note that despite being EPSEM, this second design is definitely not an SRS, as all possible combinations of observation units are not equally likely to be sampled. Historically EPSEM samples were preferred due to computing limitations; now having an EPSEM property is not as important and often we *want* to oversample certain subgroups in order to increase precision.

2.3 Design-based (randomization-based) inference

In design-based theory for sampling (also called randomization-based theory), the outcome being measured is assumed to be fixed, that is, is not a random variable. Randomness instead comes from the *selection indicators* – a random variable that indicates whether each unit is included in the sample. In probability sampling, we start with a set of N primary sampling units that taken together are the finite population of interest (denoted U). Given a sampling scheme (e.g., using feature(s) as described earlier), one could enumerate all possible samples that could be drawn from U. Across possible samples, unit i's outcome measurement is the same, but the *selection indicator* δ_i (a 0–1 indicator) varies. Of course, only one sample will be drawn, and for most sampling schemes actually enumerating all possible samples is not necessary (and would be prohibitive). But this concept of randomness coming entirely from repeated sampling is the key basis of design-based inference for probability samples.

An important by-product of probability sampling is that each observation unit has a known, non-zero probability of being included into the sample. For a given sampling scheme, each possible sample s has a known probability $P(s)$ of being chosen, and thus by aggregating across the possible samples, the *selection (inclusion) probability*, π_i for an individual sampling unit can be calculated. Once a sample is selected, these selection probabilities are used to create *sampling weights* for each sampled unit that are the inverse of the selection probabilities, $w_i = 1/\pi_i$. These weights are then used to construct estimates for population quantities. For a detailed treatment of the construction of sampling weights, see Valliant and Dever (2018).

Descriptive statistics, like means and totals, and analytic statistics, like model parameters, are common estimands in finite population estimation. Finite population totals are the simplest target to discuss. A total of some quantity Y in the population U can be written as the sum of the values over the set of sample units, s, and the sum over the nonsample units $\bar{s}$:

$$t_U = \sum_{i \in s} y_i + \sum_{i \in \bar{s}} y_i \equiv t_s + t_{\bar{s}}$$

Of course, the nonsampled sum, $t_{\bar{s}}$, is unobserved, and instead t_U is estimated by a weighted sum of the sample observations:

$$\hat{t}_U = \sum_{i \in s} w_i y_i$$

Means or proportions, which are special cases of means, are generally estimated as $\hat{\bar{y}} = \sum_s w_i y_i / \sum_s w_i$ where $\sum_s w_i$ functions as an estimator of the number of units in the population, N. Several software packages will either compute survey weights or analyze complex survey data or both, including the R survey package (Lumley, 2014), Stata,[1] SAS,[2] and SUDAAN.[3]

There are many strengths to design-based inference. The use of random selection removes any potential for bias by the investigator, for example, by selecting "approachable" looking individuals to take a survey. This ensures that probability samples are free from selection bias, assuming complete response is achieved. Additionally, under design-based inference one can always obtain an unbiased estimator of the population total for any outcome of interest (and an estimate of its variance) without having to posit a model for the data.

Design-based inference is not without its drawbacks, however. Resulting estimators can be inefficient, sometimes drastically so. Alternative methods of inference are available if one is willing to make assumptions about the survey variables. For example, in the model-assisted approach, (covariate) auxiliary information about the population is incorporated into the design-based approach via a model to improve efficiency. Broadly speaking, these methods introduce a model for predicting the outcome of interest from covariate information and use this model to essentially "adjust" the design-based estimators. Perhaps the most commonly used model-assisted method is *generalized regression estimation* (GREG). For an in-depth review of model-assisted estimation see (Särndal et al., 1992). We return to the idea of model-dependent inference in section 7 in the context of nonprobability samples.

2.4 Probability samples with nonresponse

When sampling units are people, obtaining 100% response is rarely achievable. Nonresponse causes two main problems: a reduction in power (loss of efficiency) and the potential for bias. In general, for probability samples bias is the larger concern. In the United States, response rates for large government surveys have declined over the past 25 years, in some cases quite dramatically (Czajka & Beyler, 2016) and across all modes of administration (phone, face-to-face, etc., Brick & Williams, 2013; Williams & Brick, 2018). Importantly, in the presence of nonresponse, design-based inference no longer guarantees unbiased estimates.

In the presence of unit nonresponse (unit fails to respond to entire survey), the sample weights for the responding units are commonly adjusted to account for nonresponse. One commonly used type of nonresponse weighting adjustment is *poststratification*. Poststratification first divides the sampled units into subgroups based on characteristics measured in the sample – so-called *poststrata* because group membership is only known after sampling, not on the sampling frame as in stratified sampling. Using the known population size for each stratum, sample weights within each poststratum are adjusted so that estimated counts (sum of the weights) equal the population counts. Each unit in a poststratum has the same adjustment made, that is they are all up-weighted or down-weighted equally. Note, however, that an underlying assumption of this method is that the responding members of the poststratum are similar to the nonresponding members, an assumption that may or may not be true and is difficult to validate.

Imputation for nonresponse can also be used for probability samples, though this tends to be used more for item nonresponse (when a unit fails to answer a particular question), whereas nonresponse weight adjustments are used for unit nonresponse. Additionally, the complex sampling design must be considered when doing the imputation (Kim et al., 2006). Even with these techniques, however, there is no guarantee of unbiased estimates.

Growing nonresponse rates, in conjunction with rising costs of data collection, raises the question, are these probability samples still providing unbiased inference? Can probability samples be replaced by cheaper, nonprobability samples? In order to (attempt to) answer this question, we first must understand the features of nonprobability samples and the challenges of inference from such samples. As we will discuss, several of the tools from probability sampling, for example GREG estimators and poststratification, are useful for inference in nonprobability samples.

3 Types of nonprobability samples

The American Association of Public Opinion Research (AAPOR) has issued two task force reports on the use of nonprobability samples for finite population inference. Baker et al. (2010) studied the use of online Internet panels; Baker et al. (2013a, 2013b) cover nonprobability sampling generally. Baker et al. (2010) recommended on several grounds that researchers not use online panels if the objective is to accurately estimate population values. Among other reasons, they noted that (i) some comparative studies showed that nonprobability samples were less accurate than probability samples; (ii) the demographic composition of different panels can affect estimates; and (iii) not all panel vendors fully disclose their methods. Baker et al. (2013a) took a more nuanced view that inferences to a population from nonprobability samples can be valid but that the modeling assumptions needed are difficult to check.

Nonprobability surveys capture participants through various methods. The AAPOR task force on nonprobability sampling (Baker et al., 2013a) characterized these samples into three broad types:

1. Convenience sampling
2. Sample matching
3. Network sampling

Convenience sampling is a form of nonprobability sampling in which easily locating and recruiting participants is the primary consideration. No formal sample design is used. Some types of convenience samples are *mall intercepts*, *volunteer samples*, *river samples*, *observational studies*, and *snowball samples*. In a *mall intercept sample*, interviewers try to recruit shoppers to take part in a study. Usually, neither the malls nor the people are probability samples.

Volunteer samples are common in social science, medicine, and market research. Volunteers may participate in a single study or become part of a panel whose members may be recruited for different studies over the course of time. A particular instance is the opt-in web panel in which volunteers are recruited when they visit particular websites (Schonlau & Couper, 2017). After becoming part of a panel, the members may participate in many different surveys, often for some type of incentive. *River samples* are a version of opt-in web sampling in which volunteers are recruited at a number of websites. Some thought may be given to the set of websites used for recruitment with an eye toward obtaining a cross-section of demographic groups.

In *sample matching*, the members of a nonprobability sample are selected to match a set of important population characteristics. For example, a sample of persons may be constructed so that its distribution by age, race–ethnicity, and sex closely matches the distribution of the inference population. Quota sampling is an example of sample matching. The matching is intended to reduce selection biases as long as the covariates that predict survey responses can be used in matching. Rubin (1979) presents the theory for matching in observational studies. A variation of matching in survey sampling is to match the units in a nonprobability sample with those in a probability sample. Rivers (2007) describes this type of sampling matching in the context of web survey panels. Other techniques developed by Rosenbaum and Rubin (1983) and others for analyzing observational data have also been applied when attempting to develop weights for some volunteer samples.

In *network sampling*, members of some target population (usually a relatively rare one like intravenous drug users or men who have sex with men) are asked to identify other members of the population with whom they are somehow connected. Members of the population that are identified in this way are then asked to join the sample. This method of recruitment may proceed for several rounds. *Snowball sampling* (also called chain sampling, chain-referral sampling, or referral sampling) is an example of network sampling in which existing study subjects recruit additional subjects from among their acquaintances. These samples typically do not represent any well-defined target population, although they can be a way to accumulate a sizeable collection of units from a rare population.

Sirken (1970) is one of the earliest examples of network or multiplicity sampling in which the network that respondents report about is clearly defined (e.g., members of a person's extended family). Properly done, a multiplicity sample is a probability sample because a person's network of recruits is well defined. Heckathorn (1997) proposed an extension to this called *respondent driven sampling* (*RDS*) in which persons would report how many people they knew in a rare population and recruit other members of the rare population. RDS has been used in several, specialized applications. For example, Frost et al. (2006) used RDS to locate intravenous drug users; Schonlau et al. (2014) used it in an attempt to recruit an Internet panel. If some restrictive assumptions on how the recruiting is done are satisfied, probabilities of being included in a sample can be computed and used for inferences to a full rare population, but these assumptions can easily be violated (e.g., see Gile & Handcock, 2010). Because RDS is a narrow topic, we will not pursue it in this chapter.

4 Examples of nonprobability samples that have worked and have failed

Methods can always be devised for making estimates from nonprobability samples. Validating those estimates is typically difficult. Examples where nonprobability samples did not produce good estimates are fairly plentiful. Cases where they were validated to have worked well are fewer but can be found. This section reviews a few studies; Cornesse et al. (2020) cover many more. One application area where the correct answer is ultimately known is election polling from which several of our examples are taken. The sampling methods used in polls vary but are often based on volunteer panels or probability samples that have such high nonresponse that they should be treated as nonprobability samples.

An early and notorious example of a failure is the 1936 US presidential election. In pre-election polls, the *Literary Digest* magazine collected 2.3 million mail surveys from mostly middle- to upper-income respondents. Although this sample size was huge, the poll incorrectly predicted that candidate Landon would win by a landslide over the incumbent, Franklin Roosevelt. In fact, Roosevelt won the election in a landslide, carrying every state except for Maine and Vermont (Squire, 1988). As Squire noted, the magazine's respondents consisted mostly of automobile and telephone owners plus the magazine's own subscribers. This pool underrepresented Roosevelt's core of lower-income supporters. In the same election, several pollsters (Gallup, Crossley, and Roper) using much smaller but more representative quota samples correctly predicted the outcome (Gosnell, 1937).

More recent examples of polls that failed to correctly predict election outcomes are the 2015 British parliamentary election (Cowling, 2015), the 2015 Israeli Knesset election (Liebermann, 2015), and the 2014 governor's race in the US state of Maryland (Enten, 2014). The widespread failure of the British 2015 polls led to an extensive evaluation by two professional societies (Sturgis et al., 2016). There were various potential reasons for the misfires, including samples with low contact and response rates, samples based on unrepresentative volunteer panels, inability to predict which respondents would actually vote, question wording and framing, deliberate misreporting, and volatility in voters' opinions about candidates. The samples for the 2015 British polls were online or telephone polls that could not be considered probability samples of all registered voters. Demographic population totals for characteristics like age, sex, region, social grade, and working status were used to set quota sample and weighting targets. After evaluating eight putative explanations, Sturgis et al. (2016) concluded that the British polls were wrong because of their unrepresentative samples. The statistical adjustment procedures that were used did not correct this basic problem.

AAPOR did a similar evaluation of polling results in the 2016 US presidential election (Kennedy et al., 2017). In that election, most polls called the national popular vote fairly accurately – predicting that Clinton would have a plurality over Trump. However, the American system depends on the electoral college in which state-level outcomes determine the national winner. In a handful of states, polls underestimated the support for Trump, who won the majority of state electoral votes. The AAPOR panel identified three likely reasons for the inaccurate poll results:

1. Real change in vote preference during the final week or so of the campaign
2. Adjusting for overrepresentation of college graduates was critical, but many polls did not do that
3. Some Trump voters who participated in pre-election polls did not reveal themselves as Trump voters until after the election, and they outnumbered late-revealing Clinton voters

Wang et al. (2015) used a version of superpopulation modeling described in section 7.3, termed multilevel regression and poststratification (MRP), to obtain estimates of voting behavior in the 2012 US presidential election. Their sample was a highly nonrepresentative convenience sample of nearly 350,000 users of Xboxes (video gaming devices), empaneled 45 days prior to the election. They used a poststratified estimator of the proportion voting for each candidate of the form $\hat{\bar{y}} = \sum_{h=1}^{H} P_h \hat{\mu}_h$ where h is a poststratum, H is the total number of poststrata, P_h is the proportion of voters in poststratum h, and $\hat{\mu}_h$ is an estimate of the proportion voting for a candidate in that poststratum.

The large sample, combined with highly predictive covariates about voting behavior, including information about party identification and 2008 presidential election voting behavior, allowed for poststrata that were elaborate crosses of the covariates. Bayesian priors were used to stabilize parameter estimates and resulting values of $\hat{\mu}_h$. The values of P_h were estimated via probability sample exit polls from the 2008 US presidential election, themselves of very large size (over 100,000). Wang et al. (2015) showed that, despite the fact that the raw Xbox estimates were severely biased in favor of candidate Romney, reflecting its largely male and White sample composition, accurate estimates of voting behavior were obtained, based on comparisons with aggregated probability sampling polls as well as the final election result. This accuracy was due to the large sample size that allowed prediction of voting behavior among decidedly underrepresented elements of the population (e.g., older minority females), combined with the hierarchical regression modeling to stabilize predictions.

While the Xbox application gives some hope that good estimates can be made from even the poorest sample, the accuracy of estimates leans heavily on modeling assumptions that we discuss in sections 6 and 7.

5 Problems with nonprobability samples

Since nonprobability samples are often obtained in a poorly controlled or uncontrolled way, they can be subject to a number of biases when the goal is inference to a specific finite population. Several issues are listed here in the context of voluntary Internet panels, but other types of nonprobability samples can suffer from similar problems.

Selection bias occurs if the seen part of the population (the sample) differs from the unseen (the nonsample) in such a way that the sample cannot be projected to the full population. Whether a nonprobability sample covers the desired population is a major concern. For example, in a volunteer web panel, only persons with access to the Internet can join a panel. To describe three components of survey coverage bias, Valliant and Dever (2011) defined three populations, illustrated in Figure 11.1: (1) the target population of interest for the study U; (2) the potentially covered population given the way that data are collected, F_{pc}; and (3) the actual covered population, F_c, the portion of the target population that is recruited for the study through the essential survey conditions. For example, consider an opt-in web survey for a smoking cessation study. The target population U may be defined as adults aged 18–29 who currently use cigarettes. The potentially covered population F_{pc} would be those study-eligible individuals with Internet access who visit the sites where study recruitment occurs; those actually covered F_c would be the subset of the potential covered population who participate in the study. Selecting a sample only from F_c results in selection bias. The sample s is those persons who are invited to participate in

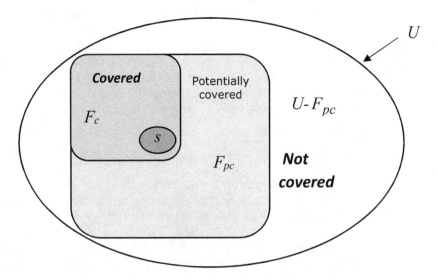

Figure 11.1 Illustration of potential and actual coverage of a target population

the survey and who actually do. The $U - F_{pc}$ area in the figure are the many persons who have Internet access but never visit the recruiting websites or who do not have Internet access at all. In many situations, $U - F_{pc}$ is vastly larger than either F_c or F_{pc}. Although we use a volunteer panel as an example, in other applications the decomposition in Figure 11.1 is still pertinent with appropriate definitions of the components.

To illustrate a case that is rife with coverage problems, we further consider surveys done using panels of persons recruited via the Internet. Table 11.2 lists percentages of persons in various European and central Asian countries that used the Internet (from any location) in a three-month period in either 2017 or 2018. The Internet could be used via a computer, mobile phone, personal digital assistant, games machine, or other devices. The percentages range from 99% in Iceland to 38% in the Kyrgyz Republic. Consequently, a survey done via the Internet would have almost total population coverage in some countries but would seriously undercover the population in others.

Access to the Internet can vary by demographic group. Table 11.3 gives the percentage of US households that have an Internet subscription of any kind in 2016 as estimated from the American Community Survey (Ryan, 2017). The ACS estimates are based on a sample of about 3.5 million households. About 18% of households had no Internet subscription, which in itself

Table 11.2 Percentages of individuals using the Internet among European and Central Asian countries. Data refer to three-month periods in 2017 or 2018.

Country	% of population	Country	% of population
Iceland	99	Slovenia	80
Liechtenstein	98	Lithuania	80
Denmark	97	North Macedonia	79
Luxembourg	97	Belarus	79
Norway	96	Kazakhstan	79
United Kingdom	95	Poland	78
Netherlands	95	Moldova	76
Sweden	92	Hungary	76
Germany	90	Croatia	75
Switzerland	90	Portugal	75
Kosovo	89	Italy	74
Estonia	89	Serbia	73
Finland	89	Greece	73
Belgium	89	Albania	72
Austria	87	Montenegro	72
Spain	86	Turkey	71
Ireland	85	Romania	71
Cyprus	84	Bosnia and Herzegovina	70
Latvia	84	Armenia	65
France	82	Bulgaria	65
Russian Federation	81	Georgia	63
Czech Republic	81	Ukraine	63
Slovak Republic	81	Kyrgyz Republic	38
Azerbaijan	80		

Source: International Telecommunication Union, World Telecommunication – ICT Development Report and database (2020). https://data.worldbank.org/indicator/IT.NET.USER.ZS

Table 11.3 Percentages of US households with Internet subscriptions; 2016 American Community Survey
Percent of households with any Internet subscription

Total households	81.9
Age of householder	
15–34 years	87.4
35–44 years	89.1
45–64 years	84.7
65 years and older	66.8
Race and Hispanic origin of householder	
White alone, non-Hispanic	83.4
Black alone, non-Hispanic	72.3
Asian alone, non-Hispanic	90.1
Hispanic (of any race)	77.1
Limited English-speaking household	
No	82.3
Yes	62.5
Metropolitan status	
Metropolitan area	82.9
Nonmetropolitan area	73.0
Household income	
Less than $25,000	58.2
$25,000–$49,999	76.9
$50,000–$99,999	89.0
$100,000–$149,999	94.6
$150,000 and more	96.4
Educational attainment of householder	
Less than high school graduate	55.7
High school graduate	71.2
Some college or associate degree	85.3
Bachelor's degree or higher	93.1

is a substantial amount of undercoverage of the full population. The coverage varies considerably by demographic group. Only 66.8% of households where the head is 65 or older have the Internet. Black non-Hispanic and Hispanic households are less likely to have access than other race-ethnicities. Households in metropolitan areas are more likely to have access. There is also a clear dependence on income and education. As income and education increase, so does the percentage of households with access. As illustrated in Dever et al. (2008), these coverage errors can lead to biased estimates for items whose means are related to groups with differential undercoverage.

Selection bias occurs when some groups are also more likely to volunteer for a panel. Bethlehem (2010) reviews this issue for web surveys. Willems et al. (2006) report that ethnic minorities and immigrant groups were systematically underrepresented in Dutch panels. They also found that, relative to the general population, the Dutch online panels contained disproportionately more voters, more Socialist Party supporters, more heavy Internet users, and fewer churchgoers. The extent of such biases varies over time as societies change but are always a cause for concern.

One approach that helps limit selection bias is to select an initial sample using what is known as address-based sampling (AAPOR, 2016). A sample of addresses is selected from a list that covers nearly 100% of a population. The sample units are then asked to join a panel. Although the initial sample has minimal coverage error, it can be degraded by nonresponse and attrition as described next.

Nonresponse of several kinds affects web panels. Many panel vendors have a "double opt-in" procedure for joining for a panel. First, a person registers his/her name, email, and some demographics. Then, the vendor sends the person an email that must be responded to in order to officially join the panel. This eliminates people who give bogus emails but also introduces the possibility of *registration nonresponse* since some people do not respond to the vendor's email. People may also click on a banner ad advertising the panel but never complete all registration steps. Finally, a panel member asked to participate in a survey might not respond.

Attrition is another problem – persons may lose interest and drop out of a panel. Many surveys oversample specific groups, for example young Black females. A panelist that is in one of these "interesting" groups may be peppered with survey requests and drop out for that reason. Another reason that some groups, like the elderly, are overburdened is that they may be over-sampled to make up for anticipated nonresponse.

Measurement error is also a worry in nonprobability surveys as it is in any survey. The types of error that have been demonstrated in some studies are effects due to questionnaire design, mode, and peculiarities of respondents. For example, the persons who participate in panels tend to have higher education levels. The motivation for participating may be a sense of altruism for some but may be just to collect an incentive for others. Some respondents speed through surveys, answering as quickly as possible to collect the incentive. This is a form of "satisficing" where respondents do just enough to get the job done (Simon, 1956). On the other hand, self-administered online surveys do tend to elicit more reports of socially undesirable behaviors, like drug use, than do face-to-face surveys. Higher reports are usually taken to be more nearly correct.

Baker et al. (2010, p. 739) list 19 studies where the same questionnaire was administered by interviewers to probability samples and online to nonprobability samples. As they noted, "Only one of these studies yielded consistently equivalent findings across methods, and many found differences in the distributions of answers to both demographic and substantive questions. Further, these differences generally were not substantially reduced by weighting."

6 The general problem of inference for nonprobability samples

Smith (1983) discusses the general problem of making inferences from non-random samples. His formulation is to consider the joint density of the population vector of an analysis variable, $\mathbf{Y} = (Y_1, Y_2, \ldots, Y_N)$, where N is the number of units in the population, and the population vector of 0–1 indicator variables, $\delta_s = (\delta_1, \delta_2, \ldots, \delta_N)$ for a sample s. The presentations of Rubin (1976) and Little (1982) on selection mechanisms and survey nonresponse are closely related. Suppose that $\mathbf{X}$ is an $N \times p$ matrix of covariates that can be used in designing a sample or in constructing estimators. The conditional density of $\mathbf{Y}$ given $\mathbf{X}$ and a parameter vector β is $f(\mathbf{Y} | \mathbf{X}; \beta)$. The density of δ_s given $\mathbf{Y}$, $\mathbf{X}$, and another unknown parameter $\mathbf{\Phi}$ is $f(\delta_s | \mathbf{Y}, \mathbf{X}; \mathbf{\Phi})$. The joint model for $\mathbf{Y}$ and δ_s is:

$$f\left(\mathbf{Y}, \delta_s | \mathbf{X}; \beta, \Phi\right) = f\left(\mathbf{Y} | \mathbf{X}; \beta\right) f\left(\delta_s | \mathbf{Y}, \mathbf{X}; \Phi\right) \tag{11.1}$$

In words, this says that the joint statistical model describing the analysis variable and whether units are in the sample can be factored into a superpopulation model for $\mathbf{Y}$ and a model for the δ_s indicators for being in the sample.

In a probability sample (without nonresponse or other missingness that is out of control of the sampler), $f(\delta_s | \mathbf{Y}, \mathbf{X}; \Phi) = f(\delta_s | \mathbf{X})$. The density $f(\delta_s | \mathbf{X})$ is the randomization distribution and is the basis for design-based inference as described in section 2. However, in a nonprobability sample, the distribution of δ_s can depend on both $\mathbf{Y}$ and an unknown parameter Φ. Depending on the application, inference can be based on either the Y-model, $f(\mathbf{Y}|\mathbf{X}; \beta)$, or the sample-inclusion model, $f(\delta_s | \mathbf{Y}, \mathbf{X}; \Phi)$, or on a combination of both. The former is the *superpopulation* approach and the latter is the *quasi-randomization* approach – both of which are described in section 7.

The fact that the second term in Expression (11.1) can depend on $\mathbf{Y}$ allows the possibility that being in the sample depends on what is to be analyzed, that is, to be *not missing at random* (NMAR). This is a worst case for inference because estimates will be biased in an unknown way, and there will usually be no way to correct the bias. For example, if an electoral poll is done, and voters' chances of participating in the poll depend on whom they will vote for, this would be NMAR. The hope is that if an extensive set of covariates $\mathbf{X}$ is available and is used to model the probability of being in the sample, then any possibility of NMAR is eliminated. In the electoral poll example, the participation probability might depend on one's age, race-ethnicity, education, income, and the person's political party, if any. By including all of these in a model for inclusion, the goal is to obtain $f(\delta_s | \mathbf{Y}, \mathbf{X}; \Phi) = f(\delta_s | \mathbf{X}; \Phi)$, which is known as *missing at random* (MAR). A few diagnostics have been devised (see section 7.5) for checking whether MAR has been achieved, but generally there is no assurance that inclusion in a nonprobability sample does not depend on any of the Y's being collected.

Estimation of model parameters often requires solving a set of estimating equations for the parameter estimates. The estimating equations can be linear in the parameters, as for linear regression or nonlinear, as for generalized linear models. In design-based finite population estimation, the estimating equations include survey weights and are estimators of types of finite population totals (Binder & Roberts, 2009). If weights are constructed for a nonprobability sample that are appropriate for estimating totals, then those weights can also be used in the estimating equations. Consequently, weight construction for nonprobability samples can play the same role in estimation as in probability sampling.

7 Approaches to inference for nonprobability samples

In any inference problem, the standard approaches involve averaging over some random process to calculate biases, variances, and other statistical properties. In design-based inference (see section 2), the random process is the drawing of the sample itself, which is controlled by the sampler. Since this method cannot be applied to nonprobability samples, models are used. One option is to model the mechanism by which units appear in the sample as being random (even though the mechanism is not controlled by the sampler). Pseudo-inclusion probabilities are estimated and used to construct weights. We term this *quasi-randomization* inference and discuss it in section 7.1. Another option is to model the variables collected in the survey as being functions of covariates. A statistical model is then used to project the sample to a target population. This is an example of *superpopulation model* or *prediction* inference described in section 7.2.

7.1 Quasi-randomization

In the quasi-randomization (QR) approach, pseudo-inclusion probabilities are estimated and used to correct for selection bias. Using the earlier notation, the goal is to estimate $f(\delta_s | \mathbf{Y}, \mathbf{X}; \Phi)$ or $f(\delta_s | \mathbf{X}; \Phi)$. Having a situation where the sample inclusion probabilities do not depend on the Y's is ideal since the nonsample Y's are unknown, but verifying that this is the case is impossible in most applications. There is some literature on estimation when nonsample data are NMAR (e.g., see Little, 2003), but the methods generally require information on nonsample units that is available only in specialized applications. Thus, the practical approach is to estimate $f(\delta_s \,|\, \mathbf{X}; \boldsymbol{\Phi})$. Next, we use $p(\mathbf{x}_i; \boldsymbol{\Phi})$ to denote the probability that a particular unit i is observed in the nonprobability sample.

Reference survey. One approach to estimating $p(\mathbf{x}_i; \boldsymbol{\Phi})$ is to use a *reference survey* in parallel to the nonprobability survey. This is described in more detail later. The reference survey can be a probability survey selected from the full population for which estimates are desired. The reference sample might also be a census that covers the entire population. The statistical approach is to combine the reference sample and the nonprobability sample and fit a model to predict the probability of being in the nonprobability sample.

A key requirement of the reference survey is that it must include the same covariates $\mathbf{x}_i$ as the nonprobability sample so that a binary regression can be fitted to permit estimation of inclusion probabilities for the volunteers. One possibility for a reference survey is to use a publicly available data set collected in a well-designed and -executed probability survey (like one done by a central government agency). Another possibility is for the survey organization to conduct its own reference survey. In the latter case, some specialized questions, beyond the usual age/race/sex/education types of demographics, can be added that are felt to be predictive of being in the nonprobability sample and of the analysis variables for the nonprobability sample. Schonlau et al. (2007) refer to these extra covariates as *webographics*. However, identifying webographics that are useful beyond the standard demographics is difficult (Lee & Valliant, 2009). Of course, another problem with conducting your own reference survey is that doing a high-quality survey with good coverage of the target population and acceptable response is expensive and may be beyond the means of many organizations.

A probability sample used as a reference survey ideally must not be subject to coverage or other types of bias. As noted in section 1, many probability samples are now subject to high nonresponse rates and are tantamount to nonprobability samples themselves. Poor-quality reference samples can lead to biased estimators of the inclusion probabilities and, consequently, biased estimators from the nonprobability sample. This is an argument for using large, well-controlled samples conducted by central governments for reference or matching samples if at all possible. For example, in a household survey in the US, the American Community Survey (www.census.gov/programs-surveys/acs/) would be a good choice for a reference.

Because the QR analysis involves both probability and nonprobability samples, we extend the earlier notation used in section 2. Denote the nonprobability sample by s_{np} and the probability sample by s_p. There are three related proposals in the literature for how to estimate $p(\mathbf{x}_i; \boldsymbol{\Phi})$. Combine the probability and nonprobability samples and let $Z_i = 1$ for nonprobability cases and $Z_i = 0$ for the probability cases conditional on being in the combined probability-nonprobability sample, $s_p \cup s_{np}$.

In the first proposal, Elliott and Davis (2005), Elliott (2009), and Elliott et al. (2010) showed that (with some assumptions), for a unit i in the nonprobability sample:

$$
\begin{aligned}
p(\mathbf{x}_i; \boldsymbol{\Phi}) &= Pr\left(i \in s_{np} \,\middle|\, \mathbf{x}_i; \boldsymbol{\Phi}\right) \\
&\propto Pr\left(i \in s_p \,\middle|\, \mathbf{x}_i\right) \frac{Pr\left(Z_i = 1 \,\middle|\, \mathbf{x}_i\right)}{1 - Pr\left(Z_i = 1 \,\middle|\, \mathbf{x}_i\right)}
\end{aligned}
\tag{11.2}
$$

That is, given values of the covariates, the probability of a unit's being in the nonprobability sample is proportional to that unit's probability of being in the probability sample. This is adjusted by the odds of being in the nonprobability sample within $s_p \cup s_{np}$. One of their key assumptions was that s_p and s_{np} were both negligibly small fractions of the population. The resulting "pseudo-weight" is given by $w_i = 1/p(\mathbf{x}_i; \boldsymbol{\Phi})$.

Note that $Pr\,(i \in s_p \mid \mathbf{x}_i)$ is not necessarily equal to the selection probability, π_i, of i in the probability sample because the covariates $\mathbf{x}_i$ may not have been used to design those selection probabilities. In the likely situation where $\mathbf{x}_i$ does not correspond precisely to the probability sample design variables, $Pr\,(i \in s_p \mid \mathbf{x}_i)$ can be estimated by regressing π_i on $\mathbf{x}_{i i}$ via beta regression (Ferrari & Cribari-Neto, 2004) in the probability sample, and predicting $Pr\,(i \in s_p \mid \mathbf{x}_i)$ for the nonprobability sample elements.

The term $P\,(Z_i = z \mid \mathbf{x}_i)$ can be estimated via logistic regression, or, to reduce model mis-specification if x_i is of high dimensionality, via least absolute shrinkage and regression operator (LASSO) (Tibshirani, 1996; LeBlanc & Tibshirani, 1998), Bayesian additive regression trees (BART) (Chipman et al., 2010), or super learner algorithms that combine estimators from numerous model fitting methods (Van der Laan et al., 2007).

Chen et al. (2019) present a second alternative for estimating $p(\mathbf{x}_i; \boldsymbol{\Phi})$ in which the probability and nonprobability samples are combined and a maximum likelihood estimate of $\boldsymbol{\Phi}$ is computed. The pseudo log-likelihood that is maximized is:

$$l(\boldsymbol{\Phi}) = \sum_{i \in s_{np}} log\, \frac{p(\mathbf{x}_i; \boldsymbol{\Phi})}{1 - p(\mathbf{x}_i; \boldsymbol{\Phi})} + \sum_{i \in s_p} \pi_i^{-1} log\left(1 - p(\mathbf{x}_i; \boldsymbol{\Phi})\right) \tag{11.3}$$

Once the estimate $\hat{\boldsymbol{\Phi}}$ is found, the pseudo-inclusion probability is estimated as $p(\mathbf{x}_i; \hat{\boldsymbol{\Phi}})$. Although Chen et al. (2019) showed that this method is theoretically sound, it does require customized programming since the method is not currently available in software packages.

A third alternative to estimating the probability of unit i's being in the nonprobability sample is used by some panel vendors. The probability (reference) and nonprobability samples are combined, and a weighted logistic regression is run to estimate $p(\mathbf{x}_i; \boldsymbol{\Phi})$ (e.g., see Valliant and Dever (2011)). This done by assigning a weight of 1 to the nonprobability cases, the probability sampling weight to the probability cases, and running a weighted logistic regression. The model predictions, thus, refer to the unconditional probability, $Pr(i \in s_{np} \mid \mathbf{x}_i)$, not a probability conditional on being in the combined sample as in Elliott et al. (2010). Chen et al. (2019) showed that this method was somewhat biased, although the bias is negligible if s_{np} is a small fraction of the population and if $Pr(i \in s_{np} \mid \mathbf{x}_i)$ is itself small for all units. However, this bias can be corrected using the transformed value

$$p_i^{\star}\left(\mathbf{x}_i; \hat{\boldsymbol{\Phi}}\right) = \frac{p\left(\mathbf{x}_i; \hat{\boldsymbol{\Phi}}\right)}{1 - p\left(\mathbf{x}_i; \hat{\boldsymbol{\Phi}}\right)}$$

See Wang et al. (2021). This corrected method is convenient since weighted logistic regression is available in survey software, and the transformation is easily programmed.

Linearization variance estimation for the QR estimators requires some complex formulas. Theoretical variance formulas for an estimator of a total or mean involve separate contributions from s_{np} and s_p (see, e.g., Chen et al., 2019; Wang et al., 2021). These variance estimators are not available in current software packages. However, a feasible alternative is to use a replication variance estimator, like the jackknife or bootstrap. As long as all steps in estimation are repeated for each replicate, the variance estimator should be approximately correct.

7.2 Superpopulation modeling

In the superpopulation (SP) modeling approach, a statistical model is fitted for a *Y* analysis variable from the sample and used to project the sample to the full population. That is, inferences are based on $f(\mathbf{Y}|\mathbf{X};\boldsymbol{\beta})$ in Expression (11.1). This approach could, of course, also be used with a probability sample. The difference here is that design-based inference, where the randomization distribution is under the control of the sampler, is not an option for a nonprobability sample. As noted in Smith (1983), the sample selection mechanism can be ignored for model-based inferences about the distribution of **Y**, if

$$f(\delta_s|\mathbf{Y},\mathbf{X};\boldsymbol{\Phi}) = f(\delta_s|\mathbf{X};\boldsymbol{\Phi}), \tag{11.4}$$

which would be the formal justification for using only $f(\mathbf{Y}|\mathbf{X};\boldsymbol{\beta})$. In Expression (11.4), *s* can denote either a probability or a nonprobability sample. There are purposive, nonprobability samples that satisfy Expression (11.4). For example, selecting the *n* units with the largest *x* values as is done by US Energy Information Administration (2016), or sampling balanced on population moments of covariates (Royall, 1970, 1971) are ignorable, nonprobability plans. However, in nonprobability samples where the selection of sample units is not well controlled, Expression (11.4) may not hold unless an extensive set of covariates can be used to model $f(\delta_s|\mathbf{X};\boldsymbol{\Phi})$.

Note that **Y** can be partitioned between the sample and nonsample units as $\mathbf{Y} = (\mathbf{Y}_s, \mathbf{Y}_{\bar{s}})$. Thus, $f(\mathbf{Y}|\mathbf{X};\boldsymbol{\beta}) = f(\mathbf{Y}_s|\mathbf{Y}_{\bar{s}},\mathbf{X};\boldsymbol{\beta})f(\mathbf{Y}_{\bar{s}}|\mathbf{X};\boldsymbol{\beta})$. If $f(\mathbf{Y}_s|\mathbf{Y}_{\bar{s}},\mathbf{X};\boldsymbol{\beta}) = f(\mathbf{Y}_s|\mathbf{X};\boldsymbol{\beta})$, then $\mathbf{Y}_s$ and $\mathbf{Y}_{\bar{s}}$ are independent conditional on the covariates, **X**. If model-based inferences are desired for $\boldsymbol{\beta}$, these can be done based only on $f(\mathbf{Y}_s|\mathbf{X};\boldsymbol{\beta})$. However, if descriptive inferences are required for the full population **Y**, then $f(\mathbf{Y}_{\bar{s}}|\mathbf{X};\boldsymbol{\beta})$ must be estimated. If this model has the same form as $f(\mathbf{Y}_s|\mathbf{X};\boldsymbol{\beta})$, then the model fitted from the sample can be used to predict values for the nonsample. This is the basis for the SP approach.

Consider the simple case of estimating a finite population total. The general idea in model-based estimation when estimating a total is to sum the responses for the sample cases and add to them the sum of predictions for nonsample cases. The key to forming unbiased estimates is that the variables to be analyzed for the sample and nonsample follow a common model and that this model can be discovered by analyzing the sample responses. An appropriate model usually includes covariates, as in the earlier $f(\mathbf{Y}_s|\mathbf{X};\boldsymbol{\beta})$, which are known for each individual sample case. The individual values of covariates may or may not be known for nonsample cases. For some common estimation methods like poststratification, only population totals of the covariates are required to construct the estimator, so that individual nonsample **X** values are unnecessary. Suppose that the mean of a variable y_i follows a linear model:

$$E_M(y_i|\mathbf{x}_i) = \mathbf{x}_i^T\beta \tag{11.5}$$

$$V_M(y_i|\mathbf{x}_i) = v_i$$

where the subscript *M* means that the expectation is with respect to the model, $\mathbf{x}_i$ is a vector of *p* covariates for unit *i* and β is a parameter vector. The term v_i is a variance parameter that does not have to be specifically defined. Given a sample *s* (either probability or nonprobability), an estimator of the slope parameter is $\hat{\beta} = \mathbf{A}_s^{-1}\mathbf{X}_s^T\mathbf{y}_s$ where $\mathbf{A}_s = \mathbf{X}_s^T\mathbf{X}_s$, $\mathbf{X}_s$ is the $n \times p$ matrix of covariates for the sample units, and $\mathbf{y}_s$ is the *n*-vector of sample *y*'s. (Weighted least squares might also be used if there were evidence of non-homogeneous model variances.) A prediction of the value of a unit in the set of nonsample units is $\hat{y}_i = \mathbf{x}_i^T \hat{\beta}$. A predictor of the population total is

$$
\begin{aligned}
\hat{t}_1 &= \sum_{i \in s} y_i + \sum_{i \in \bar{s}} \hat{y}_i \\
&= \sum_{i \in s} y_i + \left(\mathbf{t}_{Ux} - \mathbf{t}_{sx} \right)^T \hat{\beta}
\end{aligned}
\tag{11.6}
$$

where $\mathbf{t}_{Ux}$ is the total of the x's in the population and t_{sx} is the sample sum of the x's. This estimator is also equal to the general regression estimator (GREG) of Särndal et al. (1992) if the inverse selection probabilities in that estimator are all set to 1. The theory for this *prediction approach* is extensively covered in Valliant et al. (2000). If the sample is a small fraction of the population, as would be the case for most volunteer web surveys, the prediction estimator is approximately the same as predicting the value for every unit in the population and adding the predictions:

$$
\hat{t}_2 = \sum_{i \in U} \hat{y}_i = \mathbf{t}_{U_x}^T \hat{\beta}
\tag{11.7}
$$

The population mean of y can be estimated by $\hat{\bar{Y}} = \bar{X}_U^T \hat{\beta}$ where $\bar{X}_U = \mathbf{t}_{Ux} / N$, the population vector of covariate means.

The estimators in Expression (11.6) or (11.7) are quite flexible in what covariates can be included. For example, we might predict the amount that people have saved for retirement based on their occupation, years of education, marital status, age, number of children they have, and region of the country in which they live. If there is a single, categorical covariate x, then Expression (11.6) becomes a poststratified estimator. (Note that the poststrata could be the cross of multiple categorical variables, e.g., age × sex × education, so this is not as limiting as it first sounds.)

Constructing the estimator in Expression (11.6) or (11.7) would require that census counts be available for each of those covariates. Another possibility is to use estimates from some other larger or more accurate survey (e.g., Dever & Valliant, 2010, 2016). The reference surveys mentioned earlier could be a source of estimated control totals in which webographic covariates might be used.

Both Equations (11.6) and (11.7) can be written so that they are weighted sums of y's. If Expression (11.6) is used, the weight for unit i is $w_{1i} = 1 + \mathbf{t}_{sx}^T \mathbf{A}_s^{-1} \mathbf{x}_i$ where $\mathbf{t}_{sx} = \mathbf{t}_{Ux} - \mathbf{t}_{sx}$. In (7) the weight is $w_{2i} = \mathbf{t}_{Ux}^T \mathbf{A}_s^{-1} \mathbf{x}_i$. The estimated total for an analysis variable can be written as $\hat{t} = \sum_s w_i y_i$ where w_i is either w_{1i} or w_{2i}. Notice that these weights depend only on the x's, not on y. As a result, the same set of weights could be used for all estimates. It is true that a single set of weights will not be equally efficient for every y, but this situation is also true for design-based weights. A practical advantage of these SP estimates is that they can be computed using survey software like the R survey package (Lumley, 2014) or Stata (Valliant & Dever, 2018).

7.3 Multilevel Regression and Poststratification

Multilevel regression and poststratification (MRP) (Gelman & Little, 1997; Gelman, 2007) is a variation on superpopulation modeling. An elaborate set of poststrata is formed by crossing the covariates that are predictors of the survey analysis variables. Any continuous predictors are broken into categories. The intuition behind this method is that if enough finely defined cells are formed, then almost any underlying model can be approximated, regardless of how complicated. A mean or proportion is estimated as:

$$\hat{\bar{y}} = \sum_{h=1}^{G} P_h \hat{\mu}_h \qquad (11.8)$$

where P_h is the proportion of the population in poststratum (PS) h, $\hat{\mu}_h$ is the estimated mean per element in poststratum h. If the P_h are unknown, then estimates, $\hat{P}_h$, are used (e.g., see Dong et al.,2014; Zhou et al., 2016). The PS mean is estimated by a random (or mixed) effects model, which can be Bayesian or not. The general approach is to begin with the cross-classification of many covariates and dynamically decide which crosses to retain. Bayesian methods are especially useful in this regard since they can adapt the PS estimates to cases where cells have little, if any, sample. However, if sample sizes are small or zero in some poststrata, and the $\hat{\mu}_h$ for such PS are shrunk toward an overall mean, MRP can be biased if the population means in those PS are substantially different from those of the PS that are well covered. This over-shrinking can happen when, for example, the PS are defined by demographic variables and the sample frame poorly covers some combinations of the demographics (e.g., see Valliant, 2020). How to control the amount of shrinkage toward an overall mean is an unresolved topic in the Bayesian literature (Tang et al., 2018).

In cases where a linear model is used to predict y, MRP does produce unit-level weights as shown in Gelman (2007). However, when y is binary and a logistic or similar model is used at the unit level, $\hat{\bar{y}}$ cannot be written as a weighted sum of the y's. This can be a practical disadvantage if many estimates are to be made from the nonprobability sample, and a separate model must be fitted for every y.

MRP has been particularly interesting to political scientists who want to make state-level estimates based on relatively small national samples of 1,500 to 2,000 voters (Park et al., 2004, 2006; Selb & Munzert, 2011; Shapiro, 2011). An interesting application is Wang et al. (2015), mentioned in section 4, who were able to predict the outcome of the 2012 US presidential election using MRP with a sample that had gaping holes in coverage. In contrast, Buttice and Highton (2013) illustrated that strong covariates in the multilevel model and substantial variation across geographic units were necessary for MRP to perform well for both national and state-level estimates; otherwise MRP can have mediocre performance. Finally, we note that MRP estimation can be done with the R package, rstanarm (Goodrich et al., 2020).

7.4 Doubly robust estimation

When quasi-randomization and superpopulation modeling are combined to create an estimator, the combination is called *doubly robust*. There is an extensive theoretical and empirical literature on these as applied to observational data (see Scharfstein et al., 1999; Kang & Schafer, 2007; Cao et al., 2009). An estimator is doubly robust if it is unbiased or consistent when either the QR or the SP model is specified correctly.

First, pseudo-inclusion probabilities are estimated as in section 7.1. As in that section, s_{np} denotes a nonprobability sample. When the linear model in Expression (11.5) is used, the quasi-randomization weights are used to compute model-assisted weights as:

$$a_i^* = w_i \left[1 + \left(\mathbf{t}_{Ux} - \hat{\mathbf{t}}_x \right)^T \left(\mathbf{X}_{s_{np}}^T \mathbf{W} \mathbf{V}^{-1} \mathbf{X}_{s_{np}} \right)^{-1} \mathbf{x}_i / v_i \right]; i \in s_{np} \qquad (11.9)$$

where $\hat{\mathbf{t}}_x$ is the estimate of $\mathbf{t}_{Ux}$ based on the w_i quasi-randomization weights, $\mathbf{X}_{s_{np}}$ is the $n \times p$ matrix of covariates for the nonprobability sample units, $\mathbf{W} = diag\{w_i\}_{i \in s_{np}}$, $\mathbf{V} = diag\{v_i\}_{i \in s_{np}}$.

The weights in Expression (11.9) have the same form as those in a general regression estimator (Särndal et al., 1992). The $\{a^*_i\}$ weights are then used to estimate totals as $\hat{t}_y = \sum_{s_{np}} a^*_i y_i$; means are estimated as $\hat{\bar{y}} = \sum_{s_{np}} a^*_i y_i / \sum_{s_{np}} a^*_i$.

In principle, estimators constructed with these weights could be linearized and a Taylor series variance estimator used. However, both the QR and the SP distributions contribute to the variance of an estimated total or mean, complicating the calculation of an approximate variance. A more straightforward approach is replication variance estimation in which both the quasi-randomization and superpopulation estimation steps are repeated for each replicate. This will generally require customized software programming, although existing routines for GREG estimation and replication variances such as those in the R survey package or Stata will facilitate this.

7.5 Diagnostics for selection bias

Little et al. (2019), extending results in Andridge and Little (2011), propose measures to quantify the amount of selection bias present for the mean of Y estimated from a nonprobability sample, s_{np}. In particular they consider assessing the potential for selection bias due to nonignorable selection mechanisms, that is, when $f\left(\delta_{s_{np}} \middle| \mathbf{Y}_U, \mathbf{X}; \mathbf{\Phi}\right) \neq f\left(\delta_{s_{np}} \middle| \mathbf{Y}_{s_{np}}, \mathbf{X}; \mathbf{\Phi}\right)$ for all sets of nonsample units, $U - s_{np}$. In words, nonignorable selection means that the chances of being observed in the nonprobability sample can depend on the y-values, and thus the inclusion mechanism needs to be considered when making estimates. In such a case, QR or DR estimation should be used. However, if the set of available covariates is insufficient to eliminate the dependence of $f(\delta_{s_{np}} \mid \mathbf{Y}_U, \mathbf{X}; \mathbf{\Phi})$ on Y, estimates for population quantities that are unbiased or consistent will not be possible.

The general idea of the Little et al. (2019) indices is to predict the mean Y in the population under varying assumptions about the selection mechanism and then compare these means to the observed mean of Y for s_{np}. The assumptions about the selection mechanism involve an unknown sensitivity parameter ϕ that allows selection to be ignorable (depends only on $\mathbf{X}$; $\phi = 0$) or strongly nonignorable (depends entirely on Y; $\phi = 1$). Evaluating a range of ϕ values captures how sensitive estimates are to nonignorable selection, that is, how "wrong" the estimated mean of Y in s_{np} would be if selection were in fact varying degrees of nonignorable.

Effectively what the measures do is assess the selection bias present in $\mathbf{X}$, and then project that bias onto Y. Because the underlying model used by Little et al. (2019) is a normal pattern-mixture model, and they assume the linear model Expression (11.5) relates Y to $\mathbf{X}$, their bias measure only requires population totals of $\mathbf{X}$ in order to be calculated. All other necessary information comes from the nonprobability sample. This obviously requires information about the relationship between Y and $\mathbf{X}$, which is operationalized in their metrics as the observed correlation between Y and $\mathbf{X}$ in the nonprobability sample. Their measures are reflective of the magnitude of this correlation; with a strong correlation, a nonprobability sample that is highly nonignorable with respect to $\mathbf{X}$ is actually not a "bad" nonprobability sample, because we can make adjustments based on $\mathbf{X}$ that correlates strongly with Y. Andridge et al. (2019) extend the measures of Little et al. (2019) to binary Y, which are commonly encountered in practice. For binary Y, the population variance-covariance matrix is needed for $\mathbf{X}$ in addition to population totals. In the absence of this information, it can be estimated by the estimate in the nonprobability sample.

8 Conclusion

As response rates to probability samples decline and budgets shrink, more and more researchers will likely be turning to nonprobability sampling. It is therefore of the utmost importance to be aware of the limitations of nonprobability sampling and the role that high-quality probability samples play in assisting estimation from nonprobability samples. Importantly, the selection biases present in nonprobability samples cannot be assessed without having population-level auxiliary information, but with such information (from, e.g., a probability sample), methods have been developed to attempt to correct for this bias. However, as described in section 4, there are many more examples of "failed" estimates from nonprobability samples than there are success stories. As such, much more work needs to be done in this area, especially in the area of diagnostics like those in section 7.5. Sensitivity analyses conducted by producing estimates using multiple methods may also be useful as a way to assess sensitivity to unverifiable model assumptions (necessary for all estimation methods using nonprobability samples).

Notes

1 www.stata.com/
2 www.sas.com/en_us/home.html
3 www.rti.org/impact/sudaan-statistical-software-analyzing-correlated-data

References

AAPOR. (2016). *Address-based sampling*. Technical Report, The American Association for Public Opinion Research. Retrieved November 25, 2020, from www.aapor.org/Education-Resources/Reports/Address-based-Sampling.aspx

Andridge, R. R., & Little, R. (2011). Proxy pattern-mixture analysis for survey nonresponse. *Journal of Official Statistics*, *27*, 153–180.

Andridge, R. R., West, B. T., Little, R. J. A., Boonstra, P. S., & Alvarado-Leiton, F. (2019). Indices of nonignorable selection bias for proportions estimated from non-probability samples. *Journal of the Royal Statistical Society: Series C (Applied Statistics)*, *68*(5), 1465–1483. https://doi.org/10.1111/rssc.12371

Baker, R., Brick, J. M., Bates, N. A., Battaglia, M., Couper, M. P., Dever, J. A., Gile, K., & Tourangeau, R. (2013a). *Report of the AAPOR task force on non-probability sampling*. Technical Report, The American Association for Public Opinion Research.

Baker, R., Brick, J. M., Bates, N. A., Battaglia, M., Couper, M. P., Dever, J. A., Gile, K., & Tourangeau, R. (2013b). Summary report of the AAPOR task force on non-probability sampling. *Journal of Survey Statistics and Methodology*, *1*, 90–143. https://doi.org/10.1093/jssam/smt008

Baker, R., Brick, J. M., Bates, N. A., Couper, M. P., Courtright, M., Dennis, J. M., . . . Zahs, D. (2010). AAPOR report on online panels. *Public Opinion Quarterly*, *74*, 711–781. https://doi.org/10.1093/poq/nfq048

Bethlehem, J. (2010). Selection bias in web surveys. *International Statistical Review*, *78*, 161–188. https://doi.org/10.1111/j.1751-5823.2010.00112.x

Biemer, P., de Leeuw, E., Eckman, S., Edwards, B., Kreuter, F., Lyberg, L., Tucker, N. C., &West, B. E. (2017). *Total survey error in practice*. John Wiley & Sons.

Binder, D., & Roberts, G. (2009). Imputation of business survey data. In D. Pfeffermann & C. Rao (Eds.), *Handbook of statistics, sample surveys: Inference and analysis* (Vol. 29B), chapter 24. Elsevier.

Brick, J. M., & Williams, D. (2013). Explaining rising nonresponse rates in cross-sectional surveys. *The Annals of the American Academy of Political and Social Science*, *645*(36–59). https://doi.org/10.1177/0002716212456834

Buttice, M., & Highton, B. (2013). How does multilevel regression and poststratification perform with conventional national surveys? *Political Analysis*, *21*, 449–467. https://doi.org/10.1093/pan/mpt017

Cao, W., Tsiatis, A. A., & Davidian, M. (2009). Improving efficiency and robustness of the doubly robust estimator for a population mean with incomplete data. *Biometrika*, *96*(3), 732–734. https://doi.org/10.1093/biomet/asp033

Chen, Y., Li, P., & Wu, C. (2019). Doubly robust inference with non-probability survey samples. *Journal of the American Statistical Association*. https://doi.org/10.1080/01621459.2019.1677241

Chipman, H. A., George, E. I., & McCulloch, R. E. (2010). BART: Bayesian additive regression trees. *Annals of Applied Statistics*, *4*(1), 266–298. https://doi.org/10.1214/09-AOAS285

Cochran, W. G. (1977). *Sampling techniques*. John Wiley & Sons.

Cornesse, C., Blom, A., Dutwin, D., Krosnick, J., de Leeuw, E., Legleye, S., . . . Wenz, A. (2020). A review of conceptual approaches and empirical evidence on probability and nonprobability sample survey research. *Journal of Survey Statistics and Methods, 8*, 4–36. https://doi.org/10.1093/jssam/smz041

Cowling, D. (2015). Election 2015: How the opinion polls got it wrong. *BBC News*. Retrieved November 25, 2020, from www.bbc.com/ news/uk-politics-32751993

Czajka, J. L., & Beyler, A. (2016). *Declining response rates in federal surveys: Trends and implications*. Technical Report, Mathematica Policy Research.

Dever, J., Rafferty, A., & Valliant, R. (2008). Internet surveys: Can statistical adjustments eliminate coverage bias? *Survey Research Methods, 2*, 47–62.

Dever, J., & Valliant, R. (2010). A comparison of variance estimators for poststratification to estimated control totals. *Survey Methodology, 36*, 45–56.

Dever, J., & Valliant, R. (2016). GREG estimation with undercoverage and estimated controls. *Journal of Survey Statistics and Methodology, 4*, 289–318. https://doi.org/10.1093/jssam/smw001

Dong, Q., Elliott, M., & Raghunathan, T. (2014). A non-parametric method to generate synthetic populations to adjust for complex sample designs. *Survey Methodology, 40*, 29–46.

Elliott, M. (2009). Combining data from probability and non-probability samples using pseudo-weights. *Survey Practice*. https://doi.org/10.29115/SP-2009-0025

Elliott, M., & Davis, W. (2005). Obtaining Cancer Risk Factor Prevalence Estimates in Small Areas: Combining data from the Behavioral Risk Factor Surveillance Survey and the National Health Interview Survey. *Journal of the Royal Statistical Society C, 54*, 595–609. https://doi.org/10.1111/j.1467-9876.2005.05459.x

Elliott, M., Resler, A., Flannagan, C., & Rupp, J. (2010). Combining data from probability and non-probability samples using pseudo-weights. *Accident Analysis and Prevention, 42*, 530–539. https://doi.org/0.1016/j.aap.2009.09.019

Enten, H. (2014). Flying blind toward Hogan's upset win in Maryland. *FiveThirtyEight*. Retrieved November 25, 2020, from http://fivethirtyeight.com/datalab/governor-maryland-surprise-brown-hogan/

Ferrari, S., & Cribari-Neto, F. (2004). Beta regression for modelling rates and proportions. *Journal of Applied Statistics, 31*, 799–815. https://doi.org/10.1080/0266476042000214501

Frost, S., Brouwer, K., Firestone-Cruz, M., Ramos, R., Ramos, M., Lozada, R., Magis-Rodriguez, C., & Strathdee, S. (2006). Respondent-driven sampling of injection drug users in two U.S.-Mexico border cities: Recruitment dynamics and impact on estimates of HIV and syphilis prevalence. *Journal of Urban Health, 83*(6), 83–97. https://doi.org/10.1007/s11524-006-9104-z

Gelman, A. (2007). Struggles with survey weighting and regression modeling. *Statistical Science, 22*(2), 153–164. https://doi.org/10.1214/088342306000000691

Gelman, A., & Little, T. C. (1997). Poststratification into many categories using hierarchical logistic regression. *Survey Methodology, 23*, 127–135.

Gile, K., & Handcock, M. (2010). Respondent-driven sampling: An assessment of current methodology. *Sociological Methodology, 40*, 285–327. https://doi.org/10.1111/j.1467-9531.2010.01223.x

Goodrich, B., Gabry, J., Ali, I., & Brilleman, S. (2020). *rstanarm: Bayesian applied regression modeling via Stan*. Retrieved November 25, 2020, from http://mc-stan.org/rstanarm. R package version 2.19.3.

Gosnell, H. F. (1937). How accurate were the polls? *Public Opinion Quarterly, 1*, 97–105.

Heckathorn, D. D. (1997). Respondent-driven sampling: A new approach to the study of hidden populations. *Social Problems, 44*, 174–199. https://doi.org/10.2307/3096941

Kang, J. D. Y., & Schafer, J. L. (2007). Demystifying double robustness: A comparison of alternative strategies for estimating a population mean from incomplete data. *Statistical Science, 22*(4), 523–539. https://doi.org/10.1214/07-STS227

Kennedy, C., Blumenthal, M., Clement, S., Clinton, J., Durand, C., Franklin, C., . . . Wiezien, C. (2017). *An evaluation of 2016 election polls in the U.S. ad hoc committee on 2016 election polling*. Technical Report, The American Association for Public Opinion Research. Retrieved November 25, 2020, from www.aapor.org/Education-Resources/Reports/ An-Evaluation-of-2016-Election-Polls-in-the-U-S.aspx

Kim, J., Brick, J. M., Fuller, W. A., & Kalton, G. (2006). On the bias of the multiple-imputation variance estimator in survey sampling. *Journal of the Royal Statistical Society. Series B, 68*(3), 509–521. https://doi.org/10.1111/j.1467-9868.2006.00546.x

LeBlanc, M., & Tibshirani, R. (1998). Monotone shrinkage of trees. *Journal of Computational and Graphical Statistics, 7*(4), 417–433. https://doi.org/10.1080/10618600.1998.10474786

Lee, S., & Valliant, R. (2009). Estimation for volunteer panel web surveys using propensity score adjustment and calibration adjustment. *Sociological Methods & Research, 37*, 319–343. https://doi.org/10.1177/0049124108329643

Levy, P. S., & Lemeshow, S. (2008). *Sampling of Populations: Methods and Applications* (4th ed.). John Wiley & Sons.

Liebermann, O. (2015). Why were the Israeli election polls so wrong? *CNN*. Retrieved November 25, 2020, from www.cnn.com/2015/ 03/18/middleeast/israel-election-polls/

Little, R. J. A. (1982). Models for nonresponse in sample surveys. *Journal of the American Statistical Association, 77*(378), 237–250. https://doi.org/10.2307/2287227

Little, R. J. A. (2003). Bayesian methods for unit and item nonresponse. In R. Chambers & C. Skinner (Eds.), *Analysis of Survey Data*, chapter 18. John Wiley.

Little, R. J. A., West, B., Boonstra, P., & Hu, J. (2019). Measures of the degree of departure from ignorable sample selection. *Journal of Survey Statistics and Methodology*, 1–33. https://doi.org/10.1093/jssam/smz023

Lohr, S. (2010). *Sampling: Design and Analysis* (2nd ed.). Chapman & Hall/CRC Press.

Lumley, T. (2014). *Survey: Analysis of Complex Survey Samples*. R package version 3.30.

Park, D. K., Gelman, A., & Bafumi, J. (2004). Bayesian multilevel estimation with post-stratification: State-level estimates from national polls. *Political Analysis, 12*, 375–385. https://doi.org/0.1093/pan/mph024

Park, D. K., Gelman, A., & Bafumi, J. (2006). State-level opinions from national surveys: Poststratification using multilevel logistic regression. In J. E. Cohen (Ed.), *Public Opinion in State Politics*. Stanford University Press.

Rivers, D. (2007). Sampling for web surveys. In *Proceedings of the section on survey research methods*. American Statistical Association.

Rosenbaum, P., & Rubin, D. (1983). The central role of the propensity score in observational studies for causal effects. *Biometrika, 70*, 41–55. https://doi.org/10.1093/biomet/70.1.41

Royall, R. (1970). On finite population sampling theory under certain linear regression models. *Biometrika, 57*, 377–387.

Royall, R. (1971). Linear regression models in finite population sampling theory. In V. Godambe & D. Sprott (Eds.), *Foundations of Statistical Inference*. Holt, Rinehart, and Winston.

Rubin, D. (1976). Inference and missing data. *Biometrika, 63*, 581–592. https://doi.org/10.1093/biomet/63.3.581

Rubin, D. (1979). Using multivariate matched sampling and regression adjustment to control bias in observational studies. *Journal of the American Statistical Association, 74*, 318–328. https://doi.org/10.1080/01621459.1979.10482513

Ryan, C. (2017). Computer and internet use in the United States: 2016. *US Census Bureau*. Retrieved November 25, 2020, from www.census.gov/ content/dam/Census/library/publications/2018/acs/ACS-39.pdf

Särndal, C. E., Swensson, B., & Wretman, J. (1992). *Model Assisted Survey Sampling*. Springer.

Scharfstein, D. O., Rotnitzky, A., & Robins, J. M. (1999). Adjusting for nonignorable drop-out using semiparametric nonresponse models (with discussion and rejoinder). *Journal of the American Statistical Association, 94*, 1096–1146. https://doi.org/10.1080/01621459.1999.10473862

Schonlau, M., & Couper, M. (2017). Options for conducting web surveys. *Statistical Science, 32*(2), 279–292. https://doi.org/10.1214/16-STS597

Schonlau, M., van Soest, A., & Kapteyn, A. (2007). Are "webographic" or attitudinal questions useful for adjusting estimates from web surveys using propensity scoring? *Survey Research Methods, 1*(3), 155–163. https://doi.org/10.18148/srm/2007.v1i3.70

Schonlau, M., Weidmer, B., & Kapteyn, A. (2014). Recruiting an internet panel using respondent-driven sampling. *Journal of Official Statistics, 30*(2), 291–310. https://doi.org/10.2478/jos-2014-0018

Selb, P., & Munzert, S. (2011). Estimating constituency preferences from sparse survey data using auxiliary geographic information. *Political Analysis, 19*, 455–470. https://doi.org/10.1093/pan/mpr034

Shapiro, R. Y. (2011). Public opinion and American democracy. *Public Opinion Quarterly, 759*, 982–1017. https://doi.org/10.1093/poq/nfr053

Simon, H. (1956). Rational choice and the structure of the environment. *Psychological Review, 63*, 129–138.

Sirken, M. (1970). Household surveys with multiplicity. *Journal of the American Statistical Association, 65*, 257–266. https://doi.org/10.1080/01621459.1970.10481077

Smith, T. M. F. (1983). On the validity of inferences from non-random samples. *Journal of the Royal Statistical Society A, 146*, 394–403. https://doi.org/10.2307/2981454

Squire, P. (1988). Why the 1936 literary digest poll failed. *Public Opinion Quarterly, 52*, 125–133. https://doi.org/10.1086/269085

Sturgis, P., Baker, N., Callegaro, M., Fisher, S., Green, J., Jennings, W., . . . Smith, P. (2016). *Report of the inquiry into the 2015 British general election opinion polls*. Retrieved November 25, 2020, from http://eprints.ncrm.ac.uk/3789/1/Report_final_revised.pdf

Tang, X., Ghosh, M., Ha, N. S., & Sedransk, J. (2018). Modeling random effects using global – local shrinkage priors in small area estimation. *Journal of the American Statistical Association, 113*(524), 1476–1489. https://doi.org/10.1080/01621459.2017.1419135

Tibshirani, R. (1996). Regression shrinkage and selection via the lasso. *Journal of the Royal Statistical Society B, 58*, 267–288. https://doi.org/10.1111/j.2517-6161.1996.tb02080.x

US Energy Information Administration. (2016). Weekly petroleum status report. *US Department of Energy*. Retrieved November 25, 2020, from www. eia.gov/petroleum/supply/weekly/pdf/appendixb.pdf

Valliant, R. (2020). Comparing alternatives for estimation from nonprobability samples. *Journal of Survey Statistics and Methodology, 8*, 231–263. https://doi.org/10.1093/jssam/smz003

Valliant, R., & Dever, J. A. (2011). Estimating propensity adjustments for volunteer web surveys. *Sociological Methods and Research, 40*, 105–137. https://doi.org/10.1177/0049124110392533

Valliant, R., & Dever, J. A. (2018). *Survey Weights: A Step-by-step Guide to Calculation.* Stata Press.

Valliant, R., Dorfman, A. H., & Royall, R. M. (2000). *Finite Population Sampling and Inference: A Prediction Approach.* John Wiley & Sons.

Van der Laan, M. J., Polley, E. C., & Hubbard, A. E. (2007). Super learner. *Statistical Applications in Genetics and Molecular Biology, 6*(1). https://doi.og/10.2202/1544-6115.1309

Wang, L., Valliant, R., & Li, Y. (2021). Adjusted logistic propensity weighting methods for population inference using nonprobability volunteer-based epidemiologic cohorts. *Statistics in Medicine*, **40**. DOI: 10.1002/sim.9122

Wang, W., Rothschild, D., Goel, S., & Gelman, A. (2015). Forecasting elections with non-representative polls. *International Journal of Forecasting, 31*, 980–991. http://dx.doi.org/10.1016/j.ijforecast.2014.06.001

Willems, P., Vonk, T. W. E., & van Ossenbruggen, R. (2006). The effects of panel recruitment and management on research results. Retrieved November 25, 2020, from www.websm.org/db/12/12228/Web Survey Bibliography/The_effects_of_panel_recruitment_and_management_on_research_results_A_study_across_19_online_panels/

Williams, D., & Brick, J. M. (2018). Trends in US face-to-face household survey nonresponse and level of effort. *Journal of Survey Statistics and Methodology, 6*(2), 186–211. https://doi.org/10.1093/jssam/smx019

Zhou, H., Elliott, M., & Raghunathan, T. (2016). A two-step semiparametric method to accommodate sampling weights in multiple imputation. *Biometrics, 72*, 242–252. https://doi.org/0.1111/biom.12413

12

CHALLENGES OF ONLINE NON-PROBABILITY SURVEYS

Jelke Bethlehem

12.1 Introduction

Humankind has always collected data about populations. Before the nineteenth century, data collection was usually based on complete enumeration of the population. This changed in the 1800s. Because of rapidly growing populations, ever larger cities (urbanisation), more and more centralised governments, and an increasing need for information about the population, it became expensive and time consuming to completely enumerate populations. Therefore, ideas emerged to replace complete enumeration by some form of sampling. This only works if sample results can be generalised to the population (see Figure 12.1). Is it possible to select a sample from a population, analyse the data collected in the sample, draw conclusions from the analysis, and translate them into valid conclusions for the whole population? This chapter shows that the answer to this question depends on the way the sample is selected. Probability samples and non-probability samples are compared. It is shown that for probability samples it is possible to generalise, but for non-probability samples there are several issues that may prevent proper inference.

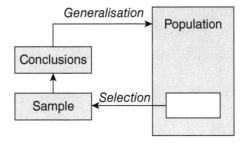

Figure 12.1   Generalisation from the sample to the population

DOI: 10.4324/9781003025245-14

12.2 The rise of probability sampling

All through history, rulers of countries have collected data to get information about the state of their countries. These data were mostly used to obtain insight in the military strength of the country and the amount of tax that could be collected. All data collection was based on integral enumeration of the population. The concept of sampling had not yet emerged.

The first sample surveys were carried out in the nineteenth century. In 1824, two newspapers in the US, the Harrisburg *Pennsylvanian* and the Raleigh *Star*, measured political preferences of voters prior to the presidential election of that year. These early surveys did not pay much attention to sampling aspects, making it difficult to establish the accuracy of the results. Such surveys were often called *straw polls*. Another example was the survey of *Literary Digest*, which was conducted during the US presidential election campaign in 1936 and based on a sample of only car and telephone owners.

The samples for these surveys were not representative, and therefore it was not possible to generalise from the sample to the population. Maybe one of the first to stress the importance of representative samples was Kiaer (1895). He proposed his *representative method*, which could be seen as a form of quota sampling. A problem of his sampling method was that the precision of estimates could not be determined.

Then there were probability surveys. The shortcomings of Kiaer's approach gave rise to discussion about its applicability. This led to new ideas about sample selection. Important was the work by Bowley (1906), who proposed to draw *random samples*. He showed that for large samples, selected at random from the population, estimates have an approximately normal distribution. Therefore, he could compute the variance of estimates and use it as an indicator of their precision. Some years later, Neyman (1934) introduced the *confidence interval* as an indicator for the precision of these estimates. This theory formed the basis for the theory of probability sampling. From the 1940s on, this became the preferred sampling method.

The confidence interval is still used nowadays to describe the *margin of error* of an estimate. Jerzy Neyman did more than invent the confidence interval. Based on an empirical evaluation of Italian census data, he could prove that the representative method failed to provide satisfactory estimates of population characteristics. As a result, this non-probability sampling technique fell into disrepute.

The classical theory of probability sampling was more or less completed in 1952 when Horvitz and Thompson (1952) published their general theory for constructing unbiased (valid) estimates. They showed that, whatever the selection probabilities are, it is always possible to construct a valid estimator. This is called the *Horvitz-Thompson estimator*. The fundamental principles of probability sampling come down to three conditions:

1. The sample must be selected by means of a probability sampling. So it must be a random sample.
2. Each person in the population must have a positive (non-zero) probability of selection.
3. All selection probabilities must be known.

If these three conditions are satisfied, it is always possible to compute unbiased estimates. It is also possible to compute variances of estimates, and therefore the precision of estimates can be determined in the form of *confidence intervals* or *margins of error*. For more about the history of survey sampling, see Bethlehem (2018, chapter 2).

And then there was the rise of online surveys starting around 1995. The internet made it possible to conduct online surveys. But is not easy, and often not possible, to draw a random sample of e-mail addresses. Therefore, researchers often could not rely on random sampling and instead applied *self-selection*. This is a form of non-probability sampling. The questionnaire is made available on the web. Respondents are those who happen to have internet, encounter the survey website, and spontaneously decide to fill in the questionnaire. On the one hand, such a survey is attractive because it allows for simple, fast, and cheap data collection, but on the other hand, it has serious methodological challenges.

The rest of this chapter compares surveys based on probability sampling with those based on non-probability sampling. For non-probability sampling, the focus is on online surveys based on self-selection.

Several simulation examples are used to show what can go wrong with self-selection online surveys. The problems with the opinion surveys for the general election in the UK in 2015 are also described (the 'British polling disaster').

12.3 An example of a probability survey

That probability sampling works can be proved mathematically. See, for example, standard books like Cochran (1977) or Bethlehem (2009). This can also be shown by simulating the process of sample selection. This section describes such a simulation. A fictitious population was constructed consisting of 100,000 people. There were five variables:

- The variable *Internet* indicated how active a person was on the internet. There were two categories: very active users and passive users. The population consisted of 1% of very active users and 99% passive users. Active users had a response probability of 0.95 and passive users had a response probability of 0.05.
- The variable *Age* in three categories: young, middle aged, and old. The active internet users consisted of 60% young people, 30% middle-aged people, and 10% old people. The age distribution for passive internet users was 40% young, 35% middle-aged, and 25% old. Typically younger people were more active internet users.
- *Voted for the National Elderly Party* (NEP). The probability of voting for this party only depended on age. Probabilities were 0.00 (for young), 0.30 (for middle-aged) and 0.60 (for old).
- *Voted for the New Internet Party* (NIP). The probability of voting for this party depended both on age and internet use. For active internet users the probabilities were 0.80 (for young), 0.40 (for middle-aged) and 0.20 (for old). For passive internet users, all probabilities were equal to 0.10. So, for active users voting for the NIP decreased with age. Voting probability was always low for passive users.

Figure 12.2 summarises the relationships between the variables. Voting for the NIP depends on two variables: *Age* and *Internet*, and voting for the NEP only depends on *Age*. The relationships between the variables were modelled somewhat stronger than they probably would be in a real-life situation. Effects were therefore more pronounced.

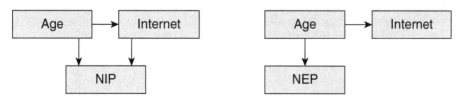

Figure 12.2 Relationships between variables

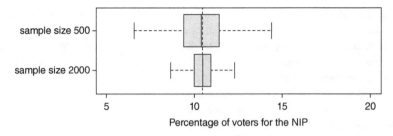

Figure 12.3   Simulation of random sampling and self-selection for the variable NIP

The simulation focuses on estimating the percentage of voters for the NIP. The population percentage is equal to 10.4%. To see how well random sampling performs, first 1,000 samples of size 500 were drawn. The sample percentage was computed for each sample. The upper part of Figure 12.3 shows the box plot of these estimates. The vertical dotted line indicates the population value to be estimated (10.4%). It is clear that the distribution is symmetric around the population value. Therefore, the sample percentage is an unbiased estimator of the population percentage.

The bottom part of Figure 12.3 shows what happens if the sample size is increased from 500 to 2,000. Again, the distribution of the sample percentage is symmetric around the population value, indicating that the estimator is unbiased. But now the variation of the values of the estimates is much smaller. This reflects the well-known rule of thumb that an estimator will be more precise if the sample size is larger.

12.4 Online surveys

Traditionally, surveys used paper questionnaires to collect data. There were three main modes of data collection: face-to-face surveys, telephone surveys, and mail surveys. Developments in information technology in the 1970s and 1980s led to the rise of computer-assisted interviewing (CAI). The paper questionnaire was replaced by a computer program asking the questions. The computer took control of the interviewing process, and it also checked the answers to the questions on the spot. Computer-assisted interviewing could also be carried out in three different modes: computer-assisted telephone interviewing (CATI), computer-assisted personal interviewing (CAPI), and computer-assisted self-interviewing (CASI).

And then came the internet. Around 1995 the first online surveys emerged. These surveys are almost always self-administered: respondents visit the survey website and complete the questionnaire by answering the questions. Online surveys became rapidly popular. This is not surprising, as online data collection has some attractive properties:

- Many people are connected to the internet, so an online survey is a simple means of getting access to a large group of potential respondents.
- Online surveys are cheap compared to other modes of data collection. No interviewers are required, and there are no travel, printing, or mailing costs.
- A survey can be set up and carried out very quickly. It is just a matter of designing a questionnaire and putting it on the internet.

So online surveys seem to be an easy, cheap, and fast means of collecting large amounts of data. Moreover, one does not have to be a survey expert to conduct an online survey. Everyone can do it. There are many software tools on the internet, some of them for free, for setting up and carrying out an online survey. A popular example is *SurveyMonkey*.

Online surveys seem attractive, but there are methodological issues. One important problem is sampling with self-selection instead of probability sampling. Self-selection is a form of non-probability sampling. It is shown in this chapter that self-selection can lead to serious estimation problems.

The importance of probability sampling was already stressed in section 12.2, as it makes it possible to compute valid (unbiased) estimates of population characteristics. Sample selection must be such that every person in the target population has a non-zero probability of selection, and all these probabilities must be known. Furthermore, probability sampling makes it possible to compute the precision of estimates.

How to select a probability sample for an online survey? The ideal situation would be to have a sampling frame consisting of e-mail addresses of all people in the target population. Then a random sample of e-mail addresses can be selected, and an e-mail can be send to the sample persons. The e-mails contain a link to the survey questionnaire. Selected persons simply click on this link to start the questionnaire.

This approach is only possible if everybody in the target population has a known e-mail address. An example is a survey conducted among students of a university, where each student has a university-supplied e-mail address and the student administration can be used as a sampling frame. Another example is an online survey among employees of a large company, where all employers have a company-supplied e-mail address.

More often there is no sampling frame of e-mail addresses. Then the sample must be selected in a different way. One approach is to first select a random sample of addresses. Next, a letter is sent to every selected address. This letter contains a link to the survey website. Respondents have to enter the link in their computer, laptop, tablet, or smartphone to start the question-naire. Another approach is to contact potential respondents by telephone (if telephone numbers are available). These two different approaches have disadvantages: they are more expensive and slower, and typing in often complex links is a source of errors.

To avoid the problems of drawing a random sample for an online survey, many survey organ-isations use self-selection. The survey questionnaire is simply put on the web. Respondents are those people who happen to have internet, encounter the survey website, and spontaneously decide to participate in the survey. Therefore, the researcher is not in control of the selection process. Participation probabilities are unknown. Hence, the principles of probability sampling cannot be applied. No unbiased estimates can be computed nor can the precision of estimates be determined. These polls are called here *self-selection surveys*. Sometimes they are also called *opt-in surveys*. A self-selection survey is a non-probability survey.

Self-selection surveys have a high risk of not being representative. Several phenomena con-tribute to this lack of representativity:

- People from outside the target population can also participate in the survey. This makes it impossible to generalise the survey results to the intended target population.
- It is sometimes possible for respondents to complete the questionnaire more than once. Even if there is a check on the IP address of the computer (the questionnaire can only be completed once on a specific computer), it is still possible for the same person to do the survey on another device (computer, laptop, tablet, or smartphone).
- Specific groups may attempt to manipulate the outcomes of the survey by calling upon the members of the group to participate in the survey and to complete the questionnaire in a way that is consistent with the objectives of the group.

- If everyone can fill in the survey questionnaire, it also becomes possible to deploy a *votebot*. This is a software tool that can automatically and repeatedly vote in an online survey. A votebot attempts to act like a human but conducts voting in an automated manner in order to influence the outcomes of a survey.

Some examples show the dangers of self-selection. The first example is the election of the 2005 Book of the Year Award (Dutch: NS Publieksprijs), a high-profile literary prize. The winning book was determined by means of an online survey. Everyone could vote by selecting one of the six nominated books or by entering the title of a different book. The winning book turned out to be the new interconfessional Bible translation launched by the Netherlands and Flanders Bible Societies. This book was not nominated, but nevertheless for an overwhelming majority (72%) it was the favourite book and therefore they voted for it. This was caused by a campaign launched by (among others) Bible societies, a Christian broadcaster, and a Christian newspaper. Although this was all completely within the rules of the contest, the group of voters could hardly be considered representative for the Dutch population.

A second example of self-selection is a series of online opinion surveys that were conducted during the campaign for the parliamentary elections in The Netherlands in 2012. A group of people tried to influence the outcomes of these surveys. By influencing the surveys, they hoped to influence the election results. The group consisted of 2,500 people. They intended to subscribe to the online opinion panel from which the surveys were taken. Their idea was to behave first as Christian Democrats (CDA). Later on, they would change their opinion and vote for the elderly party (50PLUS). They hoped this would also affect the opinion of other people. Unfortunately for them, and fortunately for the researcher, their attempt was discovered when suddenly many people at the same time subscribed to the panel. See Bronzwaer (2012) for more details about this attempt.

A third example of self-selection is an opinion survey during the campaign for the local elections in The Netherlands in 2012. A public debate was organised between local party leaders in Amsterdam. A local newspaper, *Het Parool*, conducted an online survey to find out who won the debate. Campaign teams of two parties (the Socialist Party and the Liberal-Democrats) discovered that after disabling cookies it was possible to fill in the questionnaire more than once. So the campaign teams stayed up all night and voted as many times as possible. In the morning, the leaders of these two parties had a disproportionally large number of votes. The newspaper realised that something was wrong and cancelled the poll. It accused the two political parties of manipulating the survey. It was the newspaper, however, that had conducted a bad survey (see also Bethlehem, 2014).

A fourth example is an online opinion survey during the campaign for the presidential elections in 2016 in the United States. The two main candidates were Donald Trump and Hillary Clinton. There were three debates. The third debate took place on 19 October 2016. After that debate, Breitbart News Network attempted to find out by means of a self-selection survey whether Donald Trump or Hillary Clinton had won the debate. Breitbart is a politically conservative American news, opinion, and propaganda website. Many visitors will be Republicans. Therefore, one could expect that the Republican, Donald Trump, would get more votes in the survey than the Democrat, Hillary Clinton. The left-hand side of Figure 12.4 shows the results of the survey after a couple of hours. At that moment, over 150,000 people had answered the survey question. Surprisingly, Hillary Clinton was in the lead. According to over 60% of the respondents, she had won the debate.

Breitbart claimed that the survey was infiltrated by votebots that were operated from countries such as Romania, Germany, and South Korea. Based on these votes, Hillary Clinton was

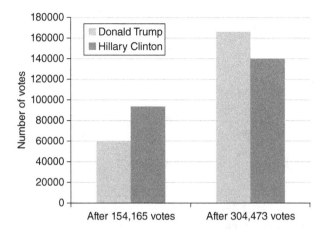

Figure 12.4   Results of the Breitbart survey after 150,000 and 300,000 votes

the overwhelming winner of the debate. Later, after 300,000 people had voted, the situation changed completely, and Donald Trump took the lead with 54% of the votes (see the right-hand side of Figure 12.4).

So, if the survey was stopped after 130,000 votes, Hillary Clinton would have been a clear winner. And after 300,000 votes, Donald Trump would have won. One must conclude this is an unreliable survey.

To obtain insight in the effects of self-selection on survey estimates, it is assumed that each person k in the target population has an *unknown participation probability* π_k, for $k = 1, 2, \ldots, N$. Bethlehem (1988) shows that the expected value of the sample mean $\bar{y}_S$ of a target variable Y is approximately equal to:

$$E(\bar{y}_S) \approx \frac{1}{N} \sum_{k=1}^{N} \frac{\pi_k}{\bar{\pi}} Y_k,$$

(12.1)

in which $\bar{\pi}$ is the mean of all participation probabilities. Hence, the bias of this estimator is approximately equal to:

$$B(\bar{y}_S) = E(\bar{y}_S) - \bar{Y} \approx \frac{R_{\pi Y} S_Y S_\pi}{\bar{\pi}},$$

(12.2)

So the magnitude of this bias depends on a number of factors:

1. The correlation $R_{\pi Y}$ between the target variable Y and participation behaviour π. A strong correlation between the values of the target variable and the participation probabilities will lead to a large bias.
2. The variation of the participation probabilities π. The more these values vary, the larger the bias will be.
3. The average participation probability $\bar{\pi}$. If people are less likely to participate in the survey, the average participation probability will be lower, and thus the bias will be larger.

To show the effects of self-selection, the simulation experiment described in section 12.3 is continued. There are active and passive users of internet in this fictitious population. Active

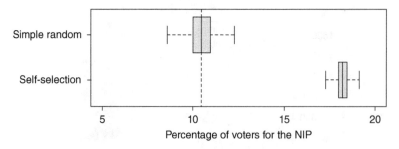

Figure 12.5   Simulation of random samples for the variable NIP

users had a participation probability of 0.95, whereas the participation probability for passive users was 0.05. So for every sample there was a random selection mechanism which included persons in the sample with probabilities equal to their participation probabilities.

Generated were 1,000 self-selection samples. The average sample size of all 1,000 samples was 1,971. Figure 12.5 shows the results of the simulation. The upper box plot contains the distribution of the estimates for random samples of fixed size 1,971. The distribution is symmetric around the population value of 10.4. There is a limited amount of variation. Clearly, the estimator is unbiased and reliable.

The lower part of Figure 12.5 shows the distribution of the estimator in case of self-selection. The distribution is symmetric, but not around the true population value. All estimates are systematically too large. So the estimator has a substantial bias. Its expected value is equal to 18.2, resulting in a bias equal to $18.2 - 10.4 = 7.8$ percentage points.

It is clear from Figure 12.5 that there are too many NIP voters in the self-selection survey. This is because internet users have a high participation probability. Typically, these people will vote for the NIP.

One can conclude that self-selection surveys can lead to biased outcomes. The problem is that estimators depend on unknown participation probabilities. Therefore, it is impossible to use such surveys for drawing valid and reliable conclusions about the population as a whole. A survey should be based on a probability sample.

Indeed, the American Association for Public Opinion Research (AAPOR) warns about the risks of self-selection (Baker et al., 2010, p. 772):

> Only when a web-based survey adheres to established principles of scientific data collection can it be characterized as representing the population from which the sample was drawn. But if it uses volunteer respondents, allows respondents to participate in the survey more than once, or excludes portions of the population from participating, it must be characterized as unscientific and is unrepresentative of any population.

Selecting a probability sample provides safeguards against various manipulations. It guarantees that sampled persons are always in the target population and that they can participate only once in the poll. The researcher is in control of the selection process.

12.5 The effect of nonresponse

If probability sampling as presented in section 12.2 is compared with non-probability sampling as described in section 12.4, the conclusion must be that it is better to prefer probability sampling, as non-probability sampling may easily lead to biased outcomes. This comparison is not completely fair. Probability sampling also can suffer from problems affecting the representativity of its outcomes. One of the most important problems is nonresponse. *Nonresponse* occurs when people in the sample do not provide the requested information. Hence, their questionnaire form remains empty.

Nonresponse has two consequences. One consequence is that the realised sample size is smaller than planned. This decreases the precision of estimates. However, if there are no other effects, valid estimates can still be obtained because computed confidence intervals still have the proper confidence level. To avoid realised samples that are too small, the initial sample size can be taken larger. For example, if a sample of 1,000 elements is required and the expected response rate is in the order of 60%, the initial sample size should be approximately 1,000 / 0.6 = 1,667.

The second, and main, problem of nonresponse is that estimates of population characteristics may be biased. This situation occurs if, due to non-response, some groups in the population are over- or underrepresented in the sample, and these groups behave differently with respect to the characteristics to be investigated. Then nonresponse is said to be *selective*.

To obtain insight in the effects of nonresponse, this phenomenon is assumed to follow the *random response model*. This model assumes every person k in the population to have an (unknown) response probability ρ_k, for $k = 1, 2, \ldots, N$. If element k is selected in the sample, a random mechanism is activated that results with probability ρ_k in response and with probability $1 - \rho_k$ in nonresponse. Bethlehem (2009, chapter 9) shows that the expected value of the response mean $\bar{y}_R$ is approximately equal to:

$$E(\bar{y}_R) \approx \frac{1}{N} \sum_{k=1}^{N} \frac{\rho_k}{\bar{\rho}} Y_k, \tag{12.3}$$

in which $\bar{\rho}$ is the mean of all response probabilities in the population. From Expression (12.3) it is clear that, generally, the expected value of the response mean is unequal to the population mean to be estimated. Therefore, this estimator is biased, where the bias is approximately equal to:

$$B(\bar{y}_R) = E(\bar{y}_R) - \bar{Y} = \frac{R_{\rho Y} S_\rho S_Y}{\bar{\rho}}, \tag{12.4}$$

where $R_{\rho Y}$ is the correlation between the values of the target variable and the response probabilities, S_ρ is the standard deviation of the response probabilities, and S_Y is the standard deviation of the target variable. From this expression of the following conclusions can be drawn:

*   The bias vanishes if there is no relationship between the target variable and response behaviour. This implies $R_{\rho Y} = 0$. The stronger the relationship between target variable and response behaviour, the larger the bias will be.
*   The bias vanishes if all response probabilities are equal. Then $S_\rho = 0$. Indeed, in this situation the nonresponse is not selective. It just leads to a reduced sample size.
*   The magnitude of the bias increases as the mean of the response probabilities decreases. Translated in practical terms, this means that lower response rates will lead to larger biases.

Response rates for general population surveys that are carried out online have a lower response rate than comparable CAPI or CATI surveys. Beukenhorst and Giesen (2010) report response rates for some online surveys of Statistics Netherlands: 21% for the Safety Monitor, 26% for the Mobility Survey, and 35% for the Health Interview Survey. Holmberg (2010) describes an experiment were respondents could choose between mail and online. Of the sample persons, only 11.8% selected the online questionnaire and 58.1% the mail questionnaire. The nonresponse was 30.1%. Those selecting the mail questionnaire did this because it was immediately available. They did not have to go to their computer, switch it on, connect to the internet, and type the appropriate link to the website.

In practice, a researcher should prefer a survey based on a probability sample. But if this survey is affected by nonresponse, one may wonder which approach is better: a probability sample with nonresponse or a self-selection sample. Both approaches will result in biased estimators. One way to look at this is to compute the worst case bias.

Expression (12.4) for the bias of the estimator under probability sampling and nonresponse can be used to compute an upper bound for the bias. Given the mean response probability $\bar{\rho}$, there is a maximum value the standard deviation S_ρ of the response probabilities cannot exceed:

$$S_\rho \leq \sqrt{\bar{\rho}(1-\bar{\rho})}. \tag{12.5}$$

This implies that in the worst case, in which S_ρ assumes its maximum value and the correlation coefficient $R_{\rho Y}$ is equal to either $+1$ or -1, the absolute value of the bias will be equal to:

$$\left|B_{max}\right| = S_Y \sqrt{\frac{1}{\bar{\rho}} - 1}. \tag{12.6}$$

This worst case value of the bias also applies in the case of self-selection. The only thing that changes is that the response probabilities $\rho_1, \rho_2, \ldots, \rho_N$ are replaced by the participation probabilities $\pi_1, \pi_2, \ldots, \pi_N$. This results in:

$$\left|B_{max}\right| = S_Y \sqrt{\frac{1}{\bar{\pi}} - 1}. \tag{12.7}$$

Using Expressions (12.6) and (12.7), several situations are compared:

- Case 1: A simple random sample is selected for a CAPI survey. The response rate is 60%. Then the worst case bias is $0.8 \subseteq S_Y$.
- Case 2: A simple random sample is selected for a telephone survey using random digit dialling (RDD). The response rate is 10%. Then the worst case bias is $3.0 \subseteq S_Y$.
- Case 3: A self-selection survey is conducted in The Netherlands. The size of the population is 12 million people (all people that can vote). The response turns out to be 120,000 respondents. Then the worst case bias is $10.0 \subseteq S_Y$.

One can conclude that the worst case bias of the self-selection survey (case 3) is 12.5 times as large as the worst case bias of the CAPI (case 1). Even in the case of the telephone survey with only 10% response (case 2), the worst case bias of the self-selection survey is still 3.3 times as large. This shows that the worst case bias of a self-selection survey will often be larger than the worst case bias of a probability survey with nonresponse. So a probability survey should be preferred, even when it is affected by nonresponse.

12.6 Reducing the bias

It is likely that a non-probability survey will result in biased estimates. And if a probability survey is affected by nonresponse, estimates will also be biased. So in both cases, researchers run the risk of drawing wrong conclusions. Therefore it is always important to correct the outcomes of a survey for the lack of representativity. The way to do this is to apply adjustment weighting.

Adjustment weighting means restoring the representativity of the survey. This is achieved by assigning weights to all respondents. In the computation of estimates, each respondent will not count for 1 anymore, but for the associated weight. Persons in underrepresented groups get a weight larger than 1, and persons in overrepresented groups get a weight smaller than 1.

To compute correction weights, auxiliary variables are required. These are variables that have been measured in the survey and for which the population distribution is available. Examples of much-used auxiliary variables are demographic variables like gender, age, education, and geographical region. Adjustment weighting will only be effective if the auxiliary variables satisfy the following two conditions:

1. They must have a strong relationship with the target variables of the survey. Together, the auxiliary variables must be able to explain the target variables. If there is no relationship, weighting will not reduce the bias of estimates for the target variables.
2. They must have a strong relationship with the response behaviour in the survey. Together, the auxiliary variables must be able to explain response/participation behaviour. If the auxiliary variables are unrelated to response/participation behaviour, adjustment weighting will not remove or reduce an existing bias.

The idea of adjustment weighting is to make the response representative with respect to the auxiliary variables. This is accomplished by computing correction weights in such a way that the weighted distribution of each auxiliary variable in the response equals the corresponding population distribution. The correction weights for underrepresented groups will be larger than 1, and those for overrepresented groups will be smaller than 1.

If it is possible to make the response representative with respect to a set of auxiliary variables, and all these auxiliary variables have a strong relationship with the target variables, the weighted response will also become (approximately) representative with respect to the target variables. Therefore, estimates based on the weighted response will be better than estimates based on the unweighted response.

To show the effects of weighting, the simulation experiment described in sections 12.3 and 12.4 is continued. Figures 12.6 and 12.7 contain the results. The upper box plot in Figure 12.6 shows the distribution of the estimator for the variable NIP if simple random samples are selected. The box plot is based on 1,000 samples of size 1,971. The distribution is symmetric around the true population value (10.4), which means the estimator is unbiased.

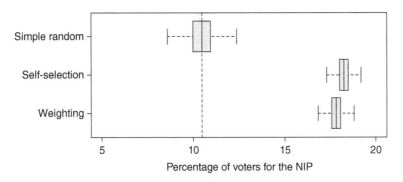

Figure 12.6 Simulation of weighting adjustment for the variable NIP

The middle box plot in Figure 12.6 shows the distribution of the estimator in case of self-selection. There are active and passive internet users in this fictitious population of 100,000 people. Active users have a high participation probability of 0.95, whereas passive users have a low participation probability of 0.05. This estimator has a serious bias. Its expected value is 18.2, which means the bias is equal to 18.2 − 10.4 = 7.8 percentage points.

For the bottom box plot in Figure 12.6, again 1,000 self-selection samples were generated. This time the results for each sample were weighted by the auxiliary age (in three categories). As can be seen in Figure 12.6, adjustment weighting only has a minimal effect here: the expected value of the estimator reduces from 18.2 to 17.8. This is still far from the true value of 10.4. So adjustment weighting did not help here. This is not surprising as there is only a weak relationship between age and participation behaviour.

Figure 12.7 shows the result of simulations with another variable: voting for the National Elderly Party (NEP). Voting for this party is largely determined by age. So weighting by age should reduce the bias. The upper box plot in Figure 12.7 shows the distribution of the estimator for simple random sampling. The expected value of this estimator is equal to the population value (25.6). So this estimator is unbiased.

The middle box plot in Figure 12.7 shows the distribution of the estimator in the case self-selection. The estimates are substantially lower. The expected value of the estimator is 24.0. So the magnitude of the bias is here 24.0 − 25.6 = −1.6 percent point.

The lower box plot in Figure 12.7 displays the distribution of the estimator after weighting by the variable age. Adjustment weighting is effective here. The bias is completely removed. So weighting works. Comparing the simulations in Figures 12.6 and 12.7, it is clear that the availability of effective auxiliary variables is of critical importance.

These simulation examples show that weighting adjustment can remove or reduce the bias of estimates. However, it should be realised that weighting adjustment is only effective if the proper weighting variables are used. If not, wrong conclusions maybe drawn from the survey. An iconic example shows what can go wrong. It is sometimes called the 'UK polling disaster'. All pre-election opinion surveys for the general election of 7 May 2015 in the UK were systematically wrong. They all predicted a neck-and-neck race between the Conservative Party and the Labour Party, but the election resulted in a comfortable majority for the Conservative Party.

The dot plot in Figure 12.8 summarises the polling disaster. It compares the predictions for the difference between the Conservative Party and the Labour Party with the true election result. The big points represent the predictions of the survey organisations just before the

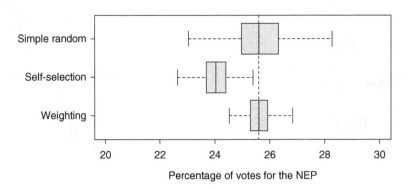

Figure 12.7   Simulation of weighting adjustment for the variable NEP

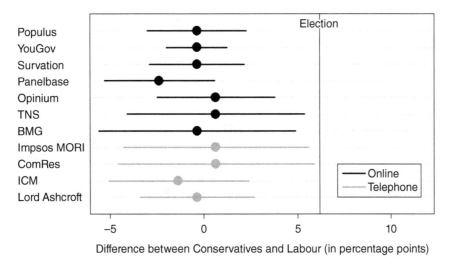

Figure 12.8 The polling disaster in the UK of 7 May 2015

election. It is clear that all differences are around zero. The vertical line represents the election result, which is a difference of 6.5 percentage points. So the Conservatives got 6.5 percentage points more than Labour. The horizontal line segments represent the margins of error of the election surveys. They assume probability samples were drawn. The election result is outside these margins. This means that all survey results differ significantly from the value to be estimated.

The poll disaster caused a lot of concern about the accuracy of the election surveys in the UK. Therefore, the British Polling Council (BPC), an association of survey organisations, decided to conduct an independent enquiry into the possible causes of the problems and to make recommendations for future polling. The inquiry panel concluded that the primary cause of the failure was the lack of representativity of the samples selected by the survey organisations. Labour voters were systematically overrepresented, and conservative voters were systematically underrepresented. Moreover, weighting adjustment procedures were not effective in reducing the bias in the predictions. See Sturgis et al. (2016) or Bethlehem (2018) for more details.

The first seven surveys in Figure 12.8 were online surveys. These surveys were based on online panels that were recruited by means of self-selection. So there was no guarantee that these panels were representative. Hence, random samples from these online panels also lacked representativity.

Four of the survey organisations in Figure 12.8 used telephone surveys. This mode of data collection is not without problems. Random samples can be generated with RDD, but response rates are very low, which may result in a serious bias.

Of course, the polling organisations attempted to remove or reduce the bias of their estimators by carrying adjustment weighting. A potentially effective weighting variable would be the vote at the previous election. This variable can only be used if it was measured properly. Measurement can be affected by recall problems. So, it is not a good idea to ask for previous voting behaviour after, say, four or five years. It is important to store voting behaviour in the panel database immediately after the corresponding election.

12.7 Conclusions

This chapter compared probability surveys with non-probability surveys. The comparison focused on online surveys. The conclusion is that online surveys based on random sampling should be preferred over online surveys based on self-selection. Although self-selection online surveys are faster and cheaper, there are serious risks of biased estimates.

If there is no nonresponse, probability surveys should always be preferred, as these surveys will not be biased. If there is nonresponse, probability surveys may also be biased. The worst case bias was introduced to compare the bias of probability and non-probability biases. It turns out that the worst case bias of self-selection bias is much larger than that of a probability surveys.

If a self-selection survey is carried out, it is of vital importance to perform some kind of weighting adjustment. This requires the availability of sufficient and effective auxiliary variables. Often this is not the case. In this case, weighting adjustment will only reduce the bias, not remove it.

Examples show that many online surveys are self-selection surveys. Therefore, one should be careful with the possibly biased outcomes. Survey reports should always document the way in which the sample was selected (at random or by means of self-selection).

The conclusions of this paper are in line with other papers comparing probability and non-probability surveys. Two examples are mentioned here. Brüggen et al. (2016) compared the accuracy of results obtained from 18 Dutch self-selection online panels with results obtained from random samples in online and face-to-face surveys. The non-probability samples yielded less accurate estimates of proportions and notably different relationships between variables than did the probability samples. Moreover, these differences were not eliminated by weighting adjustment.

MacInnes et al. (2018) describe a comparison of surveys in the US using a variety of probability and non-probability sampling methods, using a set of 50 measures and 40 benchmark variables. They found that, despite a substantial drop in response rates, probability samples for telephone and online were most accurate. Adjustment weighting using demographic variables did not change their conclusions.

References

Baker, R., Blumberg, S. J., Brick, J. M., Couper, M. P., Courtright, M., Dennis, J. M., . . . Zahs, D. (2010). Research synthesis: AAPOR report on online panels. *Public Opinion Quarterly*, 74, 711–781. https://doi.org/10.1093/poq/nfq048

Bethlehem, J. G. (1988). Reduction of the nonresponse bias through regression estimation. *Journal of Official Statistics*, 4, 251–260. www.scb.se/contentassets/ca21efb41fee47d293bbee5bf7be7fb3/reduction-of-nonresponse-bias-through-regression-estimation.pdf

Bethlehem, J. G. (2009). *Applied survey methods, a statistical perspective*. John Wiley & Sons.

Bethlehem, J. G. (2014). *Slechte peiling, gemanipuleerde uitslag* (in Dutch). http://peilingpraktijken.nl

Bethlehem, J. G. (2018). *Understanding public opinion polls*. CRC Press and Taylor & Francis. https://doi.org/10.1201/9781315154220

Beukenhorst, D., & Giesen, D. (2010). *Internet use for data collection at statistics Netherlands*. Paper presented at the 2nd International Workshop on Internet Survey Methods, Daejoeon, South Korea.

Bowley, A. L. (1906). Address to the economic science and statistics section of the British association for the advancement of science. *Journal of the Royal Statistical Society*, 69, 548–557.

Bronzwaer, S. (2012, September 13). *Infiltranten probeerden de peilingen van Maurice de Hond te manipuleren* (in Dutch). NRC. www.nrc.nl/nieuws/2012/09/13/infiltranten-deden-hackpoging-peilingen-maurice-de-hond-a1441762

Brüggen, E., Van den Brakel, J., & Krosnick, J. (2016). *Establishing the accuracy of online panels for survey research* (Discussion Paper 2016|04). Statistics Netherlands. www.cbs.nl/-/media/_pdf/2016/15/2016-dp04-establishing-the-accuracy-of-online-panels-for-survey-research.pdf

Cochran, W. G. (1977). *Sampling techniques* (3rd ed.). John Wiley & Sons.

Holmberg, A. (2010). *Using the Internet in individual and household surveys, summarizing some experiences at statistics Sweden*. Paper presented at the 2nd International Workshop on Internet Survey Methods.

Horvitz, D. G., & Thompson, D. J. (1952). A generalization of sampling without replacement from a finite universe. *Journal of the American Statistical Association, 47*, 663–685.

Kiaer, A. N. (1895). Observations et expériences concernant des dénombrements représentatives. *Bulletin of the International Statistical Institute, IX*, Book 2, 176–183.

MacInnes, B., Krosnick, J. A., Ho, A. S., & Cho, M. J. (2018). The accuracy of measurement with probability and nonprobability survey samples, replication and extension. *Public Opinion Quarterly, 82*, 707–744. http://doi:10.1093/poq/nfy038

Neyman, J. (1934). On the two different aspects of the representative method: The method of stratified sampling and the method of purposive selection. *Journal of the Royal Statistical Society, 97*, 558–606.

Sturgis, P., Baker, N., Callegaro, M., Fisher, S., Green, J., Jennings, W., . . . Smith, P. (2016). *Report of the enquiry into the 2015 British general election opinion polls*. Market Research Society and British Polling Council. http://eprints.ncrm.ac.uk/3789/1/Report_final_revised.pdf

SECTION III

Statistical modelling and simulation

13

LARGE-SCALE AGENT-BASED SIMULATION AND CROWD SENSING WITH MOBILE AGENTS

Stefan Bosse

1 Introduction

The investigation of socio-technical aspects in society, business, and industry requires accurate models and tools to test the models for validity and conformance to real-world phenomena. Commonly, field studies (surveys) and simulations are used to study effects of behaviour and networking models on populations and to determine model parameters. Field studies are performed in real-world environments, whereas simulation is performed in a closed-box virtual world.

Agent-based methods are established for modelling and studying complex dynamical systems and for implementing distributed intelligent systems, for example in traffic and transportation control (Hamidi & Kamankesh, 2018; Hox, 2017; Wang, 2005). Therefore, agent-based methods can be divided into five main classes (Baqueiro et al., 2008):

1. Agent-based modelling (ABM) – Modelling of complex dynamic systems by using the agent behaviour and interaction model $\Rightarrow$ *Physical agents*
2. Agent-based computing (ABC) – Distributed and parallel computing using mobile agents related to mobile software processes $\Rightarrow$ *Computational agents*
3. Agent-based simulation (ABS) – Simulation with physical agents to simulate distributed multi-entity systems or simulation of computational agents
4. Agent-based modelling and simulation (ABMS) – the agent model is part of the study resulting in a close modelling and simulation using the agent behaviour and interaction model
5. Agent-based spatial modelling and simulation (ABSS) – extending the simulation world with spatial data and geographical information systems

Two promising fields of current studies in computer science are data mining and agent-based modelling and simulation (Baqueiro et al., 2008). Agent-based simulation is suitable for modelling complex social systems with respect to interaction between individual entities, manipulation of the world, spatial movement, and emergence effects of groups of entities. The main advantage is the bottom-up modelling approach composing large-scale complex systems by

DOI: 10.4324/9781003025245-16

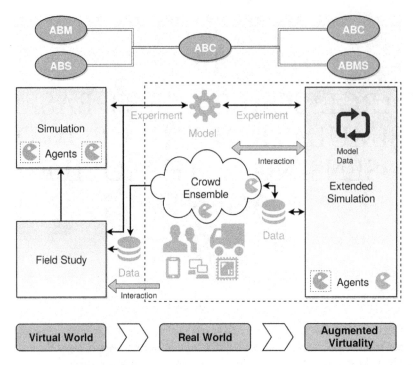

Figure 13.1 (top) The four different agent-based methods with overlapping relations – ABM: agent-based modelling, ABC: agent-based computing, ABS: agent-based simulation, and ABMS: agent-based modelling and simulation; (bottom) transition from separated field studies and simulation towards extended simulation merging real and virtual worlds

simple entity models. The main disadvantage of ABM is the (over-)simplified entity behaviour and simplification of the world the entities are acting in. Commonly, simulation is based on synthetic data or data retrieved by field studies. Many simulations and models lack the diversity existing in the real world. Commonly, sensor and model data (parameters) used in simulations (virtual world) are retrieved from experiments or field studies (real world), as shown in Figure 13.1. But there is neither a feedback from the virtual to the real world nor an interaction of the real world with the virtual world and vice versa.

ABS and ABMS are commonly constructed using collections of condition-action rules to be able to perceive and react to their situation, to pursue the goals they are given, and to interact with other agents, for example by sending them messages (Gilbert, 2004). The *NetLogo* simulator is an example of an established ABS tool that is used in the social and natural sciences (Wilensky & Rand, 2015), but it is limited to behavioural simulation only (ABM domain). In this work, a different simulation approach combining ABM, ABC, and ABS methodologies is used deploying the widely used programming language JavaScript. JavaScript is used increasingly as a generic programming language for ABC and ABS (Bosse & Engel, 2018; Calenda et al., 2016).

Mobile devices like smartphones are valuable sources for social data (Ganti et al., 2011), either by participatory crowd sensing with explicit participation of users providing first-class data (e.g., performing surveys or polls) or implicitly by opportunistic crowd sensing collecting secondary-class data, that is, traces of device sensor data delivering, for example actual position, ambient conditions, network connectivity, digital media interaction, and so on. Crowd sensing and social data mining as a data source contribute more and more to investigations of digital traces in large-scale machine-human environments characterised by complex interactions and causalities between perception and action (decision-making).

But mobile devices are not limited to being sensors. They can be used as actuators, too, by interacting with the user via chat dialogues or social media that can affect user behaviour (e.g., mobility decisions, consumer control). Moreover, mobile networks can be coupled with device and machine networks (i.e., the Internet of Things) creating augmented data and enabling advanced spatial and contextual tracking.

It is difficult to study such large-scale data collection, data mining, and their effect on societies, domestic services, and social interaction in field studies due to a lack of reliable data and complexity. Agent-based modelling of socio-technical systems is well established (van Dam et al., 2013) and can be applied for smart city management, however commonly applied in an artificial world., that is, a simulation is performed in virtual reality worlds only to derive and proof models under hard limitations. In this work, a new concept and framework for augmented virtual reality simulation is introduced that is suitable for, but not limited to, investigating large-scale socio-technical systems. Mobile agents are already used successfully in-field crowd sensing (Leppäne et al., 2017). In this work, mobile agents are used to combine in-field ubiquitous crowd sensing, for example performed by mobile devices, with simulation.

A chat bot agent (i.e., a dialogue robot) can perform dynamic and situation-aware dialogues with humans to get empirical data into the simulation and to propagate synthetic data from the simulation world into the real world. The chat bot can act as an avatar providing information for users, for example for optimised and dynamic traffic control based on real (covering actual and historical data) and simulated data (addressing future predictions).

The chat bot agents (as computational agents) can operate in both real and virtual worlds, including games, and provide a fusion of both worlds by seamless migration. Agents are loosely coupled to their environment and platform and interact with each other via tuple spaces (generative communication) and via uni-cast or broadcast signals. Mobility is provided by agent process snapshot migration between platforms.

The novel multi-agent system (MAS) based crowd sensing and simulation methodology, introduced in the next sections, is suitable for combining social and computational simulations with real-world interaction at run-time and in real time, for example by integrating crowd sensing, using mobile agents. Two classes of mobility can be modelled in the simulation: (1) social mobility on short- and long-term time scales and (2) plan-driven traffic mobility.

The crowd sensing performed by mobile agents can be used to create digital twins of real humans (with respect to the social and technical interaction model and mobility) based on individual surveys and user information collected via a chat bot dialogue.

Among the capabilities of real-time simulation, the simulation framework can create simulation snapshot copies that can be simulated in parallel in non-real time to get future predictions (simulation branches) from actual simulation states that can be back propagated into the current real-time simulation world.

The following sections introduce the agent-based methodologies addressing augmented simulation and mobile crowd sensing. Fundamental concepts enabling the augmentation of simulation is the concept of digital twin derived from survey data (off- and online) and the concept of physical and computational agents. Finally, two demonstrations and use cases are provided to show the power of the agent-based augmented simulation approach coupling real and virtual worlds.

2 Agent models and architectures

Basically, three different agent behaviour model and architecture classes can be distinguished:

1. Pure functional reactive agents
2. State-based reactive agents
3. Deliberative and knowledge-based agents, that is, corresponding to the well-known believes-desires-intention (BDI) architecture

The second class of state-based reactive agents is close to well-known programming models and can be found in ABM, ABC, and ABS domains. The *NetLogo* agent model belongs to this class, too. In the next section, the unified agent model used in this work is introduced and briefly discussed.

2.1 ATG behaviour model

Details of the unified agent model can be found in Bosse (2016, 2018), and details about the used agent processing platform *JAM* can be found in Bosse and Engel (2018).

To summarise, the agent behaviour model is purely reactive and state based, shown in Figure 13.2. An agent consists of code and private data (body variables). The code describes the agent behaviour consisting of activities executing actions. Typical actions are:

- Agent creation and termination
- Agent replication
- Agent behaviour modification (changing activities and/or transitions)
- Agent mobility
- Agent communication
- Computation

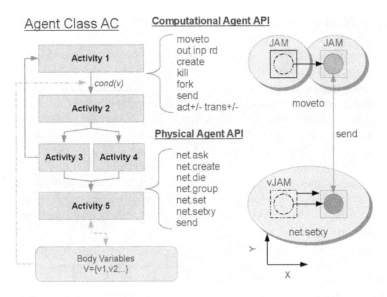

Figure 13.2 (left) Activity-transition graph (ATG) behaviour and data model of an agent for a specific class AC; (middle) physical and computational agents differ in their action set; (right) migration and communication between physical and computational agents

There are conditional and unconditional transitions between activities. The conditions access agent body variables only. Both code and data are mobile, and an agent process snapshot can migrate between two agent platforms. Activities of an agent represent intentions and micro goals, for example changing the spatial position, modifying the environment, communicating with other agents, and replicating agents. Agent processes support the concept of control path blocking, that is, the agent processing can be suspended for waiting for an event or the satisfaction of a constraint condition. Replication creates either copies of the generating agent (forking) or new agents instantiated by an agent class.

In contrast to commonly used reactive agent behaviour models, the ATG can be modified by the agent itself offering self-adaptivity. An agent can remove or add activities and transitions, providing either sub-classing (specialisation) or learning.

Agents can communicate via tuple spaces (data driven) providing generative communication and by using signal messages (agent driven), basically used by parent–child agent groups. Physical and computational agents can communicate via signals to synchronise or to exchange data.

3 Augmented virtuality

There is a significant difference between traditional closed-world simulations and simulations coupled with real-world and real-time environments (so-called human-in-the-loop simulation). Closed simulations are performed on a short time scale with preselected use cases and input data. The simulation can be processed stepwise without a relation to a physical clock. In contrast, open-loop simulation requires continuous simulation on a large time scale creating big data volumes. A relation to a physical clock is required, too.

The spatial mapping of physical on virtual worlds and vice versa is another issue to be handled. There are basically three possible scenarios and world mapping models (illustrated in Figure 13.3):

1. The real and virtual worlds are isolated (no agent/human/entity of one world is aware of the existence of humans and entities in the other world)
2. The real world is mapped on the virtual simulation world (simulating the real world with agents representing real and artificial humans or entities)
3. The virtual world extends the real world, for example by a game world, and real and virtual entities are aware of each other and can interact with each other, for example by smartphone software

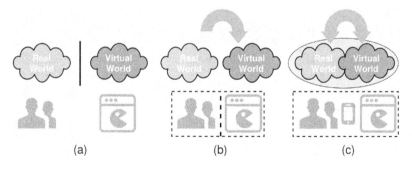

Figure 13.3 (a) Real world only deployed with humans separated from virtual world; (b) non-overlapping real and virtual worlds; (c) overlapping real and virtual worlds

In this work, real worlds can be coupled in real-time (1) unidirectionally R $\Rightarrow$ V by crowd sensing only or (2) bidirectionally R $\Leftrightarrow$ V by crowd sensing and agent-based communication interacting with technical devices (e.g., traffic signs, streetlights).

4 Virtual sensors, big data, data mining, and digital traces

According to McGrath and Scanaill (2014), a large-scale sensing application is composed of different horizontal domain layers:

1. Sensing and perception
2. Aggregation
3. Applications

Each horizontal layer is deployed with the following vertical processing layers:

1. Communication
2. Data processing
3. Security
4. Storage

Although the first vertical domain layer is represented mostly by physical sensors, all the layers can be represented by virtual sensors. A virtual sensor is a software component acting as a sensor data aggregator. Each sensor component is treated as a sensor, processing an input stream and computing an output data stream. Each physical sensor (data source) is a "data stream" transformer, too, but based on physical principles. In this work, user-provided first-class data are considered as physical sensors, too. A virtual sensor is a processing system as well as a data storage (database). In this work, virtual sensors are represented by mobile agents, performing the sensing, aggregation, and application (or delivery) of accumulated and processed sensor data. The mobility enables self-organising and adaptive mining systems controlled by environmental constraints rather than by individual users. In McGrath and Scanaill (2014), users using a smartphone app are considered as agents. This role is replaced in this work by the deployment of agents that perform tasks autonomously.

A virtual sensor consists of different components. The environment of a sensor is a set of input streams of data generated from physical or virtual sensors. The environment defines the context within which the virtual sensor operates. An aggregator processes the input streams and performs sensor data fusion, shown in Figure 13.4 (left). A filter produces a set of output streams, that is, generated by the replication of agents. Virtual sensors can be coupled in graph-like virtual networks via agent interaction (using signal messages and tuple exchange), as shown in Figure 13.4 (right). These virtual sensor networks compose processing chains (user defined or ad hoc and self-organising). Virtual sensors can operate in real-world environments (e.g., executed on mobile devices) or in virtual worlds (simulation) and are commonly related to a local context (spatial, temporal, and situation context). Agents implement the sensor data aggregator and filter function, performing fusion, storage, and communication, and represent mobile transport entities with distributed data-directed information processing. Agent processing is virtualised by a unified agent-processing platform (e.g., JAM, see section 13.9).

Digital trace data are not error-free. Even unobtrusive measures may suffer from measurement error and bias. If subjects are aware of being research subjects, this influences their communication and interaction behaviour, including answer behaviour in surveys. That is, surveys

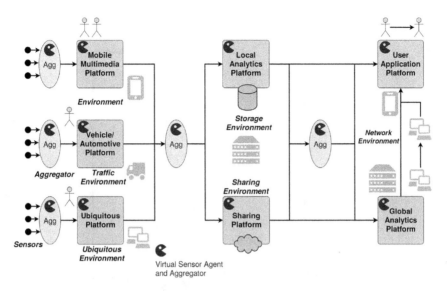

Figure 13.4 Mobile agents as virtual sensors performing sensor fusion (aggregation) connecting platform networks of virtual sensors and sensing, aggregation, and application software layers

and crowd sensing are reactive and state-based; subjects react to being researched. On the other hand, big data means the collection of data already generated. Although users are not aware of sampling this kind of data, the data is noisy and biased and highly uncorrelated.

Crowd data can be considered as natively occurring data in contrast to data from surveys and experiments and the typically associated biases through experimental effects and group effects. Computational analyses of big data offer a welcome counterpoint and potential triangulation of multi-method confirmation of key findings in experiments and surveys.

Therefore, sensor data aggregation, filtering, and fusion by such a virtual sensor architecture is vital for meaningful information derivation from large data sets collected from untrusted devices and users.

From the social science perspective, concerns about the reliability and validity of measurements have been raised in various critical papers on big data research. Although this is beyond the scope of this work, these aspects have to be addressed already on the technology and information processing level. Among the most frequently discussed issues are (1) comparatively shallow measures, (2) lack of context awareness, and (3) a dominance of automated methods of analysis (Mahrt & Scharkow, 2013; McFarland et al., 2014).

Despite the framework proposed in this work, these relevant issues have to be addressed by further investigations using and applying the agent-driven augmented virtual reality approach dealing with big data and meaningful and trustful analysis. Digital traces annotating data with additional information (e.g., trust probabilities, class of data, data source, reliability, proofs) generated by physical and virtual sensors are essential for robust data mining and decision-making. Agents are suitable for recording the data collection, interpreting and assessing the data immediately (at location), and changing data exploration strategies on environmental perception dynamically.

5 Workflow

Figure 13.5 shows the principal work and data flow of the proposed architecture, consisting of agent-based modelling (a formal mode or a software module for modelling the behaviour of

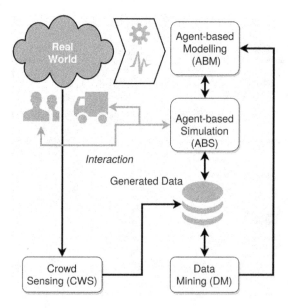

Figure 13.5 Principal work and data flow integrating agent-based crowd sensing in agent-based modelling and simulation

physical agents) as input for the agent-based simulation framework, a database containing generated input and output of the simulation, data mining (DM) modules for deriving information
from statistical weakly uncorrelated data including machine learning (ML), and crowd sensing
components. The database is continuously updated during simulation and sensing.

The ABMS relies on generated data stored in a database provided by an initial data set and
data sets derived by DM with sensor data from crowd sensing. The crowd sensing is performed
by mobile chat bot agents (computational agents). The simulation uses data from the database
as input and produces newly generated output data to the database. The data flow between the
real and virtual worlds is bidirectional, and agents can carry data generated by the simulation to
mobile devices and users in the real world.

6 Crowd sensing and surveys

The basic crowd sensing and survey architectures can be classified in

1. Centralised crowd sensing architecture with a single master instance (crowd sourcer)
2. Decentralised crowd sensing architecture with multiple master crowd sourcer instances
3. Self-organising and ad hoc crowd sensing architecture without any crowd sourcer master
   instances (Figure 13.6)

The first class is the typical web-based survey architecture. The surveys are performed with
static or dynamic forms contained in web pages. There is typically a negotiation between the
sourcer and user, or the users participating the survey are selected randomly from register databases.

The survey architecture introduced in this work relates to the second decentralised approach,
although it can be extended with a decentralised and self-organised approach, too, handled by
the same framework and mobile chat bot agents.

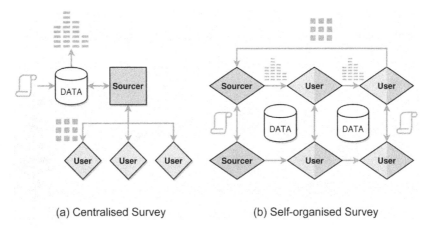

(a) Centralised Survey   (b) Self-organised Survey

Figure 13.6 Different crowd sensing and survey architectures and strategies with data sourcer and users providing data: (a) Centralised architecture and (b) decentralised and self-organised architecture with changing roles of the participants (sourcer/user of surveys and data)

Using classical data collection, the survey aims to create digital twins in the virtual world from survey participants in the real world by deriving twin behaviour model parameters from the survey answers and auxiliary sensor data (e.g., spatial position), discussed in the next section. The survey is performed by chat bot agents that can perform dynamic dialogues based on answers and context.

In this work, mobile computational agents are used to perform self-organised mobile crowd sensing for survey participation primarily on mobile devices using and chat bot agents.

The crowd sensing via mobile chat bot agents enables the interaction of real humans with agents and digital twins in the simulation world in real time and vice versa. The digital twins as well as the artificial physical agents in the simulation can interact by dynamically created (influenced) dialogues reflecting the state of the simulation world.

The survey performed by chat bot agents (computational agents) aims to create digital twins in the virtual world from survey participants in the real world by deriving twin behaviour model parameters P from the survey feedback answers F retrieved by a user dialogue D. The survey is performed by chat bot agents that can execute dynamic dialogues via a chat dialogue platform based on previous answers and context.

Mobile agents, for example chat bots, can be used to carry information from one location to another. This is typically achieved by transferring a process snapshot of the agents (including data and control state of the agent) between agent processing platforms and computing devices.

Moreover, mobile devices deployed with an agent processing platform and carrying mobile agents can be used to collect, carry, and distribute data within large regions via tuple space databases without direct communication connectivity, shown in principle in Figure 13.7. The virtual simulation world is just another region in the mobility regions of agents, and chat bots performing crowd sensing can migrate between real and virtual worlds seamlessly.

7 Digital twins

Commonly, simulation is performed with artificial agent models derived from theoretical considerations or experimental data. Augmented virtuality enables dynamic simulations with agents representing real humans (or crowds). By using crowd sensing, it is possible to create digital

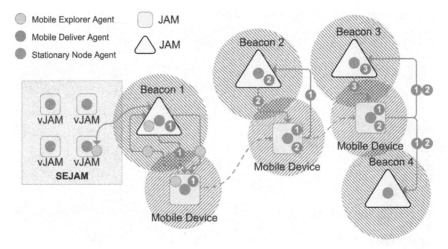

Figure 13.7   Computational agents can migrate between simulation and real-world hardware via beacons. Mobile devices can carry computational agents and extend the spatial interaction range of agents. Agents can change the mobile host devices via beacons, too.

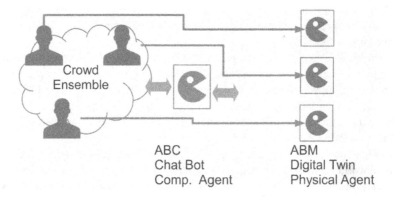

Figure 13.8   Creation of digital twins via chat bot agents from real humans

twins of real humans based on a parameterisable behaviour and interaction model. The parameters of artificial humans in the simulation represented by physical agents are collected by sensor data, that is, surveys optionally fusioned with physical sensors like GPS, performed by computational exploration and chat bot agents.

Physical agents can be equipped with a mental state based on a knowledge base enabling reasoning and deduction. The digital twins as well as the artificial physical agents in the simulation can interact with humans in the real world by dynamically created (influenced) dialogues reflecting the state of the simulation world.

The framework utilising the creation of digital twins, shown in Figure 13.8, can simulate different environments in quasi-experimental setups. Controlling all aspects of the virtual world allows an explanation of the source of structural variation in human interactions, that is, tackles the hard-to-observe mechanisms of micro-macro interactions.

A general agent behaviour model maps the environment state set E by perception P, state I, and knowledge D on plans and actions A, and can be composed of the following functions:

$$
\begin{aligned}
&ag : E \rightarrow A \\
&see : E \rightarrow P \\
&belief(\Psi) : \Psi \times P \times D \rightarrow D \\
&next(\Psi) : \Psi \times I \times D \times P \rightarrow I \\
&action(\Psi) : \Psi \times I \rightarrow A
\end{aligned}
\tag{13.1}
$$

The parameter set $\Psi = \{p_1, p_2, ..., p_i\}$ of the behaviour model (e.g., social interaction, social expectation, motivation for migration) determines individual behaviour and is derived from real humans via the chat bots.

8 Physical and computational agents

In ABM, agents represent natural and physical entities, that is, humans, animals, machines, all posing some physical interaction. The physical agents spawn a network graph with nodes representing the natural entities and their behaviour. The edges of the network graph represent social and physical interaction. In contrast, in ABC, agents represent software used for computing. These agents spawn a network graph consisting of nodes representing computers and edges representing digital communication.

The approach of augmented virtuality integrates both kinds of agents in one unified agent environment.

8.1 Physical agents

A physical agent is characterised by a behaviour consisting of social and world interaction, mobility, replication and evaluation, and cognitive capabilities. A physical agent (except robots) can only exist in simulation worlds with an abstraction of the world and the physical agent behaviour. A physical agent requires a body, that is, its own agent platform. Mobility of physical agents means mobility of the body platform carrying the agent. Physical agents can create computational agents, for example chat bot agents, originally bound to the physical agent platform node but capable of migrating to other platform nodes.

8.2 Computational agents

A computational agent is characterised by a program that performs computation, access to physical sensors, data exchange and synchronisation with other agents, mobility, replication, and learning. A computational agent is a distributed computing paradigm and can exist (and can be executed) in real and virtual simulation worlds. Computational agents require an execution platform. Mobility of computational agents means the migration of a process snapshot of the agent program. But the agent platform can be mobile itself, for example mobile host devices like smartphones.

Interaction of computational agents are based primarily on synchronised data exchange, for example using tuple spaces of signals.

Computational agents can be created by physical agents, as shown in Figure 13.9. The migration of a computational agent from a node of a physical agent to another platform (either a platform executing computational agents only or a body platform of another physical agent)

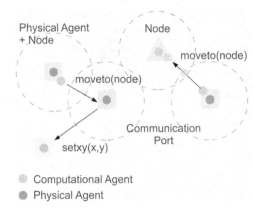

Figure 13.9 Physical and computational agents acting in one world

requires communication ports, for example virtual wireless communication channels. Only nodes with overlapping communication ranges can interact with each other, that is, computational agents are able to migrate between these nodes or communicate with each other remotely.

9 Agent-based simulation software

The following features of a simulation environment for augmented virtuality are required:

1. The simulation environment has to be capable of modelling and executing physical and computational agents with a unified programming model.
2. The simulation environment requires a network communication interface connecting to the Internet for the migration of computational agents from the virtual in the real world and vice versa.
3. The simulation environment has to provide unified virtual (logical) agent processing platforms for the processing of physical and computational agents.

The *NetLogo* simulation (Wilensky & Rand, 2015) is well known and established for modelling and simulating societies of physical agents based on a discretised patch grid world, agents with visual properties, and set iterations. But it lacks the integration of computational agents that can interact with physical agents and the real world (that is, humans via the Internet).

The migration of computational agents requires efficient process check-pointing creating code and data snapshots that can be transferred via a communication link from one to another agent processing platform. The state snapshot must contain:

- The control state (instruction pointer)
- The private data state (body variables)
- The agent behaviour code
- Environmental state information

The snapshot creation requires serialisation and deserialisation of the code and the data in host platform–independent byte code format or textual strings. Compiled code shows a strong dependency on the platform, and there is commonly no direct code-text conversion available (requiring disassembler and assembler). Interpreted languages avoid these issues but commonly lack execution performance. There are basically two exceptions: JavaScript and Lua. Both languages are always parsed on text level, commonly compiled partially to byte code, and finally processed with an additional just-in-time (JIT) compiler creating optimised native machine code at run-time. Although there is hidden byte and native code compilation, the text-code dualism is preserved, and anytime data and functions can be serialised to text and deserialised to code, too. JavaScript can be executed on a wide range of devices and in a wide range of application programs, including web browsers, making this language an ideal candidate for an agent behaviour programming language, addressing physical and computational agents.

10 Agent-based computing with the JavaScript Agent Machine (JAM)

JAM is the JavaScript Agent Machine, implemented entirely in portable JavaScript. *JAM* executes reactive agents based on the activity-transition-graph behaviour model (ATG), programmed in *AgentJS* (subset of JavaScript with some minor changes).

JAM can be executed on any JS virtual machine (VM), for example node.js, spidermonkey with web browsers, and the new low-resource machine *jvm* (based on Samsung's jerryscript and Iot.js). *Jvm* can be used on any host platform, including Android and iOS mobile devices or microcontroller-based beacons (Raspberry PI). Finally, *JAM* can be integrated in Cordova-based apps for Android and IOS devices, for example used for and performing crowd sensing with participatory and ad hoc opportunistic user interaction.

JAM agents are composed of activities performing actions (computation, interaction, mobility) and (conditional) transitions between activities based on the agent state. Activities represent short-term goals (commitments and intentions in terms of the belief-desires-intention (BDI) agent architecture). The behaviour of a reactive activity-based agent is characterised by an agent state, which is changed by activities. Activities perform perception, plan actions, and execute actions modifying the control and data state of the agent. The agent behaviour and the action on the environment is encapsulated in agent classes (see Definition 13.1), with activities representing the control state of the agent reasoning engine and conditional transitions connecting and enabling activities. Activities provide procedural agent processing by sequential execution of data processing and control statements. Agents can be instantiated from a specific class at run-time.

```
 1:  // Agent Class Constructor
 2:  function ac (p_1,p_2,..) {
 3:     // 1. Body Variables
 4:     this.v_1 = expression
 5:     this.v_2 = expression
 6:     ..
 7:     // 2. Activities
 8:     this.act = {
 9:        a_1 : function () {statements},
10:        a_2 : function () {statements},
11:        ..
12:        a_n : function () {statements}
13:     }
14:     // 3. Transitions of Activities
15:     this.trans = {
```

```
16:       aᵢ : aⱼ,
17:       aⱼ : function () {return aₓ},
18:       ..
19:    }
20:    // 4. Optional Signal Handlers
21:    this.on = {
22:       sig : function (arg,from) {statements},
23:       ..
24:    }
25:    // 5. The "Program Counter"
26:    this.next = aᵢ
27: }
```

Definition 13.1: Agent behaviour class template and constructor function in AgentJS (JavaScript)

The activity-transition graph–based agent model is attractive for fine-grained agent schedul-ing. An activity is always executed atomically, but after an activity terminates, it is a well-defined break point for agent process scheduling. An activity is activated by a transition depending on the evaluation of (private) agent data (conditional transition) related to a part of the agent's belief in terms of the BDI architecture, or using unconditional transitions (providing sequential com-position). Each agent belongs to a specific parameterisable agent class AC, specifying local agent data (only visible for the agent itself), types, signals, activities, signal handlers, and transitions. In contrast to common JavaScript objects, an *AgentJS* class definition may not use any references to free variables or functions. The *this* variable always references the agent object and can be used, for example, in transition functions, handlers, activities, and first-order functions directly.

Agent interaction in MAS is characterised by synchronisation and data exchange. *JAM* provides interaction via the tuple-space communication paradigm with a set of simple and coordinating access operations (input, output, read, remove, test), which is well accepted and an understood approach in distributed programming. Additionally, signals can be used for simple distributed one-way notifications carrying simple data. Tuple-space communication is anonymous, generative, and data-centric, whereas signals are messages directed to specific (identified) agents.

The agent input-output system (*AIOS*) is the *interface and abstraction layer* between agents pro-grammed in *AgentJS* and the agent processing platform (*JAM*), shown in Figure 13.10. Further-more, it provides an interface between host applications and *JAM*, for example a Cordova-based Android or iOS App. The *AIOS* provides computational functions, code (ATG) modification, agent control (creation, forking, termination), agent mobility, agent interaction (tuple space, signals), and APIs for other module like ML, SAT solver, and constraint programming. The *AIOS* is extensible, and additional module API can be added at run-time by the platform. An agent scheduler is used to execute multiple agents time multiplexed. Agent execution is encap-sulated in a process container handled by the *AIOS*. An agent process container can be blocked waiting for an internal system-related IO event or suspended waiting for an agent-related *AIOS* event (caused by the agent, e.g., the availability of a tuple). Both cases stop the agent process execution until an event occurs. Finally, *AIOS* provides agent resource control.

To distinguish at least trustful and not trustful agents, different agent privilege levels were introduced, providing different *AIOS* API sets, with level 0 as the lowest level that grants agent-only computational statements. They can perform negotiation to get a higher level based on protected and secured capabilities. Level 1 agents can access the common *AIOS* API operations, including agent replication, creation, killing, sending of signals, and code morphing. Level 2 agents can negotiate their desired resources on the current platform, that is, CPU time and

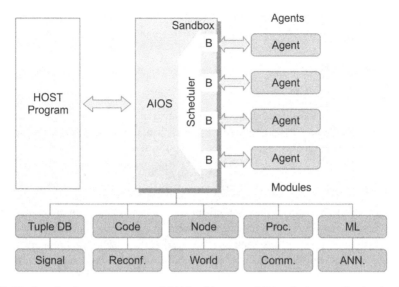

Figure 13.10   Interface between agents and *JAM* and between *JAM* and a host application by the agent input-output system (*AIOS*)

memory limits. Finally, level 3 agents are system agents with an extended API and full platform control with unlimited resources, but they are stationary (immobile) and bound to the agent platform. Physical agents in simulations are always level 3 agents.

An agent of level *n* may only create agents up to level *n*. Level 3 agents can initially only be created by the *JAM* platform. After a migration, the destination node decides about the privilege level and can lower it, for example considering the agent source being not trustful. A migrated agent can get a higher privilege level by capability-based negotiation, requiring a valid platform capability with the appropriate rights.

10.1 Physical and logical nodes

A *JAM* instance is a physical agent processing node consisting of at least one logical (virtual) *JAM* node contained in a *JAM* world. Additional logical nodes (*vJAM*) can be created at run-time. Multiple logical nodes can be connected within this world by virtual links, a prerequisite for simulation. Logical nodes can be arranged in grid networks (one-, two-, or three-dimensional) or arbitrary graphs, for example virtual mobile ad hoc networks. All logical nodes and agents are processed by the same physical instance. There is actually no benefit to parallel processing.

10.2 Connectivity and communication

Physical *JAM* nodes can be connected via arbitrary communication links using the Agent Management Port (*AMP*) protocol. *AMP* supports agent process migration, signal propagation, and general node control. Supported *AMP* ports are:

- Stream sockets
- File system pipes
- UDP sockets

- TCP sockets
- HTTP sockets
- Web sockets
- RS232 (serial interface)
- Bluetooth

Nodes are connected via loosely coupled links via negotiation and periodic check-pointing (ping-pong messages). Logical nodes are connected via virtual channel links (queues). Only logical nodes can connect to other logical nodes (either of the same physical node or of different physical nodes).

11 Agent-based simulation and computation environment for *JAM*

The *JAM* agent platform was originally used for the ABC domain to implement distributed AI systems. Testing loosely coupled distributed systems is a challenge, and the demand rose for simulation of computational agents deployed in virtual artificial worlds. Commonly, there is a large gap between real-world data processing and simulation of data processing and communication. To overcome this gap, a simulation layer was added on the top of the *JAM* platform enabling the simulation of distributed data processing by computational *JAM* agents (i.e., ABCS). Finally, the simulation layer was extended by the concept of physical agents to enable simulation of physical entities closely coupled to computational agents (i.e., ABXS).

The *SEJAM* simulator is used to create a simulation world (consisting of individuals represented by agents) that is attached to the Internet, enabling remote crowd sensing with mobile computational agents. The *SEJAM* simulator is basically a graphical user interface (GUI) on top of a *JAM* node, shown in Figure 13.11.

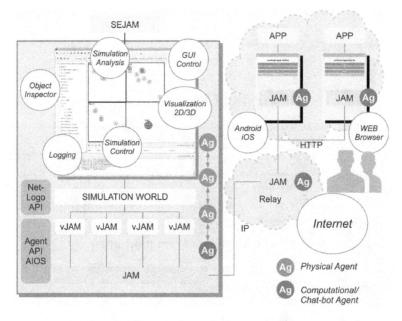

Figure 13.11 Principal concept of closed-loop simulation for augmented virtuality: (left) simulation framework based on the *JAM* platform; (right) mobile and non-mobile devices executing the *JAM* platform connected with the virtual simulation world (via the Internet) (Bosse & Engel, 2018)

The simulation world consists of multiple virtual *JAM* nodes controlled by the one physical node. Any logical node can connect to remote nodes via the Internet, for example using HTTP or UDP communication.

The entire simulation model is specified in a JavaScript/JSON objects containing:

- Agent behaviour code and visual properties (distinguishing physical and computational agents)
- Node visual properties (representing computers or physical entities)
- Communication links and resources
- Simulation parameter
- World description (spatial structure)

SEJAM supports programming and processing of physical and computational agents using the same *AgentJS* programming model. In *SEJAM*, an agent is specified by its behaviour code and visual properties (for visualisation). A physical agent can access a dedicated API only available in the simulator supporting *NetLogo* statements *create*, *ask*, and *set*. Furthermore, a two-dimensional patch-grid world can be created associating variables to patches at specific positions. Creation of a physical agent always creates always a virtual *JAM* node, too. Modification of the position of a physical agent within the simulation world moves the node together with the agent.

11.1 JAM *check-pointing*

Check-pointing creates a snapshot of the entire state of a process. A check-point of a *JAM* instance can be created for later or parallel processing by another *JAM* instance. The snapshot contains:

- All agent processes including data state and control structures
- The entire tuple space database
- The world configuration and contained all nodes
- The world and node states, the control structures including pending signals
- All agent class templates

A forked *JAM* instance snapshot can be processed by another simulator (including additional visual states) to enable co-simulation from an arbitrary simulation time point under different conditions, for example using Monte Carlo simulation, or on different time scales. The latter allows co-simulation to get future development of simulation snapshots that can be back-propagated in the parent simulation to influence the propagation of the simulation worlds with future knowledge. This is an important feature if the simulation is influenced continuously by the real world and the real world is influenced by the simulation.

12 Time machine: multi-time scale and multi-trace simulation

Coupling virtual worlds in simulation with real worlds in real time enables real-world synchronised simulation, assuming that the virtual world is related to a spatial area of the real world. The aforementioned capability of the *JAM* platform and the *SEJAM* simulator to create simulation snapshots enables the forking of simulation snapshots to predict future developments of the real-world state (Figure 13.12).

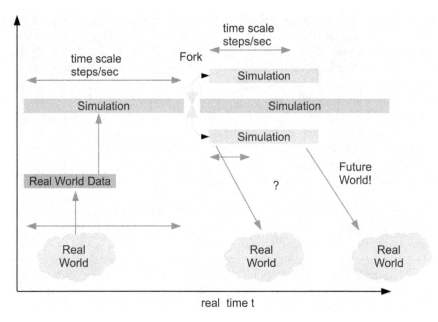

Figure 13.12 A time machine using forked simulation snapshots to predict real-world development in the future

13 A technical use case: environmental control

A simple proof-of-concept study demonstrates the capabilities of the augmented virtual simulation world for the control of technical infrastructure systems like environmental illumination.

The primary goal of this demonstrator is the control of city environments by the combination of crowd sensing with simulation to optimise environmental situations, for example to save energy or to increase people's well-being and satisfaction with domestic services. The simple demonstrator (Bosse & Engel, 2018) consists of an artificial street area with moving nodes (representing humans interacting with mobile devices or machines), beacons (access points) for sensor aggregation and distribution, and some external beacons connected to the Internet enabling the connection to mobile devices via the Internet, and finally smart light devices illuminating streets and buildings based on feedback from people and sensors, shown in Figure 13.13.

The goal of explorer agents (sent out by mobile or light devices) is information mining in the outside world via Internet-deployed agent processing platforms that can be accessed by simulation nodes and web browser apps. The collected information is passed back to the root node (e.g., a mobile device of a passenger) to assist decision-making and navigation.

The explorer agents have to estimate the position of the root node by performing sensor mining from surrounding devices they are visiting and from the outside world (far away) by asking questions answered by humans via the web app chat dialogue. The explorer asks a user for their current place and location within a region of interest and an assessment of the current light situation. Depending on the answer, a specific action is suggested.

Based on answered questions regarding the current user location, the satisfaction of ambient light condition, and an optional fusion with device sensor data (light, position, and so on), actions are directed to smart light control devices to change the light condition in streets and buildings by using mobile notification agents. The action planning is based on the crowd demands and energy-saving constraints. If action is required, mobile notification agents are sent

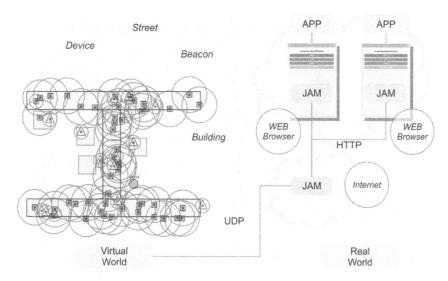

Figure 13.13   A demonstrator: (left) simulation with artificial street areas consisting of street segments and buildings, beacons (triangles, *vJAM* node), populated with stationary and mobile devices (squares, *vJAM* node). The circles around beacons and nodes show the wireless communication range. Only overlapping circles connect nodes. (Right) Crowd Sensing system with mobile apps connected to the simulation via the Internet (Bosse & Engel, 2019).

out to neighbouring nodes to change light intensity based on directed diffusion, random walk, and divide-and-conquer approaches.

The simulation with the current *SEJAM* simulator could be performed with more than 1,000 nodes, hundreds of beacons, and more than 10,000 explorer agents. Real-time values of one simulation step depends on the number of active agents to be processed, node and agent mobility (graphics and communication), and ranges from 1 ms to 1 s.

14   A simulation use case: Sakoda segregation and parameter variance by digital twins

The previous demonstrator use case was primarily used for the control of technical real-world environments by a combination of simulation and crowd sensing. The simulation results can be directly used to modify the real-world environment. The following demonstrator is primarily used to study social and socio-technical systems by ABM and ABS, combined with crowd sensing, basically to get input data for the simulation.

The MAS provides the bidirectional integration of DM via crowd sensing and ABMS (i.e., applying DM in ABMS by creating generated simulation data and applying ABMS in DM by back-propagating generated simulation data). The framework is suitable to combine social and computational simulations with real-world interaction at run-time by integrating crowd sensing, using mobile computational agents interacting with physical agents (Pournaras et al., 2015; Shah et al., 2015).

In this demonstrator, a simple social interaction model between different groups is assumed (based on Sakoda (Medina et al., 2017)). The social model expresses the social expectation at a specific location in dependence on the neighbouring population. A set of parameters $S=\{s_{i,j}\}$ expresses the social relation between individuals of the same group and between different

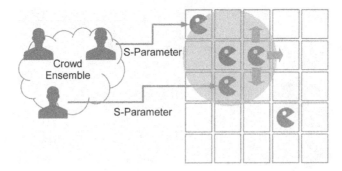

Figure 13.14 Digital twins created from crowd sensing by parametrising the Sakoda social interaction model influencing the migration mobility of individuals to improve their social expectation

groups. There are three simple states: $s_{i,j} = \{-1,0,1\}$ expressing group proximity (−1: disgusting, 0: neutral, 1: attractive), with one $s_{i,j}$ parameter for each group combination i and j. The social expectation at a specific location influences migration mobility of individuals to improve their social expectation. The parameter set S can be preselected and unique for all individuals or derived from crowd sensing via a chat bot addressing the digital twin concept (see Figure 13.14).

The Sakoda behaviour model can be applied on two different spatial and time scales resulting in different self-organising behaviour:

1. Long-time and long-range scale of mobility addressing classical segregation, for example in cities and countries
2. Short-time and short-range scale of mobility addressing, for example city mobility

14.1 Interaction model

Assuming a two-dimensional grid world that consists of places at discrete locations (x,y), an artificial agent can occupy one place of the grid. Only one agent can occupy a place. The agents can move on the grid and can change their living position. It is assumed that there are two groups related to the classes a and b of individuals. The social interaction is characterised by different attitudes (Al-Zinati & Wenkstern, 2017; Medina et al., 2017) of an individual between different and among same groups given by four parameters:

$$S = \left(s_{aa}, s_{ab}, s_{ba}, s_{bb} \right) \tag{13.2}$$

The model is not limited to two groups of individuals. The S vector can be extended to four groups (or generalised) by the matrix:

$$S_{abcd} = \begin{pmatrix} s_{aa} & s_{ab} & s_{ac} & s_{ad} \\ s_{ba} & s_{bb} & s_{bc} & s_{bd} \\ s_{ca} & s_{cb} & s_{cc} & s_{cd} \\ s_{da} & s_{db} & s_{dc} & s_{dd} \end{pmatrix} \tag{13.3}$$

The world model consists of N places x_i. Each place can be occupied by none or one agent either of group α or β, expressed by the variable $x_i = \{0, -1, 1\}$, or generalised $x_i = \{0, 1, 2, 3, 4, .., n\}$ with n groups. The social expectation of an individual i at place x_i is given by:

$$f_i(x_i) = \sum_{k=1}^{N} J_{ik} \delta_s(x_i, x_k) \tag{13.4}$$

The parameter J_{ik} is a measure of the social distance (equal one for Moore neighbourhood with distance one), decreasing for longer distances. The parameter δ expresses the attitude to a neighbouring place, given by (for the general case of n different groups):

$$\delta_s(x_i, x_k) = \begin{cases} s_{\alpha\beta} & \text{, if } x_i \neq 0 \text{ and } x_k \neq 0 \text{ with } \alpha = x_i, \beta = x_k \\ 0 & \text{, otherwise} \end{cases} \tag{13.5}$$

Self-evaluation is prevented by omitting the current place (i.e., $k \neq i$). There is a mobility factor m giving the probability for a movement.

An individual agent ag_i of any group α (class from the set of groups) is able to change its position by migrating from an actual place x_i to another place x_m if this place is not occupied ($x_m = 0$) and if $f_i(x_m) > f_i(x_i)$ and the current mobility factor m_i is greater than 0.5. Among social expectation (resulting in segregation), transport and traffic mobility has to be considered by a second goal-driven function $g(x_m)$, commonly consisting of a destination potential functions with constraints (e.g., streets). If $g_i(x_m) > f_i(x_m) > f_i(x_i)$ then the goal-driven mobility is chosen, otherwise social-driven.

$$g : (x_i, x_m, x_k, v, t) \rightarrow \mathbb{R} \tag{13.6}$$

The mobility function g returns a real value $[0,1]$ that gives the probability (utility measure) to move from the current place x_i to a neighbouring place x_m to reach the destination place x_k with a given velocity v. The g function records the history of movement. Far distances from the destination increase g values. Longer stays at the same place will increase the g level with time t. Social binding (i.e., group formation) will be preferred over goal-driven mobility.

The computation of the neighbouring social expectation values f is opportunistic, that is, if f is computed for a neighbouring node assuming the occupation of this neighbouring place by the agent if the place is free, the current original place is omitted x_i for this computation. Any other already occupied places are kept unchanged for the computation of a particular f value. From the set of neighbouring places and their particular social and mobility expectations for the specific agent, the best place is chosen for migration (if there is a better place than the current with the aforementioned condition). In this work, spatial social distances in the range of 1–30 place units are considered.

Originally, the entire world consists of individual agents interacting in the world based on one specific set of attitude parameters S. In this work, the model is generalised by assigning individual entities their own set S retrieved from real humans by crowd sensing, or at least different configurations of the S vector classifying social behaviour among the groups. Furthermore, the set of entities can be extended by humans and bots (intelligent machines) belonging to a group class, too.

Segregation effects inhibit individual movement until a different social situation enables a movement. Transportation mobility triggers movement even if there is no social enabler.

This is reflected in the extended Sakoda model by the mobility factor *m* and the goal-driven expectation function *g* that control mobility and overlays social and transportation and traffic mobility. The mobility function *g* includes random walk and diffusion behaviour, too. Constrained mobility is one major extension of the original Sakoda model presented in this work.

15 Model parameters and crowd sensing

Creation of virtual digital twins is the aim of the crowd sensing task. Crowd sensing is performed with chat bot agents. One stationary agent operates on a user device (chat moderator agent), for example a smartphone, and another mobile agent is responsible for performing the survey (either participatory with a former negotiation or opportunistic ad hoc) by providing a dialogue script consisting of questions and text. The results of the survey, a set of answered questions, are used to derive the following simulation model parameters, shown in Definition 13.2.

```
parameters = {
  group : string "a"|"b"|..,
  social-distance: number [1-100],
  mobility-distance: number [1-100],
  social-attitudes : [saa,sab,sba,sbb] | number [][],
  mobility : number [0-1],
  position : {x:number,y:number},
  destination : {x:number,y:number}
}
```

Definition 13.2: Sakoda model parameters

15.1 Survey questionnaire

Table 15.1 summarises the ad hoc mobile survey performed for twin creation by mobile chat bot agents created in the simulation world.

There are questions asking directly for the user choice of their class (poor and rich, related to agent classes A and B, respectively), which can be correct or incorrect (i.e., the user decision is highly subjective). And there are questions trying to estimate a more accurate class membership. Finally, some questions measure the social interaction radius and the mobility probability.

Qid/Variable	Type, Value, Condition	Text	Input
M1	Message	*Welcome..*	-
QSN/S	Sensors	-	{DATE, BROWSER, OS, GPS, GPS5, LOCATION, LOCATION5}
QCL/C	Question, Mutual Choice	*Who are you? Do you think you are poor or rich?*	{Poor, Rich, Do not know}

Qid/Variable	Type, Value, Condition	Text	Input
QR1 / aP	Question, Value choice, $1=QCL.answer if QCL. answer≠"Do not know"	*How do you rate your relation to people of your own group $1? Do you like (1) or dislike (−1) them?*	{−1, 0, 1}
QR2 / aN	Question, Value choice, $1=¬QCL.answer if QCL. answer≠"Do not know"	*How do you rate your relation to people of the other group $1? Do you like (1) or dislike (−1) them?*	{−1, 0, 1}
QFN/fN	Question, $1=¬QCL.answer if QCL.answer ≠ "Do not know"	*Do you have $1 friends?*	{yes, no}
QA/aG	Question, Value	*How old are you?*	[1,100]
QMS/iC	Question, Mutual Choice	*What is your monthly salary?*	{<1000, 1000–3000, 3000–5000, >5000}
QT/sA	Question, Multiple Choice	*What are your spare time activities?*	{Travelling, Sports, Education/Art, Social, Friends, Gardening, TV/Streaming}
QL/aR	Question, Text, Default=QSN. LOCATION5.CITY or QSN. LOCATION.CITY	*Where do you live [Enter ZIP Code or City Name]?*	ZIP/City
QSC/nS	Question, Value	*How many social contacts do you have?*	[1,100]
QMD/mM	Question, Mutual Choice	*Do you like to move?*	{Yes, Maybe, No}
M2	Message	*Thank you!*	–

15.2 Model parameter estimation

The model parameters of the digital twins are derived from the survey results.

15.3 Coding of categorical parameters

$$\phi(C) = \begin{cases} 0, C = \text{Do not know} \\ 1, C = \text{Poor} \\ 2, C = \text{Rich} \end{cases}, \phi(iC) = \begin{cases} 1, iC < 1000 \\ 2, iC = 1000\text{-}3000 \\ 3, iC = 3000\text{-}5000 \\ 4, iC > 5000 \end{cases}$$

$$\phi(sA) = \sum \begin{cases} 1, sA = \text{TV/Streaming} \\ 2, sA = \text{Friends} \\ 4, sA = \text{Social} \\ 8, sA = \text{Sports} \\ 16, sA = \text{Gardening} \\ 32, sA = \text{Education/Art} \\ 64, sA = \text{Travelling} \end{cases}, \phi(mM) = \begin{cases} -1, C = \text{No} \\ 0, C = \text{Maybe} \\ 1, C = \text{Yes} \end{cases}$$

(13.7)

15.4 Estimating digital twin class

- The following class estimation (a/b) bases not only on the user class selection. It uses additional survey variables

$$
class = \text{Prio}
\begin{cases}
a, \phi(C) = 0 \wedge \phi(iC) = 1 \\
a, \phi(C) = 0 \wedge \phi(sA) < 16 \\
b, \phi(C) = 0 \wedge \phi(iC) > 3 \\
b, \phi(C) = 0 \wedge \phi(sA) > 30 \\
a, \phi(C) = 1 \wedge \phi(iC) = 1 \wedge \phi(sA) < 16 \\
b, \phi(C) = 1 \wedge \phi(iC) > 2 \vee \phi(sA) > 90 \\
b, \phi(C) = 2 \wedge \phi(iC) > 2 \wedge \phi(sA) > 90 \\
a, \text{otherwise}
\end{cases}
\tag{13.8}
$$

15.5 Estimating digital twin model parameters

$$
s_{aa} = \begin{cases} aP, class = a \\ 0, class = b \end{cases}, s_{bb} = \begin{cases} 0, class = a \\ aP, class = b \end{cases}
$$

$$
s_{ab} = \begin{cases} aN, class = a \\ 0, class = b \end{cases}, s_{ba} = \begin{cases} 0, class = a \\ aN, class = b \end{cases}
\tag{13.9}
$$

$$
s_{mobi} = \begin{cases} 1, \phi(mM) = 1 \\ 0.5, \phi(mM) = 0 \\ 0.2, \phi(mM) = -1 \end{cases}, s_{sodist} = \begin{cases} 2, nS < 10 \\ 3, nS < 30 \\ 5, nS \geqslant 30 \end{cases}
$$

with $\Phi(x)$ giving the numerical code of a categorical variable (multiple choices answers are summed by a weighted code).

An ad hoc survey with 20 replies returned by users was performed via the web *JAM* app connected to a public *JAM* relay within a time interval of two hours. The survey is not representative and was used only for a proof of concept. The statistical analysis results (with coded categorical variables) are shown in Figure 13.15.

Figure 13.16 shows the class distribution from the survey (user selection) and the class estimation by the twin model shown earlier. Surprisingly, the majority shifts from rich to poor classification!

The injection of digital twins in the simulation at run-time leads to the following observations and influences on the outcome (emergence) of the entire MAS:

1. A mixed and heterogeneous agent distribution is emerging by adding variance of agent behaviour to the system, that is, there is a large set of different agent behaviour (originally the set of agent behaviour only consisted of two different parameter sets).
2. The dynamics of the segregation and group formation (creating local clusters) is strongly increased.
3. There is more agent mobility and fluctuation.
4. The time scale of non-stability (agent mobility) is extended by two or three times.
5. There is inversion of the a/b ratio of mean ensemble social expectation and suddenly appearing steps of change of the mean social expectation for one or both groups.

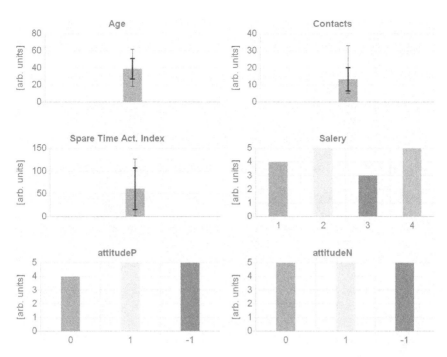

Figure 13.15   Statistics of some of the variables derived from the ad hoc mobile survey using the *JAM* app (mean, standard deviation, and minimal and maximal values are plotted for the numerical variables)

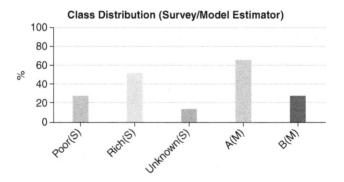

Figure 13.16   Comparison of survey classification by users (poor class relates to A, rich to B, respectively) and estimated twin class (A/B)

One important emergent measure variable is the globally averaged social expectation value (i.e., the social satisfaction measure) of agents at their current place. Surprisingly, different simulations showed totally different global satisfaction developments for class *A* and class *B* agents. Some examples are shown in Figure 13.17. Sometimes, there is a higher global social satisfaction for one class of about 40%; sometimes they are equal! It seems that the initial spatial distribution of agents determines the final stationary state of the society (agents are placed at random locations with a randomly chosen class using Monte Carlo simulation).

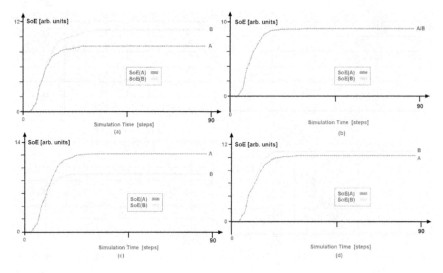

Figure 13.17 Examples of different simulation outcomes of the globally averaged social expectation value (computed by Equation 13.4) for 200 agents of class A and 200 agents B without digital twins

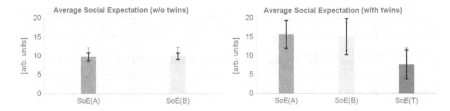

Figure 13.18 Globally averaged social expectation values for an ensemble of simulation runs with and without digital twins

The influence of digital twins injected in the simulation on the development of the social expectation measure is significant, as shown in Figure 13.19. The digital twins (200 overall) are injected in the first 100 simulation time units. The influence on the global dynamic can occur more than 200 simulations after their injection (e.g., shown in Figure 13.19 (d)). Furthermore, the digital twins with a wide range of model parameter variance can trigger steps in the social expectation measure (e.g., in Figure 13.19 (a) at 100 and 150 time units). The averaged social expectation measure of A/B agents is higher than in the experiments without digital twins (this relates clearly to a higher density of agents). But the social expectation measure of the digital twins is always significantly lower than A/B satisfaction (a result from the broad diversity and only loosely integration in clusters). Due to the low number of returned survey results, 10 digital twins were created from one parameter set derived from a survey (and placed randomly on the living areas).

Finally, Figure 13.20 shows examples of the start and end situations of the simulation world with and without digital twins. Digital twins lead to the formation of larger group clusters,

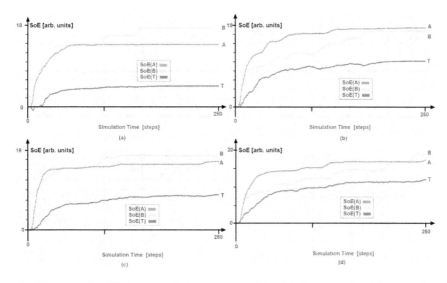

Figure 13.19 Examples of different simulation outcomes of the globally averaged social expectation value (computed by Equation 13.4) for 200 agents of class A and 200 agents B with additional 200 digital twins

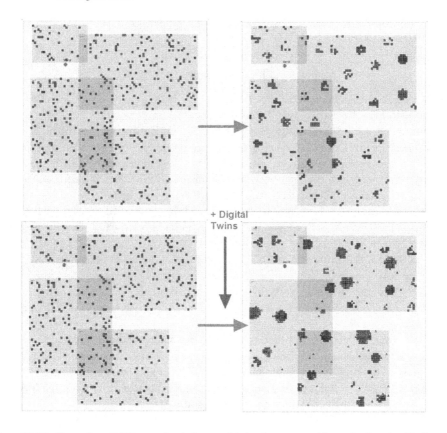

Figure 13.20 Examples of different simulation world developments without (top) and with (bottom) digital twins (triangles)

although due to broad model variance the digital twins are more spatially scattered than pure class A/B agents. The movement of agents is constrained. The simulation world is partitioned into living areas (gray areas). Agents can stay and move only in these areas.

The global averaged social expectation value (computed by Equation 13.4) increases significantly in the presence of the additional digital twins, shown in Figure 13.18. Additionally, the variance of the end stationary state of the MAS is about three times higher than without digital twins.

16 Interactive simulation: an educational tool

The previous section showed a proof-of-concept field study for augmented and real-time capable agent-based simulation. The real-time capability was in this case study not fundamental. There are other use cases (like traffic and crowd flow management) which rely significantly on the real-time capability.

Research and environmental control is only one relevant field of application for the augmented simulation approach. Education and studying human-machine interaction is another field that can profit from the features of the introduced framework.

Combining the concepts of mobile crowd sensing, agent-based simulation, and digital twin mapping of humans interacting in real time with simulation worlds can be a powerful educational tool. The aforementioned simulation of networking and segregation using digital twins derived from surveys as a pattern disturbance can be studied by students in social sciences interactively.

17 Summary

A novel approach was presented that provides an augmentation of virtual simulation worlds by using mobile computational agents and crowd sensing.

Mobile agents can be used to fuse real and virtual worlds composing augmented virtuality. The deployment of the *JAM* agent processing platform enables large-scale simulation of extended and complex socio-technical systems, for example complex traffic situations and smart wide-range traffic management, large-scale social media interaction, crowd sensing and interaction, and many more complex systems with unknown emergence behaviour.

There are basically two agent model classes covered by one unified agent model: physical and computational agents, both relying on the same unified agent behaviour programmed in JavaScript.

Physical *JAM* agents relate to the ABM/ABS domains, whereas the computational agents relate to the ABC domain. Computational agents can migrate between real and virtual worlds seamlessly. Moreover, from the point of view of social science, decision-making, opinion formation, and voting processes can be studied with a unified simulation and data mining framework.

A simple proof-of-concept study demonstrated the capabilities of the augmented virtual simulation world for the control of technical infrastructure systems like environmental illumination.

An extended field study showed the influence of digital twins created from mobile ad hoc surveys on segregation patterns and dynamics. An originally homogeneous two-class MAS was enriched with model variance by users in the real world.

The tools (the big machine) are available and the suitability could be shown with demonstrators. Future work has to find suitable research questions that can be investigated with the machine from social sciences, smart city and facility management, production and logistics environments, warehouse systems, and many more fields of applications. Additionally, real-time issues by agent interaction in real and virtual worlds differing in real-time scale have to be investigated.

One major and fundamental issue arising generally is the fusion of real and virtual worlds with respect to the temporal and spatial domains, which must be addressed in future research work. Useful temporal and spatial mappings have to be identified.

References

Al-Zinati, M., & Wenkstern, R. (2017, May). An agent-based self-organizing traffic environment for urban evacuations. In *Proceedings of the sixteenth international conference on autonomous agent and multiagent systems*. AAMAS.

Baqueiro, O., Wang, Y. J., McBurney, P., & Coenen, F. (2008). *Integrating data mining and agent based modeling and simulation*. ICDM 2009, LNAI 5633.

Bosse, S. (2016, August 22–24). Mobile multi-agent systems for the internet-of-things and clouds using the JavaScript agent machine platform and machine learning as a service. In *The IEEE 4th international conference on future internet of things and cloud*. doi:10.1109/FiCloud.2016.43

Bosse, S. (2018, September 9). Smart micro-scale energy management and energy distribution in decentralized self-powered networks using multi-agent systems. In *FedCSIS conference, 6th international workshop on smart energy networks & multi-agent systems*. IEEE.

Bosse, S., & Engel, U. (2018, November 15–30). Augmented virtual reality: Combining crowd sensing and social data mining with large-scale simulation using mobile agents for future smart cities. In *Proceedings, ECSA-5 5th international electronic conference on sensors and applications* (Vol. 4). doi:10.3390/ecsa-5–05762

Bosse, S., & Engel, U. (2019). *Real-time human-in-the-loop simulation with mobile agents, chat bots, and crowd sensing for smart cities*. Sensors (MDPI). doi:10.3390/s19204356

Bosse, S., & Pournaras, E. (2017, August 21–23). An ubiquitous multi-agent mobile platform for distributed crowd sensing and social mining. In *FiCloud 2017: The 5th international conference on future internet of things and cloud*. IEEE.

Calenda, T., Benedetti, M. D., Messina, F., Pappalardo, G., & Santoro, C. (2016). AgentSimJS: A web-based multi-agent simulator with 3D capabilities. In *WOA 2016 17th workshop "From Objects to Agents"*. *Proceedings of the 17th workshop "From Objects to Agents" co-located with 18th European Agent Systems Summer School (EASSS 2016)*.

Ganti, R. K., Ye, F., & Lei., H. (2011). Mobile crowd sensing: Current state and future challenges. *IEEE Communications Magazine, 49*, 11.

Gilbert, N. (2004). Agent-based social simulation: Dealing with complexity, In *International conference on intelligence and security informatics ISI 2008: Intelligence and security informatics* (pp. 401–412).

Hamidi, H., & Kamankesh, A. (2018). An approach to intelligent traffic management system using a multi-agent system. *International Journal of Intelligent Transportation Systems Research, 16*, 112–124.

Hox, J. J. (2017). Computational social science methodology, anyone? *Methodology, 13*(Suppl), 3–12. doi:10.1027/1614–2241/a000127

Leppäne, T., Lacasia, J. Á., Tobe, Y., Sezaki, K., & Riekki, J. (2017). Mobile crowd sensing with mobile agents. *Autonomous Agents and Multi-Agent Systems, 311*, 1–35.

Mahrt, M., & Scharkow, M. (2013). The value of big data in digital media research. *Journal of Broadcasting & Electronic Media, 57*(1), 20–33. doi:10.1080/08838151.2012.761700

McFarland, D. A., Moody, J., Diehl, D., Smith, J. A., & Thomas, R. J. (2014). Network ecology and adolescent social structure. *American Sociological Review*. http://dx.doi.org/10.1177/0003122414554001

McGrath, M. J., & Scanaill, C. N. (2014). *Sensor technologies healthcare, wellness, and environmental applications*. Apress Open.

Medina, P., Goles, E., Zarama, R., & Rica, S. (2017). *Self-organized societies: On the Sakoda model of social interactions*. Complexity.

Pournaras, E., Moise, I., & Helbing, D. (2015). Privacy-preserving ubiquitous social mining via modular and compositional virtual sensors. In *IEEE 29th international conference on advanced information networking and applications*. IEEE.

Shah, D. V., Capella, J. N., & Neuman, W. R. (2015). Big data, digital media, and computational social science: Possibilities and perils. *The ANNALS of the American Academy of Political and Social Science, 659*, 6–13. doi:10.1177/000271621557208

van Dam, K. H., Lukszo, I., & Zofia, N. (Eds.). (2013). *Agent-based modelling of socio-technical systems.* Springer Berlin.

Wang, F.-Y. (2005, September–October). *Agent-based control for networked traffic management systems.* Intelligent Transportation Systems.

Wilensky, U., & Rand, W. (2015). *An introduction to agent-based modeling modeling natural, social, and engineered complex systems with NetLogo.* MIT Press.

14

AGENT-BASED MODELLING FOR CULTURAL NETWORKS

Tagging by artificial intelligent cultural agents

Fernando Sancho-Caparrini and Juan Luis Suárez

1 Introduction

We present a model based on cultural agents, that is, human-like agents whose main framework of interactions is defined by its belonging to cultural networks. In this context, a cultural network is assumed to be made up of basic units in which an agent is connected to another agent via a cultural object. These objects are described as cultural because they contain a repository of information that may contribute to the agent's survival or sense of identity.

This chapter builds on previous work by the authors on culture and complexity (Sancho-Caparrini & Suárez, 2011; Suárez et al., 2011, 2012; Suárez et al., 2013) and cultural networks (Suárez et al., 2015; Suárez, 2020), and it attempts to design the building blocks for agent-based simulations of cultural ecosystems that will help us to understand changes that occur in cultural networks. Understanding changes that occur in cultural networks is critically important as the push for further connectivity of human life across the globe is provoking a transformation of the ways in which local and national cultural ecosystems interface. Traditionally, cultural networks presented two characteristics that are being challenged by digitization and globalization: (a) they were analogue networks in which physical contact and colocation of individuals and objects were critical for their formation and stability. But these features were not necessary for their expansion, because the combination of improvements in both travel technology and the technology to compress and codify information since the European Renaissance has made it easier for cultural networks to integrate and adapt objects from distant cultural ecosystems. And (b) they relied on cultural institutions (museums, libraries, archives, etc.), that is, socially recognized repositories of information that regulated the cultural exchanges of these networks, organizing them by serving as deposits of the memory of communities and controlling the rhythm by which novelties made it into institutional memory (Sancho-Caparrini & Suárez, 2011).

As digitization becomes one of the main economic, social, and marketing drivers of the second decade of the 21st century, ever increasing on the heels of the COVID-19 pandemic crisis, we foresee that two forces will dramatically change the nature and dynamics of traditional cultural networks. First, most traditional cultural networks are making a transition to become more and more digitally based, something that is difficult to accomplish and not strategically desirable for networks with analogue assets. Second, this digitization, even if it is partial, entails connecting (for instance, via social media) with digital platforms, which are alien to traditional

DOI: 10.4324/9781003025245-17

cultural networks but are naturalized to some of the audiences interacting with them. These platforms are heavily dependent for many of their operations on several techniques of automation and artificial intelligence algorithms (van Dijck et al., 2018) that learn from and regulate the connections among users and between these cultural objects, ultimately affecting the dynamics of these networks. The sheer number and speed of these artificial intelligence–driven interactions outpace the ability of institutions in analogue networks to perform their regulatory roles as controllers and arbiters of both memory and novelty. The connection to these artificial intelligence–based systems results in the hegemony, or pervasiveness, of impermanent or ephemeral digital cultural objects. These ephemeral digital objects are distinguished by the fact that they leave few traces of themselves in the memory of traditional institutions (i.e. museums, archives, libraries), and within the emergence of new digital networks, ephemeral digital objects remain key elements for their maintenance. Artificial intelligence–based meta cultural objects (recommender engines, creators of navigation paths, etc.) in cultural networks short circuit and circumvent traditional repositories of memory and norms, creating a rewiring of the connections that made it possible for analogue cultural networks to form, stabilize, survive, and arbitrate the network.

At the level of agents' behaviours, we have decided to focus on and simulate the role of tagging and tags in hybrid cultural networks. Tagging is crucial to digital environments because of the relations formed among agents in these ecosystems through cultural objects that are semantic (based in tagging exercises) and dynamic (the same relation does not necessarily always yield the same tags), shaping what we describe as cultural ecosystems: semantic spaces of meaning, memory and identity that serve as the scaffolding for the creation of communities.

A now well-established mechanism of participation in digital environments, tagging has become one of the main methods of interacting with digital objects such as texts, images, videos or sound. Whereas tagging happens at the level of the individual engaging in digital interactions, artificial intelligence–driven platforms harness the power of the masses participating in tagging and techniques for clustering of individuals as they form connections with objects and other individuals via tagging to control, foster and regulate the dynamics of the resulting networks. As a semantic system that helps understand the intentions of the taggers (the users or citizens in networks), platforms also cluster tags to both predict and direct their evolution and accurately predict their next behaviours. This ecosystem behaviour results in a multilevel digital ecosystem (users, objects, tags, traditional institutions, artificial intelligence–based super agents) that is predicated on the continuous naming (through tagging), creating and destroying of cultural moments (by interacting in the digital system through both tagging and non-tagging) by virtue of permanent and ephemeral tagging of the world.

The structure of the chapter is as follows: in section 2 we present the definition of cultural networks that we use, highlighting some of the features that differentiate them from other networks that we can find in other social science problems. Next, we will describe the modelling fundamentals that will support the framework proposed in this work, emphasizing its two main cornerstones: the BDI paradigm for modelling human behaviour through agents and the random surfer framework (inspired by the functioning of PageRank algorithm) for modelling the decision-making and exploration of the network by those agents. We end section 3 by presenting the concrete modelling framework that is the core of our work. In section 4, we produce a first formalization of a model that, following the presented framework, builds an evolutionary mechanism of cultural networks that approximates the complex behaviour that we can find in some real cultural networks. Here, we also show some preliminary results that have been obtained with an implementation of this model. Finally, we finish this chapter with some conclusions that can be inferred from this work as well as some lines of future research (some of which are already underway).

2 Cultural networks

For the purpose of this chapter, a cultural network is understood to be a multimodal network in which at least two types of nodes represent people and objects, respectively, and in which a cultural object or phenomenon symbolically and cognitively connects people to one another. That is, a cultural relationship is created via an object or phenomenon that semantically loads the links connecting humans through joint attention (Tomasello, 2000) with information contextually relevant to harnessing the existing environmental complexity, ultimately facilitating the cultural learning of participants within the cultural network.

Cultural networks provide the basic mechanisms required for the process of meaning making for individuals and communities; they constitute the infrastructure of symbols, tools and objects that keep communities together, providing a basis for the development of prosociality (Sancho-Caparrini & Suárez, 2011); they function as the interface used as a means to negotiate encounters between different cultures (Suárez, 2007); and they carry the requisite tools that enable cultural formations to adapt, transmute and evolve.

Understanding both the concept and the dynamics of cultural networks is critically necessary within the broader fields of digital humanities, social computing and cultural analytics. Historically, within these fields there has been a lack of recognition that cultural networks must be understood as living, responsive organisms that are leading complex processes connecting the cultural history of communities with the mechanisms of cultural evolution (Cavalli Sforza, 2007; Richerson & Boyd, 2006; Henrich, 2016; Tomasello, 2019; Inglehart, 2018). As such, it is imperative that these fields recognize that cultural networks provide the ground for the development of new tools that will uniquely position these fields to link the human past, in historical terms, with the temporal scale of the evolutionary processes of culture. Before the transition to exclusively digital cultural networks has advanced, thanks to the adoption of artificial intelligence, we urgently need to understand how digitization and artificial intelligence affect and change the traditional roles and functions that analogue and hybrid networks have served for both communities and individuals.

In this chapter, we intend to develop a model of digital cultural networks that helps us to understand how the introduction of artificial intelligence–based cultural agents affects the dynamics of these cultural networks. We will focus on the tagging of digital cultural objects as the main action of our human-type agents, while our artificial intelligence–based agents will influence subsequent iterations of the cultural network by presenting new sets of cultural objects resulting from the analysis of previous rounds of tagging and clustering by human-type agents. We will emphasize the change that the interactions through different levels of the network create when compared with the traditional cultural networks organized around canonical objects and held within centralized repositories of community memory. Importantly, we will highlight the impact that artificial intelligence surrogates and tagging have on cultural networks as these become less centralized, more ephemeral and better suited to satisfy the business models of digital platforms. Artificial intelligence surrogates and tagging also allow for the creation of constant cycles of cohesion (similar tags) and destruction (dissimilar tags or perceived absence of tags, which is another form of tagging in and of itself) of communities (both digital and analogue) through common cultural objects and the satisfaction of individual desires by targeted tagging of specific cultural objects.

3 Modelling human interactions and cultural complexity

3.1 The BDI paradigm

Although agent-based modelling provides one of the most fruitful tools for understanding complex systems (Siegfried, 2014), we still encounter unresolved difficulties in deciding how to shape the individual rules that agents must follow to obtain the purposeful design of local and global behaviour. This difficulty is found not only from an operational and functional point of view, about how to design the rules that affect the different entities that intervene in the modelling, but also from a conceptual and epistemological point of view, where the rules and their representation have an equivalence in the real world that the modeller wants to reproduce. And if this is true in the modelling of complex systems in general, it becomes especially difficult when dealing with the modelling and behaviour of systems in which the agents (or some of them) represent human beings.

Among conceptual models, the most successful in modelling human beings, the BDI architecture (Bratman, 1987, 2009; Grosz & Kraus, 1996), is based on a vision of modelling individuals as rational agents who possess certain mental attitudes: *beliefs*, *desires* and *intentions* (hence the name of the architecture) which represent, respectively, the informative, motivational and deliberative states of the agent. These mental attitudes will allow, at least conceptually, the modelling of individuals in the system as rational agents but with what we understand to be bounded rationality. The concept of bounded rationality is necessary because it includes the idea of incomplete informative states and limited intentions, which are necessary conditions to confront in any model that aims to simulate human agents. Bounded rationality is much more closely aligned to real-life situations for human beings when they are faced with making decisions in normal-life conditions. In BDI architecture:

1. *Beliefs* represents the individual's knowledge about the environment and about their own internal state;
2. *Desires* represents the goals which the individual has decided they want to achieve;
3. *Intentions* are the set of plans (sequence of actions) which the individual intends to follow to achieve their goals.

Conceptually, BDI architecture provides an approach called folk psychology, since it is based not on a physically real model of how reasoning works (at least, not in a verified way) but on how we popularly believe that the decision-making process takes place, at a high level of abstraction. Although its author, Michael Bratman, did not introduce this architecture as a practical means for the creation of multi-agent models, both he and other authors realized the potential that this architecture had for the effective construction of real models. Interestingly, shortly afterward its creation, the BDI architecture would have more influence and application within the world of computing than in the world of philosophy, where it was created. In a short period of time, the BDI architecture gave rise to a new computational paradigm with an immediate application in the specification and implementation of intelligent agents within the area of artificial intelligence (AI).

Later on, Cohen and Levesque (1990) distinguished BDI from purely reactive models by emphasizing the existence of commitments to intentions in order to achieve long-term goals, transforming the action of commitments into a critical part of the BDI model. Rao and Georgeff (1991) showed that we need suitable rational processes to decide the intentions to focus on in the long term under sets of specific circumstances. These subsequent studies have brought into real convergence areas of AI that, although intuitively close, could hardly be found together in real projects, such as agent modelling and planning, decision-making, optimization and non-classical logics (BDI logic) techniques.

Since its introduction, BDI architecture has also provided a large number of applications in practical social models (Meyer et al., 2001; Adam & Gaudou, 2015; Helbing et al., 2000), enriching many of the available multi-agent system building frameworks (commercial and free). We can find many variants and extensions to adapt it to several scenarios where specific features in the agents are needed (Singh et al., 2011; de Silva et al., 2009; Taibi, 2010).

3.2 PageRank, random surfers and recommender systems

Generically, PageRank is the name given to the various versions of a web page ranking algorithm that was designed by Larry Page and Sergey Brin when they were at Stanford University (Page et al., 1999). In addition to the impact on the world of computation that this algorithm has for the problem it solves, it has great historical, technological and social importance because its creation gave rise to the invention of Google's search engine. The algorithm provides a method to measure the importance of a web page within a system of pages, based on the quantity and quality of links pointing to it.

The problem of measuring the importance of the nodes in a network according to how they are connected to each other is an old problem that was already known and addressed from different angles within the field. At the moment of PageRank's invention there were well-known solutions, even if they were not efficient from a practical point of view, when the size of the network grew minimally. Perhaps the first known practical application of this problem is due to the economist Wassily Leontief (Harvard University, and Nobel Prize in 1971) who used it to model the functioning of an economy represented by a network in order to give a ranking between the different components of the economic system.

Along with the algebraic solutions to solve this ranking problem (Arasu et al., 2002), which include the various variants used by Google, we can find a very simple distributed solution that also provides a more extensible and inspiring solution based on the behaviour of what are called random surfers (Richardson & Domingos, 2002).

Let's assume an individual (our surfer) is surfing the network. Their way of surfing is completely random, following the existing connections: at a certain moment this surfer is in a node, then they select at random and following a uniform probability, one of the nodes that are connected to that node, and jumps to it. This is called a random walk through the network (hence the name random surfer). If we repeat this process many times and record the number of times the surfer is at each node, we can prove that the numbers at each node are proportional to the importance of the node in the network structure.

Despite some small, easily solvable drawbacks of this method, it has some clear advantages, such as:

- It is robust to changes in connections, because most walks will be minimally affected if the changes are local.
- It is easily parallelizable, just by having several surfers moving through the network simultaneously.
- It is distributed. It's easy to have several independent processes (they don't even need to be synchronized) working with different surfers.
- It is local to the topology of the network, which means that if we want to have information about the importance of a part of the network, we can originally place the surfers in that part and see the local results they produce.

In addition, it also has advantages for the generation of variants that can be interpreted as alternative analyses to the study of networks. For example:

- It is easy to consider cases where the probabilities of visiting neighbours from a node are not uniform, so there may be a preference for certain visits (if we think of a cultural network, for example the rating or tags assigned in the links).
- It is easy to introduce variants where surfers have preferences, so there may be some specialized-in-edge tags or internal characteristics of the nodes they visit.
- An importance ranking (like the one provided by the PageRank algorithm) can be obtained from a set of nodes with respect to a fixed one, making the surfer always start from a specific node.
- The importance ranking of structures larger than single nodes can be estimated by considering the visits that can be counted to a set of nodes from any other set of nodes.
- The importance ranking of edges, and not only of nodes, can also be estimated by recording the visits that they receive in random path moves.

According to the latter considerations we can use a selective surfer system as a custom ranking procedure (even from a single node) that can provide similarity measures, clustering, recommendations, etc.

3.3 A framework model of cultural networks

From the previous building blocks (the BDI paradigm as a model of intention and random surfers as a model for decentralized selection) we have built an elegant model for cultural networks that allows us to analyze and measure how the interactions between the elements of the network (human beings and cultural objects) define the structure and dynamics of the network itself as a whole.

Conceptually, the abstract framework model through which we model cultural networks is structured by several layers:

1. In the first layer we find the traditional cultural network itself, formed by the *individuals* (human-like agents) and the *cultural objects* with which they interact. Formally, it is a network where the nodes are the humans and objects, and the edges are the various interactions that can occur between them. In a first approach we consider that the network is bipartite, in the sense that the only interactions/edges between nodes are those between nodes of different types (humans/cultural objects). Since we can introduce more or fewer attributes in the nodes and we can enrich the interactions between them, we are considering a more complex computational model than the usual mathematical graph that just stores information in nodes (attributes of humans/objects) and edges (properties of the interactions that occur). It is at this level that features of the BDI paradigm can be implemented to model the dynamics of individuals in their interactions with cultural objects (or with other individuals, if we want to add that layer of possible interactions).

2. In the second layer, we find the *semantic relationships* that can be found between the attributes (information stored in nodes and edges) of the previous layer. We can consider that this second layer is a second network in which the nodes are the attributes used in the previous layer, while the relations will be defined by how those attributes are used and interpreted in that layer. In fact, this second layer can be seen as a collection of several networks that

work as projections, where we obtain a different semantic network each time we capture a specific moment an interaction happens in the model, depending on the set of relationships that we want to highlight/analyze from the previous layer.

3. A third and last layer is given by auxiliary procedures that allow us to enrich the knowledge of the network that each individual can acquire. In our framework, this personal (and inaccurate) knowledge is given by a group of surfing agents that eventually go through the network and inform individuals about the features of the observed network. We can interpret them as personalized random surfers, whose behaviour is determined by the individual's current characteristics and their relationship with the cultural objects with which they interact. Therefore, and to distinguish them from the individuals of the first layer, we will call them *cultural surrogates* (or *surrogates* in short). Their role is strictly informative, and they cannot directly modify the traditional cultural network in the first layer. From the point of view of the BDI model of individuals, surrogates are in charge of populating the beliefs of each individual. These surrogates (for instance, the algorithm of a social network that learns from the user's behaviour in order to present them personalized content or recommendations in the future) differentiate artificial intelligence–based cultural networks from traditional cultural networks in that these surrogates are very efficient in their tagging of objects for individual cultural agents. Traditional cultural networks only had cultural institutions (museums, libraries, archives) as cultural surrogates, whose functions were to generalize the memories of the traditional cultural network, while serving the whole population of the network.

Within this general framework is enough freedom to consider or to implement more or less complex models of each level of cultural networks in order to make different approaches to modelling them. We can also try a variety of approaches to test different theories about how information is organized and flows in these networks, or even how it is more or less pertinent to introduce complex models of the human being (enriching decision-making by means of more nuanced BDI models) so that certain behaviours emerge in the network.

We must note that, although we can make a static analysis of the network based on how the connections at the three levels look at a given moment in time, one of the most interesting aspects of this framework is that it is based precisely on the dynamism inherent in cultural networks. This dynamism is reflected in the actions carried out by individuals as a result of the processes determined by their own BDI model and that can replicate, for example, the usual actions of "like/dislike" in a digital social network (such as Facebook, Twitter, etc.) that an individual can perform on another individual's publication. The interaction of individuals with objects not only shapes a cultural network in any given moment, but also makes it evolve over time, producing phenomena that can be observed and measured at all three layers, such as

- Layer 1: birth/death (creation/deletion) of content (new cultural objects), birth/death (connection/disconnection) of individuals, generation of clusters of individuals/objects sharing similar characteristics, etc.
- Layer 2: dynamic grouping of interactions (e.g. certain behaviour in the network that precedes the creation/deletion of content), emergence of semantic connections between object properties, segmentation of the population based on the way they behave, etc.
- Layer 3: classification of decision patterns in the network (comparing the surrogates of individuals), complexity of the information space that individuals attend to, evolution of the characteristics of the surrogates, etc.

4 Implementation

4.1 A restricted model

Building a complete framework like the one described earlier is a difficult and long-range project. Therefore, what we present in this section is a first approach to a concrete model that follows the guidelines and fundamental ideas of the framework. It does not aim to offer all the functionalities in a complete way, but is rather a demonstration of a small agent model that replicates some of the characteristics and process dynamics that we find in some cultural networks according to our theoretical approach as described previously.

We will rely on the scenario outlined in section 2, where the interaction of human agents with cultural objects is restricted to connecting with those objects through computing affinity that generates a social semantic map, where surrogates surf the map or network looking for related objects to ensure the satisfaction of the individual in the network and, as such, their permanence in it. Thus, cultural objects are described through a set of tags. To simplify the implementation and later analysis, tags are handled among a finite and prefixed set of possibilities: T. We will denote A for the set of individuals and O for the set of cultural objects. In this model, we will assume that the individuals cannot tag the objects, but rather the tags are pre-associated to the cultural objects. For each object in O, its set of tags is given as a subset of T.

Meanwhile, individuals have a set of "preferences", P, which stores the characteristics of the ideal cultural objects that satisfy them the most. A preference of an individual will be a set $g = g^+ \cup g^-$, where g^+ and g^- are disjoint subsets of T, g^+ (resp. g^-) indicates the tags that they desire to be (resp. not to be) present in the object. The tags not in g do not affect the perceived affinity between the object and individual.

When a cultural object is presented to an individual, the latter measures how well the object fits their preferences, their affinity. We will use a simple set calculation to compute the affinity that considers the number of matches between desired and undesired tags, that is, if $a \in A$, P is their preferences, and e are the tags of the object o, then:

$$affinity(a,o) = \max_{\{g \in P\}} \left(\left| g^+ \cap e \right| + \left| g^- \cap e^c \right| - \left| g^+ \cap e^c \right| - \left| g^- \cap e \right| \right)$$

where e^c is the complementary set of e (i.e. the tags not in o). The individual calculates the affinity with o as the best of the affinities with respect to the set of their preferences. This value is always in the range $[-1,1]$. When $affinity(a,o) = 1$, the object meets exactly one of the individual's expectations, and when $affinity(a,o) = -1$, the object is at the opposite end of their expectations.

The goal of such a scenario is to demonstrate how clusters can be produced between individuals and objects through the affinity between the preferences of the former and the tags associated with the latter. This way, we have a snapshot of the structure of the cultural network that arises in this process of connecting by affinity and which corresponds to the level 1 of analysis mentioned earlier: clusters formed both in the set of individuals (by association with common objects) and in the set of objects (by association between communities of individuals).

In this context, we can consider an initial cultural network, $(A \cup O, E)$, formed by agents of A, objects of O, and connections $(a,o) \in E$ if and only if $affinity(a,o) < th_{\mathit{aff}}$ (minimum threshold of affinity). Once this network is created, we will remove the isolated nodes (from A and O), since in the dynamics to be introduced they would not play any possible role (in this dynamics objects that are exposed to individuals are selected among those connected and evaluated by other individuals, or their mutations).

Broadly speaking, the dynamic we propose follows these four general steps (repeated cyclically):

1. *Connection*: For each individual, select an object to present to them so that the individual decides (through their affinity) whether to connect them. Update the satisfaction of individuals.
2. *Birth*: Add new individuals and objects to the world, by cloning and mutation of existing ones.
3. *Oblivion*: Remove objects with lowest influence that have not been recently presented to individuals.
4. *Death*: Remove individuals and objects that have become disconnected and individuals with satisfaction below a required threshold.

Satisfaction of an individual is simulated through an accumulated function that decreases in time and increases every time the individual finds a new object of interest (high enough affinity).

In the Connection step, the selection of objects to be presented to individuals is made by using the surrogates that each individual launches to decide which objects in the network are not connected to them and could be of interest.

The Birth step tries to mimic the procedure that occurs in some cultural networks for the creation of new elements: some highly satisfied individuals invite new individuals (with similar preferences) to join the network by means of sharing or showing them some object of attraction; and, simultaneously, objects that present slight variations with respect to successful objects (high importance, for example using PageRank) are created in the network.

Since we want to maintain network capacity under some constraints, the Oblivion step produces some objects that will be forgotten. This process can be also found in many cultural networks, where cultural objects with less importance in the network and not recently used by anyone end up being forgotten.

Finally, unsatisfied individuals (represent individuals who have not found interesting information in the network) leave the network, and those elements that have become isolated are removed because it is very unlikely that they will be able to intervene in the following life cycles of the network.

The BDI architecture is being used in this approach through the following association for each individual: beliefs are given by the direct knowledge they have about their ego-network and by the information that surrogates provide them through the selection of new objects; desires are represented through individuals' preferences (static) and the attempt to maximize their satisfaction in the network (dynamic); individuals' intentions are to stay in the network, which is translated into actions through the use of surrogates looking for new information and the connection with objects that are related to their desires.

4.2 Experiments

In our example, we start with a randomly generated network of 100 individuals and 100 objects (some of these elements might be disconnected from the first step and not appear anymore), which can work with a set of 100 tags (there are 2^{100} possible different objects). The individuals have a set of 5 preferences with which they measure the affinity of the cultural objects they analyze (there are 3^{100} possible different preferences, so there are around 3^{500} possible different individuals).

Figure 14.1 Cultural network at the beginning of the simulation (individuals in dark grey, objects in light grey, and the size is proportional to their global importance in the network)

We will use an affinity threshold of 0.7 (i.e. the affinity between an object and an individual must be greater than 0.7 for a connection between them to be generated), in order to decide when an individual feels attracted to an object. We consider this is not too low so that she accepts as affinities too many different objects, nor too demanding for her desires to become the norm for her ego-network. However, we assume that the decision to make this the affinity threshold is arbitrary and can be changed to examine different scenarios.

Figure 14.1 shows an example of a network obtained with these parameters after removing the isolated nodes (those that have not reached sufficient affinity to connect to other elements).

Figure 14.2 shows the evolution that the previous network has undergone after 200 steps of the dynamics explained previously. It can be seen that the network has a very clear structure, where the following stands out:

1. Individuals of high importance (dark grey with larger size) are central to the distribution of information in the network (which is relevant to the selection process made by individual

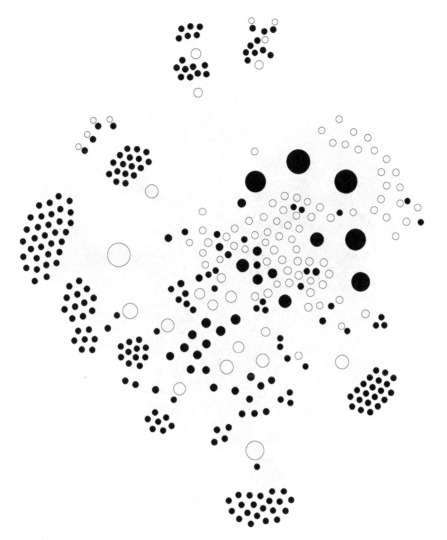

Figure 14.2 Cultural network after 200 steps of simulation (individuals in dark grey, objects in light grey, and the size is proportional to global importance in the network)

surrogates). These individuals are very active in terms of the number of objects they connect with because their preferences allow for a high number and diversity of connections.

2. Communities of individuals associate with objects of high importance to the global network (larger light grey nodes). These are individuals of lesser relative importance, with less connection capacity (perhaps more focused preferences), but who together are able to activate the importance of the objects that interest them.

3. Individuals not associated with communities, also of minor importance (dark grey, unclustered and smaller), are distributed throughout the network and serve as a support for communication between its different areas.

As an example of a Layer 2 analysis, we can build the semantic network derived from the tags of the cultural network. The relations in this new network are computed as first-level information

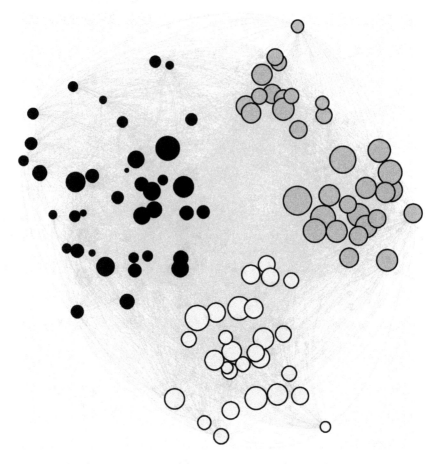

Figure 14.3 Tag distribution according to their co-occurrence similarity in the cultural network (detected communities of tags are grouped by grey shades)

in the following way: two tags are (semantically) related if they co-occur in some of the current cultural objects, and the strength of this relationship is proportional to the number of times that the tags occur together. This strength is called their co-occurrence similarity, since it measures how similar is the use of both tags (Suárez et al., 2011).

In Figure 14.3 we show the semantic network built from the cultural layer represented in Figure 14.2. In order to show the structures and hierarchy of this new layer, the position of the tags are computed through a 2D projection of the multidimensional scaling algorithm by using their co-occurrence similarity (more similar tags are shown closer), while the colour is assigned according to their community class in the network (tags with the same colour represent communities where there are more intracommunity than intercommunity relationships). Displaying both types of information simultaneously confirms that the relational structure that appears between the tags is related to their shared use by the objects in the network.

Here, the agents and objects make use of tags (which are meaningless, as our example is not supported on data from the real world) to show how the model can approximate an evolutionary behaviour of the network that emerges from the rules used by the individuals. The figures corresponding to the three layers of this new type of digitized and semi-automated cultural network are thus presented as an example of analysis of the various levels that make up the framework presented.

5 Conclusions

Traditional cultural networks are being challenged by processes of digitization and automation. Whereas those networks once implemented centralized systems of network memory that served the whole population, new automated networks proceed through multilayer mechanisms. These mechanisms aim to keep clusters of individuals together via their interaction with common cultural objects while incentivizing constant and multiple interactions to satisfy their business models. At the same time, these business models foster network mechanisms that try to satisfy the intentions and beliefs of individual agents with the highest degree of accuracy possible. It is in this level of network interactions that tagging of cultural objects by artificial intelligent surrogates is of the greatest importance.

Tagging of cultural objects by surrogates provides the speed and range of signals (tags) that individuals need to quickly decide if the presented objects satisfy their needs to a degree high enough to make those individuals or agents act on those objects by connecting to them. The reaction to those signals supplies constant information about the state of the individuals, their affinity to newly presented cultural objects (that now become mostly ephemeral even if some show a higher importance ranking as order emerges in the network) and the effectiveness of the evolving set of signals the surrogates deliver to them at each interaction. The reaction to these tags feeds the automatic mechanisms of new cultural networks and fosters an ever-active dynamic of networked culture that is less dependent on institutional repositories than on the constant feedback loop created by the various levels of individuals, connections to objects and tags describing those objects.

From the standpoint of the conceptual framework, it is interesting to see how the various extensions of the BDI paradigm can offer approaches to the modelling of specific behaviours within cultural networks, as well as to the analysis of the behaviours programmed into surrogates that can result in the formation of different types of networks.

As for specific implementations, it is important to note presently we have only presented a first, descriptive scenario to test the soundness of the proposal; in the future, we will work to implement a BDI system that allows individuals to have a richer planning system in order to realize their desires, by implementing a more diverse set of intentions. Although the model uses a simplification that only establishes interactions between individuals and cultural objects, surrogates can inform individuals about other individuals, producing a second level of interaction even in the cases where there are no direct connections between them. It may be interesting to see how to use surrogates vis-à-vis the emergence of behaviours (collaboration, altruism, etc.) between individuals.

In the implementation that we have carried out, some very basic mechanisms (based on an elementary evolution) of network transformation (birth and death of nodes and edges) are proposed, so it remains to be explored what other mechanisms related to the dynamics of cultural networks can be implemented. In relation to the analysis of cultural networks, we will analyze, in a more elaborate way, the cultural networks that are produced using different dynamics, in order to provide this skill to surrogates (even in a distributed way) so that the partial analysis they make of the network influences the individuals to whom they belong.

In order to model networks with centralized control (as is the case with digital social networks), it might be interesting to analyze how the evolution of surrogates can direct the dynamics of the cultural network in predetermined directions (for example, avoiding abandonment of the network or intervening in the type of cultural objects that are promoted within it). In this case, surrogates rely on specific individuals (e.g. learning from their past interactions) but execute algorithms (through decision-making) that are directed by an objective external to the individual.

Finally, this first implementation of the structure and dynamics of artificial intelligence–led cultural networks offers a glimpse at the differences they show in comparison with traditional cultural networks, which are dependent on centralized memory mechanisms, and the prevalence of certain cultural objects declared canonical. We think that demonstrating the behaviour of the new cultural networks being produced by digital platforms is an important first step towards adapting the managerial and institutional practices of traditional cultural networks as they connect and interact in various ways to digital ecosystems.

References

Adam, C., & Gaudou, B. (2015). *BDI agents in social simulations: A survey* (Research Report). RR-LIG-050, LIG.

Arasu, A., Novak, J., Tomkins, A., & Tomlin, J. (2002). PageRank computation and the structure of the web: Experiments and algorithms. In WWW '02: *Proceedings of the eleventh international World Wide Web conference*. Association for Computing Machinery.

Bratman, M. E. (1987). *Intention, plans, and practical reason*. Harvard University Press.

Bratman, M. E. (2009). Intention, belief, and instrumental rationality. In D. Sobel & S. Wall (Eds.), *Reasons for action*. Cambridge University Press.

Cavalli Sforza, L. L. (2007). *La evolución de la cultura*. Anagrama.

Cohen, P. R., & Levesque, H. J. (1990). Intention is choice with commitment. *Artificial Intelligence, 42*(2).

de Silva, L., Sardina, S., & Padgham, L. (2009, May). First principles planning in BDI systems. In *AAMAS '09: Proceedings of the 8th international conference on autonomous agents and multiagent systems - Volume 2* (pp. 1105–1112). AAMAS.

Grosz, B., & Kraus, S. (1996). Collaborative plans for complex group action. *Artificial Intelligence, 86*(2).

Helbing, D., Farkas, I., & Vicsek, T. (2000). Simulating dynamical features of escape panic. *Nature, 407*(6803).

Henrich, J. (2016). *The secret of our success. How culture is driving human evolution, domesticating our species and making Us smarter*. Princeton University Press.

Inglehart, R. F. (2018). *Cultural evolution. People's motivations are changing and reshaping the world*. Cambridge University Press.

Meyer, J. -J. Ch., de Boer, F. S., van Eijk, R. M., Hindriks, K. V., & van der Hoek, W. (2001). On programming KARO agents. *Logic Journal of the IGPL, 9*(2).

Page, L., Brin, S., Motwani, R., & Winograd, T. (1999). *The PageRank citation ranking: Bringing order to the Web*. Stanford InfoLab.

Rao, A. S., & Georgeff, M. P. (1991). Modeling rational agents within a BDI-architecture. In *Proceedings of the 2nd international conference on principles of knowledge representation and reasoning (KR)*. Morgan Kaufmann.

Richardson, M., & Domingos, P. (2002). The intelligent surfer: Probabilistic combination of link and content information in PageRank. In *Advances in neural information processing systems* (Vol. 14). MIT Press.

Richerson, P. J., & Boyd, R. (2006). Not by genes alone. In *How culture transformed human evolution*. The University of Chicago Press.

Sancho-Caparrini, F., & Suárez, J. L. (2011). A virtual laboratory for the study of history and cultural dynamics. *Journal of Artificial Societies and Social Simulation, 14*(4), 19.

Siegfried, R. (2014). *Modeling and simulation of complex systems: A framework for efficient agent-based modeling and simulation*. Springer.

Singh, D., Sardina, S., Padgham, L., & James, G. (2011). Integrating learning into a bdi agent for environments with changing dynamics. In T. Walsh (Ed.), *Proceedings of the twenty-second international joint conference on artificial inelligence.*IJCAI.

Suárez, J. L. (2007). Hispanic baroque: A model for the study of cultural complexity in the Atlantic world. *South Atlantic Review, 72*(1).

Suárez, J. L. (2020). Una red de redes. La red cultural del Banco de la República. In *Bogotá: Cuadernos de gestión cultural del Banco de la República*. Banco de la República. ISBN: 978-958-664-422-88

Suárez, J. L., McArthur, B., & Soto-Corominas, A. (2015). Cultural networks and the future of cultural analytics. In *2015 international conference on culture and computing*. Kyoto University.

Suárez, J. L., Sancho-Caparrini, F., & de la Rosa, J. (2011). The art-space of a global community: The network of Baroque paintings in Hispanic-America. In *2011 second international conference on culture and computing* (pp. 45–50), doi:10.1109/Culture-Computing.2011.17

Suárez, J. L., Sancho-Caparrini, F., & de la Rosa, J. (2012). Sustaining a global community: Art and religion in the network of baroque Hispanic-American paintings. *Leonardo, 45*(3).

Suárez, J. L., et al. (2013, December). Towards a digital geography of Hispanic Baroque art. *Literary and Linguistic Computing, 28*(4), 718–735. https://doi.org/10.1093/llc/fqt050

Taibi, T. (2010). Incorporating trust into the BDI architecture. *International Journal of Artificial Intelligence and Soft Computing, 2*(3).

Tomasello, M. (2000). *The cultural origins of human cognition*. Cambridge University Press.

Tomasello, M. (2019). *Becoming human. A theory of ontogeny*. Harvard University Press.

van Dijck, J., Poell, T., & de Waal, M. (2018). *The platform society*. Oxford Scholarship Online.

15

USING SUBGROUP DISCOVERY AND LATENT GROWTH CURVE MODELING TO IDENTIFY UNUSUAL DEVELOPMENTAL TRAJECTORIES

Axel Mayer, Christoph Kiefer, Benedikt Langenberg
and Florian Lemmerich

Introduction

In this chapter, we aim at bringing together techniques from computer sciences and social science methodology to efficiently find subgroups of university students that show unusual developmental trajectories in dropout intentions. In the data mining literature, efficient algorithms for subgroup discovery, a pattern mining task, are widely used for identifying subgroups with specific exceptional properties in large data sets. In the social sciences on the other hand, there are decades of research on how to model structural relations between random variables. One of the most popular and flexible methods used in this field is structural equation modeling (SEM). SEM can, for example, be used to model complex change and growth processes using (latent) growth curve models (Meredith & Tisak, 1990), growth component models (Mayer et al., 2012) or latent change models (McArdle, 2009). Some recent extensions of growth models, like growth mixture modeling (GMM, Muthén & Muthén, 2000) and structural equation model trees (SEM trees, Brandmaier et al., 2013), allow for discovering potentially latent subgroups that are distinct with regard to their growth pattern. We use an alternative to GMM and SEM trees that has similar aims but builds on algorithms from subgroup discovery and exceptional model mining (Klösgen, 1996; Leman et al., 2008) to more efficiently find the subgroups of interest in large data sets. This approach is termed *subgroup latent growth curve modeling* (SubgroupLGCM) and is similar to a recently applied approach to find subgroups in mediation models (Lemmerich et al., 2020). A key difference between SubgroupLGCM and GMM is that the former uses manifest descriptions of patterns whereas the latter builds on a latent class approach to identify unobserved subgroups. To the best of our knowledge, there is little to no overlap between SEM and pattern mining fields and we show that SEM can benefit from the algorithmic knowledge developed in other fields. Within the SEM literature there are both global (e.g., χ^2-tests of model fit) and local tests (e.g., Wald tests) that can serve as interestingness measures

DOI: 10.4324/9781003025245-18

for quantifying differences between subgroups in the algorithm, but other measures such as user-defined effect sizes can be used as well. In an illustrative example, we show how our SubgroupLGCM algorithm can be applied in the social sciences. We use data from the National Educational Panel Study in Germany, which provides longitudinal data on the development of competencies, educational processes, and educational decisions. We investigate the trajectories of university students study dropout intentions over four years and use the SubgroupLGCM algorithm to explore subgroups with exceptional trajectories. Limitations and other potential applications for computational social science are discussed.

Mining interesting subgroups and statistical models

Subgroup discovery

The discovery of interesting subgroups has a high practical relevance in many scientific disciplines and in the social sciences in particular. The well-known subgroup discovery task originating from the computer sciences (Klösgen, 1996; Herrera et al., 2011) provides a useful framework for formalizing this task. The four main components of subgroup discovery are the target variable, the subgroup description language, the interestingness measure, and the search strategy. The target variable specifies the main outcome or dependent variable of interest (e.g., successfully completing a study program), the subgroup description language informs us which combination of categorical or categorized description variables specify the subgroup under consideration (e.g., male students with a low socioeconomic status), the interestingness measure provides the criterion for identifying interesting subgroups and can for example be either an effect size measure or a statistical test (e.g., indicating that one subgroup differs significantly from the complementary subgroup with regard to study success), and the search strategy defines how the search space is explored (ranging from simple brute-force exhaustive search to more efficient search strategies like beam search or customized strategies). A challenge for subgroup discovery is that even for a moderate amount of description variables, an exponential number of subgroups can be formed via conjunctions, e.g., *Age < 18 ∧ Gender = Male*. The result of a subgroup discovery task is then a list of the subgroup descriptions that have been selected from a large pool of candidate subgroups that can be formed by the description language as the ones with the highest score according to the chosen interestingness measure. Subgroup discovery is mainly applied for exploration and descriptive induction and not for confirmatory analysis.

Exceptional model mining

The *exceptional model mining* framework (Leman et al., 2008; Duivesteijn et al., 2016) is an extension of the traditional subgroup discovery setting. The key difference is that exceptional model mining builds on a statistical model as a target concept instead of a single variable. Thus, it aims for identifying describable subgroups in the data with significantly different model parameters compared to the other instances in a pre-specified model of a specific class. As for classic subgroup discovery, subgroups can be described by a combination (conjunction) of values of categorical variables or intervals in the case of numeric variables. In exceptional model mining, we are now interested in finding interesting subgroups with respect to a specific model class, a type of model a priori picked by the analyst. For that purpose, we compare the subset of individuals in a particular subgroup (the *subgroup cover*) to the subset of persons not covered by the subgroup description (the *subgroup complement*). We consider subgroups as interesting if the parameters differ substantially depending on the model being fitted on the subgroup cover or subgroup complement instances. Such subgroups are then assigned a high score by an inter-estingness measure. As in traditional subgroup discovery, candidate subgroups with the highest scores are then identified by an efficient search algorithm.

While exceptional model mining has been used with a wide variety of statistical models (correlation, regression, Bayesian networks), in this chapter, we want to bring the exceptional model mining framework from computer science and structural equation modeling together in a joint framework. In particular, we combine exceptional model mining and latent growth curve models, a group of frequently used structural equation models, to identify subgroups of persons with unusual developmental trajectories. Before we describe the combination of both traditions, we briefly introduce the most common growth curve models and discuss existing approaches for (latent) subgroups with unusual trajectories.

Latent Growth Curve Models

In the social sciences, a popular approach to model change over time uses different kinds of latent growth curve models (LGCMs). The kinds of LGCMs can be distinguished along two different dimensions: whether they assume a predefined trajectory for every person and whether they include a measurement model for the construct of interest. Popular models with predefined trajectories are linear and quadratic LGCMs (Meredith & Tisak, 1990), whereas latent change models (McArdle, 2001; Raykov, 1999; Steyer et al., 1997) and growth component models (Mayer et al., 2012) do not make the assumption of predefined trajectories and are therefore more flexible in the shape of intra-individual development. Within the context of structural equation modeling, all these latent growth models can be modeled as so-called single-indicator models, where the developing construct is manifest (i.e., measured by a single indicator), or as multiple-indicator models (McArdle, 1988; Tisak & Tisak, 2000), where the developing construct is latent (i.e., measured by multiple indicators). In the latter case, the LGCMs also include a measurement model that relates the multiple indicators to the latent variable.

Structural equation modeling

While some latent growth models can also be specified as multilevel models, we focus on the specification in a structural equation modeling framework, because this allows for convenient incorporation of measurement models and multiple groups. The general form of a structural equation model is given by a measurement model relating manifest variables in the vector y to latent variables in the vector η and a group-specific structural model specifying structural relations among latent variables η:

$$y = v + \Lambda\eta + \varepsilon \qquad \text{Measurement model} \qquad (15.1)$$
$$\eta = \alpha + \mathbf{B}\eta + \zeta \qquad \text{Structural model} \qquad (15.2)$$

where v is a vector of measurement intercepts, Λ is a matrix of loadings, α is a vector of structural intercepts/means, $\mathbf{B}$ is a matrix of structural coefficients, ε is a vector of measurement error variables, ζ is a vector of structural residuals.

Models with predefined trajectories

Linear and quadratic LGCMs assume a predefined trajectory for every person, and in a structural equation modeling framework this is modeled by fixing the factor loadings on the latent growth factors in a certain way. These factor loadings appear in the measurement model for single-indicator models and in the structural model for multiple-indicator models. Consider an example where a single-indicator construct is measured at four equidistant time points $T = \{0, 1, 2, 3\}$. The linear LGCM includes an intercept π_0 and a slope factor π_1 and the loadings of the slope factor are defined by the time points T. The resulting model takes the form:

$$\begin{pmatrix} Y_1 \\ Y_2 \\ Y_3 \\ Y_4 \end{pmatrix} = \begin{pmatrix} 1 & 0 \\ 1 & 1 \\ 1 & 2 \\ 1 & 3 \end{pmatrix} \begin{pmatrix} \pi_0 \\ \pi_1 \end{pmatrix} + \begin{pmatrix} \varepsilon_1 \\ \varepsilon_2 \\ \varepsilon_3 \\ \varepsilon_4 \end{pmatrix} \tag{15.3}$$

$$\begin{pmatrix} \pi_0 \\ \pi_1 \end{pmatrix} = \begin{pmatrix} \mu_0 \\ \mu_1 \end{pmatrix} + \begin{pmatrix} \zeta_0 \\ \zeta_1 \end{pmatrix} \tag{15.4}$$

With this time coding, the latent intercept π_0 represents the construct of interest at the first occasion of measurement and the latent slope factor π_1 represents linear change over time. The means of the intercept and slope are μ_0 and μ_1, and their variances are $Var(\zeta_0)$ and $Var(\zeta_1)$. In this model, it is assumed that the curve for every person is a straight line, but intercepts and slope can be person-specific.

The quadratic growth model additionally includes a quadratic growth factor whose loadings are defined as the squared time points resulting in the following model equation:

$$\begin{pmatrix} Y_1 \\ Y_2 \\ Y_3 \\ Y_4 \end{pmatrix} = \begin{pmatrix} 1 & 0 & 0 \\ 1 & 1 & 1 \\ 1 & 2 & 4 \\ 1 & 3 & 9 \end{pmatrix} \begin{pmatrix} \pi_0 \\ \pi_1 \\ \pi_2 \end{pmatrix} + \begin{pmatrix} \varepsilon_1 \\ \varepsilon_2 \\ \varepsilon_3 \\ \varepsilon_4 \end{pmatrix} \tag{15.5}$$

$$\begin{pmatrix} \pi_0 \\ \pi_1 \\ \pi_2 \end{pmatrix} = \begin{pmatrix} \mu_0 \\ \mu_1 \\ \mu_2 \end{pmatrix} + \begin{pmatrix} \zeta_0 \\ \zeta_1 \\ \zeta_2 \end{pmatrix} \tag{15.6}$$

The linear slope factor now represents the instantaneous rate of change at the first occasion of measurement (Biesanz et al., 2004) and the quadratic growth factor indicates acceleration in growth. Higher-order LGCMs also exist, but these are rarely applied in the social sciences. The higher-order LGCMs are constructed using the same principles by adding growth factors to the model whose loadings are powers of time coding. For example, the cubic growth model could be obtained by adding a growth factor π_3 to the quadratic model with loadings equal to the cubed time coding.

Path models are a nice way to illustrate structural equation models, especially for somewhat more complicated models. The corresponding path diagram for the linear and the quadratic LGCMs are shown in Figure 15.1.

Models with flexible trajectories

The LGCMs considered so far have in common that the shape of the growth trajectories is predetermined by fixing factor loadings to (powers of) time coding. It has been assumed that all individuals' true growth trajectories have the same predefined shape, even though the individual values can vary. This assumption can be relaxed by using latent change models (McArdle, 2001;

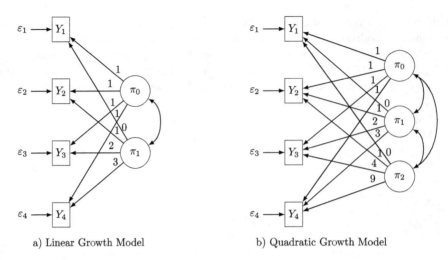

a) Linear Growth Model b) Quadratic Growth Model

Figure 15.1 Path models for a) linear and b) quadratic latent growth curve models with a single indicator per time point

Raykov, 1999; Steyer et al., 1997) and growth component models (Mayer et al., 2012). Since latent change models can be considered a special case of growth component models, we introduce the latter and show how latent change models fit in this framework.[1]

The basic idea of growth component models is to start with an explicit definition of latent growth components π_j based on well-defined variables. In single-indicator models, growth components are defined as a function of latent state variables τ_t. In multiple-indicator models, growth components are defined as a function of common latent state factors η_t (Steyer et al., 2014).

Consider again the example where a single-indicator construct is measured at four equidistant time points and let τ_t denote the corresponding latent state variables. A possible definition of growth components is:

$$\pi_0 = 1\cdot\tau_0 + 0\cdot\tau_1 + 0\cdot\tau_2 + 0\cdot\tau_3$$
$$\pi_1 = -1\cdot\tau_0 + 1\cdot\tau_1 + 0\cdot\tau_2 + 0\cdot\tau_3$$
$$\pi_2 = 0\cdot\tau_0 - 1\cdot\tau_1 + 1\cdot\tau_2 + 0\cdot\tau_3$$
$$\pi_3 = 0\cdot\tau_0 + 0\cdot\tau_1 - 1\cdot\tau_2 + 1\cdot\tau_3$$

In this case, π_0 represents the construct of interest at the time point and the other growth components π_1 to π_3 are contrast variables that compare one time point versus the preceding time point. The resulting model is called a neighbor true change model (Steyer et al., 1997) because neighboring time points are compared. In general matrix notation the definition of π_j variables is:

$$\pi = C\tau, \tag{15.7}$$

and the contrast matrix C is key to defining the growth components. Unfortunately, the specification as structural equation model requires rearrangement of Equation 15.7 in such a way that $\tau = \Lambda\pi$ (cf. measurement model in Equation 15.1). Therefore to obtain the loading matrix

Λ, we need to invert the contrast matrix **C**. For our example with the neighbor true change model, this yields:

$$\Lambda = \begin{pmatrix} 1 & 0 & 0 & 0 \\ -1 & 1 & 0 & 0 \\ 1 & -1 & 1 & 0 \\ 1 & 0 & -1 & 1 \end{pmatrix}^{-1} = \begin{pmatrix} 1 & 0 & 0 & 0 \\ 1 & 1 & 0 & 0 \\ 1 & 1 & 1 & 0 \\ 1 & 1 & 1 & 0 \end{pmatrix}$$

The corresponding path diagram is shown in Figure 15.2. The model is not identified, because there are more model parameters than empirical parameters. Therefore, it cannot be estimated without additional assumptions such as that the τ-variables are measured without error. In this case, the latent growth components are deterministic functions of the observed variables. This model would then be equivalent to using trend scores (e.g., Belsky & Rovine, 1990).

The growth component model is a very flexible approach. In principle, any contrast matrix can be used to define the growth component of interest, and their correct interpretation is ensured. The only requirement is that the contrast matrix is full rank resulting in a saturated model, because otherwise it cannot be inverted. But of course users can add constraints afterwards if needed.

Multiple-indicator LGCMs

Most researchers use LGCMs that are based on a single observed variable at each time point (Leite, 2007). However, all models presented thus far can be extended to model growth of latent variables, that is, growth of common latent state factors η_t. For this purpose a measurement model relating multiple manifest indicators to the common latent state factors is added. Several researchers have emphasized advantages of using such multiple-indicator LGCMs: First, these models make it possible to test measurement equivalence across time (Chan, 1998; Ferrer

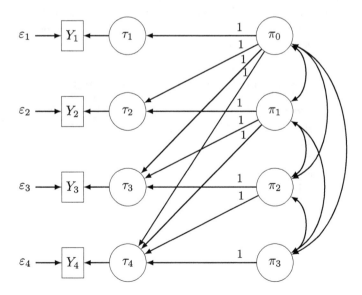

Figure 15.2 Saturated (not identified) neighbor true change model obtained via the growth components approach

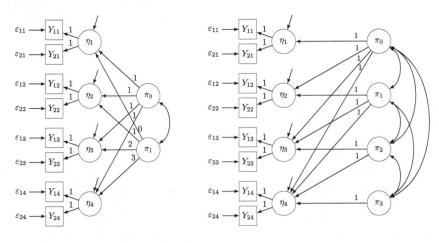

a) Multiple-Indicator Linear Growth Model   b) Multiple-Indicator Growth Component Model

Figure 15.3   Multiple-indicator version of a linear LGCM and a neighbor true change model

et al., 2008). Second, multiple-indicator LGCMs allow separating situation-specific variance from true trait change (Geiser et al., 2013; Sayer & Cumsille, 2001) and, third, they can be used to model method variance in the observed variables. Finally, using multiple indicators also has been shown to result in greater statistical power to detect individual differences in change over time (von Oertzen et al., 2010).

At least two indicator variables at each time point or precise knowledge of indicator reliability is needed in order to specify a measurement model for these latent variables. Consider our example with four equidistant time points and two parallel indicators measuring the common η_t variables. Figure 15.3 shows the multiple-indicator versions of the previously introduced linear LGCM and the neighbor true change model (omitting the true score variables).

These models consist of two parts. The first part is the measurement model for the common latent state factors η_t and the second part of the model is the linear LGCM or the neighbor true change model for the latent state factors η_t respectively.

Subgroup latent growth curve models

Oftentimes researchers are interested not only in overall or mean trajectories and interindividual differences, but also in certain subgroups that show unusual developmental trajectories. For example, researchers may be interested in gender differences, in age-group differences, or in differences between countries with regard to their trajectories. The LGCMs as presented earlier can be extended to allow for multiple groups in several ways. In this section we briefly review some existing ways to identify (latent) subgroups that have distinct trajectories. We distinguish between classic multigroup growth models, growth mixture models and tree-based growth models.

Multigroup growth models

The classic way of modeling multiple groups in structural equation modeling is a simultaneous analysis of the model in several groups (Jöreskog, 1971). In these models, the grouping variable needs to be specified a priori by the researcher usually based on substantive considerations.

This extends the measurement model and the structural model of the SEM (cf. Equations 15.1 and 15.2) and allows the parameters to be group-specific. In the context of multigroup growth models, it is usually meaningful to have not only a group-invariant measurement model, but also a group-specific structural model so that the parameters of the growth curves can be different across groups. The general complete model then is:

$$\mathbf{y} = \mathbf{v} + \Lambda\eta + \varepsilon \qquad \text{Group-invariant measurement model} \qquad (15.8)$$

$$\eta = \alpha_g + \mathbf{B}_g\eta + \zeta \qquad \text{Group-specific structural model} \qquad (15.9)$$

where the parameters are the same as earlier, but some of them can be group-specific denoted by the subscript g. In linear and quadratic LGCMs, the means and variances for the latent growth factors can then be different across groups. Similarly, for the growth component and true change models, each group can have their distinct means and variances of the latent growth components resulting in different group-specific growth patterns and trajectories.

Growth mixture models

Another related way of modeling subgroups in SEM is growth mixture modeling (Muthén & Muthén, 2000). The key difference compared to multigroup growth models is that the grouping variable in GMM is an unobserved categorical variable. The values of this variable are called latent classes, and one of the challenges in this approach is to decide on the number of classes (Nylund et al., 2007). GMM is basically a combination of finite mixture modeling (McLachlan & Peel, 2000) and SEM applied to growth curve models. A closely related approach has been termed group-based trajectory modeling (Nagin, 1999, 2005). The inclusion of mixture models allows for investigating unobserved classes of trajectories. The model equations are the same as for the multigroup models (cf. Equations 15.8 and 15.9) except that for the latent classes the subscript c is usually used instead of g to indicate that group-membership is not observed. In addition, a model equation for the latent classes is added that potentially allows predicting class membership based on covariates. The most common choice for the latent class model is a multinomial logit model, but others are possible as well. Growth mixture models and finite mixture models, in general, are a powerful tool but can be difficult to estimate because of statistical and numerical issues such as multiple local maxima of the likelihood or numerical instabilities (Muthén, 2002). However, Martin and von Oertzen (2015) found evidence that GMM outperforms simpler clustering methods.

Tree-based growth models

More recently, structural equation modeling has also been combined with tree-based approaches (Brandmaier et al., 2013) and random forests (SEM forests, Brandmaier et al., 2016). In essence, the SEM trees approach allows for fitting a SEM with different parameters in the leaves of a clustering tree. This approach thereby also makes it possible to investigate subgroups with unusual developmental trajectories by letting the means and variances of the growth factors vary across leaves. The SEM trees are built using algorithms and statistical tests from the literature on model-based recursive partitioning (e.g., Zeileis et al., 2008). Brandmaier et al. (2013) illustrated their approach using a linear growth model, and Brandmaier et al. (2017) demonstrated an application of SEM trees in combination with quadratic LGCMs.

In contrast to multigroup SEM, tree-based growth models do not require the pre-specification of the grouping variable. Instead, the final grouping is determined by the statistical algorithm and multiple tests for split points in the clustering tree. For these tests either likelihood ratio tests or score-based methods can be used. In contrast to GMM, the grouping in tree-based methods is not latent but a result of the statistical approach and represents a combination of observed values of covariates that define the leaves of the tree.

There is some recent work on investigating the performance of LGCM-based SEM trees (Usami et al., 2019), on extending the tree-based methods to nonlinear models (Stegmann et al., 2018), and on comparing growth mixture modeling and tree-based methods. For example, Usami et al. (2017) compare tree-based models and mixture models for latent change scores in a simulation and find that tree-based models are more sensitive to model misspecification.

Subgroup discovery and latent growth modeling

In the following, we introduce another exploratory approach for finding subgroups that are distinct with regard to their growth pattern. This SubgroupLGCM approach builds on multi-group structural equation models and exceptional model mining. SubgroupLGCM has similar aims like growth mixture modeling and tree-based growth models but builds on the latest algorithms from exceptional model mining to efficiently find the subgroups of interest in large data sets. In contrast to GMM, SubgroupLGCM uses manifest grouping variables and is in that respect similar to SEM trees. It also does not require the pre-specification of grouping variables and searches for interesting growth patterns in the search space by means of (statistical) algorithms. However, the algorithm for finding the interesting subgroups is different from SEM trees. While SEM trees use tree-based algorithms, SubgroupLGCM uses algorithms from subgroup discovery and exceptional model mining in a pattern- or rule-based mining tradition.

This approach makes it possible to use a wide variety of interestingness measures and established algorithms from that field. A key advantage of our approach is that effect sizes and specialized statistical tests can be used as interestingness measures and that efficient search algorithms allow for testing a large number of subgroup description variables.

General approach

Our SubgroupLGCM framework features four main components: (i) the latent growth curve model of interest, (ii) the subgroup description language, (iii) the interestingness measure, and (iv) the search strategy. In principle, all aforementioned growth curve models can be integrated into SubgroupLGCM. The latent growth curve model is specified as a two-group model with an invariant measurement model and a group-specific structural model (cf. Equations 15.8 and 15.9); that is, the LGCM is fitted simultaneously in the potentially interesting subgroup characterized by the subgroup description language (the subgroup cover) and in the remaining part of the sample (the subgroup complement). Then the interestingness measure quantifying whether the subgroup is interesting is computed and saved. Interestingness measures can either be statistical tests that compare the subgroup and its complement or can be effect sizes that quantify differences between the two groups (see later). This procedure is repeated for a large number of potentially interesting subgroups. If a brute force search algorithm is used, all possible subgroups are investigated. However, in many cases the search space is too big, and more efficient algorithms are needed such as beam search or customized search algorithms that focus on certain interesting parts of the search space and neglect less promising parts. In the end, the most interesting subgroups with respect to the interestingness measure score are reported as the result.

Interestingness measures

A key part of SubgroupLGCM is the specification of suitable interestingness measures. Such measures are scoring functions that aim to quantify how interesting a subgroup is supposedly to the data analyst. In principle, interestingness as a concept is inherently subjective. However, in exceptional model mining approaches including SubgroupLGCM typically such subgroups are deemed interesting, for which the model parameters derived from the subgroup differ meaningfully from those derived from the complement, that is, from the group of all instances not contained in a subgroup. By choosing and/or adapting interestingness measures, we can make the selection process focus on specific parameters or subgroup statistics.

In growth curve models, the most interesting parameters for finding subgroups are arguably the means and the variances of the latent growth factors or latent growth components in the structural model. To find subgroups that are exceptional with respect to the growth trajectories, we propose different types of interestingness measures. All proposed interestingness measures are computed based on the two-group LGCMs. Let the mean values of the growth components $\pi_0 \ldots \pi_k$ in the subgroup cover and its complement be denoted by μ_0^{sg} to μ_k^{sg} and μ_0^{compl} to μ_k^{compl}, respectively. We distinguish between two groups of interestingness measures that we can use for the selection of interesting subgroups.

The first group of interestingness measures allows for a principled, statistically guided selection of subgroups. That is, the question whether a subgroup is interesting (exceptional) is determined by a statistical test on the parameters of the model. Choosing a specific statistical test and a null hypothesis defines a scoring function for subgroup discovery – the higher the significance (the lower the p-value), the higher the subgroup score. Note that statistical tests are not interpreted in the usual way in terms of testing a null hypothesis, in particular if no corrections for multiple testing are applied. They rather serve as a tool to obtain an interestingness measure. Therefore, results should be interpreted as exploratory findings that are potentially interesting and can be further explored. In our setting, we can use Wald tests, likelihood ratio tests, or score tests on different null hypotheses to define interestingness measures. For example, we can compute a Wald test in each two-group growth model with the null hypothesis that all means of the growth factors are the same in the subgroup and its complement. Then, one divided by the p-value of the test can then be used as an interestingness score, mapping the highest scores to the subgroup with the most significant test outcomes. Since the tests in all subgroups have the same degrees of freedom, we can also use the Wald χ^2 test statistic instead of the (inverted) p-value as interestingness measure, which is numerically more stable and avoids potential underflow of p-values. As another example of an interestingness measure, we can apply a Wald test to assess the more specific hypothesis that the mean of the linear growth factor in a linear LGCM is the same in the subgroup and its complement. Then, the interestingness of a subgroup only depends on the linear growth factor and not on the intercept or potentially higher-order factors. The same procedure can be adjusted and tailored to specific research questions. For example, if researchers are interested in finding subgroups that are inhomogeneous in their growth trajectories, they could use the variances of the growth factors in their statistical test. Additionally, we can also limit the direction of the parameter deviation in the subgroup, for example, by considering only those subgroups as interesting for which the mean or the variance are higher (not lower) than in its complement.

A second group of interestingness measures is less rigorous but allows for exploring candidates for interesting subgroups in an interactive and iterative process. Recall that results should be interpreted as exploratory findings to serve as starting points for further research. For these measures, we typically trade off the amount of deviation in the subgroup parameters derived from a subgroup with the size of the subgroup (i.e., the number of instances in the subgroup cover). That is, we can choose to focus on selecting those subgroups in which some or all parameters are substantially different even if they only cover few instances, or we can focus on subgroups with more instances at the potential cost of stronger deviations in the parameters.

Formally, this is achieved by computing the score of each subgroup as $n^a \cdot \Delta$, where n is the number of instances in the subgroup cover, Δ is a distance measure, and a is a user-chosen parameter that allows weighting between these two factors (cf. Klösgen, 1996; Leman et al., 2008). For a single parameter of interest, Δ can be computed as the difference between the parameter in the subgroup and its complement; for multiple parameters of interest, for example, the total variation distance or the sum of element-wise squared differences between the parameter vectors derived from the subgroup and its complement can be used. To identify interesting subgroups in latent growth curve models, we have multiple options, depending on the type of subgroup we want to identify: For example, we can just compare the mean of a particular growth factor in the subgroup and its complement. Alternatively, we can use the distances (e.g., measured by the sum of squared differences) in means of growth factors between the subgroup and its complement to find subgroups with exceptional trajectories. Or we can use standardized differences between growth factors. Any such parameter or derived quantity can serve as an interestingness measure in a SubgroupLGCM analysis, and the researcher can choose which one is most interesting for a particular application in hand or even try several in an exploratory way.

To avoid redundancy in the result set, that is, the occurrence of many similar subgroups in the result, measures can be adapted by generalization-aware modifications (see, e.g., Grosskreutz et al., 2010; Lemmerich et al., 2020). By doing so, we take the raw interestingness score of each subgroup but subtract from it the maximum interestingness score from its subgroup generalizations – for example, a subgroup described by A alone is a generalization of a subgroup described by $A \wedge B$ – to calculate its final score used for subgroup selection.

Empirical example

We use data from the National Educational Panel Study (NEPS; Blossfeld & von Maurice, 2011) to illustrate the use of the SubgroupLGCM approach in applied settings. NEPS is a multi-cohort longitudinal study aimed at examining lifelong educational processes. We will investigate trajectories of university students' dropout intention during four years of studies. Using the SubgroupLGCM approach, we identify several subgroups that exhibit exceptional trajectories of dropout intention compared to the complement of the sample. A substantive and a statistical interestingness measure will be applied, resulting in different sets of subgroups. As stated previously, differing formulations of the interestingness measure cater to different research needs.

Dropout in higher education

Dropout from a university's study program is defined as the termination without obtaining an academic degree (Heublein, 2014). In Germany, about 28% of university students drop out from their bachelor degree programs (Heublein & Schmelzer, 2018). The number of students dropping out differs from major to major. For example, only 14% of students aiming for a teaching position (German: "*Lehramt*") quit their study program early, while 54% of students in math programs drop out. In this sense, a student's intention to drop out can be understood as a criterion of overall study success (Kuh et al., 2007). Both theoretical and empirical previous work emphasized the link between dropout intention and actual dropout (Bean & Metzner, 1985; Bäulke et al., 2018; Mashburn, 2000; Cabrera et al., 1993). As dropout intention precedes actual dropout, identifying subgroups with exceptional trajectories of dropout intention can help to create tailored intervention and prevention programs.

First-generation students. First-generation students are often considered vulnerable to obstacles in everyday academic life and thus more likely to anticipate academic failure (Janke et al., 2017). The "first-generation" refers to a non-academic background of both parents and is often linked to a lower sense of belonging in academia (Stephens et al., 2012a; Stephens et al., 2012b). For example, Stebleton et al. (2014) found that first-generation students report a lower rating of belonging and greater levels of depression, and recently, Marksteiner et al. (2019) proposed an intervention to support first-generation students' sense of belonging. In the literature, first-generation students are often compared to continuing-generation students who have at least one parent with an academic background. However, specific combinations of parental educational background, for example, only one parent vs. both parents with academic background, are usually not further examined. The SubgroupLGCM approach allows us to investigate the relation between parents' educational background and students' dropout intention by exploring all possible combinations of educational backgrounds.

Difference among majors. Intrinsic motivation and life aspirations have been shown as an important predictor of students' performance, whereas extrinsic life aspirations are linked to negative study success (Janke & Dickhäuser, 2019). In a recent study, Yu and Levesque-Bristol (2018) found that the extent of self-determination varies across majors, possibly explaining the high variation of dropout and dropout intention. We use SubgroupLGCM to explore possible influences of desired final qualifications (e.g., bachelor, state examination) on trajectories of students' dropout intention.

Method

Sample. To illustrate the SubgroupLGCM approach, we use data from the National Educational Panel Study in Germany (Blossfeld & von Maurice, 2011). NEPS is a multi-cohort longitudinal study aimed at examining lifelong educational processes. For our example, we use data from the Starting Cohort 5 (first-year students). Within the first-year students cohort, students' dropout intention was assessed four times, each about one year apart (i.e., after the first, second, third, and fourth year of studies). The total sample size was $N = 17,910$. We used full information maximum likelihood to account for missing data in the analysis.

The primary goal of our chapter is to illustrate the SubgroupLGCM approach as a means to identify interesting subgroups with exceptional trajectories in educational processes. For didactic purposes, we restrict ourselves to dropout intention as outcome, to an exploratory set of nonlinear contrasts, and to a limited set of subgroup description variables.

Measures

Dropout intention. The scale "dropout intention" consists of three items:

Y_{1t}: I've often thought about dropping out.
Y_{2t}: If I could choose again, I would opt for another field of study.
Y_{3t}: I am seriously thinking of completely abandoning the studies.

The items are coded on a Likert scale ranging from 1 = *does not apply at all* to 4 = *applies completely*, and t denotes the measurement occasion with $t = 1, \ldots, 4$. We used these three positively worded items as indicators of a common latent state variable η_t using a η-congeneric

Table 15.1 Descriptive statistics for subgroup description variables

Education mother	Education father
basic voc. training (N = 6715)	basic voc. training (N = 4752)
Bachelor/Master/Diploma (N = 3514)	Bachelor/Master/Diploma (N = 4576)
full maturity certificate (s.c.) (N = 1606)	Diploma (FH) (N = 2317)
Diploma (FH) (N = 1208)	Doctorate/Habilitation (N = 986)
full maturity certificate (N = 549)	full maturity certificate (s.c.) (N = 877)
other (N = 1359)	other (N = 1181)

Gender	Final qualification
male (N = 5801) female (N = 9252)	Bachelor (N = 10,854)
	state examination (*Lehramt*) (N = 367)
	Bachelor (*Lehramt*) (N = 1883)
	state examination (N = 1428)
	Diplom/Magister (N = 45)
	Arts qualification (N = 19)
	other (N = 10)

Year of Birth
Median = 1990 (1st quantile = 1989; 3rd quantile = 1991; Min = 1946; Max = 1994)

measurement model. Note that all individuals are first assessed in their first semester; that is, the time variable t represents time since the start of the study program. The reliability of the dropout intention was McDonald's ω_H = .79.

Subgroup description variables. As potential constituting variables of exceptional subgroups, we investigate sociodemographic variables (i.e., gender, year of birth), the educational background of the student's father and mother, as well as the intended final qualification of the study program. Table 15.1 provides a descriptive overview of values and frequencies of these subgroup description variables.

Subgroup latent growth component model

We formulated a multistate model of students' dropout intention using our newly developed subgroupsem package (https://github.com/langenberg/subgroupsem) which builds on lavaan 0.6–6 (Rosseel, 2012) and pysubgroup 0.6.1 (Lemmerich & Becker, 2018).[2] The latent state variables η were specified with a time-invariant measurement model. To deal with correlated measurement error variables across time points between the three dropout intention indicators, we added method factors to the multistate model as suggested by Pohl et al. (2008). The measurement model for the multistate model with method factors are shown in Figure 15.4.

Next, we defined the contrasts of interest as:

$$\pi_1 = \frac{1}{4} \cdot \eta_1 + \frac{1}{4} \cdot \eta_2 + \frac{1}{4} \cdot \eta_3 + \frac{1}{4} \cdot \eta_4 \tag{15.10}$$

$$\pi_2 = -1 \cdot \eta_1 + 1 \cdot \eta_4 \tag{15.11}$$

$$\pi_3 = -3 \cdot \eta_1 + 1 \cdot \eta_2 + 1 \cdot \eta_3 + 1 \cdot \eta_4 \tag{15.12}$$

$$\pi_4 = -1 \cdot \eta_2 + 1 \cdot \eta_3 \tag{15.13}$$

which translates to a contrast matrix:

$$
C = \begin{pmatrix}
\frac{1}{4} & \frac{1}{4} & \frac{1}{4} & \frac{1}{4} \\
-1 & 0 & 0 & 1 \\
-3 & 1 & 1 & 1 \\
0 & -1 & 1 & 0
\end{pmatrix}
\tag{15.14}
$$

The values of the first growth component *overall mean* π_0 are the true scores of students' average dropout intention over all four years of studies. In the subgroup analysis, this variable reflects the group-specific overall dropout intention and can help to detect subgroups with overall low (or high) dropout intentions. The latent variable *change from first to fourth year* π_1 represents a contrast between the true dropout intention after the first year versus after the fourth year. A positive score on this variable would mean that dropout intention was higher after the fourth year compared to the first. The growth component *overall change after first year* π_2 represents a contrast between the true dropout intention after the first year and the average dropout intention in the years 2 to 4. This variable can be used to identify subgroups, for example, where overall dropout intention decreases significantly after the first year. Last, the growth component *change from third to fourth year* π_3 would lead to identify subgroups with exceptional changes of dropout intention late in their studies.

Interestingness measures. In our analysis, we apply two interestingness measures to illustrate how their formulation can lead to different results. In applied settings, the interestingness measure should be considered with care and according to the research questions.

Statistical test of growth components. For our first interestingness measure, we compare the means of the growth components from subgroups and their corresponding complements and test their differences for statistical significance using a Wald test. The formal interestingness

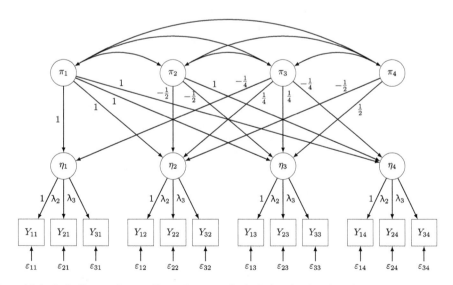

Figure 15.4   Path diagram for our illustrative example depicting the time-invariant measurement model for drop-out intention η_t for timepoints $t = 1, 2, 3, 4$ and the growth components of interest π_0 to π_3. Method factors for the second (i.e., Y_{2t}) and third (i.e., Y_{3t}) item are not shown in this figure

measure in this case is the test statistic of the Wald test. This interestingness measure yields an examination of a very broad variety of exceptional trajectories as it comprises comparisons on four growth components simultaneously. For example, an exceptional trajectory can consist of moderate differences on all four growth components or only one extreme difference on one growth component. In addition, the statistical test implicitly takes the size of the subgroup into account (e.g., estimation is more unreliable in small samples), which likely results in small subgroups with large effects or large subgroups with not so large effects. Note that we use a generalization-aware modification of the Wald test in order to account for redundancies in the most interesting subgroups. Hence, the reported interestingness measures in this section are not raw Wald test statistics, but modifications.

Absolute difference in overall dropout intention. As the second interestingness measure, we chose the absolute difference in means of the first growth component, this is, the absolute difference in the overall level of dropout intention over four years. Such an interestingness measure can be of substantial interest to identify subgroups of students, which are more likely to anticipate academic failure. However, the absolute difference is not a statistical test and, thus, such an interestingness measure tends to reveal very small subgroups with extreme differences.

Results

Statistical test of growth components. In our first subgroup analysis, we used a Wald test statistic for the means of the growth components as interestingness measure. Table 15.2 shows the description of the first five subgroups ordered by the magnitude of their interestingness measure. Additionally, Figure 15.5 shows the respective trajectory of dropout intention within each of the five subgroups compared to their corresponding complement group. In Appendix A, Table 15.A1 shows the means and variances of the growth components for the five subgroups. Note that in the following presentation we did not consider corrections of the Type 1 error for multiple testing.

The first subgroup consisted of male students, born in 1991 or later, and have a mother with an advanced academic degree (i.e., doctorate/habilitation) and contained $N = 56$ students.

Students in this subgroup exhibited trajectories of dropout intention different from the complement with regard to all four growth components. The overall level of dropout intention over four years was lower ($\alpha_0^{sg} = 1.544$, $SE = 0.086$; $\mu_0^{compl} = 1.714$, $SE = 0.007$) and showed less

Table 15.2 Description of subgroups for statistical interestingness measure

Subgroup	Subgroup description	Value	Size	Measure
1	Gender	male	56	46.446
	Education (mother)	Doctorate/Habilitation		
	Year of birth	after or in 1991		
2	Final qualification	State examination (*Lehramt*)	671	21.242
3	Education (father)	No certificate	128	18.929
4	Year of birth	before 1988	2606	17.046
5	Education (father)	Diploma or equivalent	215	16.007
	Education (mother)	Full maturity certificates (second cycle)		

Note: Interestingness measure is generalization-aware modification of Wald test statistic.

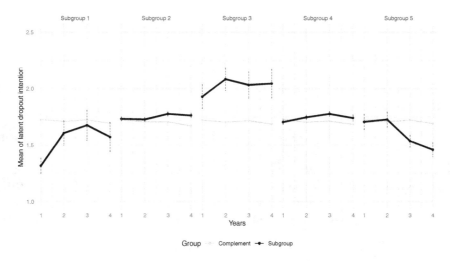

Figure 15.5 Latent trajectories of drop-out intention in the five subgroups for the Wald test-based interestingness measure. The black line shows the trajectory in the respective subgroup and the
gray line shows the trajectory in the corresponding complement group. Dashed lines indicate
standard error within each subgroup and time point

variance ($\sigma_0^{2;sg}$ = 0.336, SE = 0.084; $\sigma_0^{2;compl}$ = 0.485, SE = 0.007) in the subgroup. While
dropout intention slightly decreased in the complement group between the first and fourth
year, it significantly increased for the first subgroup (α_1^{sg} = 0.254, SE = 0.102; μ_1^{compl} = −0.034,
SE = 0.011). Again, the variance of this change was smaller in the subgroup ($\sigma_1^{2;sg}$ = 0.247,
SE = 0.101; $\sigma_1^{2;compl}$ = 0.791, SE = 0.018). Similarly, the first subgroup exhibited a strong
increase in dropout intention after the first year compared to all years thereafter, whereas the rest
of the sample showed a slight decrease with considerable variation (μ_2^{sg} = 0.902, SE = 0.228;
μ_2^{compl} = −0.052, SE = 0.024; $\sigma_2^{2;sg}$ = 1.434, SE = 0.532; $\sigma_2^{2;compl}$ = 4.268, SE = 0.092). On the
last growth component, which indicates a change between the third and fourth year, both the
subgroup and the complement had a non-significant mean change (μ_3^{sg} = 0.069, SE = 0.110;
μ_3^{compl} = 0.012, SE = 0.008), but still with considerable variance ($\sigma_3^{2;sg}$ = 0.279, SE = 0.119;
$\sigma_3^{2;compl}$ = 0.380, SE = 0.010).

The second subgroup consisted of students striving for a state examination in education (i.e.,
Lehramt in German) and contained N = 3671 students. Students in this subgroup exhibited
trajectories of dropout intention different from the complement with regard to all four growth
components. The overall level of dropout intention over four years was higher (μ_0^{sg} = 1.751,
SE = 0.014; μ_0^{compl} = 1.702, SE = 0.007) and showed more variance ($\sigma_0^{2;sg}$ = 0.527, SE = 0.016;
$\sigma_0^{2;compl}$ = 0.469, SE = 0.008) in the subgroup. While dropout intention slightly decreased in the
complement group between the first and fourth year, it did not increase significantly for the
second subgroup (μ_1^{sg} = 0.031, SE = 0.022; $\mu_1^{2;compl}$ = −0.054, SE = 0.012). The variance of this
change was smaller in the subgroup ($\sigma_1^{2;sg}$ = 0.716, SE = 0.034; $\sigma_1^{2;compl}$ = 0.810, SE = 0.021).

The second subgroup exhibited a non-significant increase in dropout intention after the first
year compared to all years thereafter, whereas the rest of the sample showed a slight decrease with
considerable variation (μ_2^{sg} = 0.071, SE = 0.050; μ_2^{compl} = −0.088, SE = 0.027; $\sigma_2^{2;sg}$ = 4.178,
SE = 0.182; $\sigma_2^{2;compl}$ = 4.277, SE = 0.104). On the last growth component, which indicates a
change between the third and fourth year, the subgroup had a significant mean change, whereas
the rest of the sample did not have a significant change (μ_3^{sg} = 0.049, SE = 0.017; μ_3^{compl} = 0.001,

$SE = 0.009$), but still with considerable variance ($\sigma_3^{2;sg} = 0.387$, $SE = 0.021$; $\sigma_3^{2;compl} = 0.377$, $SE = 0.012$).

The third subgroup consisted of students whose fathers finished their educational career without a certificate and contained $N = 128$ students. Students in this subgroup exhibited trajectories of dropout intention different from the complement with regard to all four growth components. The overall level of dropout intention over four years was higher ($\mu_0^{sg} = 2.023$, $SE = .086$; $\mu_1^{compl\ 1} = 1.708$, $SE = 0.007$) and showed more variance ($\mu_2^{2;sg} = 0.709$, $SE = 0.119$; $\sigma_0^{2;compl} = 0.478$, $SE = 0.007$) in the subgroup. While dropout intention slightly decreased in the complement group between the first and fourth year, it did not increase significantly for the third subgroup ($\mu_1^{sg} = 0.115$, $SE = 0.141$; $\mu_1^{compl} = -0.034$, $SE = 0.011$). The variance of this change was bigger in the subgroup ($\sigma_1^{2;sg} = 0.934$, $SE = 0.267$; $\sigma_1^{2;compl} = 0.783$, $SE = 0.018$). The third subgroup exhibited a non-significant increase in dropout intention after the first year compared to all years thereafter, whereas the rest of the sample showed a slight decrease with considerable variation ($\mu_2^{sg} = 0.372$, $SE = 0.245$; $\mu_2^{compl} = -0.053$, $SE = 0.024$; $\sigma_2^{2;sg} = 1.873$, $SE = 0.816$; $\sigma_2^{2;compl} = 4.229$, $SE = 0.092$). On the last growth component, which indicates a change between the third and fourth year, both the subgroup and the complement had a non-significant mean change ($\mu_3^{sg} = -0.051$, $SE = 0.119$; $\mu_3^{compl} = 0.012$, $SE = 0.008$), but still with considerable variance ($\sigma_3^{2;sg} = 0.579$, $SE = 0.173$; $\sigma_3^{2;compl} = 0.378$, $SE = 0.010$). The results for subgroups 4 and 5 are summarized in Table 15.A1.

Absolute difference in overall dropout intention. As a second interestingness measure, we investigated the mean deviation of the first growth component between subgroups and their complements; that is, the difference in the overall level of dropout intention over four years. Table 15.3 shows the description of the five subgroups with the largest difference on the first growth component. Additionally, Figure 15.6 shows the respective trajectory of dropout intention within each of the five subgroups compared to their corresponding complement group. In Appendix A, Table 15.A2 shows the means and variances of the growth components for the five subgroups.

The first subgroup consisted of students whose father did not have an educational certificate and contained $N = 128$ students. Students in this subgroup exhibited trajectories of dropout intention different from the complement, especially with regard to the first growth component. The overall level of dropout intention over four years was higher ($\mu_0^{sg} = 2.023$, $SE = 0.086$; $\mu_0^{compl} = 1.708$, $SE = 0.007$) and showed more variance ($\sigma_0^{2;sg} = 0.709$, $SE = 0.119$; $\sigma_0^{2;compl} = 0.478$, $SE = 0.007$) in the subgroup. While dropout intentions slightly decreased in the complement group between the first and fourth year, there was no significant change for the first subgroup ($\mu_1^{sg} = 0.116$, $SE = 0.141$; $\mu_1^{compl} = -0.034$, $SE = 0.011$). Again, the

Table 15.3 Description of subgroups for substantive interestingness measure focusing on overall dropout intention over four years

Subgroup	Subgroup description	Value	Size	Measure
1	Education (father)	No certificate	128	0.315
2	Gender	male Doctorate/Habilitation 1990/1991	55	0.246
	Education (mother) Year of birth			
3	Gender	female	122	0.191
	Education (mother)	No certificate		
4	Education (mother) Final qualification	Doctorate/Habilitation	50	0.187
		State examination (*Lehramt*)		
5	Education (mother) Year of birth	No certificate before 1988	68	0.148

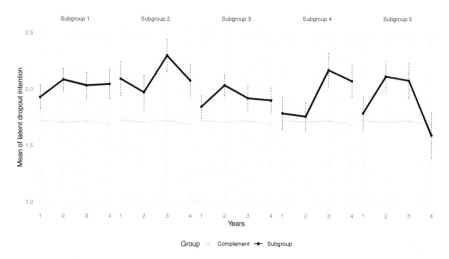

Figure 15.6 Latent trajectories of drop-out intention in the five subgroups for the substantive interesting-ness measure focusing on overall drop-out intention over four years. The black line shows the trajectory in the respective subgroup and the gray line shows the trajectory in the corresponding complement group. Dashed lines indicate standard error within each subgroup and time point

variance of this change was larger in the subgroup ($\sigma_1^{2;sg} = 0.934$, $SE = 0.267$; $\sigma_1^{2;compl} = 0.783$, $SE = 0.018$). Similarly, the first subgroup did not exhibit a significant change in dropout intentions after the first year compared to all years thereafter, whereas the rest of the sample showed a slight decrease with considerable variation ($\mu_2^{sg} = 0.373$, $SE = 0.248$; $\mu_2^{compl} = -0.053$, $SE = 0.024$; $\sigma_2^{2;sg} = 1.873$, $SE = 0.816$; $\sigma_2^{2;compl} = 4.229$, $SE = 0.092$). On the last growth component, which indicates a change between the third and fourth year, both the subgroup and the complement had a non-significant mean change ($\mu_3^{sg} = -0.051$, $SE = 0.119$; $\mu_3^{compl} = 0.012$, $SE = 0.008$), but still with considerable variance ($\sigma_3^{2;sg} = 0.579$, $SE = 0.173$; $\sigma_3^{2;compl} = 0.378$, $SE = 0.010$).

The second subgroup consisted of male students, born in 1990 or 1991, and have a mother with an advanced academic degree (i.e., doctorate/habilitation) and contained $N = 55$ students. Students in this subgroup exhibited trajectories of dropout intention different from the complement, especially with regard to the first growth component. The overall level of dropout intention over four years was higher ($\mu_0^{sg} = 2.110$, $SE = 0.110$; $\mu_0^{compl} = 1.711$, $SE = 0.006$) and showed more variance ($\sigma_0^{2;sg} = 0.552$, $SE = 0.123$; $\sigma_0^{2;compl} = 0.483$, $SE = 0.007$) in the subgroup. While dropout intentions slightly decreased in the complement group between the first and fourth year, there was no significant change for the second subgroup ($\alpha_1^{sg} = -0.015$, $SE = 0.172$; $\mu_1^{compl} = -0.033$, $SE = 0.011$). The variance of this change was larger in the complement ($\sigma_1^{2;sg} = 0.721$, $SE = 0.268$; $\sigma_1^{2;compl} = 0.790$, $SE = 0.018$). Similarly, the second subgroup did not exhibit a significant change in dropout intentions after the first year compared to all years thereafter, whereas the rest of the sample showed a slight decrease with considerable variation ($\mu_2^{sg} = 0.075$, $SE = 0.474$; $\mu_2^{compl} = -0.050$, $SE = 0.024$; $\sigma_2^{2;sg} = 6.493$, $SE = 2.095$; $\sigma_2^{2;compl} = 4.252$, $SE = 0.092$). On the last growth component, which indicates a change between the third and fourth year, the subgroup had a non-significant mean change ($\mu_3^{sg} = 0.328$, $SE = 0.144$; $\mu_3^{compl} = 0.011$, $SE = 0.008$) with considerable variance ($\sigma_3^{2;sg} = 0.649$, $SE = 0.236$; $\sigma_3^{2;compl} = 0.378$, $SE = 0.010$).

The third subgroup consisted of female students whose mother did not have an educational certificate and contained $N = 122$ students. Students in this subgroup exhibited trajectories of dropout intention different from the complement, especially with regard to the first growth component. The overall level of dropout intention over four years was higher ($\mu_0^{sg} = 1.926$, $SE = 0.078$; $\mu_0^{compl} = 1.711$, $SE = 0.007$) and showed more variance ($\sigma_0^{2;sg} = 0.554$, $SE = 0.092$; $\sigma_0^{2;compl} = 0.483$, $SE = 0.007$) in the subgroup. While dropout intentions slightly decreased in the complement group between the first and fourth year, there was no significant change for the third subgroup ($\mu_1^{sg} = 0.057$, $SE = 0.126$; $\mu_1^{compl} = -0.034$, $SE = 0.011$). The variance of this change was larger in the subgroup ($\sigma_1^{2;sg} = 0.825$, $SE = 0.187$; $\sigma_1^{2;compl} = 0.788$, $SE = 0.018$). Similarly, the third subgroup did not exhibit a significant change in dropout intentions after the first year compared to all years thereafter, whereas the rest of the sample showed a slight decrease with considerable variation ($\mu_2^{sg} = 0.322$, $SE = 0.273$; $\mu_2^{compl} = -0.052$, $SE = 0.024$; $\sigma_2^{2;sg} = 3.679$, $SE = 1.005$; $\sigma_2^{2;compl} = 4.256$, $SE = 0.092$). On the last growth component, which indicates a change between the third and fourth year, both the subgroup and the complement had a non-significant mean change ($\mu_3^{sg} = -0.113$, $SE = 0.116$; $\mu_3^{compl} = 0.013$, $SE = .008$) with considerable variance ($\sigma_3^{2;sg} = 0.514$, $SE = 0.168$; $\sigma_3^{2;compl} = 0.380$, $SE = 0.010$).

The results for the subgroups 4 and 5 are summarized in Table 15.A2.

Discussion

Summary

In this work, we presented a new framework that combines latent growth curve models with subgroup discovery and exceptional model mining. This SubgroupLGCM approach was introduced as an alternative to growth mixture modeling and structural equation model trees. It enables flexibly and efficiently finding interpretable subgroups with exceptional trajectories in large data sets. The researcher can specify the particular growth model of interest (e.g., linear and quadratic LGCMs, growth component models), the subgroup description variables that are used to find relevant subgroups, the interestingness measure (e.g., statistical measures or effect size measures), and the search algorithm. This exploratory data mining approach can help researchers to better understand heterogeneity in growth trajectories and to generate hypotheses for future research.

Limitations

It is important to emphasize that SubgroupLGCM is an exploratory approach in line with the data mining mantra of *iterative* and *interactive* analysis and should not be misunderstood as a way to confirm hypotheses. Especially when effect sizes are used as interestingness measures, the results are potentially specific for the sample under consideration and may not generalize to a wider population. Nevertheless, the approach can be very useful for finding small and potentially interesting subgroups that are worth being investigated in subsequent studies.

When we use statistical measures as interestingness measures, the exploratory nature of the approach is less pronounced, because the size of the subgroups is implicitly taken into account. Still, our approach does not test a priori hypotheses but uses statistical measures to explore subgroup differences. The tests and test statistics used in the SubgroupLGCM should be assessed with considerations of multiple testing. That is, in principle one can use p-values as interestingness measures as well, but care must be taken with regard to their interpretation since a large set of candidates is tested in the search process.

A typical issue in subgroup discovery and exceptional model mining is redundancy of results. That is, our approach typically finds multiple redundant subgroups in the set of top results. Redundancy refers to the fact that if a particular subgroup has a high score on the interestingness measure, then specializations (i.e., subgroups of this subgroup) tend to have high scores as well, but their added insights are often limited. In our empirical example, we employed a generalization-aware approach (Batal & Hauskrecht, 2010; Grosskreutz et al., 2010; Lemmerich et al., 2013) as an established and effective solution to this problem. However, our framework could also incorporate alternative techniques for avoiding redundant subgroups, such as iterative mining (Lavrač et al., 2004), or explicit algorithms for subgroup set discovery, such as diverse subgroup set discovery (Van Leeuwen & Knobbe, 2012). Note, however, that all these methods for avoiding redundancy – including our approach – are not, or only loosely, based on theoretical statistical properties but rather are pragmatic hands-on solutions that have been proven useful in a wide variety of pattern mining applications (cf. Herrera et al., 2011).

Our current search algorithm and implementation have been proven to be sufficiently efficient for moderately large data sets. Note, however, that the number of candidate subgroups that can be formed as conjunctions grows exponentially with the number of potential subgroup description variables. Thus, for very large data sets, the runtime of the search for the most relevant subgroups can become problematic. Within our framework, the main computational cost lies in fitting the LGCM for each subgroup using SEM software. Depending on the interestingness measure, omitting the computation of standard errors, model fit measures, or additional information can save a considerable amount of time. Also, using information from previous runs as starting values can decrease the required computational time. Additionally, heuristic search algorithms such as beam search (Lavrač et al., 2004) allow for balancing between runtime and result quality via meta-parameters. Furthermore, the employed search algorithms function in principle as *anytime algorithms*, that is, the search can be stopped at any time and the best results up to this point can be retrieved by a data analyst. Nonetheless, the authors of this work see a strong potential for future research in this area that could substantially improve the runtime of search algorithms, for example by introducing pruning into the search (Wrobel, 1997; Grosskreutz et al., 2008).

Acknowledgment

This work was supported by the Excellence Initiative of the German federal and state governments (RWTH PrepFund project).

This chapter uses data from the National Educational Panel Study (NEPS): Starting Cohort First-Year Students, doi:10.5157/NEPS:SC5:9.0.0. From 2008 to 2013, NEPS data was collected as part of the Framework Program for the Promotion of Empirical Educational Research funded by the German Federal Ministry of Education and Research (BMBF). As of 2014, NEPS is carried out by the Leibniz Institute for Educational Trajectories (LIfBi) at the University of Bamberg in cooperation with a nationwide network.

Notes

1 LGCMs with predefined trajectories can also be considered a special case of growth component models. See Mayer et al. (2012) for details.
2 The complete code for our example is given in https://github.com/langenberg/MayerKiefer LangenbergLemmerich2020_CSS_Handbook

References

Batal, I., & Hauskrecht, M. (2010). A concise representation of association rules using minimal predictive rules. In *Joint European conference on machine learning and knowledge discovery in databases* (pp. 87–102). Springer.

Bean, J. P., & Metzner, B. S. (1985, December). A conceptual model of nontraditional undergraduate student attrition. *Review of Educational Research, 55*(4), 485–540. doi:10.3102/00346543055004485

Belsky, J., & Rovine, M. J. (1990). Patterns of marital change across the transition to parenthood: Pregnancy to three years postpartum. *Journal of Marriage and the Family, 52*(1), 5–19.

Biesanz, J. C., Deeb-Sossa, N., Aubrecht, A. M., Bollen, K. A., & Curran, P. J. (2004). The role of coding time in estimating and interpreting growth curve models. *Psychological Methods, 9*, 30–52.

Blossfeld, H.-P., & von Maurice, J. (2011). Education as a lifelong process. *Zeitschrift für Erziehungswissenschaft, 14*(2), 19–34. doi:10.1007/s11618-011-0179-2

Brandmaier, A. M., Prindle, J. J., McArdle, J. J., & Lindenberger, U. (2016). Theory-guided exploration with structural equation model forests. *Psychological Methods, 21*, 566.

Brandmaier, A. M., Ram, N., Wagner, G. G., & Gerstorf, D. (2017). Terminal decline in well-being: The role of multi-indicator constellations of physical health and psychosocial correlates. *Developmental Psychology, 53*(5), 996.

Brandmaier, A. M., von Oertzen, T., McArdle, J. J., & Lindenberger, U. (2013). Structural equation model trees. *Psychological Methods, 18*, 71.

Bäulke, L., Eckerlein, N., & Dresel, M. (2018, October). Interrelations between motivational regulation, procrastination and college dropout intentions. *Unterrichtswissenschaft, 46*(4), 461–479. doi:10.1007/s42010-018-0029-5

Cabrera, A. F., Nora, A., & Castaneda, M. B. (1993, March). College persistence: Structural equations modeling test of an integrated model of student retention. *The Journal of Higher Education, 64*(2), 123. doi:10.2307/2960026

Chan, D. (1998). The conceptualization and analysis of change over time: An integrative approach incorporating longitudinal mean and covariance structures analysis (LMACS) and multiple indicator latent growth modeling (MLGM). *Organizational Research Methods, 1*, 421–483.

Duivesteijn, W., Feelders, A. J., & Knobbe, A. (2016). Exceptional model mining. *Data Mining and Knowledge Discovery, 30*(1), 47–98.

Ferrer, E., Balluerka, N., & Widaman, K. F. (2008). Factorial invariance and the specification of second-order growth models. *Methodology, 4*, 22–36.

Geiser, C., Keller, B., & Lockhart, G. (2013). First versus second order latent growth curve models: Some insights from latent state-trait theory. *Structural Equation Modeling, 20*, 479–503.

Grosskreutz, H., Boley, M., & Krause-Traudes, M. (2010). Subgroup discovery for election analysis: A case study in descriptive data mining. In *International conference on discovery science* (pp. 57–71). Springer.

Grosskreutz, H., Rüping, S., & Wrobel, S. (2008). Tight optimistic estimates for fast subgroup discovery. In *Joint European conference on machine learning and knowledge discovery in databases* (pp. 440–456). Springer.

Herrera, F., Carmona, C. J., González, P., & Del Jesus, M. J. (2011). An overview on subgroup discovery: Foundations and applications. *Knowledge and Information Systems, 29*(3), 495–525.

Heublein, U. (2014, October). Student drop-out from German higher education institutions. *European Journal of Education, 49*(4), 497–513. doi:10.1111/ejed.12097

Heublein, U., & Schmelzer, R. (2018). *Die Entwicklung der Studienabbruchquoten an den deutschen Hochschulen. Berechnungen auf Basis des Absolventenjahrgangs 2016* (Tech. Rep.). Deutsches Zentrum für Hochschul-und Wissenschaftsforschung (DZHW).

Janke, S., & Dickhäuser, O. (2019). Different major, different goals: University students studying economics differ in life aspirations and achievement goal orientations from social science students. *Learning and Individual Differences, 73*, 138–146. doi:10.1016/j.lindif.2019.05.008

Janke, S., Rudert, S. C., Marksteiner, T., & Dickhäuser, O. (2017, August). Knowing one's place: Parental educational background influences social identification with academia, test anxiety, and satisfaction with studying at university. *Frontiers in Psychology, 8*. doi:10.3389/fpsyg.2017.01326

Jöreskog, K. G. (1971). Simultaneous factor analysis in several populations. *Psychometrika, 36*(4), 409–426.

Klösgen, W. (1996). Explora: A multipattern and multistrategy discovery assistant. In *Advances in knowledge discovery and data mining* (pp. 249–271). American Association for Artificial Intelligence.

Kuh, G. D., Kinzie, J., Buckley, J. A., Bridges, B. K., & Hayek, J. C. (2007). *Piecing together the student success puzzle: Research, propositions, and recommendations.* Jossey-Bass.

Lavrac̆, N., Kavšek, B., Flach, P., & Todorovski, L. (2004, February). Subgroup discovery with cn2-sd. *Journal of Machine Learning Research, 5*, 153–188.

Leite, W. L. (2007). A comparison of latent growth models for constructs measured by multiple items. *Structural Equation Modeling, 14*, 581–610.

Leman, D., Feelders, A., & Knobbe, A. J. (2008). Exceptional model mining. In *European conference on machine learning and knowledge discovery in databases.* Springer.

Lemmerich, F., & Becker, M. (2018). Pysubgroup: Easy-to-use subgroup discovery in python. In *Joint European conference on machine learning and knowledge discovery in databases* (pp. 658–662). Springer.

Lemmerich, F., Becker, M., & Puppe, F. (2013). Difference-based estimates for generalization-aware subgroup discovery. In *Joint European conference on machine learning and knowledge discovery in databases* (pp. 288–303). Springer.

Lemmerich, F., Kiefer, C., Langenberg, B., Cacho Aboukhalil, J., & Mayer, A. (in press). Mining exceptional mediation models. In *International symposium on methodologies for intelligent systems* (pp. 318–328). Springer.

Marksteiner, T., Janke, S., & Dickhäuser, O. (2019, August). Effects of a brief psychological intervention on students' sense of belonging and educational outcomes: The role of students' migration and educational background. *Journal of School Psychology, 75*, 41–57. doi:10.1016/j.jsp.2019.06.002

Martin, D. P., & von Oertzen, T. (2015). Growth mixture models outperform simpler clustering algorithms when detecting longitudinal heterogeneity, even with small sample sizes. *Structural Equation Modeling, 22*, 264–275.

Mashburn, A. J. (2000, November). A psychological process of college student dropout. *Journal of College Student Retention: Research, Theory & Practice, 2*(3), 173–190. doi:10.2190/u2qb-52j9-ghgp-6lee

Mayer, A., Steyer, R., & Mueller, H. (2012). A general approach to defining latent growth components. *Structural Equation Modeling, 19*, 513–533. doi:10.1080/10705511.2012.713242

McArdle, J. J. (1988). Dynamic but structural equation modeling of repeated measures data. In R. Cattell & J. Nesselroade (Eds.), *Handbook of multivariate experimental psychology* (pp. 561–614). Plenum.

McArdle, J. J. (2001). A latent difference score approach to longitudinal dynamic structural analysis. In R. Cudeck, S. du Toit, & D. Sörbom (Eds.), *Structural equation modeling: Present and future* (pp. 341–380). Scientific Software International.

McArdle, J. J. (2009). Latent variable modeling of differences and changes with longitudinal data. *Annual Review of Psychology, 60*, 577–605.

McLachlan, G. J., & Peel, D. (2000). *Finite mixture models.* John Wiley & Sons. http://dx.doi.org/10.1002/0471721182

Meredith, M., & Tisak, J. (1990). Latent curve analysis. *Psychometrika, 55*, 107–122.

Muthén, B. O. (2002). Beyond SEM: General latent variable modeling. *Behaviormetrika, 29*, 81–117.

Muthén, B. O., & Muthén, L. K. (2000). Integrating person-centered and variable-centered analyses: Growth mixture modeling with latent trajectory classes. *Alcoholism: Clinical and Experimental Research, 24*(6), 882–891.

Nagin, D. S. (1999). Analyzing developmental trajectories: A semiparametric, group-based approach. *Psychological Methods, 4*, 139–157.

Nagin, D. S. (2005). *Group-based modeling of development.* Harvard University Press.

Nylund, K. L., Asparouhov, T., & Muthén, B. O. (2007). Deciding on the number of classes in latent class analysis and growth mixture modeling: A monte Carlo simulation study. *Structural Equation Modeling, 14*, 535–569.

Pohl, S., Steyer, R., & Kraus, K. (2008). Modelling method effects as individual causal effects. *Journal of the Royal Statistical Society: Series A, 171*, 41–63.

Raykov, T. (1999). Are simple change scores obsolete? An approach to studying correlates and predictors of change. *Applied Psychological Measurement, 23*, 120–126.

Rosseel, Y. (2012). LaVan: An R package for structural equation modeling. *Journal of Statistical Software, 48*(2), 1–36. http://dx.doi.org/10.18637/jss.v048.i02

Sayer, A. G., & Cumsille, P. E. (2001). Second-order latent growth models. In L. M. Collins & A. G. Sayer (Eds.), *New methods for the analysis of change.* Washington, DC: American Psychological Association.

Stebleton, M. J., Soria, K. M., & Huesman, R. L. (2014, April). First-generation students' sense of belonging, mental health, and use of counseling services at public research universities. *Journal of College Counseling, 17*(1), 6–20. doi:10.1002/j.2161-1882.2014.00044.x

Stegmann, G., Jacobucci, R., Serang, S., & Grimm, K. J. (2018). Recursive partitioning with nonlinear models of change. *Multivariate Behavioral Research, 53*, 559–570.

Stephens, N. M., Fryberg, S. A., Markus, H. R., Johnson, C. S., & Covarrubias, R. (2012a). Unseen dis-advantage: How American universities' focus on independence undermines the academic performance of first-generation college students. *Journal of Personality and Social Psychology, 102*(6), 1178–1197. doi:10.1037/a0027143

Stephens, N. M., Townsend, S. S., Markus, H. R., & Phillips, L. T. (2012b, November). A cultural mis-match: Independent cultural norms produce greater increases in cortisol and more negative emotions among first-generation college students. *Journal of Experimental Social Psychology, 48*(6), 1389–1393. doi:10.1016/j.jesp.2012.07.008

Steyer, R., Eid, M., & Schwenkmezger, P. (1997). Modeling true intraindividual change: True change as a latent variable. *Methods of Psychological Research Online, 2*, 21–33.

Steyer, R., Mayer, A., Geiser, C., & Cole, D. (2014). A theory of states and traits – revised. *Annual Review of Clinical Psychology, 10*. (Advance online publication) doi:10.1146/annurev-clinpsy-032813-153719

Tisak, J., & Tisak, M. S. (2000). Permanency and ephemerality of psychological measures with application to organizational commitment. *Psychological Methods, 5*, 175–198.

Usami, S., Hayes, T., & McArdle, J. (2017). Fitting structural equation model trees and latent growth curve mixture models in longitudinal designs: The influence of model misspecification. *Structural Equation Modeling, 24*, 585–598. doi:10.1080/10705511.2016.1266267

Usami, S., Jacobucci, R., & Hayes, T. (2019). The performance of latent growth curve model-based struc-tural equation model trees to uncover population heterogeneity in growth trajectories. *Computational Statistics, 34*, 1–22.

Van Leeuwen, M., & Knobbe, A. (2012). Diverse subgroup set discovery. *Data Mining and Knowledge Discovery, 25*(2), 208–242.

von Oerzen, T., Hertzog, C., Lindenberger, U., & Ghisletta, P. (2010). The effect of multiple indicators on the power to detect inter-individual differences in change. *British Journal of Mathematical and Statistical Psychology, 63*, 627–646.

Wrobel, S. (1997). An algorithm for multi-relational discovery of subgroups. In *European symposium on principles of data mining and knowledge discovery* (pp. 78–87). Springer.

Yu, S., & Levesque-Bristol, C. (2018, July). Are students in some college majors moreself-determined in their studies than others? *Motivation and Emotion, 42*(6), 831–851. doi:10.1007/s11031-018-9711-5

Zeileis, A., Hothorn, T., & Hornik, K. (2008). Model-based recursive partitioning. *Journal of Computa-tional and Graphical Statistics, 17*, 492–514.

APPENDIX

Tables of results

Table 15.A1 SubgroupLGCM results for the Wald test–based interestingness measure showing means and variances of growth components for subgroups and respective complement

Parameter	Subgroup 1 SG Estimate	SE	Complement Estimate	SE	Subgroup 2 SG Estimate	SE	Complement Estimate	SE	Subgroup 3 SG Estimate	SE	Complement Estimate	SE
μ_0	1.544	0.086	1.714	0.007	1.751	0.014	1.702	0.007	2.023	0.086	1.708	0.007
μ_1	0.254	0.102	−0.034	0.011	0.031	0.022	−0.054	0.012	0.115	0.141	−0.034	0.011
μ_2	0.902	0.228	−0.052	0.024	0.071	0.050	−0.088	0.027	0.372	0.245	−0.053	0.024
μ_3	0.069	0.110	0.012	0.008	0.049	0.017	0.001	0.009	−0.051	0.119	0.012	0.008
σ_0^2	0.336	0.084	0.485	0.007	0.527	0.016	0.469	0.008	0.709	0.119	0.478	0.007
σ_1^2	0.247	0.101	0.791	0.018	0.716	0.034	0.810	0.021	0.934	0.267	0.783	0.018
σ_2^2	1.434	0.532	4.268	0.092	4.178	0.182	4.277	0.104	1.873	0.816	4.229	0.092
σ_3^2	0.279	0.119	0.380	0.010	0.387	0.021	0.377	0.012	0.579	0.173	0.378	0.010

Parameter	Subgroup 4 SG Estimate	SE	Complement Estimate	SE	Subgroup 5 SG Estimate	SE	Complement Estimate	SE
μ_0	1.743	0.017	1.708	0.007	1.607	0.043	1.712	0.007
μ_1	0.036	0.036	−0.045	0.012	−0.246	0.087	−0.031	0.011
μ_2	0.150	0.056	−0.084	0.026	−0.396	0.192	−0.048	0.024
μ_3	0.030	0.021	0.010	0.009	−0.191	0.062	0.014	0.008
σ_0^2	0.529	0.020	0.476	0.008	0.301	0.040	0.483	0.007
σ_1^2	0.720	0.047	0.800	0.020	0.807	0.145	0.785	0.018
σ_2^2	3.493	0.208	4.385	0.100	4.269	0.735	4.221	0.093
σ_3^2	0.354	0.026	0.381	0.011	0.437	0.010	0.379	0.011

Table 15.A2 SubgroupLGCM results for the substantive interestingness measure showing overall dropout intention over four years for subgroups and respective complement

| Parameter | Subgroup 1 | | | | Subgroup 2 | | | | Subgroup 3 | | | |
| | SG | | Complement | | SG | | Complement | | SG | | Complement | |
	Estimate	SE	Estimate	SE	Estimate	SE	Estimate	SE	Estimate	SE	Estimate	SE
μ_0	2.023	0.086	1.708	0.007	2.110	0.110	1.711	0.006	1.926	0.078	1.711	0.007
μ_1	0.116	0.141	−0.034	0.011	−0.015	0.172	−0.033	0.011	0.057	0.126	−0.034	0.011
μ_2	0.373	0.245	−0.053	0.024	0.075	0.474	−0.050	0.024	0.322	0.273	−0.052	0.024
μ_3	−0.051	0.119	0.012	0.008	0.328	0.144	0.011	0.008	−0.113	0.116	0.013	0.008
σ_0^2	0.709	0.119	0.478	0.007	0.552	0.123	0.483	0.007	0.554	0.092	0.483	0.007
σ_1^2	0.934	0.267	0.783	0.018	0.721	0.268	0.790	0.018	0.825	0.187	0.788	0.018
σ_2^2	1.873	0.816	4.229	0.092	6.493	2.095	4.252	0.092	3.679	1.005	4.256	0.092
σ_3^2	0.579	0.173	0.378	0.010	0.649	0.236	0.378	0.010	0.514	0.168	0.380	0.010

| Parameter | Subgroup 4 | | | | Subgroup 5 | | | |
| | SG | | Complement | | SG | | Complement | |
	Estimate	SE	Estimate	SE	Estimate	SE	Estimate	SE
μ_0	1.948	0.107	1.712	0.007	1.894	0.116	1.712	0.007
μ_1	0.284	0.158	−0.034	0.011	−0.194	0.243	−0.033	0.011
μ_2	0.637	0.419	−0.051	0.024	0.420	0.465	−0.050	0.024
μ_3	0.411	0.117	0.011	0.008	−0.037	0.131	0.013	0.008
σ_0^2	0.439	0.109	0.484	0.007	0.606	0.165	0.484	0.007
σ_1^2	0.433	0.188	0.791	0.018	1.358	0.540	0.788	0.018
σ_2^2	3.264	1.292	4.260	0.092	5.555	2.394	4.249	0.092
σ_3^2	0.219	0.120	0.380	0.010	0.156	0.169	0.380	0.010

16

DISAGGREGATION VIA GAUSSIAN REGRESSION FOR ROBUST ANALYSIS OF HETEROGENEOUS DATA

Nazanin Alipourfard, Keith Burghardt and Kristina Lerman

1 Introduction

Social data are often highly heterogeneous, coming from a population composed of diverse classes of individuals, each with their own characteristics and behaviors. As a result of heterogeneity, a model learned on population data may not make accurate predictions on held-out test data or offer analytic insights into the underlying behaviors that motivate interventions. To illustrate, consider Figure 16.1, which shows data collected for a hypothetical nutrition study measuring how the outcome, body mass index (BMI), changes as a function of daily pasta calorie intake. Multivariate linear regression (MLR) analysis finds a negative relationship in the population (dotted line) between these variables. The negative trend suggests that – paradoxically – increased pasta consumption is associated with lower BMI. However, unbeknownst to researchers, the hypothetical population is heterogeneous, composed of classes that varied in their fitness level. These classes (clusters in Figure 16.1) represent, respectively, people who do not exercise, people with normal activity level, and athletes. When the data are disaggregated by fitness level, the trends within each subgroup are positive (dashed lines), leading to the conclusion that increased pasta consumption is in fact associated with a higher BMI. Recommendations for pasta consumption arising from the naive analysis are opposite to those arising from a more careful analysis that accounts for the confounding effect of different classes of people. The trend reversal is an example of Simpson's paradox, which has been widely observed in many domains, including biology, psychology, astronomy, and computational social science (Chuang et al., 2009; Kievit et al., 2013; Minchev et al., 2019; Blyth, 1972).

Social scientists analyze heterogeneous data with underlying structure (classes) using mixed effects models (Winter, 2013). This variant of linear regression uses random intercepts to model differences between classes and random slopes to model differences in regression coefficients within classes. Mixed effects models are used to describe non-independent observations of data from the same class, and they can even handle trend reversal associated with Simpson's paradox. Mixed effects models assume that classes are specified by a categorical variable, which can be constructed by disaggregating or binning data on an existing variable (Alipourfard et al., 2018a). In practice, however, these classes may not be known a priori or be related to multiple variables. Instead, they must be discovered from data, along with the trends they represent. Many methods

DOI: 10.4324/9781003025245-19

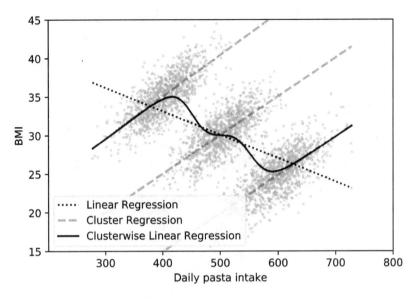

Figure 16.1   Heterogeneous data with three latent classes. The figure illustrates Simpson's paradox, where a negative relationship between the outcome and the independent variable exists for population as a whole (dotted line) but reverses when the data is disaggregated by classes (dashed lines).

already exist for finding latent classes within data; however, they have various shortcomings. Unsupervised clustering methods disaggregate data regardless of the outcome variable being explained. In reality, distinct outcomes may be best described by different clusterings of the same data. Recent methods have tackled Simpson's paradox by performing supervised disaggregation of data (Alipourfard et al., 2018b; Fabris & Freitas, 2000). However, these methods disaggregate data into subgroups using existing features and thus are not able to capture effects of latent classes (i.e., unobserved confounders). Additionally, they perform "hard" clustering, but assigning each data point to a unique group. Instead, a "soft" clustering is more realistic as it captures the degree of uncertainty about which group the data belong to. To address these challenges, we describe disaggregation via Gaussian regression[1] (DoGR), a method that jointly partitions data into overlapping clusters and estimates linear trends within them. This allows for learning accurate and generalizable models while keeping the interpretability advantage of linear models. The proposed method assumes that the data can be described as a superposition of clusters, or components, with every data point having some probability of belonging to any of the components. Each component represents a latent class, and the soft membership represents uncertainty about which class a data point belongs to. We use an expectation maximization (EM) algorithm to estimate component parameters and component membership parameters for the individual data points. DoGR jointly updates component parameters and regression coefficients, weighing the contribution of each data point to the component regression coefficients by its membership parameter. The joint learning of clusters and their regressions allows for discovering the latent classes that explain the structure of data.

Our framework learns robustly predictive and interpretable models of data. In validations on synthetic and real-world data, DoGR is able to discover hidden subgroups in data even in analytically challenging scenarios, where subgroups overlap along some of the dimensions, and identify interesting trends that may be obscured by Simpson's paradox, including scenarios where the trends in data show Simpson's reversal. We show that our method achieves performance comparable to or better than state-of-the-art algorithms but in a fraction of the time, making it suitable for big data analysis.

2 Background

Regression is one of the most widely used methods in data analysis due to its flexibility, interpretability, and computational scalability (Fox, 1997). The most popular regression method uses linear models to learn the relationship between predictor variables (also known as fixed effects or features) and the outcome variable. However, linear models make assumptions about the data that are often violated by real-world data. One of these assumptions is independence of observations. In reality, however, observations may come from groups of similar individuals, violating the independence assumption. To account for individual differences within such groups, mixed effects or multilevel models were developed (McLean et al., 1991). These models assume that similar individuals, or data samples, come from the same class, and that classes are specified by some categorical variable (Winter, 2013). In some cases, this variable can be created by binning a continuous variable and disaggregating data by these bins (Alipourfard et al., 2018a). However, existing methods do not work when differences between groups or individuals cannot directly be described by observed variables or features. In this chapter, we describe a method that captured differences between groups as latent confounders (i.e., latent clusters) that are learned from data. Our work improves the utility of linear models in the analysis of social data by controlling for these clusters. A number of previous works have attempted to tackle the issue of latent confounders. Clusterwise linear regression (CLR) (Späth, 1979) starts with initial clusters and updates them by reassigning one data point to another partition that minimizes a loss function. The method is slow, since it moves one data point at each iteration. Two other methods, Weighted Clusterwise Linear Regression (WCLR) (da Silva & de Carvalho, 2017) and Fuzzy Weighted Clusterwise Linear Regression (FWCLR) (da Silva & de Carvalho, 2018), improve on CLR by using k-means as their clustering method. These methods were shown to outperform CLR and other methods, such as K-plane (Manwani & Sastry, 2015). In conditional linear regression (Calderon et al., 2018), the goal is to find a linear rule capable of achieving more accurate predictions for just a *segment* of the population, by ignoring outliers. One of the larger differences between their method and ours is that conditional linear regression focuses on a small subset of data, while we model data as a whole, similar to CLR, WCLR, FWCLR, and K-plane. The shared parameter λ across all clusters in WCLR and FWCLR makes these methods perform poorly if clusters have different variance, as we will show in our results section. Other methods have combined Gaussian mixture models and regression to create algorithms similar to our own (Sung, 2004; Ghahramani & Jordan, 1994). We call these methods *Gaussian mixture regression* (*GMR*). In contrast to these methods, however, we can capture relationships between independent and outcome variables through regression coefficients, which previous methods were unable to do. We also use *weighted least squares* to fit our model, which makes it less sensitive to outliers (Cleveland & Devlin, 1988).

Causal inference has been used to address the problem of confounders, including latent confounders (Louizos et al., 2017), and to infer the causal relationship between features and outcomes (Bareinboim & Pearl, 2016; Ranganath & Perotte, 2018; Wang & Blei, 2018). One difficulty with causal inference, however, is that the focus is traditionally on one intervention (Ranganath & Perotte, 2018). Taking into account synergistic effects of multiple features is not well understood, but has been attempted recently (Ranganath & Perotte, 2018; Wang & Blei, 2018). With adequate data sets, these can help infer causal relationships between multiple causes, but certain causal assumptions are needed, which might not correspond to reality. In contrast, regression offers us the opportunity to understand relationships between each feature and an outcome, regardless of the data set, even if we cannot make causal claims.

3 DoGR method

Let $D = \{d_1, d_2, d_3, \ldots, d_N \mid d_i = (x_i, y_i) \in R^p \times R\}$ be a set of N observations, or records, each containing a real-valued outcome y_i of an observation i and a vector of p independent variables, or features $[x_{i,1}, x_{i,2}, \ldots, x_{i,p}]$. Regression analysis is often used to capture the relationship between each independent variable and the outcome. Specifically, MLR estimates regression coefficients $\beta_0, \beta_1, \ldots, \beta_p$ by minimizing the residuals of $y = \beta_0 + \beta_1 x_1 + \beta_2 x_2 + \ldots + \beta_p x_p$ over all observations. However, parameters learned by the MLR model may not generalize to out-of-sample populations, as they can be confounded by Simpson's paradox. We can call this the "robustness" problem of regression.

As discussed in the introduction, Figure 16.1 illustrates this problem with synthetic data. The MLR model trained on the aggregate data gives $BMI = intercept\ 0.61x$. This suggests a negative relationship (red dotted line) between the independent variable $x = Daily\ pasta\ intake$ and the outcome BMI. However, there are three components each with a positive trend. Indeed, applied separately to each component, MLR learns the proper positive relationship (dashed line) between $Daily\ pasta\ intake$ and BMI: $BMI = \beta_0 + \beta_1 x$, where β_0 is cluster's intercept, and β_1 is coefficient: 1.03, 1.08, 0.97. Associations learned by the MLR model trained on the population-level data are not *robust* or *generalizable*. This could explain the *reproducibility problem* seen in many fields (Pashler & Wagenmakers, 2012; Smaldino & McElreath, 2016), where trends seen in some experiments cannot be reproduced in other experiments with different populations. While the underlying groups within the population may be the same, the later experiments may oversample some of the groups during data collection. As a result, MLR trained at the population level may find a different association between independent variable and the outcome. However, identifying each group (cluster) and analyzing it separately reveals the same trends in the new data. In summary, disaggregating heterogeneous data and performing cluster-wise regressions will identify *robust* and *generalizable* relationships in data.

3.1 Model specification

The goal of this work is to learn robust and reproducible trends through a regression model that accounts for the latent structure of data, for example, the presence of three clusters in data shown in Figure 16.1. Our model jointly *disaggregates* the data into K overlapping subgroups, or components, and performs *weighted linear regression* within each component. We allow components to overlap in order to represent the uncertainty about which component or subgroup an observation belongs to.

We use capital letters to denote random variables and lowercase letters their values. We model the independent variable X of each component k as a multivariate normal distribution with mean $\mu_k \in R^p$ and covariance matrix $\Sigma_k \in \mathbb{R}^{p \times p}$:

$$f_X^{(k)} \sim N\left(\mu k, \Sigma_k\right) \tag{16.1}$$

In addition, each component is characterized by a set of regression coefficients $\beta_k \in \mathbb{R}^{p+1}$. The regression values of the component k are:

$$\hat{Y}^{(k)} = \beta_{k,0} + \beta_{k,1}X_1 + \beta_{k,2}X_2 + \ldots + \beta_{k,p}X_p \tag{16.2}$$

with $y - \hat{y}^{(k)}$ giving the residuals for component k. Under the assumption of normality of residuals (DeSarbo & Cron, 1988), Y has a normal distribution with mean $\hat{Y}^{(k)}$ and standard deviation σ_k:

$$f_{Y|X}^{(k)} \sim N\left(\hat{Y}^{(k)}, \sigma_k\right), \tag{16.3}$$

where $\hat{Y}^{(k)}$ is defined by Equation 16.2. Under the assumption of *homoscedasticity*, in which the error is the same for all X, the joint density is the product of the conditional (Equation 16.3) and marginal (Equation 16.1) densities:

$$f_{X,Y}^{(k)}(x,y) = f_{Y|X}^{(k)}(y|x) f_X(x) = \varphi\left(y; \hat{y}^{(k)}, \sigma_k\right) \varphi(x; \mu_k, \Sigma_k) \tag{16.4}$$

Multiplication of $f_{Y|X}(y|x) f_X(x)$ can be converted to a normal distribution $f_{X,Y}^{(k)}(x,y)$ comes from $N\left(\mu_k', \Sigma_k'\right)$, where $\mu_k' = \left[\mu_k^{(1)} . \mu_k^{(2)}, \ldots, \mu_k^{(d)}, \hat{y}^{(k)}\right]$ and $\Sigma_k' = \begin{bmatrix} \Sigma_k & 0 \\ 0 & \sigma_k \end{bmatrix}$ is a block matrix.

3.2 Model learning

The final goal of the model is to predict the outcome, given independent variables. This prediction combines the predicted values of outcome from all components by taking the average of the predicted values, weighed by the size of the component. We define ω_k as the weight of the component k, where $\Sigma_k w_k = 1$. We can define the joint distribution over all components as $fX,Y(x,y) = \sum_{k=1}^{K} wk \times f_{X,Y}^{(k)}(x,y)$.

Then the *log-likelihood* of the model over all data points is:

$$l = \sum_{i=1}^{N} log\left(\sum_{k=1}^{K} \omega k \times f_{X,Y}^{(k)}(x_i, y_i)\right) \tag{16.5}$$

The formula here is same as the *Gaussian mixture model*, except that the target y_i is a function of x_i. To find the best values for parameters $\theta = \left\{\omega_k, \mu_k, \Sigma_k, \beta_k, \sigma_k | 1 \le k \le K\right\}$, we can leverage the *expectation maximization* (EM) algorithm. The algorithm iteratively refines parameters based on the expectation (E) and maximization (M) steps.

3.2.1 E-step

Let's define $\gamma_{i,k}$ (*membership parameter*) as the probability that data point i belongs to component k. Given the parameters θ_t of last the iteration, the membership parameter is:

$$\gamma_{i,k} = \frac{\omega_k \times f_{X,Y}^{(k)}(x_i, y_i)}{\sum_{k'} \omega_{k'}' \times f_{X,Y}^{(k')}(x_i, y_i)} \tag{16.6}$$

Thus, the E-step disaggregates the data into clusters, but it does so in a "soft" way, with each data point having some probability of belonging to each cluster.

3.2.2 M-step

Given the updated membership parameters, the M-step updates the parameters of the model for the next iteration as θ_{t+1}:

$$\omega_k = \frac{\sum_i \gamma_{i,k}}{N}$$

$$\mu_k = \frac{\sum_i \gamma_{i,k} x_i}{\sum_i \gamma_{i,k}}$$

$$\Sigma_k = \frac{\sum_i \gamma_{i,k} (x_i - \mu_k)(x_i - \mu_k)^T}{\sum_i \gamma_{i,k}}$$

In addition, this step updates regression parameters based on the estimated parameters in θ_t. Our method uses *weighted least squares* for updating the regression coefficients β_k for each component, with γ as weights. In the other words, we find β_k that minimizes the *weighted sum of squares* (*WSS*) of the residuals:.

$$WSS(\beta_k) = \sum_i \gamma_{i,k} \left(y_i - \left(\beta_{k,0} + \beta_{k,1} x_{i,1} + \ldots + \beta_{k,p} x_{i,p} \right) \right)^2.$$

Using the value of β_k, the updated σ_k would be:

$$\sigma_k = \frac{\sum_i \gamma_{i,k} \left(y_i - \hat{y}_i^{(k)} \right)^2}{2}$$

Intuitively, μ_k shows us where in $\mathbb{R}^p$ the center of each subgroup k resides. The further a data point is from the center, the lower its probability to belong to the subgroup. The covariance matrix Σ_k captures the spread of the subgroup in the space $\mathbb{R}^p$ relative to the center μ_k. Regression coefficient β_k gives low weight to outliers (i.e., is a *weighted* regression) and captures the relationship between X and Y near the center of the subgroup. Parameter σ_k tells us about the variance of the residuals over the fitted regression line, and ω_k tells us about the importance of each subgroup.

3.3 Prediction

For test data x, the predicted outcome is the weighted average of the predicted outcomes for all components. The weights capture the uncertainty about which component the test data belongs to. Using Equation 16.3, the best prediction of outcome for component k would be $Y^{(k)}$, which is the mean of *conditional outcome value* of the component k:

$$\hat{y} = \sum_{k=1}^{k} \omega_k \times \left(\beta_{k,0} + \beta_{k,1} x_1 + \ldots + \beta_{k,p} x_p \right) \tag{16.7}$$

The solid line in Figure 16.1 represents the predicted outcome $\hat{y}$ as function of x. The solid line is the weighted average over the dashed lines.

4 Data

We apply our method to synthetic and real-world data sets, including the large social data sets described later.

The *Synthetic* data consist of two subgroups, with the same mean on *x*, but different variances, as shown in Figure 16.2. The variance of *x* for the top component is 600 and for the bottom component is 100. The number of data points in the bottom component is 3,000 and in the top component 2,000. The *y* value for the bottom component is $y = 200 + x$ and the top component it is $y = 800 + x$, with 20 as variance of residual.

The *Metropolitan* data come from a study of emotions expressed through Twitter messages posted from locations around Los Angeles County (Lerman et al., 2016). The data contains over six million geo-referenced tweets from 33,000 people linked to US census tracts through their locations. The demographic and socioeconomic characteristics of tracts came from the 2012 American Fact Finder.[2] A tract is a small region that contains about 4,000 residents on average. The tracts are designed to be relatively homogeneous with respect to socioeconomic characteristics of the population, such as income, residents with bachelor's degree or above, and other demographics. Of the more than 2,000 tracts within this Los Angeles County, 1,688 were linked to tweets.

Emotional *valence* was estimated from the text of the tweets using Warriner, Kuperman, and Brysbaert (WKB) lexicon (Warriner et al., 2013). The lexicon gives valence scores – between 1 and 9 –, which quantify the level of pleasure or happiness expressed by a word, for 14,000 English words. Since valence is a proxy for the expressed happiness, the data allow us to investigate the social and economic correlates of happiness. We use valence as the outcome in data analysis.

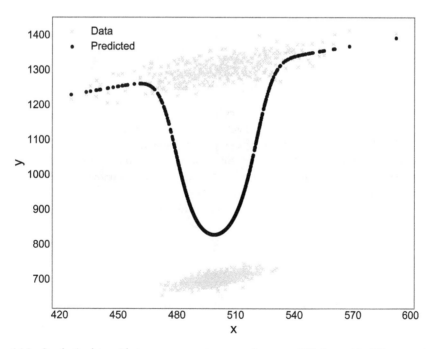

Figure 16.2 Synthetic data with two components centered on *x* = 500, but with different variances. Lighter points are data, and darker points are predicted outcomes made by our method.

The *Wine Quality* data combine two benchmark data sets from the UCI repository[3] related to red and white wines (Cortez et al., 2009). The data contain records for about 4,898 white wine and 1,599 red wine samples of wine quality and concentrations of various chemicals. *Quality* is a score between 0 and 10, and is typically around 5. Our goal is to model wine quality based on physicochemical tests. Note that the type of wine (red or white) is only used to evaluate the learned components.

The *New York City Property Sale* data[4] contain records of every building or building unit (such as an apartment) sold in the New York City property market over a 12-month period, from September 2016 to September 2017. We removed all categorical variables like *neighborhood* and *tax class*. We use each property's *borough* to study relevance of the components to different neighborhoods in NYC; however, we do not use it in analysis. The outcome variable is *sale price*, which is in million dollars, and it ranges from 0 to 2,210.

The *Stack Overflow* data set contains data from a question-answer forum on the topic of computer programming. Any user can ask a question, which others may answer. We used anonymized data representing all answers to questions with two or more answers posted on Stack Overflow from August 2008 until September 2014.[5] We created a user-focused data set by selecting at random one answer written by each user and discarding the rest. To understand factors affecting the length of the answer (the outcome, which we measure as the number of *words* in the answer), we use features of answers and features of users. Answer features include the number of *hyperlinks*, and *lines of code* the answer contains, and its *Flesch readability* score (Kincaid et al., 1975). Features describing answerers are their *reputation*, *tenure* on Stack Overflow (in terms of *percentile* rank), and experience, that is, the total *number of answers* written during their tenure. We also use activity-related features, including *time since previous answer* written by the user, *session length*, giving the number of answers the user writes during the session, and *answer position* within that session. We define a session as a period of activity without a break of 100 minutes or longer. The features *acceptance probability*, *reputation*, and *number of answers* are only used to evaluate the learned components.

4.1 Preprocessing

When variables are linearly correlated, regression coefficients are not unique, which presents a challenge for analysis. To address this challenge, we used variance inflation factor (VIF) to remove multicollinear variables. We iteratively remove variables when their VIF is larger than five. For example, in the Metropolitan data, this approach reduced the number of features from more than 40 to six, representing the number of residents within a tract who are *White*, *Black*, *Hispanic*, and *Asian*, as well as the percentage of adult residents with a *graduate* degree or with incomes *below poverty* line. Table 16.1 represents information about all data sets.

Table 16.1 Data sets and their characteristics

Data set	Records	Features	After VIF	Outcome
Synthetic	5,000	1	1	Y
Metropolitan	1,677	42	6	Valence
Wine Quality	6,497	11	5	Quality
NYC	36,805	7	4	Sale price
Stack Overflow	372,321	13	5	Answer length

4.2 Finding components

As a first step in applying DoGR to data for qualitative analysis, we need to decide on the number of components. In general, finding the appropriate number of components in clustering algorithms is difficult and generally requires ad hoc parameters. For Gaussian mixture models, the *Bayesian information criterion* (*BIC*) is typically used. We also use BIC with k ($p^2 + 2p + 3$) parameters, where k is number of components and p is number of independent variables. Based on the BIC scores, we choose five components for Metropolitan data. In our explorations, using three or six components gave qualitatively similar results, but with some of the components merging or splitting. With the same procedure, the optimal number of components for *Wine Quality* and *NYC* and *Stack Overflow* data is four.

5 Results

Due to the unique interpretability of our method, we first use it to describe meaningful relationships between variables in the real-world data ("Qualitative Results"). We then show how it compares favorably to competing methods ("Quantitative Results").

5.1 Qualitative results

We use a *radar chart* to visualize the components discovered in the data. Each polygon represents the mean of the component, μ, in the feature space. Each vertex of the polygon represents a feature, or dimension, with the length giving the coordinate of μ along that dimension. For the purpose of visualization, each coordinate value of μ was divided by the largest coordinate value of μ across all components. The maximum possible value of each coordinate after normalization is one. The mean value of the outcome variable within each component is shown in the legend, along with 95% confidence intervals.

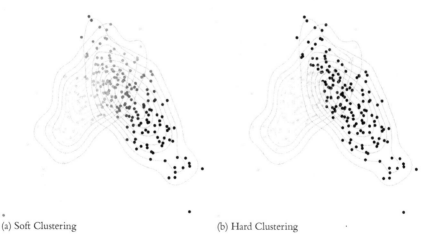

(a) Soft Clustering   (b) Hard Clustering

Figure 16.3   The difference between hard and soft clustering for data analysis. Assuming we have two clusters (dark and light), in hard clustering, the uncertainty of cluster assignment is not tractable in data analysis phase (e.g., studying the coefficients of the independent variables), since all the data points have one of the main cluster shades (b). However, with soft clustering, we can get the approximated coefficient for each individual data point (like the whole range from light to dark in (a)), separately.

Our method also estimates the regression coefficients, which we can compare to MLR. We computed the p-value assuming coefficients in DoGR are equal to MLR. If β_0 and β_1 are two coefficients to compare, and $\sigma_{\bar{\beta}_0}$ and $\sigma_{\bar{\beta}_1}$ are the *standard errors* of each coefficient, then the z-score is $z = \frac{\beta_0 - \beta_1}{\sqrt{\sigma_{\bar{\beta}_0}^2 + \sigma_{\bar{\beta}_1}^2}}$ from which we can easily infer the p-value assuming a normal distribution of errors (Paternoster et al., 1998).

We demonstrate the power of DoGR to give novel insights into data. While other methods exist for disaggregating heterogeneous data, most partition the data into disjoint groups, using hard assignment of data points to clusters, and then fit regression lines to each group separately. The main difference between DoGR and these other methods is that our method is more flexible in giving information for analytical purposes. Figure 16.3 shows schematic representation of the *coefficients* in heterogeneous data. Each latent confounder has a unique coefficient and we represent them using one of two shades: dark and light. Each data point could be a member of any cluster at the same time (with different membership values), and as a result, each data point could have a unique coefficient. The hard clustering methods are not able to offer this difference in coefficients. In Figure 16.3b, each data point has a fixed coefficient (dark or light), while in Figure 16.3a, each individual data point has a different coefficient based on its relative position from the center of the clusters. In the following sections, we apply DoGR to a variety of heterogeneous data and show the insights the method produces.

5.1.1 Metropolitan

Figure 16.4 visualizes the components of the Metropolitan data and reports regression coefficients for two variables. Interestingly, the data are disaggregated along ethnic lines, perhaps reflecting segregation within the Los Angeles County (Figure 16.5 represents the Los Angeles County tracts). The *dotted* component consists of census tracts with many highly educated White residents. It also has highest valence (5.86), meaning that people post the happiest tweets from those tracts. The *dot-dot-dash* component, is ethnically diverse, with large numbers of White, Asian, and Hispanic residents. Its valence (5.80) is only slightly lower than that of the *dotted* component. The *dash-dot* component has largely Asian and some Hispanic neighborhoods that are less well-off, but with slightly lower valence (5.76). The *dashed* and *solid* components represents tracts with the least educated and poorest residents. They are also places with the lowest valence (5.74 and 5.72, respectively). Looking at the regression coefficients, education is positively related to happiness across the entire population (*All*), and individually in all components, with the coefficients significantly different from MLR in four of the five components, *suggesting this trend was a Simpson's paradox*. However, the effect is weakest in the most and least educated components. Poverty has no significant effect across the entire population, but has a negative effect on happiness in poorest neighborhoods (*solid*). Counter-intuitively, regression coefficients are positive for two components (*dotted* and *dash-dot*). It appears that within these demographic classes, the poorer the neighborhood, the happier the tweets that originate from them.

5.1.2 Wine quality

Figure 16.6 visualizes the disaggregation of the Wine Quality data into four components. Although we did not use the type of wine (red or white) as a feature, wines were naturally disaggregated by type. The *dash-dots* component is almost entirely (98%) composed of

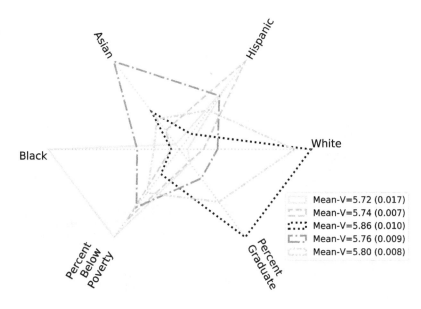

	mean	std	% Below Poverty	% Graduate
			β	β
All	5.78	0.098	0.0000	0.0028
dotted	5.86	0.092	0.0063★★★	0.0016★
dot-dot-dash	5.80	0.077	0.0002	0.0030
dash-dot	5.76	0.080	0.0018★★★	0.0050★★★
dashed	5.74	0.073	0.0001	0.0056★★★
solid	5.72	0.117	−0.0008★★★	0.0001★★★

★ p-value ≤ 0.05; ★★★ p-value ≤ 0.001

Figure 16.4 Disaggregation of the Metropolitan data into five subgroups. The radar plot shows the relative importance of a feature within the subgroup. The table report regression coefficients for two independent variables *Percent Below Poverty* and *Percent Graduate* for multivariate regression (MLR) of aggregate data and separately for each subgroup found by our method.

high-quality (average quality = 6.02) white wines. All the wines in the *solid* component are white (average quality = 5.91), while the *dashed* component is composed mostly (85%) of red wines with average quality 5.60. The lowest-quality (*dotted*) component, with average quality equal to 5.36, contains a mixture of red (43%) and white (57%) wines. In other words, we discover that in higher-quality wines, the type of wine can be determined with high accuracy simply based on its chemical components. Low-quality wines appear less distinguishable based on their chemicals. We find *Chlorides* have a negative impact on quality of wine in all components (not shown), *Sugar* has positive impact on high-quality white wines and red wines and negative impact on low-quality wines. Surprisingly, *Free Sulfur Dioxide* has a positive impact on high-quality white wines but a negative impact in other components. These findings may be important to wine growers and capture subtleties in data that commonly used MLR does not.

Figure 16.5   Map of Los Angeles county. The shading represents the component for the tract. Components match the components of Figure 16.4. Majority Asian neighborhoods are represented by ++, majority Black neighborhoods oo, affluent areas | |, ethnically diverse areas \\, and majority Hispanic (East Los Angeles) neighborhoods //.

5.1.3 NYC property sales

The mean sale price of all properties in New York City (NYC) property sales data is $1.31 million. The mean price, however, hides a large heterogeneity in the properties on the market. Our method tamed some of this heterogeneity by identifying four components within the sales data. Figure 16.7 shows that these components represent large commercial properties (*dash-dot*), large residential properties (*dashed*), mixed commercial/residential sales (*dotted*), and single-unit residential properties (*solid*).

Table 16.2 shows what percentage of each component is made up of New York City's five boroughs. Large commercial properties (*dash-dot* component), such as office buildings, are located in Brooklyn and Manhattan, for example. These are the most expensive among all properties, with an average price of more than $12 million. The next most expensive type of property are large residential buildings (*dashed* component) – multi-unit apartment buildings. These are also most likely to be located in Manhattan and Brooklyn. Small residential properties (*solid* component) – most likely to be single-family homes – are the least expensive, on average

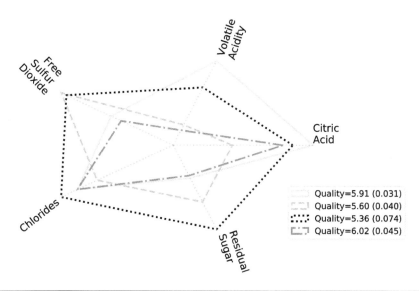

	Wine	Quality	Citric Acid	SO2	Sugar
	mean	*std err*	β	β	β
All			0.1044	−0.0008	−0.0175
dash-dot	6.02	0.023	0.4299	0.0173★★★	0.4272★★★
solid	5.91	0.016	−0.1545★★	−0.0001	−0.0156
dashed	5.6	0.020	−0.0968	−0.0024	0.3227★★★
dotted	5.36	0.037	0.3039★★	−0.011★★★	−0.004★★★
★ p-value ≤ 0.05; ★★★ p-value ≤ 0.001					

Figure 16.6 The value of the center of each component (μ) for four components of the Wine Quality data. The *dash-dot* and *solid* components are almost entirely white wines, and the *dashed* component is composed mostly (85%) of red wines. The lowest-quality and smallest – *dotted* – component is a mixture of red (43%) and white (57%) wines.

Table 16.2 DoGR components and the boroughs that make up each component (rows might not add up to 100% due to rounding)

Component	Manhattan	Bronx	Brooklyn	Queens	Staten Island
dash-dot	**17%**	20%	**41%**	17%	5%
dashed	**41%**	22%	**26%**	10%	1%
dotted	8%	9%	**65%**	15%	3%
solid	0%	13%	**37%**	**33%**	16%
All	3%	13%	40%	30%	14%

half a million dollars, and most likely to be located in Brooklyn and Queens, with some in Staten Island.

Regressions in this data set show several instances of Simpson's paradoxes. Property price in population-level data increases as a function of the number of *residential units*. In disaggregated data, however, this is true only for the *dashed* component, representing apartment buildings. Having more residential units in smaller residential properties (*dotted* and *solid* components)

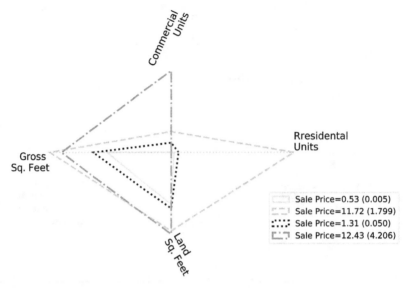

	Sale Price		Resid. Units	Commer. Units	Gross Sq. Feet	Land Sq. Feet
	mean	*std err*	β	β	β	β
All	1.31	0.079	0.036	0.039	2.681	0.595
dash-dot	12.43	2.143	0.000	0.218	8.842	−1.956
dashed	11.72	0.916	0.078	1.008	5.329	−6.652
dotted	1.31	0.026	−0.142	−0.900	0.591	−0.348
solid	0.53	0.004	−0.039	0.000	0.124	0.089

all significant: p-value ≤ 0.001

Figure 16.7 The value of center (μ) for four components of NYC data. The numbers in legends are average price of the component's real estate and is in millions of dollars.

lowers their price. This could be explained by smaller multi-unit buildings, such as duplexes and row houses, being located in poorer residential areas, which lowers their price compared to single-family homes. Another notable trend reversal occurs when regressing on lot size (*land square feet*). As expected, there is a positive relationship in the *solid* component with respect to lot size, as single-family homes built on bigger lots are expected to fetch higher prices in the New York City area. However, the trends in the other components are negative. This could be explained the following way. As land becomes more expensive, builders are incentivized to build up, creating multi-story apartment and office buildings. The more expensive the land, the taller the building they build. This is confirmed by the positive relationship with *gross square feet*, which are strongest for the *dash-dot* and *dashed* components. In plain words, these components represent the tall buildings with a small footprint that one often sees in New York City.

5.1.4 Stack Overflow

As our last illustration, we apply DoGR to Stack Overflow data to answer the question of how well we can predict the length of the answer a user writes, given the features of the user and the answer.

DoGR splits the data into four clusters, as shown in Figure 16.8. The *dotted* and *dashed* components contain most of the data, with 47% and 39% of records respectively. The radar plot shows the relative strength of the features in each component, while the table above the plot shows features characterizing each discovered group. Except for *Percentile tenure*, these features were not used by DoGR and are shown to validate the discovered groups.

The *dash-dot* component (5% of data) contains very active (longer *Session length*) users, who meticulously document their answers with many *lines of code* and *URLs*, so we can label them "power users." These are among the longest (high *words*) and more complex (low *readability*) answers in the data, and they also tend to be high quality (high *acceptance probability*). Surprisingly, this group has newer users (lower *percentile tenure*), but they have high reputation (*answerer reputation*) and wrote more answers previously (higher *number of answers*). These users, while a minority, give life to Stack Overflow and make it useful for others. *Dash-dot* component users have more *code lines* within shorter answers. This is in contrast to other groups, which tend to include more lines of code within longer answers. The brevity of *dash-dot* users when documenting code is an example of a trend reversal.

Another interesting subgroup is the *solid* group (8% of data), which is composed of "veterans" (high *percentile tenure*), who write easy-to-read answers (high *readability*) that are documented with many *URLs*. These users have a relatively high *reputation*, but they are selective in the questions they answer (lower *number of answers* than for the *dash-dot* users). Interestingly, tenure (*percentile*) does not have an effect on the length of the answer for these *solid* users, while it has positive effect in other groups (i.e., more veteran users write longer answers). The negative effect of *URLs* on the length of the answer suggests that these users use *URLs* to refer to existing answers.

The *dashed* (39%) and *dotted* (47%) components contain the vast majority of data. They are similar in terms of user *reputation*, tenure (*percentile*) and experience (*number of answers*), as well as the quality of the answers they write (*acceptance probability*), with the *dashed* component users scoring slightly higher on all the measures. The main difference is in the answers they write: *dashed* users do not include *URLs* in their answers, while *dotted* users do not include *code*. Another difference between these groups is that *dotted* users have longer answers than *dashed* users, but as their answers become longer, they also become more difficult to read (lower *readability*). In contrast, longer answers by *dashed* users are easier to read. Overall, we find intuitive and surprising results from data that are largely due to DoGR's interpretability.

5.2 Quantitative results

We compare the performance of DoGR to existing state-of-the-art methods for disaggregated regression: the three variants of CLR, WCLR (da Silva & de Carvalho, 2017), FWCLR (da Silva & de Carvalho, 2018), and GMR (Sung, 2004). We use MLR, which does not disaggregate data, as baseline.

5.2.1 Prediction performance

For the prediction task, we use 5×5-fold nested cross-validation to train the model on four folds and make predictions on the out-of-sample data in the fifth fold. As hyperparameters, we use values of k between one and six as potential number of components for all methods. For WCLR and FCWCLR, we set $\alpha = \{0.001, 0.01, 0.1, 10.0, 100.0, 1000.0\}$, and for FWCLR we set $m = \{1.1, 1.5, 2.0, 3.0\}$. We use grid search to find best hyperparameters. Table 16.3 presents results on our data sets and synthetic data. To evaluate prediction quality, we use *root*

	Size	Acceptance probability	Answerer reputation	Number of answers	Percentile tenure
dashed	39%	0.26	338.17	16.02	0.43
dotted	47%	0.24	314.35	14.56	0.42
solid	8%	0.33	492.19	20.65	0.47
dash-dot	5%	0.32	784.62	40.21	0.40

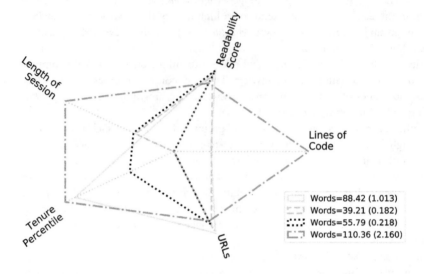

Words=88.42 (1.013)
Words=39.21 (0.182)
Words=55.79 (0.218)
Words=110.36 (2.160)

	Words		Codes	Readab.	Percnt.	URLs
	mean	std	β	β	β	β
All	54.91	0.102	0.29	0.048	5.61	17.11
dashed	39.21	0.093	0.43	0.112	6.09	0
dotted	55.79	0.111	0.00	−0.175	2.64	3.62
solid	88.42	0.517	0.17	−0.467	−0.22	−86.20
dash-dot	110.36	1.102	0.20	0.341	20.45	12.87

★ *Italicized effects are not significant*

Figure 16.8 Disaggregation of Stack Overflow data into subgroups. The outcome variable is length of the answer (number of words). The radar plot shows the importance of each features used in the disaggregation. The top table shows average values of validation features, while the bottom table shows regression coefficients for the groups.

mean square error (RMSE) and *mean absolute error (MAE)*. When comparing the quality of cross-validated predictions across methods, we use the Kruskal-Wallis test, a non-parametric method to compare whether multiple distributions are different (Kruskal & Wallis, 1952). When distributions were significantly different, a pairwise comparisons using the Tukey-Kramer test was also done as a post hoc test to determine if mean cross-validated quality metrics were statistically different (McDonald, 2014). Prediction results are shown in Table 16.3. We use ★ to indicate statistically significant ($p < 0.05$) differences between our method and other methods. Bolded values differ significantly from others or have lower standard deviation. Following (da Silva & de Carvalho, 2018), we use lower deviation to denote more consistent predictions.

WCLR and FWCLR do not perform well in Synthetic data, because the variances of the two components are different, which these methods do not handle. This is a problem that exists in an arbitrary number dimensions; we observe in higher dimensions the gap between performance of FWCLR and our method *increases*.

For Metropolitan data, there is no statistically significant difference between methods: all cluster-based regression methods outperform MLR on the prediction task. This shows that any method that accounts for the latent structure of data helps improve predictions. For Wine Quality data, while the null hypothesis of equal performance of GMR and DoGR cannot be rejected, our method has a smaller standard deviation in both data sets. We were not able to

Table 16.3 Results of prediction on five data sets. Asterisk (★) indicates results that are significantly different from our method (p-value < 0.05). The bolded results have smaller standard deviation among the best methods with same mean of error.

Method	RMSE ($\pm\sigma$)	MAE ($\pm\sigma$)
Synthetic		
MLR	294.88 ($\pm$ 1.236)★	288.35 ($\pm$ 0.903)★
WCLR	261.14 ($\pm$ 3.370)★	232.76 ($\pm$ 2.682)★
FWCLR	261.27 ($\pm$ 4.729)★	233.05 ($\pm$ 3.772)★
GMR	257.36 ($\pm$ 4.334)	219.15 ($\pm$ 3.567)
DoGR	**257.32 ($\pm$ 3.871)**	**219.11 ($\pm$ 3.106)**
Metropolitan		
MLR	0.083 ($\pm$ 0.0061)	0.062 ($\pm$ 0.0033)
WCLR	0.083 ($\pm$ 0.0029)	0.062 ($\pm$ 0.0024)
FWCLR	**0.082 ($\pm$ 0.0044)**	**0.061 ($\pm$ 0.0021)**
GMR	0.083 ($\pm$ 0.0043)	0.061 ($\pm$ 0.0023)
DoGR	0.083 ($\pm$ 0.0052)	0.061 ($\pm$ 0.0031)
Wine Quality		
MLR	0.83 ($\pm$ 0.018)★	0.64 ($\pm$ 0.015)★
WCLR	0.83 ($\pm$ 0.013)★	0.64 ($\pm$ 0.011)★
FWCLR	0.80 ($\pm$ 0.013)★	0.63 ($\pm$ 0.009)★
GMR	0.79 ($\pm$ 0.017)	0.62 ($\pm$ 0.014)
DoGR	**0.79 ($\pm$ 0.014)**	**0.62 ($\pm$ 0.011)**
NYC		
MLR	13.36 ($\pm$ 7.850)	2.20 ($\pm$ 0.064)★
FWCLR	13.14 ($\pm$ 7.643)	1.76 ($\pm$ 0.321)★
DoGR	**11.88 ($\pm$ 9.109)**	**1.40 ($\pm$ 0.222)**
Stack Overflow		
MLR	60.69 ($\pm$ 1.118)	37.74 ($\pm$ 0.152)
FWCLR	60.47 ($\pm$ 0.960)	37.25 ($\pm$ 0.794)
DoGR	60.68 ($\pm$ 1.298)	37.62 ($\pm$ 0.314)

successfully run GMR and WCLR on NYC data, due to exceptions (returning null as predicted outcome) and extremely long run time, respectively. It took three days for FWCLR and four hours for our method to finish running on NYC data. Our method has significantly lower MAE compared to FWCLR. We were also not able to successfully run GMR and WCLR on Stack Overflow data for the same reasons. It took six days for FWCLR to run one round of cross-validation, after which we stopped it.

Therefore, the mean reported in the table for FWCLR is the average of five runs, while for MLR and DoGR it is the average of 25 runs. Due to this discrepancy, we did not highlight any of the results in bold.

5.2.2 Run time

To compare the run time of all algorithms, we performed one round of cross-validation (not nested) for each method. The same machine (4-GB RAM, 3.0-GHz Intel CPU, Windows OS) was used for time calculation. The available code for WCLR and FWCLR methods are in R while the other methods are written in Python. Table 16.4 presents the run time in minutes. The slowest method is WCLR, while the fastest one is MLR. WCLR and FWCLR are sensitive to size of data, perhaps due to the many hyperparameters they need to tune. To find the best hyperparameters for GMR and DoGR, we ran the methods six times, while WCLR requires 36 runs and FWCLR 144 runs. Beside the NYC and Stack Overflow data sets for which exceptions occur in GMR, the run time of DoGR is twice that of GMR. GMR throws exception possibly because of a singular covariance matrix. While our method is similar in spirit to GMR, our method is more stable, as shown on the NYC and Stack Overflow data. In addition, our method is interpretable, as it directly computes regression coefficients, while GMR represents relationships between variables via the covariance matrix. Covariance values are not guaranteed to have the same sign, let alone magnitude, as regression coefficients. Regression is therefore necessary to understand the true relationships between variables. Mathematically, GMR and *unweighted* regression can be converted to one another using linear algebra. It is not clear, however, whether the equivalence also holds for weighted regression.

6 Discussion

In this chapter, we introduce DoGR, which softly disaggregates data by latent confounders. Our method retains the advantages of linear models, namely their interpretability, by reporting regression coefficients that give meaning to trends. Our method also discovers the

Table 16.4 Run time (in *minutes*) of one round of cross-validation (non-nested). MLR took less than a minute for all data sets; "failed" indicates that the method could not run on the data due to exceptions. We time out WCLR exceeding sufficient amount of time to show the order of performance. Numbers in bold indicate the fastest algorithm.

Dataset	WCLR	FWCLR	GMR	DoGR
Synthetic	6.46	0.68	**0.76**	1.4
Metropolitan	37	9	**2**	4
Wine Quality	180+	36	**9**	16
NYC	600+	232	failed	**10**
Stack Overflow	–	7,200+	failed	**170**

multidimensional latent structure of data by partitioning it into subgroups with similar characteristics and behaviors. While alternative methods exist for disaggregating data, our approach is unique because it produces interpretable regressions that are computationally efficient. We demonstrate the utility of our approach by applying it to real-world data, from data on wines to data on answers in a question-answer website. We show that our method identifies meaningful subgroups and trends, while also yielding new insights into the data. For example, in the wine data set, it correctly separated high-quality red wines from white, and also discovered two distinct classes of high-quality white wines. In the Stack Overflow data, it helped us identify important users like "veterans" and "power users."

There are a few ways forward to improve our method. Currently, it is applied to continuous variables, but it needs to be extended to categorical variables, often seen in social science data. Moreover, real data is often nonlinear; therefore, our method needs to be extended to nonlinear models beyond linear regression. In addition, to improve prediction accuracy, our method could include regularization parameters, such as ridge regression or LASSO. However, already in its current form, DoGR can yield new insights into data.

Notes

1 http://github.com/ninoch/DoGR
2 http://data.census.gov
3 https://archive.ics.uci.edu/ml/datasets/wine+quality
4 www.kaggle.com/new-york-city/nyc-property-sales
5 https://archive.org/details/stackexchange

References

Alipourfard, N., Fennell, P. G., & Lerman, K. (2018a). Can you trust the trend? Discovering Simpson's paradoxes in social data. In *Proceedings of the eleventh ACM international conference on web search and data mining* (pp. 19–27). ACM.

Alipourfard, N., Fennell, P. G., & Lerman, K. (2018b). Using Simpson's paradox to discover interesting patterns in behavioral data. In *Twelfth international AAAI conference on web and social media*. AAAI.

Bareinboim, E., & Pearl, J. (2016). Causal inference and the data-fusion problem. *Proceedings of the National Academy of Sciences, 113*, 7345–7352.

Blyth, C. R. (1972). On Simpson's paradox and the sure-thing principle. *Journal of the American Statistical Association, 67*(338), 364–366.

Calderon, D., Juba, B., Li, Z., & Ruan, L. (2018). Conditional linear regression. In *Thirty-second AAAI conference on artificial intelligence*. AAAI.

Chuang, J. S., Rivoire, O., & Leibler, S. (2009). Simpson's paradox in a synthetic microbial system. *Science, 323*(5911), 272–275.

Cleveland, W. S., & Devlin, S. J. (1988). Locally weighted regression: An approach to regression analysis by local fitting. *Journal of the American Statistical Association, 83*(403), 596–610.

Cortez, P., Cerdeira, A., Almeida, F., Matos, T., & Reis, J. (2009). Modeling wine preferences by data mining from physicochemical properties. *Decision Support Systems, 47*(4), 547–553.

da Silva, R. A., & de Carvalho, F. D. A. (2017). On combining clusterwise linear regression and k-means with automatic weighting of the explanatory variables. In *International conference on artificial neural networks* (pp. 402–410). Springer.

da Silva, R. A., & de Carvalho, F. D. A. (2018). On combining fuzzy c- regression models and fuzzy c-means with automated weighting of the explanatory variables. In *2018 IEEE international conference on fuzzy systems (FUZZ-IEEE)* (pp. 1–8). IEEE.

DeSarbo, W. S., & Cron, W. L. (1988). A maximum likelihood methodology for clusterwise linear regression. *Journal of classification, 5*(2), 249–282.

Fabris, C. C., & Freitas, A. A. (2000). Discovering surprising patterns by detecting occurrences of Simpson's paradox. In *Research and development in intelligent systems XVI* (pages 148–160). Springer.

Fox, J. (1997). *Applied regression analysis, linear models, and related methods.* Sage Publications, Inc.

Ghahramani, Z., & Jordan, M. I. (1994). Supervised learning from incomplete data via an EM approach. In *Advances in neural information processing systems* (pp. 120–127). Neural Information Processing Systems Foundation.

Kievit, R., Frankenhuis, W. E., Waldorp, L., & Borsboom, D. (2013). Simpson's paradox in psychological science: A practical guide. *Frontiers in Psychology, 4*, 513.

Kincaid, J. P., Fishburnea, J., Rogers, R. L., & Chissom, B. S. (1975). *Derivation of new readability formulas (automated readability index, fog count and Flesch reading ease formula) for navy enlisted personnel.* Technical Report, U.S. Navy.

Kruskal, W. H., & Wallis, W. A. (1952). Use of ranks in one-criterion variance analysis. *Journal of the American Statistical Association, 47*(260), 583–621.

Lerman, K., Arora, M., Gallegos, L., Kumaraguru, P., & Garcia, D. (2016). Emotions, demographics and sociability in twitter interactions. In *Proceedings of the international AAAI conference on web and social media* (Vol. 10). AAAI.

Louizos, C., Shalit, U., Mooij, J. M., Sontag, D., Zemel, R., & Welling, M. (2017). Causal effect inference with deep latent-variable models. In I. Guyon, U. V. Luxburg, S. Bengio, H. Wallach, R. Fergus, S. Vishwanathan, & R. Garnett (Eds.), *Advances in neural information processing systems* (Vol. 30, pp. 6446–6456). Curran Associates, Inc.

Manwani, N., & Sastry, P. (2015). K-plane regression. *Information Sciences, 292*, 39–56.

McDonald, J. (2014). *Handbook of biological statistics* (3rd ed.). Sparky House Publishing.

McLean, R. A., Sanders, W. L., & Stroup, W. W. (1991). A unified approach to mixed linear models. *The American Statistician, 45*(1), 54–64.

Minchev, I., Matijevic, G., Hogg, D., Guiglion, G., Steinmetz, M., Anders, F., . . . Scannapieco, C. (2019). Yule-Simpson's paradox in galactic archaeology. arXiv preprint arXiv:1902.01421.

Pashler, H., & Wagenmakers, E. (2012). Editors' introduction to the special section on replicability in psychological science: A crisis of confidence? *Perspectives on Psychological Science, 7*(6), 528–530.

Paternoster, R., Brame, R., Mazerolle, P., & Piquero, A. (1998). Using the correct statistical test for the equality of regression coefficients. *Criminology, 36*(4), 859–866.

Ranganath, R., & Perotte, A. J. (2018). Multiple causal inference with latent confounding. arXiv preprint: 1805.08273.

Smaldino, P. E., & McElreath, R. (2016). The natural selection of bad science. *Royal Society Open Science, 3*(9), 160384.

Späth, H. (1979). Algorithm 39 clusterwise linear regression. *Computing, 22*(4), 367–373.

Sung, H. G. (2004). *Gaussian mixture regression and classification.* PhD thesis, Rice University.

Wang, Y., & Blei, D. M. (2018). The blessings of multiple causes. arXiv preprint: 1805.06826.

Warriner, A. B., Kuperman, V., & Brysbaert, M. (2013). Norms of valence, arousal, and dominance for 13,915 English lemmas. *Behavior Research Methods, 45*(4), 1191–1207.

Winter, B. (2013). A very basic tutorial for performing linear mixed effects analyses. arxiv preprint arXiv:1308.5499.

SECTION IV

Machine learning methods

17

MACHINE LEARNING METHODS FOR COMPUTATIONAL SOCIAL SCIENCE

Richard D. De Veaux and Adam Eck

1 Introduction

The social science researcher is often faced with the problem of trying to predict an individual's (or group's) behavior from a collection of other measured variables of their state. For example, given a person's age, gender, income, occupation, location, and education, who are they most likely to vote for in the next election? When the outcome, as here, is a category – the possible candidates they will vote for – we refer to it as a *classification* problem. We might also want to predict a quantitative outcome; for example, the amount of money the same person would give to their candidate of choice given the same input variables. In this case we call the problem a *regression* problem. The input variables (e.g., occupation and education) are referred to as across various disciplines as independent variables, covariates, predictors, or attributes; the outcome variable (e.g., candidate or donation amount) is referred to as the response, dependent variable, or label.[1] The cases that couple the input variables with an associated outcome are referred to as observations, individuals, instances, or examples.[2]

Both classification and regression problems are examples of *supervised learning* – where the values of the response variable are known. In the election voting example, the researcher fits a model from a sample of individual's voting intentions, then the learned model is applied to predict the outcome in another situation, possibly the general election. Often the researcher fits several models and either chooses the best among them based on their performance or averages some or all of them in what's called an *ensemble model*.

By contrast, sometimes we want to group observations together simply by virtue of their values on a set of variables. For example, given age, gender, income, occupation, and education, are there clusters of similar individuals that we can identify? This is an example of an *unsupervised learning* problem (covered in later chapters in this volume) where no response variable is involved.

A *model* is a well-defined mathematical object that can be expressed via formulas with unknown *parameters* (constants). The parameters in the model are estimated using the data to give the best predictions to the data at hand. An *algorithm* is the computational procedure that searches for and finds the best estimates. For example, in a simple linear regression model, the model is a straight line of the form: $\hat{y}_i = b_0 + b_1 x_i$ and the algorithm might be a closed form

DOI: 10.4324/9781003025245-21

solution or a grid search for the optimal b_0 and b_1 that maximize a certain criterion (in this case least squares).

A model is a function $y = f(x_1, x_2, \ldots, x_p) + \varepsilon$ that can be used both to understand the relationship between the predictors (the x_i) and the response y, ultimately to predict y from a given set of x_i. This is an impossibly hard problem if there are no restrictions on the form of the function f. Thus, nearly all the statistical and machine learning models restrict the search by placing constraints on the form of f. For example, a multiple regression model assumes that the function is a linear function of the x_i (or re-expressions of them). A neural network is traditionally a series of sigmoidally transformed linear combinations of the predictor variables, and a decision tree is a set of logical rules that relate the predictor variables to the response variable. Models can be very complex, but they can always be written down (at least recursively). Fitting complex models to data that require intensive computation are often referred to as *machine learning* or *statistical learning*.

Many models can be used for either classification or regression, with some modification. Classical statistical models, like multiple linear regression, tend to be *transparent*. Their formulas reveal the variables that drive the prediction, and even though they are not necessarily causal, they can be used to readily understand the underlying relationships among the variables, making attribution to the inputs possible. Many modern, machine learning algorithms, by contrast, tend to be opaque *black boxes*. The advantage of these methods lies in their often-superior predictive ability, but it may be difficult, if not impossible, to extract the relationships underlying the model. Researchers must decide for themselves whether they are more interested in prediction or attribution, for there is often a trade-off between the two.

Of course, models are not the only piece in the research investigation. After defining a problem of interest, the researcher must collect appropriate data to be used to fit a model. A model is only as good as the data on which it is based. Although the Internet has made data collection easier, it has also made it more difficult to ensure that the data are representative of the group on which the researcher may want to make inference. An important consideration is the data source, the method the data were collected, the motivation behind the data collection, and the quality of the data. Even if the source of the data is a reliable one, considerable effort is often required to clean and prepare the data for modeling. Finally, the researcher must communicate the results of the models to others in ways that are useful.

In this chapter, we will briefly outline the entire process from data collection to results communication, but we will focus on the most common models for classification and regression. Section 2 describes the overall process of supervised machine learning, starting with data collection, tidying and cleaning, fitting a model, and finally evaluating the quality or performance of the learned model. Section 3 presents classical linear models of regression and classification along with their modern variants of the LASSO and elastic net. Section 4 introduces some simple methods for prediction such as k-nearest neighbor and naïve Bayes. Section 5 concerns tree-based models and introduces the ideas of bootstrap aggregation and boosting, two modern methods for model enhancement. Section 6 discusses neural networks and deep learning. Section 7 serves as a summary.

2 Supervised machine learning process

2.1 Data collection

As with any quantitative method, the supervised machine learning process (illustrated in Figure 17.1) begins with data that describe the real-world phenomenon one wishes to understand.

Figure 17.1 Supervised machine learning process flowchart

For the computational social scientist, these data could come from many sources, such as (1) surveys and interviews conducted with participants, (2) sensors measuring real-world events, such as continual measurements of weather or traffic, (3) data collected about processes (sometimes called paradata [Kreuter, 2013]), such as people's browsing behaviors on the Internet, (4) administrative data collected by government agencies, such as census records of geographic areas, (5) information derived from other data, such as sentiment scores from social media posts, or (6) information sold by third-party vendors.

To build a model predicting a response variable from a collection of predictors, the data must include both observations of the response (e.g., voting preferences or political donations) and the associated values of the predictor variables used in making predictions (e.g., age, education level, annual income) for each case. Supervised learning cannot discover patterns relating input variables to outcomes without coupled examples of both. As a general rule of thumb, more observations lead to better models by providing more information for learning, but this depends on how well the collected observations cover the range of possible combinations of values of input variables, whether all of the input variables are actually relevant to determining the outcome, and the noise inherent (and often unavoidable) in the data collection process. As a result, more collected data does not always produce better learning (a view sometimes referred to as *big data hubris* [see, e.g., De Veaux et al., 2016]), and data quality is always a concern. GIGO (garbage in garbage out) is always true, no matter how sophisticated the algorithm or type of model used during machine learning.

Continuing our election example from the introduction, imagine that we have conducted a poll of a nationally representative random sample of voters. Each respondent's answers to the poll represent an observation, which consists of both who they intend to vote for (the categorical response) and personal information such as their age and income as numeric predictors and education level, gender, and occupation as categorical predictors. Then we are ready to begin the supervised machine learning process of discovering patterns between personal characteristics (predictors) and voting preferences (response).

2.2 Data processing

Real-world data almost never arrive ready for immediate use in model building. Typically, the data need to be put into rectangular form if they do not arrive that way, a process often referred to as *tidying* the data. We can visualize our illustrative example poll data as a rectangular form like a spreadsheet, where each row is an observation, and the columns hold the response and predictor variables. Many, but not all, machine learning programs require the data to be in such a form.

The next step is to *clean* the data, a process also called *data wrangling*, or *munging*. What tasks are performed in the cleaning stage often depend on both the type of model one wishes to fit and the algorithm used to fit the model. For example, some algorithms cannot use observations with missing values. So, either those observations must be removed from the data set (reducing the amount of data available for learning), missingness needs to be treated as its own distinct category (the validity of which depends on whether the data are missing at random), or, if the missing values are missing completely at random, they can be imputed based on the information contained in other observations (e.g., using the median for continuous data or the mode for categorical data, or predicting the missing values using a separate imbedded learning process).

If numeric predictor variables have different ranges of values, such as when one variable has range [0, 1] and another has range [−100, 1,000], then it may be wise to *scale* the variables so they are comparable. Variables can be *normalized* so that they are all converted to the range [0, 1] or *standardized* to have a mean of 0 and a standard deviation of 1. One commonly used normalization method is min-max normalization, where each value is converted to the range [0, 1] as:

$$Value = \frac{Orignal\ Value - Min}{Max - Min}$$

so that original values closer to the minimum become near 0, and values closer to the maximum become near 1. In our election example, if our oldest respondent was 82 and our youngest respondent was 18, then the normalized value would be 0.375 for a respondent with an age of 42, indicating that they are in the lower half of the range of ages in the data set.

Standardization of variables involves converting the value to have mean 0 and standard deviation 1:

$$Value = \frac{Original\ Value - Mean}{Standard\ Deviation}$$

The resulting value is called a *z-score*. The *z*-score tells how many standard deviations from the mean each value lies. In our running election example, if the mean income were $60k with a standard deviation of $10k, then a respondent with income $80k would have an income *z*-score of +2.0 (i.e., two standard deviations above the mean).

Some types of models (e.g., neural networks) require that categorical variables be converted to numeric values. If a categorical predictor has only two possible values (e.g., true/false, yes/no), then one value can be set to 0 and the other value set to 1 (sometimes referred to as the reference value). In our election example, if gender is restricted to only the values male and female, then we might set male = 0 and female = 1. Alternatively, we can set the values to −1 and 1 (say male = −1 and female = 1), which then eliminates the reference value and compares both levels to the mean. The resulting variable is called an *indicator*, or *dummy variable*.

For categorical variables with more than two possible values, the most commonly used process for conversion to numeric values is *one-hot encoding*, where all but one of the possible categories is assigned a new indicator variable that takes value 1 if the original category was the corresponding value, else it takes value 0. If there are *k* possible values, this results in *k−1* indicators. The last category becomes the reference value.[3] For our election example, if the categorical *Education* predictor has four possible values: *Some High School*, *High School Diploma or GED*, *Some College*, and *College Degree*, we could construct three indicators for *Education*. Table 17.1 demonstrates how values would be assigned to these new variables for different observations. The *k*th category (here *College Degree*) has value 0 for all variables and becomes the reference value. With two categories, only one variable is needed. In fact, creating two indicators would be redundant, as the two variables would be linearly dependent (perfectly predicted from each other).

Table 17.1 One hot encoding of education categorical variable into three numeric variables

Education	SomeHS	HSorGED	SomeCollege
Some High School	1	0	0
High School Diploma or GED	0	1	0
Some College	0	0	1
College Degree	0	0	0

2.3 Feature creation and elimination

Rarely are the collected predictor variables exactly the right ones needed to build the model. The researcher can combine existing variables into new ones. For example, if we have financial information on an individual including *amount of debt* and *income*, we could create a new variable *debt.to.income.ratio* by taking their ratio. The creation of new variables is called *feature creation*. There are both manual and automatic methods for creating new variables. Many algorithms create new variables that are not directly observable, called *latent variables*. This is the case, for example, in methods such as principal components, factor analysis, partial least squares, and neural networks, among others. The latent variables may be of interest in their own right, or they may just be convenient constructs to improve the model accuracy or stability.

On the other hand, most data sets will also contain predictors that are not relevant for the task at hand. Including them may deteriorate the predictions on future data by building a model that is too complex. The choice between a model that doesn't contain enough predictors and one that is too complex is known generically as Occam's razor, after the 14th-century Franciscan friar William of Ockham who preferred the simplest possible explanations for divine miracles. Similarly, a quote describing the balance between parsimony and accuracy, often attributed to Albert Einstein,[4] states, "Everything should be as simple as possible, but no simpler." The search for the right balance is known as the bias-variance trade-off in statistics and is part of *model selection*. Many statistics have been proposed to guide the researcher to the optimum balance of simplicity and complexity, including adjusted R^2, Mallows C_p, Akaike's information criterion (AIC), and the Bayesian information criterion (BIC).

2.4 Cross-validation

However, another way to attempt to choose the right-sized model is based on training multiple versions of a model (with different sizes or other settings) and selecting the best one. Here, part of the data set, called the *training set*, is used to fit (or train) the model. Another set, called the *test set*, is used to evaluate the model after it has been fit. The test set is not used in any way during the model building and so its performance is seen as an indication of how well the model will do on new data. Sometimes a third set, called a *validation* or *tuning set*, can be used to guide the model selection within a model type. For example, the decision of which variables to include in a multiple regression could be based on which provide the best fit to the tuning set.

Observations used for evaluation in the validation and test sets are kept separate from the training set because when we evaluate a model, we want to know how well it generalizes to observations that were not used during learning, instead of how well the model simply memorizes information. Generalization, rather than memorization, represents whether the model truly learned patterns relating predictor variables and response outcomes, rather than simply remembering combinations seen during fitting. As a result, higher generalization implies better predictions when the model is applied to previously unseen data when it is used in practice. However, when the model is applied to new data, it will almost never perform as well as the test set, as a test set randomly chosen from the original data is more like the training data than it will be like a newly obtained data set. This is part of the problem of *reproducibility*.

Since both validation and test sets are used for evaluating a model, it is important to understand the differences between the two. The validation data are available to model fitting to create the best possible model, in order to tune the complexity of the model. In our election example, validation data would consist of voters for whom we know their expected votes against which we can compare the predictions of our model so that we can evaluate how well our model has learned so far. Different models will use validation data in different ways. For example, some models (e.g., neural networks) might use validation data to decide when the model can stop training, possibly because it has converged to an optimal predictive ability or because further training is actually making performance worse by *overfitting* to nuances that are present in the training data but do not generalize in the validation set (e.g., by random chance, male voters in the training set are more likely to prefer candidate X but not so in the larger population). Other models (e.g., decision trees) might use validation data to reduce the complexity of the model after the model has been fit, so that simpler patterns relating predictors and outcomes can be found.

Test data, on the other hand, are assumed to not be available during training and are the ultimate data for which we aim to make predictions. In our election example, these represent voters for whom we want to predict their intended votes. These predictions would be made after the model is fit and put into practice. Only if a model truly represents patterns that generalize beyond its training set will the model achieve good performance on the test set. For some real-world problems, the test data is collected *after* the model is fit (e.g., predicting customers' purchasing habits), while in others, data is set aside for evaluation and withheld from the model fitting process (e.g., evaluating whether it is possible to predict who will respond to a survey based on data from a previously collected social science study).

Observations from the total data set can be split into training, validation, and test sets in several ways. The simplest manner is to simply randomly select a large percentage (e.g., 60%) of data for the training set, then either use the rest for validation (if the test set will be collected later) or split the remaining data between validation and test sets (e.g., 20% each). Here, we need to balance the amount of data used for learning (from which machine learning will discover patterns) with the amount of data used to evaluate the models (too little data is not representative of the total population). There are no agreed-upon rules of thumb for choosing the proportions for the three sets.

An alternative method for splitting data that better achieves this balance is to use *k-fold cross-validation* where *k* models are fit instead of only one, so that each observation can be used in each of the training, validation, and test (if present) sets. In this method, the total data set is first split into *k* sets of equal size. If the test data are collected later,[5] then for the first model, the first bin is used as validation data and the remaining *k−1* bins are used as training data. Then for the second model, the second bin is used as validation data, and the remaining *k−1* bins are used as training data. This pattern continues until all *k* models have been trained and each observation has been in a validation set exactly once and in a training set *k−1* times. With this method, now the type of model can be assessed on more data since all data points are used in validation (instead of a small percentage) and the overall performance of all *k* models can be compared. The trade-off is that the models are not independent, so statistical comparisons are trickier, and more time is required since *k* models are fit instead of only one, which is problematic for some computationally expensive models (e.g., deep neural networks).

2.5 Model fitting

The process of fitting a model depends on both the type of the model the researcher desires and the algorithm chosen to fit the model. We describe popular types of models and related algorithms in sections 3–6. Notably, some algorithms fit a model by only considering each data point in the training set exactly once (e.g., the CART algorithm for fitting decision tree models), while others incrementally revise a model by continually looping through the training set until another pass would provide no more improvement (e.g., the backpropagation algorithm for fitting neural network models). Model fitting can be a time-consuming process.

2.6 Model evaluation

Models learned during supervised machine learning can be evaluated in several different ways, and the choice of which evaluation measure to use depends on the type of outcome (categorical vs. numeric), the balance in the distribution of outcome values, and the cost of mispredictions.

It is important to note that ideally all assessment should be done via cross-validation.

For classification problems where the outcome variable is categorical, the most common evaluation measures are (higher values are better for each):

- *Accuracy*, which measures the proportion of instances in the evaluation set for which the correct response was predicted.
- *Recall*, which measures for a reference response outcome value (e.g., "Candidate X" outcomes), what proportion of all observations with that response were correctly predicted. When the response has only two possible values, this measure is also referred to as *sensitivity* (or the true positive rate), whereas the equivalent measure for the opposite response value is referred to as *specificity* (or the true negative rate).
- *Precision*, which measures for a reference response value what proportion of the observations that received prediction were indeed correctly predicted. The measure is related to the notion of "crying wolf" – if a model makes a particular prediction, is it likely to be correct?
- *Area under the curve* (*AUC*), which measures the likelihood that the model's predictions were better than random guessing, independent of the underlying distribution of outcome values. It is calculated as the integral of the receiver operating characteristic (ROC) curve, which plots the false positive rate against the true positive rate.

Accuracy is the most commonly cited evaluation measure since it measures overall performance across all data. In our election example, this would measure how often the correct preferred candidate was predicted amongst all voters. Overall accuracy can be misleading, however, especially in the cases of unbalanced costs or when one case is much more frequent than the other. For example, fraudulent credit card transactions are fairly rare (less than 1% of all transactions), so simply predicting that all transactions are honest gives an overall accuracy of more than 99% but is useless. When the cost of a false negative is more expensive than the cost of a false positive (e.g., cancer diagnosis), then recall/sensitivity is a useful measure of performance since this measure focuses on the true positive rate. Likewise, when the cost of a false positive is higher than a false negative, than either precision (which focuses on how often a positive prediction was correct) or specificity (which focuses on the true negative rate) are good choices of performance. In all cases, the AUC can be a good choice given its independence of the outcome distribution. Typically, a research should consider several different measures of performance depending on the actual context of the problem.

For a regression problem where the response variable is quantitative, the typical assessment is the sum of the squared differences between the response and the predictions on an evaluation set, called the *sum of squares error* (SSE) :

$$SSE = \sum_{i=1}^{n} \left(y_i - \hat{y}_i \right)^2$$

To normalize this measure, it is usually divided by the sample size, n, and the square root taken, to get the measure back to the original units of the response variable, resulting in the *root mean square error* (RMSE):

$$RMSE = \sqrt{\frac{SSE}{n}}$$

While accuracy for either classification or regression is desired, it is also important to take into account more intangible qualities of the model. Were the data on which the model was based reliable? Were they representative of the populations that the researcher may want to study? Do the variables used to predict the response "make sense"? Was the model useful for solving the original question of interest? The art of model building is based not only on performance measures, but also on intangibles of domain knowledge that each researcher brings to the table.

3 Linear models for regression and classification

The least squares solution for fitting a linear function of the form:

$$y = \beta_0 + \beta_1 x_1 + \beta_2 x_2 + \ldots + \beta_p x_p + \varepsilon$$

through data was discovered by Gauss and Legendre in the late 18th century. There is still some controversy over who found the solution first. Legendre published it first, which outraged Gauss who claimed he had known about the result years earlier (see, e.g., Plackett, 1972; Stigler, 1981). In future publications, Gauss referred to the method as "my method" (*meine methode*) or at best "our method" (*principium nostrum*). In any case, it received its most famous application by Galton, who, in studying inheritable traits (eugenics), used the one variable version to predict the heights of male children from their parents (Galton, 1886). Upon discovering that tall parents, on average, gave birth to sons who were taller than the mean, on average, but not as extraordinary as their parents, he called the result a "regression towards mediocrity" and we have been stuck with the term "regression" for fitting straight lines to data ever since.

A common misconception of linear regression is that it can fit only straight lines (or higher dimensional analogues, called hyperplanes). However, the term linear refers only the equation being linear *in the parameters*, and the input variables can be of any form whatsoever. So an equation of the form:

$$y = \beta_0 + \beta_1 \sin\left(x_1\right) + \beta_2 e^{3x_2} + \beta_3 x_3^3 + \varepsilon$$

is still a linear regression, because the equation is linear in the β's and the estimates can be found by a straightforward matrix solution. (It would be nonlinear if, for example, one of the terms had been $e^{\beta_2 x_2}$ where the *parameter* β_2 now appears nonlinearly.) The fact that the inputs can themselves be very general gives multiple linear regression enormous flexibility to fit a wide variety of phenomena. Multiple regression provides some of the basis on which many machine learning algorithms are built. In many types of models, parameters are estimated by "least squares," that is, if we denote the estimates of each β_i by b_i, then the set $(b_1, b_2, \ldots, b_p)$ minimizes the residual sum of squares: $SSE = \sum_{i=1}^{n} (y_i - \hat{y}_i)^2.$

Although the response variable must be quantitative, the predictor variables need not be. For example, suppose we want to model the risk of lung disease by exposure to radon at different levels.[6] Consider a simple linear regression model:

$$y = \beta_0 + \beta_1 x_1 + \varepsilon$$

where y is the probability of developing lung disease and x_1 is the exposure to radon (in pico-curies per liter – pCi/L), then the coefficient β_1 would estimate the *average* increase per pCi/L over all population groups. A better model might estimate the risk differentially for smokers and non-smokers. Instead of splitting the data into two groups, an indicator variable for smoker can be introduced:

$$x_2 = \begin{cases} 1 & \text{if smoker} \\ 0 & \text{otherwise} \end{cases}$$

and the equation becomes:

$$y = \beta_0 + \beta_1 x_1 + \beta_2 x_2 + \varepsilon$$

which is actually two equations (depending on whether the individual is a smoker):

$$y = \begin{cases} (\beta_0 + \beta_2) + \beta_1 x_1 + \varepsilon & \text{if smoker} \\ \beta_0 + \beta_1 x_1 + \varepsilon & \text{otherwise} \end{cases}$$

Now the term β_1 still describes the average risk per pCi/L for both groups, but β_2 adjusts the intercept for the smoking group. However, as is often the case in social science, predictor variables can have *differential* effects on the response depending on the level of other variables. These effects are averaged out unless an *interaction term* is included to account for the differential effect. In our model we can add a third term:

$$y = \beta_0 + \beta_1 x_1 + \beta_2 x_2 + \beta_3 x_1 x_3 + \varepsilon$$

which, after substituting the value $x_3 = 0$ for the non-smokers and $x_3 = 1$ for smokers, leads to the two equations:

$$y = \begin{cases} (\beta_0 + \beta_2) + (\beta_1 + \beta_3) x_1 + \varepsilon & \text{if smoker} \\ \beta_0 + \beta_1 x_1 + \varepsilon & \text{otherwise} \end{cases}$$

Now both the intercept and slope are "adjusted" for the smoking group. The model might look something like Figure 17.2.

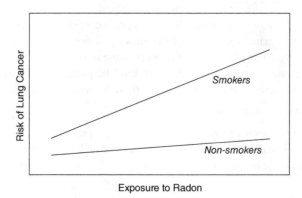

Figure 17.2 Model with an interaction term for smoker by exposure (x_1x_3) allowing for both different intercepts and slopes for the two groups

Interaction effects can appear in machine learning models either explicitly, as here in multiple regression, or automatically, as in decision trees and neural networks.

3.1 Model selection

One of the challenges of a linear regression (as in many machine learning models) is the choice of which predictor variables to include. Typically, in large data sets there are many more candidate predictors available than will persist in a final model. It is often not even possible to estimate the model with all predictors. This is especially true when one considers re-expressions of the predictors. For example, with 100 original predictor variables, if one considers including re-expressions such as square root, reciprocal, log, or other such transformations, as well as products and ratios of the variables, the number of resulting predictors can easily swamp the number of observations.

Standard model selection methods, including stepwise selection, search for the subset of variables that gave the highest predicted performance. Many of the classical methods have internal measures of performance that are used instead of cross-validation. For both, the goal is to avoid overfitting and to balance accuracy to the data with model complexity.

Forward stepwise search starts with no variables in the model and then first selects the variable that has the highest correlation with the response. It then computes the partial correlations of the response with all the remaining predictors and selects the one with the highest. It continues in this way until a criterion is reached. The most common criteria are a p-value threshold or the variables themselves or some variant of the information criteria (such as AIC, C_p, or BIC), which can be thought of as a weighted average of residual sum of squares plus a penalty for complexity of the general form:

$$SSE + \lambda C \tag{17.1}$$

where SSE is the residual sum of squares, C is a measure of the "complexity," or size, of the model and λ is a tuning parameter that adjusts the balance between the two. This "Occam's razor" choice is a guiding principle and the quest of model selection.

For many machine learning models, such internal information measures may not exist since they are usually based on some kind of asymptotic theory. In practice, then, they are often supplanted by cross-validation as discussed earlier (cf. section 2.4). In machine learning, the process of selecting variables (and thus deleting others) is known as *feature elimination*.

3.2 Biased regression

The simple least squares model discussed previously is unbiased in the sense that if the model is correctly specified, the solution is guaranteed to estimate the parameters in the model unbias-edly. In 1970 Arthur Hoerl and Robert Kennard introduced *Ridge Regression* (Hoerl & Ken-nard, 1970) in which no "features" are eliminated, unlike stepwise methods, but instead, all the predictor variables are included in the model. However, unlike the full least squares regres-sion model, the coefficients are "shrunk" toward 0. Instead of minimizing the residual sum of squares, *SSE*, ridge minimizes the *SSE* plus a term that "penalizes" large coefficients. (For this to make sense, it is usually a good idea to standardize all the variables so the coefficients are comparable.) Ridge can be shown to minimize directly a function of the form (Equation 17.1), where *C* is replaced by the sum of the squares of the (standardized) coefficients:

$$SSE + \lambda \, ||\, b\, ||^2 = \sum_{i=1}^{n} (y_i - \hat{y}_i)^2 + \lambda \sum_{j=1}^{p} b_j^2 .$$

Smaller values of λ allow larger values of $||\, b\, ||^2$ resulting in more complex models. The choice of λ is typically found by cross-validation. In the machine learning literature, this process is closely related to *regularization*. It also has a Bayesian justification.

Although it has some nice theoretical properties, ridge regression was never widely used in practice. In recent years however, variants of ridge, in particular the LASSO (Tibshirani, 1996) and the elastic net, have gained much popularity both in theory and in practice. The LASSO makes what seems like a simple change to the ridge criterion, using the sum of the absolute values of the coefficients instead of their squares in the complexity term:

$$SSE + \lambda \, ||\, b\, || = \sum_{i=1}^{n} (y_i - \hat{y}_i)^2 + \lambda \sum_{j=1}^{p} |\, b_j \, | .$$

The elastic net combines both by minimizing

$$SSE + \lambda_1 \, ||\, b\, || + \lambda_2 \, ||\, b\, ||^2 = \sum_{i=1}^{n} (y_i - \hat{y}_i)^2 + \lambda_1 \sum_{j=1}^{p} |\, b_j \, | + \lambda_2 \sum_{j=1}^{p} b_j^2 .$$

While these changes don't seem profound, the introduction of the absolute value makes the LASSO act as a combination of selection and shrinkage by eliminating some terms (like step-wise) and shrinking others (like ridge). It has proved to be very useful in cases with a large number of potential predictor variables. The elastic net offers some further benefits but acts very similarly to the LASSO.

The behavior of the LASSO can be explained as using *stagewise* regression. In stepwise regression we choose the variable (let's say x_1) that is most correlated with the response y as the first step. We then enter this variable into the model and find the predictor variable most correlated with the residuals. We repeat until no predictor adds "significantly" (as judged by various criteria) to the model. In stagewise regression we start the same, but rather than fitting the entire least squares coefficient of x_1, we only use αb_1 where α is a small constant. So, for example, if the first step indicated the variable x_1 as the most correlated with y, instead of fitting

$\hat{y} = b_0 + b_1 x_1$, we would fit only $\hat{y} = b_0 + \alpha b_1 x_1$ and then find the variable most correlated with the residuals of that model. It very well might be the case that x_1 is still the most correlated with those residuals, in which case we would add another αb_1 times x_1 to the model. This is continued until another variable is finally more correlated in which case both now enter the model.

An example based on a LASSO fit to the equation

$$y = 5 + 9x_1 x_2 - 5x_3 + 10x_4 + 5x_5 + 20x_3^2 + \varepsilon$$

is shown in Figure 17.3. In this case, x_4 is entered first. After a few initial steps, the estimated equation is $\hat{y} = 11.54 + 0.26x_4$, with an R^2 value of 0.022. The algorithm finds x_4 to be most correlated with the residuals, and so small increments of its coefficient are added until x_5 is the variable most correlated with the residuals at which point (left graphic in Figure 17.3) it is entered. The equation is now $\hat{y} = 9.55 + 4.18x_4 + 0.05x_5$. Here the steps in x_4 are reduced (and the line for x_4 appears less steep). Almost immediately x_3^2 enters and shortly thereafter x_1 and then x_2 are added. The last variable to be chosen is $x_1 x_2$. Now the equation stands at $\hat{y} = 14.64 + 1.92x_1 + 1.67x_2 - 10.47x_3 + 6.98x_4 + 2.60x_5 + 10.55x_3^2 + 0.03x_1 x_2$. At this point, the model continues, adding small increments to each variable's coefficients until either an internal (like AIC) or an external (a cross-validated R^2 for example) cross-validation measure is optimized. Here, the algorithm used AIC to stop just before entering a large pool of variables (shown as a cluster of variable paths to the right of about 275 on the x-axis). Had the algorithm continued to the end, it would have reached the least squares solution on all 65 variables (10 main effects, 10 quadratic terms, and 55 two-way interactions). However, by stopping early, it chose a more parsimonious model with only the intercept and seven terms:

$$\hat{y} = 5.52 + 7.60x_1 x_2 - 4.77x_3 + 9.48x_4 + 4.71x_5 + 10.55x_3^2 + 0.26x_1 + 0.24x_2$$

The coefficients of all the entered variables are smaller (shrunk) compared to their magnitudes in either the full least squares solution or the true function. This is a feature of ridge, LASSO, and the elastic net. It can be interpreted in the Bayesian framework as well. The idea of taking small steps toward a model solution is related to *boosting*, discussed in section 4.2.

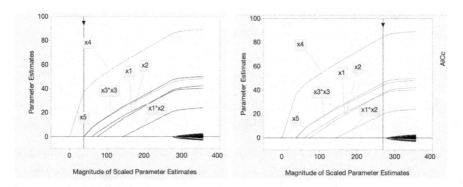

Figure 17.3 The left graphic shows the Lasso path stopped early, just as variable x_5 is first entered. The graphic on the right shows the solution found by internal cross-validation using the AIC criterion. Notice that the algorithm stops just short of entered a large number of variables shown as a cluster of paths to the right of the black line. The values at the end of each path correspond to the full least squares solution. (Graphic created from JMP (copyright) software).

3.3 Feature creation

With large numbers of potential predictor variables, it is likely that some of them will be strongly correlated. This results in an increase in the variance of the coefficients and instability of the model. We've seen that stepwise selection deals with it by eliminating predictors and ridge regression attempts to solve the problem by shrinking the coefficients of the original predictors, but there are other methods that create new variables from the old. This *feature creation* often reduces the number of variables, not by elimination, but by combining the original variables into fewer new variables, resulting in a lower dimensional space of the predictor variables.

In linear feature creation, k new variables denoted z_j are formed as linear combinations of the original x_i:

$$z_j = \alpha_{1j}x_1 + \alpha_{2j}x_2 + \ldots + \alpha_{pj}x_p .$$

To reduce the dimension, k is chosen to be less than (and often much less than) p. The z_j can then be used in a regression to predict y, possibly in a linear regression:

$$\hat{y}_i = b_0 + b_1 z_1 + \ldots + b_k z_k .$$

The choice of the α in the creation of the new variables distinguishes a variety of methods.

One of the most popular feature creation methods is *principal components*. The principal components z_j are defined so that the first principal component finds the linear combination of the predictors (suitably normalized) with the highest variance. (If you think of the data as forming an ellipse in p dimensions, this direction is the major axis). The subsequent components are the directions of highest variance that are orthogonal to all previous components. This is repeated until all p components are found. The hope of principal component analysis is that most of the total variance in the predictors and thus the information they contain can be approximated by using only the first few components. It's the same goal used in algorithms for file compression. Although the response variable plays no part in the selection of these components, the hope of principal component regression is that the response variable is well approximated by a linear regression on some subset of these new variables. There are many variants of principal components with slightly different criteria, or constraints, including factor analysis, multidimensional scaling, and partial least squares.

3.4 Nonlinear models

One way to relax the linear constraint of multiple regression is to allow smooth, rather than linear, functions of the predictors. A model of the form:

$$y = s_1(x_1) + s_2(x_2) + \ldots + s_p(x_p) + \varepsilon,$$

is called a *generalized additive model* (*GAM*) (cf. Hastie &Tibshirani 1990). The functions $s(\cdot)$ are smooth functions, fit by scatterplot smoothers (a running average would be a naïve version of such a smooth function). Model fitting is done via a technique from numerical analysis called backfitting. Each of the functions $s(\cdot)$ can be visualized by plotting $s_i(x_i)$ against x_i in a simple scatterplot.

GAMs alleviate the need to find re-expressions of the predictors by modeling each of the predictor's contributions with a scatterplot smoother. It is even possible to include surfaces of the form $s(x_i, x_j)$. The problem is that the modeler needs to specify which pair to include. It is often too computationally intensive to search over all $\binom{p}{2}$ possible pairs, and higher-order terms would be too costly to consider.

Another smoothing-based method called projection pursuit regression (ppr) is an attempt to combine feature selection with an additive model. A ppr model is of the form:

$$y = s_1\left(z_1\right) + s_2\left(z_2\right) + \ldots + s_k\left(z_k\right) + \varepsilon,$$

where the z_j are themselves linear combinations of the x_i. Typically, as in principal component regression, the number of terms k is chosen to be small and usually by cross-validation. The resulting model is quite flexible, although it can be difficult to interpret a smooth function of a arbitrary linear combination of predictors. Probably for this lack of interpretability, projection pursuit regression has never been used as widely used or cited. A quick look at the Google Scholar citations for the original ppr paper shows 2,800 citations[7] as compared to over 32,000 for the original LASSO paper.[8]

Ironically, if the smooth functions in the ppr model are constrained to be of one form, say sigmoidal functions, then the resulting model is exactly the same as an artificial neural network with a single hidden layer (cf. section 6.1). Consider the model:

$$\hat{y} = \theta_2 + w_{21}\sigma_1(z_1) + w_{22}\sigma_2(z_2) + \ldots + w_{2k}\sigma_k(z_k).$$

Here, $z_j = w_0 \theta_1 + w_{1j} x_1 + \ldots + w_{pj} x_p$ are called the neurons in the "hidden layer," and the $\sigma(\cdot)$ are sigmodal (S-shaped) functions such as a logistic or hyperbolic tangent function. Recently other forms of functions have become popular, although unlike project pursuit regression they are always restricted to be of a certain form. The nonlinear functions $\sigma(\cdot)$ are called *activation functions*. The result is that the neural network is capable of learning nonlinear relationships between the predictors and the response. Both projection pursuit and neural networks are capable of approximating any reasonable function, but both share the disadvantage of a lack of interpretability.

It is instructive to look closer at the difference between the projection pursuit model and the neural network. In both models, the latent variables (the z_j) are *linear* functions of the original (standardized) variables x_i. They are not restricted to have any special meaning as in principal components. They are simply found in an interative search that minimizes the sum of the squared residuals (or equivalently the mean squared error). For projection pursuit, the "regression" is then just a sum of smooth functions on the z_j. There are no restrictions on those functions, other than their being reasonably smooth. For neural networks, they have a specific parametric form, usually an S-shaped (sigmoidal) function. Because both ppr and neural networks can approximate any reasonable function, both need to be regularized in some way to avoid overfitting.

Another approach to nonlinearity is the use of *support vector machines* (SVMs) (Boser et al., 1992; Cortes & Vapnik, 1995), which first transform the original observation $\boldsymbol{x}$ to a different set of nonlinear features $\boldsymbol{z}$ using a function $\phi(\cdot)$ chosen by the researcher, then learn a set of weights $\boldsymbol{w}$ and intercept/bias θ that accurately predict the outcome variable:

$$\phi\left(\boldsymbol{x}\right) = z_1, z_2, \ldots, z_m = \boldsymbol{z}$$
$$\hat{y} = \theta + w_1 z_1 + w_2 z_2 + \ldots + w_m z_m$$

Different from the feature creation approaches described in section 3.3, this transformation is often nonlinear and results in a *higher*, rather than lower, dimensional vector than the original observation x (i.e., $m > p$). The goal here is to remap the original observation x to a new space z where either (1) the categories we intend to predict in a classification problem can be easily separated by a hyperplane (i.e., a line of more that two dimensions) or (2) the numeric outcomes in a regression problem fall close to a hyperplane and linear regression can be successfully applied. Common choices of the function $\phi(\cdot)$ include radial basis functions or polynomials of a chosen order d. The primary difference between this model and a neural network is the remapping of the original observation in an SVM follows a function $\phi(\cdot)$ chosen by the researcher for their particular data, whereas in a neural network, the first hidden layer learns such a remapping.

To mitigate the complexities of creating new features that have higher dimensionality than the original data, the weights and intercept in an SVM are not fit using least squares methods. Instead, a convex optimization problem is solved that finds the optimal set of weights and intercept, given a training set. For regression problems, the optimal set of weights results in a linear regression that is as close as possible to the outcomes in the training set. For classification problems, the optimal set of weights maximizes the *margin* of the resulting hyperplane, where the margin measures the distance of the closest observation in the training set to the hyperplane represented by the weights and intercept. In this way, the SVM fits a separator between outcome categories that is as distant as possible from all observations in the training set, implying maximal certainty in the predictions of the model and less overfitting.

4 k-nearest neighbors and Bayesian learning

4.1 k-nearest neighbors

One of the simplest approaches to supervised machine learning is the *k-nearest neighbor* algorithm (Cover & Hart, 1967), which requires no fitting at all (it is a type of *lazy learning*). Predictions are made simply by comparing an instance x to a historical set S (i.e., the training set) and using the k observations in S that are the most similar to x to determine what prediction to make.

For classification problems, the prediction for x is the *majority response outcome* amongst those k most similar observation in S. For example, say we have a voter for whom we want to predict their preferred candidate and we choose $k = 3$. Amongst the three nearest neighbors in S (i.e., other voters) for x, two intend to vote for Candidate X and the other intends to vote for Candidate Y. Then, the model would predict that x will also vote for Candidate X since that response was the most common amongst the $k = 3$ neighbors.

On the other hand, for regression problems, the prediction for x is the *average of the response outcomes* for the k most similar observation in S. For example, say the three nearest neighbors of voter x intend to donate \$1,000, \$200, and \$300 to their preferred candidates, then we would predict that x will donate \$500, which is the average of those three responses.

Clearly, one of the key hyperparameters to the k-nearest neighbor algorithm is the value to choose for k, the number of neighbors to include in the prediction. Higher values of k are appropriate when there is much local variance in the data set that should be smoothed by considering multiple responses when making a prediction for x, whereas smaller values of k are appropriate when observations in S are relatively dissimilar so that the prediction only consults relevant neighbors.

The other key hyperparameter to the k-nearest neighbor algorithm is the similarity (or distance) measure used to find the k nearest neighbors to a given instance. When the input variables are all numeric, typical similarity measures include cosine similarity or involve Manhattan or Euclidian distances. When the input variables are all categorical, then common similarity measures include Jaccard similarity or involve Hamming distances (cf. Chapter 19 describing the use of similarity measures for clustering in unsupervised learning). Choosing k and the appropriate distance measure are the main challenges for the implementation of k-nearest neighbors.

4.2 Bayesian learning

Sometimes researchers want to model the relationships between input variables and outcomes as conditional probabilistic relationships. This allows the researcher to answer questions such as what is the probability of a response outcome o given an observation $\boldsymbol{x}$ (i.e., $P(o \mid \boldsymbol{x})$)?

One of the most popular methods for creating models that can answer such a question is *Bayesian learning*, whose models are called *Bayesian networks* (cf. Neapolitan, 2003). In particular, these models consist of fitting conditional probability functions relating the relationships between predictor variables with both (1) other predictor variables (e.g., $P(x_i \mid x_j)$), and (2) the response outcomes (e.g., $P(x_i \mid o)$). The probability of each response is also modeled (i.e., $P(o)$). For categorical predictor variables and/or responses, a common approach to fitting these functions is through frequentist counting to establish discrete distributions, although more elaborate distributions can also be used (e.g., fitting to a Gaussian distribution for numeric input variables). Once these functions are fit, then a prediction is made using Bayes rule:

$$P(o|\boldsymbol{x}) = \frac{P(\boldsymbol{x}|o)P(o)}{P(\boldsymbol{x})}$$

In the simplest and most common form, called the *naïve Bayes* model, the input variables are all assumed to be independent so that the joint probability:

$$P(\boldsymbol{x}|o) = P(x_1|o) \times P(x_2|o) \times \ldots \times P(x_n \mid o)$$

which implies that no conditional relationships between predictor variables are required to be modeled. Although this assumption is almost always violated in practice, naïve Bayes models often still give good performance and have been the basis for many useful machine learning applications (e.g., predictions about words used in text documents, such as email spam filtering). In our election example, a naïve Bayes model would learn both conditional probabilities describing how often a voter has different demographics data (e.g., education, race, gender), given which candidate they prefer, and the proportions of voters preferring each candidate. This information would then be combined with Bayes rule to predict for a given voter, with what probability they prefer each candidate.

5 Decision trees and ensembles

5.1 Decision trees

Often the relationships of predictor variables that give rise to different responses can be described with simple rules: e.g., *if* a person has at least a bachelor's degree *and* lives in a large city *then* they are likely to vote for Candidate Y. Supervised machine learning algorithms that discover such rules from data are called *decision tree algorithms*, since such rules can be graphically displayed as decision trees, illustrated in Figure 17.4. A decision tree model consists of *nodes* (illustrated by rectangles) specifying which predictor variable is currently being consulted to make a prediction, whereas each value of the corresponding predictor variable is represented

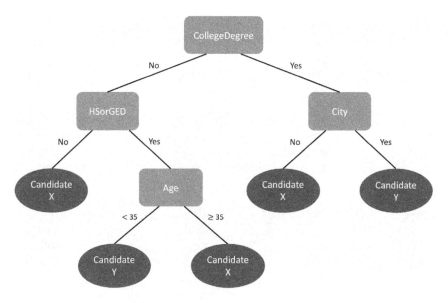

Figure 17.4   Decision tree example

by a branch (illustrated by an line) pointing from the predictor variable's node to either (1) the next predictor variable to consider during the prediction (forming an *and* relationship) or (2) an outcome (illustrated by ovals) that the model prescribes should be predicted. Popular decision tree algorithms include classification and regression trees (CART, Breiman et al., 1984) and C4.5 (Quinlan, 1993).

To make a prediction with a decision tree model for a particular observation of predictor values, one simply starts at the top of the tree (called the root node), which determines which predictor to consider first. The value of that predictor is consulted in the data point, which determines which branch to follow. The next node in the tree then specifies what predictor is consulted next, and the process continues until a response is reached at the bottom of the tree. That response is then the prediction made by the model for the current observation. When the decision tree is being fit by an algorithm, an important restriction is that each predictor only appears *once* along any path from the root node to a response, guaranteeing that a prediction can be made for any observation.

The graphical nature of decision trees makes them very transparent and easy to understand once one knows how to interpret them. Each path from the root node to a response defines a single *if . . . and . . . then . . .* rule described at the start of this subsection. For example, the rightmost path in Figure 17.4 defines precisely the aforementioned rule *if* a person has at least a bachelor's degree *and* lives in a large city *then* they will vote for Candidate Y since it first consults the CollegeDegree predictor, takes the Yes branch, then reaches the location City predictor, takes the Yes branch, and finally reaches the Candidate Y response. Any observation that matches this rule will result in a prediction of Candidate Y, regardless of the values of the other predictors. Alternatively, another path in Figure 17.4 defines the rule *if* a person has a high school diploma as their highest degree *and* they are at least 35 years old *then* they will vote for Candidate X.

Decision trees are fit by choosing predictors that are used to split the training set into smaller partitions until all of the observations in a partition have similar responses. For classification problems, that means that all observations in each partition share the same response.[9] For regression problems, that means that the *SSE* between the responses of each observation in the partition and the average response in the partition is minimized.

During fitting, partitions are created by grouping observations based on their values for a chosen predictor. If the chosen predictor is categorical, then one partition is made for each value of that predictor. If the chosen predictor is numeric, then two partitions are created – one that contains all observations whose value for that predictor is *below* a determined threshold, and a second that contains all observations whose value is *equal to or above* that threshold. For instance, the age predictor of our election example might group all observations that are younger than 35 years old and group all that are at least 35 years old. The specific predictor used to create partitions, as well as the threshold used for numeric predictors, is chosen based on the highest average response homogeneity across the resulting partitions, weighted by the size of the partition. Different fitting algorithms measure response homogeneity using different but nearly identical measures – the Gini index for CART and Shannon's entropy *H* for C4.5 and its variants (e.g., ID3). By selecting predictors in this manner, the fitting algorithms minimize the height of the tree (i.e., the number of predictors that one needs to consider while making a prediction), favoring shorter *if . . . and . . . then . . .* rules according to Occam's razor.

At the beginning of fitting, the first predictor chosen to partition the entire training set is placed as the top (root) of the decision tree. This predictor can be interpreted as being the *most significant* in determining the predicted response since its values are most predictive of the response. A branch is then added to the tree for each possible value of the chosen predictor, and the corresponding partition is filtered down each branch of the tree. The same process is then applied to each branch – another predictor is chosen to further partition the corresponding training data, its branches are added to the tree, and the smaller new partitions are filtered down each new branch. These later predictors appear in decreasing order down the tree based on their importance in predicting the response, since they are only considered when certain combinations of values for more significant predictors co-occur. Once a categorical predictor is used in the tree, it is no longer considered later down its branches since all observations that were filtered to that part of the tree share the same value for that predictor, but quantitative predictors can be split repeatedly. The leaves of the tree (at the bottom levels) occur whenever all of the observations have similar responses, so that one response can be accurately predicted. Importantly, if a predictor was erroneously included in the data set and is not actually predictive of the response, a decision tree algorithm can discover this fact, which will cause such a predictor to not appear in the tree at all. Thus, decision tree models organically perform feature elimination and reveal which predictors are *unrelated* to outcomes of interest.

Different fitting algorithms for decision trees differ in how they address some of the challenges in making predictions for real-world data. For example, CART handles missing values for predictor attributes by determining how similarly each predictor further partitions the training data, and it uses other predictors as surrogates when one's value is missing. C4.5, on the other hand, creates copies with partial weights of observations with missing values that are filtered down all possible values of that predictor.

5.2 Ensemble methods

Researchers, especially time series forecasters, have long known that prediction by averaging many models can reduce the bias of a single model. Much as a president solicits opinions from their advisors before making a decision, an *ensemble* of models can provide a more robust prediction by combining the "opinions" of many models. The variance of the predictions will decrease simply by virtue of averaging results, and the risk of choosing a bad model is mitigated as well. Researchers can build several models, based on different assumptions or exploring different parts of the data set, and then report an average of the predictions, possibly a weighted average with the weights based on some confidence level of the model. Recently, researchers have averaged many different COVID-19 models to more accurately forecast infections.[10] In the last quarter century, two very different methods called *bagging* and *boosting* have revolutionized model building in machine learning via two very different methods of building ensembles.

5.2.1 Bagging

A larger sample size (assuming reliable data) is always better but usually cost prohibitive. But, one can learn a great deal about the behavior of statistics based on one sample of the data by *bootstrapping* the data (Efron, 1979). Assuming the sample to be representative of the population, the bootstrap sample essentially creates a pseudo-population with an infinite number of copies of each data point and then samples at random from that. Practically, the bootstrap sample is a sample of the same size as the original data, obtained by randomly sampling the data *with replacement*. It was discovered in the 1970s, and then proved later, that the sampling distributions of statistics derived from bootstrap samples can provide good approximations to the theoretical sampling distributions and thus can provide confidence intervals and other summaries from a single sample. Hence the idea of picking oneself up by one's bootstraps.

Bagging (*bootstrap aggregating*) is a simple idea based on creating many slightly different model realizations by applying the same model (usually small trees) to many bootstrap samples of the data. The resulting predictions are then the average of the predictions over the collection of trees for a quantitative response, or the modal (majority vote) conclusion of the ensemble for a categorical response. In the latter case, percentages for each category can also be obtained from the ensemble frequencies.

Unfortunately, in many cases, a strong predictor will dominate the initial split and make the trees quite similar even though they are based on different samples. Leo Breiman (2001) introduced a further random element to the process to increase diversity. He suggested that at every split, only a small fraction of the predictor variables be allowed to be considered for splitting. Let's suppose we have 500 predictor variables, with only five predictors actually important for the model. By restricting to 10% of the predictors, there will be many splits that are essentially random, because none of the five will be in the selected 10%. It turns out that this doesn't really "hurt" the model, and the advantage of letting less important variables into the model overwhelms any disadvantage. This is especially true in the case of correlated predictors. Suppose that in a political district, a tree model is attempting to predict voting patterns. And suppose further that *Income* is the predominant variable and the first split in most bootstrap samples of the district. *Age* might never show up in the model because once *Income* enters, there is no extra information given by the *Age* of the voter. By sampling the predictors, for a significant percentage of splits *Income* is prohibited from splitting and *Age* is chosen instead. When looking at the number of splits across all the trees, *variable importance* can be obtained and, in this case, both *Income* and *Age* will appear.

This ensemble of bootstrapped sampling of trees together with random sampling of predictors at every split is called a *random forest*.

5.2.2 Boosting

Two computer scientists, Freund and Schapire (1997), introduced a simple algorithm that upended the machine learning world. The algorithm was the positive answer to the question posed by Kearns and Valiant as to whether a series of weak learners (like small trees) can create a strong learner. Shortly thereafter, Freund and Schapire extended this idea of *boosting* and invented a more flexible algorithm called AdaBoost (adaptive boosting) which has led to a virtual industry of innovation in machine learning.

The idea of AdaBoost is simple. Start with a weak learner (think of a small decision tree with only one or two splits) trying to predict two responses (say -1 and $+1$). It should do slightly better than pure guessing. For the observations that it gets wrong, give those observations more weight and then pass the data to another small tree. Again, give the observations that this tree gets wrong to a third tree and repeat the process n times. At the end, add all these trees up, weighting them by a function of their overall error rate.

In many examples, it was shown that AdaBoost outperformed many more complicated algorithms. In an influential paper, Friedman et al. (2000) discovered that AdaBoost could be explained as *stagewise* regression (like the LASSO) with a particular loss function (the exponential). Once that was discovered, it led to trying different loss functions (e.g., SSE and its variant Huber loss that is less sensitive to outliers) and different boosting paths. This basic idea of adding many weak learners together has led to many variations using different weak learners (tree and neural networks), and virtually any model can be boosted to increase prediction accuracy.

In particular, the popular *gradient boosting* (Friedman, 2001) algorithm focuses on fitting multiple weak learners to directly optimize the aforementioned loss functions. Instead of training new weak learners to make accurate predictions on the observations that were previously incorrectly predicted (as in AdaBoost), gradient boosting trains new weak learners to predict the *amount of correction* needed to offset the errors of the prior learners *on all observations*. Then, if the predictions of the new weak learners are added to the predictions made by the prior weak learners, the correct total prediction is made. For instance, in our campaign donation regression example, say that the first m weak learners predict donations that are \$100, \$550, and $-\$300$ off from the correct donations for the first three observations in the training set. Then, the next weak learner will be fit to predict those errors so that its predictions added to the first m learners calculates a correct total sum (instead of taking a weighted average of the weak learners each predicting the same outcome, as in AdaBoost). By predicting the errors made by the previous weak learners, each new learner is following the gradient of the loss function to optimize it as quickly as possible, hence the name gradient boosting.

6 Deep learning

Over the last decade, many of the improvements in supervised machine learning have advanced a category of models called *deep learning*. These improvements have enhanced not only the predictive ability of computers, but also the range of data that computers can learn from and problems to which machine learning can be applied. At its core, deep learning is an extension of *artificial neural networks*, henceforth referred to simply as neural networks. Before we discuss different types of deep learning models, it is helpful to understand what a neural network model is. Then, we will introduce the concept of deep neural networks and their important hyperparameters that can be tuned to improve learning performance, followed by a description of two popular types of deep networks: convolutional neural networks (commonly used with image and video data) and recurrent neural networks (commonly used with sequential data, such as text and audio).

6.1 Artificial neural networks (ANNs)

Neural networks, sometimes also called feedforward networks or multilayer perceptrons, are machine learning models that loosely resemble biological neural networks such as the human brain. Neural networks are very powerful machine learning models, theoretically capable of approximating the true relationships between predictors and response for a wide range of real-world problems to any arbitrary degree of precision. For this reason, they are sometimes referred to as the *universal approximator* (Cybenko, 1989; Hornik, 1991). In practice, neural networks often perform quite well, even if they do not achieve perfect performance. The fundamental drawbacks of neural network models include (1) their lack of transparency, as it is difficult to interpret the model after it is fit to understand why it makes specific predictions, and (2) the amount of computation time required to fit an accurate model.

Neural networks are collections of individual units called *neurons* that each performs some relatively small calculations to transform a set of input signals into an output signal. Neurons are interconnected so that the outputs of some neurons become the inputs to other neurons, allowing information processed in one neuron to benefit downstream neurons. In particular, neurons are organized into *layers*, where the neurons in the first layer take their inputs from the predictor variables, then the outputs of the first layer's neurons are the inputs to the second layer, etc. until the final layer outputs the ultimate prediction of the neural network. For this reason, the final layer is referred to as the *output layer*, while all other[11] layers are referred to as *hidden layers* (because their activities are obscured between the inputs and outputs of the network as a whole). An example neural network model with two hidden layers and one output layer for our election prediction example is illustrated in Figure 17.5.

In a typical neural network, the neurons in hidden layers are represented by a standard logistic regression model (as described in section 3.4). For neurons in the first layer, the input variables x_i are the predictor variables, whereas for neurons in later layers, the inputs to a neuron are the outputs of all of the neurons in the previous hidden layer. Fitting a neural network involves learning a suitable set of weights w and biases/intercepts θ for each neuron in the network.

The neurons we choose to put in the output layer depend on the type of supervised learning problem being modeled. For a binary classification problem where there are only two possible responses (e.g., yes or no, candidate X or Y), the output layer consists of a single neuron whose activation function $\sigma(\cdot)$ is the logistic, and its output can be interpreted as the probability that a reference response (e.g., yes, candidate X) is the correct prediction. This output layer is equivalent to a logistic regression on the outputs of the final hidden layer. For a multinomial

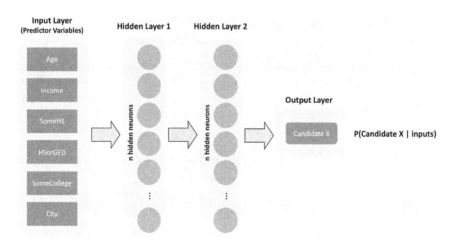

Figure 17.5 Artificial neural network example (with two hidden layers and one output layer)

classification problem where there are three or more possible responses (e.g., candidate X, Y, or Z; what numeric digit was handwritten in an image), then the output layer consists of one neuron for each possible response. Instead of a nonlinear activation function $\sigma(\cdot)$, each output neuron instead outputs its linear combination of weights and inputs z_j, which are taken together into a softmax function to determine a probability distribution describing the likelihood that each response is the correct one that should be predicted (where a single prediction is made corresponding to the output neuron with the largest z_j output). This output layer is equivalent to a multinomial regression on the outputs of the final hidden layer. When the response is a numeric prediction and the supervised learning problem is a regression, the output layer consists of a single neuron that only performs a linear regression of the outputs of the final hidden layer.

Of note, it is possible for neural networks to be used for *multilabel learning* (see, e.g., Zhang & Zhou, 2014) where more than one type of response is predicted simultaneously for a single observation. For example, we might want to simultaneously predict both which candidate a person is likely to vote for and how much they will donate to that candidate's campaign. In this setting, the neural network is adapted to include multiple output layers (one for each type of response being predicted), where each output layer takes as input the outputs of the final hidden layer in the network. In this way, information about the relationships between the predictors and one type of response can be used to fit the neural network's weights in a way that is also beneficial to the other type(s) of responses. As a result, the predictive accuracy of the neural network model can be greater than if each type of response were fit to their own individual models.

Fitting the weights and biases/intercepts of the neurons in a neural network model is typically performed using the backpropagation algorithm, which is a type of stochastic gradient descent that incrementally makes small changes to the parameters to the model as it continually loops through the observations in the training set. These changes continue until either (1) a specific number of iterations through the training set, called *epochs*, have occurred, (2) the parameters of the network model converge and no longer change with continued epochs, or (3) a performance measure called a loss function (measuring the error in the network's predictions on the training or validation set, typically SSE or cross-entropy) increases for the validation set from a previous minimum value, which indicates that the neural network is starting to overfit the training data (using its large number of parameters to memorize nuances in the training data that do not generalize to the validation set).

6.2 Deep neural networks (DNNs)

Conceptually, a deep neural network is simply an artificial neural network with a large number of hidden layers. Initially, the deep learning revolution of the late 2000s and early 2010s was led less by improvements in mathematics or methodology behind their learning and more by the wide availability of computer hardware that could finally enable training neural networks with many layers in a reasonable amount of time. Indeed, neural networks have gone through phases of popularity throughout the history of artificial intelligence: first being developed in the 1940s, then growing and waning in popularity every 10–20 years, often where new methods were developed, then paused until powerful enough computers were available to fully exploit those methods so that applications of increasingly complex neural network methods could be realized.

The primary advantage of increasing the number of layers in a neural network is it allows the model to learn *increasing levels of abstraction* while discovering patterns that relate predictors to responses. This is similar to human learning, where we might organize concepts in hierarchical levels of abstraction to help us know what to do in different situations. In particular, neurons in the first hidden layer learn how to create new features (through their weights and activation functions) that combine the values of the predictors in a way that is meaningful for making a downstream prediction. Likewise, neurons in later hidden layers learn how to exploit the features learned in the previous layer to create higher-level features. For instance, in image recognition problems where the goal is to predict what objects are present in an image, the early layers of the neural network frequently learn how dots within the images (called pixels, which are the predictor variables) organize into lines of different orientations, while the later layers frequently learn how lines organize into shapes and how shapes organize into objects (not unlike our own visual processing). Similarly, in natural language processing problems where the goal is to make predictions about a piece of text, the early layers in the network might learn how sequences of characters form relevant words, then later layers might learn how sequences of words form relevant phrases.

Interestingly, deep neural networks make extensive use of unsupervised learning during supervised learning. In particular, only the desired outputs of the neurons in the final output layer are known during learning; it is not known *a priori* what the outputs of any other neurons should be. Instead, the neural network performs unsupervised learning to discover patterns that lead to increasing levels of abstraction through the different hidden layers in support of the supervised learning of the output layer. This revelation was one of the initial key contributions of deep learning research. Notably, all of this occurs automatically through similar stochastic gradient descent fitting methods as those used for traditional neural networks.

However, the study of deep neural networks has also led to several very important advancements beyond traditional neural networks. First, additional activation functions $\sigma(\cdot)$ used to transform the linear combinations of weights, biases, and inputs z_i into nonlinear outputs have been proposed, with the simple *rectified linear unit (ReLU)*:

$$ReLU(z_i) = \begin{cases} z_i \text{ if } z_i > 0 \\ 0 \quad \text{else} \end{cases}$$

becoming one of the most popular. In particular, the derivative of this activation function is very quick to calculate (compared to more complex activation functions such as the sigmoid or hyperbolic tangent), which speeds up gradient calculations during fitting. Additionally, ReLU does not squash many inputs to a very small range of outputs (e.g., in the tails of the sigmoid function), which helps prevent what is known in the neural network literature as the *vanishing gradient problem*, where it is difficult to fit a model for such inputs.

Second, new methods of regularization have been developed for deep neural networks to help avoid the increasing risk of overfitting as more layers add more parameters to the model. One of the most popular is the use of *dropout* (Hinton et al., 2012). Dropout operates by randomly leaving out neurons during the training process so that only some weights and biases/intercepts are considered each time the model is updated using stochastic gradient descent. The appropriateness of this approach might seem counterintuitive – afterall, if the benefit of deep learning is larger models for more abstraction, why not always update the full model during training? Instead, the benefit is to spread feature recognition across neurons so that no neuron simply memorizes information related only to particular observations in the training set (which would reduce model generalization).

Third, the study of deep neural networks has also led to improvements in the algorithms used for fitting the underlying model, partly to account for the higher dimensionality of the model (i.e., more layers = more weights = more parameters). In particular, variants of stochastic gradient such as the Adam optimizer (Kingma & Ba, 2015) better fit combinations of weights and biases/intercepts to find the *globally* optimal combinations, instead of becoming stuck in *local* optima that do better than similar parameters but not the best overall.

6.3 Deep learning hyperparameters

Learning a deep neural network for a supervised learning task leaves several important hyperparameters for the researcher to choose. In the following, we describe these hyperparameters and offer some rules of thumb for settings, although the best values depend strongly on the particular data being learned, so it is common to do a grid search over several possible combinations combined with cross-validation to find the best combination for the problem at hand.

First, with regard to the underlying model, the researcher must choose the *number of layers* to include in their model (i.e., how many levels of abstraction are best for this particular problem?), as well as the *number of neurons* in each layer (i.e., how many features are needed at each level of abstraction?). Common settings for the number of neurons are either equal numbers across all layers or decreasing in count deeper into the model.

After a model (i.e., a particular organization of neurons) is chosen, additional hyperparameters are critical to the learning process. For instance, the *learning rate* determines how aggressively the fitting algorithm updates the parameters of the model: a higher learning rate might cause the model to converge more quickly and thus take less time for training, whereas a lower learning rate causes more conservative changes to the model and often slower convergerence to better parameters. Commonly, the optimal learning rate decreases as the number of layers in the network increases: values around 0.01–0.1 often work well for traditional neural networks (1–2 layers), wheres values around 0.00001–0.001 often work well for deep neural networks. The *number of epochs* to use during training determines the maximum number of times that the weights in the network will be updated: more epochs produce more changes, but also take more time to operate. For lower learning rates, it is often better to use more epochs due to the slower convergence of the weights. Often more important than the number of epochs is a special count that is frequently called *patience*, which determines for how many epochs training should continue after a new best performance (i.e., minimal loss) is achieved on the validation set. During these subsequent epochs, the fitting algorithm is trying to find a better set of weights than what was already achieved, and it gives up if better weights are not found quickly enough so that training does not continue too long. The value to use for patience depends largely on how much the weights change each epoch, but values of 25–50 epochs are not uncommon, as they strike a balance between optimistically hoping for improvement with not wasting time training more than is beneficial to the neural network.

Finally, recent advancements in deep learning have produced new types of models (called *neural architectures* in the machine learning literature) that go far beyond simply extending the number of layers in the neural network. In the following, we discuss two of the most important such models: convolutional and recurrent neural networks.

6.4 Convolutional neural networks (CNNs)

One of the most popular forms of deep neural networks is the *convolutional neural network* (*CNN*). CNNs are the state of the art in making predictions involving image and video data, such as identifying whether something of interest occurs within a photo. CNNs exploit spatial relationships in data (e.g., nearby pixels in images and video) to simplify the connections needed between neurons. This greatly reduces the number of weights needed when compared with fully connected models where all neurons from one layer are connected to the next. For example, imagine that we are trying to predict the type of animal pictured in an image. Here, the predictors are the pixels (i.e., dots) in an image, and the responses are the different types of animals of interest that might be in the image. The distinguishing features of an animal are likely going to be located within small areas of the image: determining the shape of an animal's ears (one possible feature learned by the neural network) only requires considering a small set of pixels that make up the ear of the animal that are physically near each other. A pixel from far away from the ear pixels is then not related to determining the animal's ear shape. As a consequence, the hidden neurons that might ultimately learn to identify the presence of different types of ear shapes do not need to consider far separated pixels, but instead only small regions of the picture at a time. Similarly, if we are trying to identify whether a house is in an image, we need only consider groups of pixels near each other to learn to identify the presence of a roof in the image.

Convolutional neural networks are designed to consider such spatial relationships through a special type of layer called a convolutional[12] layer. This type of layer effectively passes a sliding window across the input so that only predictors within the window are considered by the corresponding neurons, while all other predictors are ignored. The window slides[13] across the entire set of predictors so that all predictors are considered with their neighbors and no predictors are fully ignored. Convolutional layers contain several important hyperparameters that govern their learning:

1. the *kernel size*, which is the size of the sliding window (often a square) and needs to be appropriately matched to the size of the distinguishing features in the predictors,
2. the *stride*, which is how far to shift the window each time it slides (often less than the kernel size so that the windows overlap),
3. any *padding* to use, which appends zeros to the predictors so that the chosen kernel size and stride fit the dimensions of the predictors (i.e., the height and width of the input image), and
4. the *number of filters*, which is the number of features to learn within the sliding windows.

The output of a convolutional layer is a set of values for each filter (i.e., feature) across all locations of the sliding window.

Multiple convolutional layers can be stacked together in order to produce increasing levels of abstraction from predictors: as described previously, the first convolutional layer typically identifies the presence of lines within the images (and sometimes the presence of certain colors), while the next layer might identify the presence of shapes made up of lines, then later layers might identify more complex shapes or objects. Notably, these abstractions happen as a by-product of the organization of the CNN into layers and are not deliberately caused by the researcher employing the model.

Alternatively, a second type of layer unique to CNNs is the *pooling layer*, which combines information across nearby windows locations. In this way, information is aggregated across spatial regions, expanding the number of predictors considered together to indicate abstract features deeper in the neural network. The most common type of pooling used is *max pooling*, which only retains the largest values across nearby windows (useful for indicating whether some feature occurred in at least one of the locations), while *average pooling* is sometimes used, which averages values across nearby locations (useful as a summary statistic). Hyperparameters for pooling layers include number of windows to combine, as well as the aforementioned stride and padding.

Rather than creating a new CNN from scratch (including deciding what combinations of layers to use, as well as the hyperparameters to use in each layer), it is common practice in the application of supervised machine learning to reuse existing models that have performed well previously. Pretrained models can be downloaded for popular deep learning software packages (cf. section 7) and used directly by the researcher without having to do any training at all! For example, if a researcher is interested in determining whether certain entities exist in an image, previous winners of the popular ImageNet competition (Russakovsky et al., 2015) are capable of identifying over 1,000 categories of entities – ranging from household and workplace objects to types of plants and animals – with greater accuracy than people. This includes models such as ZFNet (Zeiler & Fergus, 2014) and VGG-16 (Simonyan & Zisserman, 2015) that do not have high computational requirements (e.g., only needing small amounts of memory), as well as more accurate models such as Inception (Szegedy et al., 2015) that require more computational infrastructure.

Alternatively, if a researcher only needs to identify a small number of entities (that may or may not be part of the 1,000+ categories of ImageNet), it is also possible to either retrain existing models – a process known as *transfer learning* since prior information for one task is transferred to a different prediction task or reuse the organization of the model (its layers and their hyperparameters), with all new parameters learned from scratch.

Finally, not only can CNNs be used to identify whether something is present in an image (a task called *image classification*), they can also be used to determine *where* in an image each entity exists (a task called *image segmentation*). These two types of problems differ in the outputs of the output layer. Image classification models only have one output per category of interest that indicates whether that category is present, whereas image segmentation models output has outputs for each category of interest at the pixel level: whether each pixel belongs to each category of interest. Image segmentation models thus learn much more information about their images and hence might require more time to train, more training data to adequately learn, and possibly more sophisticated models. Popular image segmentation models include UNet (Ronneberger et al., 2015) and Mask CRN (He et al., 2017).

Potential applications of CNNs for computational social science are numerous. For instance, researchers interested in understanding the daily lives of individuals or collective social behaviors could use images posted to social media as predictors of both the behaviors exhibited in the images and future behaviors. Automatically identifying the content of images could also be used to reduce respondent burden in surveys, especially for research related to diaries that record respondent behaviors over time (e.g., daily eating habits), allowing respondents to simply upload pictures (e.g., of their plate each meal) instead of answering numerous questions about their experiences. Finally, aerial images could also be processed by CNNs to automatically identify locations of interest for creating sampling frames for identifying individuals to study, ranging from finding possible archeological sites in remote areas to counting green energy production locations (e.g., windmills, solar panels) in an area to produce population estimates.

6.5 Recurrent neural networks (RNNs)

A second popular type of deep neural network model is the recurrent neural network, which specializes in making predictions about sequences of observations $x = x^1, x^2, \ldots, x^n$ instead of individual observations. For instance, natural language processing applications where a computer identifies the meaning of textual data written in natural human language involves processing sentences that are sequences of words, which in turn are sequences of characters. Likewise, audio prediction (e.g., voice recognition) often involves processing speech, which is a sequence of sounds such as syllables and pauses.

Recurrent neural networks differ from both feedforward networks (e.g., Figure 17.5) and convolutional neural networks in that they remember information across the different input observations $x^1, x^2, \supset, x^n$ that comprise a sequence. Fundamentally, this is the result of a unique feature of RNNs: the output of the neurons in a given layer from the previous observation $\sigma\left(z_j^{t-1}\right)$ are appended as additional inputs x_i^t to each of the neurons of the same layer when computing their outputs for the current observation $\sigma\left(z_j^t\right)$. By remembering the most recent outputs of neurons, features identified from previous observations in the sequence can contribute to the identification of later features (e.g., patterns from the combination of syllables or characters forming important words). To enable the RNN to discover patterns between two observations that are far apart in time within sequences, advanced types of RNNs use special neurons that also contain a small memory to remember information separate from their most recent outputs.

Recurrent neural networks differ from CNNs in that they do not introduce new types of network layers, so they have fewer unique hyperparameters. On the other hand, they do offer novel forms of neurons that enhance the ability of the network to remember information over longer periods of time, as well as identify more sophisticated nonlinear relationships between observations over time. These types of neurons include long-short term memory (LSTM) neurons (Hochreiter & Schmidhuber, 1997) and gated recurrent unit (GRU) neurons (Cho et al., 2014), which have achieved some of the state-of-the-art performances in sequence prediction problems.

Similar to CNNs, RNNs can also be used for multiple types of unique supervised machine learning problems. *Sequence classification* problems occur whenever the RNN makes a single prediction for an entire sequence of inputs, such as predicting the primary sentiment expressed in a sentence of text. In contrast, *sequence labeling* problems occur whenever the RNN produces a prediction for each observation in a sequence. In between these two problems are *sequence-to-sequence* prediction problems, where the RNN creates a sequence of predictions for a sequence of inputs (possibly fewer predictions than inputs), such as automatically translating from one natural language to another. One of the most popular type of sequence-to-sequence models is the *encoder-decoder* whereby one RNN is used to encode a sequence of inputs into some fundamental set of concepts (e.g., the underlying ideas referenced by words and phrases in one language) and a second RNN decodes those concepts into a set of outputs (e.g., the words and phrases in another language that express the same underlying ideas).

Potential applications of RNNs to computational social science are numerous. Analysis of social media posts naturally involve sequences of characters and words, possibly unlocking even greater understanding of people's daily condition, attitudes, and behaviors with minimal data collection burden. Similarly, voice recognition could enable better analysis of audio data with less human processing effort, greatly expanding the types of data available to computational social scientists. As more data is collected in real time through sensors (e.g., smartphones and wearable devices), RNNs could be used to identify relevant human activities and events from sequences of sensor data. Finally, data collection itself occurs as a sequence of actions (e.g., respondents answering successive questions on surveys, interviewers incrementally reaching out to potential respondents for interviews), for which RNNs could be used to make predictions about the data collection process itself that could lead to better data collection by expanding data *quantity* (especially in an era with very low survey response rates) and enhancing data *quality* (e.g., adaptive surveys that encourage respondents to complete surveys rather than drop out of the study).

Before concluding our discussion of RNNs, it is worth noting that recent advancements in deep learning have produced a new type of deep neural network called transformers (Vaswani et al., 2017) that are demonstrating even greater performance on applications of supervised machine learning to sequential data, especially natural language processing. As these models become more mature, they could replace RNNs on similar applications for computational social scientists.

7 Discussion

Overall, supervised machine learning has much to offer computational social scientists. Classification models can be used to predict categorical outcomes, such as which candidate a person might prefer in an upcoming election (based on intrinsic characteristics of the voter) or whether a geographical area will likely soon see a spike in COVID-19 cases during the ongoing pandemic. Likewise, regression models can be used to predict numeric outcomes, such as how much money the same voter might contribute to the campaign of their preferred candidate, or counts of the incidence of COVID-19 in the same geographic area.

Many types of classification and regression models exist, such as linear regression models, k-nearest neighbors and Bayesian networks, decision trees and their ensembles, as well as artificial and deep neural networks. Each model type has its own strengths and weaknesses, and no model dominates all others in terms of performance. Models such as linear regression, decision trees, and to some extent random forests and other ensembles are more transparent, allowing a researcher to inspect their weights or nodes (or other parameters) to understand why they make their predictions, offering both new insights into the problem being studied and potential trust in those predictions. Other models, such as neural networks and SVMs, typically offer greater predictive accuracy at the expense of less information about how they make their predictions. Specialized models also exist for specific types of data, such as convolutional neural networks for image and video data, as well as recurrent neural networks for sequential data such as audio or text. Models are powerful, but as George Box famously said, "All models are wrong, but some are useful" (Box, 1976).

Many useful software packages are available to enable social science researchers to fit such models for their given data sets. For example, in the Python programming environment, the scikit-learn[14] library (Pedregosa et al., 2011) provides implementations of most of the types of models discussed in this chapter, whereas the Tensorflow[15] (Abadi et al., 2015) and PyTorch[16] (Paszke et al., 2019) libraries are the state-of-the-art software for fitting deep neural networks. Furthermore, in the R programming environment, linear regression models are built into the R software (using the glm function) (R Core Team, 2019), whereas the rpart[17] (Therneau & Atkinson, 2018) package offers the CART decision tree algorithm and random forests are enabled through the randomForest[18] (Liaw & Wiener, 2002) package, artificial neural networks are offered through the neuralnet[19] (Fritsch et al., 2019) and nnet[20] (Venables & Ripley, 2002) packages, and the MXNet[21] (Chen et al., 2015) and tensorflow[22] (Abadi et al., 2015) packages enable R to connect to external software for constructing deep neural networks.

In terms of computational hardware, most modern laptops and desktops have sufficient processing power and memory to construct many of the models described in this chapter, although using distributed computing (e.g., a cluster) can offer substantial speed improvements or scale better to big data sets. For deep learning models, graphical processing units (GPUs, also typically known as discrete video cards) provide specialized hardware that can drastically accelerate model fitting and prediction. That is because this hardware performs linear algebra much more efficiently than a regular computer processor (CPU) does, and linear algebra represents the majority of the operations performed during modeling fitting and prediction with neural networks. It is not uncommon for model fitting to be approximately 30 times faster with a GPU than a CPU (e.g., what takes one day of computation time on a CPU takes less than one hour on a GPU), allowing for the construction of more complex models in less time. State-of-the-art GPUs that work well for fitting deep neural networks can be purchased for as low as $500, although more expensive hardware exists for further speedups and compatibility with larger models (by offering more memory).

For more information about supervised machine learning, many great resources and textbooks exist. Some recommendations include *Elements of Statistical Learning* (Hastie et al., 2009) and its companion *An Introduction to Statistical Learning (With Applications in R)* (James et al., 2013), *Machine Learning* (Mitchell, 1997), *Pattern Recognition and Machine Learning* (Bishop, 2006), and *Deep Learning* (Goodfellow et al., 2016).

Notes

1 Because the predictors are often correlated, the term independent variables can be confusing. We will use response and predictor variables.
2 In medical studies they are participants, and in surveys they might be referred to as respondents.
3 Other codings are possible to avoid reference values.
4 There are many such inspiring quotes falsely attributed to Einstein: https://championingscience.com/2019/03/15/everything-should-be-made-as-simple-as-possible-but-no-simpler/#:~:text=%E2%80%9CEverything%20should%20be%20made%20as,of%20how%20to%20conduct%20science.g
5 If a test set is taken from the originally collected data, then one bin separate from the validation set is used as a test set and only $k-2$ bins are used for the training set.
6 For simplicity we will describe a linear model, although a logistic regression model, using the log odds of the probability of disease, is preferred.
7 https://scholar.google.com/scholar?hl=en&as_sdt=0%2C22&q=Projection+Pursuit+regression&btnG=
8 https://scholar.google.com/scholar?hl=en&as_sdt=0%2C22&q=robert+tibshirani+lasso&oq=L
9 In practice, the following process often stops when *nearly all* of the observations share the same response to avoid overfitting. How *nearly all* is determined is a hyperparameter to the algorithm.
10 https://delphi.cmu.edu/covidcast/?date=20100420&signalType=value&mode=overview
11 Sometimes the predictor variables are referred to as a special *input layer* of a neural network, although they are not represented by neurons, unlike the other layers.
12 Named for the type of mathematical operation that enables its "sliding window" operation.
13 In practice, this sliding window is implemented in a neural network as one neuron for each possible window location and filter combination, where the neurons for all locations corresponding to the same filter share the same set of weights since they are ultimately trying to discover the same features (e.g., lines, shapes) in each location.
14 https://scikit-learn.org/stable/index.html
15 www.tensorflow.org/
16 https://pytorch.org/
17 https://cran.r-project.org/web/packages/rpart/rpart.pdf
18 https://cran.r-project.org/web/packages/randomForest/randomForest.pdf
19 https://cran.r-project.org/web/packages/neuralnet/neuralnet.pdf
20 https://cran.r-project.org/web/packages/nnet/nnet.pdf
21 https://mxnet.apache.org/versions/1.5.0/api/r/index.html
22 https://tensorflow.rstudio.com/

References

Abadi, M., et al. (2015). *Tensorflow: Large-scale machine learning on heterogenous systems.* Software available from tensorflow.org.

Bishop, C. (2006). *Pattern recognition and machine learning.* Springer.

Boser, B. E., Guyon, I. M., & Vapnik, V. N. (1992). A training algorithm for optimal margin classifiers. In *Proceedings of the fifth annual workshop on computational learning theory (COLT'1992)* (pp. 144–152). Association for Computing Machinery.

Box, George, E. P. (1976). Science and statistics, *Journal of the American Statistical Association*, 71(356), 791–799.

Breiman, L. (2001). Random forests. *Machine Learning*, 45(1), 5–32.

Breiman, L., Friedman, J. H., Olshen, R. A., & Stone, C. J. (1984). *Classification and regression trees*. Wadsworth.

Chen, T., et al. (2015). MXNet: A flexible and efficient machine learning library for heterogeneous distributed systems, *CoRR*, abs/1512.01274. The arXiv database.

Cho, K., van Merrienboer, B., Gulcehre, C., Bahdanau, D., Bougares, F., Schwenk, H., & Bengio, Y. (2014). Learning phrase representations using RNN encoder-decoder for statistical machine translation. In *Proceedings of the 2014 conference on empirical methods in natural language processing (EMNLP'2014)* (pp. 1724–1734). Association for Computational Linguistics.

Cortes, C., & Vapnik, V. (1995). Support-vector networks. *Machine Learning*, 20, 273–297.

Cover, T. M., & Hart, P. E. (1967). Nearest neighbor pattern classification. *IEEE Transactions on Information Theory*, 13(1), 21–27.

Cybenko, G. (1989). Approximation by superpositions of a sigmoidal function. *Mathematics of Control, Signals, and Systems, 2*, 303–314.

De Veaux, R., Hoerl, R., & Snee, R. (2016). Big data and the missing links. *Statistical Analysis and Data Mining*, 9(6), 411–416.

Efron, B. (1979). Bootstrap Methods: Another Look at the Jackknife. *The Annals of Statistics, 7*(1), 1–26.

Freund, Y., & Schapire, R. E. (1997). A decision-theoretic generalization of on-line learning and an application to boosting. *Journal of Computer and System Science*, 55(1), 119–139.

Friedman, J. H. (2001). Greedy function approximation: A gradient boosting machine. *The Annals of Statistics*, 29(5), 1189–1232.

Friedman, J. H., Hastie, T., & Tibshirani, R. (2000). Additive logistic regression: A statistical view of boosting. *The Annals of Statistics*, 28(2), 337–407.

Fritsch, S., Guenther, F., & Wright, M. N. (2019). *Neuralnet: Training of neural networks*. Retrieved from https://CRAN.R-project.org/package=neuralnet

Galton, F. (1886). Regression towards mediocrity in hereditary stature. *The Journal of the Anthropological Institute of Great Britain and Ireland*, 15, 246–263.

Goodfellow, I., Bengio, Y., & Courville, A. (2016). *Deep learning*. MIT Press.

Hastie, T., & Tibshirani, R. (1990). Generalized Additive Models, Taylor & Francis.

Hastie, T., Tibshirani, R., & Friedman, J. (2009). *The elements of statistical learning*. Springer.

He, K., Gkioxari, G., Dollar, P., & Girshick, R. (2017). Mask R-CNN. In *Proceedings of the 2017 IEEE international conference on computer vision (ICCV'2017)* (pp. 2980–2988). Institute for Electrical and Electronics Engineers. doi:10.1109/ICCV.2017.322

Hinton, G. E., Srivastava, N., Krizhevsky, A., Sutskever, I., & Salakhutdinov, R. R. (2012). *Improving neural networks by preventing co-adaptation of feature detectors*. arXiv:1207.0580. Retrieved from http://arxiv.org/abs/1207.0580.

Hochreiter, S., & Schmidhuber, J. (1997). Long short-term memory. *Neural Computation*, 9(8), 1735–1780.

Hoerl, A., & Kennard, R. W. (1970). Ridge regression: Applications to nonorthogonal problems. *Technometrics*, 12(1), 69–82.

Hornik, K. (1991). Approximation capabilities of multilayer feedforward networks. *Neural Networks*, 4(2), 251–257.

James, G., Witten, D., Hastie, T., & Tibshirani, R. (2013). *An introduction to statistical learning (with applications in R)*. Springer.

Kingma, D. P., & Ba, J. L. (2014). *Adam: A method for stochastic optimization*. arXiv:1412.6980. Retrieved from http://arxiv.org/abs/1412.6980

Kreuter, F. (2013). *Improving surveys with para data: Analytic uses of process information*. John Wiley & Sons, Inc.

Liaw, A., & Wiener, M. (2002). Classification and regression by random forest. *R News*, 2(3), 18–22.

Mitchell, T. M. (1997). *Machine learning*. WCB/McGraw-Hill.

Neapolitan, R. E. (2003). *Learning Bayesian networks*. Prentice-Hall, Inc.

Paszke, A., et al. (2019). PyTorch: An imperative style, high-performance deep learning library. *Advances in neural information processing systems* (Vol. 32, pp. 8024–8035). Curran Associates, Inc.

Pedregosa, F., et al. (2011). Scikit-learn: Machine learning in python. *Journal of Machine Learning Research*, 12, 2825–2830.

Plackett, R. L. (1972). Studies in the history of probability and statistics. XXIX: The discovery of the method of least squares. *Biometrika, 59*(2), 239–251.

Quinlan, J. R. (1993). *C4.5: Programs for machine learning*. Morgan Kaufmann Publishers, Inc.

R Core Team. (2019). *R: A language and environment for statistical computing*. R Foundation for Statistical Computing. Retrieved from www.R-project.org/

Ronneberger, O., Fischer, P., & Brox, T. (2015). *U-Net: Convolutional networks for biomedical image segmentation*. arXiv:1505.04597. Retrieved from https://arxiv.org/abs/1505.04597

Russakovsky, O., et al. (2015). ImageNet large scale visual recognition challenge. *International Journal of Computer Vision, 115*(3), 211–252.

Simonyan, K., & Zisserman, A. (2015, May 7–9). Very deep convolutional neural networks for large-scale image recognition. In *Proceedings of the 3rd international conference on learning representations (ICLR'2015)*. Retrieved from https://arxiv.org/abs/1409.1556

Stigler, S. M. (1981). Gauss and the invention of least squares. *The Annals of Statistics, 9*(3), 465–474.

Szegedy, C., et al. (2015). Going deeper with convolutions. In *Proceedings of the 2015 IEEE conference on computer vision and pattern recognition (CVPR'2015)* (pp. 1–9). Institute for Electrical and Electronics Engineers. doi:10.1109/CVPR.2015.7298594

Therneau, T., & Atkinson, B. (2018). *rpart: Recursive partitioning and regression trees*. Retrieved from https://CRAN.R-project.org/package=rpart

Tibshirani, R. (1996). Regression shrinkage and selection via the lasso. *Journal of the Royal Statistical Society. Series B. Wiley, 58*(1), 267–288.

Vaswani, A., et al. (2017). Attention is all you need. In I. Guyon, U. V. Luxburg, S. Bengio, H. Wallach, R. Fergus, S. Vishwanathan, & R. Garnett (Eds.), *Advances in neural information processing systems* (Vol. 30, pp. 5998–6008). Curran Associates, Inc.

Venables, W. N., & Ripley, B. D. (2002). *Modern applied statistics with S.* (4th ed.). Springer. ISBN 0-387-95457-0

Zeiler, M. D., & Fergus, R. (2014). Visualizing and understanding convolutional neural networks. In D. Fleet, T. Pajdla, B. Schiele, & T. Tuytelaars (Eds.), *Computer vision – ECCV 2014* (pp. 818–833). Springer International Publishing.

Zhang, M.-L., & Zhou, Z.-H. (2014). A review on multi-label learning algorithms. *IEEE Transactions on Knowledge and Data Engineering, 26*(8), 1819–1837.

18

PRINCIPAL COMPONENT ANALYSIS

Andreas Pöge and Jost Reinecke

1 Basic concepts and history of principal component analysis

The concept of *principal component analysis* (PCA) is mostly credited to Karl Pearson (1901) and, later, to Harold Hotelling (1933), who developed a technique to reduce the complexity of a given set of variables. To achieve this goal, PCA constructs uncorrelated so-called principal components (PCs) as linear combinations of the original variables that successively have maximum variance. Certain uncorrelated principal components are then chosen so that the number of components is lower than the number of initial variables and so that data approximation is adequate with regard to the preservation of maximum overall variance. This approach offers the possibility of reducing the complexity of large data sets while minimizing the loss of information. The procedure can be seen as a transformation of the data into a space with fewer dimensions. Sometimes the principal components themselves are the focus of research and sometimes they are used for further data analyses (e.g., *regression analysis* or *cluster analysis*). PCA shares its main goal of reducing complexity with the method of *factor analysis* (FA), and these two methods use similar mathematical calculations; however, PCA and FA differ in some respects, the importance of which is a matter of controversy within the scientific community. The most important difference might be that PCA is a more adaptive, explorative, and descriptive method and, unlike FA, does not necessarily require a distinct model.

Because PCA originated in the late 19th century, it is considered a rather "old" method of analyzing data. Karl Pearson (1901) and later Harold Hotelling (1933) developed the technique now known as PCA based on the earlier mathematical foundations of *singular value* and *eigen decomposition* of matrices (see Beltrami, 1873; Eckart & Young, 1936; Hilbert, 1904; Jordan, 1874; Schmidt, 1907; Smithies, 1938; Sylvester, 1889; Weyl, 1912). It is worth mentioning that from the outset PCA and FA (Thurstone, 1931) were developed in connection with each other. PCA was enhanced by Girshick (1936, 1939) and Anderson (1963), who worked on the inferential statistics of sample PCs as maximum likelihood estimates of the population PCs and analyzed sample coefficients and variances in PCA. Although further important contributions came from Rao (1964) and Gower (1966), it was not until the development of modern computers at the end of the 20th century that PCA became broadly available for data analysis. As with many other statistical analysis procedures, especially those dealing with large data sets, the calculations require considerable computational power. Today, these computational problems

DOI: 10.4324/9781003025245-22

have been overcome, and the past few decades have seen the widespread use of PCA in many scientific fields.

2 Formalization

The starting point of PCA is to find a linear function of a given set of p variables $x_1, \ldots, x_p$ with maximum variance, where a_1 is the vector of p constants $a_{11}, \ldots, a_{1p}$ (Jolliffe, 2002):

$$y_1 = a_1'\mathbf{x} = a_{11}x_1 + a_{12}x_2 + \cdots + a_{1p}x_p = \sum_{j=1}^{p} a_{1j}x_j. \tag{18.1}$$

Further, stepwise linear functions $a_2'\mathbf{x}, \ldots, a_p'\mathbf{x}$ can be formulated with the additional restriction that all these derived variables $y_1, \ldots, y_p$ are uncorrelated and successively maximize variance. The kth derived variable $y_k = a_k'\mathbf{x}$ is the kth principle component (PC) and a_k is the vector of coefficients or loadings for the kth PC. In general:

$$\mathbf{y} = \mathbf{A}'\mathbf{x}, \tag{18.2}$$

with y as the vector of the PCs $y_1, \ldots, y_p$ and A' as the transposed orthogonal matrix

$$\mathbf{A}' = \begin{pmatrix} a_{11} & \cdots & a_{p1} \\ \vdots & & \vdots \\ a_{1p} & \cdots & a_{pp} \end{pmatrix}$$

Equivalently, in some textbooks the complete $n \times p$ data matrix $\mathbf{X}$ of n observations on p variables x is considered. Equation 18.2 can then be written as:

$$\sum_{j=1}^{p} a_j x_j = X\,a, \tag{18.3}$$

or, when all PCs are merged columnwise, as:

$$y = XA \tag{18.4}$$

$$\Leftrightarrow \begin{pmatrix} y_{11} & \cdots & y_{1p} \\ \vdots & & \vdots \\ y_{n1} & \cdots & y_{np} \end{pmatrix} = \begin{pmatrix} x_{11} & \cdots & x_{1p} \\ \vdots & & \vdots \\ x_{n1} & \cdots & x_{np} \end{pmatrix} \begin{pmatrix} a_{11} & \cdots & a_{1p} \\ \vdots & & \vdots \\ a_{p1} & \cdots & a_{pp} \end{pmatrix}$$

The criterion to obtain the PCs is maximum variance. For the first PC it is therefore necessary to search for a vector a_1 that will satisfy the following equation:

$$\text{var}(y_1) = \text{var}(a_1'\mathbf{x}) = a_1' \Sigma\, a_1 \overset{!}{=} \max \tag{18.5}$$

with Σ as the population covariance matrix of the vector of random variables $\mathbf{x}$.[1]

With the constraint that a_1 has unit length (i.e., $a_1'\,a_1 = 1$) and with the help of the technique of Lagrange multipliers, it can be shown that, as the solution, the PC coefficient a_1 is the *eigenvector* corresponding to the largest *eigenvalue* $\lambda_1 = \text{var}(a_1'\,x) = a_1'\,\Sigma a_1$ of the covariance matrix Σ.

In general, given a known population covariance matrix Σ (or a sample covariance matrix S) of the vector of random variables x, the kth PC $y_k = a'_k\, x$, where a_k is an eigenvector of Σ corresponding to its kth largest eigenvalue λ_k. If the eigenvector a_k is chosen to have unit length ($a'_k\, a = 1$), then the variance of the kth PC equals the eigenvalue λ_k (for a derivation see, e.g., Jolliffe, 2002, pp. 4 sqq.). The eigenvalues $\lambda_1, \ldots, \lambda_p$ of the $(p \times p)$ covariance matrix Σ can be obtained by finding solutions for:

$$\det\left(\Sigma - \lambda \mathbf{I}\right) = 0. \tag{18.6}$$

The following equation holds for the eigenvectors a of the eigenvalues $\lambda_1, \ldots, \lambda_p$:

$$\Sigma a_j = \lambda_j \mathbf{I} a_j = \lambda_j a_j, \quad \text{for } j = 1,\ldots,p. \tag{18.7}$$

With Equation 18.5 and the orthogonality of $A\left(AA' = A'A = I\right)$ it follows that:

$$
\begin{aligned}
& A'\Sigma A = \Lambda \\
\Leftrightarrow \quad & \Sigma A = A\Lambda \\
\Leftrightarrow \quad & \Sigma = A\Lambda A'
\end{aligned} \tag{18.8}
$$

with Λ as diagonal matrix of the eigenvalues $\lambda_1, \ldots, \lambda_p$ of the population covariance matrix Σ

$$\Lambda = \begin{pmatrix} \lambda_1 & & \\ & \ddots & \\ & & \lambda_p \end{pmatrix}$$

and A as the matrix of loadings

$$A = \begin{pmatrix} a_{11} & \cdots & a_{1p} \\ \vdots & & \vdots \\ a_{p1} & \cdots & a_{pp} \end{pmatrix}$$

Also, because of the orthogonality of A, x can be retrieved back from y without a loss of information:

$$
\begin{aligned}
& \mathbf{y} = \mathbf{A'x} \\
\Leftrightarrow \quad & \mathbf{Ay} = \mathbf{AA'x} \\
\Leftrightarrow \quad & \mathbf{Ay} = \mathbf{Ix} \\
\Leftrightarrow \quad & \mathbf{Ay} = \mathbf{x}.
\end{aligned} \tag{18.9}
$$

It has to be mentioned that commonly the variables that form the linear functions in Equation 18.2 are centered by the use of their means $x^{\star}_{ij} = x_{ij} - \bar{x}_j$. Centering does not change the covariance between variables (in contrast to standardization); therefore, the solution is not affected by this procedure.

To understand the mathematical procedures of PCA it is helpful to look first at a graphical interpretation. For the sake of simplicity, we can inspect the unrealistic case of only two variables. (This empirical example is described in more detail in Section 3.) To visualize data, a scatter plot of both variables is presented in Figure 18.1. It shows the amount of water (x_1) and carbohydrates (x_2) contained in 100 selected cakes and pies as well as pizzas. All data points were mean-centered, and because of this centering, the origin lies in the middle of the plot.

As both variables are correlated, a point cloud with an elliptical shape can be seen. In a scatter plot, the variables are the orthogonal basis of the coordinate system. The aim of the PCA is to find a new orthogonal basis for the coordinate system with axes that successively express maximum variance and are linear combinations of the variables. The first axis (PC) must express the maximum account of variance and therefore lies closest to all points in the point cloud. The second component must express the maximum of the remaining variance and is orthogonal to the first component, which means it stands at an angle of 90 degrees relative to the first one. In Figure 18.1, the new axes or components are plotted as dashed lines. Based on the new axes/components, all data points can now be described with new coordinates. A flip of the signs can occur but is not relevant for the result. We can see that most of the variation in the example data can be expressed with the first component, since the point cloud now stretches out mainly on the first PC. The variation on the second component is less, which is evident from the fact that the extent of the point cloud is much smaller.

Although it is possible to extract p PCs on the basis of p initial variables and to reproduce all the overall variance, it would be desirable to explain most of the variation in x with only m PCs where $m < p$. The aim of the PCA is to reduce the dimensionality of data sets with minimum loss of information. To determine how many PCs should be extracted, one important

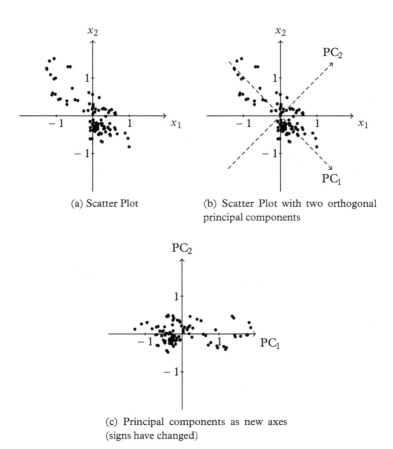

(a) Scatter Plot

(b) Scatter Plot with two orthogonal principal components

(c) Principal components as new axes (signs have changed)

Figure 18.1 Amount of water (x_1) and amount of carbohydrates (x_2) in 100 observations (cakes and pies and pizzas; mean-centered values)

measure is the proportion of total variance that a PC accounts for. The overall variance of a p-dimensional data matrix is the sum of the diagonal elements of its covariance matrix (these are the variances). Hence, the sum of diagonal elements of a quadratic matrix is defined as its trace, and the overall variance can be expressed as tr(Σ). We know that the variance of the kth PC equals the eigenvalue λ_k. Therefore, the proportion of total variance a PC accounts for (π_j) is:

$$\pi_j = \frac{\lambda_j}{\sum_{j=1}^{p} \lambda_j} = \frac{\lambda_j}{\text{tr}(\Sigma)}. \tag{18.10}$$

To decide how many PCs should be retained, often the cumulative amount of variance is taken into account. It is a common practice to look at all the PCs that cumulatively account for at least 70% to 80% of the overall variance.

Often the eigenvalues and/or the proportions of variance are visualized by plotting them against the number of components in a so-called *scree plot* (Cattell, 1966). The graph usually shows a strong decrease with the first components that is less steep as the number of PCs gets higher (for an example, see Figure 18.2 in Section 3). To identify an adequate number of PCs, it is necessary to find the point where a sharp bend is visible (*elbow criterion*). All other PCs starting with this point can be omitted. Unfortunately, in practice the scree plot often shows more than one sharp bend. It is advisable to further inspect all solutions with different numbers of PCs that might be suitable in such a case.

2.1 Singular value decomposition

As shown earlier, the PCs can be obtained by conducting an *eigen decomposition* (sometimes called *spectral decomposition*) of the covariance (or correlation) matrix (Σ or R). Such a decomposition is possible only if Σ (or R) is diagonalizable. That means Σ (or R) is a square matrix and similar to a diagonal matrix. Alternatively, the PCs can be computed by performing a *singular value decomposition* (SVD), which is a generalization of the eigen decomposition. The SVD has some computational advantages and provides higher numerical accuracy (Jolliffe, 2002, pp. 44 sqq.). Therefore, this method is often used by statistical software.

2.2 Correlation matrices

In practice, PCAs are often done by using the correlation matrix R instead of the covariance matrix of a given set of variables. Analyses of covariance matrices might cause problems if the units of the variables and their variances differ strongly. Since the variance depends on the unit of a variable, the PCs are sensitive to the scale of the variables. This might be undesirable, and standardization of the variables can be a solution. Often, the following standardization is used:

$$z_{ij} = \frac{x_{ij} - \bar{x}_j}{s_j}. \tag{18.11}$$

The data matrix X is replaced by the standardized matrix Z. Because the covariance matrix of a standardized data set equals the correlation matrix R, the PCA is then based on a correlation matrix. Equation 18.2 in this case looks like:

$$Za_k = \sum_{j=1}^{p} a_{jk} z_j. \tag{18.12}$$

Although standardization is a rather simple transformation, the two approaches lead to different results. The pairs of eigenvector and eigenvalues of the covariance matrix Σ cannot be converted to the corresponding pair of the correlation matrix R. Therefore, the PCs based on the covariance matrix and the PCs based on the correlation matrix neither are the same nor directly related to each other. Moreover, because the sum of diagonal elements of the correlation matrix equals the number of variables p, the proportion of total variance accounted for by the kth PC is the eigenvalue λ_k divided by p. In most cases, to achieve an adequate data approximation using the correlation PCA, a higher number of PCs is needed than if the covariance PCA is used (see Jolliffe & Cadima, 2016, p. 6). As a criterion for the number of relevant PCs in a correlation PCA, it is reasonable to look at the proportion of total variance as well. As a rule of thumb, all PCs that express 70% to 90% of the total variance should be taken into account. An additional rule of thumb advises that all PCs with an eigenvalue $\lambda_i > 1$ should be considered. The rationale for this is that standardized variables have a variance of 1, and only those PCs having a higher variance than one single variable should be respected (Kaiser, 1960). Of course, the scree plot can also be analyzed in a correlation PCA (Cattell, 1966). Also, a so-called *parallel test* is available (Horn, 1965) that compares the empirical eigenvalues to simulated eigenvalues based on random data of the same size.

2.3 Rotation

A procedure that can help to simplify the interpretation of the results is the so-called rotation. The matrix A that contains the coefficients respective loadings is multiplied with a rotation matrix T:

$$\mathbf{B} = \mathbf{AT}. \tag{18.13}$$

The matrix B then contains the rotated PC loadings. The entries for T can be seen as rotation angles that are cosine or sine. Different rotation matrices can be used depending on a chosen simplicity criterion. For example, if T is an orthogonal matrix, a multiplication produces an orthogonal rotation of the axes. Often in this case the varimax criterion is used, which demands maximization of the summed-up variances of the squared loadings of each PC. The variance reaches a maximum if the squared loadings are near 0 or near 1. After such a rotation, the solution is easier to interpret because the loadings on the rotated components are either very high or very low. It is important that no variance be lost with a rotation. Sometimes – and often with FA – the restriction of orthogonal axes is loosened. This can improve the interpretation of loadings, but a correlation matrix of the PCs or factors is also needed and must be interpreted. Although a rotation may lead to a simplified interpretation of the results with the variance explanation unchanged, there are some disadvantages. For example, successive maximization of the variance of the PCs is not preserved. Instead, the proportion of variance per PC is more evenly distributed after a rotation. Furthermore, if in a solution with q PCs an additional PC is taken into account, the rotated components might differ more than the unrotated components do (see Jolliffe & Cadima, 2016, p. 11; Wolff & Bacher, 2010, p. 352 sqq.).

2.4 Visualization of the results

An important and common way to visualize the results of a PCA is the biplot of the PCs (Gabriel, 1971). Usually, the first two PCs are primarily taken into account because they are the most relevant ones, but sometimes the inspection of other pairs of PCs can be useful too.

The biplot shows the data points with their "new" coordinates in the space that is spanned by the orthogonal PCs (see Figure 18.3 of the example in Section 3). Often, the original variables are additionally plotted as vectors in the biplot. The cosines of the angles between the variable vectors themselves as well as between the variable vectors and the PCs correspond to their correlations. In such a biplot, points that are close together have similar scores on all variables. The distances between the transformed observations equal approximately the Euclidean distances between the observations themselves. Therefore, the biplot is a useful tool, especially to identify homogeneous groups and outliers (Schlittgen, 2009, p. 269 sqq.). In R, the package `ggbiplot` can be used to produce high-quality outputs.

3 Empirical example

As an example of the use of PCA, we analyzed data from the Food and Nutrient Database for Dietary Studies 2015–2016 of the U.S. Department of Agriculture (USDA, 2018). We used the built-in function prcomp()[2] of the statistical software R 3.6.0 (R Core Team, 2019), which is available with no additional packages (see Kassambara, 2017). The data set contains the amount of different nutrients per 100 grams of 50 selected cakes and pies (id numbers 101–150) and 50 pizzas (id numbers 501–550). In detail, we analyzed six variables:

- `Water_g` – Amount of water (in grams)
- `Prot_g` – Amount of protein (in grams)
- `Carb_g` – Amount of carbohydrate (in grams)
- `Sug_g` – Amount of sugars (in grams)
- `Fib_tot_g` – Amount of dietary fiber (in grams)
- `Fat_tot_g` – Amount of fat (in grams)

The task was to reduce these six dimensions to a minimum number and at the same time preserve maximum variability of the data. Because all the variables have the same unit (gram), it

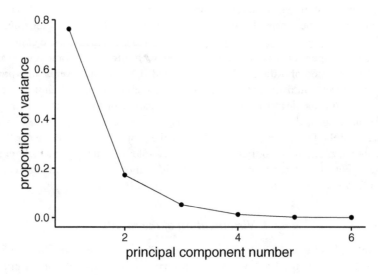

Figure 18.2 Screeplot of the example data

was advisable to use covariance PCA in this example. The built-in R function `prcomp()` gave the following summary of its calculations:

```
Importance of components:
                          PC1     PC2     PC3     PC4     PC5     PC6
Standard deviation     17.4668  8.2948 4.57332 2.20675 0.68190 0.13895
Proportion of Variance  0.7624  0.1719 0.05227 0.01217 0.00116 0.00005
Cumulative Proportion   0.7624  0.9344 0.98662 0.99879 0.99995 1.00000
```

To obtain the eigenvalues that express the variances accounted for by the PCs, the standard deviations had to be squared by hand:

```
[1] 305.0878640 68.8037693 20.9152275 4.8697450 0.4649868 0.0193076
```

One can see that the first PC accounts for 76.24% of the overall variance in the sample. This already indicates a rather good approximation with only one single PC. The second PC accounts for 17.19% of the overall variance and is therefore less meaningful. Together, the first two PCs express 93.44% of the overall variance and are (more than) sufficient to describe the variation in the data. The scree plot[3] (see Figure 18.2) visualizes the same information by plotting the proportion of variance dependent on the number of PCs. A bend at two PCs is clearly visible, indicating a possible solution with only one PC, but another bend appears with three PCs, pointing toward the two-PC solution. The scree plot confirms the finding that either one or two PCs might be appropriate in this example.

The R function `prcomp()` additionally gives the following results:

```
Standard deviations (1,.., p=6):
[1] 17.4667646  8.2948038  4.5733169  2.2067499  0.6818994  0.1389518
```

```
Rotation (n x k) = (6 x 6):
                 PC1          PC2          PC3          PC4         PC5          PC6
Water-g    -0.46930489  0.726707989  0.05248234 -0.12181999  0.03397491 -0.48259675
Prot-g     -0.14661370 -0.315172731 -0.26317922  0.71886464  0.01127811 -0.54130740
Carb-g      0.57360548  0.007338751 -0.49381635 -0.43071683  0.00384651 -0.49146365
Sug-g       0.65138510  0.481729137  0.33650622  0.47588765  0.06137206  0.01274628
Fib-tot-g  -0.02702240 -0.037322270 -0.04506777 -0.02301778  0.99680571  0.04116169
Fat-tot-g   0.06481769 -0.372896604  0.75422820 -0.23638455  0.03627057 -0.48030553
```

The standard deviations of the PCs are repeated, and we can see the matrix of the PC loadings (somewhat unusually called rotation here). The eigenvectors are the columnwise merged loadings. The loadings in the first PC are positive with respect to "carbohydrate," "sugars," and "fat" and negative with respect to "water," "protein," and "fiber." The highest loadings are allocated to the variables "sugars," "carbohydrate," and "water" and therefore mainly affect the first PC. The second PC has positive loadings for "water," "carbohydrate," and "sugars" and negative loadings for "protein," "fiber," and "fat." This PC has the highest loadings in "water" and "sugars."

Looking at the biplot[4] in Figure 18.3, we can see a homogeneous group of points in the lower left of the plot. These are the pizzas (id numbers 501–550), which all contain a comparatively high amount of water and low amount of sugars and carbohydrate (PC1) in conjunction with a high amount of protein (PC2). The points belonging to cakes and pies are more widely

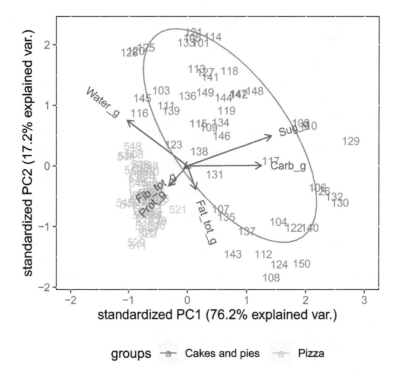

Figure 18.3   Biplot of 50 cakes and pies (id numbers 101–150) and 50 pizzas (id numbers 501–550) in the two-dimensional subspace spanned by the first two principal components (PCs)

scattered, indicating a higher variability regarding their nutrients. If we look at the first PC, the cakes and pies have higher amounts of sugars and carbohydrate compared with the pizzas. The distribution of points for the second PC mainly shows a lower amount of protein.

It is interesting to look at some single data points as well. On the far right side of the plot, for example, the data point with id number 129 ("Cake, angel food, with icing or filling") obviously differs from all the other cakes and pies in that it has an extremely high amount of carbohydrate and sugars with a low amount of water. Above left in the plot is a group of three "fruity" cakes and pies with id numbers 120, 125, and 128 (respectively, "Pie, raspberry cream"; "Pie, squash"; and "Cheesecake with fruit") showing a high amount of water and low amounts of carbohydrate and sugars. As a final example, the data point for the pizza with id number 521 ("Pizza, no cheese, thick crust") is nearest and therefore most similar to the 50 cakes and pies with regard to the six nutrients analyzed. This finding obviously makes sense, since a pizza without cheese and with a thick crust strongly resembles a pie or a cake.

4 A comparison of PCA and FA

Although PCA and *exploratory factor analysis* (EFA or FA) share the general goal of reducing complexity by reducing the dimensionality of a given data set (and many researchers see them as very similar to each other), they do involve different approaches. FA is mostly credited to Charles Spearman (1904) and Louis Thurstone (1947), who were active in psychometrics and developed models to explain correlations between tests having one or multiple factors. Hauser and Goldberger (1971) implemented so-called latent variables (i.e., factors) into the framework of *path analysis* to overcome the assumption of error-free measurements. This concept was extended by Karl Jöreskog (1969, 1973), who developed a general model to fit systems of linear equations including latent variables (for *confirmatory factor analysis*, see Reinecke & Pöge, 2019).

The starting equations of PCA and FA differ from one another: Whereas PCA expresses the PCs as linear equations of the (centered) *original variables* (see Equations 18.1 and 18.2), FA tries to express a set of manifest variables $x_1, \ldots, x_j$ via linear combinations of latent *factor variables* $p_1, \ldots, p_q$:

$$
\begin{aligned}
x_1 &= a_{11}p_1 + a_{12}p_2 + \cdots + a_{1q}p_q + \varepsilon_1 \\
x_2 &= a_{21}p_1 + a_{22}p_2 + \cdots + a_{2q}p_q + \varepsilon_2 \\
&\vdots \qquad \vdots \qquad \vdots \qquad \ddots \qquad \vdots \qquad \vdots \\
x_j &= a_{j1}p_1 + a_{j2}p_2 + \cdots + a_{jq}p_q + \varepsilon_j
\end{aligned}
\tag{18.14}
$$

with a_{jq} as the factor loadings and ε_j as measurement error terms. In matrix notation, this is:

$$
\mathbf{x} = \mathbf{p}\mathbf{A}' + \boldsymbol{\varepsilon}.
\tag{18.15}
$$

Assumptions for Equations 18.14 and 18.15 are that $E(\boldsymbol{\varepsilon}) = \mathbf{0}$ and $E(\mathbf{p}\boldsymbol{\varepsilon}') = \mathbf{0}$. This formalization has, of course, implications in terms of the way the results have to be interpreted. In the behavioral sciences, for example, we often interpret latent factors as "higher-order" attitudes or characteristics that cause individuals to answer to the manifest variables in a special way. Moreover, the specified error terms allow a modeling of measurement errors for each single variable.

With these equations, FA formulates a definite model to express j variables x with a smaller number of q latent factors. In contrast, in most applications a model for PCA is neither needed nor formulated (see Jolliffe, 2002, p. 151). Because the linear equations for the PCs do not contain error terms, they formulate an exact way to calculate them on the basis of the analyzed variables. The PCs are exact linear functions of $\boldsymbol{x}$. In FA, the factors are not exact functions of the variables, and the factor scores have to be estimated and cannot be calculated exactly.

Another aspect in comparing PCA and FA is related to the covariance matrix $\boldsymbol{\Sigma}$ as the basis for both types of analyses. Whereas PCA tries to maximize variance and therefore concentrates on the diagonal elements of the covariance matrix, FA concentrates more on the off-diagonal elements that are the covariances between the variables (see Jolliffe, 2002, p. 158). Partly because of this, a single variable PC is possible in PCA, whereas in FA a factor must contribute to at least two variables.

Furthermore, FA requires that the diagonal elements of the correlation matrix $\boldsymbol{R}$ (*communalities*) be estimated prior to the factorization. This is necessary because the diagonal elements do not equal 1 owing to the specified error variances. Often, squared multiple correlations (smc) are used as initial values with which the factorization of $\boldsymbol{R}$ is performed. On basis of the solution of the factorization, the communalities are then recomputed. In most statistical software programs, an iterative algorithm is implemented that does this factorization repeatedly until the communalities no longer change. Although its convergence has not been proved, this procedure works out quite well in practice. Some statistical software programs (e.g., SPSS) perform FA in a way that also sets the number of factors to the number of PCs identified by a preceding PCA by means of the Kaiser (1960) criterion (eigenvalue $\lambda_i > 1$). Although the PCs often give an adequate initial solution in FA, it is not a given that this holds universally. An alternative criterion to determine the number of factors in FA is to extract all factors with positive eigenvalues after the first factorization Guttman (1954). Overall, the indicated appropriate number of factors and PCs may differ relevantly between PCA and FA with the same data set.

With all these differences in mind, however, the results of PCA in practical applications (in this case, correlation PCA with rotation) are often very similar to the results of FA with an orthogonal rotation. Most of the time the coefficients retained from PCA and the factor loadings of the FA do not differ much for the same data set. Nevertheless, in the social sciences and psychology, for example, the PCA approach is theoretically inferior in most applications. The omission of measurement errors usually cannot be justified. In general, one should not use PCA if latent constructs or factors are of interest and should be analyzed (see Widaman, 1993). If PCA is used in the field of factor analysis, researchers should be aware of the differences between these two analytical procedures.

5 Software

As mentioned earlier, the use of PCA has become widespread in many disciplines. Because of its popularity, nearly all the major statistical software programs offer PCA, and users can choose from a variety of different PCA implementations. Such modules or functions are implemented in Stata, SPSS, MATLAB, and SAS, for example, and R includes several PCA functions, such as the aforementioned built-in functions `prcomp()` and `princomp()`.[5]

Notes

1 For a linear combination c' X generally holds var(c' X) = c' Σc), with **X** as a column vector of n random variables ($X_1, \ldots, X_n$), c as a column vector of n scalars ($c_1, \ldots, c_n$) and Σ as covariance matrix of **X** (Johnson & Wichern, 2007, pp. 75 sqq.).
2 Another built-in alternative is the R function `princomp()` that computes the results based on the spectral decomposition approach (see section 2.1). The function prcomp() uses the singular value decomposition method instead and delivers slightly better numerical results. Because of this advantage we decided to analyze the example data with `prcomp()`.
3 We used the function `ggscreeplot()` of the R package `ggbiplot`.
4 We used the function `ggbiplot()` of the R package `ggbiplot`.
5 Users can also decide to use, among others, the function `PCA()` from the package `FactoMineR`, the function `dudi.pca()` from the package `ade4`, the function `epPCA()` from the package `ExPosition`, and the function `principal()` from the package `psych`.

References

Anderson, T. W. (1963). Asymptotic theory for principal component analysis. *The Annals of Mathematical Statistics, 34*(1), 122–148. https://doi.org/10.1214/aoms/ 1177704248

Beltrami, E. (1873). Sulle funzioni bilineari. *Giornale di Matematiche, 11*, 98–106.

Cattell, R. B. (1966). The scree test for the number of factors. *Multivariate Behavioral Research, 1*(2), 245–276.

Eckart, C., & Young, G. (1936). The approximation of one matrix by another of lower rank. *Psychometrika, 1*, 211–218. https://doi.org/10.1007/bf02288367

Gabriel, K. R. (1971). The biplot graphic display of matrices with application to principal component analysis. *Biometrika, 58*(3), 453–467. https://doi.org/10.1093/biomet/58.3.453

Girshick, M. A. (1936). Principal components. *Journal of the American Statistical Association, 31*(195), 519–528. https://doi.org/10.1080/01621459.1936.10503354

Girshick, M. A. (1939). On the sampling theory of roots of determinantal equations. *The Annals of Mathematical Statistics, 10*(3), 203–224. https://doi.org/10.1214/aoms/ 1177732180

Gower, J. C. (1966). Some distance properties of latent root and vector methods used in multivariate analysis. *Biometrika, 53*(3–4), 325–338. https://doi.org/10.1093/ biomet/53.3–4.325

Guttman, L. (1954). Some necessary conditions for common-factor analysis. *Psychometrika, 19*(2), 149–161. https://doi.org/10.1007/bf02289162

Hauser, R. M., & Goldberger, A. S. (1971). The treatment of unobservable variables in path analysis. *Sociological Methodology, 3*, 81–117. https://doi.org/10.2307/270819

Hilbert, D. (1904). Grundzüge einer allgemeinen Theorie der linearen Integralgleichungen. (Erste Mitteilung). *Nachrichten von der Königl. Gesellschaft der Wissenschaften zu Göttingen. Mathematisch-physikalische Klasse, 1*, 49–91.

Horn, J. L. (1965). A rationale and test for the number of factors in factor analysis. *Psychometrika, 30*(2), 179–185. https://doi.org/10.1007/bf02289447

Hotelling, H. (1933). Analysis of a complex of statistical variables into principal components. *Journal of Educational Psychology, 24*(6), 417–441. https://doi.org/10.1037/ h0071325

Johnson, R., & Wichern, D. (2007). *Applied multivariate statistical analysis* (6th ed.). Prentice Hall.

Jolliffe, I. T. (2002). *Principal component analysis* (2nd ed.). Springer.

Jolliffe, I. T., & Cadima, J. (2016). Principal component analysis: A review and recent developments. *Philosophical Transactions of the Royal Society A: Mathematical, Physical and Engineering Sciences, 374*(2065). https://doi.org/doi.org/10.1098/rsta.2015.0202

Jordan, C. (1874). Sur la réduction des formes bilinéaires. *Comptes rendus de l'Académie des sciences de Paris, 78*, 614–617.

Jöreskog, K. G. (1969). A general approach to confirmatory maximum likelihood factor analysis. *Psychometrika, 34*(2), 183–202. https://doi.org/10.1007/bf02289343

Jöreskog, K. G. (1973). A general method for estimating a linear structural equation system. In A. S. Goldberger & O. D. Duncan (Eds.), *Structural equation models in the social sciences* (pp. 85–112). Seminar Press.

Kaiser, H. F. (1960). The application of electronic computers to factor analysis. *Educational and Psychological Measurement, 20*(1), 141–151. https://doi.org/10.1177/ 001316446002000116

Kassambara, A. (2017). *Practical guide to principal component methods in R: PCA, M (CA), FAMD, MFA, HCPC, factoextra*. STHDA.

Pearson, K. (1901). On lines and planes of closest fit to systems of points in space. *The London, Edinburgh, and Dublin Philosophical Magazine and Journal of Science, 2*(11), 559–572. https://doi.org/10.1080/14786440109462720

R Core Team. (2019). *R: A language and environment for statistical computing*. R Foundation for Statistical Computing. www.R-project.org/

Rao, C. R. (1964). The use and interpretation of principal component analysis in applied research. *Sankhya: The Indian Journal of Statistics, Series A, 26*(4), 329–358.

Reinecke, J., & Pöge, A. (2019). Confirmatory factor analysis. In P. Atkinson, S. Delamont, A. Cernat, J. W. Sakshaug, & R. A. Williams (Eds.), *SAGE research methods foundations*. https://doi.org/10.4135/9781526421036889599

Schlittgen, R. (2009). *Multivariate Statistik*. Oldenbourg.

Schmidt, E. (1907). Zur Theorie der linearen und nichtlinearen Integralgleichungen. I Teil: Entwicklung willkürlichen Funktionen nach Systemen vorgeschriebener. *Mathematische Annalen, 63*, 433–476.

Smithies, F. (1938). The eigen-values and singular values of integral equations. *Proceedings of the London Mathematical Society, 43*, 255–279. https://doi.org/10.1112/plms/s2-43.4.255

Spearman, C. (1904). "General Intelligence", objectively determined and measure. *The American Journal of Psychology, 15*, 201–292. https://doi.org/10.2307/1412107

Sylvester, J. J. (1889). On the reduction of a bilinear quantic of the *n*th order to the form of a sum of *n* products by a double orthogonal substitution. *Messenger of Mathematics, 19*, 42–46.

Thurstone, L. L. (1931). Multiple factor analysis. *Psychological Review, 38*(5), 406–427. https://doi.org/10.1037/h0069792

Thurstone, L. L. (1947). *Multiple-factor analysis; a development and expansion of the vectors of mind*. University of Chicago Press.

U.S. Department of Agriculture, Agricultural Research Service (Ed.). (2018). *USDA food and nutrient database for dietary studies 2015–2016*. www.ars.usda.gov/nea/bhnrc/ fsrg

Weyl, H. (1912). Das asymptotische Verteilungsgesetz der Eigenwerte linearer partieller Differentialgleichungen (mit einer Anwendung auf die Theorie der Hohlraumstrahlung). *Mathematische Annalen, 71*, 441–479.

Widaman, K. F. (1993). Common factor analysis versus principal component analysis: Differential bias in representing model parameters? *Multivariate Behavioral Research, 28*(3), 263–311. https://doi.org/10.1207/s15327906mbr2803_1

Wolff, H.-G., & Bacher, J. (2010). Hauptkomponentenanalyse und explorative Faktorenanalyse. In C. Wolf & H. Best (Eds.), *Handbuch der sozialwissenschaftlichen Datenanalyse* (pp. 333–365). VS.

19

UNSUPERVISED METHODS

Clustering methods

Johann Bacher, Andreas Pöge and Knut Wenzig

1 Introduction

The basic aim of all clustering methods is to assign objects to groups (clusters) according to similarities in their specific characteristics. Two objects assigned to the same cluster should share similar specified characteristics (variables, patterns, symbols, etc.), whereas two objects allocated to different clusters should be less similar. Objects might be cases of either a data matrix or variables. For example, countries (cases) might be classified in clusters according to their values in selected variables. Alternatively, variables might be clustered into groups, so that cluster 1 contains variable $X1$, $X2$, and $X4$, cluster 2 variables $X3$, $X5$, etc. In most applications, cases are clustered. Therefore, these two terms (objects, cases) will be used here synonymously.

The development of clustering methods has varied in intensity and innovation since the 1960s when they first became popular. For example, Ward proposed his well-known minimum variance method in 1963. The 1970s saw a flurry of textbooks on the subject (e.g., Everitt, 1974; Hartigan, 1974; Jardine & Sibson, 1971), which tended to focus on algorithms to generate the clusters and proposed some formal criteria to decide the number of clusters. However, several problems remained unsolved at the end of this first period of intensive development (Everitt, 1979). They included the selection of appropriate variables and appropriate clustering methods, the determination of the number of clusters, and the evaluation of the clustering results. A further practical problem was the limited computer capacity at the time. In the 1980s, with the increase in computer capacity, cluster analysis techniques were included in standard statistical packages.

In the 1990s, inroads were made into addressing these early problems. This period was marked by the development of so-called model-based and probabilistic clustering techniques (e.g., Fraley & Raftery, 1999; Vermunt & Magidson, 2000) on the one hand and density clustering methods (Ester et al., 1996) on the other.

Today, in the early 21st century, with huge advancements in computer capacity and capability, elaborate and computationally intensive methods have become the norm (Wierzchoń & Kłopotek, 2018; Zgurovsky & Zaychenko, 2020) and the literature has exploded (Murtagh, 2016). Clustering methods are available in most statistical software packages, as well as in machine-learning software and data-mining packages such as RapidMiner. The most comprehensive collection of clustering methods is available in the software package R (Leisch & Gruen, 2020).

DOI: 10.4324/9781003025245-23

This article provides an overview of clustering methods and covers the following topics:

- Steps toward an appropriate cluster solution
- Clustering methods
- Criteria to determine the number of clusters
- Methods to validate cluster solutions
- Computer programs
- Application
- Summary and recommendations

An in-depth insight into the discussed topics is provided by the excellent handbook by Hennig et al. (2016) and the reader by Wierzchoń and Kłopotek (2018).

2 Steps toward an appropriate cluster solution

In order to arrive at an appropriate cluster solution, the following steps are necessary:

1. *Selection of appropriate variables, cases, and clustering method.* The selection of appropriate variables and cases is a substantive decision that depends on the research question. Sometimes researchers can collect variables and cases by themselves, but in many applications, the data already exist and the researchers merely have to select the variables. From a formal perspective, the variables should be able to differentiate between the clusters. However, whether this is the case can only be judged a posteriori after completing the next steps. The selection of an appropriate clustering method depends on the selected data (size, measurement level of variables) and the researcher's assumption of what the cluster should look like.
2. *Running the cluster analysis.* Sometimes the selected method is not available in the researcher's statistical package, making it necessary for him/her to familiarize him-/herself with a new computer program.
3. *Selection of one or more appropriate cluster solutions.* Sometimes, only one cluster solution comes into consideration for subsequent steps, but very often, there is more than one appropriate cluster solution for further consideration.
4. *Validation of cluster solution(s).* The selected cluster solutions are validated using external and internal techniques. If more than one cluster solution remains after step 3, this step should help to make a final decision.
5. *Final decision for a specific cluster solution.* If one cluster solution meets formal and substantive criteria, this cluster solution is selected and the resulting classification can be used. If this is not the case, the researcher can return to step 1 and opt to select additional variables or to exclude variables, and/or to choose a different clustering method.

The application of these steps will be demonstrated in section 8.

3 Clustering methods

There are different ways to classify clustering methods (e.g., Saxena et al., 2017). One prominent distinction (Saxena et al., 2017) is between *hierarchical* and *partitioning techniques* (see Figure 19.1). *Hierarchical methods* can be further divided into divisive and agglomerative methods. *Divisive hierarchical methods* start with the assumption that all objects belong to one large cluster and divide the clusters stepwise until each object builds a distinct cluster. In contrast,

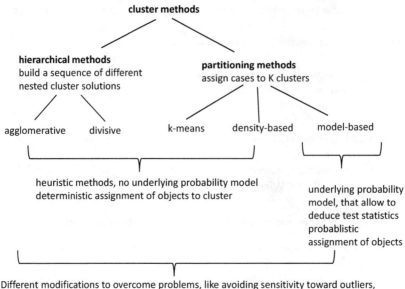

cluster methods

hierarchical methods
build a sequence of different
nested cluster solutions

partitioning methods
assign cases to K clusters

agglomerative   divisive   k-means   density-based   model-based

heuristic methods, no underlying probability model
deterministic assignment of objects to cluster

underlying probability
model, that allow to
deduce test statistics
probablistic
assignment of objects

Different modifications to overcome problems, like avoiding sensitivity toward outliers,
detection of outliers, assignment to more clusters, Bayes estimation etc.

Figure 19.1   Overview of clustering methods

agglomerative hierarchical methods assign each case to a distinct cluster at the beginning and then combine the clusters stepwise until all cases belong to one large cluster. *Partitioning techniques* start with a given number of clusters K and assign the cases iteratively to these K clusters by minimizing or maximizing a certain criterion. The most popular partitioning technique is *k-means clustering*.

In order to demonstrate the logic of *hierarchical methods*, it is important to compute a similarity or dissimilarity matrix for the cases. A large number of similarity and dissimilarity measures exists. They are well documented in most textbooks (e.g., Bacher et al., 2010; Everitt et al., 2001).

For *quantitative variables*, product and distance measures can be distinguished. The most prominent product measure is *Pearson's correlation* coefficient:

$$s_{ij} = \frac{\sum_{l=1}^{m}\left(x_{il} - \overline{x}_i\right)\left(x_{jl} - \overline{x}_j\right)}{\left(\sum_{l=1}^{m}\left(x_{il} - \overline{x}_i\right)^2 \sum_{l=1}^{m}\left(x_{jl} - \overline{x}_j\right)^2\right)^{1/2}}$$

Pearson's correlation coefficient is a similarity measure. A higher value indicates a greater similarity between two objects.

Prominent examples of distance measures are the Euclidean distance and the city-block distance, which can be derived from the general *Minkowski metric* for two cases i and j:

$$d_{ij} = \left(\sum_{l=1}^{m}\left|x_{il} - x_{jl}\right|^p\right)^{1/p}$$

For $p = 1$ the Minkowski metric results in the city-block distance, sometimes denoted as L1 metric, for $p = 2$ the Euclidean distance, also denoted as L2. Distance measures are dissimilarity measures.

If the variables have another nonquantitative measurement level, distance and product measures are available, too. Especially for dichotomous variables, numerous measures have been developed that differ as to how the presence and absence of an attribute is evaluated. Already in the 1970s, Gower (1971) proposed a similarity measure for variables with mixed measurement levels. If cases are clustered, the measures are computed for each pair of cases in contrast to the usual analysis whereby the correlation coefficient is computed for pairs of variables.

An example of a dissimilarity matrix is given in Table 19.1. A higher value indicates a larger dissimilarity. In the example, objects 5 and 6 with a value of $d(5,6) = 1$ have the smallest dissimilarity; they are the most similar of the six objects. The largest dissimilarity occurs for objects 1 and 6 ($d(1,6) = 44$). These objects are the least similar of the six objects.

Agglomerative methods start with the assumption that each object/case builds a cluster. For n cases, there are n clusters. The algorithms search the pair of clusters with the smallest dissimilarity and agglomerate them into one cluster. The number of clusters reduces to $n-1$ and a new dissimilarity matrix is computed; therefore, the dissimilarity between two clusters has to be defined (see later). Afterward, the aforementioned steps are repeated until all cases build one large cluster. The process is usually reported in an agglomeration schedule (see Table 19.2) and graphically visualized in a dendrogram (Figure 19.2). *Divisive methods* follow the opposite principle and start with one large cluster that contains all cases. This large cluster is split stepwise into subclusters until each case builds a cluster.

Table 19.2 reports the *agglomeration schedule of single linkage* for the dissimilarity matrix of Table 19.1. At the beginning, each object builds one cluster. $C1=\{1\}$, $C2=\{2\}$, ..., $C6=\{6\}$. In

Table 19.1 Dissimilarity matrix for six objects

	1	2	3	4	5	6
1	0					
2	10	0				
3	30	20	0			
4	38	28	8	0		
5	43	33	13	5	0	
6	44	34	14	6	1	0

Note: Table was generated by the authors.

Table 19.2 Agglomeration schedule for dissimilarity matrix in Table 19.1

Stage	Cluster combined		Coefficients (agglomeration level v_k)
	Cluster 1	Cluster 2	
1	5	6	1.000
2	4	5	5.000
3	3	4	8.000
4	1	2	10.000
5	1	3	20.000

Note: The cluster analysis was performed with IBM SPSS (version 26), module CLUSTER.

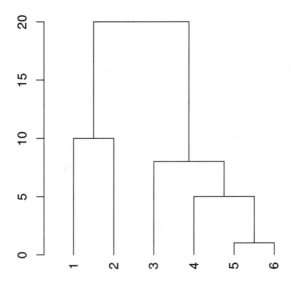

Figure 19.2   Dendrogram for the agglomeration schedule of Table 19.2 (result for single linkage)

the first step, the nearest cases 5 and 6 are combined at a level of 1.0. Now we have five clusters: $C1=\{1\}$, $C2=\{2\}$, ..., $C5=\{5, 6\}$. In the next step, the cluster with case 4 and the cluster with case 5 (and 6, not reported) are combined at a level of 5.0, and so on. The *dendrogram* (Figure 19.2) reports the process graphically. Objects 5 and 6 are combined at a low level; the next object, 4, is assigned to this cluster, afterward object 3. In the next step a new cluster is formed by objects 1 and 2, and finally the two clusters $C1=\{3,4,5,6\}$ and $C2=\{1,2\}$ are combined into one cluster. The length of the line where two clusters merge represents the dissimilarity that occurs after the two clusters are combined. It corresponds to the agglomeration level in the agglomeration schedule.

The agglomeration methods differ in how they compute the new dissimilarities after two clusters are combined. Three main approaches exist (Everitt et al., 2001, pp. 55–67):

- *Single linkage*. In a specific step, the new dissimilarities between a cluster k and the new cluster (i, j), which agglomerates clusters i and j, is computed as: $d_{k(ij)} = \min(d_{ki}, d_{kj})$. This procedure results in clustering whereby each object of a cluster has at least one nearest neighbor within the cluster with a dissimilarity less than/equal to the reported agglomeration level v_k at a certain step. Due to this property, single linkage is also referred to as the nearest neighbor method. It is able to produce chains and to find outliers.
- *Complete linkage*. The new dissimilarities between a cluster k and the new cluster (i, j) are computed as: $d_{k(ij)} = \max(d_{ki}, d_{kj})$. This procedure results in a clustering where the dissimilarities between all objects of a cluster are less than/equal to the reported agglomeration level v_k at a certain step. Due to this property, complete linkage is known as the furthest neighbor method, because the furthest object in a cluster is a neighbor. Complete linkage results in very homogenous clusters. The structure of the cluster is unimportant.
- *(Weighted) average linkage*. The new dissimilarities between a cluster k and the new cluster (i, j) are computed as a weighted average. Different formulas are used.

The aforementioned Ward's method can be seen as a special agglomerative method. It requires quantitative variables and uses squared Euclidean distance. At a certain step, those two clusters are combined that minimize the sum of squares within clusters.

K-means methods do not require a similarity or dissimilarity matrix to be computed. Rather, the number of clusters and a starting configuration must be specified at the outset. The starting configuration can be generated randomly or empirically with another cluster or statistical method. It is also possible to use results or theoretical considerations. The results may depend on the starting values and the ordering of the cases.

K-means clustering assigns the cases to K clusters so that the within-cluster variation $SSE(K)$ ("sum of squares of error") is minimized:

$$SSE(K) = \sum_{i=1}^{n}\sum_{k=1}^{K} w_{ik} \sum_{l=1}^{p}\left(x_{il} - \bar{x}_{kl}\right)^2 \rightarrow \min$$

where
w_{ik} = membership function ($w_{ik} = 1$ if case i belongs to cluster k, else 0)
x_{ij} = value of case i in variable l
$\bar{x}_{kj}$ = mean of cluster k in variable l

Table 19.3 reports the result of k-means clustering for a data set with 25 cases. In the example, a cluster solution with three clusters was computed. The means of cluster 1 and cluster 2 in variable $x1$ are similar (1.97 and 2.01). Hence, the two clusters do not differ with respect to $x1$. However, they do differ in $x2$. The mean of cluster 1 is 2.62, whereas cluster 2 has a mean of 1.27. In contrast, cluster 3 differs from cluster 1 and 2 in $x1$, and from cluster 1 in $x2$, too.

Density-based clustering (Ester et al., 1996; Schubert et al., 2017). K-means clustering tends to build spherical clusters (Steinley, 2016) and is sensitive to outliers (Kaufman & Rousseeuw, 1990, p. 117) like every procedure that works with the sum of squares. Density-based clustering overcomes this problem. It can detect clusters of different shapes. It assumes that areas of higher and lower density exist in the data space and requires the definition of two parameters: the radius ε and the number of points *NPts* that should occur within the radius of objects that build a region with high density. Figure 19.3 reports the results of density-based clustering.

Hierarchical methods, k-means, and density-based clustering methods are all *heuristic methods*. They use no underlying statistical model, like a normal distribution, and hence they are unable to deduce model-based measures to select a specific cluster solution and to evaluate this solution. They usually require decisions by the user that are ambiguous. For example, DBSCAN requires the definition of the minimal number of cases that should belong to a cluster and is very sensitive to this specification. If we increase the number of points *NPts* in the previous example, more objects are labeled as outliers even if they seem to be close to a cluster.

Table 19.3 Results of k-means clustering

Cluster centers				Test statistics				
				Cluster K	SSE	ETA²	PRE	FMAX
	Cluster			1	18.19	0.0%		
	1	2	3	2	8.86	51.3%	51.3%	24.24
N	6	9	10	3	4.10	77.5%	53.7%	37.81
x1	1.97	2.01	1.00	4	2.67	85.3%	34.8%	40.65
x2	2.62	1.27	1.29	5	1.69	90.7%	36.8%	48.85
				6	1.39	92.4%	17.7%	45,93

Note: k-means clustering was performed with IBM SPSS (version 26), module QUICK CLUSTER, option UPDATE. The test statistics are computed via additional syntax. Data are generated by the authors.

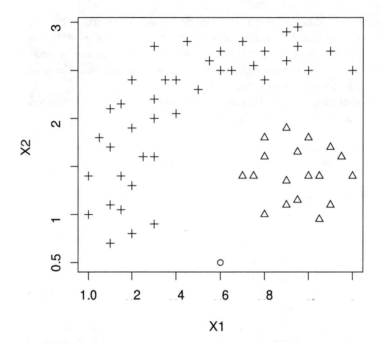

Figure 19.3   Graphical results of DBSCAN

Note. The solution was generated with R-function HDBSCAN from the package DBSCAN. The number of points *NPts* was set to 5. The cases of cluster 1 are drawn with crosses. The cases of cluster 2 are drawn with triangles. One case (circle) is detected as an outlier. Even without the outlier, the K-means solution with 2 clusters would not differentiate between the two geographic shapes.

Model-based clustering methods use an underlying statistical model. They assume that a mixture of probability distributions underlies the analyzed data. In the case of quantitative data, a mixture of normal distributions is usually assumed. In model-based clustering methods the general model is:

$$f(X / \theta_K = \{\theta_1, \theta_2, ..., \theta_K,\}, K) = \prod_{k=1}^{K} f(X / \theta_k) \, p_k$$

where
$f(X / \theta_k)$ = joint distributions of the variables X in cluster k. The distribution depends on the parameters θ_K
p_k = proportion of cluster k

If all variables are dichotomous, the *latent class model* evolves. If all variables are quantitative, we arrive at the *latent profile model*. Both models were proposed by Lazarsfeld and Henry (1968) in the 1960s. The approach includes *finite mixture models* (McLachlan & Peel, 2005), which assumes in its classical approach that the observed distribution is a mixture of K p-dimensional normal distributions with a mean vector μ_k and variance-covariance matrix Σ_k (Everitt et al., 2001, pp. 120–122). Nowadays, adequate software is available, like LatentGold (see section 7), and it is possible to analyze variables of a mixed measurement type.

The primary objectives in the model-based clustering method are to estimate the parameters θ_K of the conditional distributions and the number K of the clusters. Due to the assumption of probability distributions, statistically based measures are available. Information measures are most frequently used for this purpose (see section 5).

4 Modifications and recent developments

The methods described previously can be regarded as prototypes that have been modified in several ways, especially in recent years. Some of these modifications are now described:

- *Enhanced hierarchical methods for large data sets.* Hierarchical methods require the computation and storage of a dissimilarity matrix and therefore need considerable computer memory. Consequently, enhanced hierarchical methods have been developed to handle large data sets, like BIRCH or CURE (Saxena et al., 2017).
- *Using other measures of central tendency instead of the mean in k-means.* Clustering methods exist that use medians (k-median clustering, Bradley et al., 1996), modes (K-modes clustering, Huang, 1998), or representative data points (k-medoids clustering, Kaufman & Rousseeuw, 1990, pp. 68–123) instead of means.
- *Using other distance measures in k-means.* K-means clustering uses squared Euclidean distances and consequently the centers are sensitive to outliers. Therefore, the use of the city-block distance instead of the squared Euclidean distance was proposed. For instance, k-medoids clustering minimizes: $F(K) = \sum_{i=1}^{n}\sum_{k=1}^{K} w_{ik} \sum_{l=1}^{p} |x_{il} - m_{kl}|$, where m_{kl} is a representative data point.
- *Detection and elimination of outliers.* Another way to avoid dependence on outliers is to detect and eliminate them (Hautamäki et al., 2005). The iterative k-means procedure (Holmgren et al., 2020) is one example.
- *Assignment of cases to more than one cluster.* Some cases are difficult to assign to a single cluster. They may be located between two clusters. Hence, it may be reasonable to assign them to two or even more clusters. Fuzzy clustering methods (Jain & Dubes, 1988, pp. 130–133) are one approach that allows multiple assignment.
- *Bayes estimation methods.* In accordance with the general trend toward Bayesian statistics, Bayes estimation methods have been introduced for clustering techniques. One cluster program that has fully implemented a Bayes approach is AutoClass (Bacher et al., 2010, pp. 439–446).

5 Criteria to determine the number of clusters

The *determination of the number of clusters* is critical in clustering methods. Generally, the user must decide the number of clusters. Most implementations of cluster methods in software packages provide formal criteria. Some implementations have automatized the decision and propose a certain cluster solution. However, these suggestions depend on the specified parameters and if these parameters are changed, the number of cluster changes, too. Therefore, even in these cases, the proposed cluster solution should be validated (see the next section). It might be the case that a different solution is more appropriate than that proposed. Further criteria, which are not used in the automatic proposal, are relevant. These further criteria might be interpretability, comprehensibility (small number of clusters is preferred), and minimal cluster size (each cluster should have at least a certain number of cases).

The available formal criteria depend on the clustering methods. For *hierarchical clustering methods* the number of clusters is commonly fixed graphically. The user sets the number of clusters equal to the number of "hills" in the dendrogram. In Figure 19.2, two hills can be seen. Another graphical method is the inverse scree test (Lathrop & Williams, 1989), sometimes called the elbow test. Similar to explorative factor analysis, a scatter plot is generated. The number of clusters defines the x-axis, the value of the agglomeration schedule the y-axis (see Figure 19.4).

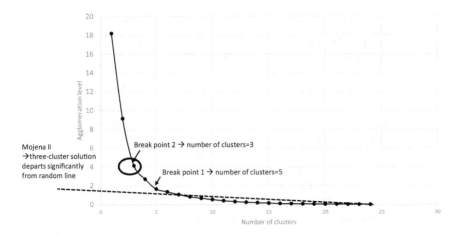

Figure 19.4 Scree diagram generated for agglomerative hierarchical clustering method

The diagram is read from right to left, starting with the highest number of clusters. Moving left, one stops when the first break point ("elbow") is observed. The number of clusters is set equal to the number of clusters where the first break point occurs. In Figure 19.4, the first break point occurs for five clusters. For a large data set, this procedure can result in a high number of clusters. In this case, one can continue and look for the next break point. In our example, five clusters might be acceptable and the number is not too high. The example indicates a further break point at three clusters. Hence, we can conclude that two cluster solutions are appropriate. Mojena (1977) formalized the decision based on the scree diagram. One of his criteria is to estimate a regression line until K clusters, to predict the value for $K-1$ clusters based on the results of this regression line and to test whether the empirical value significantly departs form the predicted value. Mojena proposes a threshold of 2.75 for the standardized residuals for K clusters from a regression line from 1 to $K-1$ clusters. In Figure 19.4, the significant departure occurs for three clusters.

For *k-means clustering*, it is obvious to use the sum of squares of error and some derived measures to determine the number of clusters. For this purpose it is necessary to generate a series of k-means solutions. We recommend starting with one cluster as the lowest value and set the highest value as one that would not be expected from a substantive perspective, e.g., 10 to 20 clusters. The decision for a cluster solution might now be based on:

- Explained variance $(ETA_K^2 = 1 - \dfrac{SSE_K}{SSE_1})$: the user defines a threshold in advance, starts with $K=1$ cluster and selects the first solution with K clusters that meets this threshold.

- PRE statistic $(PRE_K = 1 - \dfrac{SSE_K}{SSE_{K-1}})$: the user selects the solution with K clusters if PRE_K is large and the following PRE for $K+1$, $K+2$ are small.

- FMAX statistic $(FMAX_K = \dfrac{(SSE_1 - SSE_K)/(K-1)}{SSE_K/(n-K)})$: the user selects the cluster solution with the highest F value.

In Table 19.3, FMAX suggests a five-cluster solution, whereas we can observe a clear drop after three clusters for PRE (from 53.7% to 34.8%). ETA^2 already reaches a high level of 77.5% for three clusters. Hence, it might be useful to further analyze a three- and a five-cluster solution. It is also possible to draw a scree diagram for the different criteria mentioned earlier. If FMAX statistics are used as the y-axis, for example, the solutions with the highest peak are selected. If a modified method is used, alternative measures can be used. We will demonstrate the use of this graphical method later for information criteria.

Density-based clustering methods propose a certain number of clusters. Therefore, the user does not need to decide the number of clusters at first. However, s/he must test validity. One or more alternative solutions may be more appropriate. In addition, as already mentioned, the solution depends on the specified parameter.

Model-based clustering methods have the advantage that the underlying statistical probability model enables the deduction of formal criteria. On the one hand they make it possible to run chi-square-based tests, like likelihood-ratio (LR) test; on the other information criteria are available. In order to select a certain cluster solution, it is necessary to generate a series of possible solutions. Again, we recommend starting with $K=1$.

The LR test is defined as

$$LR(K, K-1) = LL_{K-1} - LL_K,$$

where
LL_x = log-likelihood function for a solution with x clusters.

The LR statistic makes it possible to test whether a solution with K clusters significantly improves a solution with $K-1$ (or $K-x$) clusters. Wolfe (1970) proposed a modification for the LR statistic. From a theoretical point of view, the LR statistic or its modification by Wolfe has a chi-square distribution. Results by McLachlan and Peel (2005) and McLachlan and Basford (2000) suggest that this is unfortunately mostly not the case. Therefore, the bootstrap method is recommended nowadays.

Information measures are most frequently used to decide the number of clusters. Popular information measures are

$$AIC_K = -2LL_K + 2m_K$$
$$BIC_K = -2LL_K + m_K \log(n)$$
$$CAIC_K = -2LL_K + m_K (\log(n) + 1)$$
$$AIC3_K = -2LL_K + 3m_K$$

where
LL_K = value of the log-likelihood function that maximizes $LL = \sum_{i=1}^{n} w_i \ln(f(X_i / \theta_k))$
m_k = number of parameters that must be estimated
n = number of cases

The underlying idea behind these measures is to correct for the fact that more clusters will automatically provide a better fit. Again, a scree diagram can be drawn. The most appropriate solution is the solution with the lowest value (inverse peak, see Figure 19.5).

An evaluation study (Fonseca & Cardoso, 2007) suggests that AIC3 performs best for categorical data, whereas BIC performs best for quantitative (metric) variables. AIC has a tendency to select too many clusters (McLachlan & Peel, 2005, p. 220). For mixed scaled variables, the integrated completed likelihood criterion $ICL - BIC$ (Biernacki et al., 2000) outperforms. It is defined as

$$ICL - BIC = BIC + 2EN(S)$$

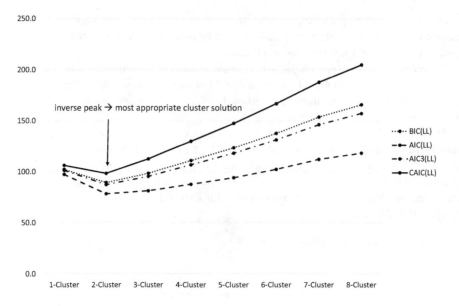

Figure 19.5 Scree diagram generated for different information measures (results from model-based clustering)

and additionally integrates the entropy of the probability of class membership $EN(S_K) = -\sum_{i=1}^{n}\sum_{k=1}^{K}\pi(k\,/\,i)\,\log(\pi(k\,/\,i))$.

According to McLachlan and Peel (2005, pp. 217–220) $ICL - BIC$ outperforms in the case of quantitative variables, too. Akogul and Erisoglu (2016) report that the Kullback information criterion (KIC) performs best for quantitative variables. KIC is defined as

$$KIC_K = -2LL_K + 3\big(m_K + 1\big)$$

and differs from AIC3 only by adding 3. In a further paper, the authors (Akogul & Erisoglu, 2017) propose using an analytic hierarchy process (AHP) that combines different information measures. This procedure is similar to the consensus method proposed in Bacher et al. (2010).

6 Criteria to validate a cluster solution

After the decision for one or more possible cluster solutions, the selected solutions must be evaluated or rather validated. Validation involves (Everitt et al., 2001, pp. 180–196; e.g., Jain & Dubes, 1988; Wierzchoń & Kłopotek, 2018):

1. *Formal internal validation of the selected solutions.* An index is computed that measures the homogeneity of the clusters of the different solutions. If only one solution is evaluated, thresholds must be defined in order to be able to judge whether the solution can be accepted. If more than one solution is validated, one speaks of a relative validation. In this case, the solutions with the highest formal validity can be selected.
2. *Stability test.* Cluster analysis requires decisions where the user is uncertain which decision is correct. These uncertain decisions should have no or only a small influence on the results. Therefore, this criterion is labeled also as robustness.

3. *Interpretability*. This is the most important criterion. Ideally, formal validation and the stability test result in a decision for a certain cluster solution. If this solution should be used for further analysis, the clusters must be substantively interpretable. It must be possible to give the clusters substantive meaningful names. Sometimes it may occur that this is not possible for all clusters.
4. *Validation by external criteria*. Interpretation very often results in the specification of hypotheses about the association of one or more clusters with other variables, for example "Cluster *C1* is associated with variable *Z*." It may also be possible that these hypotheses exist in advance. The researcher expects certain clusters and associations. In very rare cases, it might be possible to use another classification for validation. The task in this step is to test whether the hypotheses hold.

In the last two decades, many coefficients for formal validation have been proposed (Liu et al., 2010; Satre-Meloy et al., 2020). One frequently used coefficient for formal validation is the silhouette coefficient SC. SC reports how much the objects of one cluster differ from the objects of the cluster that is closest to them. The SC for one object *i*, cluster *k*, and finally the cluster solution *K* is defined as

$$SC(i) = \frac{b(i) - a(i)}{\max(b(i), a(i))}, \ SC(k) = \frac{1}{n_k} \sum_{i=1}^{n_k} SC(i) \text{ and } SC(K) = \frac{1}{n} \sum_{k=1}^{K} n_k SC(k),$$

where
$b(i)$ = average distance of object *i* to all objects in its nearest cluster.
$a(i)$ = average distance of object *i* to all other objects in the cluster to which object *i* belongs.

Different distance measures can be used and will result in different scores. If the clusters are well separated, *SC(K)* should be large. Kaufman and Rousseeuw (1990, p. 88) propose the following threshold values:

```
0.71 ≤ SC(K) ≤ 1.00 strong structure
0.51 ≤ SC(K) ≤ 0.70 reasonable structure
0.26 ≤ SC(K) ≤ 0.50 weak structure (could be artificial,try ad-
                         ditional methods)
     SC(K) ≤ 0.25      no substantial structure
```

A further frequently cited index is the Dunn index (Kaufman & Rousseeuw, 1990, p. 171). Similar to *SC(K)*, higher values of the Dunn index indicate a better separation. Recent literature recommends to use at least one of these indices to determine the number of clusters, for example by drawing a scree diagram for the silhouette coefficient for different cluster solutions and selecting the solution with the highest silhouette coefficient. Several further indices are available for this task.

In order to compare different cluster solutions, the Rand index is available (Everitt et al., 2001, pp. 181–183). The Rand index depends on the marginal distributions of the classification. Therefore, the adjusted (or corrected) Rand index is recommended. It corrects for purely random agreement and is able to discriminate good solutions. Thresholds are *RAND* > 0.7 (Frabioni & Saltstone, 1992). For the Hubert-Arabie Adjusted Rand index, Steinley (2004) gives the following thresholds:

```
0.90 < adj.Rand          excellent recovery
0.80 < adj.Rand ≤ 0.90   good recovery
0.65 < adj.Rand ≤ 0.80   moderate recovery
       adj.Rand ≤ 0.65   poor recovery.
```

7 Software

Modules in standard statistical software and special, stand-alone software programs are available for cluster analysis. A short and narrative overview will be provided here because the implementation and availability of a program can change during a program upgrade.

IBM SPSS (version 24.0 and above, www.ibm.com/analytics/spss-statistics-software) offers three procedures for clustering: agglomerative hierarchical methods, k-means clustering, and model-based clustering (TSC, two-step cluster). TSC is a hierarchical (divisive) model-based program. It starts with one cluster and splits the clusters as long as the increase in the BIC or AIC change falls below a certain threshold (Bacher et al., 2004). It enables users to handle outliers and to analyze variables with mixed measurement levels. However, ordinal variables have to be treated as nominal scaled variables.

STATA (version 15 and above, www.stata.com/) offers agglomerative hierarchical methods and k-means and model-based clustering similar to IBM SPSS. Model-based clustering is available via generalized structural equation models and corresponds to the described approach. In addition, *k*-median is available, as are special modules for computing the silhouette coefficients and adjusted R.

R offers the most powerful implementation for clustering methods. Leisch and Gruen (2020) provide an overview.

LatentGold (www.statisticalinnovations.com/latent-gold-5-1/) is a stand-alone software that enables model-based clustering. Variables with different measurement levels can be used. Correct standard errors are computed for complex sample designs (like multistage sampling). Bayes elements are integrated in order to avoid local minima and degeneration of solutions. The same models are available in *MPLUS* (www.statmodel.com/).

A comparison by Kent et al. (2014) between TSC and LatentGold favors LatentGold. This result corresponds to Bacher et al. (2004). Rodriguez et al. (2019) compare nine clustering methods that are implemented in R. The studied methods cover all discussed types of clusters. They found a small difference if the dimensionality of the data is small (Rodriguez et al., 2019).

8 Application

We reanalyze data from the Austrian Social Survey (SSÖ) from 2018 (Hadler et al., 2019), which are described in more detail in Eder et al. (2020).[1] The authors use this data set of 1,200 respondents aged 18 and above to analyze their positional, moral, and emotional subjective recognition with the aim of identifying social groups that feel unrecognized. With the help of eight dichotomized indicator items, the authors perform model-based clustering (latent class analysis) and select a solution with four classes. The indicators are shown in Figure 19.6. Their analyses were performed with the statistical software R and the package poLCA.

The first class (cluster) is described as "almost entirely recognized," the second class as "positionally recognized but emotionally unrecognized," the third class as "emotionally recognized but positionally unrecognized," and the fourth class as "poorly recognized." The profile of the four clusters is visualized in a diagram by the authors.

The authors validated their interpretation with a multinomial logistic regression. The four clusters were used as dependent variables. Variables deduced from theory were used as independent variables. The multivariate analysis confirms the interpretation.

Hence, the following criteria are fulfilled:

- Formal internal validity (the four-cluster solution has the lowest BIC and entropy-R-squared is sufficient high).

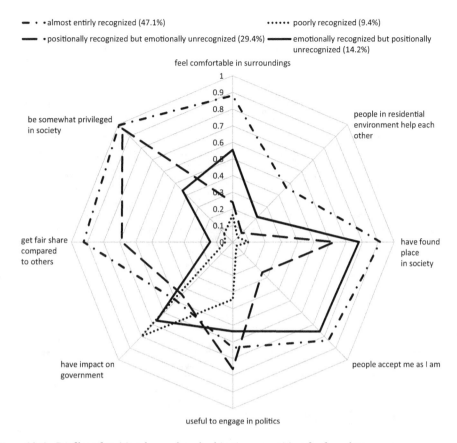

Figure 19.6 Profiles of positional, moral, and subjective recognition for four clusters

- Interpretability is given.
- Validity by external criteria is given.

Relative validity and stability were not tested. This is not necessary, especially if all or nearly all criteria suggest a four-cluster solution. Nonetheless, we will perform a relative internal validity test and test stability. For this purpose, we applied another computer program, namely Latent-Gold 5.0, and computed up to 10 clusters. The information measures (see Table 19.4) suggest a four-cluster solution (BIC, CAIC) and a six-cluster solution (AIC3). Some simulation results (see earlier) suggest AIC3 for categorical variables. Therefore, we further analyze the four- and six-cluster solution to come to a final decision.

Table 19.5 reports the results of internal validity tests. The four-cluster solution results in a slightly higher silhouette coefficient and Dunn index than the six-cluster solution. The average weighted evidence prefers the four-cluster solution, too. According to the thresholds for the silhouette coefficient, this is a weak cluster solution and further tests should be conducted.

Stability was tested by varying the measurement level of the variables. The use of the non-dichotomized indicator items defined as continuous variables leads to computational problems in LatentGold and cannot be further analyzed. Defining these indicator items as ordinal, the BIC suggests a seven- and the CAIC a five-cluster solution, whereas the AIC3 does not indicate a solution within one to 10 clusters. To remain comparable to the aforementioned

Table 19.4 LatentGold output (eight indicators, nominal scale type, missing values excluded)

Classes	LL	BIC(LL)	AIC3(LL)	CAIC(LL)	Entropy-R^2 [a]
1	−5379.1005	10814.0638	10782.2009	10822.0638	----
2	−5028.8155	10176.3396	10108.6309	10193.3396	0.6589
3	−4933.6455	10048.8454	9945.2910	10074.8454	0.6763
4	−4891.8868	10028.1737	9888.7735	10063.1737	0.6586
5	−4864.1043	10035.4545	9860.2085	10079.4545	0.6391
6	−4848.3874	10066.8666	9855.7749	10119.8666	0.6536
7	−4839.4093	10111.7561	9864.8186	10173.7561	0.6822
8	−4832.7305	10161.2443	9878.4611	10232.2443	0.6333
9	−4825.9397	10210.5083	9891.8793	10290.5083	0.6538
10	−4820.3521	10262.1789	9907.7041	10351.1789	0.7069

Note: a) Entropy-R^2 (Vermunt & Magidson, 2013, p. 70) measures the explained variance for a cluster solution with K clusters. The results were generated with LatentGold version 5.0. Calculation was done by the authors. Data are taken from Social Survey Austria 2018 (Hadler et al., 2019), which is freely available at AUSSDA (https://aussda.at/).

Table 19.5 Results of further internal validity tests

	Internal validity		
Cluster	SC (K)	DUNN	AWE
4r	0.2937	0.6919	– [a]
4l	0.2956	0.6891	11274.24
6r	0.2766	0.6489	– [a]
6l	0.2766	0.6397	11788.93

Note: r = poLCA, l = LatentGold, SC was computed using city-block distance.

a) AWE (approximate weight of evidence, Vermunt & Magidson, 2013, p. 71) not available in poLCA. Calculation was done by the authors. Data are taken from Social Survey Austria 2018 (Hadler et al., 2019), which is freely available at AUSSDA (https://aussda.at/).

solutions, we test the stability of four- and six-cluster solutions based on the ordinal scale type (see Table 19.6). All solutions seem to be somewhat stable, whereby the solutions based on the dichotomized indicator are very similar between poLCA and LatentGold. However, the Rand index and especially the adjusted Rand index indicates bigger differences between the solutions based on the original ordinal indicators and the dichotomized solutions. All values for the four-cluster solution are above the quoted thresholds and we can regard the solutions as stable. For the six-cluster solution, the adjusted Rand index falls under the threshold of 0.65 and the recovery is poor.

Finally, we checked the interpretability of a six-cluster solution with dichotomized indicators. It is possible to describe the class profiles as follows: Class 1 (40.3%): "positionally recognized but morally and emotionally unrecognized"; class 2 (23.4%): "almost entirely recognized"; class 3 (14.6%): "positionally recognized but emotionally unrecognized"; class 4 (8.8%): "emotionally and morally recognized but positionally unrecognized"; class 5 (8.5%): "somewhat recognized, somewhat unrecognized"; and class 6 (4.6%): "poorly recognized." The interpretability is not as clear as that for the four-class solution, as the additional classes do not add substantial improvements. In summary, our additional analysis supports the authors' decision.

Table 19.6 Rand indices and adjusted Rand indices

	4l	4r		6l	6r
4r	0.9984		6r	0.9987	
	(0.9960)			(0.9967)	
4l ord	0.8710	0.8708	6l ord	0.7700	0.7695
	(0.7142)	(0.7139)		(0.3809)	(0.3801)

Note: r: poLCA, l: LatentGold, l ord: Latent Gold, ordinal indicators. First line Rand index, second line adjusted Rand index. Calculation was done by the authors. Data are taken from Social Survey Austria 2018 (Hadler et al., 2019), which is freely available at AUSSDA (https://aussda.at/).

9 Summary and recommendations

In the last two decades, a large variety of cluster algorithms and criteria for selecting and validating cluster solutions have been developed. This development focuses on computer science and informatics. The innovations are partially used in applied science. It is difficult to predict which innovations will become established.

Therefore, we can recommend using only those methods that are well documented. It is important to read the definition and computation criteria because they may have the same name but in fact differ in computation method.

Among the discussed methods, we prefer – where appropriate – to use model-based methods because they have a statistical base. Exceptions are a small data set or geographical data. For the first case, hierarchical methods are recommended; for the second, density-based clustering methods can be considered.

The aforementioned innovations may help to solve some of the problems that were mentioned by Everitt (1979). Sometimes, the picture may become unclear when more measures are used. In our experience, the main reason for this unsatisfactory situation is missing substantive theory that enables valid variables and expected clusters to be deduced. As long as this theory is lacking, some cluster analysis problems will remain unsolved.

10 Appendix: data sets and syntax for examples

The used data sets and the syntax are available at doi:10.5281/zenodo.5031638 [1.8.2021].

Note

1 We would like to thank Robert Moosbrugger as one of the authors for his help in preparing the data for analysis.

References

Akogul, S., & Erisoglu, M. (2016). A comparison of information criteria in clustering based on mixture of multivariate normal distributions. *Mathematical and Computational Applications*, *21*(3), 34. https://doi.org/10.3390/mca21030034

Akogul, S., & Erisoglu, M. (2017). An approach for determining the number of clusters in a model-based cluster analysis. *Entropy*, *19*(9), 452. https://doi.org/10.3390/e19090452

Bacher, J., Pöge, A., & Wenzig, K. (2010). *Clusteranalyse*. Oldenbourg Wissenschaftsverlag GmbH. https://doi.org/10.1524/9783486710236

Bacher, J., Wenzig, K., & Vogler, M. (2004). *SPSS TwoStep Cluster – a first evaluation*. Lehrstuhl für Soziolo-gie, WISO-Fakultät, Universität Erlangen-Nürnnberg. Retrieved from www.ssoar.info/ssoar/handle/document/32715

Biernacki, C., Celeux, G., & Govaert, G. (2000). Assessing a mixture model for clustering with the integrated completed likelihood. *IEEE Transactions on Pattern Analysis and Machine Intelligence, 22*(7), 719–725. https://doi.org/10.1109/34.865189

Bradley, P. S., Mangasarian, O. L., & Street, W. N. (1996). Clustering via concave minimization. In *Pro-ceedings of the 9th international conference on neural information processing systems* (pp. 368–374). MIT Press.

Eder, A., Moosbrugger, R., & Hadler, M. (2020). An enquiry in the importance of positional, moral and emotional recognition for social integration in Austria. *Österreichische Zeitschrift Für Soziologie, 45*(2), 213–233. https://link.springer.com/article/10.1007/s11614-020-00415-y

Ester, M., Kriegel, H.-P., Sander, J., & Xu, X. (1996). A density-based algorithm for discovering clusters in large spatial databases with noise. In *Proceedings of the 2nd ACM international conference on knowledge discovery and data mining (KDD)* (pp. 226–231). AAAI Press.

Everitt, B. (1974). *Cluster analysis. Reviews of current research* (Vol. 11). John Wiley & Sons.

Everitt, B. (1979). Unresolved problems in cluster analysis. *Biometrics, 35*(1), 169–181.

Everitt, B., Landau, S., & Leese, M. (2001). *Cluster analysis* (4th ed.). Arnold Publishers.

Fonseca, J. R. S., & Cardoso, M. G. M. S. (2007). Mixture-model cluster analysis using information theo-retical criteria. *Intelligent Data Analysis, 11*(2), 155–173. https://doi.org/10.3233/IDA-2007-11204

Frabioni, M., & Saltstone, R. (1992). The WAIS-R number-of-factors quandary: A cluster analxtic approach to construct validation. *Educational and Psychological Measurement, 52*(3), 603–613.

Fraley, C., & Raftery, A. E. (1999). MCLUST: Software of model-based cluster analysis. *Journal of Clas-sification, 16*(2), 297–306.

Gower, J. C. (1971). A general coefficient of similarity and some of its properties. *Biometrics, 27*(4), 857–871.

Hadler, M., Höllinger, F., & Muckenhuber, J. (2019). *Social Survey Austria 2018 (SUF edition)*. https://doi.org/10.11587/ERDG3O

Hartigan, J. (1974). *Clustering algorithms*. John Wiley & Sons.

Hautamäki, V., Cherednichenko, S., Kärkkäinen, I., Kinnunen, T., & Fränti, P. (2005). Improving K-means by outlier removal. In A. Kaarna, H. Kalviainen, & J. Parkkinen (Eds.), *Lecture notes in computer science: Vol. 3540. Image analysis* (Vol. 3540, pp. 978–987). Springer-Verlag. https://doi.org/10.1007/11499145_99

Hennig, C., Meila, M., Murtagh, F., & Rocci, R. (Eds.). (2016). *Chapman & Hall/CRC handbooks of mod-ern statistical methods. Handbook of cluster analysis*. CRC Press a Chapman & Hall book.

Holmgren, J., Knapen, L., Olsson, V., & Masud, A. P. (2020). On the use of clustering analysis for identi-fication of unsafe places in an urban traffic network. *Procedia Computer Science, 170*, 187–194. https://doi.org/10.1016/j.procs.2020.03.024

Huang, Z. (1998). Extensions to the k-means algorithm for clustering large data sets with categorical values. *Data Mining and Knowledge Discovery, 2*, 283–304.

Jain, A. K., & Dubes, R. C. (1988). *Algorithms for clustering data. Prentice-Hall advanced reference series*. Pren-tice Hall.

Jardine, N., & Sibson, R. (1971). *Mathematical taxonomy*. John Wiley & Sons.

Kaufman, L., & Rousseeuw, P. J. (1990). *Finding groups in data*. John Wiley & Sons. https://doi.org/10.1002/9780470316801

Kent, P., Jensen, R. K., & Kongsted, A. (2014). A comparison of three clustering methods for finding subgroups in MRI, SMS or clinical data: Spss TwoStep cluster analysis, latent gold and SNOB. *BMC Medical Research Methodology, 14*, 113. https://doi.org/10.1186/1471-2288-14-113

Lathrop, R. G., & Williams, J. E. (1989). The Sahpe of the inverse scree test for cluster analysis. *Educational and Psychological Measurement, 50*(2), 325–330.

Lazarsfeld, P. F., & Henry, N. W. (1968). *Latent structure analysis*. Mifflin.

Leisch, F., & Gruen, B. (2020). *CRAN task view: Cluster analysis & finite mixture models*. JKU. https://cran.r-project.org/web/views/Cluster.html

Liu, Y., Li, Z., Xiong, H., Gao, X., & Wu, J. (2010). Understanding of internal clustering validation meas-ures. In *IEEE international conference 13.12.2010–17.12.2010* (pp. 911–916). https://doi.org/10.1109/ICDM.2010.35

McLachlan, G. J., & Basford, K. E. (2000). *Mixture models: Inferences and application to clustering*. Marcel Dekker.

McLachlan, G. J., & Peel, D. (2005). *Finite mixture models. Wiley series in probability and statistics Applied probability and statistics section*. John Wiley & Sons. Retrieved from http://gbv.eblib.com/patron/Full-Record.aspx?p=219004 https://doi.org/10.1002/0471721182

Mojena, R. (1977). Hierarchical grouping methods and stopping rules: An evaluation. *The Computer Journal, 20*(4), 359–363. https://doi.org/10.1093/comjnl/20.4.359

Murtagh, F. (2016). A brief history of cluster analysis. In C. Hennig, M. Meila, F. Murtagh, & R. Rocci (Eds.), *Chapman & hall/CRC handbooks of modern statistical methods. Handbook of cluster analysis* (pp. 21–30). CRC Press a Chapman & Hall book.

Rodriguez, M. Z., Comin, C. H., Casanova, D., Bruno, O. M., Amancio, D. R., Costa, L. d. F., & Rodrigues, F. A. (2019). Clustering algorithms: A comparative approach. *PloS One, 14*(1), e0210236. https://doi.org/10.1371/journal.pone.0210236

Satre-Meloy, A., Diakonova, M., & Grünewald, P. (2020). Cluster analysis and prediction of residential peak demand profiles using occupant activity data. *Applied Energy, 260*, 114246. https://doi.org/10.1016/j.apenergy.2019.114246

Saxena, A., Prasad, M., Gupta, A., Bharill, N., Patel, O. P., Tiwari, A., . . . Lin, C.-T. (2017). A review of clustering techniques and developments. *Neurocomputing, 267*, 664–681. https://doi.org/10.1016/j.neucom.2017.06.053

Schubert, E., Sander, J., Ester, M., Kriegel, H. P., & Xu, X. (2017). DBSCAN revisited. *ACM Transactions on Database Systems, 42*(3), 1–21. https://doi.org/10.1145/3068335

Steinley, D. (2004). Properties of the Hubert-Arabie adjusted rand index. *Psychological Methods, 9*(3), 386–396. https://doi.org/10.1037/1082-989X.9.3.386

Steinley, D. (2016). K-mediods and other criteria for crisp clusters. In C. Hennig, M. Meila, F. Murtagh, & R. Rocci (Eds.), *Chapman & hall/CRC handbooks of modern statistical methods. Handbook of cluster analysis* (pp. 55–66). CRC Press a Chapman & Hall book.

Vermunt, J. K., & Magidson, J. (2000). *Latent GOLD user's guide*. Statistical Innovations Inc.

Vermunt, J. K., & Magidson, J. (2013). *Technical guide for latent GOLD 5.0: Basic, advanced, and syntax*. Statistical Innovations Inc.

Ward, J. H. (1963). Hierarchical grouping to optimize an objective function. *Journal of the American Statistical Association, 58*(301), 236–244. https://doi.org/10.1080/01621459.1963.10500845

Wierzchoń, S. T., & Kłopotek, M. (2018). *Modern algorithms of cluster analysis. Studies in big data* (Vol. 34). Springer-Verlag. http://search.ebscohost.com/login.aspx?direct=true&scope=site&db=nlebk&AN=1670339

Wolfe, J. H. (1970). Pattern clustering by multivariate mixture analysis. *Multivariate Behavioral Research, 5*(3), 329–350. https://doi.org/10.1207/s15327906mbr0503_6

Zgurovsky, M. Z., & Zaychenko, Y. P. (2020). *Big data: Conceptual analysis and applications* (Vol. 58). Springer International Publishing. https://doi.org/10.1007/978-3-030-14298-8

20

TEXT MINING AND TOPIC MODELING

Raphael H. Heiberger and Sebastian Munoz-Najar Galvez

1 Introduction

In the digital age, texts are available in unprecedented quantities. Since the beginning of textual mass production with Gutenberg's printing press (arguably a decisive step in the development of a differentiated modern society (Luhmann, 1995)), the rise of literacy, and, more recently, the inventions of personal computers and the World Wide Web, we have seen a sheer explosion of textual information. Nowadays, everybody is constantly exposed to text, and most people are producers themselves. Textual traces are therefore ubiquitous and can be found in blogs and articles on the web, social media posts and comments, messages of all sorts, e-books, and digital representations of vast (physical) libraries. As a persistent, ubiquitous feature of social life in contemporary societies, textual data constitutes an important part of computational social science (Lazer et al., 2009; Heiberger & Riebling, 2016).

The vast collections of textual traces (*corpora*) often exceed what an individual could read, if such was their only occupation, in an entire lifetime. Researchers trying to utilize such massive text sources, hence, rely on methods stemming from information retrieval (Manning et al., 2008). Most information retrieval tools share the idea to summarize text by reducing its dimensions and yet keep its relevant information (Evans & Aceves, 2016). One relatively early attempt to handle large amounts of textual data was proposed by Deerwester et al. (1990). The widely applied 'latent semantic analysis' (LSA), basically a factor analysis on documents and terms, may be seen as an intellectual 'grandfather' of modern topic models.

LSA paved the way for modern topic modeling, which will be the focus of this paper. As LSA, topic models aim to extract main themes from large corpora. Topics are directly derived from the documents by probabilistic algorithms and consist of words that co-occur across documents. No labeled training data is needed, which is why topic models are generally classified as *unsupervised machine learning* (Jordan & Mitchell, 2015). The possibility to detect thematic patterns "automatically" has proven to be very reliable in practical applications (Landauer, 2007) and has important applications to the social sciences in particular (McFarland et al., 2013; DiMaggio et al., 2013; Grimmer & Stewart, 2013), for instance to trace the development of public discourses (Farrell, 2016) or paradigm shifts in academia (Munoz-Najar Galvez et al., 2020).

Despite the usefulness and popularity of topic models, there exist substantial doubts as to how to assess their validity (Denny & Spirling, 2018). Or, as Chang et al. (2009) put it in a

DOI: 10.4324/9781003025245-24

seminal paper on that issue: is the output of topic models "like reading tea leaves"? One of the main problems is how to choose an appropriate number of topics K, which can alter interpretations considerably and, hence, challenge the quality of any substantial result from topic models. Given its importance, much work has been devoted to that question (Mimno et al., 2011; Grimmer & Stewart, 2013; Roberts et al., 2016). While there cannot be a "right" number, we can make informed choices based on statistical metrics. However, it is much less understood how researchers' choice of K depends on *preprocessing steps* (PS) of the corpus (Denny & Spirling, 2018; Jockers & Mimno, 2013). Such "cleaning" efforts precede almost all topic models and include, for instance, removing stopwords (Schofield et al., 2017a) or reducing the size of a vocabulary by stemming (Schofield & Mimno, 2016). Despite the common use of PS, the steps are typically not discussed, yielding problems to reproduce results and undermining topic models scope (Fokkens et al., 2013). Given the importance of the choice of K and the inevitability of PS, this contribution seeks to investigate how preprocessing affects (i) the choice of K and (ii) the quality of a topic model, that is, its predictive power (Wallach et al., 2009b; Mimno et al., 2011; Roberts et al., 2016) and consistency (Wallach et al., 2009a; Schofield et al., 2017b). Resting on ample tests and empirical results we provide several practical recommendations for researchers which PS affect suitable ranges of K and which PS improve topic models.

For that purpose, the chapter begins with an overview of existing literature applying topic models in social science. This is followed by an overview of structural topic models, after which we present our methodological setup to test the influence of PS on topic models. We close by deriving several practical recommendations for researchers using topic models from our empirical results.

2 Topic models in social science

The increased availability of textual data has already yielded numerous studies from many areas of social sciences. A multitude of communications, interactions, historical events, memoirs, biographies, newspapers, and scientific writings are under consideration. For all accounts, it is essential to have in mind that "the more tightly coupled a text is to social moves in the game of interest, the stronger the inferences that can be made" (Evans & Aceves, 2016, p. 24).

Methodologically, we can differentiate between supervised and unsupervised machine learning tools to analyze large corpora (Jordan & Mitchell, 2015). Although our contribution focuses on methodological aspects of topic modeling, an unsupervised method, a brief glimpse at supervised methods may help to understand topic models' challenges and advantages. Supervised machine learning needs labeled input, often manually coded by researchers. The codes may stem from theories, assumptions, or prior arguments. The trained data can then allow researchers to automatically derive classifications for many more documents and predict labels for unlabeled instances. Thus, supervised methods' input is labeled text with codes that identify some categories of interest, for instance sentiments or ideology. Regressions may be fed with text features to predict an outcome like movie reviews (Joshi et al., 2010). Other predefined text categories include collective sentiments, which can be used to predict stock returns (Tetlock, 2007; Bollen et al., 2011). More sophisticated methods linking training to test data apply deep learning frameworks, for instance, Iyyer et al. (2014) to infer the political position of sentences.

While supervised models can be fruitfully applied in social science, they always need pre-labeled data which is expensive, labor intensive, and, sometimes, simply not available. In such instances, unsupervised methods come into play. Unsupervised models detect underlying patterns and structures in unlabeled data. Thus, researchers use the output of unsupervised methods, among other things, to learn how texts may be classified, instead of feeding the computer with coded text. Unsupervised methods like topic models utilize the co-occurrence of terms in documents to estimate latent thematic dimensions underlying textual data (Jordan & Mitchell, 2015). The derived dimensions can yield valuable insights for social scientists. They allow researchers to investigate textual data "so broad that an entire team of researchers working for several years could only map a fraction of all the texts, transcripts, or archives that define them" (Bail, 2014, p. 469).

One area in which topic models are a valuable source is shifts of public discourse. For instance, DiMaggio et al. (2013) traced changes in newspaper articles reporting on the National Endowment for the Arts in the U.S. Bonilla and Grimmer (2013) used latent Dirichlet allocation (LDA) topic models to document how media and public allocated their attention to terror threats after the U.S. government implemented terror alerts. Examining a specific public discourse with comments on TED talks hosted on YouTube, Schwemmer and Jungkunz (2019) find that only a few talks address social inequalities, and if they do, theyreceive more negative commentary than do others.

The political arena is *per se* characterized by the availability of text due to speeches, party manifestos, and parliamentary debates. Many studies in that area exploit textual data. Utilizing press releases of the U.S. Senate, Grimmer and Stewart (2013) show that aligned, more ideological senators are more likely to participate and, hence, shape policy debates. His findings provide one cause for the increasingly polarized discourse in the U.S. Farrell (2016) also focuses on polarization. Using written and verbal texts produced by climate change countermovements, he shows that corporate funding influences the actual thematic content and discursive prevalence. Based on German parliamentary debates, Geese (2019) traces positions of parties and legislators in regard to the sensitive issue of migration during the "refugee crisis". Fligstein et al. (2017) investigate minutes of the U.S. Federal Open Market Committee. Using topic models, they find that the Federal Reserve's framework of macroeconomic theory prevented policymakers from relating to bubbles on the housing market, subprime mortgages, and related financial instruments. The Federal Reserve was therefore unable to react to the unexpected situation.

Another important area of studies using textual data focuses on the workings of science itself. A seminal paper on hot and cold topics in science stems from Griffiths and Steyvers (2004), in which they show how topic models help to reveal scientific trends. Retrieving information from large-scale corpora has also yielded valuable insights in the reconstruction of the history of a scientific field by investigating ebbs and flows in computational linguistics (Anderson et al., 2012). Marshall (2013) explored themes and shifts within the discipline of demography in England and France. She found an alignment of each country's cultural and institutional setting to the way each country frames its decline in fertility. In addition, Evans and Foster (2011) explained scientists' choice of research strategy, while Shi et al. (2015) enabled researchers to model the process of scientific discovery.

Besides using topics to describe and trace discourses, topic models can also be employed to derive metrics representing textual properties. Bail (2016) uses a coefficient of discursive variation to predict that advocacy organizations maximize public attention if they diversify the discursive content of their messages up to a certain degree. Making use of a representative sample of U.S. dissertations in education, Munoz-Najar Galvez et al. (2020) investigate topics' contribution to academic careers. In particular, they compute the empirical entropy of topic proportion in each dissertation to measure the document's specialization and study the relation of this property to employability.

This short account is somewhat eclectic and does not aim to provide a comprehensive overview, for such see, for instance, Evans and Aceves (2016). Yet, the rich literature applying topic models shows the importance of assessing their validity. All of the aforementioned studies, implicitly or explicitly, had to make preprocessing decisions and deal with the issue of selecting the number of topics K. Therefore, the remainder of this chapter examines how common preprocessing steps affect the choice of K and quality of topics. For that purpose, we will use the same sample as in Munoz-Najar Galvez et al. (2020).

3 Using (structural) topic models

Topic models provide users with the ability to represent large corpora by their latent dimensions derived from statistical distributions of words and documents, which makes them a method for automated content analysis. The main idea of topic models is to summarize a collection of text documents (the corpus) by reducing their dimensions while preserving relevant thematic information. Topic models are guided by probabilistic properties of words and documents and no further "input" (like labeled texts) is needed.[1] During the iterative topic model process, a set of documents is assigned to meaningful themes (i.e., the *topics*). These topics are directly derived from the documents by probabilistic algorithms and rely on the notion that words co-occurring in and across documents describe meaningful topics.

The pioneering work by Blei et al. (2003) proposed the use of the *latent Dirichlet allocation* probability distribution as the basis for estimating topics. In this generative model, each topic is a probability distribution over words, and each document is modeled as a mixture of different topics (each a multinomial distribution over words) in different proportions. Given a desired number of topics K and a set of D documents containing words from a vocabulary V, LDA models infer K topics, which are each a multinomial distribution over words V. Thus, the topics are a mixture of words V with probability β for each word (mentioned earlier), which gives us each word's association to each topic. The intuition is straightforward: the more often words co-occur in documents, the higher the probability that they constitute a topic.

At the same time, a document is also considered a mixture of topics, so that a single document can be assigned to multiple themes. The topic proportions are given by parameter θ. By design, all topics occur within each document, however, the proportion of θ gives us the strength of connection between a topic (itself an ordered vector of words) and a document. Finally, it is important to note that the sampling process of LDA draws for each topic and each document from an eponymous Dirichlet distribution. Hence, the same multinomial distribution is used for all documents in a corpus.

Many varieties of the LDA algorithm have been proposed, some accounting for local word order instead of pure "bag-of-words" (Griffiths et al., 2005), some making use of document dependencies like citations or hyperlinks (Chang & Blei, 2010), and yet others that claim to utilize the temporal order of documents (Blei & Lafferty, 2006).

In this chapter, we apply *structural topic models* (STM), a variation of probabilistic topic models designed explicitly for use in social research (Roberts et al., 2014). Its key feature is that it enables researchers to incorporate document metadata and utilize document-specific information (e.g., year, source, etc.) to improve the estimation of topics. These are the covariates of a document d are denoted as X_d. As with an LDA topic model, each document is still assumed to contain a mixture of K topics and words are aligned to topics with a certain probability β. As opposed to the conventional LDA model, the topic proportions θ in a STM depend on a logistic-normal generalized regression, such that $\theta \sim LogisticNormal(X_d, \Sigma)$. That means that for each word, a topic is drawn from the *specified* distribution of a document based on its covariates values X_d (not a uniform distribution across all documents like in classic LDA). This provides a measure of topic prevalence by X_d, the covariate used (for instance, prevalence over time). It has been argued that including the date of a document is especially useful to model (changing) discourses (Farrell, 2016). In addition to topic prevalence, the metadata can be used to estimate topical content. The content side of the STM allows the researcher to use categorical variables to model the probability distribution over words in each topic. Allowing content to vary on covariates opens up the possibility of analyzing, for instance, gender differences in framing the same topics (for an example, see Roberts et al., 2014, p. 1078).

In short, conditioning the word and document distribution by employing additional information about the documents allows the STM to base a word's topic assignment on a document-specific distribution, not only – as in the regular LDA – on a general distribution that is the same for all documents. It has been shown that the incorporation of covariates improves the results of the topic quality substantially (Roberts et al., 2014, 2016). Or in the words of its developers, "These additional covariates provide a way of 'structuring' the prior distributions in the topic model, injecting valuable information into the inference procedure". In addition, the STM solves another technical issue in finding the optimal starting parameters and providing consistent results by a "spectral initialization" (Roberts et al., 2016).

Summing up, topics are the result of iterative learning steps derived from a *two-step clustering approach*: our model learns the mixture of topics that make up each document and the words that belong to each topic via successive updates to two sets of prior multinomial distributions, (i) one of documents over topics and (ii) one of topics over words. As with grounded theory, topics allow multiple interpretations depending on the perspective we use to look at them (Inglis & Foster, 2018). Topics do not provide a "deterministic" reduction of dimensions. Rather, it is – used on its own – an exploratory approach (like most unsupervised learning tools).

4 Influence of preprocessing decisions on the chosen number and quality of topics

4.1 Decisions while preparing textual data

Working with textual data is messy, in the sense that large portions of an unprocessed vocabulary may contain little to no information, conditional on the research question. According to *Zipf's law*, the frequency distribution of words resemble a power law, meaning that any word is inversely proportional to its rank in the frequency table (Manning et al., 1999). Thus, few words like "the", "can", "non", and so on appear very often. Because all texts contain those stopwords, they are of relatively little value to extract meanings and themes. One common preprocessing step is therefore the removal of stopwords. While the removal of most common stopwords seems obvious, an extended custom list of stopwords can also decrease the quality of a topic model (Schofield et al., 2017a). In addition, extending stopwords is time consuming and decisions are often hard to reproduce. Thus, the first *preprocessing step* (PS) we test is to remove a short list of stopwords or use an extended list. As *default*, we used the snowball stopword list from the stopwords package in R and a custom list containing time-related words ("year", "january", etc.), numbers ("one", "tenth", etc.) and miscellaneous subject-related words ("examine", "study", etc.).

Another very common PS is to reduce the size of a vocabulary by limiting all words to root form. If the process is rule based, it is called *stemming* (Manning et al., 2008). Among the most popular of its kind is the Porter stemmer (Porter, 1980). Words with the same root (e.g., "statistical", "statistics", "statistic") are thereby conflated to a single word ("statist"). While stemmers are commonly used in topic models, no empirical evidence is found that stemming improves model quality (Schofield & Mimno, 2016).

Another popular tool to reduce different forms of words to the same base is *lemmatization*. This strategy is dictionary based and not rule based. Lemmatizers use a dictionary in which standardized word forms are linked to grammatical forms (for instance, singular-plural, grammatical endings like "-ing"). While the method is less likely to overconflate, it depends on the availability of a dictionary and is much more expensive computationally. Thus, we compare as *second PS* stemming and lemmatizing the corpus, and, given evidence that reducing the vocabulary does not improve model quality (Schofield & Mimno, 2016), we will also compare both to a corpus with no stemmers or lemmas. We use the R package by Rinker (2018) to implement this second PS.

The third and last PS is using ngrams to concatenate words appearing next to each other in a text (Jurafsky & Martin, 2000). Bigrams (two-grams) consist of neighboring words, trigrams of three, and so on. For instance, "United States" is a bigram. Not combing both to "United_ States" would lead to less information since each word on its own transports a different meaning. There exist different methods to find the most meaningful and frequent ngrams in a text, yet results are rather similar. We will use the "lambda" method proposed by Blaheta and Johnson (2001) as implemented in quanteda (Benoit et al., 2018).

Combining the choices of each PS – stopwords, stemming, ngrams – yields 12 different setups. An overview of the model varieties is given in Table 20.1. We assess them in terms of quality of topics and approximate the number of K. In total, we will therefore compare 120 Ms. We run models in the range $K = [10, 100]$ with step 10 resting on previous validation procedures presented in Munoz-Najar Galvez et al. (2020), which results in a choice of $K = 60$. In the respective paper, we used extended stopwords, Porter stemming, and trigrams.

4.2 Metrics

As with other techniques to reduce dimensions of data (e.g., cluster analysis), a permanent challenge is (i) to choose an appropriate number of dimensions K, although the number of relevant themes is not known a priori, and (ii) to assess the quality of the extracted dimensions. A low value of K might render models coarse; a high value could result in a model that is too complex. The choice of K is a widely recognized issue in topic modeling (e.g., Chang et al., 2009; Wallach et al., 2009a; McFarland et al., 2013; Rule et al., 2015).

Table 20.1 Overview of model varieties

Model abbreviation	Word reduction	Stopwords	Ngrams
lemma_def_bi	Lemmas	Default	Bigrams
lemma_def_tri	Lemmas	Default	Trigrams
lemma_ext_bi	Lemmas	Extended	Bigrams
lemma_ext_tri	Lemmas	Extended	Trigrams
none_def_bi	None	Default	Bigrams
none_def_tri	None	Default	Trigrams
none_ext_bi	None	Extended	Bigrams
none_ext_tri	None	Extended	Trigrams
port_def_bi	Porter	Default	Bigrams
port_def_tri	Porter	Default	Trigrams
port_ext_bi	Porter	Extended	Bigrams
port_ext_tri	Porter	Extended	Trigrams

A number of metrics have been developed to guide researchers' choice of K, foremost *semantic coherence* (Mimno et al., 2011) and *exclusivity* (Roberts et al., 2014, 2016). The semantic coherence of a topic is computed by calculating the frequency with which high-probability topic words tend to co-occur in documents. However, semantic coherence alone can be misleading since high values can simply be obtained by very common words of a topic that occur together in most documents. To account for the desired statistical discrimination between topics, we consider a topic's exclusivity. This measure provides us with the extent to which the high-probability words of a topic are distinct to it. Both exclusivity and coherence complement each other and, hence, are examined in concert to give us an impression of whether topics represent word distributions in documents and provide at the same time differentiated latent thematic dimensions.

The developers of STM recommend that researchers look for the "semantic coherence-exclusivity frontier" – namely the specification after which allowing for more topics fails to produce models that dominate others in terms of semantic coherence and exclusivity (Roberts et al., 2014, p. 7). Thus, what we are looking for is when both indicators build a *plateau*, that is, they do not improve (much) with higher K's. This gives us an upper limit for a reasonable K.

Finding a suitable range for K is a challenging interpretive task. Semantic coherence and exclusivity can aid in this endeavor but, ultimately, a researcher will want topics that allow for a substantive interpretation. Another strategy that aids researchers in this task is to look for topics that appear constantly across different specifications of the value of K. We can think of that as a test whether topics are "inherited" from model to model as K grows.

For that purpose, we employ two metrics, *variety of information* (VI) and *redundancy*. VI measures the similarity between two sets of clusters and computes the distance between these partitions (Meila, 2003). In topic modeling, it is used to compare topic assignments for documents (Wallach et al., 2009a). That is, each document is assigned to its maximum topic. Those assignments are then checked across different K.

Redundancy is a metric we introduced to the context of model validation in order to formalize the following intuition: we want to select a model that produces topics that appear again in many other models with different specifications of K (Munoz-Najar Galvez et al., 2020). Redundancy is a measure of local clustering for bipartite networks (Latapy et al., 2008) that ranges from 0 to 1, where one is complete redundancy. A bipartite network has two modes; nodes can connect across modes but not within their own mode. A node is redundant in a bipartite network when its removal would not affect the shared neighborhood of nodes in the alternate mode.

We construct a bipartite network with two kinds of nodes: models and topic groups. Models connect to a topic group when one of its topics is assigned to the topic group by the Topic-Check algorithm. TopicCheck (Chuang et al., 2015) is a tool that allows up-to-one mapping of topics across models. In our bipartite network, a model is redundant when it connects to many topical groups that, in turn, connect to many other models. We can then interpret a redundant model as one with topics that align with the discoveries of many other specifications.

Finally, we will assess the predictive quality of topics by using *held-out likelihood* (LL). This is "a measure of predictive power to evaluate comparative performance", in this case among models that allow for different numbers of topics (Stewart, 2015, p. 24). We first subset 10% of documents and "hold out" half of the words in them. We then evaluate the likelihood of the held-out words. Higher likelihoods indicate a more predictive model. In general, LL is rising linear with K (more topics, more predictive power).

In sum, our experimental setup seeks to test the influence of PS on topic models. We first test with *exclusivity* and *coherence* whether PS yield different ranges of suitable K. Second, we investigate if and how PS affect the consistency (i.e., topics' redundancy) and predictability of topic models. Both aspects combined assess the "quality" of topic models, since exploratory studies – for which topic models are often used – lose a lot of appeal if they change with *K*.

4.3 Results

Comparing exclusivity and coherence in search for a suitable *K* yields rather different results across PS. The plateaus differ along all three dimensions, that is, we find various optima if we compare one horizontally (same stemming procedure, different stopwords and ngrams) or vertically (different stemmers). For the least reduced PS (none_(def)_(bi)) we would choose *K* = (60: 80), where both exclusivity and coherence form a plateau. Only changing the decision to use bigrams *and* trigrams (none_(def)_(tri)) shifts coherence to the right and we would argue for *K* = (80: 90). Implementing a stemmer (stem_(def)_(bi)) would also yield different results with a first plateau appearing at *K* = 40, while using a lemmatizer (stem_(def)_(bi)) would underline our choice of *K* = (60: 80).

In general, our results reveal that the use of bigrams or trigrams considerably change both exclusivity and coherence. That is somewhat surprising, since the kind of ngrams used is a decision that is rarely discussed by researchers doing topic models. A second take-away from our first test is that the choice of stemmers yields varying *K*'s too. Lemmatization especially alters results of coherence. Finally, we find that the choice of stopword removal has the least impact, confirming results on topic coherence by Schofield et al. (2017a).

Our second objective is to estimate the *consistency* of topics across *K*. In line with other studies (Wallach et al., 2009a; Schofield et al., 2017b), we use consistency as an indicator for the quality of a topic model. Thus, which decisions during PS yield the most consistent topics so that topics are inherited across *K*?

To answer this question, we use redundancy and VI explained earlier. Figure 20.2 shows the redundancy of topics for each PS for models with 10 to 100 topics. It is initially clear that all models find topics that align with the majority of topics discovered by other models with higher *K*. However, we see some moderate differences between PS. The least modified sample (none_(def)_(bi)) is located among the PS with the lowest redundancy. The highest values of redundancy can be found, in contrast, for (none_def_tri), (none_ext_tri), and (port_def_tri). Thus again, using trigrams in addition to bigrams changes the topical space. It is a striking result that the PS with the best performances (highest consistency) all use trigrams. Instead, lemmatization does not seem to improve redundancy, neither do most of the solutions using Porter stemming. Also, employing extended stopword lists does not enhance consistency; for some instances it even impairs results (e.g., port_def_tri vs. port_ext_tri).

Using VI, we can now explore how different PS relate to each other in terms of consistency, or in other words, which PS yield similar results. The greater the VI, the greater the *dissimilarity* between two topic-document assignments (Wallach et al., 2009a). Hence, we fix *K* and compare how close or distant the document classification is between PS. While similarity decreases with growing *K* as expected, we find the darkest spots at the same rasters in each subplot (Figure 20.3). Across *K* the most similar pairs are between extended and default stopwords and their respective counterparts, that is, port_def_bi and port_ext_bi, port_def_tri, and port_ext_bi, and so on. Thus, the least impact on topics has, again, stopword removal, underlining previous findings (Schofield et al., 2017a). That means, at the same time, that decisions in the other two PS *change* topic-document assignments.

Finally, we use held-out likelihood to assess the predictive quality of different PS. Because the trend is the same for all PS (more topics, higher likelihood), we summarize results in boxplots.

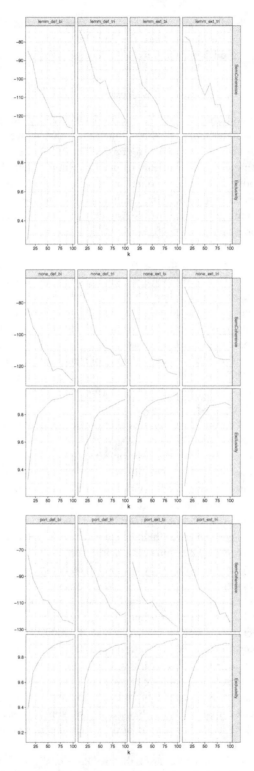

Figure 20.1a–c   Plots for semantic coherence (upper panel) and exclusivity (lower panel) across *K* and PS

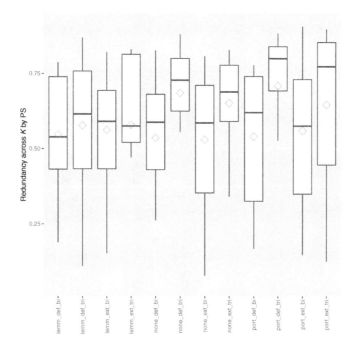

Figure 20.2 Redundancy of models in the model-topical group bipartite network. Dots depict the mean redundancy for all *K*

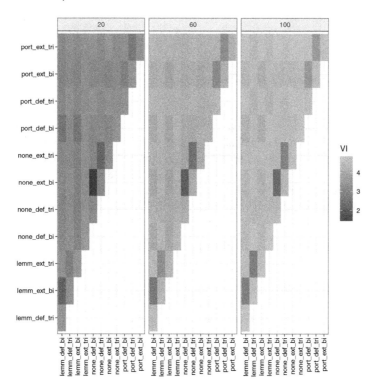

Figure 20.3 The variation of information between different preprocessing steps

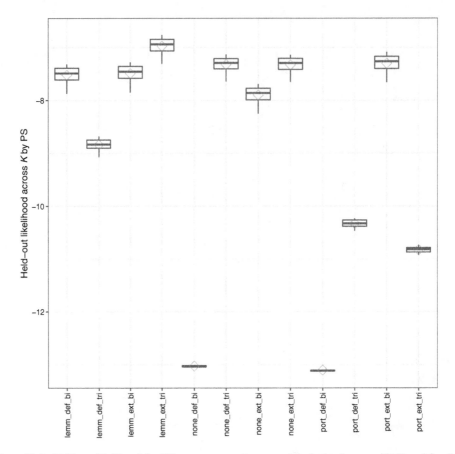

Figure 20.4 Held-out likelihood for different preprocessing steps; dots depict the mean likelihood for all *K*

Figure 20.4 reveals apparent differences. The "baseline" (none_def_bi) performs much weaker than most and builds with port_def_bi the rear-end. We find highest predictive power for lemm_ext_tri, none_ext_tri, and none_def_tri, underlining the importance of trigrams. However, using trigrams in combination with Porter stemming performs badly. Another pattern that Figure 20.4 reveals is that extended stopwords increase the performance for most PS, for example lemm_ext_tri vs. its counterpart with only default stopwords.

5 Discussion

Selecting the number of topics *K* is one of the most problematic choices in topic modeling and is recognized by many scholars (McFarland et al., 2013; Wallach et al., 2009a; Farrell, 2016; Roberts et al., 2016). At the same time, almost all topic models rest on preprocessed texts, in particular the removal of stopwords, some sort of stemming, and ngrams (Schofield et al., 2017b). The influence of these PS on the crucial decision to choose a final model with a certain number of topics is, however, mostly unknown. With the exception of Denny and Spirling (2018), the link between PS decisions and selection of *K* remains widely unexplored.

We can derive several practical recommendations for researchers using topic models: first, PS change the range of suitable *K* substantively. Thus, decisions made during cleaning the corpus are wide ranging, although only a few researchers discuss their PS. Our results strongly suggest that researchers spell out details of PS. Second, we find across all metrics that the decision to use up to trigrams changes the choice of *K*. In addition, trigrams yield more predictive and more consistent results. Therefore, it seems advisable to include trigrams and not only use bigrams. A third recommendation based on our empirical results is that, in contrast to ngrams, the expense of generating extended stopword lists is improving neither predictive power nor consistency. The same holds, to a somewhat lesser extent, for reducing vocabulary by lemmatizing or stemming. While stopwords and stemmers or lemmas *do* change the corridor of suitable *K*, they do not improve quality of topics in terms of consistency or predictive power. Hence, a third derivative of our extensive investigation of PS is to refrain from using (work-intensive) extended stopwords and rule-based or dictionary-based reductions of vocabulary. If interpretation affords the removal or conflation of certain terms, it can still be done *after* running the topic models (Schofield et al., 2017b).

However, our contribution is based on a specific sample. Future research may seek to extend the sample on other text genres. Providing our code may facilitate such undertakings.[2] Despite the focus on an academic text sample, our framework presents a general way for researchers to cope with the challenges of selecting *K* and assessing the consistency and predictive power of topic solutions. To improve reproducibility of topic models, we suggest that researchers spell out PS decisions. To extend models' scope, researchers might want to test different numbers of *K* and compare results, especially if the objective is to interpret topics in a substantial way. Using different metrics and, hence, perspectives presented in this paper may support such efforts.

Notes

1 However, there are hyperparameters that can be used to control different aspects of initialization and model convergence.
2 The R-code of this project can be found at https://github.com/RapHei/Handbook_CSS_TM.

References

Anderson, A., McFarland, D., & Jurafsky, D. (2012). Towards a computational history of the ACL: 1980–2008. In *Proceedings of the ACL-2012 special workshop on rediscovering 50 years of discoveries, ACL'12* (pp. 13–21). Association for Computational Linguistics.

Bail, C. A. (2014). The cultural environment: Measuring culture with big data. *Theory and Society, 43*(3–4), 465–482.

Bail, C. A. (2016). Cultural carrying capacity: Organ donation advocacy, discursive framing, and social media engagement. *Social Science €3 Medicine, 165*, 280–288.

Benoit, K., Watanabe, K., Wang, H., Nulty, P., Obeng, A., Miller, S., & Matsuo, A. (2018). quanteda: An R package for the quantitative analysis of textual data. *Journal of Open Source Software, 3*(30), 774.

Blaheta, D., & Johnson, M. (2001). Unsupervised learning of multi-word verbs. In *Proceedings of the ACL 2001 workshop on collocation: Computational extraction, analysis and exploitation* (pp. 54–60). Association for Computational Linguistics (ACL).

Blei, D. M., & Lafferty, J. D. (2006). Dynamic topic models. In *Proceedings of the 23rd international conference on machine learning* (pp. 113–120). Association for Computational Machinery (ACM).

Blei, D. M., Ng, A. Y., & Jordan, M. I. (2003). Latent Dirichlet allocation. *The Journal of Machine Learning Research, 3*, 993–1022.

Bollen, J., Mao, H., & Zeng, X. (2011). Twitter mood predicts the stock market. *Journal of Computational Science, 2*(1), 1–8.

Bonilla, T., & Grimmer, J. (2013). Elevated threat levels and decreased expectations: How democracy handles terrorist threats. *Poetics, 41*(6), 650–669.

Chang, J., & Blei, D. M. (2010). Hierarchical relational models for document networks. *Annals of Applied Statistics, 4*(1), 124–150. Publisher: Institute of Mathematical Statistics.

Chang, J., Gerrish, S., Wang, C., Boyd-graber, J. L., & Blei, D. M. (2009). Reading tea leaves: How humans interpret topic models. In Y. Bengio, D. Schuurmans, J. D. Lafferty, C. L. I. Williams, & A. Culotta (Eds.), *Advances in neural information processing systems* (Vol. 22, pp. 288–296). Curran Associates, Inc.

Chuang, J., Roberts, M. E., Stewart, B. M., Weiss, R., Tingley, D., Grimmer, J., & Heer, J. (2015). TopicCheck: Interactive alignment for assessing topic model stability. In *Proceedings of the 2015 conference of the North American chapter of the association for computational linguistics: Human language technologies* (pp. 175–184). Association for Computational Linguistics (ACL).

Deerwester, S., Dumais, S. T., Furnas, G. W., Landauer, T. K., & Harshman, R. (1990). Indexing by latent semantic analysis. *Journal of the American Society for Information Science, 41*(6), 391–407.

Denny, M. J., & Spirling, A. (2018). Text preprocessing for unsupervised learning: Why it matters, when it misleads, and what to do about it. *Political Analysis, 26*(2), 168–189. Publisher: Cambridge University Press.

DiMaggio, P., Nag, M., & Blei, D. (2013). Exploiting affinities between topic modeling and the sociological perspective on culture: Application to newspaper coverage of U.S. government arts funding. *Poetics, 41*(6), 570–606.

Evans, J. A., & Aceves, P. (2016). Machine translation: Mining text for social theory. *Annual Review of Sociology, 42*(1), 21–50.

Evans, J. A., & Foster, J. G. (2011). Metaknowledge. *Science, 331*(6018), 721–725.

Farrell, J. (2016). Corporate funding and ideological polarization about climate change. *Proceedings of the National Academy of Sciences, 113*(1), 92–97.

Fligstein, N., Stuart Brundage, J., & Schultz, M. (2017). Seeing like the fed: Culture, cognition, and framing in the failure to anticipate the financial crisis of 2008. *American Sociological Review, 82*(5), 879–909. Publisher: SAGE Publications Inc.

Fokkens, A., van Erp, M., Postma, M., Pedersen, T., Vossen, P., & Freire, N. (2013). Offspring from reproduction problems: What replication failure teaches Us. In *Proceedings of the 51st annual meeting of the association for computational linguistics* (Vol. 1, Long Papers, pp. 1691–1701). Association for Computational Linguistics.

Geese, L. (2019). *Immigration-related speechmaking in a party-constrained parliament: Evidence from the 'refugee crisis' of the 18th German Bundestag (2013–2017)*. German Politics and Routledge.

Griffiths, T. L., & Steyvers, M. (2004). Finding scientific topics. *Proceedings of the National Academy of Sciences, 101*(Suppl. 1), 5228–5235.

Griffiths, T. L., Steyvers, M., Blei, D. M., & Tenenbaum, J. B. (2005). Integrating topics and syntax. In L. K. Saul, Y. Weiss, & L. Bottou (Eds.), *Advances in neural information processing systems* (Vol. 17, pp. 537–544). MIT Press.

Grimmer, J., & Stewart, B. M. (2013). Text as data: The promise and pitfalls of automatic content analysis methods for political texts. *Political Analysis, 21*(3), 267–297.

Heiberger, R. H., & Riebling, J. R. (2016). Installing computational social science: Facing the challenges of new information and communication technologies in social science. *Methodological Innovations, 9*, 1–11.

Inglis, M., & Foster, C. (2018). Five decades of mathematics education research. *Journal for Research in Mathematics Education, 49*(4), 462–500. Publisher: National Council of Teachers of Mathematics.

Iyyer, M., Enns, P., Boyd-Graber, J., & Resnik, P. (2014). Political ideology detection using recursive neural networks. In *Proceedings of the 52nd annual meeting of the association for computational linguistics* (Vol. 1, Long Papers, pp. 1113–1122). Association for Computational Linguistics.

Jockers, M. L., & Mimno, D. (2013). Significant themes in 19th-century literature. *Poetics, 41*(6), 750–769.

Jordan, M. I., & Mitchell, T. M. (2015). Machine learning: Trends, perspectives, and prospects. *Science, 349*(6245), 255–260.

Joshi, M., Das, D., Gimpel, K., & Smith, N. A. (2010). Movie reviews and revenues: An experiment in text regression. In *Human language technologies: The 2010 annual conference of the North American chapter of the association for computational linguistics, HLT'10* (pp. 293–296). Association for Computational Linguistics.

Jurafsky, D., & Martin, J. H. (2000). *Speech and language processing*. Prentice Hall.

Landauer, T. K. (2007). *Handbook of latent semantic analysis*. Lawrence Erlbaum Associates. Google-Books-ID: jgVWCuFXePEC.

Latapy, M., Magnien, C., & Vecchio, N. D. (2008). Basic notions for the analysis of large two-mode networks. *Social Networks, 30*(1), 31–48.

Lazer, D., Pentland, A., Adamic, L., Aral, S., Barabasi, A.-L., Brewer, D., . . . Alstyne, M. V. (2009). Computational social science. *Science*, *323*(5915), 721–723.

Luhmann, N. (1995). *Social systems*. Stanford University Press. Google-Books-ID: zVZQW4gxXk4C.

Manning, C. D., Manning, C. D., & Schitze, H. (1999). *Foundations of statistical natural language processing*. MIT Press. Google-Books-ID: YiFDxbEX3SUC.

Manning, C. D., Raghavan, P., & Schitze, H. (2008). *Introduction to information retrieval*. Cambridge University Press. Google-Books-ID: t1PoSh4uwVcC.

Marshall, E. A. (2013). Defining population problems: Using topic models for cross-national comparison of disciplinary development. *Poetics*, *41*(6), 701–724.

McFarland, D. A., Ramage, D., Chuang, J., Heer, J., Manning, C. D., & Jurafsky, D. (2013). Differentiating language usage through topic models. *Poetics*, *41*(6), 607–625.

Meila, M. (2003). Comparing clusterings by the variation of information. In B. Scholkopf & M. K. Warmuth (Eds.), *Learning theory and Kernel machines, lecture notes in computer science* (pages 173–187). Springer.

Mimno, D., Wallach, H. M., Talley, E., Leenders, M., & McCallum, A. (2011). Optimizing semantic coherence in topic models. In *Proceedings of the conference on empirical methods in natural language processing* (pp. 262–272). Association for Computational Machinery (ACM).

Munoz-Najar Galvez, S., Heiberger, R., & McFarland, D. (2020). Paradigm wars revisited: A cartography of graduate research in the field of education (1980–2010). *American Educational Research Journal*, *57*(2), 612–652.

Porter, M. (1980). An algorithm for suffix stripping. *Program*, *14*(3), 130–137. Publisher: MCB UP Ltd.

Rinker, T. W. (2018). *Textstem: Tools for stemming and lemmatizing text*. Retrieved from http://github.com/trinker/textstem

Roberts, M. E., Stewart, B. M., & Airoldi, E. M. (2016). A model of text for experimentation in the social sciences. *Journal of the American Statistical Association*, *111*(515), 988–1003.

Roberts, M. E., Stewart, B. M., Tingley, D., Lucas, C., Leder-Luis, J., Gadarian, S. K., . . . Rand, D. G. (2014). Structural topic models for open-ended survey responses. *American Journal of Political Science*, *58*(4), 1064–1082.

Rule, A., Cointet, J.-P., & Bearman, P. S. (2015). Lexical shifts, substantive changes, and continuity in State of the Union discourse, 1790–2014. *Proceedings of the National Academy of Sciences*, *112*(35), 10837–10844.

Schofield, A., Magnusson, M., & Mimno, D. (2017a). Pulling out the stops: Rethinking stopword removal for topic models. In *Proceedings of the 15th conference of the European chapter of the association for computational linguistics* (Vol. 2, Short Papers, pp. 432–436). Association for Computational Linguistics.

Schofield, A., Magnusson, M., Thompson, L., & Mimno, D. (2017b). Understanding text pre-processing for latent Dirichlet allocation. In *Proceedings of the 15th conference of the European chapter of the association for computational linguistics* (Vol. 2, pp. 432–436). Association for Computational Linguistics.

Schofield, A., & Mimno, D. (2016). Comparing apples to apple: The effects of stemmers on topic models. *Transactions of the Association for Computational Linguistics*, *4*, 287–300.

Schwemmer, C., & Jungkunz, S. (2019). Whose ideas are worth spreading? The representation of women and ethnic groups in TED talks. *Political Research Exchange*, *1*(1), 1–23. Routledge. https://doi.org/10.1080/2474736X.2019.1646102

Shi, F., Foster, J. G., & Evans, J. A. (2015). Weaving the fabric of science: Dynamic network models of science's unfolding structure. *Social Networks*, *43*, 73–85.

Stewart, B. M. (2015). *Three papers in political methodology*. Retrieved July 17, 2015, from T16:52:37Z.

Tetlock, P. C. (2007). Giving content to investor sentiment: The role of media in the stock market. *The Journal of Finance*, *62*(3), 1139–1168.

Wallach, H. M., Mimno, D. M., & McCallum, A. (2009a). Rethinking LDA: Why priors matter. In *Advances in neural information processing systems* (pp. 1973–1981). Association for Computational Machinery (ACM).

Wallach, H. M., Murray, I., Salakhutdinov, R., & Mimno, D. (2009b). Evaluation methods for topic models. In *Proceedings of the 26th annual international conference on machine learning* (pp. 1105–1112). ACM.

21

FROM FREQUENCY COUNTS TO CONTEXTUALIZED WORD EMBEDDINGS

The Saussurean turn in automatic content analysis

Gregor Wiedemann and Cornelia Fedtke

1 Introduction

Text, the written representation of human thought and communication in natural language, has been a major source of data for social science research since its early beginnings. While quantitative approaches seek to make certain contents measurable, for example through word counts or reliable categorization (coding) of longer text sequences, qualitative social researchers put more emphasis on systematic ways to generate a deep understanding of social phenomena from text. For the latter, several qualitative research methods such as qualitative content analysis (Mayring, 2010), grounded theory methodology (Glaser & Strauss, 2005), and (critical) discourse analysis (Foucault, 1982) have been developed. Although their methodological foundations differ widely, both currents of empirical research need to rely to some extent on the interpretation of text data against the background of its context. At the latest with the global expansion of the internet in the digital era and the emergence of social networks, the huge mass of text data poses a significant problem to empirical research relying on human interpretation. For their studies, social scientists have access to newspaper texts representing public media discourse, web documents from companies, parties, or NGO websites, political documents from legislative processes such as parliamentary protocols, bills and corresponding press releases, and for some years now micro-posts and user comments from social media. Computational support is inevitable even to process samples of such document volumes that could easily comprise millions of documents.

Although automatic methods of content analysis and text mining already have been employed in social and political science for decades, for a long time their application was restricted to rather simplistic methods of quantifying word usage (Wiedemann, 2013). Especially qualitatively oriented researchers remained skeptical about computational methods since they do not seem to contribute to a deeper understanding of expressed contents (ibid.).

Fortunately, natural language processing (NLP), a subfield of computer science and artificial intelligence (AI) research, made remarkable progress in recent years improving computational capabilities to represent semantics. The rapid evolvement in neural networks for so-called *deep learning* with big data currently revolutionizes the way natural language is processed in computer science. Of particular interest is the representation of meaning in the form of high-dimensional,

DOI: 10.4324/9781003025245-25

dense vectors, so-called *embeddings*, which we will discuss in more detail in this article. For applied sciences like empirical social research, this new development bears a huge potential to address concerns about the suitability of previously existing automatic content analysis approaches. However, the earlier development also has shown that the transfer and adaptation of state-of-the-art models from computer science into social science applications can take quite a long time. For instance, it took about 15 years for the machine learning approach of topic modeling from the publication of a seminal paper (Blei et al., 2003) to enter the standard toolbox of the social sciences (Maier et al., 2018). Other NLP methods with an even longer history such as supervised text classification with logistic regression or support vector machines are still rarely used (Wiedemann, 2019).

Grimmer and Stewart (2013) argue in a widely cited review article about automatic content analysis, "all quantitative models of language are wrong, but some are useful" (p. 269f). Their usefulness should be evaluated regarding their ability to perform social science tasks such as document categorization, the discovery of new useful categorization schemes and the measuring of theoretically relevant quantities from large collections. Regarding this claim, it is interesting to reflect on the evolution of computational models for text throughout the last decades, especially on their capability to represent certain semantics. It is still true for each human-written text that its "data generation process [. . . remains] a mystery – even to linguists" (ibid.) and, hence, we cannot know whether some newer computational model is more correct than its predecessor. However, we can evaluate the fit between computational models and basic linguistic theories to assess their suitability to perform social science tasks. The hypothesis underlying this chapter is that computational models of semantics eventually converge towards basic linguistic models of semantics and, thus, comply much better with basic theoretical assumptions of many of today's text-based empirical research methodologies. Especially the compliance of the new embedding-based models with the methodological assumptions underlying social research may pave the way for exciting new research opportunities. In this light, we strive to answer two questions: (1) how do models of computational semantics relate to linguistic structuralism as the provenance of many modern text research methods, and (2) how may the recent advancements impact automatic content analysis in the social sciences?

We will start our argumentation in section 2 with a brief discussion of theoretical foundations of linguistic structuralism by Ferdinand de Saussure along with an illustrative example about the semantic change of the term "Goldstück" (English: gold piece). This example was selected because it vividly demonstrates the rapid evolvement of its meaning from a positively connoted term to a hate speech expression in German social media communication. The fourth section then introduces a recent turning point in natural language processing: models of latent space semantics and embedding semantics that, as we argue, to some extent replicate the linguistic turn of the humanities and social sciences on a technical level. This argument, again, is illustrated with the empirical example of the term "Goldstücke" to reveal the potentials and limitations of the individual computational methods. Eventually, as we conclude in the final section, computational semantics 'after the Saussurean turn' enables semantic text search and context-sensitive automatic coding, which offers exciting opportunities for the integration of qualitative and quantitative empirical social research.

2 Linguistic Semantics

2.1 Linguistic structuralism

Due to his book *Cours de linguistique générale* (1916), Ferdinand de Saussure is considered the founder of linguistic structuralism. With his works, Saussure paved the way for a new, systematic analysis of language. Decades later, his theory became the decisive preparatory groundwork for the *linguistic turn* in the social sciences and humanities. The linguistic turn describes a paradigmatic shift towards methodological research "approaches that assume that knowledge is structured by language and other sign systems" (Wrana, 2014, p. 247, own translation). This basic assumption significantly influenced qualitatively oriented empirical social research, and especially (poststructuralist) discourse research in the second half of the 20th century. Saussure's structural model presents language as an interrelation between individual elements that are organized by differences. In the social sciences, these interrelationships became a subject of research as a proxy to study social reality (cp. Posselt & Flatscher, 2018, p. 211; Angermüller, 2007, p. 161). Besides the central assumption of language as a system of differences, two further conceptual differentiations are introduced that are essential for our considerations – the differentiation of language into *langue* and *parole*, and the linguistic sign as a composition of the *signifier* and the *signified*.

The differentiation of language into langue and parole is the starting point of Saussure's theory and essential to structuralist language analysis. Langue describes the system of language and its rules as a social institution, while parole refers to the act of speaking, that is, the concrete use of language. Those two mutually depend on each other because the language system only exists when language is actually used, and conversely, language use can only lead to successful communication if it follows the rules of a commonly shared language system. Saussure, thus, specifically states that langue is either social or does not exist (cf. Saussure, 2001, p. 20). However, according to Saussure, only langue is systematic and therefore suitable as a subject of research. Pierre Bourdieu sharply criticizes this privilege of langue over parole, pointing to Saussure's neglect of not just the usage of language but also of its historicity, materiality, and social embedding (Bourdieu, 2003).

The conceptualization of language as a system of linguistic signs, in which each element does not a priori have a fixed and objective meaning but rather receives this meaning only through the difference to other elements, represents a radical break with essentialist traditions (cf. Posselt & Flatscher, 2018, p. 207). The rejection of signs as 'positive' elements leads to the core idea of structuralism, which states that the position of a sign in the structured language system is relevant to determine its meaning. Referring to the game of chess, Saussure illustrates this idea: "The value of the individual figures depends on their respective position on the chessboard, just as in language each element has its value through its positional relationship to other elements" (Saussure, 2001, p. 105; own translation).

As in chess, there are also rules in language when it comes to determining the meaning of signs. Hereby, the guiding principle is the distinction between syntagmatic and paradigmatic relationships. Syntagmatic relationships exist between successive elements of a text sequence, for example the sentence "He paid five gold pieces". Due to their sequential order and specific relative positions in a sentence, the individual words in their role as linguistic signs are given a certain syntactic function, such as subject, predicate, and object, as well as a certain semantic function, such as the fact that gold pieces can be used by someone to pay. A paradigmatic relationship exists, in contrast, between elements of different sentences that are functionally interchangeable while retaining the same context. The sentence "He paid five gold coins", for example, together with the previous example, establishes a paradigmatic relationship between gold pieces and gold coins as a means of payment (cf. Saussure, 2001, p. 147f.).

But what are signs anyway? For Saussure, a sign is composed of two sides and arises in the link of a concept with a sound-image (Saussure, 2001, p. 78). The sound-image, also called signifier, is primarily the psychological representation of a word (cf. Saussure, 2001, p. 77). The signified, on the other hand, is the hearer's impression of that sound, also called the concept. In the course of the linguistic turn, this definition has been extended to "describe the signifier as the form that the sign takes and the signified as the concept to which it refers" (Chandler, 2007, p. 18). This interpretation includes the acoustic representation of the spoken word as well as its written representation as a sequence of characters of an alphabet into the notion of the signifier, which was important especially for the methodological foundations of empirical social research with text. An essential aspect is that precisely this connection between signifier and signified is arbitrary, though neither random nor necessary (cf. Saussure, 2001, p. 79). Instead, the connection is socially constructed and, thus, not fixed. Consequently, signs can change their meaning, with the result that language cannot transport meaning unambiguously. The assignment of meaning therefore always arises through the act of interpretation against the background of a language system as well as the context of an utterance.

Following empirical research methodologies rooted in structuralism, one needs to take these assumptions into account when social reality is to be examined based on language data, whether as a mental concept, spoken language, or written text. In this respect, automatic content analysis faces a severe problem because it can only observe the surface of language, that is, the signifier level. For a computer, it is impossible to interpret what meaning is actually to be conveyed in a given text. However, a human interpretation of the linguistic surface form can be encoded in a semantic model by a process of operationalization of the signified, that is, the concept level as the actual study objective. Therefore, it is crucial for the support of empirical social research to determine to what extent computer algorithms are able to represent ambiguous surface structures together with their linguistic contexts to disambiguate their (interpreted) meaning.

2.2 Levels of semantics

Given that signifier and signified are only arbitrarily linked in the language system (langue), the context of their use (parole) is decisive in order to be able to deduce the meaning of a sign. Especially for qualitative text analyses, it is important to look at statements in their respective context to validly interpret them. Thereby, context can refer to very different things. In general, this can be a historical linguistic context, which corresponds roughly to what Saussure describes

Table 21.1 Three levels of semantics for "Goldstücke" (Eng. translation in square brackets)

Semantic level	Example
Word (1)	**Goldstücke** [gold pieces]
Sentence (2)	*Sind doch alles **Goldstücke**, diese Menschen, die wir geschenkt bekommen haben.* [They are all **pieces of gold**, these people that we have been given as gifts.]
Discourse (3)	*Das darf doch gar nicht sein. Sind doch alles **Goldstücke**, diese Menschen, die wir geschenkt bekommen haben. Eines steht immer mehr fest – Wenn Europa und insbesondere Deutschland bereits vor zwei Jahren eine effektive Grenzsicherung betrieben hätte, wäre unsere Gesellschaft nicht noch um 50 Milliarden € reicher, sondern auch viel sicherer.* [This is impossible. They are all **pieces of gold**, these people that we have been given as gifts. One thing is becoming increasingly clear – if Europe, and Germany in particular, had already implemented effective border control two years ago, our society would not only be €50 billion richer but also much safer.] (Anonymized Facebook user, 28 April 2017, commenting on a German news article from DER SPIEGEL about a suspected Islamist terrorist)

with langue as the actual subject of synchronic linguistics. More specifically, context can also refer to a surrounding text unit or a contemporary social debate.

To systematize the origin of meaning, linguists generally distinguish between word and sentence meaning while discourse theory further introduces the notion of discourse meaning (Pêcheux et al., 1995, p. 102). The meaning of a sign can change, therefore, depending on the context level from which it is looked at. This can be illustrated vividly with the example of the German term "Goldstücke". In Table 21.1, an example is given for each of the three levels. On the level of the word (1) we only see the string "Goldstücke". Due to the current German language system, most readers will associate this string with the concept of shiny metallic coins, which were used as means of payment in earlier times. Another meaning would be a metaphorical compliment to another person. If the individual word is considered in a concrete sentence, not only the sentence itself carries a certain meaning. The sentence context also modifies the meaning of the individual word. In example (2), one can deduce that the term is intended to designate a group of people. According to the conventional interpretation of the language system, persons with this designation are attributed to a positive esteem. However, this interpretation changes drastically when a broader context is considered. At the level of discourse meaning (3), what has been said before must be included in the interpretation. This can refer to actually present text, previous statements in a dialogical exchange of texts, or even a broad social debate that has been conducted across many participants and texts. In the example, the context of discourse makes it clear that the term "gold pieces" is used in a derogatory way to refer to refugees who came to Germany in large numbers in 2015 in an attempt to seek asylum.

The repeated use of the word "gold pieces" (parole) in this particular sense would be capable of altering its meaning in the linguistic system (langue) by adding a third meaning to the inventory of its aforementioned senses. In general, this points to the phenomena of polysemy and synonymy in language. The same word (represented in written language by the same character string) can take on several meanings or be linked to different mental concepts due to the characteristic of polysemy. On the other hand, synonymy describes the phenomenon that a mental concept can be expressed by different linguistic signifiers. These characteristics of language result in the heterogeneity and diversity with which similar thoughts can be expressed, which as a whole shape social reality, but also make the study of this reality through text such a complex endeavor.

3 In search for gold: an illustrative example

Due to its ambiguity and context-dependency, the interpretation of language use for empirical research is a demanding task for analysts. Computational models are capable of encoding the semantics of natural language with varying degrees of complexity to make it accessible to human interpretation. To illustrate these differences, we present the capabilities of different algorithmic models along with a selected example from German social media communication.

In June 2016, the chairman of the German Social Democrats (SPD) and president of the European Parliament Martin Schulz made an influential public statement about the increase of people seeking asylum in Germany at that time: "What the refugees bring to us is more valuable than gold. It is the unwavering belief in the dream of Europe. A dream that was lost to us at some point" (Riemer, 2016, own translation). In German social media communication, especially in debates of right-wing Facebook groups and commentators, this quotation was quickly altered into the sarcastic aggravation that refugees themselves are "more valuable than gold". Eventually, this culminated in a substantial semantic change of the term "Goldstücke". Originally, the German reference dictionary Duden describes two regular meanings: a gold coin deemed to be legal tender, or metaphorically a very appreciated person or object (Duden, 2020). In social media, it rapidly became a derogatory term to mock migrants that frequently occurred in hate speech contexts (Fedtke & Wiedemann, 2020).

To reveal the semantic capabilities of different computational models, we investigate the semantic shift of the term "gold pieces" in social media compared to a reference corpus of standard language use. Our social media corpus contains roughly 360,000 user comments downloaded from German Facebook pages operated by major German mass media outlets such as Spiegel Online or Tagesschau.[1] Comments and replies to comments were crawled via the Facebook API from about 3,000 discussion threads during a time range of five months in 2017. Threads were selected only if the corresponding official post text of the mass media account contained at least one term of a list of filter keywords.[2] This key term filter was applied to retrieve a corpus of (potentially) controversial topics around refugees, migration, and discrimination. For our analysis, we split the user comments into roughly two million sentences to investigate the usage of terms in their sentence context.

In a previous study, this corpus was examined to analyze the dynamics of hate speech and counter-speech in German social media (Fedtke & Wiedemann, 2020). As one outcome, the new way of using the word "gold pieces" was particularly striking. Accordingly, the corpus serves us in this chapter as a basis for a closer examination of this shift in meaning. We contrast the new use of the word "gold pieces" in social media with a thematically nonspecific corpus of Wikipedia articles. For this reference corpus, we combined two standardized corpora from the Leipzig Corpora Collection, each containing one million sentences randomly sampled from Wikipedia in 2014 and in 2016 (Quasthoff et al., 2014).

4 Three challenges in automatic content analysis

In light of the linguistic principles discussed earlier, three challenges for automatic content analysis can be derived. *First*, to comply with the principle of syntagmatic relations between words, a computational text model should be able to take the sequentiality of text for adequate meaning representation into account. *Second*, the principle of paradigmatic relation requires a model to capture linguistic phenomena such as polysemy and synonymy concerning a specific usage context. *Third*, content analysis requires a representation of meaning for different semantic levels.

To meet these challenges, in our view it is essential that a model is able to separate a linguistic surface form, for example a fixed character string as a representative for a sign, from its corresponding meaning representation. However, since the first attempts to use computers for content analysis in social and communication studies, researchers relied mostly on word retrieval and frequency counts that are strictly confined to the surface form. The French philosopher and linguist Michel Pêcheux pointed to a tautological problem for the endeavor to infer understanding of texts based on such a technology: automatic searches for word surfaces "presuppose a knowledge of the very result we are trying to obtain" (Pêcheux et al., 1995, p. 121). Put another way, one must already know which meaning is communicated with a word to validly quantify its usage in texts. From quantification alone, however, one cannot learn about any meaning or change of it. This problem explains a lot of the discomfort qualitatively oriented social scientists expressed for decades when being confronted with research narratives based on computational analysis (for an early critique see Kracauer, 1952).

With Saussure's distinction of signifier and signified, Pêcheux argues that discourse has to be studied by observing language within its contexts of production and its use with as few presumptions as possible. Approaches that just count character sequences assigned to categories suffer from the underlying false assumption of a bi-unique relation between signifier and signified. They are, thus, to be considered as "pre-Saussurean" (Pêcheux et al., 1995, p. 65). Along with our illustrative example, we will discuss opportunities and limitations of two "pre-Saussurean" semantic representations widely used in automatic content analysis: string patterns and the vector space model.

4.1 String pattern matching

The most basic form of computational semantic representation is also the most widely used in social science contexts: sequences of alphabet characters, referred to as a string, serve as query input for a matching procedure on some target text encoded as a string as well. Strings can be of arbitrary lengths and, thus, represent single words, multi-word units, phrases, sentences, or entire documents. For instance, a target document can be split at punctuation marks into sentences, and sentences can be split into isolated words at whitespace characters. The pattern matching algorithm can then check how often a query string, for example a keyword, occurs in a given target text. More complex extensions to this approach combine queries for individual words to word lists, so-called dictionaries, in which each term of a dictionary category is a representative for a more abstract concept (e.g. positive or negative sentiment). Dictionary terms can further be combined with certain rules (e.g. by AND, OR, NOT conditions) or regular expressions to match a desired observation in target texts. Among other things, regular expressions allow using wildcard characters and character classes (e.g. numbers or word characters) to look for. Such dictionaries are the basis for most automatic content analyses from the early document categorizations in media studies (Stone et al., 1966) to nowadays widely conducted sentiment analyses (e.g. Young & Soroka, 2012).

With regard to our example, Table 21.2 shows potential information that can be obtained automatically within this paradigm. We see that after splitting our corpora into sentences and words, Wikipedia contains more terms (word tokens) and a richer vocabulary (word types). For both corpora, we can measure how often we observe the occurrence of the exact character string "Goldstück" (singular), its plural form "Goldstücke", or its diminutive ("Goldstückchen"). Since the matching is for exact character strings only, query variations spelled with an initial lowercase letter produce drastically different results. The last query pattern, the regular expression "(?i)Goldstück.*| Goldmünze.*" matches a more complex pattern of words

Table 21.2 Frequencies of textual entities, character strings, and regular expression patterns in the two example corpora

Pattern	Absolute		Relative	
	Wikipedia	Facebook	Wikipedia	Facebook
Sentences	2,000,050	2,056,795	–	–
Tokens	39,387,827	27,863,340	–	–
Types	1,560,839	492,660	–	–
Goldstück	18	47	0.46	1.69
Goldstücke	31	276	0.79	9.91
Goldstückchen	0	80	0.00	2.87
goldstück	0	0	0.00	0.00
goldstücke	0	13	0.00	0.47
(?i)Goldstück.* | Goldmünze.*	146	494	3.71	17.73

beginning with Goldstück or its synonym term Goldmünze (gold coin) followed by any potential suffix while ignoring letter casing for any match. In total, we can observe quite large differences in absolute frequencies between the two sources. Also, nonstandard spelling variations occur only in Facebook. Yet, absolute numbers are hard to interpret regarding the different corpus sizes. Computing a relative measure, such as frequency per million words, shows that there is significant overuse of "Goldstück" and especially of the plural form "Goldstücke" in social media.

From our theoretical perspective, the important characteristic is the underlying assumption that each matching of a query in a target text is identical with one predefined meaningful event. In other terms, the Saussurean distinction of signifier and signified is bluntly ignored, as soon as meaning simply collapses with its linguistic surface form. It is impossible to learn about how these quantitative differences relate to actual semantics just from frequencies alone. Although string query patterns retain the sequential order of text, they are mostly restricted to the word level and do not contain any abstract representation of meaning to capture polysemy

Table 21.3 Keyword in context display for the target term "Goldstücke"

Corpus	Left context	Keyword	Right context
Wikipedia	samt dem Großgrundbesitz für 275 500	*Goldstücke*	, wobei ein Teil des Kaufpreises
	[along with the large land estate worth 275 500 of]	[*gold pieces*]	[where as part of the price]
	tausend "Goldmännchen", kleine	*Goldstücke*	mit eingravierten menschlichen Figuren aus der
	[thousand "little men of gold", small]	[*gold pieces*]	[with engraved human figures from the]
	Die letzten behandelt er bedächtlich wie	*Goldstücke*	; keine verfehlt das Ziel.
	[the last he treated cautiously like]	[*gold pieces*]	[; none misses the target.]
	Straßburg gegen eine Zahlung von 130.000	*Goldstücke*	und eine lebenslange Rente von 9.000
	[Straßbourg at a payment of 130,000]	[*gold pieces*]	[and a life annuity of 9,000]
	, die unter dem Namen „	*Goldstücke*	" vertrieben werden.
	[, those by the name of "]	[*gold pieces*]	[" being distributed.]
Facebook	und Massenschlägereien meinen da sind die	*Goldstücke*	sehr aktiv aber leider nicht wirklich
	[mean . . . and mass brawls, there are]	[*gold pieces*]	[very active but unfortunately not really]
	hat, allerdings gibt es wirklich	*Goldstücke*	unter den Leuten, die hier
	[have, however there are truly]	[*gold pieces*]	[among those people that here]
	Kannst ja paar	*Goldstücke*	haben vielleicht denkst dann anders:
	[You can [have] a couple of]	[*gold pieces*]	[maybe then you change your mind]
	Kohls	*Goldstücke*	und ihr Neid auf Alles und
	[Kohls']	[*gold pieces*]	[and their jealousy of everything and]
	Für Merkel und den Altparteien ihre	*Goldstücke*	25 Mrd.
	[For Merkel's and the old-parties']	[*gold pieces*]	[25 billion.]

or synonymy. To learn about actual differences in usage contexts and corresponding semantic change, we need to read closely each matching example of the search query. In Table 21.3, a so-called keyword in context (KWIC) list is given for five matches from each corpus that displays six tokens to the left and the right of each occurrence of an examined key term. The sample reveals that in Wikipedia "gold pieces" is utilized in the context of a means of payment, while in Facebook the term presumably designates a group of persons. To further validate this hypothesis, the analyst is set back to the method of qualitative reading of many more samples.

4.2 Vector space model

More elaborated methods of text mining and automatic content analysis are based on the idea to convert texts into some numeric representation ready for statistical analysis (Grimmer & Stewart, 2013, p. 272). For this, the complexity of natural language must be severely reduced. The two most severe simplification assumptions are that meaning can be observed through frequency counting of isolated word surface forms (statistical semantics hypothesis), and that word order in sentences or documents is not relevant to encode their meaning (bag of words hypothesis) (cp. Turney & Pantel, 2010). In the vector space model (VSM), each context unit (e.g. a sentence or document) of a given text collection is converted into a vector containing a count value for each word of a defined vocabulary. The vocabulary may comprise all distinct word types occurring in the text collection. This way, the entire corpus can be represented as a so-called document-term matrix (DTM) with n rows, the number of documents in the collection, and m columns, the number of word types in the vocabulary (e.g. 2,000,050 sentences and 1,560,839 distinct words for the Wikipedia corpus, cp. Table 21.2). A variant of the VSM is the term-term matrix (TTM). In $m \times m$ dimensions, the TTM encodes how often (or how significantly) two words co-occur in the same context window such as left/right neighborhood, sentence, or document throughout the entire collection.

Computationally such large data objects are hard to process and suffer from information sparsity.[3] Thus, the complexity of the original texts needs to be reduced even further. Typical measures are to restrict the vocabulary (e.g. ignoring less frequent terms) or to aggregate different word surface forms into one single form, for example counting each occurrence of an inflected form or the plural "Goldstücke" as an observation of the corresponding lemma form (this preprocessing step is called lemmatization). Of course, substantial information is lost from the text during this process of abstraction. However, proponents of automatic content analysis argue that enough information for certain analysis types such as thematic categorization, document similarity, or the study of word semantics is preserved. For the latter, co-occurrence analysis (also referred to as collocation analysis if conducted for direct neighboring contexts) strives to extract typical context words that co-occur with a given target word based on a statistical test of the TTM frequencies. From this analysis, co-occurrence graphs of typical usage contexts of words can be drawn for visual inspection.

Figure 21.1 contrasts co-occurrence graphs for our example target word "Goldstücke" in the two corpora based on a sentence context window and a log-likelihood test for significance. For complexity reduction, all words have been preprocessed to their lemma form with lower casing. By this step, we lost the information that the plural form is much more likely to occur in the Facebook corpus than the corresponding singular form and, hence, may be associated with a particularly interesting usage context. Yet, the graphs reveal very distinct contexts for the two sources. In Wikipedia, we see terms from a bakery context, as well as a range of other terms that first seem somewhat unrelated but actually stem from sentences of board game instructions. In Facebook, we also see a context of bakery terms and a set of terms related to politics and

Figure 21.1 Co-occurrence graphs based on Wikipedia (above) and Facebook (below): starting with the term "goldstück", its top five co-occurrence terms and again their co-occurrences are displayed. Edge thickness represents its significance strength

the migration discourse in Germany. Words such as "Fachkraft" (skilled worker) and "hoch-qualifiziert" (highly qualified), for instance, point to debates about skill levels of the migrant workforce. However, to be able to validly interpret the actual meaning behind these word pairs, again we need to closely read (a sample of) sentence structures containing them.

In contrast to basic string matching, the VSM is much more flexible to encode meaning for content analysis. Due to its severe reduction of complexity of natural language during the conversion of words or text sequences into DTMs or TTMs, a representation of different semantic levels for complex analysis setups can be achieved easily. This flexibility comes at the expense of the loss of all information from sequentiality, that is, word order. However, the numeric 'bag-of-words' encoding of text allows for the use of advanced statistics to reveal meaningful structures. In terms of Saussurean structuralism, a statistically significant co-occurrence of two words in the same context window can be interpreted as a syntagmatic relation between those words (e.g. "Kohls"[4] and "Goldstücke" frequently occur next to each other). Similar patterns of syntagmatic relations, that is, small distances in the vector space of the TTM, can be interpreted as a paradigmatic relation between those words (e.g. "Goldstück" and "Fachkraft" seem to be used often in a similar sentence context). However, the major drawback of string matching also remains for representations of words in the VSM. Still, word meaning is collapsed with its surface form. Thus, specific usage contexts signaling distinct word senses are not separated in lexicometric statistics. Even statistically significant patterns of surface forms that appear quite similar at the first glance, such as the semantic relation of "Goldstück" and "Kuchen" [cake] in both of our example data sets, may actually relate to drastically different contents.

5 The 'Saussurean turn' in automatic content analysis

The earlier examples demonstrated that Pêcheux's criticism applies to a range of computational text analysis approaches widely used to date. The shortcoming of meaning representations collapsed into surface forms not only affects empirical social science but also sets an upper bound to the performance of many inference tasks in NLP. For this reason, language models that allow a separation of the meaning from its surface form while incorporating sequential and contextual information were studied in computer science. In the following, we sketch two major model types from this development which we, in analogy to the earlier methodological turn in the social sciences, interpret as the 'Saussurean turn' in automatic content analysis.

5.1 Latent space models

The idea that meaning should not be identical with observable variables in the data paved the way for the success of latent variable models in NLP. A first attempt by Deerwester et al. (1990), called 'latent semantic analysis', utilized the idea of singular value decomposition (SVD), a matrix factorization approach that allows for compression of the information contained in the high-dimensional, sparse DTM. LSA results in a lower-dimensional matrix representation of the original text that keeps the largest possible variance of the data. This way, the information encoded in document-wise counts of the several thousands of vocabulary words can be reduced to a vector of typically $K = 50$, 100, or 300 dimensions. In this latent vector space, semantically similar documents are placed near to each other due to correlation patterns of the vocabulary they contain. As a result, documents can be retrieved as similar, not necessarily because they contain a large overlap in their observable vocabulary, but because they share a certain latent meaning that stems from semantically related terms. Although LSA was successfully applied for document retrieval, it did not gain much attention in social science applications because the latent dimensions resulting from SVD are hardly interpretable in a meaningful way. This changed with "pLSA", the probabilistic reformulation of the approach by Hofmann (1999), and "latent Dirichlet allocation" by Blei et al. (2003), who combined the pLSA idea with a Bayesian statistical framework. Also referred to as the first 'topic model', LDA especially attracts a lot of attention in computational social science nowadays. The model contains two latent variables, a document-topic distribution θ and a topic-term distribution φ to model the thematic composition of a text collection. Most probable terms of each of the K term distributions in φ (usually) form semantically coherent groups that can be interpreted as topics. Topic distributions in θ contain information about how large the proportion of a certain topic in every single document of the collection is. With this information, contents of very large collections can be analyzed thematically as well as with respect to collection metadata such as topic distribution over time, across different authors, or publications (Blei, 2012). The adaptation of topic models in the social sciences has led to research on best practices for their use as well as on solutions to the reliability problem of the seminal model (Maier et al., 2018).

Regarding our illustrative example, we used LDA to compute one model with $K = 200$ topics from a new corpus combining both the Wikipedia and the Facebook source. To keep the thematic usage of the term gold pieces distinguishable by source, we replaced each occurrence of the term with "goldstück_wiki" in the first source, and "goldstück_fb" in the second source. Further, lemmatization, lowercase reduction, and stopword removal were applied as preprocessing steps.

Table 21.4 displays the top 20 terms of the three topics with the highest probability of our target term in the two sources. Since "goldstück" itself is not overly frequent in both corpora, it is not among the top 20 terms shown in the table. However, the list of topic terms reveals six distinguishable thematic contexts, three for each source, which further enlightens the semantic shift in social media compared to the standardized text source. While the finance context dominates the use in Wikipedia, Facebook users tend to use the term when they express their opinion about migration and the welfare system.

Regarding the three challenges to automatic content analysis, latent topic models still are based on the DTM representation suffering from a complete loss of word order. Since the goal is to infer unobservable latent variables as an explanation for thematic coherence of entire texts, topic models are also restricted to operate on the document level of semantics only. However, compared to earlier more simple approaches, for the first time, they introduce a separation of meaning representation encoded in latent variables from the linguistic surface form of words used in a text. Since the model assigns a probability to each term of the vocabulary for each topic, any single term such as gold pieces can have a greater or lesser influence on each topic. This implicitly allows capturing the polysemic nature of terms to some extent.

5.2 Static word embeddings

In the adaptation of Saussure's notion of paradigmatic word relations for statistical semantics, Harris (1954) stated his famous distributional hypothesis that words that occur in similar contexts tend to have a similar meaning. Based on this assumption, language models that strive to encode word meaning by observing statistical word co-occurrence patterns in empirical language data were developed in computational linguistics. A very successful approach to distributional semantics is so-called word embedding vectors computed by artificial neural networks. Latent semantic models reduce the dimensionality of the vocabulary to represent the meaning of entire documents as a vector. Word embedding models, in contrast, learn meaningful low-dimensional vectors for each word of the vocabulary by observing their neighboring context words in a large text collection. Popular models such as word2vec (Mikolov et al., 2013) and GloVe (Pennington et al., 2014) result in vectors for which the proximity of words in their vector space indicates their semantic relatedness, for example similarity. As in Saussure's chess analogy, an embedding model tries to find a positioning of all the words to each other to optimally

Table 21.4 Top 20 topic terms of the three topics with the highest probability of "Goldstücke" in Wikipedia and Facebook (Eng. translation in brackets). The word lists reveal thematic contexts around the term. Topic labels originate from manual interpretation.

Source	Wikipedia			Facebook		
Label	Money	Routine	Order	Migration	Opinion	Welfare
1	million [million]	tage [days]	grund [reason]	papier [paper]	passen [fit]	arbeiten [work]
2	euro [euro]	nächst [next]	einverstanden [agreed]	bundeswehr [federal armed forces]	schön [nice]	bekommen [get]
3	pro [per]	schön [nice]	ha [hectare]	wertvoll [valuable]	weltbild [world view]	geld [money]
4	rund [about]	woche [week]	heißen [called]	ausweis [ID]	echt [real]	arbeit [work]
5	mio [million]	abend [evening]	erlauben [allow]	bringen [bring]	gut [good]	job
6	betragen [amount]	stunde [hour]	strafrecht [criminal law]	gold	voll [full]	verdienen [earn]
7	milliarde [billion]	wochenende [weekend]	überdenken [review]	handy [cell phone]	klappen [work out]	rente [pension]
8	zahlen [pay]	essen [food]	vortäuschen [pretend]	schnell [fast]	raus [out]	wohnung [apartment]
9	jährlich [annual]	tag [day]	hinrichtung [execution]	identität [identity]	glauben [believe]	hartz [welfare]
10	us-dollar	nacht [night]	weide [meadow]	paß [passport]	halt [just]	rentner [retiree]
11	kosten [cost]	paar [pair]	angemessen [adequate]	verlieren [lose]	hirn [brain]	arbeitslos [unemployed]
12	insgesamt [total]	täglich [daily]	acker [acre]	holen [fetch]	lustig [funny]	leisten [afford]
13	dollar	weisheit [wisdom]	unsicher [insecure]	kontrollieren [control]	richtig [right]	lebensunterhalt [subsistence]
14	verkaufen [sell]	traum [dream]	gelten [apply]	bw	denken [think]	empfänger [receiver]
15	dm	brot [bread]	zschäpe	gefälscht [faked]	bitten [ask]	arbeitsplatz [job]
16	mrd [billion]	löffel [spoon]	aufhalten [impede]	überprüfen [check]	bisschen [a little]	bezahlen [pay]
17	höhe [amount]	lecker [delicious]	asiat [asian]	rein [clean]	ok	mindestlohn [minimum wage]
18	monat [month]	ruhen [rest]	abwertung [devaluation]	behörde [authority]	sorry	verdient [earn]
19	schätzen [estimate]	nah [near]	geltung [application]	prüfen [check]	passend [fitting]	vermieter [landlord]
20	knapp [scarce]	schaukel [swing]	schlumpf [smurf]	smartphone	maul [yap]	arbeiter [worker]

describe the language use it is presented with during its training phase. But, instead of the two-dimensional chessboard, it typically uses between 50 and 300 dimensions to position its elements and encode different aspects of meaning along with these dimensions. This way, it is not only the relative proximity of words that implies their meaning. To some extent, vector arithmetic can also be applied to reveal more complex semantic properties than solely word similarity. For instance, the vector operation 'king' – 'man' + 'woman' yields 'queen' as the closest vector indicating that some notion of gender is encoded in the model. Kozlowski et al. (2019) use this property of word2vec embeddings to their approach of the "geometry of culture". The main idea is to investigate cultural patterns simply by studying distances of words in an embedding model trained on a large corpus of texts representative for some base population (e.g. millions of US-American newspaper articles from one decade). The embedding vectors for music genres, sports, or professions can be projected along with gender, class, or ideological dimensions through the relative word distance to opposite terms of an imagined continuum (e.g. male-female, rich-poor, or liberal-conservative). The approach can reveal interesting cultural connotations especially in a diachronic perspective, for example the feminization of the occupation "journalist" in the second half of the 20th century (ibid.). In natural language processing, the use of word embeddings pretrained on very large generic corpora drastically improved the state of the art for almost any inference task due to the circumstance that they allow for some form of knowledge transfer in machine learning. For instance, a sentiment classifier presented a sentence containing the attribute 'good' during training already knows something about other sentences containing closely related terms such as 'great' or 'awesome' (Rudkowsky et al., 2018).

Embedding models can be trained on very large, generic data sets to encode general linguistic knowledge or with a domain-specific data set to capture particular aspects of a subset of the language system. For our gold piece example, we show the results for two embedding models. Since word embedding models require a lot of text to learn vectors from, we computed a word-2vec model based on the entire German Wikipedia, and a GloVe model based on our entire Facebook corpus instead of our previously used samples.[5]

Table 21.5 shows a list of the nearest neighbors of "Goldstück" ranked by cosine similarity in the two embedding models. We can see easily that the Wikipedia list is dominated by semantically equivalent terms from the context of means of payment or treasure. The closest 15 terms can be regarded as more or less synonymous with gold pieces. In Facebook, however, we see terms such as "Facharbeiter", "Asylant" [asylum seeker], or "Neubürger" [new citizen]. In fact, these terms are used by right-wing commentators in Facebook to belittle refugees sarcastically. In this sense, they become synonymous with gold pieces which can automatically be revealed by the model. This way, word embeddings solve the synonymy problem of natural language to some extent by effectively separating word surface forms from their meaning.

5.3 Contextualized word embeddings

Saussure's dualism of the linguistic sign implies an arbitrary connection between the mental concept and a corresponding linguistic pattern, which results in the aforementioned synonymy problem. Conversely, linguistic patterns such as words can be assigned to distinct mental concepts. Since static word embeddings still mingle all different senses of a word surface form into one vector, this polysemy problem of natural language requires an extension of embedding semantics. Our gold piece example has already shown that the meaning of the term is quite different in our two sources. To represent the sense as a means of payment vs. a sarcastic reference to refugees, actually, two vectors would be required. For empirical analysis, it is impractical to assume a fixed sense inventory, since we do want to find out about different (new) usage

Table 21.5 The 25 terms with highest cosine similarity to "Goldstück" (descending) in Wikipedia and Facebook (Eng. translations in brackets)

Rank	Wikipedia		Facebook	
1	*Goldstück [gold piece]*	1	*goldstück [gold piece]*	1
2	Münze [coin]	0.63	fachkraft [skilled worker]	0.42
3	Goldbarren [gold bar]	0.62	facharbeiter [skilled worker]	0.37
4	Silbermünze [silver coin]	0.59	mutti [mommy]	0.36
5	Goldmünze [gold coin]	0.59	asylant [asylum seeker]	0.34
6	Schmuckstück [jewelry]	0.54	merkel	0.34
7	Geldstück [coin]	0.53	neubürger [new citizen]	0.32
8	Geldschein [banknote]	0.52	traumatisiert [traumatized]	0.32
9	Silberstück [silver piece]	0.51	unsere [our]	0.32
10	Silberbarren [silver bar]	0.50	volksvertreter [representative]	0.31
11	Juwel [jewel]	0.50	einzelfall [single case]	0.31
12	Taler [thaler]	0.50	kerl [guy]	0.30
13	Banknote [banknote]	0.50	kanzlerin [chancellor]	0.30
14	Dukaten [ducat]	0.50	schulz	0.30
15	Schatz [treasure]	0.50	migrant	0.29
16	Gold [gold]	0.50	ronny	0.28
17	Goldschatz [treasure of gold]	0.49	flüchtling [refugee]	0.28
18	Edelstein [gem]	0.48	wir [we]	0.27
19	Schatulle [casket]	0.48	unserer [our]	0.27
20	Kostbarkeit [preciousness]	0.48	gast [guest]	0.27
21	Goldklumpen [nugget]	0.48	unser [our]	0.27
22	Truhe [chest]	0.47	billig [cheap]	0.27
23	Schatztruhe [treasure chest]	0.47	wertvoll [valuable]	0.26
24	Papiergeld [paper money]	0.47	wirtschaftsflüchtling [economic migrant]	0.26
25	Silberschatz [treasure of silver]	0.47	goldjungs [golden boys]	0.26

contexts in the first place. To deal with this context-dependency of meaning, contextualized word embeddings have been developed as the recent major milestone in NLP. Contextualized word embedding models such as ELMO (Peters et al., 2018) or flair (Akbik et al., 2018) combine static word embeddings with an embedding representation of the surrounding context for each word in a text sequence, which allows an embedding of the same word surface form to vary slightly depending on its left and right neighboring terms. The most recent innovation are language models based on the transformer neural network architecture such as BERT (Devlin et al., 2019). Transformer networks create contextualized word embeddings without relying on precomputed static embeddings as an initial layer of word meaning representation. Instead, the entire model is pretrained on very large text collections to learn about language regularities. In its deep architecture, it produces embeddings on each network layer that encode complex syntactic and semantic information. For the BERT model, Wiedemann et al. (2019) show that its last embedding layer places the same word into separable regions of the vector space along with their different sense contexts. This suggests that some internal mechanism of word sense disambiguation is performed by the model automatically. The incorporation of long context sequences for word embeddings is so successful that newer models based on BERT even outperform the average human performance for many natural language inference tasks such as reading comprehension, question answering, and text classification (Liu et al., 2019).

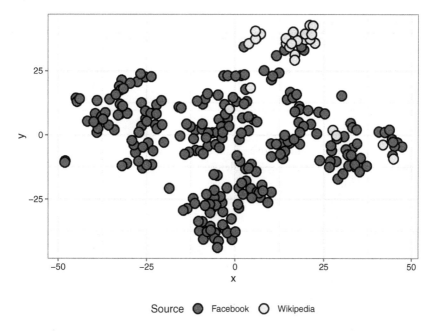

Figure 21.2   Two-dimensional t-SNE projection (Maaten & Hinton, 2008) of contextualized word embeddings in Wikipedia and Facebook. Each point represents one occurrence of "Gold-stücke" in a specific sentence. The closer the points, the more similar is their contextual meaning

For our example case, we use a BERT model pretrained on German newspaper data to create contextualized word embeddings for all occurrences of "Goldstücke" in a combined corpus of our Wikipedia and Facebook source. Figure 21.2 displays a two-dimensional projection of the 768-dimensional embedding vectors. In this plot, the proximity of points indicates the semantic similarity of their usage contexts. Embeddings from Wikipedia are mainly placed in a separate region in the upper part of the projection grouping the contexts around the act of payment. Other regions of the projection reveal distinct derogatory contexts of "gold pieces", for instance accusations of sexual violence in the bottom center.

The clustering or projection of contextualized embeddings allows for a semantic grouping and quick visual inspection of patterns of similar usage contexts. Moreover, information about polysemy and synonymy of terms captured with contextual embeddings can drastically improve classifiers for the automatic coding of text. To automatically code the context of accusations of sexual violence as one specific form of hate speech against refugees in social media would require only a few training examples for a BERT-based text classifier. As an integral part of the transformer neural network architecture, the way of encoding semantics by contextual embeddings also retains the information from the sequential order of the text. Finally, yet importantly, the aggregation of word embeddings allows, depending on the network architecture, to compute sentence or document embeddings, thus, a flexible encoding of different semantic levels.

6 Conclusion

In this chapter, we derived three challenges for automatic content analysis based on structuralist linguistic principles that were highly influential for the development of text-based empirical

Table 21.6 Summary of linguistic challenges addressed by computational text models

Challenge	String matching	Vector space model	Latent semantic model	(Contextualized) Embeddings
Sequentiality	yes	no	no	yes
Semantic levels	no	yes	no	yes
Sign dualism	no	no	(yes)	yes

social research. Along with an illustrative example, we showed that widely used computational methods actually struggle to meet these challenges.

Table 21.6 summarizes how these challenges are addressed by computational models of increasing complexity. For the less complex models, information from the sequentiality of text is only retained when retrieving words as consecutive strings directly. Word order information is lost in the 'bag-of-words' approach of the VSM and the latent semantic model based on it. Second, a flexible encoding of semantics from varying levels of granularity is only possible with the VSM in which the vectors can easily represent different context units such as sentences, documents, or entire collections. The latent semantic model, in contrast, is only meaningfully defined for the document level, since documents are considered as a mixture of topics. The Saussurean dualism of the linguistic sign can be operationalized in computational models by separating a meaning representation from its linguistic surface form, that is, the character string representing a word or a word sequence. In part, this is realized by latent semantic models such as the LDA topic model, which models the same word contributing with varying share to each topic. This way, a high proportion of a word in two or more thematically distinct topics is a hint for its polysemic character. The automatic, unsupervised detection of such meaningful thematic coherence between words that abstracts from the isolated, ambiguous word surface form constitutes the success of topic modeling in the social sciences (Maier et al., 2018).

Regarding our posed challenges, the latest paradigm shift in NLP towards contextualized word embeddings in combination with deep neural networks (DNN) can be seen as a major step forward for computational content analysis. This way of modeling natural language allows taking word order into account. It also can represent semantics on higher levels than words through various methods of aggregating word embeddings. Last but not least, embeddings consequently realize Saussure's sign duality. A semantic concept can be interpreted as some specific region in the embedding vector space that may contain several, distinct terms referring synonymously to it. The contextualization of embeddings further allows for the same linguistic sign to refer to distinct regions in the vector space, thus modeling the polysemy of words.

To further elaborate the analogy between linguistic structuralism and embedding models from NLP, we can again look at the distinction between langue and parole. Language models such as word2vec and BERT need to be trained on very large text collections to encode their knowledge about semantics and language structure in an embedding vector space. Hereby, training data fits the notion of parole, the actual language use. Based on this empirical data, a language model is learned that can be viewed as an approximation of langue, the language system that originally generated the training data.

What's in it for computational social sciences? In contrast to earlier automatic approaches, the new DNN models are particularly appealing for qualitatively oriented social research. In empirical research with text, we do not look for signifiers as an end in itself but as references to underlying ideas and concepts. Contextualized embeddings, eventually, will enable researchers to conduct semantic searches, that is, to search for meaning instead of word surface forms. Like our illustrative example revealed, with the help of embedding semantics we can discover the shift of meaning of the term "Goldstücke" from a compliment, or means of payment, to a set of sarcastic, derogatory accusations against refugees in social media. In combination with active learning (Wiedemann, 2019) where the machine and the content analyst fruitfully interact for automatic text coding, the new NLP-based language models will enable us to study social discourse with sophisticated depth in qualitative terms while retaining the advantages of quantitative analysis at large scale. Michel Pêcheux, to our knowledge the earliest advocate for a research program towards automatic discourse analysis (1969), would probably have been very excited about this 'Saussurean turn' in automatic content analysis.

Notes

1 See https://spiegel.de, and https://tagesschau.de
2 The keyterm list contains the following German word stems (translation, respective explanations are given in square brackets): afd [AfD, a German right-wing radical party], afrika [Africa], anschlag [attack], asyl [asylum], ausländ* [foreign], flucht [escape], flücht* [refugee], frau [woman], humanit* [humanitarian], islam [Islam], kopftuch [headscarf], missbrauch [abuse], muslim [Muslim], nazi [Nazi], npd [NPD, a German right-wing extremist party], rassis* [racism], schleier [scarf], sexuell [sexual], sudan [Sudan], syr* [Syria], terror [terror], vergewalt* [rape].
3 The absolute majority of cells in each row of such a matrix contains 0 values since only a few terms of the m-length vocabulary occur in each single document.
4 A reference to the former German chancellor Helmut Kohl.
5 We decided for the GloVe model for our Facebook corpus because it performs significantly better than word2vec for smaller data sets.

References

Akbik, A., Blythe, D., & Vollgraf, R. (2018). Contextual string embeddings for sequence labeling. In *Proceedings of the 27th international conference on computational linguistics* (pp. 1638–1649). Association for Computational Linguistics. http://aclweb.org/anthology/C18-1139

Angermüller, J. (2007). Was fordert die Hegemonietheorie? Zu den Möglichkeiten und Grenzen ihrer methodischen Umsetzung. In M. Nonhoff, E. Laclau, & C. Mouffe (Eds.), *Diskurs – radikale Demokratie – Hegemonie. Zum politischen Denken von Ernesto Laclau und Chantal Mouffe* (pp. 159–172). Transcript.

Blei, D. M. (2012). Probabilistic topic models: Surveying a suite of algorithms that offer a solution to managing large document archives. *Communications of the ACM, 55*(4), 77–84.

Blei, D. M., Ng, A. Y., & Jordan, M. I. (2003). Latent Dirichlet allocation. *Journal of Machine Learning Research, 3*, 993–1022. www.cs.princeton.edu/~blei/papers/BleiNgJordan2003.pdf

Bourdieu, P. (2003). The production and reproduction of legitimate language. In P. Bourdieu, J. B. Thompson, & G. Raymond (Eds.), *Language and symbolic power* (pp. 43–65). Harvard University Press.

Chandler, D. (2007). *Semiotics: The basics.* Routledge.

Deerwester, S., Dumais, S. T., Furnas, G. W., Landauer, T. K., & Harshman, R. (1990). Indexing by latent semantic analysis. *Journal of the American Society for Information Science, 41*(6), 391–407. https://doi.org/10.1002/(SICI)1097-4571(199009)41:6%3C391::AID-ASI1%3E3.0.CO;2-9

Devlin, J., Chang, M.-W., Lee, K., & Toutanova, K. (2019). BERT: Pre-training of deep bidirectional transformers for language understanding. In *Proceedings of the 2019 conference of the North American chapter of the association for computational linguistics: Human language technologies (long and short papers)* (Vol. 1, pp. 4171–4186). Association for Computational Linguistics. https://doi.org/10.18653/v1/N19-1423

Duden. (2020). *Goldstück.* www.duden.de/rechtschreibung/Goldstueck

Fedtke, C., & Wiedemann, G. (2020). Hass- und Gegenrede in der Kommentierung massenmedialer Berichterstattung auf Facebook: Eine computergestützte kritische Diskursanalyse. In P. Klimczak, C. Petersen, & S. Breidenbach (Eds.), *Soziale Medien? Interdisziplinäre Zugänge zur Onlinekommunikation* (pp. 91–120). Springer. https://doi.org/10.1007/978-3-658-30702-8_5

Foucault, M. (1982). *The archaeology of knowledge.* Pantheon Books.

Glaser, B. G., & Strauss, A. L. (2005). *Grounded theory: Strategien qualitativer Forschung* (2nd ed.). Huber.

Grimmer, J., & Stewart, B. (2013). Text as data: The promise and pitfalls of automatic content analysis methods for political texts. *Political Analysis, 21*(3), 267–297. https://doi.org/10.1093/pan/mps028

Harris, Z. (1954). Distributional structure. *Word*, *10*(23), 146–162.

Hofmann, T. (1999). Probabilistic latent semantic indexing. In *SIGIR'99, proceedings of the 22nd annual international ACM SIGIR conference on research and development in information retrieval* (pp. 50–57). ACM. https://doi.org/10.1145/312624.312649

Kozlowski, A. C., Taddy, M., & Evans, J. A. (2019). The geometry of culture: Analyzing the meanings of class through word embeddings. *American Sociological Review*, *84*(5), 905–949. https://doi.org/10.1177/0003122419877135

Kracauer, S. (1952). The challenge of qualitative content analysis. *Public Opinion Quarterly*, *16*(4), 631–642. www.jstor.org/stable/2746123

Liu, Y., Ott, M., Goyal, N., Du, J., Joshi, M., Chen, D., . . . Stoyanov, V. (2019). RoBERTa: A robustly optimized BERT pretraining approach. *CoRR*, *abs/1907.11692*.

Maaten, L. van der, & Hinton, G. (2008, November). Visualizing data using t-SNE. *Journal of Machine Learning Research*, *9*, 2579–2605.

Maier, D., Waldherr, A., Miltner, P., Wiedemann, G., Niekler, A., Keinert, A., . . . Adam, S. (2018). Applying LDA topic modeling in communication research: Toward a valid and reliable methodology. *Communication Methods and Measures*, *12*(2–3), 93–118. https://doi.org/10.1080/19312458.2018.1430754

Mayring, P. (2010). Qualitative content analysis. In U. Flick, E. V. Kardorff, & I. Steinke (Eds.), *A companion to qualitative research* (pp. 266–269). Sage.

Mikolov, T., Chen, K., Corrado, G., & Dean, J. (2013). Efficient estimation of word representations in vector space. In Y. Bengio & Y. LeCun (Chairs.), *1st International conference on learning representations (ICLR)*.

Pêcheux, M. (1969). *Analyse automatique du discours*. Dunod.

Pêcheux, M., Hak, T., & Helsloot, N. (Eds.). (1995). *Automatic discourse analysis*. Rodopi.

Pennington, J., Socher, R., & Manning, C. D. (2014). GloVe. Global vectors for word representation. In *Empirical methods in natural language processing (EMNLP)*. www.aclweb.org/anthology/D14-1162

Peters, M., Neumann, M., Iyyer, M., Gardner, M., Clark, C., Lee, K., & Zettlemoyer, L. (2018). Deep contextualized word representations. In *Proceedings of the 2018 conference of the North American chapter of the association for computational linguistics (NAACL)* (pp. 2227–2237). ACL. https://doi.org/10.18653/v1/N18-1202

Posselt, G., & Flatscher, M. (2018). *Sprachphilosophie: Eine Einführung* (2nd ed.). UTB: Vol. 4126. Facultas.

Quasthoff, U., Goldhahn, D., & Eckart, T. (2014). Building large resources for text mining: The Leipzig corpora collection. In C. Biemann & A. Mehler (Eds.), *Theory and applications of natural language processing. Text mining* (pp. 3–24). Springer. https://doi.org/10.1007/978-3-30819-12655-5_1

Riemer, S. (2016, June 11). "Was die Flüchtlinge uns bringen, ist wertvoller als Gold". *Rhein-Neckar-Zeitung*. www.rnz.de/nachrichten/heidelberg_artikel,-Heidelberg-Was-die-Fluechtlinge-uns-bringen-ist-wertvoller-als-Gold-_arid,198565.html

Rudkowsky, E., Haselmayer, M., Wastian, M., Jenny, M., Emrich, Š., & Sedlmair, M. (2018). More than bags of words: Sentiment analysis with word embeddings. *Communication Methods and Measures*, *12*(2–3), 140–157. https://doi.org/10.1080/19312458.2018.1455817

Saussure, F. de. (1916). *Cours de linguistique générale*. Payot.

Saussure, F. de. (2001). *Grundfragen der allgemeinen Sprachwissenschaft* (C. Bally, & A. Sechehaye, Eds., 3rd ed.). De Gruyter.

Stäheli, U. (2000). *Poststrukturalistische Soziologien. Einsichten. Themen der Soziologie*. Transcript.

Stone, P. J., Dunphy, D. C., Smith, M. S., & Ogilvie, D. M. (1966). *The general inquirer: A computer approach to content analysis*. MIT Press.

Turney, P. D., & Pantel, P. (2010). From frequency to meaning: Vector space models of semantics. *Journal of Artificial Intelligence Research*, *37*, 141–188. www.jair.org/media/2934/live-2934-4846-jair.pdf

Wiedemann, G. (2013). Opening up to big data: Computer-assisted analysis of textual data in social sciences. *Historical Social Research*, *38*(4), 332–357.

Wiedemann, G. (2019). Proportional classification revisited: Automatic content analysis of political manifestos using active learning. *Social Science Computer Review*, *37*, 135–159. https://doi.org/10.1177/0894439318758389

Wiedemann, G., Remus, S., Chawla, A., & Biemann, C. (2019). Does BERT make any sense? Interpretable word sense disambiguation with contextualized embeddings. In *Proceedings of the 15th conference on natural language processing (KONVENS)* (pp. 161–170). German Society for Computational Linguistics & Language Technology.

Wrana, D. (2014). Linguistic turn. In D. Wrana, A. Ziem, M. Reisigl, M. Nonhoff, & J. Angermüller (Eds.), *Suhrkamp-Taschenbuch Wissenschaft: Vol. 2097. DiskursNetz: Wörterbuch der interdisziplinären Diskursforschung* (1st ed., pp. 247–248). Suhrkamp.

Young, L., & Soroka, S. (2012). Affective news: The automated coding of sentiment in political texts. *Political Communication, 29*(2), 205–231. https://doi.org/10.1080/10584609.2012.671234

22

AUTOMATED VIDEO ANALYSIS FOR SOCIAL SCIENCE RESEARCH[1]

Dominic Nyhuis, Tobias Ringwald, Oliver Rittmann, Thomas Gschwend and Rainer Stiefelhagen

1 Introduction: Moving beyond the analysis of digitized text

The widespread digitization has profoundly impacted research practices in the social sciences. The ubiquity of digital data has enabled research projects on scales that were almost inconceivable a mere 30 years ago. As human coding is often no longer a viable option to deal with the immense amounts of data, scholars have begun to embrace methodological innovations that aim to automate the transposition of digitized information into data points. Among the most successful and most widely employed techniques is the automated analysis of text, which has become a staple of social science research (Grimmer & Stewart, 2013; Lucas et al., 2015; Wilkerson & Casas, 2017). But even though text mining has yielded crucial insights in a number of disciplinary subfields, scholars have yet to appreciate the full potential of the universal digitization for the social sciences.

While some studies have recently started using techniques for the automated analysis of still images (Haim & Jungblut, forthcoming; Peng, 2018; Williams et al., 2020; Zhang & Pan, 2019), almost no social science contributions have adopted tools for the automated analysis of other forms of digitized media, such as audio or video recordings. Not only do these data promise new and valuable insights, our perspective on some social phenomena clearly remains incomplete when we disregard visual information. The most obvious example is social media research. Our focus on textual information has severely hampered our understanding of these platforms, where ideas are frequently expressed as images and videos and where the visual cues arguably dominate the textual ones.

Studying the visual cues of social media posts underlines the need for embracing automated tools to make sense of the vast amounts of data that are continuously generated on these platforms. While previous studies have analyzed social media imagery using manual classification (Kharroub & Bas, 2016; Neumayer & Rossi, 2018; Rose et al., 2012), these efforts are limited by the size of the data and the costs of human coders. These problems are compounded by the fact that we are typically interested in multiple dimensions of digitized media, further increasing the need for human coders, thus limiting the amount of material that can be covered.

While social scientists have so far resisted adopting tools for studying images and video data, tremendous progress in computer science has been made to analyze this type of data using automated systems. The aim of this chapter is to highlight some of these potentials and to encourage

DOI: 10.4324/9781003025245-26

researchers to make greater use of the available techniques for analyzing digitized media. This chapter focuses on the automated analysis of video footage, but the underlying methods are similar across the different data types, not least due to the similarity of still images and videos. In either case, machine learning is used to classify images or video data based on a sample of human-coded training data.

To showcase the possibilities, section 2 begins with an overview of typical scenarios and tools for classifying video footage. Section 3 provides a summary of current research in the social sciences to give a sense of the type of research question that can be explored with video data. Section 4 illustrates a case study in greater detail. Section 5 concludes with a discussion of some conceptual and methodological challenges and research perspectives.

2 The state of the art in automated video analysis

The core objective of machine learning is to automate data analysis. Machine learning replaces the need for human coders who would otherwise have to perform mundane and repetitive tasks. This is especially true for high-bandwidth data such as videos, which require human annotators to be attentive for long stretches of time while – depending on the specific coding task – paying attention to the audio and video tracks at once.

The tasks in automated video analysis are highly diverse, and a multitude of subtasks depend on the desired characteristics and the intended usage of such systems. Common tasks are the detection of humans or generic objects (object detection), localization of body parts (pose estimation), detection of higher-level actions (activity recognition), and identification and tracking of humans (person re-identification) based on certain features such as face, gait, or appearance.

Ever since Krizhevsky and colleagues (2012) have shown the enormous potential of deep neural networks for image classification, the research on automated video analysis has shifted towards deep convolutional neural networks (CNNs). We will introduce the aforementioned concepts in the context of CNNs, as they usually outperform other approaches (Wang et al., 2011).

At a fundamental level, automated video analysis can be thought of as the analysis of a series of images. A basic classification task might consist of predicting a certain class label from a pre-defined list of possible classes for a single image or a series of images. Object detection extends this setup by also predicting the location of an object in the form of a rectangular bounding box. One of the earliest CNN-based methods in the area of object detection was the region-based CNN (R-CNN; Girshick et al., 2014). R-CNN has a two-stage object detection pipeline: First, region proposals, that is, a set of bounding boxes, are generated through a selective search algorithm (Uijlings et al., 2013). In the second stage, these regions are classified with a CNN as belonging to a class from a list of possible classes or as background in cases where the region does not contain an object.

Due to the slow inference speed of R-CNN, multiple improvements to the region proposal and classification stage have been proposed in Fast R-CNN (Girshick, 2015) and Faster R-CNN (Ren et al., 2015). As even Faster R-CNN is too slow for real-time inference, recent research has shifted towards anchor box-based predictions instead of region proposals. Anchor box-based detection architectures directly regress coordinates of bounding boxes and do not require a separate region proposal stage. Research has also looked into more efficient CNN backbone architectures such as MobileNet (Howard et al., 2017) and SqueezeNet (Iandola et al., 2016), specifically designed for use on mobile devices. Examples of real-time detection frameworks are the single-shot multibox detector (SSD; Liu et al., 2016) and YOLO (Redmon et al., 2016; Redmon & Farhadi, 2017).

The recent Mask R-CNN (He et al., 2017) extends the idea of Faster R-CNN and predicts a fine-grained segmentation mask in addition to the coarse object bounding box. This results in more detailed object contours as generic rectangular regions often contain a large number of non-object pixels.

Regarding humans in video footage, fine-grained predictions are often done in the form of pose estimation (Cao et al., 2019; Wei et al., 2016). In this case, several key points on the human body, such as joints, eyes, and ears, are predicted and merged into a full skeleton. This can be done in 2D (image space) or in 3D (world space) based on triangulation from multiple single views or depth cameras. Specialized pose estimation focuses on fine-grained detection of sub-parts of the human body, such as hands, which can deliver precise information about gestures.

All of these techniques can be applied to single frames of a video and tracked over time, that is, an object can be tracked in a video by applying object detection at every frame and connecting the resulting bounding boxes based on the overlap between the individual frames. For a higher-level understanding of videos – such as activity recognition – still images are insufficient, as they do not contain temporal context. In order to exploit the high performance of single-image classification networks, Donahue and colleagues (2015) proposed extracting single-image CNN features at specific time steps in videos and passing them to a long short-term memory (LSTM) module (Hochreiter & Schmidhuber, 1997). LSTMs are commonly used for sequence processing, as they can encode and propagate states over multiple time steps and capture long-term dependencies within the input data.

CNNs are also commonly used for person (re-)identification. Here, the task is usually defined as retrieving similar images from a gallery given a single query image. For example, in a surveillance task, the query could be the image of a suspect, while the gallery consists of footage from a surveillance camera. As there are an unknown number of identities in the gallery, (re-)identification differs from a normal classification task. Instead, models in this area predict the similarity between two inputs based on a metric such as Euclidean distance. One of the most popular works was published by Schroff and colleagues (2015), who use CNNs to learn a compact feature embedding for an input image. During training, embeddings from images showing the same person are optimized to be closer than embeddings from images showing different persons.

Given the increasing popularity of automated video analysis, several software solutions have been published in recent years. One of the most popular open source solutions for pose estimation is OpenPose,[2] which offers a multitude of different pose-related solutions such as body and hand keypoint estimation in 2D and 3D. For standard image classification tasks, many pretrained models are available for commonly used CNN architectures. Oftentimes, the ImageNet data set (Deng et al., 2009) is used for pretraining, as it offers a diverse set of 1,000 different classes that cover most objects found in everyday life. Similarly, deep learning frameworks such as PyTorch (Pasczke et al., 2019) offer pretrained solutions for object detection, semantic segmentation, instance segmentation, and action recognition.[3] Even if these models are not trained on a class required for a specialized prediction task, they can still be used as a starting point for fine-tuning, thus easing the training process and reducing the need for additional training data.

3 Current applications in the social sciences

Even though tools for the automated analysis of video data are well established in computer science, and even though there is great potential to advance social science research with video data in a number of areas, efforts to apply computer vision in empirical social research are rare. To provide an overview of this nascent research field, it is helpful to distinguish between the audio and visual components of video recordings. While we have seen some analyses of still images (Haim & Jungblut, forthcoming; Peng, 2018; Zhang & Pan, 2019), the analysis of moving images is virtually nonexistent in the social sciences. By contrast, analyses of audio data have been somewhat more common.

In a series of papers, Dietrich and colleagues study audio recordings of political speech, where vocal pitch is taken as an indicator for the emotional intensity of speakers. Analyzing speeches in the US House of Representatives, Dietrich et al. (2019) find that female legislators exhibit greater variation in vocal pitch when they address women. Dietrich and Juelich (2018) analyze the vocal pitch of Hillary Clinton and Donald Trump during the televised debates in the 2016 Presidential election campaign. The authors find that candidates' vocal pitch is related to the content of their speech, in that candidates addressing core party issues exhibit higher standardized vocal pitch. Additionally, Dietrich and colleagues have analyzed the vocal pitch during oral arguments before the US Supreme Court, which famously only publishes audio recordings of their deliberations, but does not allow video cameras in the court room. Dietrich et al. (2019) find that the Justices signal their eventual vote choice during oral argument. The Supreme Court deliberations are also analyzed by Knox and Lucas (forthcoming). Based on a general speech classifier, the authors train a model to detect skepticism in the utterances of the Justices (Knox and Lucas forthcoming).

While analyses of audio recordings have been – comparatively – more common in the recent social science literature, a few studies have also analyzed video recordings. For example, Dietrich presents analyses of video footage from the US House of Representatives (forthcoming, 2015). In these contributions, Dietrich is interested in how the increasing polarization in the US political system manifests in the behavior of legislators on the House floor. He argues that as the polarization has intensified, legislators have become less likely to interact with their counterparts from the opposing party – they are literally less likely to cross the aisle. To test this behavioral upshot of the changing political landscape, the author studies video footage from the House of Representatives that is published by C-SPAN. Dietrich specifically focuses on the video segments during the proceedings when legislators take a roll call vote. During voting, C-SPAN shows an overhead shot of the plenary floor. To proxy the interactions between legislators, Dietrich relies on a fairly simple technique that compares the pixels in the overhead shots, where more dissimilarity between two frames is taken as an indicator of more movement on the House floor. Assuming that crossing the aisle – moving across the screen to interact with members of the opposing party – creates greater dissimilarity between the frames, Dietrich confirms that the stability of the frames in the overheard shots has gone up over time.

While the work by Dietrich is a good example of how video recordings can inform political research in diverse and unexpected ways, a more natural application is presented by Joo and colleagues (2019). The authors conduct an exploratory analysis to assess whether machine learning is useful for automatically classifying video recordings of political actors. Studying footage from the first televised debate between Hillary Clinton and Donald Trump during the 2016 presidential election campaign, the authors manually code a variety of nonverbal candidate behaviors. Next, they extract facial and pose characteristics of the candidates from the footage using standard libraries, among them OpenPose, introduced in the previous section (Cao et al., 2019). Based on these features, the authors train a neural network to predict the manual codes. Overall, their model performs reasonably well, suggesting that automated video analysis may greatly decrease the need for manual labor in this research area, opening up enormous potentials for large-scale comparative work.

While these initial applications of automated video analysis in the social sciences show great promise, there is a lot of room for additional research. First, much of the work using audio and video data is exploratory and descriptive in nature, while these tools have yet to be incorporated into more conventional research programs with an explanatory interest. Second, applications of computer vision in the social sciences have not yet made full use of the tools that have been developed in recent years and that have become more easily accessible to interested researchers as highlighted in the previous section. Third, digitized video recordings are available in many areas that have not yet found their way into social science applications. What is more, the published studies have occasionally discarded relevant parts of the data. Specifically, none of the studies included in the overview have integrated audio and video data to make the most of the available data. While the video or audio component is not always available or relevant for the research question, some of the studies on political speech could easily benefit from adding the video component of the footage. To further highlight the potentials of automated video analysis for empirical social research, the next section will discuss an application from legislative politics in greater detail.

4 A sample application: Analyzing parliamentary video footage

In a move to increase the transparency of parliamentary activities, many legislatures have allowed third-party cameras into the plenary chamber or have begun publishing video recordings of the plenary proceedings themselves (Ryle, 1991). Over time, these efforts have become more technologically sophisticated and, nowadays, digitized video footage of parliamentary proceedings is available on many parliamentary websites.

For researchers interested in legislative politics, these data hold an enormous potential. In addition to enabling analyses of parliamentary behaviors that are not recorded in the minutes of the plenary proceedings, such as legislator attendance or interactions, parliamentary video footage is characterized by several features that make it particularly suitable for an automated analysis. Most importantly, video footage of parliamentary proceedings is more uniform than footage generated in other contexts, say, videos from traditional or social media. Knowing what is contained in a collection of videos greatly simplifies the classification task. First and foremost, we do not need to distinguish between relevant and irrelevant footage. For example, if we were interested in protest imagery on social media, a key task would be to identify the relevant footage before moving to the analysis. But even beyond selecting the relevant footage, videos of parliamentary proceedings are more uniform than video footage in other contexts, which means that building a classification scheme and applying it to the videos is easier and more robust. For example, in the application presented here, we gauge the dynamics of plenary attendance from the parliamentary video footage. To this end, we build a model to identify the legislators that are visible in the videos. This task is comparatively straightforward, as the number of legislators is small, such that collecting training footage for the identification is simple and the classification accuracy is high.

The video footage of the plenary proceedings that is published by many parliamentary administrations typically focuses on the speaker. Such data are well suited for studying questions about legislative speech. For example, analyses of the vocal pitch in audio recordings of political speech (Dietrich et al., 2019) could easily be supplemented with video footage, as the video track contains additional cues about the nonverbal characteristics of political speech, such as facial expressions and body movements. In addition to shots of the speaker, some parliamentary administrations intersperse their videos with shots of the full plenary, either to make the footage – marginally! – more captivating or to bridge sequences in the proceedings when no speaker addresses the plenary. This is exploited in the contribution by Dietrich (forthcoming), who studies the overhead shots from the US House of Representatives. While the work

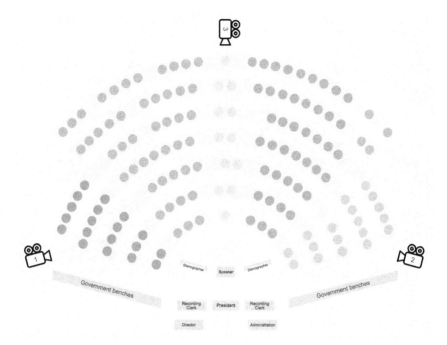

Figure 22.1　Camera locations in the Landtag Baden-Württemberg

Note: The layout of the plenary chamber was adopted from the official seating chart of the Landtag.

by Dietrich constitutes an excellent example of how these occasional shots of the plenary can inform research on legislative politics, the utility of this type of footage is nonetheless limited. Some of the most interesting questions on legislator behavior require a continuous record of the plenary proceedings and not just the occasional and often somewhat haphazardly inserted shots of the plenary chamber.

To advance such a research program, we have collaborated with the *Landtag Baden-Württemberg*, a large German state-level parliament, to provide us with continuous footage of the plenary proceedings. The parliamentary administration records the plenary chamber with three cameras, as displayed in Figure 22.1, one focusing on the speaker (camera 3) and two focusing on the plenary (cameras 1 and 2). The footage that is published by the administration predominantly consists of footage of the speaker from camera 3, along with occasional sweeps across the plenary. Hence, most of the footage from cameras 1 and 2 is never published and typically deleted. To study interactions in the *Landtag*, we have been able to secure the footage from cameras 1 and 2 for one year between July 2018 and July 2019. Specifically, the following analysis is based on footage from 31 plenary sessions, ordinarily lasting from mid-morning to well in the evening. The sheer size of the data, 31 days with about 8–10 hours of video material per camera and day ($31 \times 2 \times 9 = 558$ hours or roughly 23 days), highlights the need for automating the analysis, as the cost for manually coding the material would be prohibitive – not to mention the human suffering caused by having to watch 23 straight days of plenary proceedings.

The footage allows studying a variety of questions about legislative behavior. For the sample application, we analyze which legislators are present in the plenary chamber at any given time. This is more of a validation exercise and does not make use of the full potential of this data for research on legislative politics. We briefly highlight some areas where future research could build on these preliminary analyses at the end of this section. It should be stressed, however, that even studying the ebbs and flows of plenary attendance is valuable in its own right and that this information is not available from the official parliamentary records otherwise. While some assemblies have legislators sign in when they enter the building or take attendance at the beginning of the session, to the best of our knowledge, no legislature in the world records whether legislators are actually present in the plenary chamber as the day progresses or whether they are attending a committee meeting, meeting with colleagues, or working in their offices.

Capturing the patterns of parliamentary attendance from the video recordings involves two steps. In the first step, we employ a neural network to detect the faces in the videos (detection). In the second step, another neural network is used to assign the names of the legislators to the detected faces (identification). For the identification step, we build a training data set containing photos and video clips of the legislators, so the model can learn the facial features of the legislators. Both steps are standard tasks in computer vision, and robust tools have been developed that perform face detection and face identification with high levels of accuracy. For the detection part, the TinyFace architecture of Hu and Ramanan (2017) was used, as it offers accurate detections even for barely visible faces. The identification part was solved by an ImageNet pretrained ResNet-18 model (He et al., 2016), which we fine-tuned with our legislator data set. Given the small number of legislators – currently, the *Landtag* has 143 seats – the classification is correct in 99.7 percent of cases based on a holdout validation set.

For the validation step, we present two aggregate perspectives on the resulting attendance data. One, we study plenary attendance over the course of the day; two, we investigate plenary attendance by type of parliamentary procedure. For the first perspective, Figure 22.2 displays the average share of legislators that were detected in the video footage in all 31 sessions. The figure distinguishes between a morning and an afternoon session, as the *Landtag* takes a lunch break for about an hour around 12:30am. To combine the attendance figures from the individual

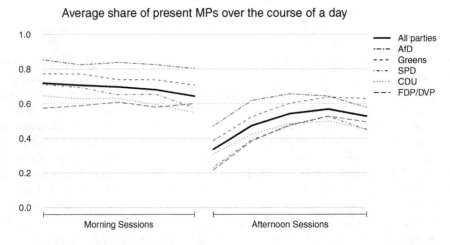

Figure 22.2 Average share of detected legislators in the *Landtag* over the course of the day

Note: The figure displays the average share of legislators that attended the plenary sessions over the course of the day across all 31 sessions in the analysis. To combine the figures from the different sessions, the morning and afternoon sessions were split into five equally sized segments each. In addition to the overall average attendance shares in the 10 segments, the figure displays the values for the five parties that were represented in the *Landtag* at the time of the investigation.

sessions, the morning and afternoon sessions were split into 10 equally sized segments, five in the morning and five in the afternoon. In addition to the overall average, Figure 22.2 displays the attendance averages for the five parties with a parliamentary representation at the time of the investigation.

The results generally support conventional wisdom about legislative politics. Attendance is noticeably lower in the afternoon than in the morning, which speaks to the quip, "there is no greater secret than the spoken word in the plenary after 2pm" (Hohl, 2017, p. 18; translation by the authors). Interestingly, however, there is a clear uptick in attendance as the afternoon progresses, albeit not to the same levels as in the morning, which seems to belie the idea of an irrelevant parliamentary afternoon. Figure 22.2 suggests that while legislators tend to hang out at lunch too long, we do not find that attendance decreases as the session moves into the evening hours. Two factors may help explain this somewhat surprising finding. One, compared with many national parliaments, where legislative sessions can easily run past midnight, the *Landtag* typically finishes its business in the early evening, making it less burdensome for legislators to stay until the end. Two, the *Landtag* meets comparatively infrequently, making attending the individual sessions more important. This proposition is supported by the high levels of attendance overall.

The party-level averages are similar to the grand mean. Notably, the new right-wing populist party AfD, which entered the *Landtag* for the first time in 2016, exhibits the highest attendance levels. This observation nicely aligns with existing research, which has suggested that the AfD values public appeals in the plenary over substantive work in the committees (Ruhose, 2019; Schroeder et al., 2018).

The second way to assess the validity of the attendance data is to split the observations by type of parliamentary procedure. In this case, we should expect legislators to attend in greater numbers when the stakes are high. To examine this proposition, Figure 22.3 distinguishes between the six main plenary procedures in the Landtag Baden-Württemberg. In addition to government declarations, typically delivered by the prime minister, and ordinary legislative debates, the rules of procedure offer four plenary procedures that can be subsumed under the heading of parliamentary control instruments: urgent debates, major interpellations, oral questions, and the question hour. They differ in terms of the kind of issue that they address. Oral questions and the question hour are scheduled on a regular basis. They allow legislators to pose short oral questions on different topics, which are answered by members of the executive. By contrast, major interpellations and urgent debates need to be explicitly requested, and they dedicate an entire segment of the legislative session to just one issue when the topic is of general importance or urgency.

Figure 22.3 strongly supports the idea that the stakes of the debate influence plenary attendance. The figure shows the attendance distributions by the five parties under the six plenary proceedings, along with the proceeding-specific average values, indicated by the dashed lines. Comparing the four control instruments, we find that urgent debates and major interpellations trigger average attendance values well over 60 percent, whereas oral questions and the question hour only result in an average attendance around 40 percent. Interestingly, there is a notable gap between the mean attendance values of the AfD and the other parties during oral questions and the question hour. Again, this observation nicely complements existing research which has highlighted how AfD members focus their efforts on government control and critique (Schroeder et al., 2018).

In summary, both perspectives on plenary attendance show high levels of face validity. Beyond highlighting how accurate computer vision has become for detecting and identifying faces, these preliminary analyses pave the way for future research on legislative politics

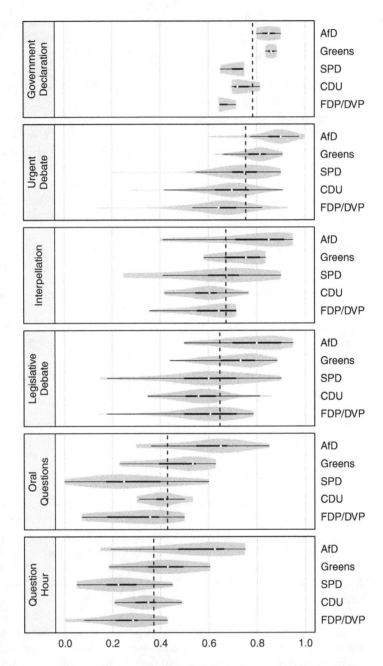

Figure 22.3 Share of detected legislators per party in the *Landtag* by type of parliamentary procedure

Note: The figure displays the share of party representatives that were detected in the six types of plenary procedures across all 31 sessions. For example, between 60 and 100 percent of the AfD legislators attended the urgent debates. The dashed vertical lines represent the mean attendance by parliamentary procedure. The six parliamentary procedures are government declaration (*Regierungsinformation*), urgent debate (*Aktuelle Debatte*), interpellation (*Große Anfrage*), legislative debate (*Beratung*), oral questions (*Regierungsbefragung*), and question hour (*Fragestunde*).

using automated video analysis. Without going into unnecessary detail, at least four research perspectives could be pursued with the footage introduced earlier. First, the aggregate figures have clearly shown how plenary attendance reflects political importance. The analysis could be extended to study political importance attributions for specific issues among parties or individual legislators. Second, the data speak to a research agenda on the determinants of legislator efforts with a particular emphasis on plenary attendance (Arnold et al., 2014; Bernecker, 2014; Besley & Larcinese, 2011). The video footage can provide a more nuanced perspective on plenary attendance by moving beyond the coarser measures based on absences during roll call votes. Third, a broad literature has analyzed the networks among legislators. Lacking a direct measure for legislator interactions, these contributions have typically focused on proxy measures, such as bill co-sponsorships (Bratton & Rouse, 2011; Cho & Fowler, 2010; Fowler, 2006). Building on the preliminary analyses presented here, it is possible to study interactions and networks in the parliamentary arena more directly. Fourth, the footage could also be reanalyzed to study questions beyond the presence or absence of legislators. For instance, one could train models to assess the focus of attention or reactions of legislators in the plenary. In combination with the legislator IDs, such a model could inform a number of research questions, for example on how female/male legislators react to female/male speakers or on how members of the political mainstream react to speakers by the AfD and vice versa. Overall, we hope that these brief comments highlight how computer vision can advance our understanding of social phenomena and, in the present case, our understanding of legislative politics.

5 Conclusion: Potentials and challenges for the application of computer vision in social research

Computer vision promises to be a key tool for empirical social research that could impact research in a number of subfields. Current applications have barely scratched the surface of what is possible with automated video analysis. Not only have many of the available tools not yet been adopted for social science research, there is also a lot of untapped potential on the data side. Digitized video footage is created and published in a variety of settings, and there are numerous applications beyond the obvious use cases of video data from social and traditional media. For example, political scholars could learn a lot about deliberative practices from video recordings in committee settings. Existing research on this question has relied on video recordings of committee deliberations that were analyzed with painstaking manual coding procedures (e.g., Nullmeier et al., 2008; Weihe et al., 2008). Automated video analysis could support and expand such efforts by enabling a comparative perspective with high reliability at low cost. Another major area for the application of automated video analysis in the social sciences is in the study of video footage that is explicitly collected for the purpose of that research. Qualitative research on video data frequently does not study footage "from the wild", but analyzes videos that were shot for the purpose of coding actor behaviors in a second step (Heath et al., 2010). Automated video analysis promises to be a disruptive force in this field by enabling research projects on much larger scales.

Despite the undeniable value of computer vision for social science research, scholars face a number of challenges in bringing the available tools to real-world applications. First, in some research applications, the first step is choosing which material to include in the study. Particularly when studying footage from social or traditional media, only a – potentially small – subset of the footage might be relevant for the research problem. In principle, the same tools we use for classifying the data can also be used for distinguishing between the relevant and the irrelevant material. For example, in a research application on political protests, we can use neural networks to classify whether a segment contains protest footage.

Second, real-world applications of computer vision in the social sciences are often more complex than the case studies in computer science. Whereas applications in computer science tend to zero in on one particular problem, real-world applications need to deal with multiple problems at once. Following up on the case study outlined in the previous section, we might not only be interested in detecting and identifying legislators, but we might also be interested in classifying their parliamentary behaviors, which would require additional classification steps. While this is technically possible, the ambiguities associated with a research project increase as more classification steps are added, in our case from face detection to face recognition to activity recognition.

Third, the simplest way to conduct automated video analysis is to rely on pretrained models to assign the footage to common categories of interest. The downside of using out-of-the-box solutions is that the categories are often too blunt to speak to our research questions. Therefore, to improve the results, it is often preferable to train a model for the specific research problem, which means having to manually code a portion of the material to ensure that the categories for the classification fit the research problem.

Fourth, privacy considerations and formal privacy rules and regulations are an important factor to consider when analyzing real-world video footage using automated video analysis. In light of the many applications of computer vision for the purposes of law enforcement, the general public has become increasingly aware of these technologies and wary of the possibilities for their use and abuse. Therefore, along with stricter rules on other forms of big data analysis, it is likely that computer vision will continue to be a controversial technology, potentially resulting in stricter limitations on its use. At the very least, privacy laws, such as the European General Data Protection Regulation, frequently mandate the storage of the resulting data on secured servers, creating added levels of difficulty when engaging with video data.

These challenges notwithstanding, we hope that this chapter has highlighted the potentials of automated video analysis for the social sciences and how the available computer vision tools might support research in diverse areas.

Notes

1 We are grateful to Morten Harmening, Felix Münchow, and Marie-Lou Sohnius for excellent research assistance. Funding for this project was provided by the *Deutsche Forschungsgemeinschaft* through the *Sonderforschungsbereich 884* "The Political Economy of Reforms".
2 Available at https://github.com/CMU-Perceptual-Computing-Lab/openpose
3 Available in the torchvision package at https://pytorch.org/vision/stable/index.html

References

Arnold, F., Kauder, B., & Potrafke, N. (2014). Outside earnings, absence, and activity: Evidence from German parliamentarians. *European Journal of Political Economy, 36*, 147–157.

Bernecker, A. (2014). Do politicians shirk when reelection is certain? Evidence from the German parliament. *European Journal of Political Economy, 36*, 55–70.

Besley, T., & Larcinese, V. (2011). Working of shirking? Expenses and attendance in the UK parliament. *Public Choice, 146*(3), 291–317.

Bratton, K., & Rouse, S. M. (2011). Networks in the legislative arena: How group dynamics affect cosponsorship. *Legislative Studies Quarterly, 36*(3), 423–460.

Cao, Z., Hidalgo, G. M., Simon, T., Wei, S.-E., & Shekh, Y. (2019). *OpenPose: Realtime multi-person 2D pose estimation using part affinity fields*. IEEE Transactions on Pattern Analysis and Machine Intelligence.

Cho, W. K. T., & Fowler, J. H. (2010). Legislative success in a small world: Social network analysis and the dynamics of Congressional legislation. *Journal of Politics*, 72(1), 124–135.

Deng, J., Dong, W., Socher, R., Li, L.-J., Li, K., & Fei-Fei, L. (2009). ImageNet: A large-scale hierarchical image database. In *IEEE conference on computer vision and pattern recognition*. IEEE.

Dietrich, B. J. (2015). If a picture is worth a thousand words, what is a video worth? In R. X. Browning (Ed.), *Exploring the C-SPAN archives: Advancing the research agenda* (pp. 241–263). Purdue University Press.

Dietrich, B. J. (forthcoming). Using motion detection to measure social polarization in the U.S. House of Representatives. *Political Analysis*.

Dietrich, B. J., Enos, R. D., & Sen, M. (2019). Emotional arousal predicts voting on the U.S. Supreme court. *Political Analysis*, 27(2), 237–243.

Dietrich, B. J., Hayes, M., & O'Brien, D. Z. (2019). Pitch perfect: Vocal pitch and the emotional intensity of congressional speech. *American Political Science Review*, 113(4), 941–962.

Dietrich, B, J., & Juelich, C. L. (2018). When presidential candidates voice party issues, does Twitter listen? *Journal of Elections, Public Opinion and Parties*, 28(2), 208–224.

Donahue, J., Hendricks, L. A., Guadarrama, S., Rohrbach, M., Venugopalan, S., Saenko, K., & Darrell, T. (2015). Long-term recurrent convolutional networks for visual recognition and description. In *IEEE conference on computer vision and pattern recognition*. IEEE.

Fowler, J. H. (2006). Connecting the congress: A study of cosponsorship networks. *Political Analysis*, 14(4), 456–487.

Girshick, R. (2015). Fast R–CNN. In *IEEE international conference on computer vision*. IEEE.

Girshick, R., Donahue, J., Darrell, T., & Malik, J. (2014). Rich feature hierarchies for accurate object detection and semantic segmentation. In *IEEE conference on computer vision and pattern recognition*. IEEE.

Grimmer, J., & Stewart, B. M. (2013). Text as data: The promise and pitfalls of automatic content analysis methods for political texts. *Political Analysis*, 21(3), 267–297.

Haim, M., & Jungblut, M. (forthcoming). Politicians' self-depiction and their news portrayal: Evidence from 28 countries using visual computational analysis. *Political Communication*.

He, K., Gkioxari, G., Dollár, P., & Girshick, R. (2017). Mask R–CNN. In *IEEE international conference on computer vision*. IEEE.

He, K., Zhang, X., Ren, S., & Sun, J. (2016). Deep residual learning for image recognition. In *IEEE conference on computer vision and pattern recognition*. IEEE.

Heath, C., Hindermarsh, C. J., & Luff, P. (2010). *Video in qualitative research: Analysing social interaction in everyday life*. Sage.

Hochreiter, S., & Schmidhuber, J. (1997). Long short-term memory. *Neural Computation*, 9(8), 1735–1780.

Hohl, K. (2017). *Agenda politics im parlament: Das themen- und tagesordnungsmanagement der opposition im landtag von NRW*. Springer VS.

Howard, A. G., Zhu, M., Chen, B., Kalenichenko, D., Wang, W., Weyand, T., Andreetto, M., & Adam, H. (2017). *Mobilenets: Efficient convolutional neural networks for mobile vision applications*. arXiv:1704.04861.

Hu, P., & Ramanan, D. (2017). Finding tiny faces. In *IEEE conference on computer vision and pattern recognition*. IEEE.

Iandola, F., Hang, S., Moskewicz, M. W., Ashraf, K., Dally, W. J., & Keutzer, K. (2016). *SqueezeNet: AlexNet-level accuracy with 50x fewer parameters and <0.5 MB model size*. arXiv:1602.07360.

Joo, J., Bucy, E. P., & Seidel, C. (2019). Automated coding of televised leader displays: Detecting nonverbal political behavior with computer vision and deep learning. *International Journal of Communication*, 13, 4044–4066.

Kharroub, T., & Bas, O. (2016). Social media and protests: An examination of Twitter images of the 2011 Egyptian revolution. *New Media and Society*, 18(9), 1973–1992.

Knox, D., & Lucas, C. (forthcoming). A dynamic model of speech for the social sciences. *American Political Science Review*.

Krizhevsky, A., Sutskever, I., & Hinton, G. E. (2012). *ImageNet classification with deep convolutional neural networks*. Advances in Neural Information Processing.

Liu, W., Anguelov, D., Erhan, D., Szegedy, C., Reed, S., & Fu, C.-Y. (2016). SSD: Single shot multibox detector. In *European conference on computer vision*.

Lucas, C., Nielsen, R., Roberts, M., Stewart, B. M., Storer, A., & Tingley, D. (2015). Computer-assisted text analysis for comparative politics. *Political Analysis*, 23(2), 254–277.

Neumayer, C., & Rossi, L. (2018). Images of protest in social media: Struggle over visibility and visual narratives. *New Media and Society*, 20(11), 4293–4310.

Nullmeier, F., Pritzlaff, T., Weihe, A. C., & Baumgarten, B. (2008). *Entscheiden in Gremien: Von der Videoaufzeichnung zur Prozessanalyse.* VS Verlag für Sozialwissenschaften.

Pasczke, A., Gross, S., Massa, F., Lerer, A., Bradbury, J., Chanan, G., . . . Chintala, S. (2019). *Pytorch: An imperative style, high-performance deep learning library.* Advances in Neural Information Processing.

Peng, Y. (2018). Same candidates, different faces: Uncovering media bias in visual portrayals of Presidential candidates with computer vision. *Journal of Communication, 68*(5), 920–941.

Redmon, J., Divvala, S., Girshick, R., & Farhadi, A. (2016). You only look once: Unified, real-time object detection. In *IEEE conference on computer vision and pattern recognition.* IEEE.

Redmon, J., & Farhadi, A. (2017). YOLO9000: Better, faster, stronger. In *IEEE conference on computer vision and pattern recognition.* IEEE.

Ren, S., He, K., Girshick, R., & Sun, J. (2015). *Faster R-CNN: Towards real-time object detection with regional proposal networks.* Advances in Neural Information Processing Systems.

Rose, J., Mackey-Kallis, S., Styles, L., Barry, K., Biagini, D., Hart, C., & Jack, L. (2012). Face it: The impact of gender on social media images. *Communication Quarterly, 60*(5), 588–607.

Ruhose, F. (2019). *Die AfD im Deutschen Bundestag: Zum Umgang mit einem neuen politischen Akteur.* Springer.

Ryle, M. (1991). Televising the house of commons. *Parliamentary Affairs, 44*(2), 185–207.

Schroeder, W., Weßels, B., & Berzel, A. (2018). Die AfD in den landtagen: Bipolarität als Struktur und Strategie: Zwischen parlaments und 'bewegungs'-orientierung. *Zeitschrift für Parlamentsfragen, 49*(1), 91–110.

Schroff, F., Klenichenko, D., & Philbin, J. (2015). Facenet: A unified embedding for face recognition and clustering. In *IEEE conference on computer vision and pattern recognition.* IEEE.

Uijlings, J. R. R., Van de Sande, K., E. A., Gevers, T., & Smeulders, A. W. M. (2013). Selective search for object recognition. *International Journal of Computer Vision, 104*(2), 154–171.

Wang, H., Kläser, A., Schmid, C., & Liu, C.-L. (2011). Action recognition by dense trajectories. In *IEEE conference on computer vision and pattern recognition.* IEEE.

Wei, S.-E., Ramakrishna, V., Kanade, T., & Sheikh, Y. (2016). Convolutional pose machines. In *IEEE conference on computer vision and pattern recognition.* IEEE.

Weihe, A. C., Pritzlaff, T., Nullmeier, F., Felgenhauer, T., & Baumgarten, B. (2008). Wie wird in politischen Gremien entschieden? Konzeptionelle und methodische Grundlagen der Gremienanalyse. *Politische Vierteljahresschrift, 49*(2), 339–359.

Wilkerson, J., & Casas, A. (2017). Large-scale computerized text analsis in political science: Opportunities and challenges. *Annual Review of Political Science, 20*, 529–544.

Williams, N. W., Casas, A., & Wilkerson, J. D. (2020). *Images as data for social science research.* Cambridge University Press.

Zhang, H., & Pan, J. (2019). CASM: A deep-learning approach for identifying collective action events with text and image data from social media. *Sociological Methodology, 49*(1), 1–57.

INDEX

Note: Page numbers in *italics* indicate a figure and page numbers in **bold** indicate a table on the corresponding page.